COMMON KNOWLEDGE

Common Knowledge

Knowledge

**A READER'S
GUIDE TO
LITERARY
ALLUSIONS**

David Grote

GREENWOOD PRESS
NEW YORK • WESTPORT, CONNECTICUT • LONDON

Library of Congress Cataloging-in-Publication Data

Grote, David.
  Common knowledge.
  1. Allusions—Dictionaries. I. Title.
PN43.G68   1987   803   87-10710
ISBN 0-313-25757-4 (lib. bdg. : alk. paper)

British Library Cataloguing in Publication Data is available.

Library of Congress Catalog Card Number: 87-10710
ISBN: 0-313-25757-4

First published in 1987

Greenwood Press, Inc.
88 Post Road West, Westport, Connecticut 06881

Printed in the United States of America

The paper used in this book complies with the
Permanent Paper Standard issued by the National
Information Standards Organization (Z39.48-1984).

10 9 8 7 6 5 4 3 2 1

Contents

Introduction _____

This book is intended to be a companion for the general reader, a guide to common literary allusions. It is an attempt to present in one place the fundamental names in mythology, theater, literature, religion, history, and popular culture that reasonably educated persons might be expected to know in order to understand most general literature. That is, it is a guide to names that have been the common coin of both literary and public discourse, in some cases for years, in others for centuries.

The fundamental criterion for inclusion is that, in the course of general reading, the name is likely to be mentioned in works that are not about the character or figure named. Someone is "as melancholy as Hamlet," or a lawsuit is "a David and Goliath contest," or someone else revives "Phoenix-like, from the ashes of his earlier defeat." This is a dictionary of such names.

The names are primarily those of characters from literature and of figures from the Bible and Greek and Roman mythology. In addition, a number of names of historical figures are also included, particularly when they have so completely entered our culture that they too became common subjects for literature. Finally, also included are a number of names of significant events, such as the Crucifixion, concepts, such as the Noble Savage, or stories, such as the principal parables of Jesus, which have become proverbial to both the general reader and writer and are generally known by a common identifying name.

It is my hope that, armed with this work, *Bartlett's Familiar Quotations*, and a good biographical dictionary, the general reader or undergraduate student could understand the allusions in practically any non-specialist material she or he is likely to read.

USE

One of the unique elements of this book is that its entries are the names themselves, not the authors or the works from which they come. Although this is a companion to literature in general, it is not a companion to literature in the sense of the admirable Oxford or Cambridge Companions or their imitators and competitors. It is concerned not with authors nor with works, nor with theories of literature, but rather with the characters from those works that seized the memory of readers (or audiences) and became a part of the common consciousness of our culture. Hence, you will find here discussions of the major characters in Shakespeare's plays, but nothing about Shakespeare's life or Shakespearean scholarship and criticism.

Another unique element is that it is a companion to literature *in general*. It includes figures from mythology, but it is not a dictionary of mythology. It includes figures from the Bible, but it is not a Bible dictionary. And so on. There are numerous specialized reference works in such fields, with far more detail than could be included in such a work as this and which will be of considerably more use to the student within a particular field. But, as any general reader has learned when faced with an unfamiliar allusion, a Bible dictionary is of no help if you do not already know that the name comes from the Bible, nor is a companion to French literature helpful if you do not already know that the author and the work from which the name comes are both French.

Where such specialist reference books are intended to be the final word in their fields or to provide a refresher course with significant details for the advanced scholar and teacher, this book is intended to be a book of first resort. In a sense, it is a book to help when readers do not quite know where to start looking.

Thirdly, the information presented in each entry is designed to answer one, and only one, question: With what trait, activity, or type is this name usually associated? Or, phrased another way: Why would anyone mention this figure to begin with? Included are more than 4,000 names that the reader is likely to find not just mentioned but mentioned for an illustrative purpose in other works aimed not at the specialist but at the general reader. In some cases, this may be a physical trait, in others a personality trait, in still others some activity, and in still others it may be a famous saying. Thus, while some entries may give a brief summary of plot, others will not. Each entry, I hope, includes enough information so that the reader may quickly grasp why the allusion was originally made and, if more information is desired, will know where to find more information about it.

In no case is an entry intended to be an explanation or a critical commentary on the original for the reader engaged in study of the original. It will attempt to summarize what the general educated public has thought of Stephen Dedalus, for example, not what Joyce thought of him or what scholars now believe Joyce should have thought of him, or what I believe other scholars should have believed about him. At the same time, however, it may be a great help to the reader of Joyce's work, by explaining a number of Joyce's allusions to *other* works.

A number of names of historical figures are included, but the criteria for selecting them was the same as that for characters drawn from works of literature. That is, no attempt has been made to include the "important" figures of history.

Rather, every attempt has been made to include those who became so completely identified with some character type or activity that their names are synonymous with some trait or their activities have entered the world of legend. Thus, Ben Franklin is here for his kite and for Poor Richard, while James Madison is not because, despite his historical importance, his persona never quite penetrated the public consciousness. In many cases, of course, legend and fact are inseparable, and the legend preceded our discovery of the historical facts in relation to the figure involved. We now know that Troy was ''real,'' but it is the legend of Troy that fascinated us and in fact made us become interested in the search for the real Troy. Much the same criterion has been used to determine those historical figures to be included here. In many such entries, no attempt has been made to explain anything more than the legend or the standard literary description; those wishing more complete or factual biographies can pursue the point in encyclopedias or biographical dictionaries and historical studies.

Similarly, the names of prominent saints are also included, some legendary, some carefully verified by historians, but all are associated in some vivid and memorable way with a unique event, trait, or personality.

CRITERIA

More specifically, the following criteria were used to determine the entries:

1. The name has become synonymous with a character type. This includes such figures as Harlequin, Jezebel, Samson, Romeo, Lothario, Svengali, and Uriah Heep.
2. The name has preempted other uses. This includes those characters who were so vivid that no one else now dare use the name unless intending a direct allusion, such as Scarlett, Blanche, or Alice.
3. The figure's story has been retold by numerous writers throughout the ages. This includes such figures as Odysseus, Don Juan, Cleopatra, Troilus, Napoleon, and Lizzie Borden.
4. The character is referred to in common catch-phrases, such as the Oedipus complex, Fabian campaigns, or a Peter Pan syndrome, or it is clearly known as the source of common sayings.
5. The name entered the language in a usage that remained after the general public lost all interest in the figure concerned. This includes such terms as the Trilby, bowdlerization, or Dundreary whiskers, all of which are drawn from the name of a character or personage.
6. The figure is a common subject of other artistic media, such as famous paintings or musical compositions. This includes such figures as Venus, Daphnis and Chloe, Till Eulenspiegel, and St. Sebastian.
7. The figure is the source for commonly used personal names. This includes such figures as Abigail, Ezra, Veronica, and Flora.
8. The character is a principal figure in a work generally regarded as a fundamental work. This includes such characters as Hamlet, Lear, Stephen Dedalus, Violetta, Elizabeth Bennet, and Swann.

9. The character was a model much admired or imitated in its time. This includes such
   figures as Werther, Tamberlaine, Orlando, and Hawkshaw.

No limitations have been placed on sources for such figures. Many come from
mythology and the Bible, others come from history and literature, but many
others come from folklore, comic strips, opera, the movies, or some of the more
disreputable forms of popular literature. Wherever such names began, they became a part of our common culture for more than a brief moment in time. It is
that common cultural heritage that, in a sense, I hope to define and make available
to the general reader at a time when education, on either side of the Atlantic,
has rejected its role in the maintenance of such a common culture.

ENTRIES

Each entry includes the following information:

Name

This is the name as it is most commonly used or identified. Where a figure
is known only by a single name, that name of course is listed. Where the figure
has both a Christian name and a surname, the primary entry is made under the
most commonly used name; for example, Jo March is almost always called only
Jo, and thus, information about her is entered under "Jo." However, as allusions
may be made in many forms, the name is also cross-referenced under other parts
of the name; for example, under "March," the entry will indicate "*See* Jo."
Similarly, Sam Weller is entered primarily under Weller, with a cross-reference
under "Sam," because allusions tend to be to his full name but are occasionally
made only to the Christian name.

When several characters from the same family are known from a single work,
they are entered together under the family surname, with each individual name
highlighted in boldface. However, every effort has been made to also indicate
cross-references under various Christian names where needed.

When a figure may be known by several different names, or may have several
common nicknames, the complete entry is made only under what is judged to
be the primary name, with cross references under various common alternates or
nicknames. In the case of Greek and Roman mythology, the most ancient name
is presumed to be the primary name; that is, entries are primarily under the
Greek name, even though the Roman may actually have been used more often,
due to the ease of transliteration from Latin. Hence, "Ulysses" is cross-referenced to "Odysseus," where the actual entry will be given.

When allusions are sometimes made to several different figures using the same
name in several unrelated sources, all such citations are given under the single
name, numbered and arranged historically. Thus, some eight separate citations
are listed under "Isabella," with the earliest one listed first.

When figures share a common name but are often known by distinguishing modifiers, the names may be listed separately. Hence, the entry for "John" is immediately followed by separate entries for "John, Don; John, Little; John, Prester; John, St.; John Henry"; etc. Since these entries are immediately adjacent to the central entry for John, they are not cross-referenced within the entry for John itself.

In many instances, the same name may appear in many forms, due to its appearance in several different languages or changes in spelling that have occurred over the years, or even common nicknames. Such variants are listed at the end of each citation following the notation *See also*. Thus, the citation for Catherine will conclude with "*See also* Cathy; Kate; Katharine." *See also* the Note on Spelling below.

Source

This is the primary source in which the name first appeared or in which the name was widely transmitted. It will include the name of the work, the author, if known, and the date of publication or first performance.

References to the Bible are to the most complete version of a particular story or to the earliest citation dealing with the figure; for example, some parables are repeated in several Gospels, but if they appear in *Matthew*, which comes first in the Bible, *Matthew* is the source listed. Citations are given only to the chapter, not to specific verses.

For figures in mythology or folklore, the identification is "Greek legend," "British folklore," etc. No attempt has been made to trace stories to specific collectors, scholars, or variants unless the story is commonly associated with that source, because such information lies outside the purview of this work.

Similarly, dating is done only in terms of when the work became available to people who might allude to it. This is done only in order to provide a historical context for the citation, not to settle academic disagreements. For example, although research may often establish that a work was "written" some years before it was "published," the date given here is the publication date because that is the earliest moment at which others would have begun to allude to the characters in the work. For plays, the date given is the date of public performance, not the date of publication, which may have occurred many years later, as with Shakespeare.

For those works written and circulated before the invention of printing, no date is given; all such works are "classics" that became widely available at about the same time, during the fifteenth century. If it seriously matters to you whether Ovid might have known about Daphnis and Chloe, you are already reading primary sources and will not need this dictionary.

In the case of Shakespeare, I have simply accepted the date on which most reference works seem to agree, without reference to the most current scholarship and the academic wars associated with it, or, in those few cases in which that agreement is missing, I have selected a mean date around which most theories cluster.

In the case of Dickens and other nineteenth-century novelists whose works appeared as serials over several years, I have used the date at which the serializations began rather than the date at which the complete work was published in hard-covers. In some few cases in which a work consists of several distinct works that appeared over a number of years, such as *Remembrance of Things Past* or *The Ring of the Niebelung*, I have listed inclusive dates for the entire work rather than try to distinguish which specific piece of information comes from which specific volumes. For characters appearing in series and serials, the date at which the series began is the only date given.

Dates given for historical figures are the date of death only, not only because this is often the only verifiable date but also because one can be reasonably sure that, whatever the person might have been famous for, he or she was usually famous for it by that date, a claim which is rarely possible at any earlier time in life and never at birth.

Citation

This is a brief explanation of that for which the figure is most commonly noted. Such entries are necessarily brief, and all brevity leads to generality. To those readers looking up citations for favorite characters, such citations will always be disappointing, and I apologize in advance to the Dickensians, the Janeites, the Proustians, the Holmesians, and the Shakespeareans, as well as to the theologians and scholars. Almost all of the figures here cited do more, say more, and are interesting for more than is here described. That additional information lies outside the scope of this work. All that is intended here is an explanation of why the name might be alluded to in works addressed to persons who are not already devotees or advanced students.

Additional information

Additional information is indicated in two ways. First, in the course of the explanation, other names will often be mentioned. If entries exist under those names, this will be indicated by an asterisk (*) following the name. Secondly, additional information may be found under names preceded by the notations *See* or *See also*.

Nicknames and alternate names are listed following *Also called*. If additional entries exist for some of these nicknames, these will be indicated by the asterisk as well.

A NOTE ON SPELLING

Even for common English names, spelling is wildly variable. It was only in the late nineteenth century, after the rise of universal education, that surnames were standardized, and Christian names even today are spelled at the whim of the parent or of the author. Hence, it has often been necessary to make an editorial decision as to the way in which an entry will be spelled, with the result that some, perhaps many, allusions will be found that use different spellings of the same name.

This problem is magnified when dealing with names from foreign languages, for allusions are sometimes made to the name as in the original language and sometimes to an Anglicized version of the name. The problem is increased exponentially when dealing with names from foreign languages that also have foreign alphabets, particularly Greek, Russian, and the ancient Hebrew; some writers transliterate the names (often with multiple spellings), while others translate them, and still others use an English or American equivalent. A general reader is likely to come across any of these contradictory spellings in the course of general reading.

For the purposes of this dictionary, the following spelling decisions were made:

For Greek and Roman names, I have used the most common transliterations rather than the most current or most "accurate." In most cases, this has meant the Latinate and Victorian version of the name. Contemporary scholarship has for the most part rejected these spellings, for reasons that are not always clear, especially by adopting *os* for the Latinate *us*, *ai* for *ae*, and *k* for *c*, but as there is no consistency in these new adoptions and since the overwhelming number of allusions will have been made by non-scholars and older writers who learned the Latinate forms, the choice of spelling seemed obvious in almost all cases. Where there is no overwhelmingly dominant spelling (Gaea/Gaia, for example), I have simply placed the entry under one and a cross-reference under the other.

For Biblical names, I have used the spellings of the King James Version. Where multiple spellings exist in that translation, or in a few extremely rare cases in which common usage has almost completely replaced that spelling with a modern version, I have provided cross-references.

For Arthurian legend, I have used the spelling in the Penguin edition of Malory as the most widely available version, except in rare cases such as "Guinevere" and "Lancelot," both of which are clearly dominant modern spellings.

For French and German names, I have used the common French or German spelling, with cross-references indicated only where this might not be immediately apparent to the reader faced with a rare Anglicized spelling.

For Russian names, I closed my eyes and pointed, trying to select the version of the name that seemed to be most commonly used during years of reading. This means, unfortunately, that there is no immediately visible consistency; just as usage has given us Chekhov and Tchaikovsky, so usage has given us Nikolai for some characters and Nicholas for the Czar, and our choice of Lopahin, Lopakin, or Lopakhin. The spelling selected here is the one that seemed most common or familiar after many years of general reading, or, barring that, the one that seemed simplest. In those cases, such as Lopahin, where the variant spellings would immediately follow each other, variants have not been cross-referenced, on the assumption that the spelling variation would be immediately obvious to the reader. Nicknames and patronymics make particular problems with Russian names; however, usage tends to select the simplest name and hence tends to concentrate on the surname, or on the nickname where such a name exists. Thus, there is an entry to Natasha and a cross-reference under the family name Rostov, but there is no entry under Ilyanova, Ilyanovna, Rostova, or Rostovna, any of which might be more "accurate." When the patronymic might commonly be used in English, it is of course included and cross-referenced. In the case of multiple family members, male and female both are entered under the male form of the family name unless the female form is overwhelmingly dominant (Anna Karenina, for example).

With the exceptions noted, however, every effort has been made to cross-reference all common spellings of a name. Even so, there will be some that are missing, for which I can only note that most such variations should be immediately clear if the reader glances at other nearby entries.

ACKNOWLEDGMENTS

A complete bibliography of works consulted for such a dictionary would take almost as much space as the dictionary itself. The primary sources for the entries here are of course the works cited in the entries. But the failures of memory and the exigencies of time naturally required considerable consultation of other reference sources. Hence, I should like to acknowledge my debt to: the *Oxford Companion* series, especially those volumes for English, American, French, Classical, and Children's Literature; Haydn and Fuller's *Thesaurus of Book Digests*; and Magill's *Cyclopedia of Literary Characters*. Also important were *Cassell's Encyclopedia of Literature, Chambers Biographical Dictionary, Harper's Bible Dictionary*, the *Contemporary Authors* series, the *Dictionary of Literary Biography* series, *The World Encyclopedia of Comics*, the Penguin Dictionary series, particularly the *Dictionary of Saints*, Ferguson's *Signs and Symbols in Christian Art*, Balanchine's *Complete Stories of the Great Ballets*, Shipley's *Guide to the World's Great Plays*, Brooks and Marsh's *Complete Directory to Prime Time Network TV Shows*, Halliwell's *Filmgoer's Companion*, Fellner's *Opera Themes and Plots*, Buxton and Owen's *The Big Broadcast*, and Hart's *The Popular Book*.

Numerous other works were consulted, often with surprise at how difficult it had become to verify or even trace so many figures that had become bywords in our culture. In this search, considerable help was provided by many unnamed and unsung aides, the librarians at the San Francisco Public Library and the San Francisco State University Library, for whose help I am more than grateful.

Finally, I must express my overwhelming gratitude to my wife, Susan, for her willingness to aid in the research (which replaced the all but obligatory cadre of graduate students normally used for such projects), to prod her memory as well as mine for entries to be included, sources to be verified, and ways to express information more clearly and accurately, and for her skill in the picking of nits.

Having noted that, I feel obligated to add that this is a personal work. The editorial decisions, the summaries and citations, and the errors, if such exist, are not the work of a committee or a collection of experts. This is a book for the general reader compiled by a general reader, and the selections and exclusions, as well as the interpretations and biases inherent in such selections and exclusions, are the result of years of that general reading. I have tried to be descriptive, rather than prescriptive; that is, I have tried to include those figures and information (or misinformation) that people who wrote for a literate, but still general, audience tend to have known, rather than those things such people ought to have known.

Nonetheless, there will be many significant omissions. As I was preparing this final version, for example, I decided, with great regret, to eliminate some minor characters from a play by Shaw. Two days later, I picked up a current British magazine and found them mentioned not in the drama pages but in the financial column, precisely the kind of verification of their penetration into the general culture that affected so many of my editorial decisions. Even so, I decided not to restore them. For that writer, they were obviously common knowledge; in my opinion, they were not. I have tried to make that opinion as broad as possible, and I have consulted numerous lists of "great" and "important" and "influential" works to test and modify my opinion, but it is still only one person's opinion.

COMMON
KNOWLEDGE

A

Aaron. (1) In the Bible, *Exodus*, brother of Moses* and first high priest of Israel.* He made the Golden Calf* that Moses destroyed on his return from Mt. Sinai* with the Ten Commandments.* (2) In Shakespeare's play *Titus Andronicus* (1592), Aaron the Moor, a villain who delights in villainy for its own sake, even repenting at his own death any good he might have done inadvertently. *See also* Titus Andronicus; Lavinia; Tamora. (3) *See* Slick, Aaron.

Aase. In Henrik Ibsen's play *Peer Gynt* (1867), Peer Gynt's* long-suffering yet always loving mother.

Abas. In Greek mythology, a man changed into a lizard for mocking Demeter.*

Abdiel. In John Milton's poem *Paradise Lost* (1667), the only one of Satan's* seraphim* to refuse to join Satan's revolt.

Abdul Abulbul Amir. In an anonymous nineteenth-century song, the bravest of the ''sons of the Prophet''; he always led the charge, but he met his match in a Russian he challenged over an accidentally stubbed toe.

Abe, Honest. *See* Lincoln, Abraham.

Abednego. *See* Shadrach.

Abel. In the Bible, *Genesis*, the second son of Adam* and Eve,* a shepherd, who was murdered by his brother Cain.* (2) *See* Rima; Sheba.

Abélard. *See* Héloïse.

Abigail. In the Bible, *I Samuel* xxv, wife of Nabal.* She prevents David* from murdering Nabal by telling David that God intends David to be king; later she marries David. Her continual references to herself as ''thine handmaid'' led to general usage of her name for a woman-in-waiting.

Abijah. *See* Asa.

Abiram. In the Bible, *Numbers* xvi, one of the leaders, with Dathan,* of a revolt against Moses;* God swallowed him up in the earth.

Abishag. In the Bible, *I Kings*, a beautiful woman brought in to nurse the aged David;* Solomon* later used her as an excuse to kill Adonijah.*

Abner. In the Bible, *I Samuel* xiv, captain of Saul's* army in the war against the Philistines;* later, in *II Samuel* ii–iii, he led a revolt against David,* then either changed sides or pretended to change sides again, only to be assassinated by Joab.*

Abner, Li'l. In the American newspaper cartoon *Li'l Abner* (beg. 1934), a handsome, slow-witted hillbilly caught by and married to the gorgeous Daisy Mae.* *See also* Dogpatch; Yokum.

Abraham. In the Bible, *Genesis*, husband of Sarah* and father of Isaac.* God commanded him to sacrifice his son; as he was about to kill the boy, God sent him a ram to use instead and blessed Abraham for his faith. *See also* Hagar; Ishmael; Midian.

Abram. A name sometimes used for Abraham.*

Absalom. In the Bible, *II Samuel*, a son of David.* Renowned for his beauty, he also killed Amnon,* David's firstborn, in revenge for Amnon's rape of Absalom's sister Tamar.* Later, he engineered a coup that drove David out of Jerusalem* and, in the eventual climactic battle of the civil war, was killed after he caught his hair in the limb of a tree. *See also* Ahitophel.

Absolute. In R. B. Sheridan's play *The Rivals* (1775), **Anthony** is the bluff, strong-willed father; **Jack** is the young hero who impersonates a poor young ensign in order to win the love of Lydia Languish.* *See also* Malaprop, Mrs.

Abou ben Adhem. In Leigh Hunt's poem *Abou ben Adhem* (1838), a man who sees an angel* in a dream making a list of those who love God; since his name is not included, he prays that he may be known as one who loves his fellow man, and an angel appears showing his name has been added at the head of the list.

Acantha. In Greek mythology, a nymph* loved by Apollo* and changed into the acanthus flower.

Acestes. In Virgil's *Aeneid*, a man who shot an arrow with such speed that it caught fire from the air's friction.

Achaeans. Historically, one of the tribes of ancient Greece; the name was often used for all the Greeks.

Achates. In Virgil's *Aeneid*, a faithful friend of Aeneas.*

Acheron. In Greek mythology, the river of woe, one of the five rivers of Hades.*

Achilles. In Homer's *Iliad*, the greatest of all Greek warriors at the siege of Troy,* but also the most proud. The *Iliad* begins when Achilles sulks over a social slight given by Agamemnon* and withdraws from the fighting; no matter how badly the battle goes, he refuses to return until his friend Patroclus,* wearing Achilles's own armor, is killed. From that moment, he becomes an unbeatable fighter, killing great numbers of Trojans; he eventually kills Hector,* the greatest Trojan warrior, and in his wrath refuses to return the body, dragging it in the dirt three times around Troy. Non-Homeric legend said that his mother Thetis* dipped Achilles in the River Styx,* which made him invulnerable except for the heel by which she held him. He then died when either an arrow or a sword hit his heel; hence, an Achilles heel is a secret, deadly weak spot. Legend also has it that Thetis tried to keep him out of the Trojan War by disguising him as a girl. *See also* Briseis; Diomedes; Iphigenia; Neoptolemus; Peleus; Polyxena; Troilus.

Achitophel. In John Dryden's poem *Absalom and Achitophel* (1681), Ahitophel.*

Acis. In Greek legend, a young man who loved Galatea* but was killed by Polyphemus,* who also loved her.

Acres, Bob. In R. B. Sheridan's play *The Rivals* (1775), the timid, friendly country squire who finds himself maneuvered into a comic duel he has no will to fight.

Actaeon. In Ovid's *Metamorphoses*, a hunter who saw Artemis* naked and refused to leave, so that she changed him into a stag, after which he was killed and eaten by his own hunting dogs.

Ada. *See* Lester.

Adam. (1) In the Bible, *Genesis*, the first man, whose rib was used by God to make Eve,* the first woman, and who lived in the Garden of Eden* until he ate the fruit of the Tree of Knowledge and was driven out to live a life of work and pain. *See also* Abel; Cain; Lilith; Seth. (2) In Shakespeare's play, *As You Like It* (1599), the dedicated old servant who despite age and infirmity serves his young master Orlando* faithfully.

Adams, Nick. In several stories by Ernest Hemingway, beginning in the collection *In Our Times* (1925), a prototypical American young man growing up, surviving WWI, and generally finding mental recuperation in dealing with nature, particularly fishing and hunting.

Addie. *See* Bundren.

Adeline. *See* Hulot.

Ades. A name sometimes used for Pluto.*

Adler, Irene. In Arthur Conan Doyle's story *A Scandal in Bohemia* (1891), a beautiful, intelligent woman, the only person ever to outwit Sherlock Holmes* and always referred to by him as "*the* woman."

Admetus. In Greek legend, a man who, when hearing that his allotted life was up, searched for a substitute to die in his place, eventually allowing his wife Alcestis* to die for him; also, one of the Argonauts.*

Admirable Crichton, The. *See* Crichton.

Adolphe. In Benjamin Constant's novel *Adolphe* (1815), a sensitive young man whose conflict with conventionality leads him to try a romantic conquest, which he soon finds constrains him as much as other aspects of society and leads to unhappiness while his beloved is alive and desolation when she dies.

Adonijah. In the Bible, *I Kings* i–ii, the fourth son of David;* as the eldest son still living, he thought to inherit the kingdom, but he was passed over in favor of Solomon,* who later had him killed.

Adonis. In Greek legend, a youth of such great beauty that the goddess Aphrodite* fell in love with him; he was killed by a wild boar, and anemones took their color from his blood. In some stories, he was revived by Persephone,* who so admired him that he had to spend half the year with her in Hades* and half above ground with Aphrodite, thus sometimes symbolizing winter and summer. *See also* Myrrha.

Aegeus. In Greek legend, the father of Theseus.* When his son had gone to fight the Minotaur,* he arranged for the ship that returned to raise a white sail if Theseus was safe and a black one if he had been killed. Theseus forgot and left the black sail in place; Aegeus then leapt from the cliff into the sea (now called the Aegean).

Aegisthus. In Greek legend, the lover of Clytemnestra* and murderer of her husband Agamemnon;* he was later murdered in revenge by Agamemnon's son Orestes.* In Aeschylus's play *Agamemnon*, he is a bully without much dignity, and most other versions follow this characterization. *See also* Atreus; Electra.

Aeneas. In Homer's *Odyssey*, a great warrior of Troy.* In Virgil's *Aeneid*, when Troy falls, he escapes, bearing his father Anchises* on his back, and eventually reaches Italy, where he becomes the father of the Roman people. Along the way, he meets and deserts Dido,* the Queen of Carthage, who commits suicide when he leaves; he also makes a famous trip through Hades.* *See also* Achates; Aphrodite; Ascanius; Cerberus; Creusa; Diomedes; Euryalus; Helenus; Lavinia; Misenus; Nisus; Palinurus.

Aeolus. In Greek mythology, the god of the winds.

Aesculapius. In Greek mythology, the physician for the Argonauts* and the god of healing and medicine.

Aesop. The apochryphal writer, thought to be a slave, to whom most Greek and Latin fables are ascribed; hence, a storyteller and moralist who teaches by illustrative fables.

Affery. *See* Flintwitch.

Agamemnon. In Greek legend, the brother of Menelaus* and commander of the Greek forces in the Trojan War.* In Homer's *Iliad*, his taking of Briseis* sends Achilles* out of the battle and almost loses the war. After the war, he takes Cassandra* for his personal mistress, which ensures the curses of the gods on him and his family. In Aeschylus's play *Agamemnon*, he returns to Greece, where his wife Clytemnestra* and her lover Aegisthus* murder him, as a result of which his children Orestes* and Electra devote themselves to avenging him. In general, he is described as a short-tempered, headstrong, bluff warrior. *See also* Chryseis; Chrysothemis; Iphigenia.

Agatha, St. In Christian legend, a female martyr usually represented with a pair of shears, as she was killed by having her breasts cut off.

Agathon. Historically, an Athenian playwright from whom no complete works remain; Plato's *Symposium* occurs in his home. He is also ridiculed in Aristophanes' play *Thesmophoriazusae* as a flamboyant transsexual who refuses to help defend Euripides.

Agave. In Euripides's play *The Bacchae*, mother of Pentheus* and leader of the female worshippers of Dionysus;* when her son spies on their secret rites, she helps the women tear him to pieces and then displays his head.

Aggerawayter. *See* Cruncher.

Aglaya. In Dostoevsky's novel *The Idiot* (1868), a pampered, beautiful young woman, virginal but complex, betrothed to the "idiot" Prince Myshkin;* the combination of her jealousy and his sense of unworthiness ends the relationship. *See also* Prokofievna, Lizaveta.

Agnes. (1) In Molière's play *The School for Wives* (1662), the ward of Arnolphe,* who has raised her to be ignorant and innocent in hopes that she will become a perfect wife for him; among other things, she believes babies come through the ear. (2) In Charles Dickens's novel *David Copperfield* (1849), Wickfield's* daughter, who loyally cares for him in his decline; the despicable Uriah Heep* plans to marry her, but his plan is foiled. After David Copperfield's* first wife dies, he realizes that Agnes would have been the perfect wife and marries her. (3) In Henrik Ibsen's play, *Brand* (1866), Brand's* wife; when she is ill, she forces him to make the choice he demands of his followers and to leave her to die in order to follow his higher duty. *See also* Einar.

Agnes, St. In Christian legend, a young girl who refused to marry. She was placed in a brothel, was then thrown into a fire which refused to burn her, and was finally beheaded. She is patron saint of virgins. In folklore it was said that a dream on St. Agnes's Eve (January 20) would reveal the person one was destined to marry.

Agoracritus. In Aristophanes's play *The Knights*, a sausage seller who is judged to be ideally suited for political office because he is the most vulgar, dishonest, and ignorant man available. *See also* Cleon; Demos.

Agramante. In Ariosto's *Orlando Furioso* (1516), the great Saracen warrior who threatens Charlemagne's* forces until he is finally overcome by Orlando.*

Agrippa. *See* Herod.

Aguecheek, Sir Andrew. In Shakespeare's play *Twelfth Night* (1599), a cowardly, gullible country gentleman who is tricked into a comic duel with Viola;* he is generally portrayed as very tall, thin, and pale. *See also* Belch, Sir Toby.

Ah Sin. In Bret Harte's poem *Plain Language from Truthful James* (1870), the original "heathen Chinee," an inscrutable Chinese immigrant who manages to outcheat the white men who try to cheat him.

Ahab. (1) In the Bible, *I Kings*, the husband of Jezebel* and a king of Israel* who did more wickedness before the Lord than any other king; he hounded the prophets, especially Elijah,* and when he was killed in battle in Samaria, dogs lapped up his blood. (2) In Herman Melville's novel *Moby-Dick* (1851), the obsessed captain of the ship *Pequod** who pursues Moby Dick,* the Great White Whale, even to the destruction of himself and all his crew. He has one leg made of whalebone, replacing one that was bitten off by the whale, and a livid scar running the length of his face. He is killed when he is caught in a harpoon line that binds him onto the side of the whale. *See also* Ishmael; Pip; Queequeg; Starbuck; Stubb.

Ahasuerus. (1) In the Bible, *Esther*, a Persian king who marries Esther* and, at her instigation, saves the Jews from annihilation. He is generally identified with the historical Xerxes.* *See also* Vashti. (2) In Christian legend, the Jew who ridiculed Jesus* on the way to the Crucifixion* and told Him to go faster, in punishment for which he was condemned to wander the world until His Second Coming.* *Also called* The Wandering Jew. *See also* Samuel.

Ahitophel. In the Bible, *II Samuel*, the manipulator behind Absalom's* revolt against David;* he committed suicide when the revolt failed. *Also called* Achitophel.*

Aias. A name sometimes used for Ajax.*

Aida. In Verdi's opera *Aida* (1871), an Ethiopian princess who, now a slave of the Egyptian princess Amneris,* must choose between love of Radames* and love of her country. Eventually she joins her lover in his tomb.

Aimwell. In George Farquhar's play *The Beaux' Stratagem* (1707), an impoverished young noble hunting for a rich heiress to marry, which he finds in the modest Dorinda;* in alternate months, he trades places with his friend Archer,* each playing the other's servant.

Ajax. (1) In Greek legend, one of the bravest and strongest Greek warriors in the Trojan War.* His most famous activity, however, occurred not in battle but after the death of Achilles* when, angered because Odysseus* was awarded the dead man's armor, he went mad and slaughtered the Greek sheep and cattle. In Sophocles's play *Ajax*, he recovers his senses and is so mortified that he commits suicide. *Also called* Aias. (2) In Greek legend, a different Greek warrior in the Trojan War, who dragged Cassandra* away from Athena's* altar and raped her during the sack of the city; shipwrecked on the way home, he boasted of his swim to shore and was drowned by Poseidon* for his arrogance.

Aladdin. In *The Arabian Nights*, a poor young man who finds a magic lamp which, when rubbed, produces a genie* that grants him three wishes.

Albany. In Shakespeare's play *King Lear* (1605), Goneril's* essentially kind husband; revolted by her behavior, he eventually repudiates her.

Alberich. In Richard Wagner's opera *Das Rheingold* (1869), a misshapen, greedy dwarf who, by forswearing love forever, is able to forge a ring from the Rhine gold that will give the wearer power to rule the world. He uses it to amass a fortune until Wotan* and Loge* trick him and take the ring, whereupon he issues the curse on the ring and its wearers that will lead to all the later tragic events in the *Ring* cycle. *See also* Brünnhilde; Fafner; Niebelung; Siegfried; Sieglinde, Siegmund; Valkyrie.

Albert. (1) Most English allusions will be to the historical Prince Albert (d. 1861), husband of Queen Victoria.* (2) *See* Johnny.

Albertine. In Marcel Proust's novels *Remembrance of Things Past* (1913–27), the dark-haired girl with whom the narrator Marcel* falls in love while a young man and with whom he conducts an extended but intermittent affair as she matures, marries someone else, and divorces; she is eventually revealed to be a lesbian but nonetheless contemplates marriage with Marcel, which is prevented when she is killed by a fall from a horse.

Albion. In British legend, the son of Poseidon* who came to Britain and taught the inhabitants to build ships; no Greek references to such a god are known. The name is also given to the island of Great Britain.

Albrecht. In the ballet *Giselle* (1841), the romantic prince who disguises himself as a peasant to court Giselle,* only to lose her when his lie is exposed and then to have her return as a spirit and save him from the revenge of the Wilis.*

Alceste. In Molière's play *The Misanthrope* (1666), the misanthrope; a man who rejects all forms of hypocrisy and makes many enemies by his social rigidity, he eventually goes away into the country to live isolated from society after his rejection by the beautiful Célimène.*

Alcestis. In Greek mythology, the loving wife of Admetus;* she agreed to die in his place. In some versions, she was brought back from Hades* by Heracles.*

Alcides. A name sometimes used for Heracles.*

Alcinous. In Homer's *Odyssey*, king of the Phaeacians to whom Odysseus* narrates his adventures before finally returning to Greece.

Alcmena. In Greek legend, mortal mother of Heracles* after her liaison with Zeus.* *See also* Amphitryon.

Alcyone. *See* Halcyone.

Alden, John. In Henry Wadsworth Longfellow's poem *The Courtship of Miles Standish* (1858), a young scholar who courts Priscilla* for another man (Standish*), until she says "Speak for yourself, John," and they realize they love each other.

Alden, Roberta. In Theodore Dreiser's novel *An American Tragedy* (1925), a poor factory girl who is killed by her lover Clyde Griffiths* after she tells him she is pregnant.

Aldrich, Henry. In the American radio series *The Aldrich Family* (beg. 1939), a wholesomely bumbling, innocent, and endearing American teenager.

Alecto. In Greek mythology, one of the Furies;* in Virgil's *Aeneid*, her intervention stirs up the war between the Latins and Aeneas.*

Alexander. Historically, the great Greek king (d. 323 B.C.) whose armies established an empire holding all the known world except India; in legend, he is also noted for cutting the Gordian Knot.* *See also* Bucephalus; Roxana; Thaïs.

Alexandra. *See* Nicholas.

Alexas. (1) In Shakespeare's play *Antony and Cleopatra* (1606), a witty attendant of Cleopatra.* *See also* Charmian. (2) In John Dryden's play *All For Love* (1677), Cleopatra's* eunuch, an inveterate political schemer and liar.

Alexis. *See* Carrington.

Alexis, St. In Christian legend, a wealthy Roman who forsook his wealth to live in poverty and who returned unrecognized to his father's house to live there as a servant.

Alfredo. *See* Germont.

Alger, Horatio. Historically, the author (d. 1899) of numerous novels; in common usage, his name has come to stand for all his heroes, poor but honest boys whose virtues and work ethic lead them to success, a symbol of people who pull themselves up by their own bootstraps.

Algernon. (1) In Oscar Wilde's play *The Importance of Being Earnest* (1895), a fashionable wit who pretends to be his friend Jack Worthing's* nonexistent brother in order to meet Cecily;* aside from numerous aphorisms, he is also noted for his use of the imaginary friend Bunbury.* *See also* Bracknell, Lady. (2) In Daniel Keyes's story *Flowers for Algernon* (1959), an experimental mouse who competes in intelligence with Charley.*

Ali. Historically, Mohammed's* cousin and son-in-law (d. 661) whose eyes were synonymous with beauty. The name is so common that many Westerners use it to signify any or all Arabs.

Ali Baba. In *The Arabian Nights*, the Persian woodcutter who discovers a great treasure by finding the secret cave of the Forty Thieves and opening it with the secret password, "Open, Sesame."

Alice. (1) In stories by Lewis Carroll beginning with *Alice in Wonderland* (1865), the intelligent, adventurous, and strong-willed young girl whose adventures begin when she falls down a rabbit hole; these include food which makes her change size and a trial for no particular charge at which she is condemned. For other experiences, *see* Caterpillar; Cheshire Cat; Dormouse; King of Hearts; Mad Hatter; March Hare; Mock Turtle; Queen of Hearts; Tweedledum; White Rabbit; William, Father. (2) In August Strindberg's play *The Dance of Death* (1900), Edgar's* long-tyrannized wife who taunts him on his deathbed. (3) *See* Munro.

Allah. The most common transliteration of the Arabic name for God.

Allan-a-Dale. In British folklore, Robin Hood's* minstrel.

Allen, Barbara. In the British and American ballad, a young woman in love. In dozens of variants, Barbara sees or allows her lover to die, sometimes in spite, and then dies of remorse herself. A rose grows out of his grave, a briar from hers, the two usually twining together.

Allworthy, Squire. In Henry Fielding's novel *Tom Jones* (1749), the just, virtuous, and thus gullible country gentleman who raises the orphan Tom Jones,* throws him out when his actions are misrepresented, and then is reconciled to him and makes him his heir. *See also* Blifil; Square; Thwackum.

Almanzor. In John Dryden's play *The Conquest of Granada* (1670), the epitome of the Restoration hero of serious drama.

Almaviva, Count. (1) In Beaumarchais's play (1775) and Rossini's opera (1816) *The Barber of Seville*, an ardent young noble in love with Rosine.* He later reappears in Beaumarchais's play (1784) and Mozart's opera (1786) *The Marriage of Figaro*, now married and a bored, aging roué. *See also* Figaro.

Almayer. In Joseph Conrad's novels *Almayer's Folly* (1895) and *An Outcast of the Islands* (1896), **Kaspar** is an unsuccessful trader in Malaya, deserted by his wife and wasting away as an opium addict, the quintessential weak white man destroyed by the tropics. His daughter **Nina** is a half-caste; educated as a European but outcast in European Singapore society, she returns to the jungle, marries a native, and refuses any further contact with whites.

Alonya. In Dostoevsky's novel *Crime and Punishment* (1866), the miserly pawnbroker murdered by Raskolnikov.*

Alphonse and Gaston. In the American newspaper cartoon *Alphonse and Gaston* (beg. 1902), two comic Frenchmen, noted particularly for their overexaggerated politeness.

Althaea. *See* Althea.

Althea. (1) In Ovid's *Metamorphoses*, mother of Meleager,* who was promised to live as long as a particular log remained unburned; in a fit of anger, she shoved the log into the fire, and he died. *See also* Oeneus. (2) Among seventeenth-century English poets, especially Lovelace, an idealized female lover.

Alving. In Henrik Ibsen's play *Ghosts* (1881), **Helen** is the tragic wife and mother; although her husband had been a drunk and a profligate, when she tried to run away to Manders,* he sent her back to her husband for the sake of her son Osvald. After she sends the child away to protect his idea of his father, her husband finally dies. **Osvald** returns, an artist who has lost his joy in life, suffering from a mistaken love for his father and an inherited venereal disease. He tries to revive himself through a marriage with the maid, but she is revealed to be his illegitimate sister, whereupon he goes mad.

Alyosha. *See* Karamazov.

Amadís de Gaul. In Vasco de Loveira's romance *Amadís de Gaul* (1508), the knightly hero, one of the fundamental exemplars of chivalrous romance.

Amalthea. In Greek legend, a Cretan princess who nursed the infant Zeus* on goat's milk. *See also* Melissa.

Amanda. *See* Elyot; Wingfield.

Amaryllis. In Roman literature, a stereotypical name for a shepherdess, often used for an attractive, natural maid in pastoral poems of later years.

Amazon. In Greek legend, a race of female warriors; at various times they were said to cut off one of their breasts in order to handle their bows more easily, to kill all their male children, and to fight as allies of the Trojans.* *See also* Antiope; Bellerophon; Hippolyta; Penthesilea; Theseus.

Amfortas. In Richard Wagner's opera *Parsifal* (1882), the wounded king whose pain sends Parsifal* on his quest of the Holy Grail.

Amintor. In Beaumont and Fletcher's play *The Maid's Tragedy* (1610), the honorable man who is ordered by the king to marry Evadne,* whom he does not love, only to discover later that she is the king's mistress. Torn between his real love Aspatia, his duty to the king, and his own honorable code of revenge for the destruction of his honor, he repudiates Evadne, accidentally kills Aspatia, and then commits suicide.

Amneris. In Verdi's opera *Aida* (1871), the Egyptian princess, jealous of the love between Aida* and Radames.*

Amnon. In the Bible, *II Samuel*, David's* eldest son; he rapes his half-sister Tamar* and is in turn killed by his half-brother Absalom.* *See also* Jonadab.

Amos. In the Bible, *Amos*, a herdsman who prophesied Israel's* downfall for her greed and oppression of the poor.

Amos 'n' Andy. In the American radio series (beg. 1928), and TV series (beg. 1951) ''Amos 'n' Andy'', **Andy** was a rather slow-witted black man, and **Amos**, his friend, was a more intelligent, hardworking cabdriver working his way into the lower middle class, but they are almost always referred to together. Early references are to their wit, humor, charm, and immense popularity; in the late sixties, they came to be used as a derogatory reference to all of the worst aspects of caricatured black stereotypes. *See also* Kingfish.

Amphitrite. In Roman mythology, the wife of Neptune.*

Amphitryon. In Greek mythology, husband of Alcmena;* in the most widely used source, Plautus's play *Amphitryon*, while Amphitryon is away, Zeus* takes on his form and sleeps with Alcmena, thereby fathering Heracles,* which produces much comic mystification when Amphitryon returns and finds that he has apparently been in two places at once.

Amy. In Louisa May Alcott's novel *Little Women* (1868), the sister who dreams of becoming an artist. *See also* Beth; Jo; Meg. (2) *See* Robsart, Amy.

Amyris. In Greek legend, a man who knew the truth of the future but who was thought by his listeners to be a fool.

Ana, Doña. In Mozart's opera *Don Giovanni* (1787), the woman whose seduction by Don Juan* leads to the death of the Commendatore,* her father. (2) In the *Don Juan in Hell* sequence from G. B. Shaw's play *Man and Superman*

(1905), the female nemesis from whom Don Juan* tries to escape by going to Hell.* *See also* Whitefield, Ann.

Ananias. (1) In the Bible, *Acts* v, a convert who sold his lands and promised to give the proceeds to Peter* but kept back part of the profits for personal use; God struck him and his wife Sapphira* dead for trying to lie to God. (2) In the Bible, *Acts* ix, a Christian in Damascus* who restored Paul's* sight after Paul had been blinded by his vision. (3) In the Bible, *Acts* xxiii, the high priest in Jerusalem* who arrested and persecuted Paul. (4) In Ben Jonson's play *The Alchemist* (1610), a quarrelsome fundamentalist Puritan.

Anastasia. (1) Historically, a daughter of Czar Nicholas* II of Russia; she entered twentieth-century folklore after her apparent assassination (1917) when many women surfaced in Europe and America claiming to be her in order to claim the Romanov fortunes that still existed outside Russia. She eventually became the subject of a popular play and movie and is often referred to both as a symbol of the tragedy of the Russian nobility after the communist revolution and as a symbol of fraudulent impersonations by fortune hunters. (2) *See also* Nastasia.

Anatol. In Arthur Schnitzler's play *Anatol* (1893), a shallow, if witty, lover, followed through a series of casual affairs.

Anaxarete. In Ovid's *Metamorphoses*, a cold-hearted beauty who was unmoved even when one of her rejected lovers hanged himself at her front door; she was turned to stone by Aphrodite.*

Anchises. In Greek mythology, a man of such beauty that the goddess Aphrodite* slept with him; the result of their union was the hero Aeneas.* His escape from burning Troy* as an old man on the back of his son is one of the most widely known passages from Virgil's *Aeneid*.

Ancient Mariner. *See* Mariner, Ancient.

Andrei. (1) The Russian form of Andrew.* (2) *See* Bolkonsky.

Andrew. (1) In the Bible, *Matthew*, Peter's* brother, and with Peter, the first of the twelve Apostles;* in *John* i, he is indicated as the one who brings Peter to Jesus.* He is normally depicted with a cross in the shape of the letter X, on which he was crucified, and which in legend appeared to the kings of the Picts and the Scots before a great battle and thus became the national emblem of Scotland. He is the patron saint of both Scotland and prerevolutionary Russia. (2) *See* Aguecheek, Sir Andrew; Ferrara, Andrew. (3) *See also* Andy.

Andrew, St. Andrew* the Apostle.

Andrews, Joseph. In Henry Fielding's novel *Joseph Andrews* (1742), a virtuous, handsome, and exceedingly simple young man who unwittingly finds himself involved in amorous adventures he neither desires nor understands. *See also* Fanny.

Andrews, Pamela. In Samuel Richardson's novel *Pamela* (1740), the virtuous servant girl who, after repelling numerous assaults on her virtue by the young squire Mr. B————,* manages to get him to marry her.

Androcles. In Christian legend, a runaway Roman slave who pulled a thorn from a lion's paw; he was later captured and thrown to the lions in the arena, where the same lion recognized and refused to eat him.

Andromache. In Greek legend, the wife of Hector* and mother of Astyanax;* in Homer's *Iliad*, one of the most noted scenes is Hector's last farewell to her before the battle in which he is killed. In Euripides's play *The Trojan Women*, she sees Astyanax taken from her arms to his death. *See also* Helenus; Pyrrhus.

Andromeda. In Greek legend, daughter of Cassiopeia* and a beautiful maiden chained to a rock to be sacrificed to a sea monster but rescued by Perseus,* who married her; after her death, she was changed into a constellation. *See also* Phineus.

Andronicus, Titus. *See* Titus Andronicus.

Andy. *See* Amos 'n' Andy; Handy Andy; Hardy, Andy.

Angel. In the Bible, a heavenly servant of God. Angels take many forms, sometimes merely human and sometimes, as in Ezekiel's* vision, having multiple faces, wings, and calf's feet. In Christian usage, they are almost always human in appearance, with the addition of wings, and wearing white robes. Although generally depicted as young men in Renaissance art, since the nineteenth century, most popular representations have shown them as women, except for the cherubim,* who are depicted as young boys with wings. Angels participate in many significant events in the Bible, including the announcement to Mary* that she would conceive the child Jesus;* the rescue of Shadrach,* Meshach, and Abednego in the fiery furnace and of Daniel* in the lion's den; the wrestling match with Jacob;* and the killing of the troops of Sennacherib.* One was recognized by Balaam's* ass. In folklore, all the sins and good deeds of humanity are entered in a book by the ''Recording Angel,'' Satan* was also said to have been an angel until he was cast out of Heaven,* most prominently noted from John Milton's poem *Paradise Lost*. Other angels whose names are known include Azaziel,* Azrael,* Belial,* Gabriel,* Israfel,* Michael,* and Raphael.* *See also* Archangel; Seraphim.

Angelica. (1) In Ariosto's *Orlando Furioso* (1532), a Chinese princess who drives Orlando* mad with love; she also is enchanted and is offered for sacrifice, but is saved by Rogero,* who forgets his true love and gives her his magic ring, which she uses to make herself invisible and leave him. She then nurses back to health the Saracen Medoro, whom she takes back to Cathay. (2) In William Congreve's play *Love for Love* (1695), the clever young woman loved by Valentine.*

Angelo. In Shakespeare's play *Measure for Measure* (1604), the rigid and puritanical deputy who, left in charge when the Duke leaves the city, arrests and condemns the young Claudio* for impregnating his fiancée. Angelo offers to drop the charges if Claudio's sister Isabella* will sleep with him; she refuses, then agrees, but substitutes Angelo's rejected lover, whom he is then forced to marry.

Anitra. In Henrik Ibsen's play *Peer Gynt* (1867), a seductive dancing girl who also robs Peer Gynt.*

Ann. (1) *See* Whitefield, Ann. (2) *See also* Ana, Doña; Anna; Anne; Anya.

Anna. *See* Christie, Anna; Karenina, Anna; Odintsov, Anna. (2) *See also* Ana, Doña; Anne; Anya.

Anna Livia Plurabelle. In James Joyce's novel *Finnegan's Wake* (1939), Earwicker's* wife, a remarkably complex symbolic character of many shapes, in some allusions a symbol of symbolic characters. At various times she is Eve,* Iseult,* Isis,* a consistent personification of love, and, most complexly, a river.

Anne. (1) *See* Boleyn, Anne; Elliot; Frank, Anne. (2) *See also* Ann; Anna; Anya.

Anne, Lady. (1) In Shakespeare's play *Richard III* (1592), the woman who succumbs to Richard III's* wooing despite her knowledge that he had had her much-loved husband murdered. (2) *See* Boleyn, Anne.

Annie, Little Orphan. (1) In the American newspaper cartoon *Little Orphan Annie* (beg. 1924), a little orphan girl, noted for her optimism, her dog Sandy, and the style of drawing that never showed any irises inside her eye circles; also the subject of the musical comedy *Annie* (1977). *See also* Warbucks, Daddy. (2) *See also* Little Orphant Annie.

Annunciation. In Christian usage, the announcement made to Mary* that she would bear the Son of God; in the religious calendar, this is celebrated on March 25. Occasionally, the term is also applied to the announcement that Jesus* had been born given to the shepherds* in the fields.

Anse. *See* Bundren.

Anselm, St. Historically, an English bishop and theologian (d. 1109) canonized for his philosophical writings and great spirit. His symbol is a ship, his day is April 21.

Antaeus. In Greek legend, a powerful giant wrestler who was invincible as long as he maintained contact with the earth; Heracles* strangled him after lifting him off the ground.

Anthony, Mark. *See* Antony, Marc.

Anthony, St. Historically, a hermit saint (d. 356), noted for his fervent resistance to all temptations of the flesh, depicted in numerous paintings. He is also often the saint to whom one goes for help in finding lost items; his day is January 17.

Antichrist. In the Bible, *I John* ii, an opponent who endangered the Church, soon developed in theology and folklore into the great opponent who would lead the forces of evil at Armageddon,* identified with the Beast,* and often applied as well to anyone who posed a significant threat to the true Christian religion.

Antigone. In Greek legend, a daughter of Oedipus.* In Sophocles's play *Antigone*, she violates Creon's* command and buries her brother Polynices,* because it is the "right" thing to do, and she forces Creon to execute her for the crime. As such, she is often used as a symbol of the individual in opposition to the power of the state or the upholder of universal truth as opposed to the expediencies of political necessity. In *Oedipus at Colonnus*, she is her blind father's guide. *See also* Eteocles; Haemon; Ismene.

Antinous. In Homer's *Odyssey*, the most arrogant and cruelest suitor of Penelope* and the first to be killed by Odysseus.*

Antiope. In Greek legend, a queen of the Amazons,* sometimes the sister of Hippolyta* and sometimes another name for Hippolyta.

Antipholus. In Shakespeare's play *The Comedy of Errors* (1593), twin brothers, long separated, who accidentally find themselves in the same city and, after much comic confusion, are eventually reunited. *See also* Dromio.

Ántonia. *See* Shimerda, Ántonia.

Antonio. A name much used by English writers for Italian characters. Allusions to the name are generally to Antonio, the actual merchant in Shakespeare's play *The Merchant of Venice* (1596), whose pound of flesh has been promised to Shylock;* however, allusions also are made to the captain who risks his life to help Sebastian* in Shakespeare's play *Twelfth Night* (1599), and to the subversive brother of Prospero* in Shakespeare's play *The Tempest* (1611). *See also* Changeling, The.

Antony, Marc. Historically, Julius Caesar's* adopted son who failed and died (30 B.C.) in the civil war with Octavius;* in literature, especially Shakespeare's play *Antony and Cleopatra* (1606) and John Dryden's play *All For Love* (1677), he is a tragic lover who sacrifices his honor and the possibility of becoming Emperor of Rome for his love of Cleopatra.* References to his oration are to the speech he makes at Caesar's funeral in Shakespeare's play *Julius Caesar* (1599), which begins, "Friends, Romans, countrymen, lend me your ears" and is built around the ironic refrain that "Brutus* is an honorable man." *See also* Enobarbus; Caesar, Augustus; Octavia.

Antrobus. In Thornton Wilder's play *The Skin of Our Teeth* (1942), **George** is a symbolic Everyman* character—inventor, philosopher, artist, and father of the family but tempted by the sins of the flesh. **Mrs. Antrobus** is the tenacious mother, willing to sacrifice anyone or anything to protect her children, while their son **Henry** represents Cain* and all the destructive tendencies of humankind, and their daughter **Gladys** has a baby after she is raped. *See also* Sabina.

Anya. (1) In Anton Chekhov's play *The Cherry Orchard* (1904), Ranevskaya's* virginal daughter who falls in love with the student Trofimov.* *See also* Gaev; Varya. (2) *See also* Anna.

Aphrodite. In Greek mythology, the goddess of love, called Venus* by the Romans. Said to be the daughter of Zeus* and Dione,* she was also said to be the daughter of Thalassa,* the sea, or to have sprung full-grown from the sea foams. She was married to Hephaestus* but was known for her numerous affairs, the most noted of which were those with Ares,* who was caught in flagrante delicto with her in a net by Hephaestus; with Anchises,* which made her the mother of Aeneas;* and with Adonis.* After Paris* chose her as the most beautiful of the goddesses, she tried to interfere in the Trojan War* on the Trojan side but she was defeated by the combined opposition of Hera* and Athena.* For other participations in the affairs of mortals, *see* Anaxarete; Dryope; Galatea; Glaucus; Phaon; Pygmalion; Psyche. *Also called* Astarte;* Cytherea; Eriboea; Paphia; Pelagia; Pontia. *See also* Diomedes; Dryope; Hermaphroditus; Phryne; Rose.

Apley, George. In John P. Marquand's novel *The Late George Apley* (1937), a perfectly proper, upper-class, old line Bostonian, neither too bright nor too ambitious and ultimately undistinguished.

Apollo. In Greek, and later in Roman, mythology, the god of the sun, music, poetry, and manly youth and beauty; often portrayed holding a lyre, or simply as an ideal male beauty, and as such the subject of numerous ancient statues. He was the son of Zeus* and Leto* and twin brother of Artemis.* He was also often noted as a god of prophecy, particularly in relation to his oracle* at Delphi.* Hermes* stole his sacred cattle at birth, and Odysseus's* men later killed and ate some of the same herd, for which Apollo drowned them. He also sent a plague to the Greeks when they refused to surrender his priestess Chryseis,* thereby setting in train the events that kept Achilles* out of battle in Homer's *Iliad*, and he tried to protect Orestes* from the Furies.* For other participations in the affairs of mortals, *see* Cassandra; Hyacinthus; Laomedon; Niobe; Phlegyas. For his amorous adventures, *see* Acantha; Chione; Clytia; Creusa; Daphne; Marpessa. He is sometimes identified with Helios,* the sun. *Also called* Cynthius; Delius; Phoebus. *See also* Battus; Daedalion; Hyacinthus; Ion; Midas; Phaeton.

Apollonia, St. Historically, a Christian martyr (d. 249) who walked into the flames voluntarily rather than renounce her faith. Also, her teeth were knocked out before her death, which led to her association with toothaches. Her symbol is a forceps holding a tooth, her day is February 9.

Apollyon. (1) In the Bible, *Revelation* ix, the god of the bottomless pit. (2) In John Bunyan's *Pilgrim's Progress* (1678), a winged dragon with whom Christian* battles for half a day in the Valley of Humiliation.

Apostles, The. In the Bible, the first twelve disciples of Jesus.* According to *Matthew*, they were Peter,* Andrew,* two men called James,* John,* Philip,* Bartholomew,* Thomas,* Matthew,* Thaddeus,* Simon,* and Judas.* Nathaniel* is mentioned only in *John* and is thought to be another name for Bartholomew, and Jude* is listed in *Luke* in place of Thaddeus. In *Acts*, Matthias* was selected to replace Judas. Paul* is often called Paul the Apostle for his work in spreading the religion, although he did not convert until after the Crucifixion.*

Apothecary. In Shakespeare's play *Romeo and Juliet* (1595), a pitiful wretch who sells Romeo* the poison with which he kills himself.

Apple, The. (1) In Christian legend, the fruit of the forbidden Tree of Knowledge, never specifically identified in *Genesis*, which Eve* ate at the serpent's* urging and then gave to Adam* to eat, resulting in their expulsion from the Garden of Eden.* (2) *See* Eris; Hesperides; Iduna.

Aquinas. *See* Thomas, St.

Arachne. In Ovid's *Metamorphoses*, a mortal girl who challenged Athena* to a weaving contest; when Athena ripped up her cloth, she hanged herself and was changed into a spider.

Aram. In the Bible, *Genesis* x, a son of Shem.*

Aram, Eugene. In Edward Bulwer-Lytton's novel *Eugene Aram* (1832), the over-reaching scientist who accidentally kills a man in order to further his experiments and is executed.

Aramis. In Alexandre Dumas's novel *The Three Musketeers* (1844), one of the Three Musketeers, noted for his religious tendencies and his taste for black, simple dress. *See also* Athos; D'Artagnan; Porthos.

Ararat, Mt. *See* Flood, The.

Arc, Joan of. *See* Jeanne d'Arc.

Arcadia. Historically, a mountainous region of Greece, in legend noted as the home of Pan* and generally seen as an ideal land of rustic simplicity and happiness, populated by beautiful shepherdesses and romantic shepherds playing on pipes, most notably in Philip Sidney's romance *Arcadia* (1590).

Arcas. In Greek legend, a king of Arcadia* who almost killed his mother Callisto* when she was changed into a bear; he was later changed into the constellation Ursa Minor.

Arcati, Madame. In Noel Coward's play *Blithe Spirit* (1941), the practical, bicycle-riding medium, notable for her tweedy, English schoolmistress solidity in place of the usual mediumistic hocus-pocus.

Archangel. In Christian lore, superior angels* who deal directly with God and lead or supervise other angels; according to *Revelation*, there are seven, but throughout the Bible, only four are given names: Gabriel,* Michael,* Raphael,* and Uriel.*

Archer. In George Farquhar's play *The Beaux' Strategem* (1707), one of the two beaux; he disguises himself as a servant and develops a lively comic romance with the vivacious Cherry.* *See also* Aimwell.

Archer, Isabel. In Henry James's novel *The Portrait of a Lady* (1881), an initially unworldly American girl of great beauty who goes to Europe, is admired by many men, and eventually marries the aesthete Gilbert Osmond.* Although disillusioned by the more sordid aspects of accepted society life, she manages to maintain a ladylike existence.

Archer, Lew. In numerous novels by Ross MacDonald (beg. 1951), a tough, honest, and sensitive private detective in the Los Angeles area.

Archimago. In Edmund Spenser's poem *The Faerie Queene* (1590), a villain who assumes many disguises to lure knights and ladies into sin. *See also* Duessa.

archy. In a series (1916–30) of unrhymed, uncapitalized, and unpunctuated poems by Don Marquis, a cockroach who observes the world and writes his reports by leaping headfirst onto the typewriter keys; he is madly in love with mehitabel* the cat, but the love is unrequited.

Arcite. *See* Palamon.

Arden, Enoch. In Tennyson's poem *Enoch Arden* (1864), a fisherman who is shipwrecked and presumed lost, so that his wife Annie marries his friend. Years later, when he returns, rather than upset Annie, he decides not to reveal himself and leaves with a broken heart.

Arden, Forest of. In Shakespeare's play *As You Like It* (1599), the forest to which the exiled Duke Senior* and his followers, and later Rosalind,* go to live an idyllic existence.

Ardennes, Wild Boar of. *See* Wild Boar of Ardennes.

Ares. In Greek mythology, the god of war, called Mars by the Romans. In Greek sources, he tends to be hot-tempered and even dishonorable, but the Romans depict him with greater dignity and honor. Perhaps because of his occupation in warfare, he has a minimal lore. His most notable amorous adventure is with Aphrodite,* for which he is publicly humiliated when Hephaestus* catches them in a net. His most noted military appearance is in Homer's *Iliad*, where he fights on the Trojan* side and is wounded by the mortal Diomedes,* and also is captured by Otus,* who keeps him sealed in a jar for thirteen months. *Also called* Quirinus. *See also* Eris; Melanippe; Panic; Phobos.

Arethusa. In Ovid's *Metamorphoses*, a nymph* whom Artemis* changes into a sacred stream in order to prevent a river god from seducing her.

Argan. In Molière's play *Le Malade imaginaire* (1673), the quintessential hypochondriac. *See also* Diafoirus; Toinette.

Argives. In Homer's *Iliad*, one of the names used for the Greeks.

Argonauts. In Greek legend, Jason* and his 55 followers on the ship Argo, who ventured in search of the Golden Fleece.* They included Admetus,* Aesculapius,* Euryalus,* and, for a time, Heracles.* *See also* Hypsipyle.

Argos. (1) In Greek legend, a part of Greece in which was the kingdom ruled by Agamemnon.* *See also* Danaus. (2) In Greek legend, a herdsman set to guard Io* by the jealous Hera* because he had eyes all over his body; after Hermes* killed him, his eyes were placed in the peacock's tail.

Ariadne. In Greek legend, the daughter of King Minos* of Crete. She told Theseus* the secret of the Labyrinth,* gave him the ball of yarn that he used to find his way out, and eloped with him, only to be deserted by him on the island of Naxos in favor of her sister Phaedra.* Some sources say she later married the god Bacchus.* *See also* Minotaur.

Aricie. In Jean Racine's play *Phèdre* (1677), the young woman preferred by Hippolyte.*

Ariel. In Shakespeare's play *The Tempest* (1611), Prospero's* spirit servant.

Arion. In Greek legend, a poet who, when thrown overboard by sailors trying to rob him, was carried to shore by a dolphin who liked his singing.

Ark. (1) In the Bible, *Genesis* vi–ix, the ship which God ordered Noah* to build in order to survive the great Flood* and in which Noah took two of every animal in order to repopulate the earth. (2) In the Bible, *Deuteronomy* x, the Ark of the Covenant, which Moses* built to carry the Ten Commandments;* eventually David* and Solomon* built a temple in Jerusalem* to house it permanently.

Arkadina, Irina. In Anton Chekhov's play *The Sea Gull* (1896), an aging, great, but egotistical, self-centered actress, unable to establish a sincere relationship with either her lover Trigorin* or her son Constantin,* which eventually helps push the latter to suicide.

Arkady. *See* Kirsanov.

Arlequino. *See* Harlequin.

Armado. In Shakespeare's play *Love's Labour's Lost* (1595), the braggart Spaniard.

Armageddon. In the Bible, *Revelation*, the final battle between the forces of darkness and light. *See also* Second Coming.

Armstrong, Jack. In the American radio series "Jack Armstrong" (1933–51), the "All-American Boy."

Arnold, Dr. Historically, headmaster of Rugby school (d. 1842), noted for his redefinition of the English public school curriculum and practice, and for his portrayal in Thomas Hughes's novel *Tom Brown's Schooldays* (1857), as the strict, ideal schoolmaster.

Arnolphe. In Molière's play *The School For Wives* (1662), the jealous old man who tries to maneuver his ward Agnes* into becoming his wife.

Arrowsmith. In Sinclair Lewis's novel *Arrowsmith* (1924), the dedicated doctor/researcher who finds that his integrity makes him a misfit in the medical world, until eventually he finds happiness only in his private laboratory in the Vermont woods.

Arsinoé. (1) In Greek legend, the nurse of Orestes;* she saved him from being murdered by Aegisthus* by substituting her own son in the bed of Orestes. (2) In Molière's play *The Misanthrope* (1666), the jealous prude.

Artaxerxes. In the Bible, *Ezra* vii, the King of Persia who allowed Ezra* and the Jews to return to Israel.*

Artemis. In Greek mythology, daughter of Zeus* and twin sister of Apollo,* called Diana* by the Romans. Goddess of the moon and of hunting, and sometimes mentioned as goddess of childbirth, she is portrayed with a bow, silver arrows, the moon, deer, and/or the cypress tree. Often called the virgin huntress, she is not noted for her own amorous adventures, sleeping with Endymion,* for example, only in his dreams. Her appearances in the affairs of mortals are often associated with the protection of chastity. *See* Arethusa; Britomartis. For other significant appearances, *see* Actaeon; Iphigenia; Niobe; Oeneus; Chione. *Also called* Astarte;* Cynthia;* Delia; Hecate;* Luna;* Selene. *See also* Oreades.

Artful Dodger. In Charles Dickens's novel *Oliver Twist* (1837), the clever young pickpocket who introduces Oliver Twist* to the criminal Fagin.*

Arthur. In British legend, most completely codified in Malory's *Morte d'Arthur*, a great king of Britain. As a youth, he pulled out a sword magically imbedded in a stone. By means of his sword Excalibur,* with which he was invincible, he unified the land and brought all the knights together in Camelot,* where they sat as equals at the Round Table. His queen Guinevere* eventually betrayed him in an affair with Lancelot,* and in the civil war that resulted, Arthur was killed and his body was carried away by the Lady of the Lake* to Avalon,* from which he will someday return; hence his title as the "once and future king." For his knights, *see* Balin; Bedivere; Dinadan; Gaheris; Galahad; Gareth; Gawain; Kay; Mordred; Pellinore; Pelleas; Percival; Tristram. *See also* Connecticut Yankee; Dagonet; Ector; Galapas; Igraine; Merlin; Morgan le Fay; Red Cross Knight; Roland, Childe; Uther Pendragon.

Arviragus. *See* Dorigen.

Asa. In the Bible, *I Kings* xv, a king of Judah* who destroyed all the idols set up by his father Abijah and drove the sodomites from the land.

Ascalaphus. In Greek legend, the son of Acheron.* He told Pluto* that Persephone* had eaten after she had been forbidden to do so, and he was changed into an owl by Demeter* as a result.

Ascanius. In Virgil's *Aeneid*, the son of Aeneas.*

Ascension. In the Bible, *Acts* i, Jesus's* actual ascent into Heaven,* occurring 40 days after His Resurrection.*

Ashenden. In Somerset Maugham's novel *Ashenden* (1927), a morally neutral, unromantic, technician spy, one of the first such in popular literature.

Asher. In the Bible, *Genesis* xxxv, a son of Jacob* and Zilpah* and father of one of the twelve tribes of Israel.*

Ashley. *See* Wilkes, Ashley.

Ashley, Lady Brett. In Ernest Hemingway's novel *The Sun Also Rises* (1926), a beauty who is also an alcoholic, flagrantly promiscuous, bitchy, and yet somehow oddly childlike and touching, a signal member of the Lost Generation.* *See also* Barnes, Jake.

Ashton, Lucy. In Walter Scott's novel *The Bride of Lammermoor* (1819), a young woman who goes mad and dies on her wedding night when she is forced to marry a man she does not love. *See also* Lucia.

Asmodeus. In the Bible, in the Apochrypha, *Tobit*, the demon of vanity; he causes Sara's* first seven husbands to die before the eighth, Tobias,* with the angel Raphael,* drives him out to Egypt.

Aspatia. In Beaumont and Fletcher's play *The Maid's Tragedy* (1619), a woman who bears great sorrows with patience; when her lover marries another, she disguises herself as a man and challenges him to a duel in which she is killed.

Assumption. In Christian legend, the ascent of Mary's* soul into Heaven,* followed three days later by her body's ascent.

Asta. In a series of movies, beginning with *The Thin Man* (1934), the unpredictable terrier belonging to Nick and Nora Charles.*

Astarte. A Phoenician goddess of fertility, sexual love, and the moon, sometimes mentioned in Greek writings and identified with Aphrodite* and/or Artemis.* *Also called* Ishtar.*

Astolfo. In Ariosto's *Orlando Furioso* (1532), a knight who takes a fabulous journey on the Hippogriff* to the land of Prester John* and to the moon, where he finds the lost wits of Orlando,* which he returns to restore him to sanity.

Astraea. In Roman mythology, the goddess of justice, often seen as a symbol of purity or innocence.

Astrophel. In Philip Sidney's poem *Astrophel and Stella* (1591), the disappointed yet still passionate lover of Stella.*

Astrov. In Anton Chekhov's play *Uncle Vanya* (1900), a depressed doctor who allows his practice and his plans for his dream of reforestation to decline while in love with Helena Serebryakov;* when she leaves, he remains with the hope that he can resume his old life. *See also* Sonya.

Astyanax. In Greek legend, and particularly in Euripides's play *The Trojan Women*, the young son of Hector* and Andromache;* he is saved from the sack of Troy* only to be murdered at Odysseus's* command, for fear he might avenge his father and the city when he grows up. *See also* Talthybius.

Atala. In Chateaubriand's novel *Atala* (1801), a Christian Indian maiden who, unable to fulfill her vow to become a nun because of her love for a brave, kills herself; her burial near a mountain stream is a much admired passage.

Atalanta. In Ovid's *Metamorphoses*, an athletic girl who desires perpetual virginity. When a marriage is proposed, she races the suitor; if he loses, he is put to death. Finally one, with the help of Venus,* outruns her by throwing golden apples in her path, which she stops to pick up, and he marries her. This may or may not be the same Atalanta to whom Meleager* gave the head of the Calydonian Boar.* *See also* Hesperides.

Ate. A name sometimes used for Eris.*

Athaliah. In the Bible, *II Kings* xi, the daughter of Jezebel.* When her son died, she killed all the remaining descendants of the royal house of Judah* and ruled as queen. One child, however, was saved; a rebellion formed around him, and she was killed.

Athalie. In Jean Racine's play *Athalie* (1691), Athaliah.*

Athena. In Greek mythology, goddess of wisdom, skilled crafts, and warfare, called Minerva* by the Romans; special protector of the city of Athens, she is usually represented in armor and helmet, carrying a shield, or with the owl, or with her special tree, the olive,* and she is often described as "grey-eyed." One of the most prominent of all the gods in literature, she is supposed to have been born when her mother Metis* was swallowed by Zeus* and Athena emerged full-grown from his head. She is reputed to have caused the Trojan War* when Paris* did not select her as the most beautiful of all goddesses, and she served as a consistent guide and meddler on the Greek side in that war, as well as the protector of Odysseus* and his family during his odyssey. She also acquitted Orestes* when he was tried for the murder of his mother. *Also called* Pallas; Parthenos; Tritonia. *See also* Ajax; Arachne; Ipthime; Tiresias; Tydeus.

Athene. *See* Athena.

Athos. In Alexandre Dumas's novel *The Three Musketeers* (1844), one of the musketeers, a nervy noble in disguise whose dark secret is a bad marriage. *See also* Aramis; D'Artagnan; Porthos.

Atlantis. In Plato's *Kritias*, a legendary kingdom destroyed by a great earthquake and flood. The story has been retold in countless versions, the most influential being Ignatius Donnelly's *Atlantis* (1882), almost all of which see it as a kingdom of peace and beauty. The country has been sited in countless places, and in some versions it is even thought to be a city still in existence with highly evolved or super-technical humans able to live under the sea.

Atlas. In Greek mythology, a Titan* who was said to hold the world on his shoulders; also, father of the Pleiades.* *See also* Perseus.

Atreus. In Greek legend, a noble who fed his brother Thyestes* his own son and, as father of Agamemnon,* founded the family that would provide some of the most persistently used stories of family discord and tragedy in all literature. *See also* Aegeus; Aegisthus; Ariadne; Cassandra; Clytemnestra; Electra; Helen; Hermione; Hippodamia; Hippolytus; Iphigenia; Menelaus; Orestes; Phaedra; Theseus.

Atropos. *See* Fates.

Attila. Historically, leader of the Huns* (d. 453) when they invaded Europe, the epitome of barbarianism and brutality.

Auberon. *See* Oberon.

Aucassin. *See* Nicolette.

Audrey. In Shakespeare's play *As You Like It* (1599), the stupid, homely, dirty, but good-hearted country girl who marries Touchstone.*

Augean Stables. In Greek legend, the sixth labor of Heracles;* they contained 3,000 cattle and had not been cleaned for 30 years, and hence stand for something incredibly filthy.

Augeus. *See* Augean Stables.

Augustine, St. Historically, a bishop (d. 604) and great theologian; his popular reputation derives from a profligate youthful life which he renounced upon baptism to enter a monastic life, recounted in his *Confessions*. *See also* Monica, St.

Augustus. *See* Caesar, Augustus.

Aurelia. In Goethe's novel *Wilhelm Meister's Apprenticeship* (1796), a woman who, when deserted by her lover Lothario,* takes in the child of Wilhelm Meister's* mistress Mariana* and cares for it.

Aurelius. *See* Dorigen.

Aurelius, Marcus. Historically, emperor of Rome (d. 180), noted primarily as the author of his *Meditations*, one of the finest statements in history of a personal philosophy and of the Stoic outlook in particular.

Aurora. In Greek mythology, the goddess of the dawn. *Also called* Eos; Hespera. *See also* Cephalus; Tithonus. (2) *See* Leigh.

Autolycus. (1) In Greek mythology, a son of Hermes* and a famous thief who stole the cattle of Sisyphus.* *See also* Chione. (2) In Shakespeare's play *The Winter's Tale* (1610), a charming, witty thief and con man, one of Shakespeare's most popular characters, especially in the nineteenth century.

Avalon. In Malory's *Morte d'Arthur*, the island to which the dying Arthur* is taken, there to await his ultimate return; often used for a land of happiness and peace.

Avdotya. *See* Dounia.

Aviragus. *See* Dorigen.

Ayesha. (1) Historically, the favorite wife of Mohammed;* she lost her necklace in a dubious fashion, as a result of which legend says Moslem women have been maintained in seclusion since. (2) In H. Rider Haggard's novel *She* (1887), the name of She-Who-Must-Be-Obeyed.*

Azazil. In John Milton's poem *Paradise Lost* (1667), the standard-bearer of Satan's* force of rebel angels.*

Aziz. In E. M. Forster's novel *A Passage to India* (1924), a sensitive and intelligent Indian who is accused of attempted rape by an Englishwoman and comes to represent the irreconcilable cultural differences and problems of British colonialism in India. *See also* Moore, Mrs.; Malabar Caves; Quested, Adela.

Azrael. In Jewish and Moslem mythology, the angel* who separates the soul from the dead body, often referred to as the Angel of Death.

Azucena. In Verdi's opera *Il Trovatore* (1853), the gypsy woman, the ultimate operatic gypsy.

B

B———, **Mr.** *See* Andrews, Pamela.

Baal. In the Bible, the false god of the Phoenicians, generally associated with greed, pestilence, and evil, and the source for many names of devils,* such as Beelzebub.*

Baba, Ali. *See* Ali Baba.

Baba, Hajji. *See* Hajji Baba.

Babberley, Fancourt. In Brandon Thomas's play *Charley's Aunt* (1892), the genial student who is forced to impersonate Charley's Aunt* from Brazil.

Babbitt. In Sinclair Lewis's novel *Babbitt* (1922), a middle-American real estate salesman who, after a momentary fling with liberal opinions, returns to the unthinking small-town boosterism of his acquaintances; hence, an uncultured, small-minded, and money-oriented American businessman.

Babe. *See* Bunyan, Paul.

Babel, Tower of. In the Bible, *Genesis* xi, a great tower by means of which men tried to reach Heaven;* God destroyed the tower and, as punishment, gave mankind different languages to create confusion among them.

Babs. *See* Babberley, Fancourt.

Babu. In Hindu, a title of respect; among Westerners, it came to be applied insultingly to any semi-educated Indian.

Babylon, Whore of. *See* Scarlet Woman, The.

Bacchae. Historically, priestesses of Dionysus.* In Euripides's play *The Bacchae*, they become so frenzied that they tear apart Pentheus,* who has penetrated their rites disguised as a woman. *Also called* Bacchantes; Maenads. *See also* Agave.

Bacchantes. *See* Bacchae.

Bacchus. In Roman mythology, the god of wine; although roughly equivalent to Dionysus,* he is usually depicted as much more jovial—a jolly, fat little drunkard. He is sometimes said to have married Ariadne.* *See also* Silenus.

Backbite. In R. B. Sheridan's play *The School for Scandal* (1777), a scandalmonger. *See also* Sneerwell, Lady.

Bacon, Friar. In Robert Greene's play *Friar Bacon and Friar Bungay* (1589), a scholar/magician who, through his servant's stupidity, sleeps through the secret of wisdom spoken by his brass bust. Based on folklore concerning the historical Francis Bacon.

Badger. In Charles Dickens's novel *Bleak House* (1852), **Bayham** is a doctor who takes great pride in the fact that **Mrs. Badger's** previous husbands were a Navy captain and a scientist.

Baggins, Bilbo. In J. R. R. Tolkien's novel *The Hobbit* (1937), a gentle hobbit* who ventured from home and stole a magic ring that would have made the wearer all-powerful, but declined to ever use it for such a purpose, ultimately bequeathing it to his cousin Frodo.*

Bagnet. In Charles Dickens's novel *Bleak House* (1852), a retired soldier, bluff, hearty, and admiring of his wife, whom he calls The Old Girl. When he becomes upset, he always tells her to tell them what he thinks.

Bagstock, Major. In Charles Dickens's novel *Dombey and Son* (1846), the retired major who introduces Dombey* to Edith,* becomes the unrequited subject of Miss Tox's* affections, and always discusses himself in the third person with an apparently endless series of nicknames.

Bailey, Beetle. In the American newspaper cartoon *Beetle Bailey* (beg. 1950), an Army private noted for his less-than-enthusiastic participation in military life.

Bailey, Harry. In Chaucer's *Canterbury Tales*, the host of the inn who organizes the storytelling contest.

Bajazet. (1) In Jean Racine's play *Bajazet* (1672), a Turkish prince imprisoned by his brother. When he is released by Roxane,* he tries to take the throne but spurns her love in favor of another; she then allows him to be strangled by a gang of mute assassins. (2) *See also* Bajazeth.

Bajazeth. (1) In Christopher Marlowe's play *Tamburlaine the Great* (1586), the emperor of the Turks who, when defeated by Tamburlaine,* is exhibited in a cage until, humiliated, he kills himself by smashing his head against the bars. (2) *See also* Bajazet.

Baker St. In numerous stories by Arthur Conan Doyle and others, Sherlock Holmes* and Dr. Watson* share quarters at 221B.

Balaam. In the Bible, *Numbers* xxii, a prophet who was met by an angel* which he failed to recognize until the ass on which he was riding refused to advance and spoke to Balaam.

Balan. *See* Balin.

Balder. *See* Baldur.

Baldur. In Scandinavian mythology, god of the summer sun; he could be harmed only by mistletoe, a twig of which pierced his heart.

Balfour, David. In R. L. Stevenson's novel *Kidnapped* (1886), the honorable young man who is almost cheated out of his inheritance by the kidnapping arranged by his greedy, miserly uncle. *See also* Breck, Alan.

Balin. In Malory's *Morte d'Arthur*, Balin and his brother Balan are knights of Arthur's* court who, failing to recognize each other's armor, fight and kill each other. In Tennyson's *Idylls of the King* (1885), the story is retold with Balin enraged by jealousy and Balan thinking him a demon.

Balius. In Homer's *Iliad*, one of the immortal horses of Achilles.* *See also* Xanthus.

Balthasar. (1) In Shakespeare's play *Romeo and Juliet* (1595), the servant who tells Romeo* that Juliet* has died. (2) In Shakespeare's play *The Merchant of Venice* (1596), the name used by Portia* in disguise. (3) *See also* Balthazar.

Balthazar. In Christian legend, one of the Magi.* (2) *See also* Balthasar.

Bambi. In Felix Salten's novel *Bambi* (1929), a fawn who grows to maturity in the forest, an especially common symbol of sentimental gentleness and purity owing to Walt Disney's* movie cartoon version (1942).

Bandersnatch. In Lewis Carroll's poem *Jabberwocky* (1872), a hypothetical beast that one should shun because it is "frumious."

Banquo. In Shakespeare's play *Macbeth* (1605), the noble friend who is murdered because witches prophesied his children would sit on Macbeth's* throne and whose ghost appears at Macbeth's banquet. *See also* Fleance; Weird Sisters.

Banshee. In Irish and Scottish folklore, a female spirit whose wailing foretells a death.

Baptist. *See* John the Baptist.

Baptista. In Shakespeare's play *The Taming of the Shrew* (1593), the wealthy father who refuses to allow his gentle daughter Bianca* to marry until after her sister Kate* the shrew is wed.

Barabas. (1) In Christopher Marlowe's play *The Jew of Malta* (1589), the Jew who, when his fortune is taken, avenges himself by arranging the death of the governor's son and then of his own daughter who has rejected him. He then betrays Malta to the Turks and is eventually killed, cursing mankind, in a trap he arranged himself. (2) *See also* Barabbas.

Barabbas. (1) In the Bible, *Matthew* xxvii, the murderer whose release was demanded of Pilate* by the mob in place of Jesus.* (2) *See also* Barabas.

Barbara, Major. In G. B. Shaw's play *Major Barbara* (1905), a young woman who tries to save the souls of the poor through the Salvation Army; disillusioned with that institution when her father Undershaft* gains its favor by donating wealth she thinks immorally gained, she converts to her father's brand of capitalism which feeds the bodies of the poor before their souls. *See also* Cusins.

Barbara, St. In Christian legend, a great beauty whose father tried to kill her; she was miraculously transported from his attack, but he denounced her to the authorities, who tortured her. When she still refused to renounce her faith, her father was ordered again to kill her; he succeeded and was struck by lightning. Thus, she became the patron saint of those seeking safety from lightning and those involved with explosives, such as miners and artillery gunners. Her symbol is a tower, her day is December 4.

Barbara Allen. *See* Allen, Barbara.

Barbie. An extremely popular American doll (beg. 1959); although designed primarily as a model for a large line of fashionable doll clothes, her sleek plastic body and long blonde hair became synonymous with a plastic, expressionless, unindividualized American beauty and in some circles came to be seen as a model that stereotyped females as mindless and superficial.

Barbour. In the American radio serial "One Man's Family" (1932–59), the typical American family experiencing the vicissitudes of life.

Bardell, Mrs. In Charles Dickens's novel *Pickwick Papers* (1836), Pickwick's* landlady who mistakes his enquiry about a servant for a proposal of marriage and later sues him for breach of promise. When he refuses to pay the judgement and goes to debtor's prison, her lawyers in turn send her to the same prison for failure to pay their fees. *See also* Dodson and Fogg.

Bardolph. In several of Shakespeare's plays, beginning with *Henry IV, Part I* (1597), a red-nosed, hot-tempered, foul-mouthed drunkard, an associate of Falstaff* in various crimes and ludicrous adventures who is eventually hanged for theft in France. *See also* Pistol.

Barkis. In Charles Dickens's novel *David Copperfield* (1849), a simple carter who woos Peggotty* with the persistent message, "Barkis is willin'."

Barleycorn, John. In folk usage, whiskey.

Barnabas. In the Bible, *Acts*, a Christian who traveled widely as Paul's* companion; he vouched for Paul to early Christians who remembered Paul's earlier attacks on Christians.

Barnaby. *See* Rudge.

Barnacle. In Charles Dickens's novel *Little Dorrit* (1855), the family who control the Circumlocution Office and guarantee that nothing ever gets done.

Barnardine. In Shakespeare's play *Measure for Measure* (1604), a prisoner who, without care, sees death as no more than a drunken sleep.

Barnes, Jake. In Ernest Hemingway's novel *The Sun Also Rises* (1926), the journalist, emasculated by a war wound, in love with Lady Brett;* also noted for saying, "Isn't it pretty to think so?"

Barnhelm, Minna von. *See* Minna.

Barnwell, George. In George Lillo's play *The London Merchant* (1731), an apprentice who is seduced by a famous courtesan and is encouraged to rob his employer and kill his uncle; often cited as the first example of domestic tragedy in European theater.

Bart, Lily. In Edith Wharton's novel *The House of Mirth* (1905), a beautiful young woman who tries to flirt her way to luxury and is eventually sacrificed on the altar of social convention. When a married man becomes infatuated with her, his wife sets up a campaign that eventually ends in Lily's disgrace, poverty, and death. *See also* Dorset.

Bartholo, Don. In Beaumarchais's play *The Barber of Seville* (1775), the elderly, suspicious guardian who locks his ward Rosine* away from all men and tries to marry her himself to control her inheritance. In *The Marriage of Figaro* (1784), he returns in an attempt to blackmail Figaro.* *See also* Almaviva.

Bartholomew. (1) In the Bible, one of the twelve Apostles;* he is generally depicted holding a butcher's knife. Tradition says he was martyred in Armenia, although the method varies. His day is August 24, on which a great pleasure fair was traditionally held in London until 1855. On that date in 1572, the French tried to massacre the Protestant Huguenots. (2) *See* Cokes, Bartholomew.

Bartholomew, St. Bartholomew* the Apostle.

Bartleby. In Herman Melville's story *Bartleby the Scrivener* (1853), a mysterious legal clerk who, when asked to do anything other than copy, always answers "I would prefer not to."

Bartolo, Dr. In Mozart's opera *The Marriage of Figaro* (1786), Don Bartholo.*

Bashmachkin. In Gogol's story *The Overcoat* (1842), a poor and meek clerk who scrimps for months to get a new overcoat, which is stolen; unable to secure help in finding it, he freezes to death. His ghost returns and snatches overcoats from strangers until it takes one that fits from the Certain Important Personage who would not help him.

Basilio, Don. In Rossini's opera *The Barber of Seville* (1816), Don Bazile.*

Baskerville. In Arthur Conan Doyle's novel *The Hound of the Baskervilles* (1902), the lord of the manor who is threatened by a mysterious curse; most references are to the gigantic hound of the Baskervilles which is supposed to haunt the family. *See also* Holmes, Sherlock.

Bassanio. In Shakespeare's play *The Merchant of Venice* (1596), the young lover who must choose the right casket in order to win Portia's* love; his wooing is also the reason Antonio* borrows the money from Shylock.*

Bassarides. A name sometimes used for the Bacchae.*

Bates, Miss. In Jane Austen's novel *Emma* (1816), a good but extremely garrulous and boring woman, particularly on the subject of her niece Jane Fairfax.* Her mother Mrs. Bates is very deaf.

Bates, Norman. In the movie *Psycho* (1960), a disturbed young man who adopts his dead mother's personality and murders beautiful young women who register at his remote motel; noted particularly for an often imitated "shower scene," in which he stabs a woman.

Bath, Wife of. *See* Wife of Bath.

Bathsheba. (1) In the Bible, *II Samuel* xi, the beautiful wife of Uriah;* David* lusted after her and had Uriah placed in the van in battle so that he might be killed, after which David married her, and she gave birth to Solomon.* (2) *See* Everdene, Bathsheba.

Bathshua. A name sometimes used for Bathsheba.*

Battus. In Ovid's *Metamorphoses*, a shepherd who witnessed the theft by Hermes'* of Apollo's* cattle; when he broke his promise not to tell, he was turned to stone.

Baucis. In Ovid's *Metamorphoses*, wife of Philemon.* They entertained Zeus* so well that their home was changed into a temple; since they desired to die together, they were turned into companion trees.

Bayard. In Ariosto's *Orlando Furioso* (1532), the magic horse given by Charlemagne* to Rinaldo* and used in many mock-heroic works as a name for any horse or for any character who is blindly reckless.

Bazarov. In Turgenev's novel *Fathers and Sons* (1862), the arrogant and antihumanitarian nihilist who believes completely in the power of the intellect. His father not only does not understand him but does not care about his attitudes, doting on anything his son does. *See also* Kirsanov; Odintsov, Anna.

Bazile, Don. In Beaumarchais's play *The Barber of Seville* (1775), a music teacher who carries messages of love from Almaviva* to the beautiful Rosine* while pretending to do so for Bartholo.*

Bears, Three. *See* Goldilocks.

Beast, The. (1) In the Bible, *Revelation* xiii, a powerful beast from the sea that can make war on the saints; those who serve it are given a mark, and its number is 666. It is variously interpreted as the Roman Empire or as the Antichrist.* (2) *See* Beauty.

Beatitudes. In the Bible, *Matthew* v, a collection of the sayings of Jesus* in the form of "Blessed are. . . . " *See also* Sermon on the Mount.

Beatrice. (1) In Dante's poem *Vita Nuova*, the "glorious lady of the mind," a beautiful young girl whom Dante loved ideally from afar and who inspired his poetry; in his poem *Divine Comedy*, he is ultimately united with her in Heaven.* (2) In Shakespeare's play *Much Ado About Nothing* (1598), the sharp-tongued spinster who is tricked into falling in love with Benedick;* she also demands that he kill his best friend Claudio* when her cousin Hero* is slandered, but eventually she marries him when order is restored. (3) *See* Cenci. (4) *See also* Beatrix.

Beatrice-Joanna. In Thomas Middleton's play *The Changeling* (1622), a degenerate young beauty who has her fiancé murdered in order to avoid the wedding; then, when she is betrothed to the man she loves, she is forced instead to spend the wedding night with the murderer De Flores.*

Beatrix. (1) *See* Esmond. (2) *See also* Beatrice.

Beau Brummel. *See* Brummel, Beau.

Beauty. In a fairy tale told by Perrault (1697), a beautiful and gentle maiden who volunteers to live with a terrible beast in exchange for her father's life; when she accepts the Beast, he reveals himself to be a prince.

Beaver. *See* Cleaver.

Becket, Thomas à. Historically, the Archbishop of Canterbury assassinated at the altar at the behest of Henry II* in 1170; he was canonized in 1173, and his tomb soon became an important site for pilgrims, such as those in Chaucer's *Canterbury Tales*. He also quickly came to symbolize the separation of personal conscience and religion from the power of the state and, as such, has appeared in numerous works, most notably the modern plays *Murder in the Cathedral* by T. S. Eliot (1935) and *Becket* by Jean Anouilh (1960).

Beckmesser. In Richard Wagner's opera *Die Meistersinger* (1868), the music critic, noted for his sharp tongue and his inflexible devotion to rules. *See also* Sachs, Hans.

Becky. *See* Sharp, Becky; Thatcher.

Bede. In George Eliot's novel *Adam Bede* (1859), **Adam** is a carpenter who, quick to judge others, drives off the young noble whom he finds kissing Hetty,* the woman he loves. In spite of her pregnancy, she refuses to marry him, and he later learns tolerance and forgiveness as he defends her when she is accused of murdering her child. His father **Matthias** is an idler and drunkard who drowns while drunk; his mother **Lisbeth** is devoted and partial to her son. *See also* Morris, Dinah.

Bede, Venerable. Historically, a priest and scholar (d. 735) noted for his humility, his wisdom, and his history of ancient England.

Bedivere. In Malory's *Morte d'Arthur*, the only knight to survive Arthur's* last battle; he is ordered to throw Excalibur* into the lake, fails twice, and finally follows the order. He then places Arthur on the barge that carries him away to Avalon.*

Bedlam. In English usage, a corruption of Bethlehem,* actually the hospital of St. Mary* of Bethlehem in London, famous as a home for lunatics; hence, a name for madness or chaos and, in such names as Tom o'Bedlam, a generic name for lunatics.

Beelzebub. A devil;* in the Bible, *Matthew* xii, the name is given to "the prince of devils," and in Milton's poem *Paradise Lost* (1667), he is second in command to Satan.* Generally, this is one of the standard names given to Satan by preachers in America.

Behemoth. In the Bible, *Job* xl, a great beast, now thought to be the hippopotamus, but generally used to signify any gigantic, powerful creature.

Belch, Sir Toby. In Shakespeare's play *Twelfth Night* (1599), an obstreperous fat drunkard devoted to carousing; he sets in motion the plot against the puritanical Malvolio* and arranges the duel between Aguecheek* and Viola.* *See also* Feste; Maria; Olivia.

Belial. Originally a Hebrew phrase meaning worthlessness, but the phrase "sons of Belial" was not translated in the King James Bible. As a result, Belial has come to signify the personification of evil and is used as a name for various demons and for the Devil* himself. In John Milton's poem *Paradise Lost* (1667), he is a fallen angel* devoted to lust who tries to convince the others to be less conspicuous in their rebellion, on the assumption that they can continue in vice unharmed if God is not forced to take notice of them.

Belinda. (1) A name much used by English Restoration writers for a young woman of fashion, as in William Congreve's play *The Old Bachelor* (1693), in John Vanbrugh's play *The Provok'd Wife* (1697), and in Alexander Pope's poem *The Rape of the Lock* (1712), where her petulant rage when a lock of her hair is cut by a lover sets in motion the mock-heroics of the poem. (2) *See also* Bellinda.

Bell, Adam. In English folklore, a famous archer.

Bella. *See* Wilfer.

Bellafront. In Thomas Dekker's *The Honest Whore* (1604), a courtesan who repents and becomes an exemplary wife.

Bellair. In George Etherege's play *The Man of Mode* (1676), a poet and dandy who outwits his father and marries Emilia,* the woman his father had hoped to wed.

Bellamy. In the British television series "Upstairs, Downstairs" (beg. 1972), also seen in the United States (beg. 1974), a prototypical upper-class family whose fortunes are followed from approximately 1900 to 1930. Among the many members were the honorable but somewhat stuffy father, a member of Parliament; the elegant **Lady Bellamy**, who died on the Titanic; **James**, a rather weak-willed son who is left disheartened and confused by World War I; and the beautiful young cousin **Georgina**. *See also* Hudson; Rose.

Bellaston, Lady. In Henry Fielding's novel *Tom Jones* (1749), a sensual noblewoman who becomes Tom Jones's* lover, supports him in London, and tries to prevent Tom's reunion with Sophia Western* by arranging a marriage for her.

Bellerophon. In Greek legend, grandson of Sisyphus,* slayer of the Chimers,* and a conqueror of the Amazons.* He was killed during his attempt to fly to heaven* on his winged horse Pegasus.*

Bellinda. (1) In George Etherege's play *The Man of Mode* (1676), Dorimant's* mistress, who has no objections to her lover's marriage as long as she can continue their affair in secret. (2) *See also* Belinda.

Bellona. In Roman mythology, goddess of war, sometimes identified as the wife of Mars,* sometimes as his sister.

Belshazzar. In the Bible, *Daniel*, king of Babylon whose feast was interrupted by a finger writing a message on the wall saying "mene, mene, tekel, upharsin," which Daniel* translated as meaning the days of the kingdom were numbered and the king had been weighed and found wanting. On the night of the translation, Belshazzar was killed and Darius* conquered the kingdom.

Belvidera. In Thomas Otway's play *Venice Preserved* (1682), the noble and loyal wife of Jaffier;* she remains faithful despite her husband's apparent abuse of her, and, after he is executed, she dies of grief on seeing his ghost.

Belzebub. *See* Beelzebub.

Benbow. In William Faulkner's novel *Sanctuary* (1931), the old-fashioned Southern lawyer who tries to defend Lee Goodwin.* *See also* Popeye.

Benedetto, Don. In Ignazio Silone's novel *Bread and Wine* (1937), the liberal priest whose sacramental wine is poisoned by supporters of Mussolini. *See also* Spina.

Benedick. In Shakespeare's play *Much Ado About Nothing* (1598), a witty soldier and supposed woman-hater who is tricked into falling in love with the sharp-tongued Beatrice.* To prove his love, she demands that he kill his best friend Claudio,* but fortunately a ruse prevents that, and he marries her. The name is sometimes used for any confirmed bachelor who finally marries.

Benedict, St. Historically, the sixth-century founder of the Benedictine order, one of the most influential monastic orders of Christian history. He is patron saint of Europe, his symbol is a broken cup, and his day is July 11.

Ben Hur. In Lew Wallace's novel *Ben Hur* (1880), a Jewish noble wrongly accused of attempting to murder a Roman governor. Sent to the galleys, he saves the commander. Later, he is taken to Rome where he becomes a great charioteer, defeating and killing his nemesis Messala* in a great race. He returns to Israel* where he and his family are converted to Christianity at the Crucifixion.*

Benjamin. In the Bible, *Genesis*, the youngest son of Jacob* and Rachel* and founder of one of the twelve tribes of Israel;* Rachel died giving birth to him.

Benjy. *See* Compson.

Bennet. In Jane Austen's novel *Pride and Prejudice* (1813), **Elizabeth** is a spirited, witty, and very intelligent young woman prejudiced against proud young men like Darcy* and against self-satisfied young men like the clergyman Collins* whose proposal she refuses. As circumstances develop, she realizes that she has been mistaken and gradually comes to love Darcy, eventually marrying him. **Mrs. Bennet** is a silly woman with little interest in anything but her daughters' marriages. **Mr. Bennet** is a gentle eccentric who spends most of his time in his library to avoid his wife and daughters, except for Elizabeth. Her sisters include **Jane**, a beauty who is prevented from marrying her love Mr. Bingley* by his sisters, who think she is beneath their family, and **Lydia**, a flighty young girl who runs away with the worthless officer Wickham.* *See also* de Bourgh; Charlotte.

Beowulf. In the anonymous poem *Beowulf*, the great hero who kills the monster Grendel* and then later also kills Grendel's mother in an underwater battle; he returns to his home and becomes a king. In his old age, a dragon attacks the kingdom; he kills it, but it also kills him.

Berenice. (1) In Jean Racine's play *Bérénice* (1679), a Judean queen in love with Titus,* now Roman Emperor. The love is so strong that she rejects the love of another king, even though she knows that Titus must reject her as well for political reasons. (2) *See* Brown, Berenice. (3) *See also* Bernice.

Beret. *See* Hansa.

Bergamo. *See* Gotham.

Bergerac, Cyrano de. *See* Cyrano.

Berinthia. In John Vanbrugh's play *The Relapse* (1696), an attractive but unscrupulous widow who lures Loveless* back into infidelity and tries to entice his wife into the same sin.

Bernadette, St. Historically, a French peasant girl (d. 1879) whose series of visions of the Virgin Mary* established the spring at Lourdes as a major pilgrimage site. She eventually became a nun and lived a life of self-effacing simple faith.

Bernard, St. (1) Historically, a priest (d. 1081) who founded hospices for travelers in the Alps; no verifiable connection with the famous dogs of that name is known. Patron saint of mountaineers, his day is May 23. (2) Historically, Bernard of Clairvaux, founder (d. 1153) of the Cistercian Order, noted for his eloquent calls for the Crusades. His symbol is a beehive, his day is August 20.

Bernardo. In Shakespeare's play *Hamlet* (1600), an officer on guard who sees the ghost of Hamlet's* father.

Bernice. (1) In the Bible, *Acts* xxv, granddaughter of Herod* and incestuous sister of Herod Agrippa. *See also* Paul. (2) *See also* Berenice.

Berowne. In Shakespeare's play *Love's Labour's Lost* (1595), a witty young lord who sees wisdom in the study of women, delighting in rhapsodic wordplay and verbal flirtation, and who eventually falls in love with Rosaline.*

Berserker. In Scandinavian legend, a wild warrior who fought with frenzied and uncontrolled fury.

Bertha, Big. In English slang of World War I, a gigantic German cannon.

Bertie. *See* Wooster, Bertie.

Bertram. (1) In Shakespeare's play *All's Well That Ends Well* (1602), a self-centered and pompous young noble who runs away rather than marry Helena,* whom he thinks is beneath him. He is tricked into consummating the marriage, but still he refuses to recognize her worth until she is reported dead, after which she is restored and he is reconciled to her. *See also* Parolles; Roussillon, Countess of. (2) *See also* Bertie.

Bertram. In Jane Austen's novel *Mansfield Park* (1814), **Sir Thomas** is an emotionally reserved baronet who rejects his ward Fanny Price* when she refuses to marry a man he considers more suitable for her than his son Edmund. **Lady Bertram** is an indolent and spoiled beauty. Their son **Tom** is headstrong and worldly until sobered by a severe illness. **Edmund**, the second son, is sober and intent on a religious life. Their two daughters **Maria** and **Julia** are equally spoiled and self-centered and each runs away with a man, Maria deserting a husband, disgracing themselves and the family. *See also* Crawford; Norris, Mrs.

Bess. (1) In Dubose Heyward's novel *Porgy* (1925) and especially in Gershwin's opera *Porgy and Bess* (1935), a beautiful woman who, trying to escape the violent gambler Crown, becomes the lover of the crippled Porgy.* When he is arrested for killing Crown, she is lured away by the dope dealer Sportin' Life.* (2) *See also* Elizabeth.

Beth. (1) In Louisa May Alcott's novel *Little Women* (1868), the frail and gentle sister who contracts scarlet fever and eventually dies. *See also* Amy; Jo; Meg. (2) *See also* Elizabeth.

Bethel. In the Bible, *Genesis* xxviii, the site of Jacob's* dream of the ladder, also noted for its spring; the name means ''house of God.''

Bethesda. In the Bible, *John* v, the pool at the Sheep's Gate of Jerusalem* whose waters healed the sick; Jesus* performed one of His miracles here, restoring the sight of a blind man whom no one would help into the water.

Bethlehem. In the Bible, the village in which Jesus* was born. His parents Joseph* and Mary* had to go there to be counted in a great census, but since there were no rooms available in the inn, they stayed in a stable, where Jesus was laid in a manger and where the shepherds* and the Magi* came to honor Him.

Bette. In Balzac's novel *Cousin Bette* (1847), an envious spinster who hides her malice and greed behind a mask of kindly eccentricity. When a man she loves leaves her for her niece, she weaves a subtle plot that destroys most of the Hulot* family, but her true feelings are never revealed to them. *See also* Creval; Steinbock; Marneffe, Mme.

Beulah. In the Bible, *Isaiah*, Isaiah's* name for the Promised Land.* In John Bunyan's *Pilgrim's Progress*, this is the point at which the pilgrims see the Heavenly City.

Beuno, St. *See* Winifred, St.

Beverley, Constance de. *See* Constance.

Beverley, Ensign. In R. B. Sheridan's play *The Rivals* (1775), the alias used by Jack Absolute.*

Bezukov, Pierre. In Tolstoy's novel *War and Peace* (1865), a count's illegitimate son who unexpectedly inherits a fortune that makes him a center of social interest. Fat and awkward, he is essentially interested only in finding peace and living the good life, but he has great difficulty deciding what that life might be, trying numerous methods at random, including philanthropy, society, wine, Freemasonry, ''modern'' farming, and wartime self-sacrifice. The most vivid incident comes when he wanders into the confusion of the battle of Borodino. Although he loves Natasha* from afar, he is easily maneuvered into marrying the beautiful Hélène, who is unfaithful and with whom he has a painful married life. After her death he marries Natasha. *See also* Bolkonsky; Kuragina, Hélène; Rostov.

Bianca. (1) In Shakespeare's play *The Taming of the Shrew* (1593), the sweet, gentle, younger sister of the shrew Kate.* *See also* Baptista; Hortensio; Lucentio. (2) In Shakespeare's play *Othello* (1604), a courtesan who loves Cassio* and is ridiculed by him behind her back. (3) In Thomas Middleton's play *Women Beware Women* (1621), a sweet and gentle girl who elopes with Leantio.* She is abducted by the duke and, as a result of her passion for him, becomes a lascivious and evil manipulator, eventually encouraging her husband's murder and then attempting to poison a cardinal as well. *See also* Isabella; Livia.

Biblis. In Ovid's *Metamorphoses*, a woman who falls in love with her twin brother and is changed into a fountain.

Biff. *See* Loman.

Big Brother. In George Orwell's novel *1984* (1949), the dictator noted for his all-pervasive image and the slogan ''Big Brother is watching you!''

Big Daddy. In Tennessee Williams's play *Cat On a Hot Tin Roof* (1955), the domineering patriarch of a degenerating Southern plantation family. *See also* Brick; Maggie.

Bigelow, Billy. In Rodgers and Hammerstein's musical play *Carousel* (1945), a carnival barker and small time con man who marries the naive Julie* and is killed in a robbery. *See also* Liliom.

Bigger Thomas. *See* Thomas, Bigger.

Bildad. In the Bible, *Job*, one of Job's* friends who deserts him.

Bilhah. In the Bible, *Genesis* xxx, the maid whom Rachel* encouraged her husband Jacob* to sleep with when Rachel was barren; she became the mother of Dan* and Naphtali.*

Bilko, Sgt. In the American TV series "The Phil Silvers Show" (1955–59), a raucous con man and loud-mouthed, bossy Army sergeant.

Billee, Little. In George du Maurier's novel *Trilby* (1894), a delicate and innocent art student who loves Trilby* but is shocked by her life. He almost dies of shock when she disappears, then recovers when she is found, only to die when she dies. His name may in turn be a reference to a British folk ballad. *See also* Svengali.

Billy the Kid. Historically, William Bonney (d. 1881), a gunman in the American West who entered legend as the quintessential outlaw-rebel.

Bingley. In Jane Austen's novel *Pride and Prejudice* (1813), a good-natured bachelor who loves Jane Bennet;* their marriage is prevented by his sister Caroline's snobbishness until the courtship is successfully renewed when Darcy* starts to court Elizabeth.

Birdseye, Miss. In Henry James's novel *The Bostonians* (1886), the gentle old woman who dies peacefully following her long life devoted to humanitarian causes. *See also* Chancellor, Olive.

Birotteau. In Balzac's novel *César Birotteau* (1837), **César** is an honest, self-made businessman who finds initial success through his skill and hard work but whose trust in the integrity of others leads to his bankruptcy and death. His wife **Constance** is both attractive and intelligent and has a better business sense, with which she tries to save her husband from his own childishness in business matters, never wavering in her devotion to him despite numerous attempts on her own honor. Their daughter **Constance** inherits the attractiveness and integrity of her parents and, despite the loss of her dowry, eventually attains her desire of a home free of social pretension. *See also* Tillet, Ferdinand du.

Bishop's Candlesticks. In Victor Hugo's novel *Les Misérables* (1862), a famous episode in which Valjean* tries to steal a pair of candlesticks and is forgiven by the bishop who discovers him, thereby encouraging him to reform his life.

Black Beauty. In Anna Sewell's novel *Black Beauty* (1877), a gentle horse passed through a number of vicious owners and handlers until finally reaching a family that treats him well.

Blackpool, Stephen. In Charles Dickens's novel *Hard Times* (1854), a poor but honest weaver who loses his factory job by refusing to join either strikers or strike-breakers, then is framed for a robbery and dies after falling into an open mine shaft on his way home to clear himself of the charges. *See also* Bounderby; Gradgrind; Rachel.

Blanche. *See* Dubois, Blanche.

Blanche, Anthony. In Evelyn Waugh's novel *Brideshead Revisited* (1945), the mannered, witty, "artistic" homosexual friend of Sebastian at Oxford. *See also* Marchmain; Ryder, Charles.

Blandings, Mr. In Eric Hodgins's novel *Mr. Blandings Builds His Dream House* (1946), a representative postwar American middle-class male trying to cope with the rigors of suburbia.

Blandish, Miss. In James Hadley Chase's novel *No Orchids for Miss Blandish* (1939), a woman kidnapped and raped by a criminal gang. Her name is often cited for the brutality of the work itself, shocking as well as best-selling in its day, and as a prime example of the "cheap" thriller.

Blandois. In Charles Dickens's novel *Little Dorrit* (1855), the "cruel gentleman with slender white hands," a Frenchman who murders his wife, escapes to England, and there blackmails Mrs. Clennam,* only to be killed when the old Clennam house collapses about him.

Blas, Gil. In Le Sage's novel *Gil Blas* (1715), a humble peasant who is waylaid on his way to school, beginning a series of adventures with high and low in eighteenth-century society, in the course of which he becomes a first-class rogue of wit and imagination.

Blepyrus. In Aristophanes's play *Ecclesiazusae*, the husband of Praxagora;* he is happy when the women take over the government because he thinks he will no longer have to work.

Blifil. In Henry Fielding's novel *Tom Jones* (1749), the hypocritical half-brother of Tom Jones;* he tells numerous lies about Tom from behind a mask of religious purity and honesty. *See also* Allworthy, Squire.

Bligh, Capt. Historically, a British sea captain (d. 1817). The mutiny of his crew after a trip to Tahiti and his amazing crossing of much of the Pacific in an open boat were the subjects of Nordhoff and Hall's novels *Mutiny on the Bounty* (1932) and *Men Against the Sea* (1934) and several movie versions, in which Bligh came to represent egotistical tyranny and unnecessarily cruel authority. *See also* Christian, Fletcher.

Blimp, Col. In British newspaper editorial cartoons by David Low (beg. 1934), a bald old soldier with drooping walrus mustache, given to self-contradictory aphorisms, usually delivered while wearing a towel in a steambath. The character soon became synonymous with unthinking military attitudes, as well as with insular British characters in general.

Blondie. *See* Bumstead.

Bloom. In James Joyce's novel *Ulysses* (1922), **Leopold** is the Jewish businessman and husband whose daily routine sends him searching for something unusual in a world all too ordinary. His wife **Molly**, an occasional singer, is a sensual, emotional woman who escapes boredom through a series of love affairs; her long monologue which concludes the novel is one of the most famous works of the twentieth century—a long stream-of-consciousness reverie in which she touches on all aspects of her past and dreams, including some vivid sexual experiences. *See also* Dedalus, Stephen.

Blue Bird of Happiness. In Maurice Maeterlinck's play *The Blue Bird* (1908), the spirit of happiness sought by the children in the play but which always flies off to be pursued again when it is found.

Blue Boy. In a painting by Gainsborough (1770), a boy dressed in a blue suit, often cited as a symbol of painting and of culture in general.

Bluebeard. In the fairy tale as told by Perrault (1697), a nobleman who married repeatedly, killing each of his wives. *See also* Fatima; Gilles de Rais.

Bluffe, Capt. In William Congreve's play *The Old Bachelor* (1693), the cowardly bully.

Bluntschli. In G. B. Shaw's play *Arms and the Man* (1894), an officer who climbs into Raina's* bedroom to hide during a retreat. He is distinguished by his practical and antiromantic attitude toward war and is often known as the Chocolate Soldier because he kept chocolate rather than ammunition in his cartridge case. *See also* Sergius.

Boadicea. Historically, a queen of a British tribe who led a revolt against the Romans, committing suicide when it failed in 61. She appears in numerous English works, with numerous spellings, as an early exemplar of British patriotism.

Boanerges. In the Bible, *Mark* iii, a name meaning "sons of thunder" given to James* and John.*

Boaz. In the Bible, *Ruth*, the man who allowed Ruth* to glean his fields, whereupon he recognized her good qualities and married her.

Bobadill. In Ben Jonson's play *Every Man In His Humour* (1598), a vain, braggart, yet cowardly soldier, distinguished among such characters for his sense of decorum.

Bobby. In British slang, a policeman, probably from Robert Peel, who organized the London Metropolitan Police in 1828.

Bobchinsky. In Gogol's play *The Inspector General* (1836), a stupid, greedy local squire, usually paired with Dobchinsky, an identically stupid and greedy neighbor, as examples of indistinguishables. *See also* Klestakov.

Boche. In British and French slang of World War I, the Germans.

Boffin. In Charles Dickens's novel *Our Mutual Friend* (1864), **Noddy** is "The Golden Dustman," a cheerful, simple, and honest illiterate who inherits a fortune. He takes in Bella Wilfer* and, concerned by her materialism, puts on a particularly convincing pretense of miserliness and greed to convince her of her fault, then returns the fortune happily when the real beneficiary is revealed. His wife **Henrietta** is a cheerful woman who lavishes love on all around her. *See also* Wegg, Silas.

Bois-Guilbert, Brian de. In Walter Scott's novel *Ivanhoe* (1820), the Knight Templar who falls in love with the Jewess Rebecca,* kidnaps her, and then deserts her when she is tried for witchcraft. He is killed by Ivanhoe.*

Boldwood. In Thomas Hardy's novel *Far From the Madding Crowd* (1874), the patient middle-aged bachelor whose continual frustrations in his courtship of Bathsheba Everdene* lead to his mental derangement and the murder of her husband Sergeant Troy.*

Boleyn, Anne. Historically, Henry VIII's* second wife and the mother of Elizabeth* I. She was a beautiful young girl for whom he divorced his first wife; his conflict with the Pope over this issue led to the establishment of the Church of England. When Anne failed to deliver a male heir, Henry charged her with adultery, divorced her, and had her beheaded (1536). The subject of numerous plays, historical novels, and other works, she is usually portrayed as a beautiful but thoughtless girl who is made a victim of politics and Henry's self-centeredness.

Bolingbroke. Historically, Henry IV* of England; his most noted appearance under this name is in Shakespeare's play *Richard II*.

Bolkonsky. In Tolstoy's novel *War and Peace* (1865), one of the principal families in the work. **Nikolai** is the father, an eccentric and tyrannical landowner, passionately attached to his estate and refusing to abandon it in the face of the French. His son, Prince **Andrei** is a sensitive and brave soldier, much honored in society as well as in the Army. He is almost killed at Austerlitz but survives and, when his first wife dies in childbirth, eventually becomes engaged to Natasha.* Humiliated by her near seduction by Kuragin,* he breaks the engagement, refuses any contact with her, and retires to his father's estate. He eventually rejoins the army when Napoleon* invades, and he is fatally wounded; accident brings him again to Natasha and reconciles them before his death. His sister **Marya** is driven into intense religiosity by her father's methodical interference with all attempts at courtship of her because he wants her as his nurse and companion. After her father's death, she gradually forsakes her life as a recluse and marries Nikolai Rostov.*

Bon, Charles. In William Faulkner's novel *Absalom, Absalom* (1936), a handsome, dashing Civil War hero and friend of Henry Sutpen.* He is engaged to Henry's sister, even though it is rumored that he is her illegitimate half-brother. He is murdered when Henry realizes he is also part Negro.

Bonaparte. *See* Napoleon.

Bonaventure, St. Historically, a theologian (d. 1274) of great intellect and simple habits. His symbol is a cardinal's hat from the story that, when the legates brought him his hat, he had them hang it on a tree since his hands were wet and dirty. His day is July 15.

Bond, James. In numerous novels by Ian Fleming, beginning with *Casino Royale* (1953), and numerous movies (beg. 1964), the ultimate super-spy noted for his skill, imagination, and derring-do, for his skill at seduction, and in the movies, for his alliance with flamboyant technology. His identifying marks were his code name 007, his martinis "shaken, not stirred," his skill at baccarat, and his Beretta pistol.

Bonduca. *See* Boadicea.

Bones, Brom. In Washington Irving's story *The Legend of Sleepy Hollow* (1819), a sturdy Dutch farmer who disguises himself as the Headless Horseman* in order to frighten Ichabod Crane* away from the girl he loves.

Boniface. In George Farquhar's play *The Beaux' Stratagem* (1707), the landlord of the inn who claims to live on ale. He is an unscrupulous rogue, but the name became generic for pub landlords in England for many years. *See also* Cherry.

Booby, Lady. In Henry Fielding's *Joseph Andrews* (1742), a lascivious lady who lusts after Joseph Andrews,* her footman, and who fires him when he rejects her advances, later falsely accusing him of a crime to prevent his marriage to his true love.

Boojum. In Lewis Carroll's poem *The Hunting of the Snark* (1876), a dangerous type of snark;* it causes the Baker to "softly and suddenly vanish away."

Boon. *See* Hogganbeck, Boon.

Boone, Daniel. Historically, an American woodsman and explorer (d. 1820) who helped open up Kentucky to settlers. Much folklore grew up around him, and he is often depicted as a mythological great hunter and Indian fighter.

Boop, Betty. In numerous American movie cartoons (1931–39), a singing heroine with enormous round head and eyes atop a tiny but exaggeratedly curvaceous body, noted for naive sensuality and her catch-phrase "boop-boop-a-doo."

Booz. *See* Boaz.

Borachio. In Shakespeare's play *Much Ado about Nothing* (1598), an egotistical villain whose plot rouses Claudio's* jealousy but who confesses reluctantly after he is overheard by the watch. *See also* Dogberry; Hero; John, Don.

Borden, Lizzie. Historically, a woman accused in 1892 of killing her father and stepmother with an ax. Although acquitted, she entered legend as one of the great American murderers, particularly from the rhyme: "Lizzie Borden took an ax and gave her mother 40 whacks. . . . ''

Boreas. In Greek mythology, the north wind.

Borgia. Historically, a powerful family in Renaissance Italy. **Rodrigo** (d. 1503) was a ruthless politician, who eventually became Pope and used papal power to further the interests of his children. **Cesare**, his most powerful son (d. 1507), was a brilliant military mind and a notorious murderer. **Lucrezia**, the daughter (d. 1519), seems to have been worst served by history, being married off by her father several times for political reasons, her husbands conveniently dying when required, until a final marriage which lasted so long that her court became a center of arts and learning. In tradition and folklore, however, she was known as a great poisoner personifying evil and sexual license. Rumors abounded of incest with both her father and her brother.

Boris. (1) A common Russian name, used in the West for a stereotypical Russian, usually big, muscular, and slow-witted. (2) *See* Godunov, Boris.

Boors. In Malory's *Morte d'Arthur*, a knight of Arthur's court who, with Galahad* and Percival,* sees a vision of the Holy Grail.*

Bosola. In John Webster's play *The Duchess of Malfi* (1613), the cynical, ruthless, yet intelligent villain, forced by the nobles who control him to do things that outrage his sense of honor. Eventually, he murders the Duchess, then, before his own death, avenges her upon her brothers who ordered her execution. *See also* Malfi, Duchess of; Ferdinand.

Boswell. Historically, the companion (d. 1795) and biographer of Dr. Johnson.* Allusions generally indicate a devoted follower who reveres his subject, collecting and saving even his daily conversations.

Bottom. In Shakespeare's play *A Midsummer Night's Dream* (1595), the weaver who plays Pyramus* in the play-within-a-play. He is a ham actor and something of an egotist who tries to play all the parts, yet he is so good-natured that no one even thinks to complain. He is also given the head of an ass by a magic spell and temporarily becomes the lover of the fairy queen Titania.* *See also* Oberon; Puck; "Pyramus and Thisbe"; Quince, Peter.

Bounderby. In Charles Dickens's novel *Hard Times* (1854), a wealthy factory owner who is vain about being a self-made man. His social position is destroyed when the source of his wealth, a respectable mother, is revealed. He also marries Louisa Gradgrind* but is capable of only a cold and loveless kind of marriage. *See also* Pegler, Mrs.; Sparsit, Mrs.

Bountiful, Lady. In George Farquhar's play *The Beaux' Stratagem* (1707), a wise and kindly woman who is an extremely effective nurse.

Bourgh, Catherine de. *See* de Bourgh.

Bovary. In Gustave Flaubert's novel *Madame Bovary* (1857), **Emma** is a young woman caught in a boring bourgeois marriage who is in search of the exalted romance and passion she has read and dreamed about. She tries two affairs, each of which is shabby and sordid as much from her inability to transcend her own materialism as from the unsuitability of her partners. Disillusioned, hopelessly in debt, and trapped in a vicious blackmail by one of the lovers, she commits suicide. Her husband **Charles** is a docile husband who loves her but is incapable of fulfilling any of her dreams. A country doctor without imagination or distinction, he is eventually destroyed by his own mediocrity as much as by her indiscretions. *See also* Dupuis; Homais; Lheureux; Rodolphe.

Bowdler. Historically, a doctor who published a "family" edition of Shakespeare in 1818. One of the leading exponents of expurgation of literature (hence, "bowdlerization") to protect the sensibilities of women and children.

Box and Cox. In J. M. Morton's play *Box and Cox* (1847), two men who share a room without knowing it, since one works days and one works nights. Eventually they discover this, with humorous consequences, and also realize that they also share proposals of marriage to the same woman.

Boxer. In George Orwell's novel *Animal Farm* (1945), the horse who responds to each revolutionary crisis by saying, "I must work harder," working until he drops in his tracks.

Boyet. In Shakespeare's play *Love's Labour's Lost* (1595), a witty courtier, noted for his bawdiness.

Boylan, Blazes. In James Joyce's novel *Ulysses* (1922), a concert manager with whom Molly Bloom* is having an affair.

Boyle. In Sean O'Casey's play *Juno and the Paycock* (1924), **"Captain" Jack** is the impractical lower-class Irishman, happy with life as long as he has money for drink and a pal to drink with. His wife **Juno** struggles mightily to maintain some semblance of practicality and stability in the family, but she is obviously being beaten down into a state of sustained anxiety. Their daughter **Mary** has the intelligence for a better life, but she lets herself get pregnant in an affair and thus loses any chance to escape by an advantageous marriage. Their son **Johnny**

has joined one of the many anti-British organizations: He is injured in a demonstration but, because he eventually informs on his compatriots, he is summarily executed by them. Jack seems to be bothered by none of this. The final image of him telling his pal Joxer* that "the world's in a terrible state of chassis" in a room where even his furniture has been repossessed is one of the most sadly comic moments in twentieth century theater.

Boythorn. In Charles Dickens's novel *Bleak House* (1852), the cantankerous and litigious but good-hearted friend of Jarndyce.*

Boy Who Cried Wolf. In Aesop's* fable, a shepherd boy who out of boredom pretends that a wolf is attacking the flock. After several times, no one pays any attention to him when the wolf really does attack.

Bozo. Historically, an American circus clown of the post-WWII years with two pointed tufts of red hair. He became so popular that his name is often applied to all clowns or to anyone acting stupidly.

Brabantio. In Shakespeare's play *Othello* (1604), the father of Desdemona* who is outraged that she has married Othello* without his consent.

Brachiano. In John Webster's play *The White Devil* (1612), a duke whose lust overwhelms all other considerations; he has his wife and his lover Vittoria's husband murdered, then is haunted by the ghosts of his victims and is poisoned. *See also* Flamineo.

Brack, Judge. In Henrik Ibsen's play *Hedda Gabler* (1890), a devious friend who tries to blackmail Hedda Gabler* into his bed, leading to her suicide. *See also* Lovborg.

Bracknell, Lady. In Oscar Wilde's play *The Importance of Being Earnest* (1895), the formidable aunt who personifies the power of manners and custom over society and all who would be a part of it. She is clearly intelligent and witty, but that often seems to pale before her awesome will and self-assurance. *See also* Algernon; Gwendolen; Worthing, Jack.

Bradamant. In Ariosto's *Orlando Furioso* (1532), Rinaldo's* sister and a great female warrior who eventually marries Rogero,* the only man able to stand against her for a day; a symbol of steadfast love in contrast to Angelica.*

Bradamente. *See* Bradamant.

Bradwardine. In Walter Scott's novel *Waverely* (1814), a noble Jacobite,* proud but pedantic, and father of Rose, the mild and faithful girl who eventually wins Edward Waverley's* love.

Brahma. In Hindu mythology, the supreme god from whom the universe is formed and of whom the universe is a manifestation—one of the triumvirate with Shiva* and Vishnu.*

Brainworm. In Ben Jonson's play *Every Man In His Humour* (1598), the mischievous servant of many disguises. *See also* Knowell.

Bramble. In Tobias Smollett's novel *Humphrey Clinker* (1771), an old bachelor, an eccentric given to passionate discussions of favorite topics, especially his health and the manners of foreign parts where he is traveling; his sister **Tabitha** is a fussy female much like him. *See also* Clinker, Humphrey.

Brand. In Henrik Ibsen's play *Brand* (1866), an uncompromising priest who demands complete self-sacrifice from himself and his followers, even abandoning his wife Agnes* in her illness on his climb up the mountain toward God. Eventually he loses all but one of his followers, the gypsy girl Gerd,* while appearing to receive Christ's* stigmata before being killed in an avalanche.

Brandon, Col. In Jane Austen's novel *Sense and Sensibility* (1811), a quiet, mature suitor of Marianne Dashwood.* He is rejected because of his age until she is horrified by her younger, more romantic suitor; they are then married.

Brasidas. Historically, a Spartan* general (d. 422 B.C.) noted in folklore for having spared the life of a mouse because it was brave enough to bite him.

Brass. In Charles Dickens's novel *The Old Curiosity Shop* (1840), **Sampson** is the dishonest lawyer who aids Quilp* in his machinations; **Sally**, his spinster sister, is even more cunning and devious and cruelly starves her servant Sophronia Sphynx.* *See also* Nell, Little.

Bray. In Charles Dickens's novel *Nicholas Nickleby* (1838), **Madeline** is the beautiful but devoted daughter who agrees to sacrifice herself for the sake of her dissolute and now invalid father **Walter** and marry the old miser Gride* in order to provide comfort for Walter in his last years; freed at the last moment by her father's death, she is rescued by Nicholas Nickleby,* whom she eventually marries.

Bray, Vicar of. *See* Vicar of Bray.

Breck, Alan. In R. L. Stevenson's novel *Kidnapped* (1886), the dashing Jacobite* rebel who rescues David Balfour* from a sinking ship, whose escape from British forces occupies much of David's adventures, and whose force of arms helps restore David to his fortune.

Brendan, St. Historically, an Irish monk (d. 577) noted for his voyages into the Atlantic Ocean.

Brennan on the Moor. In an Irish folksong, a highwayman, "bold, brave, and undaunted."

Br'er Rabbit. *See* Rabbit, Br'er.

Brett. *See* Ashley, Lady Brett.

Brewster. In Joseph Kesselring's play *Arsenic and Old Lace* (1941), the two spinsters who poison old vagrants with their elderberry wine out of kindness and bury them in their cellar but are never suspected because of their perfect "sweet little old lady" personalities. One nephew believes he is Teddy Roosevelt* and buries the bodies in "the Panama Canal"; the second, **Mortimer**, is a drama critic who discovers the crimes and eventually finds the happy solution; the third is a vicious criminal whose plastic surgeon has made him look like Frankenstein's* monster and who is humiliated to think his aunts have killed more men than he.

Brick. In Tennessee Williams's play *Cat On a Hot Tin Roof* (1955), a once glorious young athlete now an alcoholic, pining for a dead friend and wallowing in self-pity, ignoring his sensual wife Maggie,* and about to be disinherited by his father, Big Daddy.*

Brideshead. *See* Marchmain.

Bridget, Mrs. In Laurence Sterne's novel *Tristram Shandy* (1759), the perky maid with her cap set for Corporal Trim.* *See also* Wadman, Widow.

Bridget, St. *See* Brigid, St.

Bridoye. In Rabelais's *Pantagruel* (1546), a judge who decides cases by the throw of the dice.

Briggs, Miss. In William Makepeace Thackeray's novel *Vanity Fair* (1847), Becky Sharp's* respectable companion, called her "sheepdog," whose presence provides the screen for many of Becky's peccadilloes.

Brighella. In the commedia dell'Arte, the first zany,* usually a roguish servant who concocts plots for the pleasure of making them, a devotee of pleasure, particularly wine, women, and song; he is generally without scruples, often getting Harlequin* to make a fool of himself or take the blame. *Also called* Mezzetino; Scapino.*

Brigid. St. Historically, founder of the first women's religious community in Ireland, figuring in numerous legends and folklore and revered second only to St. Patrick* in Ireland.

Brinker, Hans. In Mary Mapes Dodge's novel *Hans Brinker* (1865), the brave and unspoiled Dutch teenager who takes over support of his family when his father is injured and who, with his sister, is the best skater on the Zuider Zee; his sister actually wins the silver skates, although Hans is often credited with this in many allusions.

Briscoe, Lily. In Virginia Woolf's novel *To the Lighthouse* (1927), a painter who is drawn into the Ramsay* circle by her need for the love Mrs. Ramsay provides to all and who thus gains a chance at a fulfilling life, even though she never quite becomes a great artist.

Briseis. In Homer's *Iliad*, a pretty captive given to Achilles.* When Agamemnon* claims her by his right as commander, Achilles goes to his tent to sulk, thus setting in motion most of the action of the *Iliad*. *See also* Chryseis.

Brisk, Fastidious. In Ben Jonson's play *Every Man Out of His Humour* (1599), the fashionable courtier who maintains his fashion lead by changing clothes so often no one can keep up with him.

Britannicus. Historically, a son of Claudius* and Messalina,* spurned by his father in favor of Nero* and after Claudius's death poisoned by Nero. In Racine's play *Britannicus* (1669), this murder is caused by Nero's jealousy concerning a proposed marriage.

Britomart. (1) In Edmund Spenser's poem *The Faerie Queene* (1590), a female knight and a model of chastity; she falls in love with the knight Artegall after seeing him in a magic mirror and pursues him, resisting numerous sexual temptations along the way. (2) *See* Undershaft.

Britomartis. In Greek legend, a nymph,* daughter of Zeus* and servant of Artemis,* who drowns herself to escape the attentions of Minos.*

Brittanicus. *See* Britannicus.

Brobdingnag. In Jonathan Swift's novel *Gulliver's Travels* (1726), a land of giants where Gulliver* is kept as a pet in a birdcage.

Brocklehurst. In Charlotte Brontë's novel *Jane Eyre* (1847), the strict, sanctimonious clergyman.

Brooke. In George Eliot's novel *Middlemarch* (1871), **Dorothea** (Dodo) is a sensitive girl who marries the dull cleric Casaubon* in her search for a meaningful life, then after his death renounces her fortune to marry an artist. Her sister **Celia** is a much more placid but affectionate woman. *See also* Lydgate.

Brother, Big. *See* Big Brother.

Brown, Berenice. In Carson McCullers's novel *The Member of the Wedding* (1946), the strong, motherly Negro cook with an eyepatch who acts as a surrogate mother for the young girl Frankie;* especially noted from the play version for a powerful performance of the song "His Eye Is on the Sparrow."

Brown, Charlie. In the American newspaper comic strip *Peanuts* (beg. 1950), a perfectly average, bland child, noted for baseball games he always loses, his dog Snoopy,* and the catch-phrase, "Good Grief." *See also* Lucy.

Brown, Father. In numerous stories by G. K. Chesterton (beg. 1911), a gentle priest whose simplicity, open-mindedness, and understanding of human nature allow him to solve crimes that baffle detectives.

Brown, John. Historically, an American abolitionist who first came to notice in the Kansas wars and then tried to instigate a slave uprising in the South with his raid on Harper's Ferry, for which he was hanged in 1859. He appears in numerous works as a martyr for both Christianity and the antislavery movement and in others as a wild-eyed fanatic; in both guises, he is portrayed as a very tall, patriarchal figure with a great beard.

Brown, Tom. In Thomas Hughes's novel *Tom Brown's School Days* (1857), a good-natured schoolboy who finds himself in much mischief until he is reformed by the courageous example of his roommate, after which he becomes a leader and an example for all the school. *See also* Arnold, Dr.; Flashman.

Brownie. In Scottish folklore, a fairy;* in America, the name is also used by members of the youngest branch of the Girl Scouts organization.

Brownlow. In Charles Dickens's novel *Oliver Twist* (1837), the benevolent old gentleman whose evidence rescues Oliver Twist* from jail and who never gives up his faith in Oliver even after the boy disappears; eventually, he adopts Oliver. *See also* Grimwig.

Bruin. In French folklore, the bear whom Reynard* wedges in a log filled with honey.

Brummel, Beau. Historically, a London dandy (d. 1840) who was such an important leader of fashion that his name became synonymous with the well-dressed male. His most famous innovations were clean linen and full-length trousers.

Brunhild. (1) In the anonymous *Niebelungenlied*, a daughter of Wotan* and a powerful virgin warrior until overcome by Siegfried* impersonating Gunther.* When she learns of the ruse that forced her to marry and lose her power, she arranges Siegfried's death. *See also* Gunther; Hagen; Kriemheld. (2) *See* Brünnhilde.

Brünnhilde. (1) In Richard Wagner's operas *The Ring of the Niebelung* (1869–76), a Valkyrie* who, after trying to save Siegmund's* life against her father Wotan's* command, is put to sleep within a ring of fire. After many years, she is awakened by Siegfried,* whom she promises to love eternally. Later, when Siegfried is drugged, forgets her, and marries another, she arranges his death, then repents and rides onto his funeral pyre to join him in death. (2) *See also* Brunhild.

Brute. *See* Brutus.

Brutus. (1) Historically, one of the leading men of Republican Rome (d. 42 B.C.), he helped assassinate Julius Caesar* and then committed suicide after losing the battle of Philippi. He appears in numerous works, most notably Shakespeare's play *Julius Caesar* (1599), in which he is portrayed as "the noblest Roman of them all," the only one of the conspirators who acts for the good of Rome and for his honor rather than for personal gain. It is to him that Caesar addresses the famous "Et tu, Brute?" In Dante's *Divine Comedy*, he is a traitor condemned in Hell* to dwell forever in ice. *See also* Antony, Marc; Cassius. (2) In English legend, a great-grandson of Aeneas* and first king of England.

Bucephalus. The war horse of Alexander.* When young, Alexander indicated his potential greatness by being the only man able to ride him.

Buchanan. In F. Scott Fitzgerald's novel *The Great Gatsby* (1925), **Tom** is an uncultured, wealthy young man who has an affair with the wife of a mechanic and then, in revenge for his wife's affair with Gatsby,* encourages the mechanic, who eventually shoots Gatsby. For Tom's wife, *see* Daisy.

Buck. In Jack London's story *The Call of the Wild* (1903), the intelligent but long-suffering dog who finally finds happiness by breaking away from a sled team and joining a wolf pack in Alaska.

Buckingham. Historically, a major family of English nobles who figure in numerous historical plays and novels. There is a duke of devious bent (d. 1483) allied with Somerset in Shakespeare's *Henry VI* plays (1589–92); he also appears in *Richard III* (1592) as a brilliant manipulator who puts Richard III* on the throne, only to be executed when he refuses to consent to the murder of the young princes. His son is a man of great dignity (d. 1521) who is executed for his enmity to Cardinal Wolsey in Shakespeare's play *Henry VIII* (1613). A later duke (d. 1628) appears in Alexandre Dumas's novel *The Three Musketeers* (1844) as the handsome, brilliant English government minister whose affair with the queen of France almost destroys her.

Budd, Billy. In Herman Melville's novel *Billy Budd* (1924), a young sailor who personifies simplicity, beauty, and goodness, for which he is much persecuted by the evil Claggart.* A stutterer, Billy lashes out in frustration, accidentally killing Claggart, and he is hanged by the reluctant Capt. Vere.* He is generally seen as a demonstration of the way in which a wicked world eventually destroys that which is good.

Buddenbrook. In Thomas Mann's novel *Buddenbrooks* (1901), the representative German bourgeois family whose fortunes are followed through four generations of decline. The principal figures are **Johann**, the benevolent patriarch and astute businessman; his son **Johann**, who combines business acumen and sentimental but sincere pietism; his son **Thomas**, who runs the business without imagination but with much family pride until in his forties he becomes obsessed by death and suddenly dies of a stroke; his brother **Christian**, whose childhood playfulness gradually grows into real neurosis; their sister **Toni**, who moves from one broken marriage to the next; and Thomas's son, **Hanno**, a sickly child prodigy whose death by typhoid ends the line.

Buffalo Bill. Historically, William Cody (d. 1917), an American army scout and buffalo hunter who became famous as the hero of a number of stories by Ned Buntline and then became a symbol of the American West with the European tours of his circus-like "Wild West Shows." He is usually depicted with flowing hair and mustache, wearing a white buckskin suit.

Bugs Bunny. In numerous American movie cartoons (beg. 1939), a lovable scoundrel rabbit of many disguises and endless imaginative machinations, noted for an ever-present carrot and the catch-phrase, "What's up, Doc?"

Bulba, Taras. In Gogol's novel *Taras Bulba* (1835), a Cossack chieftain, a great warrior against the Poles and defender of the Orthodox faith, who dies bravely while guarding the escape of his men against overwhelming odds.

Bull, John. In common usage, a symbol of the Englishman, first appearing in a series of satirical pamphlets in 1712 as an honest, bold, but choleric fellow, fond of his bottle and his freedom.

Bullen, Anne. *See* Boleyn, Anne.

Bulstrode. In George Eliot's novel *Middlemarch* (1871), the pious but wealthy banker who uses his money to support his public appearance of morality, eventually exposed as a humbug when the shady foundations of his fortune are revealed.

Bumble. In Charles Dickens's novel *Oliver Twist* (1837), the fat, self-important beadle who operates the almshouse where Oliver Twist* is taken and who starves and mistreats his charges to build up his pocket and his pride. He eventually meets his match when he marries Mrs. Corney,* the workhouse matron, for her fortune and is instead bullied into submission. When told that the law holds a husband responsible for his wife's actions, he answers with the famous: "If the law supposes that—the law is a ass."

Bumby, Mother. Historically, a widely known Elizabethan fortune-teller, often mentioned in plays of the time and the nominal subject of a comedy by Lyly (1594).

Bumper. In R. B. Sheridan's play *The School for Scandal* (1777), a drinking companion of Charles Surface* and the singer of "Here's to the maiden of bashful fifteen."

Bumppo, Natty. In several novels by James Fenimore Cooper, beginning with *The Last of the Mohicans* (1826), the paradigmatic American frontiersman: hardy, honest, direct, natural, a great hunter and a noble fighter respected by his enemies as well as by his allies, unable to abide the life of "civilization." *Also called* Hawkeye for his great shooting skill and Leatherstocking for his usual leggings. *See also* Chingachgook; Uncas.

Bumstead. In the American newspaper cartoon *Blondie* (beg. 1930), **Dagwood** is the bumbling, ineffectual husband and office worker, also noted for the outrageous sandwiches he eats; **Blondie** is his wife, originally something of a scatterbrain but soon becoming a sensible, model housewife.

Bunbury. In Oscar Wilde's play *The Importance of Being Earnest* (1895), an imaginary character invented by Algernon;* whenever he wished to avoid something, he would be "called away" to visit his sick friend Bunbury.

Bundren. In William Faulkner's novel *As I Lay Dying* (1930), a family of struggling Southern poor white trash. **Addie** is the overworked wife unable to find any meaning in her grinding existence, unable to find release even in sex, wanting nothing except to see her coffin before she dies; **Anse**, her husband, is shiftless, setting out on a long journey with the body, ostensibly to bury it in town, only to turn the trip into a search for false teeth and a new wife. Of their children, **Darl** is a lunatic; **Dewey** is a teenaged girl trying to find drugs to induce a miscarriage for her illegitimate pregnancy; **Cash** is a stoical carpenter crippled while trying to ferry the body across a flood; and **Jewel** is a violent foul-mouthed young man who can express positive feelings only through the horses he adores.

Bunker. In the American television series "All in the Family" (1971–83), **Archie** is the epitome of the opinionated, pig-headed, ignorant working man who became for many synonymous with loud-mouthed social and racial bigotry and for others a symbol of the American "silent majority." His wife **Edith**, called the "ding-bat," is a gentle soul, kindly but slow-witted, with her heart always in the right place.

Bunsby. In Charles Dickens's novel *Dombey and Son* (1846), Capt. Cuttle's* innocent friend, who is unwittingly caught in marriage by the imposing Mrs. MacStinger.*

Bunter. In numerous novels by Dorothy Sayers (beg. 1923), the perfect butler/valet of Lord Peter Wimsey* and an occasional aide in the investigations.

Bunter, Billy. In numerous stories by Frank Richards (beg. 1908) and in English cartoons (beg. 1939), a fat schoolboy at Greyfriars School, noted for his greed, his lies, and his pranks.

Bunthorne. In Gilbert and Sullivan's operetta *Patience* (1881), an ultrarefined poet and a caricature of the Aesthetes of the period.

Bunyan, Paul. In American/Canadian folklore, a giant lumberjack who performed numerous outrageous deeds based on his size and strength. He was accompanied by Babe, the Blue Ox, whose horns measured 42 feet across.

Buonaparte. *See* Bonaparte.

Burden, Joanna. In William Faulkner's novel *Light in August* (1932), a Southern white woman who becomes the mistress of the demented mulatto Joe Christmas;* her attempt to "improve" him depends on her own sexual dominance over him, as a result of which he kills her.

Burns, Walter. In Hecht and MacArthur's play *The Front Page* (1928), the flamboyant and rascally newspaper editor, the epitome of shameless anything-for-a-story yellow journalism.

Busiris. In Greek legend, an Egyptian tyrant who murdered strangers until he was killed by Heracles.*

Bussy D'Ambois. *See* D'Ambois, Bussy.

Busy, Zeal-of-the-Land. In Ben Jonson's play *Bartholomew Fair* (1614), a hypocritical preacher, full of Puritan rhetoric but also a glutton.

Bute. *See* Crawley.

Butler, Rhett. In Margaret Mitchell's novel *Gone With the Wind* (1936), the dashing but cynical Southern blockade runner who finds himself in love with Scarlett O'Hara,* eventually marrying her after the war when he has become a wealthy profiteer. He finally deserts her, in the movie version (1939) uttering the famous exit line, "Frankly, my dear, I don't give a damn."

Buto. In Egyptian mythology, the mother of the sun and the moon.

Buttercup. In Gilbert and Sullivan's operetta *H.M.S. Pinafore* (1878), the plump matron who many years ago had mixed up the babies and sings the famous: "I'm called little Buttercup." For most of the twentieth century, when fictional men had a dark secret in their schoolboy past, it was more often than not that they had played Buttercup in the school production.

Butterfly. In John Luther Long's story *Madame Butterfly* (1897), in David Belasco's play (1900), and especially in Puccini's opera version (1904), a naive Japanese geisha who falls in love with the American naval officer Pinkerton* only to be deserted by him when she is pregnant. When he returns to Japan married to an American, she commits suicide in one of the most famous opera deaths. Also noted for her aria "Un bel di."

Button Moulder, The. In Henrik Ibsen's play *Peer Gynt* (1867), God's representative on earth who melts down the souls of those neither good nor bad to make into buttons. *See also* Gynt, Peter.

Buzfuz. In Charles Dickens's novel *Pickwick Papers* (1836), the imposing barrister who pleads the case against Pickwick.* *See also* Bardell, Mrs.; Snubbin.

C

Cacus. In Roman legend, a three-headed giant who breathed flames and was a famous thief; he was killed after stealing some of Hercules's* cattle.

Caddy. *See* Compson.

Cade, Jack. Historically, leader of an English peasant rebellion in 1450; in Shakespeare's play *Henry VI, Part II* (1592), he utters the famous: "The first thing we do, let's kill all the lawyers."

Cadmus. In Greek legend, a prince sent to search for his sister Europa* after her abduction by Zeus.* He killed a dragon on the plain of Thebes, then sowed the dragon's teeth, each of which immediately grew into a warrior, whom he tricked by throwing a stone among them and letting them in their anger and confusion kill each other; the five remaining helped him found the city of Thebes. He is also said to have introduced the use of alphabet letters. *See also* Ino; Spartae.

Caeneus. In Greek legend, a woman allowed by Poseidon* to change her sex and who as a male became a great warrior until she offended Zeus* and was buried under a pile of pine trees.

Caesar. Historically, a title given to Roman emperors.

Caesar, Augustus. Historically, the adopted son (d. 14) of Julius Caesar* and the first Roman emperor; he appears in numerous works, usually as a wise and effective politician and administrator. *Also called* Octavius. *See also* Livia; Tiberius.

Caesar, Julius. Historically, a Roman general, conqueror of Gaul, who crossed the Rubicon* with his army and took authority in Rome, effectively ending the Republic, until his assassination in 44 B.C. He appears in numerous works (including his own *Gallic Wars*, long studied by all Latin students and beginning, "All Gaul is divided into three parts") in mixed characterization, sometimes as a great general and brilliant man, other times as a self-seeking politician and tyrant. In Shakespeare's play *Julius Caesar* (1599), he is rather arrogant and pompous. *See also* Antony, Marc; Brutus; Calpurnia; Cleopatra; Pompeia.

Caesar, Octavius. *See* Caesar, Augustus.

Caesar Augustus. *See* Caesar, Augustus.

Caesar's Wife. In Plutarch's *Lives*, Julius Caesar* divorced his wife Pompeia without determining the truth of the rumors about her adultery, saying "Caesar's wife must be above suspicion." The term is often used to indicate anyone close to an important personage whose actions might be interpreted as being done with the approval or encouragement of the famous person.

Cagliostro. Historically, a charlatan (d. 1795) who posed as a doctor and necromancer and who claimed, among other things, to have the secret of eternal youth; often synonymous with magicians, hypnotists, and anyone who claims to master the black arts.

Caiaphas. In the Bible, *Matthew* xxvi, the Jewish high priest who tried Jesus;* he is often interpreted as having engineered His conviction.

Caieta. In Virgil's *Aeneid*, the nurse of Aeneas.*

Cain. In the Bible, *Genesis* iv, first son of Adam* and Eve;* he tended the fields. In a fit of jealousy after the Lord accepted a sacrifice from his brother Abel,* who tended the flocks, and rejected his own offering of plants, he killed Abel. When the Lord asked him about Abel, he replied, "Am I my brother's keeper?," but God was not fooled and cursed Cain with a life in which no crops would grow for him, marked him so that all would know him, and sent him out to wander in the land of Nod, east of Eden.*

Caiphas. *See* Caiaphas.

Caius. *See* Cornelia.

Caius, Dr. In Shakespeare's play *The Merry Wives of Windsor* (1598), a French doctor whose fractured English leads to numerous crude puns. *See also* Evans.

Calchas. In Greek legend, a Trojan, father of Cressida,* and a great seer who joined the Greeks when he foresaw Troy's fall; his prophecies led to the importance of Achilles* in the Trojan War,* the sacrifice of Iphigenia,* and the restoration of Chryseis.* He was said to have died of grief when another seer more accurately predicted an event.

Caleb. In the Bible, *Joshua* xiv–xv, a spy sent by Moses* into the Promised Land;* for his services, Moses promised him the land of Hebron.

Calf, Fatted. *See* Prodigal.

Calf, Golden. *See* Golden Calf.

Caliban. In Shakespeare's play *The Tempest* (1611), a partly human monster, often portrayed as part fish, subdued by Prospero.* He tries to revolt, only to be disillusioned by the drunkenness of the humans he thought were gods. He is sometimes seen as a ridiculous monster, sometimes as Shakespeare's negative conception of "natural man," and in recent years rather sympathetically as a symbol of the native inhabitant oppressed by the powerful or the European. *See also* Stephano; Trinculo.

Caligula. Historically, the third Roman emperor, assassinated in 41; he figures in numerous works as a tyrant and madman of incredible cruelty. Among his most commonly reported acts were making his horse a senator, declaring himself a god, and perhaps engaging in incest with his sister, whom he later murdered. When modern writers talk about the "Decline of the Roman Empire," they generally refer to his reign, although it in fact occurred in the earliest years of the empire.

Calisto. (1) In Fernando de Rojas's novel *Celestina* (1501), a gentleman who loves Melibea,* arranges with the bawd Celestina* to seduce her, and is killed by falling from a ladder afterwards. (2) *See also* Callisto.

Callahan, Harry. *See* Dirty Harry.

Calliope. In Greek mythology, the Muse* of epic poetry and mother of Orpheus.*

Callisto. (1) In Greek legend, a huntress changed into a bear by Hera* when Zeus* falls in love with her. She is almost killed by her son Arcas* before being changed into the constellation Ursa Major. (2) *See also* Calisto.

Calpurnia. Historically, second wife of Julius Caesar.* In Shakespeare's play *Julius Caesar* (1599), she tries to keep him away from the Senate as a result of her ominous dreams. *See also* Caesar's Wife.

Calvary. In Christian usage, the name given to the hill on which Jesus* was crucified, derived from the Latin translation of Golgotha;* hence, often used to signify both a place of great suffering and the suffering itself.

Calydonian Boar. *See* Meleager; Oeneus.

Calypso. In Homer's *Odyssey*, an island queen with whom Odysseus* was shipwrecked, by whom he had two children, but with whom he refused to stay after seven years in spite of her offer of immortality.

Cama. *See* Kama.

Cambyses. In Thomas Preston's play *Cambyses* (1569), a son of Cyrus* and king of Persia, noted primarily for his bombastic rhetoric.

Camelot. In British legend, especially in Malory's *Morte d'Arthur*, the site of Arthur's* court; in legend, it has come to symbolize any place of true peace and justice.

Camenae. In Roman mythology, the Muses.*

Camilla. In Virgil's *Aeneid*, a virgin warrior queen, so swift she could run over a field without bending the blades of corn; she fought with one breast bare to free her bow arm and was killed by one of Aeneas's* men.

Camille. In Alexandre Dumas *fils*'s novel (1848) and play (1852) *The Lady of the Camellias*, a beautiful and successful Parisian courtesan who falls in love with young Duval* and then, to prevent his ruin, sacrifices herself and returns to her old life, even though it means her death by tuberculosis. Her real name was Marguerite Gautier, but she took this nickname from the white camellias she carried to indicate her availability for dalliance. Her long, exaggerated death scene was long admired and as often parodied. *See also* Violetta.

Camillo, Don. In numerous stories by Giovanni Guareschi (beg. 1950), an Italian village priest noted for his long-running conflict with the local communist mayor and for his often awkward attempts to justify this in his prayers.

Camillus, St. Historically, a mercenary (d. 1614) who, due to his own wounds and diseases, founded the Servants of the Sick after his conversion and reformed hospital treatment throughout much of Europe; the patron saint of nurses, his day is July 14.

Campion, Albert. In numerous novels by Margery Allingham, beginning with *The Crime at Black Dudley* (1929), a mild-mannered, unprepossessing detective with large glasses and a fatuous facade.

Cana. In the Bible, *John* ii, the site of a marriage feast at which Jesus* turned the water into wine, His first miracle.

Canaan. In the Bible, *Genesis* ix, the son of Ham* cursed by God when Ham saw Noah* naked and condemned to be a slave of the children of Ham's brothers; in later chapters, Canaan is listed among the nations of Africa, which led many apologists for Negro slavery to justify it as God's will. At the same time, the inhabitants of the Promised Land* before the Israelites and Joshua* conquered it were also called Canaanites, and the land of Canaan is often used synonymously with the geographical Israel.*

Canace. In Chaucer's *Canterbury Tales*, in the Squire's Tale, a paragon among women who receives from the king of Arabia a ring that allows her to understand the language of the birds and a mirror that will tell if her lover is true. Edmund Spenser continues the story in *The Faerie Queene* (1590) in which she marries a knight who proves his worth by withstanding her brother in a duel.

Candace. In the Bible, *Acts* viii, a wealthy queen of Ethiopia; her eunuch is converted by Philip.*

Candida. In G. B. Shaw's play *Candida* (1897), the beautiful, intelligent, and independent wife of the pompous minister Morell.* She is loved by the weak, childish poet Marchbanks,* but when asked to choose between the two, she chooses the one who needs her most—Morell.

Candide. In Voltaire's novel *Candide* (1759), a gentle, honest, and extremely simple young man who believes the teaching of Dr. Pangloss* that this is "the best of all possible worlds," even in the face of numerous misfortunes such as war, the Lisbon earthquake, his interrogation by the Inquisition, and his discovery of Eldorado* and subsequent loss of the wealth. Finally he realizes that life is not perfect, and he retires to cultivate his garden and live as well as possible in the circumstances. *See also* Cunegonde.

Candour, Mrs. In R. B. Sheridan's play *The School for Scandal* (1777), a hypocritical scandalmonger who claims to love only the truth.

Candy. In Terry Southern and Mason Hoffenberg's novel *Candy* (1958), a simple but voluptuous young girl who accidentally and rather innocently finds herself in numerous exotic and generally humorous sexual adventures.

Canens. In Ovid's *Metamorphoses*, a woman who grieves so much for her husband Picus* that she dissolves in tears.

Canio. In Leoncavallo's opera *Pagliacci* (1892), the clown who murders his unfaithful wife during a performance and says "la comedia è finita." He is the epitome of the sad clown. *See also* Tonio.

Canon's Yeoman, The. In Chaucer's *Canterbury Tales*, the yeoman who tells the story exposing the alchemists.

Canossa. *See* Henry.

Canute. Historically, a Danish king of England (d. 1035). In legend, he is said to have ordered the sea to fall back in order to show his courtiers how little power he had and thus indicate the folly of flattery; however, in many allusions, he is used to indicate the folly of those who think themselves all-powerful.

Capaneus. In Greek legend, one of the Seven Against Thebes;* he is killed by Zeus* for boasting that not even Zeus could stop him. *See also* Evadne.

Capitano, il. In the commedia dell'Arte, the braggart soldier who was sometimes a quick-tempered duelist but more often a coward behind his bluster. He was one of the most popular commedia character types and reappeared under many different names, such as Scaramouche,* Miles Gloriosus,* and Pasquariello.

Capp, Andy. In the English newspaper cartoon *Andy Capp* (beg. 1957), a little man noted for his ability to avoid work while living off his wife's earnings and for his devotion to drink, football, pigeons, woman chasing, and sarcasm. He is identified by his ever-present cloth cap worn so low his eyes are never visible.

Capricorn. A name sometimes used for Pan,* particularly when in the form of a goat. One of the signs of the zodiac.

Captain, The. (1) In August Strindberg's play *The Father* (1887), the father driven to madness by his wife Laura.* (2) *See* Edgar. (3) *See* Capitano, il; Miles Gloriosus.

Capulet. In Shakespeare's play *Romeo and Juliet* (1595), one of two feuding families in Verona; its most noted members are Juliet* and Tybalt.* *See also* Montague.

Cardew, Cecily. *See* Cecily.

Carey, Philip. In Somerset Maugham's novel *Of Human Bondage* (1915), a sensitive and idealistic young man with little self-confidence due to his club foot; his life is almost destroyed by his obsession with the vain and thoughtless Mildred Rogers.*

Carker. In Charles Dickens's novel *Dombey and Son* (1846), **James** is Dombey's* head clerk, a secretive man with a chilling smile who quietly destroys Dombey's business and runs off with Dombey's wife Edith,* only to be rejected by her in turn and to die by falling under a train while trying to escape Dombey's pursuit. His brother **John** is a faithful, gentle clerk who, allowed to keep his job despite an early theft, repays Dombey's kindness by trying to restore what his brother had destroyed.

Carmel. In the Bible, *I Kings* xviii, the mountain on which Elijah* overcame the 450 prophets of Baal.*

Carmen. In Prosper Mérimée's novel (1847) and Bizet's opera (1875) *Carmen*, a sensual gypsy girl who seduces the soldier Don José* into a life of crime among smugglers and then deserts him for a bullfighter, eventually to be killed by him in jealousy; generally seen as one of the most vivid representations of temperament and blazing sexual passion. *See also* Escamillo; Lucas.

Carmichael, Augustus. In Virginia Woolf's novel *To the Lighthouse* (1927), a minor poet and hanger-on who takes love from others but gives none in return.

Carpenter. A name sometimes used for Jesus* from His youthful work with His earthly father, the carpenter Joseph.*

Carraway, Nick. In F. Scott Fitzgerald's novel *The Great Gatsby* (1925), the young, sensitive, and sympathetic narrator. *See also* Buchanan; Daisy; Gatsby.

Carrie. In Theodore Dreiser's novel *Sister Carrie* (1912), a country girl of emotional nature who pursues an acting career; she is intelligent, but instinctive, and vaguely disillusioned as each success fails to match her ideal. She was particularly noted in her time for her open sexuality, and the work is often cited as a major step in the development of American realism. *See also* Hurstwood.

Carrington. In the American television series "Dynasty" (beg. 1981), a family of incredible wealth and complex, melodramatic lives. **Blake** is the handsome patriarch, and **Krystle**, his second wife, is a beautiful, sensitive, and understanding woman, but most interest revolves around his divorced wife **Alexis**, the epitome of the beautiful, wealthy, but also scheming, vicious, and heartless bitch.

Carson, Kit. Historically, an American trapper (d. 1868) and explorer, subject of much fictional and legendary literature as a quintessential frontiersman. In William Saroyan's play *The Time of Your Life* (1939), a garrulous old coot and outrageous liar claims to be him.

Carstone, Richard. In Charles Dickens's novel *Bleak House* (1852), a young man who gradually wastes his life and talent in hopes of eventual inheritance in the Jarndyce* case. *See also* Clare, Ada.

Carter, Nick. In as many as 1000 stories by John Coryell and others (beg. 1886), a heroic detective/spy of numerous disguises, penetrating intelligence, and phenomenal physical skill.

Carton, Sidney. In Charles Dickens's novel *A Tale of Two Cities* (1859), a drunken lawyer who, owing to his secret love for Lucie, substitutes himself for her lover Charles Darnay* and is guillotined during the Reign of Terror,* his last words being, "It is a far, far better thing I do than I have ever done before. . . . "

Carver. *See* Doone.

Carya. In Greek legend, a girl loved by Dionysus;* she was changed into a walnut tree after her death, from which the caryatids, female statues serving as columns of temples, derived their name.

Casanova. Historically, an Italian adventurer (d. 1798) and author of a set of memoirs whose sexual frankness made him synonymous with sexual libertinage.

Casaubon. In George Eliot's novel *Middlemarch* (1871), the unimaginative, gloomy, and vindictive clergyman and unsuccessful scholar who destroys much of Dorothea Brooke's* personality during their marriage.

Casby, Christopher. In Charles Dickens's novel *Little Dorrit* (1855), the miserly landlord who pretends to nobility and philanthropy because he can delegate all the dirty work to his manager Pancks.* For his daughter, *see* Flora.

Casca. In Shakespeare's play *Julius Caesar* (1599), one of the conspirators, generally depicted as less intelligent than the others. *See also* Brutus; Caesar, Julius; Cassius.

Casey. (1) In Ernest L. Thayer's poem *Casey at the Bat* (1888), a mighty baseball player; "there is no joy in Mudville" when, with the game in the balance, he strikes out ignominiously. (2) *See* Jones, Casey.

Cash. *See* Bundren.

Casimir, St. Historically, a Polish prince (d. 1484) canonized for his life of purity and the numerous miracles associated with his tomb; the patron saint of Poland, his day is March 4.

Caspar. *See* Milquetoast, Caspar.

Cass. In George Eliot's novel *Silas Marner* (1861), **Squire** is an inflexible landlord prone to fits of intense anger; his son **Godfrey** is the father of Eppie* and is so weak and fearful of his father that he keeps his marriage and her birth a secret; the other son **Dunstan** is a dissolute spendthrift who blackmails his brother and steals Silas Marner's* gold, only to die holding it while falling into the stone pit.

Cassandra. In Greek legend, a Trojan* princess given the power of prophecy by Apollo.* When she refused to give herself to him in return, he promised that, although she would always know the future, no one would ever believe her. In Homer's *Iliad* and in Virgil's *Aeneid*, her numerous predictions of doom for the Trojans were all ignored, making her synonymous with both ignored prophets and perpetual doomsayers. After Troy fell, she was taken as the slave/mistress of Agamemnon.* In Euripides's play *The Trojan Women*, this prompts a mad scene in which she performs a satiric wedding hymn that foretells the fall of the house of Atreus.* In Aeschylus's play *Agamemnon*, she confronts Clytemnestra* and foresees her own murder. *See also* Ajax; Eurypylus; Hecuba; Priam.

Cassio. In Shakespeare's play *Othello* (1604), the lieutenant promoted for his education rather than his experience, whom Iago* plots to remove; unable to hold his liquor, he is easily made to seem a drunkard, and then his pleas to Othello's wife Desdemona* to be reinstated are twisted into an appearance of adultery. *See also* Bianca.

Cassiopeia. In Greek legend, queen of Ethiopia and mother of Andromeda.* Her boast that she was more beautiful than the Nereids* led to the destruction of the country by a sea monster and her transformation into a constellation.

Cassius. Historically, one of the principal assassins (d. 42 B.C.) of Julius Caesar.* In Shakespeare's play *Julius Caesar* (1599), he is a practical and brave man, but he is mistrusted for his "lean and hungry look." In Dante's *Divine Comedy*, he is a traitor forever condemned to be frozen at the center of Hell* in ice as cold as his heart. *See also* Brutus; Casca; Cinna.

Cassy. In Harriet Beecher Stowe's novel *Uncle Tom's Cabin* (1852), Eliza's* mother and a slave who eventually escapes from the evil Legree* by taking advantage of his superstitions. *See also* Tom, Uncle.

Castor. In Greek legend, one of the twin sons of Leda* and Zeus.* A great horseman, after his death he joins his brother Pollux* in the constellation Gemini. *See also* Hilara; Phoebe.

Castorp, Hans. In Thomas Mann's novel *The Magic Mountain* (1924), a young engineer whose commitment to a sanitorium for treatment of his tuberculosis initates a spiritual journey through the major philosophies of European thought that culminates in a snowstorm where he has a vision of both paradise and blood sacrifice. After his release, he forgets that vision, dabbling in spiritualism and experiencing occasional glimpses of the "death wish" he finds in Romantic music.

Catch–22. In Joseph Heller's novel *Catch–22* (1961), the "catch" that means that the rules apply only when authority chooses to apply them. This takes many forms, but the most often cited is that anyone insane will be sent home from the war as soon as he asks, but anyone who asks to go home must be sane and thus cannot go home. *See also* Yossarian.

Caterpillar. In Lewis Carroll's story *Alice in Wonderland* (1865), the caterpillar sits on a mushroom smoking a waterpipe and asking terse questions of Alice.*

Catharine. *See* Catherine.

Catherine. (1) Historically, Catherine of Aragon (d. 1536), queen of England and first wife of Henry VIII,* noted primarily for being divorced by Henry and thus bringing about English Protestantism. (2) *See* Medici. (3) *See also* Cathy; Kate; Katharine.

Catherine, St. In Christian legend, an Alexandrian maiden who challenged the Roman emperor for his worship of idols, demolishing the arguments of 50 philosophers, who were executed for their failure, and emerging unharmed from the torture of a spiked wheel when the wheel disintegrated. She was finally beheaded, and milk flowed from her veins. Her emblem is the wheel, her day is November 25.

Cathleen, Countess. In W. B. Yeats's play *The Countess Cathleen* (1892), an ancient Irish countess who exhausts her resources trying to feed her people in a famine and then sells her soul to gain sustenance for them.

Cathy. (1) In Emily Brontë's novel *Wuthering Heights* (1847), the saucy and spirited daughter of Earnshaw.* Initially a close friend of the orphan Heathcliff,* she grows more arrogant and snubs him as she begins to mix with local society and eventually rejects him to marry the wealthy Edgar Linton.* She and Heathcliff maintain a passionate but spiritual attachment and, after her death in childbirth and his death many years later, their spirits are said to wander the Heights together. (2) *See also* Catherine; Kate; Katherine.

Catiline. Historically, a dissolute noble whose conspiracy to overthrow the Roman republic in 63 B.C. was exposed in Cicero's orations on the subject, thus becoming one of the fundamental illustrations of treason.

Cato. (1) Historically, a Roman consul (d. 149 B.C.) known for his rigid opposition to luxury and immorality. (2) Historically, a Roman sage (d. 46 B.C.) known as "the conscience of Rome"; in Renaissance literature, he was usually seen as a symbol of pagan virtue, as in Dante's *Divine Comedy*, where he directs Dante and Virgil on their way upward.

Cattle of Geryon. In Greek legend, cattle taken from the monster Geryon* as the tenth labor of Heracles.*

Cattle of the Sun. In Homer's *Odyssey*, cattle sacred to Apollo* but killed and eaten by Odysseus's* men, for which they were all drowned. *See also* Eurylocus; Hermes.

Caulfield, Holden. In J. D. Salinger's novel *The Catcher in the Rye* (1951), a teenaged boy who, expelled from prep school, spends a few days alone in New York before his breakdown, prompted by his own adolescent confusions and by the "phoniness" of the world he observes. He is noted as one of the most perceptive depictions of the youthful psyche, for his observations of the hypocrisy of respectable society that made him a spokesman for several youthful generations, and for his use of teenaged "vulgar" language that has made him and the book a target of censors for decades.

Cavaradossi. In Puccini's opera *Tosca* (1900), the painter and patriot whose death is accidentally brought about by his jealous lover Tosca.*

Cawdor. One of the titles held by Macbeth.*

Cécile. *See* Volanges, Cécile de.

Cecilia, St. In Christian legend, virgin wife of Valerian.* She lived three days after a clumsy attempt was made to behead her after she refused to practice idolatry. Her story is also told by the Second Nun in Chaucer's *Canterbury Tales*. She is patron saint of the organ and of music in general, although the sources of that relationship are obscure, and her feast day (November 22) is often a celebration of music, particularly in John Dryden's poem *A Song for St. Cecilia's Day* (1687), rather than a celebration of her martyrdom.

Cecily. In Oscar Wilde's play *The Importance of Being Earnest* (1895), a romantic girl who writes a fictional diary to make her life more interesting. *See also* Algernon; Gwendolen; Worthing, Jack.

Cedric the Saxon. In Walter Scott's novel *Ivanhoe* (1820), the warlike Saxon who disowns his son Ivanhoe.* *See also* Wamba.

Celestina. In Fernando de Rojas's novel *Celestina* (1501), a crafty bawd who tricks the virtuous maiden Melibea* into debauchery and is murdered for her money.

Celia. (1) In Shakespeare's play *As You Like It* (1599), Rosalind's* gentle and more traditionally feminine cousin who deserts her father and runs away with Rosalind to the Forest of Arden.* (2) In Ben Jonson's play *Volpone* (1605), the virtuous wife of Corvino.* (3) *See* Brooke.

Célimène. In Molière's play *The Misanthrope* (1666), the witty, flirtatious, beautiful, and occasionally caustic widow who rejects the misanthrope Alceste's* offer of marriage. Generally she is seen as the epitome of the shallow fashionable female more concerned with flattery and social success then true relationships. *See also* Arsinoé; Éliante.

Celmus. In Ovid's *Metamorphoses*, a playfellow of the child Zeus* who was changed into a magnet for claiming Zeus was mortal.

Cenci. Historically, a Roman family whose father tried to force the daughter Beatrice into an incestuous relationship; in revenge, she and her brother had the father killed, only to be themselves discovered, tortured, and executed in 1599. In Shelley's play *The Cenci* (1819), the daughter Beatrice is portrayed as innocent of the conspiracy and betrayed by the evil priest Orsino.*

Centaur. In Greek legend, a creature with the upper body of a man and the lower body of a horse. *See also* Chiron; Lapiths; Nessus; Pirithous; Sagittarius.

Cephalus. In Ovid's *Metamorphoses*, a handsome prince who married Procris but was stolen by Aurora,* whose love he spurned; the goddess returned him in new form to his wife, whom he seduced. When he was given his original shape, Procris felt so guilty that she ran away. Although later reconciled, she jealously spied on him until he mistook her in the woods and killed her by accident.

Cephas. A name sometimes used for Peter.*

Cerberus. In Greek mythology, the three-headed dog that guards the entrance to the underworld; Heracles's* twelfth labor was to bring him up to the earth. In Virgil's *Aeneid*, Aeneas* gets past him by giving him a cake. *See also* Hades; Pluto.

Cereno, Benito. In Herman Melville's story *Benito Cereno* (1856), the captain of a Spanish slave ship whose cargo revolts and commits numerous atrocities on the crew, the witnessing of which destroys his own spirit.

Ceres. In Roman mythology, goddess of agriculture, generally equivalent to Demeter.*

Cerynean Hind. In Greek legend, a beautiful stag with brass hoofs and golden antlers that Heracles* captured as one of his labors.

Ceyx. In Ovid's *Metamorphoses*, a man whose deep love for his wife Halcyone* was so strong that his death at sea was communicated to her in a dream; both were changed into kingfishers.

Chadband, Rev. In Charles Dickens's novel *Bleak House* (1852), a hypocritical clergyman given to flowery and discursive speech.

Chan, Charlie. In several novels by Earl Derr Biggers (beg. 1925) and in numerous movies, a chubby, genial Chinese detective noted for his "number one son" and his ability to find an ancient aphorism to fit any situation in a case.

Chancellor, Olive. In Henry James's novel *The Bostonians* (1886), the independent feminist theoretician and organizer, desolated by her protegée Verena's desertion of the cause for a man. *See also* Ransom, Basil.

Changeling, The. In Middleton and Rowley's play *The Changeling* (1623), the young man Antonio who pretends to be insane to have access to the wife of the asylum keeper.

Channing, Margo. In the movie *All About Eve* (1950), the sharp-tongued star faced with the beginning of her career's decline, noted for some of the most deliciously waspish insults ever spoken on film. *See also* Eve.

Chanticleer. (1) In French folklore, the cock who relaxes his guard after Reynard* the fox claims to have become a vegetarian, only to see the fox eat his chicks. (2) In Chaucer's *Canterbury Tales*, in the Nun's Priest's Tale, the vainglorious cock who, when praised by the fox, closes his eyes to crow some more and is captured; he then encourages the fox to brag about the escapade and escapes when the fox opens his mouth to talk. *See also* Pertelote.

Chaos. In Greek mythology, the shapeless mass that existed before the creation of the universe; sometimes portrayed as a god.

Chardon, Lucien. In several novels by Balzac, especially *Lost Illusions* (1837–43), a young man on the make in nineteenth-century Paris. He is a modest provincial poet who uses poetry as an entrée into provincial society. Following an affair with a noblewoman, he goes to Paris with the master criminal Vautrin,* where he devotes himself to a life of pleasure amid the cynical literary life of the city until his eventual suicide in prison.

Charlemagne. Historically, a king of the Franks (d. 814) and the founder of what came to be called the Holy Roman Empire. He figures in numerous medieval and Renaissance works as a great king and warrior, most notably in *The Song of Roland*, in which he is said to be 200 years old and is presiding over a court of equals when not battling with the pagan Saracens. *See also* Ganelon; Ogier; Oliver; Orlando; Roland; Paladin.

Charles. (1) Historically, a name used by two kings of England: **Charles I**, whose failure to realize the strength of the rising middle class and protestant Puritanism led to the English Civil War and his execution in 1649; and his son **Charles II** (d. 1685), who was eventually restored to the throne in 1660 after long exile during Cromwell's* dictatorship and who initiated the period of relaxed social and artistic morality known as the Restoration. Both appear in numerous works, generally as profligates more concerned with personal pleasure and privilege than good government. (2) Historically, a name used by numerous kings of France. Most literary references are to **Charles I**, known as Charlemagne;* **Charles VII**, the weak and vacillating Dauphin restored to the throne by Jeanne d'Arc,* known more for being henpecked by his mistress than for his real success at driving the English out of France and stabilizing the national economy. (3) Historically, a name used by numerous Holy Roman Emperors, the most often referred to being **Charles V** (d. 1558), also **Charles I** of Spain, who is entertained by Faustus* in Christopher Marlowe's play *Doctor Faustus* (1592) and is often depicted in English literature as the power-mad genius behind Catholic designs on England during the reign of Henry VIII.* (4) In Shakespeare's play *As You Like It* (1599), a great wrestler defeated by Orlando.* (4) *See* Surface. (5) *See also* Charlie, Bonnie Prince; Charley.

Charles, Nick and Nora. In Dashiell Hammett's novel *The Thin Man* (1934) and in several movies (beg. 1934), Nick is a tough, intelligent detective, now married to the wealthy Nora; together they came to personify the perfect couple, elegant yet casual, charming yet tough and intelligent on demand, devoted and faithful yet always able to tease each other as equals, and completely secure in their relationship. *See also* Asta.

Charley. In Daniel Keyes's story *Flowers for Algernon* (1959), a severely mentally handicapped man who undergoes an experimental operation and temporarily becomes a genius. *See also* Algernon.

Charley's Aunt. In Brandon Thomas's play *Charley's Aunt* (1892), the eccentric aunt whose support is needed for a young man's marriage and who is humorously impersonated by his male friend Babs;* noted for being from Brazil, "where the nuts come from."

Charlie, Bonnie Prince. Historically, a prince of the Stuart family (d. 1788) who claimed the English throne after the Hanoverians had been crowned. Rallying support among all the Jacobites,* especially the clans of Scotland, he attempted to take the crown by force in 1745; the revolt finally ended at the battle of Culloden in 1746, after which he escaped to Europe and eventually died a drunken wanderer. He figures in countless poems, legends, songs, and novels, most notably in works by Robert Burns and Walter Scott, usually as a gallant and brave prince, nobly fighting for a great lost cause.

Charlotta. (1) *See* Ivanovna, Charlotta. (2) *See also* Charlotte.

Charlotte. (1) In Goethe's novel *The Sorrows of Young Werther* (1774), the woman loved by Werther;* she is the perfection of femininity: faithful, kind, genteel, and compassionate. (2) In Goethe's novel *Elective Affinities* (1808), the wife who falls in love with a friend of her husband but who refuses to violate her moral code to satisfy that love until her husband's death. *See also* Edward; Ottilie. (3) In Jane Austen's novel *Pride and Prejudice* (1813), Charlotte Lucas, a woman with a gentle heart and common sense who marries the pompous Collins* after Elizabeth Bennet* has rejected him, thinking his offer far the best she is likely to receive. (4) *See* Corday, Charlotte. (5) *See also* Charlotta.

Charlus. In Marcel Proust's novels *Remembrance of Things Past* (1913–27), a baron of the Guermantes* family and a depraved homosexual, a figure of both fascination and disgust, particularly in *Cities of the Plain*, who eventually becomes senile in old age.

Charmaine. In Stallings and Anderson's play *What Price Glory?* (1924), the beautiful, playful French peasant girl fought over by Flagg* and Quirt.*

Charmian. In Shakespeare's play *Antony and Cleopatra* (1606), Cleopatra's* servant. Initially, she seems concerned only with the wittily risqué, but as she tends her mistress's body and prepares for her own suicide, she becomes tragically dignified. *See also* Alexas; Charmion; Iras.

Charmion. In John Dryden's play *All for Love* (1677), one of Cleopatra's* faithful servants who commits suicide with her. *See also* Charmian.

Charon. In Greek mythology, a minor god of Hades* who ferried the dead over the river Styx* to the underworld. He demanded pay for this, so a coin was placed in the mouth of the dead, and he was assumed to leave those not thus properly buried stranded on the shore for a hundred years.

Charybdis. In Greek mythology, a sea monster and daughter of Poseidon.* In Homer's *Odyssey*, she is more specifically a whirlpool opposite the cave of the monster Scylla,* between the two of which Odysseus* must safely pass.

Chase, Elyot. *See* Elyot.

Chasuble, Rev. In Oscar Wilde's play *The Importance of Being Earnest* (1895), a gentle clergyman quietly enamored of Miss Prism,* much given to allusions and able to adapt any sermon to any circumstance.

Chatsky. In Griboyedov's play *Woe from Wit* (1822), a Russian gentleman given to ridicule of the artificial Frenchified ways of Russian society, eventually driven out when people believe the rumor that he is insane.

Chatterley. In D. H. Lawrence's novel *Lady Chatterley's Lover* (1928), Lady Chatterley is an English gentlewoman whose husband returns paralyzed from World War I and who turns for solace to a passionate affair with her gamekeeper Mellors.* Her husband quickly becomes a symbol of both sexual and social rigidity and sterility, while she becomes a symbol of sexual freedom and natural strength. Due to the novel's use of direct sexual language, the work was long censored in England and America, thus making her name synonymous with unbridled sexuality, titillation, and pornography.

Chauntecleer. *See* Chanticleer.

Chebutykin. In Anton Chekhov's play *Three Sisters* (1901), the old, incompetent military doctor who reads only newspapers and who responds to all events by saying, "It doesn't matter."

Cheeryble. In Charles Dickens's novel *Nicholas Nickleby* (1838), two cheerful, redheaded, boisterous, and completely good brothers who give Nicholas Nickleby* a job in their firm and aid him in his problems with his uncle.

Cheevy, Miniver. In Edward Arlington Robinson's poem *Miniver Cheevy* (1910), the "child of scorn" who lives in melancholy romantic dreams and eventually becomes an alcoholic.

Cheiron. *See* Chiron.

Chélan, Abbé. In Stendhal's novel *The Red and the Black* (1830), the parish priest, maneuvered from his post for his liberal leanings, who encourages Julien Sorel* to go to school and try for a career away from his family.

Chelone. In Greek legend, a nymph* who refused to attend Zeus's wedding and was condemned to perpetual silence as a tortoise.

Ch'en. In André Malraux's novel *Man's Fate* (1933), a Chinese communist revolutionary who blows himself up in an assassination attempt which he makes in defiance of party orders. *See also* Kyo.

Cherry. In George Farquhar's play *The Beaux' Stratagem* (1707), the vivacious daughter of the landlord Boniface;* she is sent to spy on the beaux and soon falls in love with Archer.* *See also* Aimwell; Dorinda.

Cherub. One of the Cherubim.* *See also* Seraph.

Cherubim. In the Bible, *Ezekiel* x, creatures with four wings and four heads, and in other citations described variously, often as composite beasts. In Christian tradition, however, they are depicted as plump little boy angels* and, with the Seraphim,* are often said to surround the throne of God; no one seems to know precisely when or how the conception changed so drastically.

Chérubin. In Beaumarchais's play *The Marriage of Figaro* (1784), the teenaged page in love with all women, who finds himself regularly disguised as a woman to escape from crises. *See also* Almaviva; Figaro; Susanna.

Cherubino. In Mozart's opera *The Marriage of Figaro* (1786), Chérubin;* the role is always sung by a woman.

Cheshire Cat, The. In Lewis Carroll's story *Alice in Wonderland* (1865), a grinning cat who sits in a tree to talk to Alice* and then disappears without warning, its grin remaining for a while after the rest of the cat has vanished.

Chichikov. In Nikolai Gogol's novel *Dead Souls* (1846), an ambitious Russian official who, wishing to become wealthy, travels across Russia buying serfs (''souls'') who are cheap because they have died since the last census; with this paper wealth, he is then able to enter provincial society as a wealthy man and raise capital without effort until he is exposed. His escape in a sleigh gone out of control is a famous metaphor for the headlong rush of Russian society toward its eventual collapse.

Childe Harold. *See* Harold, Childe.

Childe Roland. *See* Roland, Childe.

Childers, E. W. B. In Charles Dickens's novel *Hard Times* (1854), a circus performer, billed as ''The Wild Huntsman of the North American Prairies,'' who helps Tom Gradgrind.*

Childe Waters. In an ancient British ballad, the heartless lover of Ellen, who serves disguised as his page to be near him, despite his mistreatment of her, including her giving birth in a stable tended only by his horse.

Chillingworth. In Nathaniel Hawthorne's novel *The Scarlet Letter* (1850), Hester's* husband, believed dead, who reappears as a mysterious doctor, keeping his identity secret after her adultery has been exposed. Sly and devious, he is always a lurking, evil presence, whether ministering to the sick Dimmesdale* or spying on Hester and Pearl.*

Chimène. In Pierre Corneille's play *Le Cid* (1637), the daughter of a Spanish count, who was killed by the Cid* on a point of honor; when she demands the killer be killed, the Cid offers her his sword, but, torn between her love for him and her duty to her father, she cannot kill him herself. Despite his victories against the Moors, she still demands revenge, although her love for the Cid is obvious even to the king, who sends him off to the wars in hopes that that will resolve her dilemma. *See also* Ximena.

Chimera. In Greek legend, a fire-breathing monster with a lion's head, a goat's body, and a snake's tail, killed by Bellerophon.*

Chingachgook. In James Fenimore Cooper's novel *The Last of the Mohicans* (1826), an Indian chief, stalwart friend of Natty Bumppo,* and father of Uncas,* the last Mohican.

Chione. In Greek legend, a great beauty who slept with both Apollo* and Hermes* on the same night, giving birth to Autolycus* and Philammon,* and who was killed by Artemis* for her vanity. *See also* Daedalion.

Chipping, Mr. *See* Chips, Mr.

Chips, Mr. In James Hilton's novel *Goodbye Mr. Chips* (1933), Mr. Chipping, a gentle teacher whose life was completely committed to his boys at the school and to his young wife; a sentimental depiction of the ideal teacher loved by his students and teaching far more than mere subject matter.

Chiron. (1) In Greek legend, a centaur,* famous for his knowledge and kindness, who taught mankind about medicinal herbs and instructed many heroes in social graces and skills; the only non-warlike centaur. (2) In Shakespeare's play *Titus Andronicus* (1592), one of Tamora's* sons who rape the innocent Lavinia* and then cut off her hands and cut out her tongue so she may not identify them. *See also* Demetrius.

Chloe. (1) In the Bible, *I Corinthians* i, a Corinthian Christian woman who reported dissension and possible apostasy there to Paul,* thus leading to his first epistle to them. (2) In numerous works by English Restoration poets, particularly Matthew Prior, a beautiful and beloved young woman. *See also* Euphelia. (3) In Harriet Beecher Stowe's novel *Uncle Tom's Cabin* (1852), the wife of Uncle Tom,* left on the plantation after Tom has been sold. *See also* Shelby. (4) *See* Daphnis.

Chloris. In Greek mythology, goddess of flowers. *See also* Flora.

Cho-Cho-San. The actual name of Butterfly.*

Chocolate Soldier. *See* Bluntschli.

Chremes. A name used in many Greek comedies for neighbors and similar minor characters. The most noted, in Terence's *Phormio*, is a man with two wives in different cities, more than a little afraid of the second one, Nausistrata.*

Christ. A name given to Jesus,* from the Hebrew meaning "messiah*" or "anointed one," used to signify the special mission of Jesus from God.

Christabel. In Samuel Taylor Coleridge's poem *Christabel* (1816), a beautiful maiden who is put under a spell after she recognizes an evil spirit in disguise; the poem and her fate are both unfinished.

Christian. (1) In John Bunyan's *Pilgrim's Progress* (1678), the pilgrim who sets out on a journey to Heaven,* each stage of which provides a new temptation or trial; the whole personifies the path of salvation for all Christians. *See also*

Apollyon; Christiana; Vanity Fair. (2) In Edmund Rostand's play *Cyrano de Bergerac* (1897), the handsome and brave young man who is tongue-tied with women and who persuades Cyrano* to help him court the beautiful Roxanne.* (3) *See* Buddenbrook.

Christian, Fletcher. Historically, leader of a mutiny on the ship H.M.S. *Bounty* in 1787; in Nordhoff and Hall's novel *Mutiny on the Bounty* (1932) and in several movies, he is a handsome and principled young officer who takes charge of the mutiny to save the crew from Capt. Bligh's* tyrannical brutality.

Christiana. In John Bunyan's *Pilgrim's Progress*, Part II (1684), Christian's* wife who, regretting her decision not to accompany her husband, now makes her own pilgrimage to salvation.

Christie, Anna. In Eugene O'Neill's play *Anna Christie* (1921), an "ordinary little drab." Deserted by her father, she becomes a prostitute and eventually returns to the father and the sea, where she finds a chance at love and the honest life of which she has dreamed.

Christmas, Father. A name sometimes used for Santa Claus,* particularly in Britain.

Christmas, Joe. In William Faulkner's novel *Light in August* (1932), a mulatto in the American South trapped in a life neither white nor Negro and living precariously outside all society. He eventually murders his white lover Joanna Burden,* who tries to use sex to dominate him, and he is in turn brutally mutilated and killed by the lawmen chasing him.

Christophe, Jean. *See* Jean-Christophe.

Christopher, St. In Christian legend, a man of strength whose penance was to carry travelers across a river. One day a child became so heavy he faltered, whereupon the child was revealed to be Jesus,* who explained that by carrying Him Christopher had also carried the sins of the world. He became the patron saint of all travelers, many of whom continue to wear his medal for safety even though the Church dropped his name from the Calendar of Saints in 1969.

Christopher Robin. In A. A. Milne's stories *Winnie-the-Pooh* (1926), the delicate little boy who rescues his toy bear Winnie-the-Pooh* from a number of fey adventures. *See also* Eeyore; Heffalump; Piglet; Roo.

Christopher Sly. In Shakespeare's play *The Taming of the Shrew* (1593), a drunken country fellow who, for a joke, is treated as a nobleman and is shown the play.

Christopherson, Anna. The full name of Anna Christie.*

Christy. *See* Mahon, Christy.

Chronos. In Greek mythology, god of time; distinct from Cronos,* although often spelled Cronus or Chronus.

Chryseis. In Homer's *Iliad*, a priestess of Apollo* captured in the Trojan War* by the Greeks and given to Agamemnon;* Apollo sent a plague that he refused to lift until she was returned to her father. To compensate for this loss, Agamemnon claimed Briseis* from Achilles,* provoking the quarrel that almost lost the war.

Chrysothemis. In Homer's *Iliad*, a name for Iphigenia.* (2) In Sophocles's play *Electra*, Electra's* passive sister, who argues against revenge for Agememnon's* death.

Chuffey. In Charles Dickens's novel *Martin Chuzzlewit* (1843), the old and nearly deaf and blind but faithful clerk. *See also* Chuzzlewit.

Churchill, Frank. In Jane Austen's novel *Emma* (1816), a neighbor's attractive son, whom Emma* temporarily thinks is in love with her; at least part of his attraction is the mystery he surrounds himself with in order to conceal a secret engagement to Jane Fairfax.*

Churchill, Winston. Historically, British prime minister (d. 1965) during World War II who symbolized for many the British tenacity and temperament. He is noted for his cigar, his bulldog-like appearance, his "V for Victory" sign, and his legendary oratorical skills, including "blood, sweat, and tears," which is not quite what he actually said.

Chuzzlewit. In Charles Dickens's novel *Martin Chuzzlewit* (1843), **Martin** is an eccentric, selfish old man who believes no one can be trusted due to their designs on his wealth and who nonetheless temporarily disinherits his grandson for wanting to marry Mary Graham, a girl with no wealth or future. The grandson, also called **Martin**, is equally selfish and headstrong, although he is faithful to Mary. Refusing to make up with his grandfather, he goes to America, only to find it too crude and uncivilized, and he returns to eventual restoration of fortune. **Anthony**, old Martin's brother, is a miser who has educated his son **Jonas** to consider only potential profit in any relationship, with the result that Jonas spends his time wishing his father would die and eventually tries to poison him. Although the poison fails, Anthony's death close after the attempt persuades Jonas he is a criminal, and he begins to act like one, mistreating his wife and eventually murdering Montague Tigg* to prevent being blackmailed, then poisoning himself to avoid prison. *See also* Chuffey; Gamp, Sairey; Pecksniff; Pinch, Tom; Tapley, Mark.

Cid, The. In the anonymous *Poem of the Cid*, a great Spanish hero and warrior who defeats the Moors and protects the feudal Christian order in Spain. In other works dealing with the legend, the Cid dies in battle, but his death is kept from his troops, as his body is lashed into his saddle and leads the men who follow him to victory. In Corneille's play *Le Cid* (1637), he kills Chimène's* father in a duel, offering his own life when she demands revenge; she in turn has fallen in love with him and cannot kill him but cannot allow the love to be seen, due to her own honor. The king, realizing this, sends the Cid to fight the Moors. *See also* Ximena.

Cimmeria. In Homer's *Odyssey*, a land of perpetual darkness visited by Odysseus.*

Cincinnatus. Historically, a Roman consul of great integrity who in 458 B.C. was called from his plow to lead the armies in a crisis and then, having won, refused all further authority and returned to his farm. Particularly during the eighteenth century, he became a symbol of the ideal republican and citizen; George Washington,* for example, was often called the American Cincinnatus.

Cinderella. In a fairy tale told by Perrault (1697), a pretty girl who is forced to do all the work of the household by her stepmother and ugly stepsisters; when they are invited to a ball at which the prince will choose a wife, she is left at home until her fairy godmother gives her clothes that she can wear only until the stroke of midnight. The prince loves her, but she runs away as required, leaving behind a glass slipper, which the prince tries on every woman in the kingdom until he finds her, and they are happily married.

Cinna. In Shakespeare's play *Julius Caesar* (1599), one of the conspirators. *See* also Brutus; Casca; Cassius.

Cinq-Mars. Historically, a young marquis (d. 1642) who conspired to assassinate Richelieu.* He is noted as the subject of Alfred de Vigny's novel *Cinq-Mars* (1826), in which he is eventually executed because political expediency is more important than even the king's friendship.

Cinyras. In Greek legend, a king tricked into impregnating his daughter Myrrha,* siring Adonis,* for which he committed suicide.

Circe. In Greek legend, a daughter of Helios* and an evil sorceress who murdered her husband to take his kingdom, for which she was exiled on an island. In Homer's *Odyssey*, when Odysseus* lands there, she turns all his men into swine in order to hold him. *See also* Latinus; Picus; Scylla; Telegonus.

Citizen Kane. *See* Kane.

Clack, Miss. In Wilkie Collins's novel *The Moonstone* (1868), a poor relation who spends her time rather ludicrously passing out religious tracts to the poor.

Claggart. In Herman Melville's novel *Billy Budd* (1924), a dark, mysterious, evil officer who cannot stand Billy Budd's* beauty and honesty; he falsely accuses Billy of conspiracy, and when Billy, unable to express himself, knocks him down in frustration, he hits his head and dies. *See also* Vere, Capt.

Clampett. In the American television series "The Beverly Hillbillies" (1962–71), **Jed** is a poor hillbilly who finds oil and moves to Beverly Hills, where he and his mother-in-law, called **Granny**, continue to live among the wealthy exactly as they had in the hills. His son **Jethro** is a large, simpleminded, and good-spirited boy; his daughter **Ellie Mae**, a blonde beauty unaware of her good looks.

Clara. *See* Middleton.

Clare, Ada. In Charles Dickens's novel *Bleak House* (1852), Jarndyce's* generous and gentle ward who marries Richard Carstone* and remains loyal to him despite his obsessions.

Clare, Angel. In Thomas Hardy's novel *Tess of the D'Urbervilles* (1891), an honest young man who wants to be a farmer and who marries Tess.* A victim of the double standard, he cannot forgive Tess her previous affair and deserts her. He eventually seeks a reconciliation, but she has already killed D'Urberville,* so their time together is brief.

Clare, Lady. In Walter Scott's poem *Marmion* (1808), a beautiful heiress who is pursued by Marmion* and who enters a convent to escape him after she believes her true love dead. *See also* Constance.

Clare, St. Historically, foundress (d. 1253) of the order of the Poor Clares, an order living solely on alms.

Clarence. Historically, a series of English dukes from 1362, the most noted being Richard III's* brother (d. 1478), whose death by drowning in a butt of malmsey wine is dramatized in Shakespeare's play *Richard III* (1592).

Clarissa. In Samuel Richardson's novel *Clarissa Harlowe* (1747), a delicate and modest girl who becomes fascinated with Lovelace,* an unscrupulous, fashionable man, despite her parents' protestations and elopes with him. He puts her into a brothel where she is drugged, raped, and then jailed for debt. On her release, she contemplates her coffin, refuses the repentant Lovelace, and dies of shame, a moralistic counterpoint to Richardson's Pamela Andrews.*

Claudio. (1) In Shakespeare's play *Much Ado About Nothing* (1598), a young noble who is engaged to Hero,* then renounces her at the altar when he believes she is faithless, only to eventually marry her when he learns of her innocence. *See also* Beatrice; Benedick. (2) In Shakespeare's play *Measure for Measure* (1604), the brother of Isabella.* After getting his fiancée pregnant, he is condemned to death; when his only hope is for his sister Isabella to give herself to Angelo,* he begs her to do so, but she refuses.

Claudius. (1) Historically, the fourth Roman Emperor (d. 54). He appears in numerous works, most notably as the narrator of Robert Graves's novel *I, Claudius* (1934), as a lame stammerer often taken for a fool, even after being made emperor by default after the assassination of Caligula.* He was an able administrator but apparently much misled by love of his wife Messalina.* (2) In Shakespeare's play *Hamlet* (1600), Hamlet's* stepfather and the king of Denmark. He takes the throne after murdering Hamlet's father and marrying Gertrude.* As Hamlet begins to suspect the murder, Claudius tries to arrange Hamlet's death, eventually poisoning a drink that Gertrude sips by accident and a sword tip that kills Hamlet in a duel with Laertes,* but not before Hamlet kills Claudius. He is generally portrayed as bluff, gruff, and pompous, although he is also seen praying in remorse. *See also* Polonius.

Claus, Santa. *See* Santa Claus.

Clay, Mrs. In Jane Austen's novel *Persuasion* (1818), the scheming daughter of the Elliot* family agent; her hopes to marry Sir Walter are spoiled when she is herself victimized and becomes William's mistress instead.

Cléante. A name often used in plays by Molière. In *Tartuffe* (1664), he is the sensible brother-in-law; in *The Miser* (1668) and *Le Malade imaginaire* (1673), he is the young man in love. *See also* Cléonte.

Cleaver. In the American television series "Leave It to Beaver" (1957–63), the prototypical ideal American family: modest and bland father **Ward**, understanding housewife **June**, teenaged son **Wally**, and younger son nicknamed "**Beaver**."

Clelia. (1) In Roman legend, a maiden given as hostage to Porsena, a neighboring king, who bravely escaped by swimming the Tiber; the Romans, however, returned her to her captor, who released her in recognition of her courage. (2) In Stendhal's novel *The Charterhouse of Parma* (1839), one of the great beauties of Parma. She falls in love with Fabrizio,* despite her vow never to look at him, and has his child while married to another.

Clement. (1) In the Bible, *Philippians* iv, a Christian leader at Philippi. (2) Historically, a name adopted by fourteen Popes. *See* Clement, St. (3) In Ben Jonson's play *Every Man In His Humour* (1598), a shrewd but jovial justice who eventually provides clemency for the various plotters. *See also* Brainworm; Knowell.

Clement, St. Historically, a first-century bishop of Rome, regarded now as the first Pope to follow Peter.* Legend says he was tied to an anchor and thrown into the Crimean; hence, his symbol is an anchor.

Clementine. In an American folksong, a miner's eccentric, big-footed daughter who drowns and is "lost and gone forever."

Clennam. In Charles Dickens's novel *Little Dorrit* (1855), **Arthur** is a young man returned from China who is haunted by the presentiment that there is some crime behind his family's wealth; he is bankrupted through no fault of his own and then is nursed back to life in the debtors' prison by Little Dorrit,* to whom he had earlier been attracted and whom he marries. **Mrs. Clennam**, his mother, is a cold, miserly invalid who was the real brains of the family affairs and who founded much of the family fortune on an inheritance stolen from Dorrit. *See also* Barnacle; Blandois; Doyce, Daniel; Flintwitch; Flora; Meagles; Merdle.

Cleo. *See* Clio.

Cleon. (1) Historically, an Athenian tanner who became a general and a demagogue whose opposition prevented peace in the Peloponnesian War. In Aristophanes's play *The Knights*, he is portrayed as a demagogue who is eventually removed from office by Agoracritus,* the only man cruder and more vulgar than himself, after a ludicrous debate ending in a wrestling match. *See also* Demos; Pericles. (2) In Shakespeare's play *Pericles* (1608), a cowardly friend with whom Pericles* leaves his daughter Marina.* When she grows up to be more beautiful than Cleon's own daughter, he yields to his wife Dionyza's* plot to murder Marina, foiled only when the girl is captured by pirates.

Cléonte. In Molière's play *The Bourgeois Gentleman* (1670), a young man of common birth who eventually wins Jourdain's* daughter. *See also* Cléante.

Cleopas. In the Bible, *Luke* xxiv, one of the Christians to whom Jesus* appeared on the road to Emmaus* after His Resurrection* and who did not at first recognize Him.

Cleopatra. (1) Historically, one of several ancient queens of Egypt; almost all allusions, however, are to the Cleopatra born in 68 B.C., restored to the throne by Julius Caesar,* and later the lover of Marc Antony* during his war with Octavius.* After the lost battle of Actium, Antony thought she was dead and killed himself, and she followed suit, probably to avoid being taken captive to Rome. She is generally portrayed as a beautiful seductress of great passion, usually only minimally dressed. In Shakespeare's play *Antony and Cleopatra* (1606), she is quite complex, haughty and frightened, self-centered and passionately in love with Antony, politically alert and yet often naive and unable to hold to any commitments. She kills herself by holding a poisonous asp to her bosom. In John Dryden's play *All for Love* (1677), she is somewhat less varied, a steadfast lover who allows herself to be deluded by scheming servants and is single-minded in her efforts to prevent Antony's return to his wife. In G. B. Shaw's play *Caesar and Cleopatra* (1901), she is a frightened and illiterate child whom Caesar teaches how to use her authority, beauty, and intelligence. *See also* Alexas; Charmian; Ftatateeta. (2) In Charles Dickens's novel *Dombey and*

Son (1846), the nickname for Edith's* mother, so called for her faded beauty and her time spent reclining on a chaise in the pose long associated with the historical Cleopatra.

Clerk of Oxford. In Chaucer's *Canterbury Tales*, a serious young scholar who tells the story of patient Griselda.*

Clinker, Humphrey. In Tobias Smollett's novel *Humphrey Clinker* (1771), a simple country boy who proves himself to be well-bred, honorable, devout, and heroic. *See also* Bramble.

Clio. In Greek mythology, the Muse* of history.

Clitandre. In Molière's play *The Misanthrope* (1666), a fop who courts Célimène.*

Cloe. *See* Chloe.

Clootie. A Scottish nickname for the Devil.*

Clorin. In John Fletcher's play *The Faithful Shepherdess* (1609), a shepherdess who lives faithfully by the tomb of her dead lover, her chastity a defense against all evils.

Clorinda. In Tasso's *Jerusalem Delivered* (1580), a beautiful pagan woman, suckled by a tiger, who dresses and fights as a man and is eventually killed in combat by Tancred.*

Cloten. In Shakespeare's play *Cymbeline* (1609), Imogen's* vicious, stupid stepbrother. He disguises himself in her husband Posthumus's* clothes in hopes of getting close enough to Imogen to rape her; as a result, when he is beheaded, she mistakes his body for that of her husband.

Clotho. *See* Fates.

Cloud, St. Historically, a Frankish prince (d. 560) who surrendered his claim to the throne to become a monk.

Cloudcuckooland. In Aristophanes's play *The Birds*, the land of the birds in between the gods and the earth; often used to signify any imaginary, visionary, impractical proposal.

Clouseau, Inspector. In numerous movies, beginning with *The Pink Panther* (1963), an inept Parisian police detective who solves crimes by accident, meanwhile unwittingly wreaking havoc on all around him and speaking in an absurdly incomprehensible French accent.

Clout, Colin. In John Skelton's poem *Colyn Clout* (1519), a wandering poet opposed to clerical abuses. The name was used in Edmund Spenser's poem *The Fairie Queene* (1590) for a shepherd and poet and again in his poem *Colin Clouts*

Come Home Again (1591) for a simple Irish poet who travels to the English court and is disillusioned despite his admiration for the queen herself.

Clumsey, Sir Tunbelly. In John Vanbrugh's play *The Relapse* (1696), a fat country squire tricked into imprisoning the visiting Novelty Fashion.*

Clym. *See* Yeobright.

Clytemnestra. In Greek legend, a daughter of Leda* and Tyndarus* and wife of Agamemnon.* While her husband was gone to the Trojan War,* she took Aegisthus* as her lover, and they both murdered Agamemnon on his return; her son Orestes* in turn killed her in revenge. In Aeschylus's plays *Oresteia*, she is a haughty and domineering woman but is also angry because of Agamemnon's sacrifice of their daughter Iphigenia.* After the crime, she is haunted by nightmares and pitifully pleads that her life be spared. In Sophocles's play *Electra*, she rejoices at the (mistaken) news that Orestes has been killed. *See also* Atreus; Electra; Erigone; Eumenides; Oeax.

Clytia. In Greek legend, a nymph* who pined for Apollo* and was changed to the sunflower, which always turns toward the sun.

Clytie. *See* Clytia.

Cocytus. In Greek mythology, one of the five rivers of Hades.*

Coelus. A name sometimes used for Uranus.*

Coeur de Lion. A nickname for Richard I,* the "Lion-hearted."

Cokes, Bartholomew. In Ben Jonson's play *Bartholomew Fair* (1614), a gullible gentleman who is defrauded at the fair, where he also neglects and loses his fiancée Grace Wellborn.*

Coldfield. In William Faulkner's novel *Absalom, Absalom!* (1936), a grocer who locks himself in his attic, living on food pulled up in a basket to avoid any contact with the Civil War, which he opposes. His daughter **Rosa** becomes a straitlaced spinster after she rejects a proposal from Sutpen,* whom she considers too crude, but nevertheless remains obsessed with him throughout her life. For his other daughter **Ellen**, *see* Sutpen.

Cole, Old King. In the nursery rhyme, a "merry old soul" who enjoyed his pipe, his wine, and his music.

Colin. *See* Clout, Colin.

Collins. In Jane Austen's novel *Pride and Prejudice* (1813), the pompous young clergyman whose suit is rejected by Elizabeth Bennet,* known also for his exaggerated sycophancy toward the minor nobility; he later marries her friend Charlotte.*

Colombina. *See* Columbine.

Colossus. One of the ancient Seven Wonders,* a gigantic statue either astride or beside the entrance to Rhodes harbor.

Columbine. In the commedia dell'Arte, the artful servant girl, witty, high-spirited, and coquettish, often loved by Harlequin.* *Also called* Pierrette;* Zerbinetta.

Columbus, Christopher. Historically, an Italian explorer working for Spain who discovered the islands of the Caribbean while searching for a route to the Indies in 1492. In legend, he is said to have been the only person who believed the world was round, although the view had in fact been widely accepted in intellectual circles, and to have secured funds for his voyage by a romance with Isabella,* queen of Spain.

Commandments. *See* Golden Rule; Ten Commandments.

Commendatore. In Mozart's opera *Don Giovanni* (1787), the father of Doña Ana.* He is killed when he surprises Don Giovanni* coming from her chamber; later, his statue comes to life and takes Giovanni to Hell.*

Common, Dol. In Ben Jonson's play *The Alchemist* (1610), a female cheat who joins Subtle* and Face* in their numerous frauds, playing all the female roles, including Queen of the Fairies,* as needed during each trick.

Compson. In William Faulkner's *The Sound and the Fury* (1929), a symptomatic Southern family in decay. **Jason** is the descendant of a governor and of a general but is unable to make a living, devoting himself to the classical languages and drink. His wife **Caroline** is a neurotic who confines herself to the house with odd psychosomatic illnesses while pretending to be an antebellum Southern belle. Their four children are Caddy, Quentin, Jason, and Benjy. **Caddy** is promiscuous and obsessed with her brother Quentin, whom she presses into incest. **Quentin** (also the narrator of *Absalom, Absalom!*) is deeply disturbed by the nature of his family background and commits suicide while still a student. **Jason** is petty and aggressive, a cunning, bitter redneck who purposely stays a bachelor to end the line. **Benjy** is an idiot whom his brother Jason eventually castrates and sends to an asylum. Caddy's daughter **Quentin** is a beautiful but wild child who steals family funds and elopes with a carnival worker. The novel is told in part by the characters, and Benjy's section is one of the most celebrated pieces of writing in modern American letters. *See also* Dilsey.

Comus. A Roman god of feasting and wild revelry; many sources suggest he was in fact invented by John Milton for his poem/play *Comus* (1634).

Conan. (1) In Irish legend, a rough-tempered, cantankerous companion of Finn* and a trickster who is not afraid even to return the blows of the Devil* in the underworld. (2) In numerous stories by Robert E. Howard and others (beg.

1932), a barbarian hero, without the subtlety or the debility of civilization, who fights the forces of evil with brute force.

Conchubar. In Irish legend, the great king of Ulster and uncle of Cuchulain.* He kept Deirdre* in isolation so that he might marry her; when she fell in love with Naisi, Conchubar treacherously lured him to his death, thus losing Deirdre as well. The most widely known version of the story is J. M. Synge's play *Deirdre of the Sorrows* (1910).

Concordia. In Greek mythology, the goddess of harmony and peace. *See also* Irene; Pax.

Confucius. Historically, a great Chinese philosopher and teacher (d. 471 B.C.). In American folklore, "Confucius say . . . " became a common introduction to an absurd aphorism and a catch-phrase given to stereotyped Chinese characters, due primarily to its use in numerous movies featuring Charlie Chan.*

Coningsby. In Benjamin Disraeli's novel *Coningsby* (1844), a generous and intelligent young man embodying new political ideas and ideals opposed both to unthinking Conservatism and to Utilitarianism.

Conklin, Jim. In Stephen Crane's *The Red Badge of Courage* (1895), the "tall soldier" whose death unnerves the young Henry Fleming.*

Connecticut Yankee. In Mark Twain's novel *A Connecticut Yankee in King Arthur's Court* (1889), an American factory engineer who awakes to find himself transported to Arthur's* court. His modern devices, such as matches, make him the greatest magician of the kingdom, and he uses his power as "the boss" to instigate numerous nineteenth-century social reforms.

Constance. (1) In Chaucer's *Canterbury Tales*, in the Man of Law's Tale, a Christian maiden married to the Moslem Sultan and jealously cast adrift on the sea by the Sultan's mother. (2) In Walter Scott's poem *Marmion* (1808), Constance de Beverley, a young nun who breaks her vows to follow Marmion* disguised as a page boy, until he deserts her for a more desirable heiress. She is tried by an ecclesiastical court and is buried alive in a well. (3) *See* Birotteau; Neville, Constance. (4) *See also* Constantia.

Constantia. (1) *See* Durham, Constantia. (2) *See also* Constance.

Constantin. In Anton Chekhov's play *The Sea Gull* (1896), the young poet, son of Arkadina* but ignored by her and in love with the young actress Nina,* who prefers an older man; when Nina rebuffs him a second time in favor of the life of an actress, he kills himself.

Constantine. Historically, a Roman emperor (d. 337) known primarily for proclaiming Christianity as the state religion. Legend says his conversion occurred when he saw a cross in the sky during a battle in 312. *See also* Helena, St.

Cophetua. In European legend, a king in Africa who cared for no women until falling in love at first sight with a beggar woman, whom he married and lived with happily.

Copia. In Roman mythology, the goddess of plenty.

Coppélia. In the ballet *Coppélia* (1870), a life-sized doll impersonated by Swanilda* in order to win back her lover.

Coppélius, Dr. In the ballet *Coppélia* (1870), the doll maker who builds Coppélia.*

Copperfield, David. In Charles Dickens's novel *David Copperfield* (1849), a sensitive boy who endures a miserable childhood with a tyrannical stepfather Murdstone,* a school with a bully for a headmaster, and a miserable job cleaning bottles in his stepfather's warehouse. Running away, he throws himself on the mercy of his aunt Betsey Trotwood,* who sends him to a new school. He eventually becomes a writer, mistakenly marries the childlike Dora,* and finally finds happiness with Agnes* after Dora dies. He is generally seen as the author's thinly disguised self-portrait. *See also* Creakle; Em'ly, Little; Micawber; Peggotty; Steerforth; Strong, Dr.; Traddles.

Cora. (1) A name sometimes used for Persephone.* (2) *See* Munro.

Corbaccio. In Ben Jonson's play *Volpone* (1605), the feeble, deaf, and aged miser so consumed by greed he tries to exchange wills in the absurd belief that he will outlive Volpone.*

Corcoran, Capt. In Gilbert and Sullivan's operetta *H.M.S. Pinafore* (1878), the captain of the *Pinafore* who is "hardly ever" seasick. *See also* Buttercup; Rackstraw, Ralph.

Corday, Charlotte. *See* Marat.

Cordelia. In Shakespeare's play *King Lear* (1605), Lear's* youngest daughter, the only one to honestly love him. When she refuses to make speeches about her love, Lear disinherits her. She marries the King of France and, when they then invade the country to restore her father, is captured in battle and hanged. Lear's "howl, howl, howl" is said over her body. *See also* Edmund; Goneril; Regan.

Corin. In Shakespeare's play *As You Like It* (1599), a wise and virtuous old shepherd who extols the value of simple country life.

Corineus. *See* Gog.

Corinthian Kate. In Pierce Egan's stories *Life in London* (1820), the most beautiful and adept prostitute in London.

Corinthian Tom. *See* Tom and Jerry.

Coriolanus. In Shakespeare's play *Coriolanus* (1607), a great general who is offered a Roman consulship if he obtains the approval of the masses. Unable and unwilling to conceal his scorn of the rabble, he is assumed to be a potential tyrant and is banished. He joins the Volscians in a march on Rome, but he decides, after his mother's pleading, not to sack the city and is then killed by the Volscians for making a traitorous peace. He is sometimes seen as a lesson in the pitfalls of uncontrolled pride and sometimes as a symbol of the inherent stupidity of the common citizens who destroy those better than themselves, even when they need such people. *See also* Virgilia; Volumnia.

Corleone. In Mario Puzo's novel *The Godfather* (1969), the family who epitomize the American Mafiosi. Most references are to Don Corleone in the movie version (1972), the quiet but ruthless father of the clan, noted for saying, "Make him an offer he can't refuse."

Cornelia. Historically, mother of the Gracchi.* Legend says that, when another woman bragged about her jewelry, Cornelia brought out her sons and said, "These are my jewels."

Cornelius. In the Bible, *Acts* x, a Roman centurion to whom God sent the Holy Spirit in front of Peter* and other Jews in order to demonstrate that the message of Jesus* was intended for Jew and Gentile alike.

Corney, Mrs. In Charles Dickens's novel *Oliver Twist* (1837), the self-centered and greedy workhouse matron who robs the corpse of Oliver Twist's* mother; later, she marries Bumble* and so completely dominates him that he loses all his self-satisfaction.

Cornwall. In Shakespeare's play *King Lear* (1605), a duke and husband of Regan.* Even in that family, he is noted for his cruelty. When he eventually tears out Gloucester's eyes, he is killed by a servant who rebels at this final cruelty.

Corombona, Vittoria. *See* Vittoria.

Corporal, Little. *See* Napoleon.

Corsican, The. *See* Napoleon.

Corsican Brothers. In Dion Boucicault's play *The Corsican Brothers* (1852), twins, Louis and Fabien. Louis goes to Paris and is killed in a duel, which Fabien sees psychically and which Fabien soon avenges. The play is particularly noted for its unique method of causing the ghost to appear through a special trap, called the Corsican Trap.

Cortés. *See* Cortez.

Cortez. Historically, the Spanish adventurer (d. 1547) who conquered the Aztecs in Mexico. He is the quintessential Conquistadore, alternately depicted as a brilliant military commander and leader of civilization and as a brutal and greedy colonialist who destroyed entire cultures in a single-minded quest for power and gold.

Corvino. In Ben Jonson's play *Volpone* (1605), the merchant whose greed overcomes his rampant jealousy; he tries to give his wife Celia* to Volpone* in hope of future wealth.

Cory, Richard. In Edward Arlington Robinson's poem *Richard Cory* (1897), a wealthy man who seems to have everything a person could want and yet shoots himself.

Corybantes. In Ovid's *Metamorphoses*, priests of Cybele,* noted for their knowledge of the arts; they are also said to have guarded the infant Zeus* when Cronos* tried to kill him, hiding his cries in the clash of their cymbals.

Corydon. In Virgil's *Eclogues*, a simple shepherd; the name was much used in Renaissance literature for a country swain.

Cosette. In Victor Hugo's novel *Les Misérables* (1862), an orphan daughter of the prostitute Fantine* raised by Jean Valjean;* rather than reveal her true history, Valjean separates her from her lover Marius,* then later rescues him to reunite the pair.

Cosmas, St. In Christian legend, a martyr who, with his brother Damian, worked as a doctor without charging fees; hence, patron saint of physicians. Cynics sometimes note that his day (September 27) is rarely celebrated in the modern world.

Costard. In Shakespeare's play *Love's Labour's Lost* (1595), a rustic clown who mimics the big words of the more educated characters.

Cottard, Dr. In Marcel Proust's novels *Remembrance of Things Past* (1913–27), a noted surgeon who is also a social boor much given to bad puns and gauche remarks.

Cottontail. *See* Flopsy, Mopsy, and Cottontail.

Cotys. In Greek mythology, a goddess of debauchery whose festivals were noted for their secrecy and their licentiousness.

Cotytto. A name sometimes used for Cotys.*

Count of Monte Cristo. *See* Dantes, Edmund.

Country Wife. *See* Pinchwife.

Coupeau. In Émile Zola's novel *L'Assommoir* (1877), the dependable roofer who marries Gervaise,* then, after a disabling fall, takes to drink until committed to an asylum. His wedding party's uncomprehending trip through the Louvre is a noted depiction of the barrenness of working-class life.

Coverley, Roger de. *See* de Coverley, Roger.

Covielle. In Molière's play *The Bourgeois Gentleman* (1670), the clever and outspoken servant who aids Cléonte* and stages the Turkish masquerade.

Cowardly Lion. *See* Lion.

Cox. *See* Box and Cox.

Crab. *See* Launce.

Craig, Harriet. In George Kelly's play *Craig's Wife* (1925), an outwardly devoted wife and homemaker who in fact sees her marriage only as a means to personal security and selfish satisfaction, eventually destroying her husband's friendships and driving him out of the house; a woman "who would rather see her husband smoke in hell than in her living room."

Crane, Ichabod. In Washington Irving's story *The Legend of Sleepy Hollow* (1819), a gaunt and superstitious schoolmaster who is frightened away from a prosperous marriage when pursued by what he believes is the ghostly Headless Horseman.*

Cranstoun, Lord. In Walter Scott's poem *The Lay of the Last Minstrel* (1805), a noble knight who dons the armor of the knight Deloraine,* whom he has wounded, and fights a duel in his place in order to make amends.

Cratchit, Bob. In Charles Dickens's novel *A Christmas Carol* (1843), the genial but impoverished clerk whom Scrooge* only grudgingly allows a day off on Christmas; father of Tiny Tim.*

Crawford. In Jane Austen's novel *Mansfield Park* (1814), **Henry** is the unprincipled neighbor who flirts with Fanny Price* during the amateur theatricals, is rejected by her, and runs off with Maria Bertram,* who is married to another man. His sister **Mary** is a cynical and worldly woman who loses Edmund Bertram's love when she fails to be properly upset by the elopement.

Crawley. In William Makepeace Thackeray's novel *Vanity Fair* (1847), **Capt. Rawdon** is a charming but stupid Guards officer, a gambler who marries Becky Sharp* and ignores her indiscretions until he catches her in flagrante delicto. **Sir Pitt**, his father, is an eccentric who abuses his wife, then, after her death, proposes to Becky and eventually carries on a senile affair with his butler's daughter. Sir Pitt's sister, **Miss Crawley**, is a bossy, eccentric spinster to whom the entire family toadies in hope of inheriting her fortune. **Pitt**, Rawdon's brother, is a proper, careful young man with political ambitions. Rawdon and Becky's son, also called **Rawdon**, refuses to speak to Becky, although he does send her money regularly. Sir Pitt's brother, **Rev. Bute**, is a village rector controlled by an ambitious and manipulating wife whose plan for gaining the inheritance is ruined when her shy son **James** gets drunk and smokes a pipe in front of Miss Crawley. *See also* Steyne, Marquis of.

Craye, De. *See* De Craye.

Creakle. In Charles Dickens's novel *David Copperfield* (1849), the bullying headmaster of David Copperfield's* first school who prides himself on his cane rather than his scholarship and who also goes in awe of the young Steerforth.*

Creation, The. Numerous stories of creation exist in mythology and legend, usually involving some kind of primordial warfare between gods, but almost all allusions to *the* creation are to the Bible, *Genesis* i, in which God created the world in six days, by Himself and for no stated reason, and then rested on the seventh day.

Creon. (1) In Greek legend, a king of Thebes. As Jocasta's* brother, he ruled until Oedipus* arrived to solve the riddle of the Sphynx,* whereupon he surrendered the throne. After the civil war caused by Eteocles* and Polynices,* he resumed the throne and refused to bury the body of Polynices. When Antigone* disobeyed his command and buried her brother's body, he had her executed. In Sophocles's play *Antigone*, he is the voice of reason and political expediency, as opposed to Antigone's voice of moral duty, and this depiction of him has remained constant in most later versions of the story. *See also* Haemon; Megara; Seven Against Thebes. (2) In Greek legend, a king of Corinth and father of Glauce.* *See also* Jason; Medea.

Cressida. In medieval literary legend, a beautiful woman of Troy.* In Chaucer's poem *Troilus and Criseyde* she is a demure widow who yields to the love of Troilus* lest he die of unrequited love. When her father Calchas,* who has joined the Greeks, demands her return, she is forced to stay in their camp, where she eventually yields to Diomedes.* In Shakespeare's play *Troilus and Cressida* (1602), she is a fickle, salacious strumpet who pretends to be coy with Troilus and who quite happily accepts Diomedes as her lover. *See also* Pandarus.

Creusa. (1) A name sometimes used for Glauce.* (2) In Greek legend, mother of Ion.* In Euripides's play *Ion*, she abandons the child and marries a mortal who had vowed to adopt the first child they saw, which was Ion; not recognizing her child, she tries to kill him until she is prevented by a priestess who identifies the child. (3) In Virgil's *Aeneid*, wife of Aeneas.* She is separated from her husband during the fall of Troy* and is never found; she reappears to Aeneas in a dream in which she predicts his future travails and ultimate success. *See also* Ascanius.

Creval. In several novels by Balzac, most notably *Cousin Bette* (1847), a self-important wealthy businessman who tries to seduce Adeline Hulot* in revenge for her husband's taking Creval's mistress and who later marries Mme. Marneffe.*

Crewler. In Charles Dickens's novel *David Copperfield* (1849), **Horace** is a poor clergyman; **Mrs. Crewler** is an invalid whose illness improves or worsens depending on how she feels about things happening around her. Their daughter **Sophy** is "the dearest girl in the world" who cares for all the family and eventually marries Traddles.*

Crichton. In J. M. Barrie's play *The Admirable Crichton* (1903), the efficient butler who, when his household is stranded on a desert isle, assumes command and demonstrates his natural leadership, yet insists on reverting to his servant role when rescued. *See also* Loam.

Criseyde. A name sometimes used for Cressida.*

Crispin, St. In Christian legend, a noble Roman who, with his brother Crispinian, converted to Christianity and supported themselves as shoemakers until their martyrdom. He is the patron saint of shoemakers, but he is best known among the English for his day, October 25, on which occurred the battle of Agincourt, and the stirring "St. Crispin's Day" speech in Shakespeare's play *Henry V* (1598).

Crispinian, St. *See* Crispin, St.

Crispus. In the Bible, *Acts* xviii, the leader of the synagogue at Corinth who converted to Christianity.

Croaker. In Oliver Goldsmith's play *The Good-natured Man* (1768), a perpetually gloomy man.

Crocale. In Ovid's *Metamorphoses*, Diana's* hairdresser.

Crockett, Davy. Historically, an American frontiersman and congressman (d. 1836), around whom a large body of legendary tall tales accumulated, aided in large part by his own fanciful "autobiography"; generally identified by his coonskin cap and noted for such exploits as staring down a bear when hunting without a weapon.

Croesus. Historically, the last king of Lydia, said to be the richest man in the world. When he claimed to be happy, he was told by a Greek philosopher that no man could be really happy until he ended his life happily, a point Croesus learned after his kingdom was sacked by Cyrus;* generally a symbol of unimaginable wealth.

Cromwell. Historically, the general of the rebel forces that overthrew Charles* I. He eventually became virtual dictator of England (d. 1658) during a period of strict Puritan control of government and religion, and he is usually depicted in various works as a dour, humorless symbol of puritanical fundamentalism and repression.

Cronos. In Greek mythology, a Titan,* husband of Rhea* and father of Zeus,* Demeter,* Hestia,* and Poseidon.* Cronos overthrew Uranus* and ruled as king of the Titans until defeated by the thunderbolts of Zeus; in some stories, he swallowed all his children except Zeus, who then released them by cutting him open after he was defeated. *Also called* Saturn.* Distinct from Chronos.*

Cronus. *See* Cronos.

Cross. *See* Crucifixion; Stations of the Cross.

Crowne, Lenina. *See* Lenina.

Crown of Thorns. The crown Jesus* was forced to wear at His trial and Crucifixion,* intended by his captors to be a satirical comment on his claim to be "King of the Jews."

Croy, Kate. In Henry James's novel *The Wings of the Dove* (1902), a stylish English girl who persuades Merton Densher,* the man she loves, to marry the rich but seriously ill American Milly Theale* so that they can live well after he inherits Milly's money.

Crucifixion. In the Bible, the execution of Jesus.* He was nailed to a cross and the cross was raised on Golgotha* (or Calvary*). While on the cross, he was taunted by bystanders and by the two thieves crucified alongside Him and given vinegar to drink until the ninth hour, in which He cried out to God and then died. In *John* xix, He was also stabbed in the side, but only after He was dead, although many depictions of the scene show Jesus with a bleeding wound. His death was accompanied by an earthquake.

Crummles. In Charles Dickens's novel *Nicholas Nickleby* (1838), the family operating the strolling actors' troupe that Nicholas Nickleby* joins. **Mr. Crummles** is a generous, friendly fellow and a player of the flamboyant school who cares not what the new play is about as long as there is a prominent place for the new pump he has purchased. **Mrs. Crummles** plays motherly roles, and their daughter is always referred to as the "**Infant Phenomenon**." *See also* Snevelicci.

Cruncher. In Charles Dickens's novel *A Tale of Two Cities* (1859), **Jerry** is a bank clerk who digs up bodies at night to sell to doctors and who helps Darnay* escape. He calls his wife the "aggerawayter."

Crusoe, Robinson. In Daniel Defoe's novel *Robinson Crusoe* (1719), an Englishman shipwrecked on a desert island, who industriously and imaginatively uses his resources to build a comfortable home and life. After 24 years alone, he finds the Negro Friday,* who becomes his servant, pupil, and companion.

Ctesipho. In Terence's play *The Brothers*, the young man who abducts the slave girl with whom he has fallen in love. *See also* Demea; Michio.

Cuchulain. In Irish legend, a great warrior hero, loved by many women, most noted for his single-handed repulse of the invading forces of Queen Maeve;* he eventually died at the hands of daughters of the men he had slain. *Also called* Cuthullin.* *See also* Conchubar.

Cuddie. In Edmund Spenser's poem *The Shepherd's Calendar* (1579), a simple shepherd.

Cuff, Sergeant. In Wilkie Collins's novel *The Moonstone* (1868), the amiable grizzled detective with a passion for roses who is sent to solve the mystery of the missing moonstone; generally regarded as a prototype for modern mystery detectives.

Cunegonde. In Voltaire's story *Candide* (1759), the beautiful girl who loves Candide.* Raped by an invading army, she escapes to Portugal where she becomes the mistress of two important men simultaneously, finds and loses Candide again, and then is finally reunited with him, an older, wiser, and far less beautiful woman, on his farm. *See also* Pangloss.

Cupid. In Roman mythology, the god of love, generally equivalent to Eros.* He is usually portrayed as a small boy whose arrows cause those hit by them to fall in love with the first person they see. *See also* Psyche.

Curly. (1) In Rodgers and Hammerstein's musical play *Oklahoma!* (1942), the handsome cowboy who sings "Oh, What a Beautiful Morning" and marries Laurey.* *See also* Jud. (2) *See* Stooges, Three.

Cush. In the Bible, *Genesis* x, a son of Ham* and father of Nimrod;* the name is sometimes used in other passages for the part of Africa now known as Ethiopia.

Cusins. In G. B. Shaw's play *Major Barbara* (1905), a meek but extremely intelligent Greek scholar who joins the Salvation Army to be near Major Barbara;* when he agrees to learn to be a man of business, Undershaft* takes him into the munitions factory, and he marries Barbara.

Cuthbert, St. Historically, a Scottish priest (d. 687) noted for his practical holiness and willingness to travel long distances to minister to his flock. His day is March 20.

Cuthullin. In Ossian's* poems (1762), Cuchulain.*

Cutpurse, Moll. Historically, a notorious thief and fortune-teller of Jacobean London, appearing in numerous works, most notably Middleton and Dekker's play *The Roaring Girl* (1611).

Cuttle, Capt. In Charles Dickens's novel *Dombey and Son* (1846), a retired sea captain, always wearing his laquered waterproof hat and speaking an erratic sea argot, who becomes Walter Gay's* friend. Terrified of his landlady, Mrs. MacStinger,* he takes over Solomon Gills's* shop while Gills looks for Walter and shelters Florence Dombey* there when she leaves home. *See also* Bunsby.

Cybele. The Phrygian name for Rhea.* *See also* Corybantes; Marsyas.

Cyclops. In Greek legend, a giant with a single eye in the middle of his forehead. The most famous is Polyphemus* who, in Homer's *Odyssey*, traps Odysseus* and begins to eat his crew.

Cymbeline. In Shakespeare's play *Cymbeline* (1609), an ancient king of Britain who banishes his daughter Imogen* for her love of a poor nobleman but is eventually reconciled to her after considerable complications following a Roman invasion of his kingdom. His wife the Queen is a wicked stepmother who jealously tries to poison Imogen but fails when the potion only puts her to sleep. *See also* Iachimo; Posthumus.

Cynara. In Ernest Dowson's poem *Non sum qualis eram . . .* (1896), the lover whom the poet deserts for "madder music," but whose memory makes all pleasures unsatisfactory so that he can claim, "I have been faithful to thee, Cynara!, in my fashion."

Cynosura. In Greek legend, a nurse of the infant Zeus;* she was changed into the North Star.

Cynthia. (1) A name sometimes used for Artemis.* *See also* Endymion; Dipsas. (2) In the elegies of Propertius, a beautiful, temperamental mistress with whom the poet is passionately in love, even after her death. (3) In the sixteenth through eighteenth centuries, a name much used by poets for a beautiful woman; Spenser, Lyly, and Jonson in particular used it as a metaphorical name for Queen Elizabeth* to suggest her goddess-like nature.

Cynthius. A name sometimes used for Apollo.*

Cyrano. Historically, Cyrano de Bergerac, a French soldier and poet (d. 1655). He is known primarily as the hero of Edmund Rostand's play *Cyrano de Bergerac* (1897), a poet and great swordsman with a grotesque nose, jealously protective of his sense of honor, one of the grandest embodiments of theatrical romance. Passionately in love with his cousin Roxanne,* who is in turn in love with the tongue-tied Christian,* he writes Christian's love letters to her, thus expressing the love he believes will never be requited, due to his nose. He is noted for his famous thesaurus of nose insults, for composing a complex poem while duelling, for a passionate and sad scene in which he courts Roxanne for Christian from the darkness under her balcony, and for his death scene during which Roxanne recognizes his love as he duels with Death itself.

Cyrene. *See* Simon.

Cyril, St. Historically, a missionary (d. 869) to the Slavs credited with developing both the Glagolitic and Cyrillic alphabets. Long a patron saint of several Balkan nations, in 1981 he was declared one of the patron saints of Europe; his day is February 14. *See also* Methodius, St.

Cyrus. (1) Historically, a Persian king (d. 529 B.C.) and founder of the Persian Empire, conqueror of Lydia and Babylon; generally regarded as a great king and a liberator for his willingness to respect the local customs of his various conquered states. He is mentioned admiringly in numerous passages in the Bible as the king who returned the Jews to their homeland after their exile. *See also* Belshazzar; Cambyses; Croesus; Daniel. (2) Historically, a Persian prince (d. 401 B.C.) who aided Sparta in the Peloponnesian War and in whose revolt were enlisted The Ten Thousand.*

Cytherea. A name sometimes used for Aphrodite.*

D

Daedalion. In Ovid's *Metamorphoses*, father of Chione.* When Chione was killed, Daedalion threw himself from a mountainside, but he was changed into a hawk by Apollo* before he could be killed.

Daedalus. (1) In Greek legend, a great artist and inventor of the ax, sails, and so on. After he killed Talos* in jealousy, he fled to Crete, where he built the Labyrinth* for Minos,* who then confined Daedalus there. He escaped by making wings of feathers and wax for himself and his son Icarus,* on which they flew out. (2) *See also* Dedalus, Stephen.

Dagon. In the Bible, a Philistine* deity; it is his temple that Samson* pulled down. In John Milton's poem *Paradise Lost* (1667), he is half man, half fish.

Dagonet. In Malory's *Morte d'Arthur*, Arthur's* fool.

Dagwood. *See* Bumstead.

Daisy. (1) In F. Scott Fitzgerald's novel *The Great Gatsby* (1925), the old flame of Gatsby.* When she marries Tom Buchanan,* she becomes a spoiled and bored rich woman, but she eventually revives a romance with the now wealthy Gatsby, whom she had once rejected in the belief that he had no future. Finally, she accidentally runs over a woman whose husband mistakenly kills Gatsby in revenge. (2) *See* Miller, Daisy.

Daisy, Solomon. In Charles Dickens's novel *Barnaby Rudge* (1841), a parish clerk with "rusty" clothes who is a pub regular and tells the tale of the old murder.

Daisy Mae. In the American newspaper cartoon *Li'l Abner* (beg. 1934), the voluptuous but innocent blonde woman who captures Li'l Abner* in the Sadie Hawkins'* Day Race and marries him.

Dale, Laetitia. In George Meredith's novel *The Egoist* (1879), a gentle and trustworthy tenant of Sir Willoughby Patterne;* she generally retains her amenable nature despite a life spent nursing her invalid father and doing literary hackwork. Although she initially admires Sir Willoughby, she soon realizes that his eccentricities are really egoism and self-deception and rejects his proposal, eventually accepting him only when she can obtain concessions that will control him.

Dalgarno. In Walter Scott's novel *The Fortunes of Nigel* (1822), a spendthrift and untrustworthy Scot who introduces Nigel Olifaunt* to the underworld, then informs on him, marries the moneylender Trapbois's* daughter for her money, and runs off with another man's wife; he is eventually murdered.

Dalila. In John Milton's poem *Samson Agonistes* (1671), Delilah.*

Dalloway, Mrs. In Virginia Woolf's novel *Mrs. Dalloway* (1925), a representative middle-aged, middle-class wife who has begun to question her life, especially her choice of stability and comfort in a husband rather than the unpredictability that accompanied the passion of an early romance. She is also much concerned by her sense of triviality in daily activity, her lack of feeling for her husband and family, and her fears of impending age.

Daly, Joxer. *See* Joxer.

Damascus. Historically, a major city, now the capital, of Syria; in the Bible, *Acts* ix, it is on the road to Damascus that the vision appears to Paul* which leads to his conversion. The city is also noted in medieval legend as the source of Damascus steel swords and damask silk cloth.

Damastes. A name sometimes used for Procrustes.*

D'Ambois, Bussy. In George Chapman's play *Bussy D'Ambois* (1604), an insolent, ambitious, intelligent, and proud commoner; he maneuvers his way into the French court, kills several courtiers in a grisly duel, and seduces the woman his patron desires, for which he is murdered. One of the Jacobean theater's great over-reachers.

Damian, Peter. *See* Peter, St.

Damian, St. *See* Cosmas, St.

Damocles. In Greek legend, a flatterer who said the king was the happiest man in the world, whereupon the king changed places with him, and Damocles saw hanging over his head a sword suspended by a single hair.

Damoetas. In Virgil's poems *Eclogues*, an old shepherd.

Damon. (1) In Greek legend, a philosopher whose great friend was Pythias;* various versions disagree in details, but one of the pair was condemned to death, and the other offered to die in his friend's place, so impressing Dionysus* that he freed both. (2) In Virgil's poem *Eclogues*, a simple rustic singer.

Dan. In the Bible, *Genesis* xxxv, a son of Jacob* and Bilhah* and founder of one of the twelve tribes of Israel.*

Danaan. *See* Danaus.

Danaë. In Greek legend, mother of Perseus;* she was impregnated by Zeus* in a golden shower inside the tower in which her father had imprisoned her.

Danaidae. *See* Danaus.

Danaus. In Homer's *Iliad*, a king of Argos* from whom Homer derived the name Danaans, which he applied to the Greeks. In legend, Danaus had 50 daughters, the Danaidae, who married the 50 sons of his brother and 49 of whom then murdered their husbands on their wedding night, for which they were condemned to draw water in Hades* with a sieve; the fiftieth pair, Hypermnestra* and Lynceus,* became the progenitors of all the people of Argos. Aeschylus's play *The Suppliants* deals with the time prior to their marriage, in which the women seek (and find) refuge from their suitors on the altars in Argos.

Dandin. In Racine's play *Les Plaideurs* (1668), a judge so obsessed with legalisms that he goes mad; shut up in his house, he attempts to try cases out the window and eventually tries his dog for eating a chicken, sentencing it to the galleys until moved to compassion by its puppies.

Dandin, George. In Molière's play *George Dandin* (1668), a ninny who marries an overbearing wife above his station; noted for his catch-phrase: "Vous l'avez voulu, George."

Dane, Melancholy. *See* Hamlet.

Dangle. In R. B. Sheridan's *The Critic* (1779), a stagestruck Londoner who joins Mr. Puff* at his rehearsal.

Daniel. In the Bible, *Daniel*, a prophet and wise man of the Jews during their captivity in Babylon; by successfully interpreting the dreams of Nebuchadnezzar,* he became the principal administrator of the kingdom. He also correctly interpreted the writing on the wall at Belshazzar's* feast, predicting Belshazzar's downfall. When he continued to pray to God, violating a decree of the new king Darius,* he was thrown into the lion's den, but God sent an angel* to protect him. The judge who wisely recognizes Susanna's innocence in the Apochryphal book *Susanna* may be the same Daniel.

Dantes, Edmund. In Alexandre Dumas's novel *The Count of Monte Cristo* (1844), a young man unjustly imprisoned in the infamous Chateau d'Îf, where he makes friends with an old prisoner by means of a tapping code and after years of work scrapes a passage between the cells. When the old man dies, Edmund takes his place inside the shroud, is thrown into the sea, and is saved by smugglers. Eventually, he finds the old man's fortune, reappears in Paris as the mysterious Count of Monte Cristo, the richest man in the world, and destroys the fortunes and lives of the men who connived at his imprisonment and stole the woman he loved.

Danton. Historically, a French lawyer (d. 1794) and leader in the French Revolution, the dominant radical voice in the Committee for Public Safety credited with beginning the Reign of Terror,* during which he himself was eventually executed for treason. He has been an obsessive figure in European literature, portrayed variously as the hero of the common man, the self-centered tyrant, the consummate political animal, the egalitarian betrayed, the intellectual not understood by his inferiors, and the idealist unable to cope with the machinations of the ambitious.

Danu. In Gaelic mythology, mother of all the gods.

Danvers, Mrs. In Daphne du Maurier's novel *Rebecca* (1938), the gaunt, dour, mysterious housekeeper who resents the new wife and who eventually sets fire to the house. *See also* Rebecca.

Daphne. In Greek legend, a nymph* pursued by Apollo;* her father Peneus* changed her into a laurel tree to allow her to escape.

Daphnis. (1) In Greek legend, a son of Hermes* who was reared by shepherds and who invented poetry; in some versions, he invented poetry after being struck blind when being unfaithful to a Naiad.* He was also devoted to hunting and pined away after his favorite hunting dogs died. (2) In Longus's story *Daphnis and Chloe*, Daphnis and Chloe are foundlings; although Chloe is sought by many men, she loves only Daphnis but can marry him only after he has found a unique purse of silver and they are discovered to be the long-lost children of wealthy Greeks.

Dapper. In Ben Jonson's play *The Alchemist* (1610), a clerk who wants the alchemists to make him a successful gambler.

Darby and Joan. In an old English song, first printed in 1735, an aged husband and wife; by the twentieth century, this had become a common term in Britain signifying an idealized, happy old couple.

Darcy. In Jane Austen's novel *Pride and Prejudice* (1813), a handsome and proud aristocrat who proposes to Elizabeth Bennet* but is refused because of what she sees as his overweening pride and his interference in her sister's romance with Bingley.* He meets Elizabeth again later, when she comes to understand his true nature and happily accepts a second proposal. His sisters are as haughty and interfering as Elizabeth believes him to be.

Dardanus. In Greek legend, a son of Zeus* and founder of a city that eventually grew into Troy;* he was also noted for his twelve horses, so fast no one could catch them.

Dares. In Virgil's *Aeneid*, a great boxer and companion of Aeneas.*

Darius. (1) In the Bible, *Daniel*, king of the Chaldeans and successor of Belshazzar,* apparently a regional ruler within the Persian empire ruled at the time by Cyrus;* *also called* Darius the Mede. He threw Daniel* into the den of lions, then repented and honored Daniel and his God. (2) Historically, several kings of Persia. **Darius I** (the Great) (d. 486 B.C.) expanded the empire and is most known for his two attempts to subdue the Greeks, known as the Persian Wars, and for returning the Jews to Israel* and rebuilding the temple in Jerusalem.* Legend says he became king by owning the horse that neighed first in a contest with other claimants. **Darius II** (d. 404 B.C.) interfered with varying success in the Peloponnesian War. **Darius III** (d. 330 B.C.) was defeated by Alexander.*

Dark Lady. A woman to whom many of the sonnets of Shakespeare are addressed; the debate on her true identity has consumed as much time and ink as any single topic in literature—some contend that she was, in fact, a he.

Darling. In J. M. Barrie's play *Peter Pan* (1904), the family at whose window Peter Pan* lurks in order to hear the stories. **Wendy** is the little girl who flies away with him to Never-Never-Land* to be the "mother" for all the Lost Boys, taking along her own brothers **Michael** and **John**. **Mrs. Darling** is the perfect mother, and **Mr. Darling** is an essentially genial authoritarian. In most performances, the actor playing Mr. Darling also plays Captain Hook,* suggesting perhaps a bit more Freudian complexity than Barrie intended. *See also* Nana.

Darnay, Charles. In Charles Dickens's novel *A Tale of Two Cities* (1859), a French aristocrat who, after escaping to England, returns to France to try to rescue the rest of his family and who is loved by Lucie; when he is captured, Sidney Carton,* who looks like him, takes his place on the guillotine so that he can be reunited with Lucie. For his father, *see* St. Evrémonde.

D'Artagnan. In Alexandre Dumas's novel *The Three Musketeers* (1844), a brave and honorable young man and a great swordsman who joins the King's Musketeers, becomes friends with the three musketeers Athos,* Porthos,* and Aramis,* and saves the Queen's honor.

Dartle, Rosa. In Charles Dickens's novel *David Copperfield* (1849), the insinuating and jealous woman in love with the younger Steerforth;* her lip is scarred by a hammer with which he struck her in a fit of temper and yet she continues her often humiliating passion for him.

Dasha. *See* Shatov.

Dashwood. In Jane Austen's novel *Sense and Sensibility* (1811), **Elinor** is a sensible young woman. Her sister **Marianne** is emotional and impulsive; she falls in love with the dissolute Willoughby,* who jilts her, and drives herself into serious illness, recovering only when Willoughby marries an heiress and the older and more sensible Col. Brandon* proposes to her. **Mrs. Dashwood** is warmhearted but impractical. Their half-brother **John** is cold and selfish and, under pressure from his arrogant and pretentious wife **Fanny**, refuses to give them any part of his inheritance. *See also* Ferrars; Steele, Lucy.

Dathan. In the Bible, *Numbers* xvi, one of the leaders of a revolt against Moses,* whom Dathan said had brought the Israelites out of Egypt "to kill us in the wilderness." God swallowed them up in the earth and then sent a plague killing 14,700 of their followers. *See also* Abiram.

Dauphin. Historically, the eldest son of the king of France; the most common references are to Charles,* later Charles VII, who was served by Jeanne d'Arc.* Some allusions may be to the son of Louis* XVI who was rumored to have escaped during the Revolution; one of the con men claims to be this Dauphin in Mark Twain's novel *Huckleberry Finn* (1885).

David. (1) In the Bible, *I* and *II Samuel*, a great king of Israel.* Born a shepherd boy, he was anointed while a child by Samuel.* He killed the giant Goliath* with his sling and then was brought to Saul's* court as a harpist and singer, becoming a great friend of Jonathan.* Saul exiled him, pursuing him through the hills, until Saul died and David returned as king. He built a temple to house the ark* of the covenant. When he fell in love with Bathsheba,* he arranged for her husband Uriah* to be killed in battle. His son Absalom* eventually led a revolt against him. Another son Amnon* raped his daughter Tamar.* After reunifying the kingdom, he numbered the people. He died of old age and was succeeded by his son Solomon.* A great poet and musician, he is the nominal author of most of the Psalms. Jerusalem* is sometimes called the City of David, and in *Luke* ii, Bethlehem* is also called the City of David to which Joseph* goes to be taxed. *See also* Abigail; Abishag; Abner; Adonijah; Eglah; Jesse; Rizpah.

David, St. Historically, a bishop (d. 601) and founder of monasteries, the patron saint of Wales. His symbol is a dove, and his day is March 1.

Davy Jones. In British nautical usage, the spirit of the sea; his locker is the grave of those who die at sea.

Deadeye, Dick. *See* Dick Deadeye.

Deadwood Dick. In numerous stories by Edward Wheeler and others (beg. 1877), the first masked cowboy fighter-for-justice, also noted for his all-black costume.

Dean, Ellen. In Emily Brontë's novel *Wuthering Heights* (1847), Cathy's* humble and patient servant who returns to keep house for Heathcliff.*

Deans. In Walter Scott's novel *The Heart of Midlothian* (1818), **David** is a prosperous but stern Presbyterian farmer. His youngest daughter **Effie**, spoiled, pretty, and passionate, eventually produces an illegitimate child; when the child disappears, she is tried for murder but is saved at the last moment and allowed to marry her lover Robertson.* After his death, she enters a convent. Her elder sister **Jeanie** is plain, but she is a model of affection and heroism who walks to London to plead successfully with the queen for Effie's life. *See also* Dumbiedikes; Murdockson, Meg.

Deasy. In James Joyce's novel *Ulysses* (1922), the anti-Semitic headmaster of the school in which Stephen Dedalus* teaches.

de Beverley, Constance de. *See* Constance.

Deborah. (1) In the Bible, *Genesis* xxxv, Rebecca's* nurse. (2) In the Bible, *Judges* iv, a prophetess and judge who led the Israelites in revolt against Sisera.* (3) *See* Jenkyns; Primrose.

de Bourgh. In Jane Austen's novel *Pride and Prejudice* (1813), **Lady Catherine** is the haughty, domineering, and loquacious aunt of Darcy.* Her daughter **Anne** has been so completely overwhelmed by Lady Catherine's personality that no personality of her own remains.

de Coverley, Roger. In numerous *Spectator* stories (1711–12), an eccentric, bluff, affable, and commonsensical English country gentleman, devoted to his club and his estate, seen by many as representative of the best English national character.

de Craye. In George Meredith's novel *The Egoist* (1879), a charming but untrustworthy Irish colonel.

de Croye, Countess. *See* Isabelle.

Dedalus. *See* Daedalus.

Dedalus, Stephen. In James Joyce's novels *A Portrait of the Artist as a Young Man* (1916) and *Ulysses* (1922), a sensitive and intelligent young man. In the earlier work, Stephen is a student trying to come to grips with the Irish temperament and Catholic morality, eventually repudiating both by deciding to leave the country. His father Simon is easygoing, loquacious, and shiftless, too much devoted to drink and blarney to be a success in any of his many endeavors. In the later work, recalling his distrust of his father, his guilt about his deathbed vow to his mother to be a good Catholic, and his frustration with Ireland, Stephen metaphorically searches during a single day for a spiritual father throughout Dublin, which he finds in Bloom,* who meets him in a brothel and then helps him after a drunken street brawl with British soldiers.

Dedlock. In Charles Dickens's novel *Bleak House* (1852), **Lady Dedlock** is a great beauty who had an illegitimate child (Esther Summerson*) by Captain Hawdon* before her marriage; when the lawyer Tulkinghorn* threatens to expose her past, she runs away and dies of shame and exposure at her former lover's grave. **Sir Leicester** is an insufferably proud, pompous, and stiff gentleman, yet completely in love with his younger wife, paralyzed with the shock of her past but also desperate to have her back. *See also* Rouncewell.

Dee, Judge. Historically, a seventh-century Chinese magistrate who figured in a number of fictional detective stories which were translated, adapted, and then added to in a series of novels by Robert Van Gulik (beg. 1949).

Deeds, Mr. In the American movie *Mr. Deeds Goes to Town* (1936), a quintessential American small-town man who inherits a fortune and is thought insane because he tries to give away what he does not want for his simple needs.

Defarge. In Charles Dickens's novel *A Tale of Two Cities* (1859), a wineshop keeper and radical leader of the French Revolution. **Mme. Defarge**, who is more famous, is a cold and ruthless woman who hates all aristocrats and is always in the front row at the guillotine, knitting a stitch for every head chopped off.

De Flores. In Middleton and Rowley's play *The Changeling* (1622), a man so obsessed with a woman, Beatrice-Joanna,* that he stops at nothing, even multiple murder, to spend one brief evening with her, which remains enough to him to justify all his crimes as he commits suicide.

Deianeira. In Greek legend, the second wife of Heracles.* Told by the centaur Nessus* that a garment steeped in his blood would reclaim the love of a wandering husband, she gave the garment to Heracles; it was in fact poisoned and killed her husband. In Sophocles's play *The Women of Trachis*, she is virtuous, intelligent, and loving, and she kills herself after Heracles's death.

Deidre. *See* Deirdre.

Deiphobe. In Virgil's *Aeneid*, the Cumean Sibyl* who led Aeneas* to the underworld.

Deiphobus. In Homer's *Iliad*, a son of Priam;* he marries Helen* after Paris* is killed. In Chaucer's *Troilus and Criseyde*, he brings Troilus* and Cressida* together at his home.

Deirdre. In Irish legend, a beautiful maiden who was loved by the king Conchubar,* who had her raised in solitude to prevent her loving another; nevertheless, she met and fell in love with Naisi, who carried her off. When Conchubar pretended to forgive them, they returned, Naisi was murdered, and Deirdre committed suicide. Her story figures in numerous works of the Irish revival, particularly in J. M.Synge's play *Deirdre of the Sorrows* (1910) and W. B. Yeats's play *Deirdre* (1907).

Dejanira. *See* Deianeira.

del Dongo, Fabrizio. *See* Fabrizio.

Delia. A name sometimes used for Artemis.*

Delilah. In the Bible, *Judges* xvi, a Philistine* woman who seduced Samson* and discovered that his strength came from his vow never to cut his hair. When she cut it, he was weakened, captured, and imprisoned; hence, a temptress or a woman whose demands or whose love weakens a man. *Also called* Dalila.*

Delius. A name sometimes used for Apollo.*

Deloraine. In Walter Scott's poem *The Lay of the Last Minstrel* (1805), a knight who recovers a magic book from a wizard's tomb, then is wounded in a duel with the neighboring Lord Cranstoun,* who then impersonates Deloraine in a duel that prevents a war and ends a bitter feud.

Delphi. Historically, the site of a major temple of ancient Greece, home of the most famous oracles* of Apollo,* consulted by numerous legendary and historical Greek characters and thought by the Greeks to be the center of the world. *See also* Omphalos.

Demas. In the Bible, *II Timothy* iv, a friend who deserted Paul.*

Demea. In Terence's play *The Brothers*, Micio's* brother, who raises his children by the rule of discipline and fear.

Demeter. In Greek mythology, a sister of Zeus,* the goddess of agriculture, called Ceres by the Romans. Her worship centered in Eleusis and included a number of closely guarded rites called the Eleusinian mysteries. She was the mother of Persephone,* and when the latter was abducted by Pluto,* Demeter wandered the earth in search of her, leaving the earth barren until Zeus* ordered Persephone's return. She was often said to spend part of the year in mourning whenever Persephone regularly returned to Hades,* restoring the crops each spring when she returned. She sent her priest Triptolemus* throughout the world to teach mankind how to grow grain; other interventions in mortal affairs were minimal, the most noted concerned Abas,* Erisichthon,* and Pelops.* *See also* Ascalaphus; Thesmophoriazusae.

Demetrius. (1) In the Bible, *Acts* xix, an Ephesian silversmith who raised the town against Paul* because the Christian teachings were destroying the market for images of the gods, in particular of Diana.* (2) In Shakespeare's play *Titus Andronicus* (1592), one of Tamora's* sons, both of whom rape Lavinia,* kill her husband, and cut out her tongue, and are then later killed, cooked, and fed to their mother by Andronicus.* *See also* Chiron. (3) In Shakespeare's play *A*

Midsummer Night's Dream (1595), one of the young lovers, the one preferred by Hermia's father and who follows Hermia* and Lysander* into the woods, spurning the doting Helena.* (4) In Shakespeare's play *Antony and Cleopatra* (1606), a soldier who is much concerned about Antony's obsession with Cleopatra.*

Demipho. In Terence's play *Phormio*, the pompous and miserly father. The name is also used for similar characters in some of Plautus's plays.

Demiurge. In philosophical writings by Plato, a name sometimes used for the creator of the world; in later Christian usage, it was sometimes used for any pagan god or for the Devil.*

Demogorgon. In medieval usage, a mysterious primeval god who predates all other ancient gods. In Percy Shelley's play *Prometheus Unbound* (1820), he appears as the god who overcomes Jupiter* and frees Prometheus.* *See also* Demiurge.

Demon Barber. *See* Todd, Sweeney.

Demophon. In Greek legend, a son of Theseus* and lover of Laodice* in Troy;* when on his way home, he fell in love with Phyllis,* who hanged herself when he did not return to her as he had promised.

Demos. In Aristophanes's play *The Knights*, a foolish, temperamental, and selfish old man representing the democratic people of Athens. *See also* Agoracritus; Cleon.

Demosthenes. Historically, a great Greek orator (d. 322 B.C.); legend says he learned to speak well by talking with pebbles in his mouth.

Denis, St. Historically, the first bishop of Paris, a missionary to Gaul who was beheaded c. 258. Patron saint of France, he is usually depicted carrying his head in his hands; his day is October 9.

Densher, Morton. In Henry James's novel *The Wings of the Dove* (1902), a charming journalist who marries the ill American heiress Milly Theale* in hopes of inheriting enough money at her death to marry Kate Croy,* whom he really loves. He is too sensitive to go through with this plan completely, so he confesses it to Milly, who is shocked but still leaves him the money. Nevertheless, he is so disturbed by her goodness that he is unable to bring himself to marry Kate.

Denys, St. *See* Denis, St.

Deronda, Daniel. In George Eliot's novel *Daniel Deronda* (1876), an orphan and a sensitive, intelligent man in search of his family past, at last realizing that he is Jewish and devoting himself to Jewish causes.

Desborough, Lucy. In George Meredith's novel *The Ordeal of Richard Feverel* (1859), the farmer's daughter with whom Richard Feverel* elopes and who dies of brain fever when she believes he has been killed in a duel.

Desdemona. In Shakespeare's play *Othello* (1604), a beautiful young Venetian noblewoman who falls in love with Othello* when he tells of his exotic and adventurous past, as he falls in love with her. She marries him against her father Brabantio's* wishes and then accompanies him to the wars in Cyprus. Trapped almost by accident in Iago's* plot against Othello and Cassio,* she is made to appear to be having an affair with Cassio, for which Othello kills her, usually suffocating her with a pillow in her bed. She is generally portrayed as a gentle blonde maiden, innocent and pure, a nature underlined by the famous scene in which she sings the "willow song." *See also* Emilia; Roderigo.

Des Grieux. In the Abbé Prévost's novel *Manon Lescaut* (1731), a young nobleman whose passion for the amoral Manon* leads to his loss of honor, dignity, and wealth.

Desmond, Norma. In the movie *Sunset Boulevard* (1950), the faded but egotistical silent film star who slides into insanity after her dream of a comeback evaporates and she murders her young gigolo.

Desqueyroux. In François Mauriac's novel *Thérèse* (1927), **Thérèse** is an attractive married woman who tries to poison her husband in order to marry another man, running away to Paris after the plot is discovered. **M. Desqueyroux** is a proud provincial who refuses to press charges in hopes of avoiding a scandal. Their daughter **Marie** eventually finds Thérèse in Paris, where Marie's fiancé falls in love with Thérèse, who confesses her crimes to him and returns, nearly insane, to the country to try to find salvation.

Destiny. In Greek mythology, an ancient deity who helped determine the fate of mankind and could withstand the power even of Zeus.* *See also* Fates.

Deucalion. In Greek legend, a son of Prometheus.* When the great flood* covered the earth, only he and his wife Pyrrha* survived, repopulating the earth by throwing stones over their shoulders, his becoming new men.

Devereaux, Robert. *See* Essex.

Devi. In Hindu mythology, the wife of Shiva.*

Devil. In the Jewish and Christian religions, the name given to the spirit of supreme evil; in most usage, the lower-case "devil" applies to any number of demons and other assorted malignant supernatural creatures, of which *the* Devil is the titular ruler, the Prince of Darkness, as well as the ruler of all those condemned to Hell.* In European legend and folklore, the Devil may take any shape, the most noted being the serpent that tempts Adam* and Eve,* but is usually revealed in his true shape, with horns, cloven hooves, a pointed tail, and skin or clothing of red. He is said to travel the world seeking converts, who sell him their souls in return for special powers of knowledge, witchcraft, or wealth, usually signing a contract in their own blood. He is said to be worshipped by cults that practice Black Masses, and to be served by numerous witches* and warlocks.* He is usually called Satan,* but other common names include Beelzebub,* Belial,* Clootie, Lord of the Flies,* Lucifer,* Mephistopheles, Old Nick, and Scratch. *See also* Imp; Samael.

de Winter. In Daphne du Maurier's novel *Rebecca* (1938), the mysterious, reserved, and guilt-ridden owner of Manderley* and the former husband of Rebecca.*

Diafoirus. In Molière's play *Le Malade imaginaire* (1673), a family of doctors. The father is pompous and dedicated to the knowledge of the ancients, even if it does not work; the son is incredibly stupid, unable even to repeat properly the set speeches, but he almost marries into the hypochondriac Argan's* family so that Argan will always have a doctor available. *See also* Toinette.

Diana. (1) In Roman mythology, goddess of the moon; generally equivalent to Artemis,* she also had significant associations with unique concerns of women. *Also called* Diana of the Ephesians, due to the images produced there and described in the Bible, *Acts* xiv; Diana of the Crossways, due to a common practice of placing her statues at road junctions. The name is particularly common in English poetry. *See also* Hecate; Luna. (2) *See* Merion, Diana; Vernon, Diana.

Dicaepolis. In Aristophanes's play *Acharnians* (425 B.C.), an honest farmer who makes a separate peace with the Spartans* when the Athenians will not stop the Peloponnesian War.

Dice. *See* Dike.

Dick. (1) *See* Dick and Jane; Dudgeon, Dick. (2) *See also* Richard.

Dick, Deadwood. *See* Deadwood Dick.

Dick, Mr. In Charles Dickens's novel *David Copperfield* (1849), a genial lunatic who is trying to write a history but always returns to the subject of King Charles's* head; Betsey Trotwood* often defers to him as a judge of character.

Dick and Jane. In numerous reading primers used in American schools (beg. 1920), a brother and sister who were depicted as typical children doing typical activities with their dog Spot. The simplistic writing style, such as ''See Spot run!,'' is often parodied.

Dick Deadeye. In Gilbert and Sullivan's operetta *H.M.S. Pinafore* (1878), a deformed and embittered sailor, disliked by all; he eventually deserts. He also reports Ralph Rackstraw's* romance to Captain Corcoran.*

Diddler. In James Kenney's play *Raising the Wind* (1803), a small-time swindler who lives by borrowing petty sums that he never repays.

Dido. In Roman legend, the founder and queen of Carthage. In one legend, she threw herself on the fire to avoid marriage with a neighboring king. In Virgil's *Aeneid*, she fell in love with Aeneas* when he stopped in Carthage, consummating their love in a cave during a storm on a hunting trip, and then cursed him and stabbed herself when the gods ordered him to give her up and to continue toward Italy. He saw her again on his journey through the underworld, but her spirit passed by and refused to speak to him. *Also called* Elissa.

Didymus. A name sometimes used for Thomas* the Apostle.

Diggory. (1) In Oliver Goldsmith's play *She Stoops to Conquer* (1773), a farm laborer pressed on grand occasions into table service, where he commits gauche errors. (2) *See* Venn, Diggory.

Dignam, Paddy. In James Joyce's novel *Ulysses* (1922), the friend whose funeral Bloom* attends.

Dike. In Greek mythology, the goddess of justice; also one of the Horae.*

Dillon, Matt. In the American television series "Gunsmoke" (1955–75), the town marshall of Dodge City, a brave, stolid, honest, and fatherly gunfighter/lawman.

Dilsey. In William Faulkner's novel *The Sound and the Fury* (1929), the Compson* family's quiet, faithful, female Negro servant who in actuality holds the family together, representing those who "endure."

di Luna. In Verdi's opera *Il Trovatore* (1851), the evil count who pursues and kills Manrico,* only to discover too late that they are brothers.

Dimitri. (1) In Pushkin's play *Boris Godunov* (1825), an ambitious monk who seeks the Russian throne and betrays the country to the invading Poles in order to reach his goal. *See also* Godunov, Boris. (2) *See* Karamazov; Neklyudov, Dimitri.

Dimmesdale. In Nathaniel Hawthorne's novel *The Scarlet Letter* (1850), a Puritan minister and the father of Hester's* illegitimate child; wracked by guilt, he begins to waste away physically until, at last confessing his sin publicly, he dies, a stigmata matching the "A" worn by Hester being found on his chest. *See also* Chillingworth.

Dinadan. In Malory's *Morte d'Arthur*, one of Arthur's* knights, noted for his good humor and his scorn of love as well as for his prowess.

Dinah. (1) In the Bible, *Genesis* xxxiv, a daughter of Jacob.* After she is raped by a son of Hamor, Jacob's sons pretend to agree to her marriage and peace if Hamor's men will be circumcised; then, "when they were sore," her brothers attacked and killed them all. (2) In Lewis Carroll's story *Alice in Wonderland* (1865), the real-life pet cat belonging to Alice.* (3) In American slang usage, particularly in the nineteenth century, a stereotypical name for a Negro cook, as in the folk song verse, "someone's in the kitchen with Dinah. . . ." (4) *See* Morris, Dinah.

Dindymene. A name sometimes used for Cybele.*

Dinmont, Dandy. In Walter Scott's novel *Guy Mannering* (1815), a hospitable farmer and breeder of terriers.

Diogenes. Historically, a Greek philosopher who advocated the simple life. Legend says he lived in a tub, told Alexander* the Great to stand out of his sunlight, and walked the streets in daylight carrying a lantern in search of a single honest man.

Diomed. *See* Diomedes.

Diomedes. (1) In Homer's *Iliad*, a great Greek warrior in the Trojan War,* second only to Achilles* in skill. He wounds Aeneas,* who escapes only because the gods hide him in a wall of mist, kills numerous other Trojans, and even fights and wounds the gods Ares* and Aphrodite* when they try to intervene in the battle. According to Virgil's *Aeneid*, he enters Troy in the Trojan Horse.* In Dante's *Divine Comedy*, he is the quintessential evil counselor and is changed to an eternal flame in Hell.* In Shakespeare's play *Troilus and Cressida* (1602), he escorts Cressida* to the Greeks and seduces her, although not without her own eager participation. *See also* Glaucus; Odysseus. (2) In Greek legend, the owner of a set of mares that ate human flesh; one of the labors of Heracles* was to kill the mares, which he did after killing Diomedes and feeding them his flesh.

Dione. In Greek legend, mother of Aphrodite;* the name is sometimes also used for Aphrodite.

Dionysius. (1) Historically, a tyrant of Syracuse (d. 367 B.C.) noted for his welcome of Plato and the demonstration he gave Damocles.* (2) In the Bible, *Acts* xvii, an Athenian judge converted by Paul.* (3) *See also* Dionysus.

Dionysus. In Greek mythology, the god of wine and drunkenness, called Bacchus by the Romans. He is also a god of fertility, and in many stories he dies regularly and then is reborn. He is often the god of poetic inspiration or imagination, due to the liberating influence of the wine, and for the same reason just as often a god whose votaries practice exotic, mystical, ecstatic, and/or sexually uninhibited and violent ceremonies. He takes many forms, sometimes jovial and sometimes threatening, sometimes a delicate youth and sometimes a powerful bearded warrior in a chariot drawn by tigers. The Greek drama is said to have evolved from the choric hymns sung at his spring festivals. His cult appears to have faced considerable opposition, including attempts at suppression by Pentheus* and Lycurgus.* *See also* Ariadne; Bacchae; Carya; Damon; Icarius; Satyr; Semele.

Dionyza. In Shakespeare's play *Pericles* (1608), the jealous and overbearing wife of Cleon.* When Marina,* the daughter that Pericles* left with them, grows to be more beautiful than her own daughter, she tries to have Marina killed.

Dioscuri. A name sometimes given to Castor* and Pollux.*

Dipsas. In John Lyly's play *Endymion* (1588), an evil enchantress who puts a spell on Endymion* before she is reformed by Cynthia.*

Dipsodes. In Rabelais's *Pantagruel* (1532), knights who invade Pantagruel's* homeland, whom he defeats by giving them pills that make them so thirsty that they drink too much wine and pass out. He aggravates their thirst by sprinkling salt into their open mouths and then drowns them in his urine.

Dirty Harry. In several movies, beginning with *Dirty Harry* (1971), a tough, laconic policeman who often breaks the rules in order to administer true justice. Identified by his .357 Magnum pistol and his dislike of liberals and bureaucrats, he is often interpreted as a spokesman for violent and simpleminded solutions to complex social problems.

Dis. A name sometimes used for Pluto.*

Disciples. A name sometimes used for the Apostles.*

Discordia. A name sometimes used for Eris.*

Dismas. In Christian legend, the thief who, when crucified with Jesus,* repented and was promised a place in Paradise.* *See also* Gestas.

Disney, Walt. Historically, an American cartoonist and filmmaker (d. 1966) as well as the founder of the modern theme entertainment park. His name is often used to symbolize "wholesome family entertainment," as well as a simplistic, optimistic worldview associated with such entertainment. *See also* Bambi; Mickey Mouse; Donald Duck; Snow White.

Diver. In F. Scott Fitzgerald's novel *Tender is the Night* (1933), **Dick** is an intelligent psychiatrist who is eventually destroyed by his mentally ill wife **Nicole** as they live a Lost Generation* existence on the Riviera.

Diver, Jenny. In John Gay's play *The Beggar's Opera* (1728), one of the prostitutes who love Macheath.* In Bertolt Brecht's version *The Threepenny Opera* (1928), she is Macheath's favorite and betrays him to the police. *See also* Pirate Jenny.

Dives. In Christian usage, the name of the rich man in the parable of Lazarus.* The Bible gives no name, but the usage probably comes from the Latin Vulgate, where "riches" is "dives."

Dixie. In American usage, the southern states, in particular those states that seceded to form the Confederacy during the Civil War. Popularized by Dan Emmett's song *Dixie* (1859), the term was in use long before then.

Djinn. A name sometimes used for a genie.*

Dmitri. *See* Dimitri.

Dobbin. (1) In British usage predating Shakespeare, the name given to a faithful work horse. (2) In William Makepeace Thackeray's novel *Vanity Fair* (1847), the faithful officer and friend of George Osborne;* he loves Amelia Sedley* from afar and discreetly helps her in her troubles.

Dobbs, Fred C. In B. Traven's novel *The Treasure of the Sierra Madre* (1935), a down-on-his-luck American in Mexico who discovers gold and becomes crazed with greed; perhaps better known from the movie (1948).

Dobchinsky. *See* Bobchinsky.

Dobson, Zuleika. In Max Beerbohm's novel *Zuleika Dobson* (1911), a bewitchingly beautiful young woman, said to be so lovely the statues melt when she passes by, but who cannot love any man who loves her. When she visits Oxford, she wreaks havoc among the student body, several of whom commit suicide, and then she leaves for Cambridge.

Dodger, Artful. *See* Artful Dodger.

Dodo. (1) In the Bible, *II Samuel*, a general of David's* army. (2) Historically, a South Seas bird with almost nonexistent wings that coped so poorly with the human threat that it was extinct less than 100 years after its discovery; hence, any particularly stupid person. The bird appears in Lewis Carroll's *Alice in Wonderland* (1865), in which he suggests the caucus race to dry everyone off after Alice* falls into the pool of tears. (3) *See* Brooke.

Dodson and Fogg. In Charles Dickens's novel *Pickwick Papers* (1836), the unscrupulous attorneys who counsel Mrs. Bardell* to sue Pickwick* for breach of promise and then have her imprisoned for debt when she cannot pay their bill.

Dodsworth. In Sinclair Lewis's novel *Dodsworth* (1929), **Sam** is a successful American businessman on a tour of Europe; sensible and practical, he is alternately attracted to and repelled by European culture, which he tries to understand. His wife **Frances** is a smug and spoiled woman who desperately pretends to be European and cultured and berates her husband for his insensitivity. She is eventually lured into an affair with an impoverished count which leads ultimately to her divorce.

Doe, John. An imaginary, representative person. The usage is drawn from a British legal usage, discarded in 1852, that listed Doe as plaintiff in all actions of ejectment, against the defendant the equally imaginary Richard Roe.

Dogberry. In Shakespeare's play *Much Ado About Nothing* (1598), the local constable; pompous and loquacious, he is noted for the ways in which he mangles the language. *See also* Verges.

Dogpatch. In the American newspaper cartoon *Li'l Abner* (beg. 1934), the home of the Yokums,* soon synonymous with backwoods hillbilly life.

Dolabella. (1) In Shakespeare's play *Antony and Cleopatra* (1606), an emissary from Rome who tells Cleopatra* that she will be displayed there after her surrender; this encourages her to kill herself. (2) In John Dryden's play *All For Love* (1677), a handsome young Roman whom Antony* banishes for fear he will steal Cleopatra's* love and who tries to arrange Antony's reconciliation with Rome.

Dolittle, Dr. In numerous stories by Hugh Lofting (beg. 1920), a genial and eccentric doctor who can speak the languages of most animals.

Dolly. (1) In Tolstoy's novel *Anna Karenina* (1875), a sister of Kitty* and wife of Oblonsky.* She is a plain woman who, when faced with his numerous affairs, seeks solace through absorption in the life of her children. (2) *See* Levi, Dolly; Varden.

Dolon. In Homer's *Iliad*, a Trojan* famous for his speed, captured and killed while spying on the Greek camp.

Dolores. In Swinburne's poem *Dolores* (1866), "Our Lady of Pain."

Dombey. In Charles Dickens's novel *Dombey and Son* (1846), a wealthy and cold-blooded merchant who ignores his first wife, who dies in childbirth, and his loving daughter and who devotes all his plans to the son who will share his business with him. After the son dies, he becomes even more distant and cold and eventually marries Edith,* a woman equally cold who runs away with his chief clerk Carker,* who also bankrupts Dombey. The son **Paul** is a weak and sensitive child, preoccupied with death; after an abortive attempt at education, he "grows more and more old fashioned" until he dies. The daughter **Florence** is rejected and ignored by her father, who cares little for her, although she is desperate to please him. Gentle, loving, yet strong, she nurses her brother, fends for herself, and eventually marries the young man whom her father had tried to send away to his death. *See also* Bagstock, Major; Chick; Cleopatra; Cuttle, Capt.; Gay, Walter; Nipper, Susan; Toodle; Toots; Tox, Miss.

Dominic, St. Historically, a preacher to the Albigensians (d. 1221) and the founder of the Order of Preachers, called the Dominicans. His emblems are a star and a dog with a torch, and his day is August 7.

Dominie Sampson. *See* Sampson, Dominie.

Domitius. A name sometimes used for Nero.*

Donalbain. In Shakespeare's play *Macbeth* (1605), Duncan's* younger son, who flees to Ireland after his father's murder. *See also* Malcolm.

Donald Duck. In numerous movie cartoons produced by Walt Disney* (beg. 1934), a belligerent, hot-tempered duck, also noted for the strangulated sound of his voice. *See also* Mickey Mouse.

Don John. *See* John, Don.

Don Juan. *See* Juan, Don.

Donnithorne. In George Eliot's novel *Adam Bede* (1859), **Capt. Arthur** is an impulsive but pleasant young man who seduces Hetty; * when she abandons their illegitimate child, he saves her life but leaves home disgraced and chastened. His grandfather the **Squire** is a hard-tempered old miser.

Don Quixote. *See* Quixote, Don.

Dooley, Mr. In Finley Peter Dunne's stories (beg. 1898), a talkative Irish-American saloonkeeper who observes and comments satirically on American life; known for his thick brogue, his sharp eye for the hypocrite, and for knowing only what he reads in the papers.

Doolittle. In G. B. Shaw's play *Pygmalion* (1913), **Eliza** is a Cockney flower seller who is trained by the speech consultant Higgins* to speak and act like an English gentlewoman. Her father **Alfred** is "one of the undeserving poor," a drunkard who lives without responsibilities or a job; Higgins recommends him as an original philosopher, which in turn leads him into dreaded "respectability." *See also* Pickering.

Doone. In R. D. Blackmore's novel *Lorna Doone* (1869), an outlaw clan living on the wild moors of England. **Lorna**, a ward of the clan chief Ensor since her kidnapping as a child, rebels against their savageness by falling in love with John Ridd,* whose family have long been enemies of the Doones. Among the Doones, **Carver** is the most villainous, the murderer of Ridd's father and of Lorna's closest relative.

Dora. In Charles Dickens's novel *David Copperfield* (1849), David Copperfield's* "child bride," a childlike, and often childish, helpless female who loves her husband but can do nothing for herself, dealing with all problems by shaking her curls and playing with her dog Jip. *See also* Spenlow.

Dorante. (1) In Corneille's play *Le Menteur* (1643), a handsome and intelligent young man who is unable to tell the truth about anything, even when it would be to his advantage. (2) In Molière's play *The Bourgeois Gentleman* (1670), a count who flatters M. Jourdain* in order to laugh at his gaucheries and bilk him of his money. *See also* Dorimène.

Dorcas. A name sometimes used for Tabitha.*

Dorigen. In Chaucer's *Canterbury Tales*, in the Franklin's Tale, a beautiful lady, wife of Arviragus. When Aurelius tries to seduce her, she refuses until the rocks of the seacoast should disappear; Aurelius arranges for a magician to make them disappear, and her husband insists she fulfill her part of the bargain. However, Aurelius is so impressed by the honor of the couple that he returns her untouched.

Dorimant. In George Etherege's play *The Man of Mode* (1676), an amoral, witty dandy who wins and discards several mistresses in search of a rich heiress; in many ways, he is the model for all the heroes of Restoration comedy. *See also* Bellinda; Harriet; Loveit, Lady.

Dorimène. In Molière's play *The Bourgeois Gentleman* (1670), a sensible widow who marries Dorante;* M. Jourdain* tries to impress her with extravagant musical interludes and jewelry, but she ignores him.

Dorinda. In George Farquhar's play *The Beaux' Stratagem* (1707), the modest heiress courted by Aimwell.

Doris. In Greek legend, daughter of Oceanus* and mother of the Nereids.*

Dormouse. In Lewis Carroll's story *Alice in Wonderland* (1865), a guest at the Mad Hatter's* tea party who falls asleep in his tea. *See also* Alice; March Hare.

Dorn. In Anton Chekhov's play *The Sea Gull* (1896), a middle-aged doctor, penniless yet happy with his life, who refuses to upset his satisfying existence with a love affair.

Dorotea. *See* Dorothea; Dorothy.

Dorothea. (1) *See* Brooke. (2) *See also* Dorothy.

Dorothea, St. In Christian legend, a martyr (c. 303). Legend says that the judge at her execution sarcastically asked her to send him some fruit from Paradise,* which she did. She is usually depicted with roses on her head and fruit by her side, and her day is February 6.

Dorothy. In Frank Baum's *The Wonderful Wizard of Oz* (1900), and especially in the movie (1939), a Kansas farm girl who with her dog Toto* is transported by a tornado into the magical kingdom of Oz,* where she has numerous adventures. She mets a Scarecrow,* a Tin Man,* and a cowardly Lion,* and the four follow the yellow brick road to find the wizard who can return her to her home. *See also* Em, Auntie. (2) *See also* Dorothea.

Dorrit. In Charles Dickens's novel *Little Dorrit* (1855), an impoverished family living in debtors' prison which suddenly finds itself heir to a large fortune. The father, **Mr. Dorrit**, is a gentle old man who never understands the legal reasons for his bankruptcy or his release but whose pleasant personality when he is in prison earns him the title ''Father of the Marshalsea.'' After his enrichment, he becomes extravagant, but his mind deteriorates, and he dies thinking himself back in the happy life of the prison. His daughter Amy, called **Little Dorrit** because of her tiny size, is a sensitive and sweet but extremely self-sufficient girl who holds the family together, caring for her father in prison, earning money by sewing jobwork, and then desperately trying to hold down the family extravagance after its sudden wealth. She is loved by Arthur Clennam,* whom she marries after she nurses him during his own term in debtors' prison. Her sister **Fanny** is a self-centered and scatterbrained ballet dancer whose personality leads her into society after the inheritance, where she marries Sparkler.* Her brother **Tip** is a spendthrift and layabout who can never find a job that really suits his talents. Their uncle **Frederick** is a shy clarinetist in a theater orchestra, a simple man of simple tastes. *See also* Flintwich; General, Mrs.; Maggy; Merdle; Plornish.

Dorset. (1) In Edith Wharton's novel *The House of Mirth* (1905), **George** is an unhappily married man who becomes infatuated with Lily Bart;* when his jealous wife **Bertha** realizes this, she embarks on a scandal campaign that destroys Lily, even though there is no real affair. (2) In Max Beerbohm's novel *Zuleika Dobson* (1911), a young duke who, when he hears a bird that has always foreshadowed death in his family, feels obligated to uphold tradition by drowning himself. *See also* Dobson, Zuleika.

Dotheboys Hall. In Charles Dickens's novel *Nicholas Nickleby* (1838), a foul boys school run by Squeers,* noted as a place where unwanted children are sent to be lost and are badly mistreated without being given any education. Nicholas Nickleby,* hired as a teacher, finds Smike* there and eventually aids the boys in a revolt.

Doughboy. In American slang, an infantry soldier, used primarily during World War I, although the term may date back to soldiers' bread in the Mexican-American War.

Douglas. Historically, a major family of Scottish nobility; the family figures in numerous literary works, especially in those of Walter Scott. In *Marmion* (1808), a Douglas is charged with protecting the nuns whom Lady Clare* has joined; in *The Lady of the Lake* (1810), James Douglas rebels against the king, and his daughter Ellen eventually brings peace when she finds that the young man who loves her, despite her rejection of his proposal, is the king in disguise.

Douglas, Widow. In Mark Twain's novel *Huckleberry Finn* (1885), the upright woman who is Huck Finn's* guardian in town and from whose ideas of civilization Huck runs away. *See also* Watson, Miss.

Dounia. In Dostoevsky's novel *Crime and Punishment* (1866), Raskolnikov's* devoted sister who works to support and encourage her severely disturbed brother; she is engaged to Razumihin.*

Dowd, Elwood P. In Mary Chase's play *Harvey* (1944), a genial alcoholic who spends all his time with the invisible rabbit Harvey.*

Dowling. In Henry Fielding's novel *Tom Jones* (1749), a less than honest lawyer who eventually reveals Tom Jones's true identity.

Dowsabel. An Anglicized version of Dulcibella.*

Doyce, Daniel. In Charles Dickens's novel *Little Dorrit* (1855), an uncomplaining, practical engineer whose plans for great savings and improvements are rejected by the Circumlocution Office and who eventually goes into business with Arthur Clennam.* *See also* Meagles.

Draco. Historically, an Athenian lawyer (d. 621 B.C.) whose strict "Draconian" laws, in which almost all crimes were capital offenses, became synonymous with unbending legal severity.

Dracula. In Bram Stoker's novel *Dracula* (1897), a mysterious Transylvanian count who is also a vampire* and around whose character almost all vampire lore now revolves. He appears only at night, since the light of the sun could kill him, sleeping through the day in a coffin filled with dirt from his homeland. He can turn himself into a bat; he sucks the blood of others to live, biting them on the neck; he cannot see his image in a mirror; he can be frightened away by a cross or by garlic; and he can be killed only by driving a stake through his heart. In the novel, he comes to England where he bites Lucy* and turns her into a vampire as well, until she is killed. He is finally tracked down and killed by Dr. Van Helsing* on the journey back to Transylvania. *See also* Harker.

Dragon. A mythical beast that appears in the folklore and legend of most cultures throughout the world, especially in medieval Europe, China, and Japan. Generally, the dragon was large, breathed fire, and was covered with scales. In the Bible, particularly *Revelation*, the dragon is often used to denote the forces of evil in the war against God. Most famous knights encountered and killed a dragon at some time, most notably St. George,* who is the single European most associated with the beast. Many legendary heroes kill dragons, such as Beowulf,* Siegfried,* and Heracles* in the Hesperides;* St. Margaret* also killed a dragon by making the sign of a cross inside its body. Noted dragons in legend include Apollyon* and Fafnir.* Cadmus* sowed a field with dragon's teeth, each of which turned into a warrior, and Jason* did the same when laboring for the Golden Fleece.* Medea's* chariot was drawn by dragons.

Drake, Temple. In William Faulkner's novel *Sanctuary* (1931), a college girl kidnapped and raped with a corncob by Popeye,* then imprisoned in a brothel. Although she is finally rescued, her mind is disturbed, and she is haunted and guilt-ridden for her sometime pleasure in the experience.

Drew, Nancy. In numerous novels by Carolyn Keene (beg. 1930), a wholesome American teenaged girl with an aptitude for finding and then solving mysteries.

Dreyfus. Historically, a Jewish French army captain convicted of treason in 1894. When later evidence made it clear that the treason had been committed by an officer from an old French military family, the Army nonetheless refused to free Dreyfus, thereby instigating a scandal and years of internecine political struggle among various groups in French society that soon forgot Dreyfus himself, a struggle which is all but incomprehensible to outsiders but whose scars have seriously affected French politics for almost a century. Countless allusions appear in modern French literature, but their meanings are almost as countless.

Driffield, Rosie. *See* Rosie.

Dromio. In Shakespeare's play *The Comedy of Errors* (1583), the servants, twin brothers separated at the same time as their twin masters Antipholus,* and subject to numerous comic confusions when the two pairs end up by accident in the same city. *See also* Dromo.

Dromo. In several plays by Terence, a name for a servant. *See also* Dromio.

Drozdov. In Dostoevsky's novel *The Possessed* (1867), **Lizaveta** (Liza) is a high-spirited young widow enamored of Stavrogin's* supposed ideals but disillusioned after she sleeps with him; she is ultimately beaten to death by villagers for her association with him. Her mother **Praskovya Ivanovna** is a shallow woman who has hoped to marry Lizaveta to Stavrogin. *See also* Shatov.

Drugger. In Ben Jonson's play *The Alchemist* (1610), a tobacconist who wants the alchemists to make him rich and make the Widow Pliant* love him.

Drummle. In Charles Dickens's novel *Great Expectations* (1860), a rich boy, much given to pouting, who grows into the spoiled and cruel young man who marries Estella,* to the great misery of both.

Drummond, Bulldog. In numerous novels by Sapper and others (beg. 1920), a hearty English gentleman and soldier who continually saves society from numerous foreign threats; known initially for his bluff British directness and heroic derring-do, he has more recently come to be seen as a symbol of racist jingoism and sadism.

Dryad. *See* Nymph.

Dryasdust. In prefaces to several novels by Walter Scott, an imaginary scholar with whom Scott discusses the purpose and use of history.

Dryope. In Greek legend, a woman in whose shape Aphrodite* persuaded all the women of Lemnos* to murder their husbands.

Dubedat. In G. B. Shaw's play *The Doctor's Dilemma* (1906), **Louis** is a bigamous spendthrift with an incurable disease, but he is also an artist with the promise of greatness—the epitome of the artist of great talent and little character. His beautiful wife **Jennifer** has dedicated herself to his career and devotes her love, her fortune, and her considerable charm to encouraging and supporting him. In the plot, she pleads for his life with Dr. Ridgeon, who has only enough of a new cure for one man and who uses the cure for someone else in the vain hope of marrying her. Dubedat dies rather nobly, and Jennifer remarries as he wishes, devoting her life to the joy of Dubedat's memory.

DuBois, Blanche. In Tennessee Williams's play *A Streetcar Named Desire* (1947), an unbalanced Southern belle now grown older and poorer, her family plantation sold for debts. A small-town schoolteacher fired for her nymphomania and drunkenness, haunted by the young husband who killed himself when she discovered his homosexuality, she visits her sister in New Orleans in hopes of a last chance, but her pretensions outrage Stanley Kowalski,* her brother-in-law, and she goes mad after he exposes her past to Mitch,* who has proposed to her, and then rapes her. Her exit line is, "I have always depended on the kindness of strangers." She has become a symbol of the sensitive artistic temperament destroyed by the animalistic common man, particularly within the American homosexual community.

Duchess, The. In Lewis Carroll's story *Alice in Wonderland* (1865), an ugly woman with a baby that cries constantly, perhaps because she shakes it violently throughout her lullaby. It turns into a pig when it is placed in Alice's* arms. Her cook puts pepper in everything.

Dudgeon, Dick. In G. B. Shaw's play *The Devil's Disciple* (1897), a wild young man disliked by his puritanical relatives for his sense of pleasure and his insistence on always speaking the truth. He tries to sacrifice himself by pretending to be another man, an American rebel leader wanted by the British, but he is rescued on the gallows.

Duessa. In Edmund Spenser's poem *The Fairie Queen* (1590), the female accomplice of Archimago* and a woman able to mask her ugliness by a beautiful false appearance. She generally signifies Falsehood, but more specifically the Catholic Church.

Duke, The. In Mark Twain's novel *Huckleberry Finn* (1885), a con man who joins Huck Finn* and Jim* on their raft, along with another who claims to be the long-lost Dauphin;* the two of them commit numerous frauds, the most noted being the Royal Nonesuch.*

Duke, Uncle. In the American newspaper cartoon *Doonesbury* (beg. 1970), a sometime journalist and full-time drug sampler, always wearing sunglasses and often carrying a pistol. With a long career of dubious professions, he somehow in his multiple manifestations manages to represent the many weird extremes of American social and political life in the 1970s and 1980s.

Dulcibella. A generic name used in much English poetry for a sweetheart or beautiful young girl. *Also called* Dowsabel.

Dulcinea. In Cervantes's novel *Don Quixote* (1605), the beautiful and ideal lady to whom Quixote* dedicates all his knightly exploits; she is actually only a peasant girl noted for her skill at salting pork.

Dumaine. In Shakespeare's play *Love's Labour's Lost* (1595), a witty courtier who falls in love with the equally witty Maria.*

Dumbiedikes. In Walter Scott's novel *The Heart of Midlothian* (1818), the father and **Laird** is a grasping landlord; his son, eventually the new **Laird**, is a shy and awkward suitor of Jeanie Deans.*

Duncan. In Shakespeare's play *Macbeth* (1605), the Scottish king who rewards Macbeth* and then is murdered by him and his wife. *See also* Donalbain; Malcolm.

Dundreary. In Tom Taylor's play *Our American Cousin* (1858), a dim-witted and lazy gentleman, noted for the long drooping whiskers worn by the actor who made the role famous in the United States.

Dunia. *See* Dounia.

Dunn. In G. B. Shaw's play *Heartbreak House* (1920), **Ellie** is a disillusioned young woman who plans to marry for money because only money will buy the beauty that could give her life meaning, a "modern" young woman without romance or ideals; her father **Mazzini** is poor but honest, the ineffectual good man. *See also* Mangan; Shotover, Capt.

Dunois. Historically, a French general (d. 1498) called the Bastard of Orleans for his attack with Jeanne d'Arc* driving the British out of the town. He appears in most works in which Joan also figures, most notably as the voice of pragmatism debating with Joan's voice of faith in G. B. Shaw's play *Saint Joan* (1923).

Dunstan. *See* Cass.

Dunstan St.. Historically, a Saxon churchman (d. 988) who reinvigorated the monastic system in England. Legend says that while he was working on some jewelry, he grabbed the Devil* by the nose with his pincers until the Devil promised not to tempt him further; hence, he is usually shown with pincers or tongs in his hand. His day is May 19.

Dunyasha. In Anton Chekhov's play *The Cherry Orchard* (1904), the simple maid who dresses beyond her station and pretends to be a lady in hopes of winning the attention of the sophisticated footman Yasha.*

Dupin. In Edgar Allan Poe's story *The Murders in the Rue Morgue* (1841), a French gentleman who solves an apparently insoluble mystery; generally credited as the first fictional detective.

Dupuis. In Gustave Flaubert's novel *Madame Bovary* (1857), a law clerk with whom Emma Bovary* has a particularly intense affair in hopes of finding some romantic excitement; he goes to Paris to study, never understanding what Emma really wants or needs, then returns and renews the affair which, this time, pushes her toward suicide.

D'Urberville. In Thomas Hardy's novel *Tess of the D'Urbervilles* (1891), a local noble family. **Alex** is a dissolute gentleman who relentlessly pursues Tess,* seduces her, and is ultimately murdered by her.

Durbeyfield. In Thomas Hardy's novel *Tess of the D'Urbervilles* (1891), **Jack** Durbeyfield is a lazy carter who devotes his life to leisure and drink when he realizes that his name indicates his descent from the noble D'Urbervilles.* **Joan**, his wife, is more practical and hardworking. For their daughter, *see* Tess.

Durham, Constantia. In George Eliot's novel *The Egoist* (1879), ''the racing cutter,'' a beautiful and wealthy young woman who is betrothed to Sir Willoughby Patterne* and who, when she realizes his true nature, immediately elopes with a soldier to escape the marriage.

Durward, Quentin. In Walter Scott's novel *Quentin Durward* (1823), a brave Scottish nobleman in France who joins the French army, rescues the countess Isabelle,* and saves the king's life as well. *See also* Maugrabin.

Dushyanta. In Kalidasa's *Sakuntala*, the Indian king who marries Sakuntala;* placed under a spell, he forgets her until they are reunited in heaven.

Dutchman, Flying. *See* Flying Dutchman.

Duval. In Alexandre Dumas *fils*'s novel (1848) and play (1852) *The Lady of the Camellias*, a young man who falls in love with Camille* but who is deserted by her for his own good after she meets with his father, a sensible, respectable man. *See also* Germont.

Dwarfs, Seven. *See* Seven Dwarfs.

E

E. T. In the movie *E. T.* (1982), a short, loveably ugly "extra-terrestrial" creature stranded on earth, rescued and protected by a suburban American boy until he can "phone home."

Earnest. In Oscar Wilde's play *The Importance of Being Earnest* (1895), the title pun on the name Ernest, which is the name given by Jack Worthing* to an imaginary scapegrace brother and the name he pretends to when in London because it is the only name that Gwendolen* could possibly love. *See also* Algernon.

Earnshaw. In Emily Brontë's novel *Wuthering Heights* (1847), the family which takes in the foundling Heathcliff.* **Hindley** is a jealous boy who cruelly mistreats the young Heathcliff and who dies an impoverished drunkard disgraced by Heathcliff's revenge. His son **Hareton** is raised almost as a wild animal, mistreated by Heathcliff, on whom he depends because of his father's weakness, as Heathcliff himself was mistreated, until he is civilized by the young Cathy. For Hindley's sister **Catherine**, *see* Cathy.

Earth Mother. A name often given to a primitive female goddess who appears in almost all mythologies throughout the world as the fundamental mother from whom humanity and often the earth itself are descended; in many usages, it also indicates some kind of fundamental spirit of femininity.

Earwicker. In James Joyce's novel *Finnegan's Wake* (1939), a tavern keeper whose dream state is chronicled in the work and who in the course of the dream takes on the characteristics of an Everyman* figure. *See also* Anna Livia Plurabelle.

Easter. In Christian usage, the day on which occurred the Resurrection* of Jesus,* celebrated on the first Sunday after the first full moon after the vernal equinox. Traditionally, this is one of the fundamental spring festivals, signified by a large number of baptisms and the traditional practice of wearing good, new clothes to the church services on that day.

Easy. In Captain Marryat's novel *Mr. Midshipman Easy* (1836), a young man raised to believe in Equality who finds himself in continual trouble due to his simplistic application of the theory to daily life. He joins the navy, mistakenly thinking it a place where all are equal. There he has numerous adventures, both humorous and dangerous, becomes a hero, and marries a beautiful Spanish maiden. He is one of the great boys' book heroes. *See also* Mesty.

Eatanswill. In Charles Dickens's novel *Pickwick Papers* (1836), the town in which Pickwick* observes a typical election.

Ebenezer. In the Bible, *I Samuel* vii, the name given to a stone commemorating a victory of the Israelites over the Philistines.*

Eccles. In Tom Robertson's play *Caste* (1867), a drunkard and ne'er-do-well as eager to avoid work as to cadge a drink or a smoke, for many years regarded as one of the great comic characters. His daughter **Esther** is a dancer who marries a nobleman, his other daughter **Polly** engages in teasing repartee with the tradesman Sam Gerridge,* whom she marries.

Ecclesiastes. In Christian usage, the "Preacher" whose proverbs compose the bulk of the Biblical book *Ecclesiastes*; most typical and noted of his sayings are perhaps "vanity of vanities, all is vanities," and "to everything there is a season."

Ecclesiazusae. In Aristophanes's play *Ecclesiazusae*, the women of Athens who disguise themselves as men in order to take over the assembly and give the rule of the city to women. *See also* Blepyrus; Praxagora.

Echidna. In Greek legend, a monster half woman, half snake variously given as mother of Cerberus,* of the Sphinx,* and/or of Chimera.*

Echo. In Greek legend, a daughter of Galatea;* when the handsome Narcissus* did not return her love, she pined away until she was changed into a stone that could reply but could not initiate speech.

Ector. (1) In Malory's *Morte d'Arthur*, the foster father who raises the young Arthur.* Also, a different Sir Ector is Lancelot's* brother and finds Lancelot's body. (2) *See also* Hector.

Eden. In the Bible, *Genesis* ii, the "garden" in which Adam* and Eve* were placed when God created them; when they ate the fruit of the Tree of Knowledge, He drove them out and placed a flaming sword at the entrance to keep them out. *See also* Cain; Paradise.

Edgar. (1) In Shakespeare's play *King Lear* (1605), the loyal legitimate son of Gloucester.* He is driven into hiding when his illegitimate brother Edmund* convinces his father that Edgar is plotting against him; disguised as a madman, he befriends Lear* during the storm and then cares for his blinded father, finally killing Edmund in battle. (2) In August Strindberg's play *The Dance of Death*

(1901), a contemptuous captain who lives in continual warfare with his wife Alice,* devoting even his last moments of life to destroying her chances at happiness.

Edison. Historically, an American inventor (d. 1931) of numerous items, such as the phonograph, the light bulb, and the movie camera and projector. In American folklore, he is the epitome of the self-made man who pulled himself up from adverse circumstances by his own initiative.

Edith. (1) In Charles Dickens's novel *Dombey and Son* (1846), a beautiful young woman raised to be an ornamental wife but intelligent enough to resent the situation; as a result, she becomes a cold, distant woman. When she marries Dombey,* the marriage is a cold, mercenary arrangement until, in revenge for many humiliations, she runs away with Dombey's clerk Carker.* (2) *See* Bunker.

Edmund. (1) In Shakespeare's play *King Lear* (1605), the handsome bastard son of Gloucester;* insatiably jealous and ambitious, he convinces his father that the legitimate, loving son Edgar* is plotting against him, ingratiates himself with both Goneril* and Regan* (Goneril poisons her sister to prevent her marrying Edmund), and orders Cordelia's* execution in simple maliciousness. (2) *See* Dantes, Edmund.

Edmund, St. Historically, an English king killed in 869 by the Danes. Legend says he was tied to a tree and shot full of arrows; hence, his symbol is the arrow; his day is November 20.

Edward. (1) Historically, the name of numerous kings of England. For **Edward I**, *see* Edward, St. Others of note include **Edward II**, depicted in Christopher Marlowe's play *Edward II* (1593) as a headstrong, histrionic, and dissipated monarch; **Edward V**, whose murder at the age of twelve is depicted in Shakespeare's play *Richard III* (1592), **Edward VIII**, who is sometimes seen as a figure of romance due to his abdication in 1936 to marry "the woman I love," an American divorcée. Most modern allusions are to the son of Victoria,* **Edward VII** (d. 1910), noted for his girth, his sexual affairs, his devotion to food and drink, and the relative peace and prosperity of his times, often called Edwardian. (2) In Goethe's novel *Elective Affinities* (1808), a wealthy noble who develops an uncontrolled passion for Ottilie,* whom he eventually joins in death by committing suicide. *See also* Charlotte.

Edward, St. Historically, king of England (d. 1066) whose death led to the confusion in which William* invaded England. Known for his devotion and said to be able to cure certain diseases by his touch, he is buried at Westminster Abbey. *Also called* Edward the Confessor.

Eeyore. In A. A. Milne's stories *Winnie-the-Pooh* (1926), the morose donkey who temporarily loses his tail.

Effie. *See* Deans.

Egmont. In Goethe's play *Egmont* (1788), a Flemish general who speaks out against the Spanish attempts to conquer Flanders and who is ultimately executed for treason.

Eilythyia. In Greek mythology, goddess of childbirth. *Also called* Lucina.*

Einar. In Henrik Ibsen's play *Brand* (1866), the painter who becomes a missionary when Agnes* leaves him for Brand.*

Einstein. Historically, a mathematician who developed the Theory of Relativity and the formula $E = mc^2$. In modern folklore, he is the epitome of the genius— his shaggy white hair, casual dress, and genial, distracted manner identify him as an absentminded professor who cannot be bothered with normal life because his mind is busy developing profound theories that no one else understands.

Eirene. *See* Irene.

Ekdal. In Henrik Ibsen's play *The Wild Duck* (1884), **Old Ekdal** is a former forger, now an eccentric old man who keeps a miniature forest in the attic where he "hunts" and where he keeps a wounded wild duck being nursed back to health. His son **Hjalmar** is a photographer, happily married and enchanted by his innocent daughter **Hedvig**. When Hjalmar's old friend Gregers* tells Hjalmar that **Gina**, now Mrs. Ekdal, was the mistress of Gregers's father and that Hedvig may be illegitimate, Hjalmar's happiness is destroyed. Hedvig, convinced that she must make a sacrifice to make her father love her again, shoots herself.

Elaine. (1) In Malory's *Morte d'Arthur*, "the fair maid of Astolat" who dies of unrequited love for Lancelot.* The most popular retelling is in Tennyson's poem *Elaine* (1859), in which Elaine's body floats downriver to Camelot. His poem *The Lady of Shalott*∗ tells much the same story without naming the lady. (2) In Malory's *Morte d'Arthur*, a different Elaine is the mistress of Lancelot* and mother of Galahad.*

Elam. (1) In the Bible, *Genesis* x, one of the sons of Shem.* (2) In the Bible, *Nehemiah*, one of the leaders who sealed the covenant and cleansed Jerusalem* after the return from exile in Babylon.

Elatus. In Homer's *Odyssey*, one of the suitors of Penelope.*

Eldorado. In folklore, a city of gold assumed to exist somewhere in the unexplored interior of the Americas; it was variously described as a place with buildings or streets of gold and a prince who had gold dust blown onto his body each day, making it an obsession of European explorers. As the explorers never found it, it gradually came to mean a paradisical land of wealth, peace, and happiness, as in Voltaire's story *Candide* (1759).

Eleazar. (1) In the Bible, *Exodus* vi, one of Aaron's* sons and a high priest. (2) In the Bible, *II Samuel* xxiii, one of the three mighty men of David.* (3) *See also* Eliezer.

Electra. (1) In Greek legend, daughter of Agamemnon* and Clytemnestra.* When Clytemnestra murdered Agamemnon, Electra and her brother Orestes* avenged their father. In Aeschylus's play *Choephoroe*, she is somewhat hesitant to accept the simple code of vengeance recommended by the other women. In Sophocles's play *Electra*, she initially believes that Orestes is dead and resolves to kill Clytemnestra herself despite the arguments of her sister Chrysothemis,* the duty passing to Orestes only at his last minute arrival. In Euripides's play *Electra*, she is married to a peasant; when Orestes returns to fulfill a prophecy, she must hound him into actually doing the deed. She appears in numerous additional works, sometimes vengeful, sometimes haunted with guilt, sometimes a powerful independent woman, sometimes a frustrated harridan—one of the most frequently depicted characters in Greek legend. She is often cited for the ''Electra complex,'' i.e., a daughter obsessively attached to her father while resenting her mother, a female counterpoint to the Oedipus* complex. (2) In Greek legend, one of the Pleiades.* After an affair with Zeus,* she gave birth to Dardanus,* founder of the Trojan* royal family. *Also called* Laodice.

Elf. In German folklore, one of various creatures with supernatural powers. In English usage, an elf is generally synonymous with a fairy*—light, pretty, playful, and harmless. In American usage, an elf is often merely a playful dwarf, as in the elves who are supposed to help Santa Claus* make all the toys he brings. *See also* Erl-King.

El Hakim. In Walter Scott's novel *The Talisman* (1825), the doctor, actually Saladin* in disguise, who heals Richard* the Lionhearted.

Eli. (1) In the Bible, *I Samuel* i–iv, a judge of Israel* for forty years; in his old age, he mistook Hannah's* prayers for drunkenness. Later, when the child Samuel* served him, he realized that God was calling Samuel; however, because he had overlooked the sins of his own sons, God destroyed them and allowed Israel to be defeated and the ark* lost to the Philistines,* after which Eli fell and broke his neck. (2) The nickname given to a student or graduate of Yale University, from Elihu Yale, whose donation in 1718 helped found the school.

Eliah. A name sometimes used for Elijah.*

Éliante. In Molière's play *The Misanthrope* (1666), the sincere woman whose admirable character counterbalances that of her cousin Célimène.*

Elias. A name sometimes used for Elijah.*

Eliezer. In the Bible, *Genesis* xv, a servant of Abraham,* generally presumed to be the one who found Rebecca* at the well. (2) In the Bible, *Exodus* xviii, second son of Moses.* (3) In the Bible, *II Chronicles* xx, a prophet who attacked Jehoshaphat.* *See also* Eleazar.

Eligius, St. *See* Eloi, St.

Elihu. In the Bible, *Job*, a friend who berated Job* at great length for striving against God.

Elijah. In the Bible, *I Kings*,a great prophet who heard the "still, small voice" of God. He preached against the wickedness of King Ahab* and his queen Jezebel,* contested faith with the priests of Baal,* and at least for a time rid the kingdom of all idols. Driven into the wilderness, he was fed by ravens; at his death, he was taken into Heaven* in a chariot of fire. *Also called* Eliah; Elias. *See also* Elisha.

Elinor. *See* Dashwood.

Elisabeth. (1) In the Bible, *Luke* i, the mother of John the Baptist;* she gave birth at an advanced age as a reward from God for her righteousness. While pregnant, she was moved by the Holy Spirit when visited by Mary.* (2) In Richard Wagner's opera *Tannhäuser* (1845), the beautiful noblewoman who loves and protects Tannhäuser after he proclaims the sinful joys of Venusberg.* She wastes away waiting for his return from his pilgrimage, but her pure love even after her death redeems him. (3) *See also* Elizabeth.

Elisabeth, St. Historically, a Hungarian princess (d. 1231) who renounced society after her husband's death, joined an order of nuns related to the Franciscans, and became famous for her care of the poor and ill. She is especially popular in German-speaking areas and is often signified by three crowns. Her day is November 17.

Elisha. In the Bible, *II Chronicles*, a great prophet, follower of and successor to Elijah.* When children mocked him, they were eaten by bears, and, among many miracles, he raised a boy from the dead. *See also* Gehazai.

Elissa. A name sometimes used for Dido.*

Eliza. (1) In Harriet Beecher Stowe's novel *Uncle Tom's Cabin* (1852), a Negro slave who runs away to the north to avoid having her child sold away to a different owner; her escape across the frozen Ohio River became one of the most famous moments of the nineteenth-century theater in numerous stage versions of the work. (2) *See* Doolittle; Gant. (3) *See also* Liza.

Elizabeth. (1) Historically, two queens of England. **Elizabeth I** (d. 1603), daughter of Henry VIII* and Anne Boleyn,* was an astute and dynamic queen, and the renaissance of life and literature during her reign gave the era the name Elizabethan. Often called the Virgin Queen for her refusal to marry, she is perhaps the most celebrated monarch in literature. She appears in numerous works as herself, noted for her red hair when young and her vanity when going bald as she aged; her ending of the religious persecutions imposed by Bloody Mary* and the reestablishment of Protestantism; her conflict with Mary, Queen of Scots* [the subject of Schiller's play *Maria Stuart* (1800) and Maxwell Anderson's play *Mary of Scotland* (1933)]; her possible romances with Essex* [the subject of Walter Scott's novel *Kenilworth* (1821) and Maxwell Anderson's play *Elizabeth the Queen* (1930)] and others; her relations with Drake and others of the privateers of her time; and the defeat of the Armada. She also figures metaphorically in numerous poems and plays of her day, as Gloriana* in Edmund Spenser's *The Faerie Queene* (1590), as Cynthia* in John Lyly's *Endymion* (1588), and as Oriana in other poems. Legend says she asked Shakespeare to write a play about Falstaff* in love, which became *The Merry Wives of Windsor* (1598); and in G. B. Shaw's play *The Dark Lady of the Sonnets* (1910), Shakespeare accidentally meets her, argues with her, and steals some of his best lines from her while waiting to meet his "dark lady." **Elizabeth II** began her reign in 1952 and, as she is a contemporary, most allusions to her are simply to "the Queen." (2) *See* Bennet; Elliot. (3) *See also* Bess; Beth; Bette; Elisabeth; Eliza; Lizaveta; Lizzie.

Elizabeth, St. (1) Historically, Elizabeth Seton, an American convert (d. 1821) who founded a religious community and was the first American to be canonized. (2) *See also* Elisabeth, St.

Ellen. (1) *See* Childe Waters; Dean, Ellen; Douglas; Sutpen. (2) *See also* Helen.

Ellie Mae. *See* Clampett; Lester.

Ellie May. *See* Ellie Mae.

Elliot. In Jane Austen's novel *Persuasion* (1818), **Anne** is an attractive young woman who misses numerous opportunities for happiness through her willingness to be persuaded by others; eventually, however, her true love Wentworth* returns with wealth and status and she manages to marry him at last. Her father **Walter** lives beyond his means and is inordinately proud of his family name. Her elder sister **Elizabeth** is a cold and selfish, though beautiful, woman who cannot make a suitable match. The youngest sister **Mary**, spoiled and selfish, marries the squire Musgrove.* **William** is their cousin, a charming but devious man; uninterested in marrying Elizabeth in order to keep the fortune entailed to him in the family, he marries a wealthy farmer's daughter, then, when left a widower, courts Anne and seduces Mrs. Clay* to prevent a marriage to Walter that might produce an heir and disinherit him.

Elmire. In Molière's play *Tartuffe* (1664), Orgon's beautiful, faithful wife. The subject of repeated seduction attempts by Tartuffe,* she finally convinces her husband of Tartuffe's hypocritical actions by hiding Orgon under the table on which Tartuffe tries to make love to her.

Elmo, St. In Christian legend, either a preacher to mariners in Galicia (d. 1240) or an Italian bishop martyred in the fourth century. The patron saint of mariners; the electrical discharge often seen at the top of ship masts is called St. Elmo's fire.

Elohim. In the Bible, one of the most common names for God. *See also* Jehovah; Yahweh.

Eloi, St. Historically, a French bishop (d. 660) also known as an engraver and founder of various missionary enterprises. The patron saint of metalworkers, his day is December 1. *Also called* St. Eligius.

Eloisa. *See* Héloïse.

Elsa. In Richard Wagner's opera *Lohengrin* (1850), a duke's daughter who promises to marry the mysterious unknown knight when he defends her against a charge of murdering her brother; upon their marriage night, however, she breaks her vow and asks him his name, whereupon he reveals himself as Lohengrin* but deserts her.

Elsinore. In Shakespeare's play *Hamlet* (1600), the castle in Denmark where Claudius* and Hamlet* reside and on the battlements of which Hamlet sees his father's ghost.

Elvira. (1) In Mozart's opera *Don Giovanni* (1787), a woman seduced and deserted by Don Giovanni;* she tries to warn others about him and to convince him to reform. *See also* Elvire. (2) In Noel Coward's play *Blithe Spirit* (1941), the jealous, childish, and beautiful ghost who returns to haunt her husband and his new wife and tries to kill him in order to reunite them. She is perhaps most noted for the grey makeup worn in the original production to indicate her ghostly nature.

Elvire. In Molière's play *Don Juan* (1665), Don Juan's* wife, whom he had originally abducted from a convent. Finally freed from her passion for him by his philandering, she decides to return to the convent. *See also* Elvira.

Elvsted, Mrs. In Henrik Ibsen's play *Hedda Gabler* (1890), a woman whose goal in life is to be some man's inspiration. Rejected by her husband, she saves and supports Lovborg* until he meets Hedda Gabler* and then remains as the potential rescuer of Tessman* after Hedda's death.

Elyot. In Noel Coward's play *Private Lives* (1930), an elegant and flippant divorcé who meets his ex-wife Amanda while they are both honeymooning with new spouses. He and Amanda return to Paris together and decide to remarry, realizing that their quarrels are part of their love. Their long stage fight is one of the most famous twentieth-century comic scenes.

Elysium. In Greek mythology, the home of the blessed in the afterlife, sometimes placed in Hades* and sometimes placed in the far west. *See also* Paradise.

Em, Auntie. In Frank Baum's novel *The Wonderful Wizard of Oz* (1900), the aunt with whom Dorothy* lives in Kansas; she is better known from the movie version (1939).

Emelye. *See* Emilia.

Émile. In Jean-Jacques Rousseau's novel *Émile* (1762), the orphan whose education is used to illustrate the ideal education needed to produce the natural man. *See also* Sophie.

Emilia. (1) In Chaucer's *Canterbury Tales*, in the Knight's Tale, the sister of Hippolyta;* her love is fought for in a tournament by the two brave knights Palamon* and Arcite. The story is also used in Fletcher and Shakespeare's play *The Two Noble Kinsmen* (1613). (2) In Shakespeare's play *Othello* (1604), the wife of Iago* and maid of Desdemona;* through love for her husband, she gives him Desdemona's handkerchief, then in the "willow song" scene discusses the political and social value of selective adultery. She finally exposes Iago's plot, for which she is murdered by her husband. (3) In George Etherege's play *The Man of Mode* (1676), the beautiful young woman who marries Bellair.* (4) *See* Galotti, Emilia. (5) *See also* Emily.

Emily. (1) In Thornton Wilder's play *Our Town* (1938), a representative young girl who falls in love, marries, dies in childbirth, and learns the importance of daily life when, as a spirit, she tries to revisit her past. *See also* Gibbs; Webb. (2) In William Faulkner's story *A Rose for Emily* (1930), an old woman who is discovered to have slept with the decaying body of her lover for many years. (3) *See* Em'ly, Little. (4) *See also* Emilia.

Em'ly, Little. In Charles Dickens's novel *David Copperfield* (1849), the gentle, beautiful, but unpredictable niece of Daniel Peggotty* with whom the young David Copperfield* falls in love; he grows out of this infatuation, and she runs off with Steerforth* on the eve of her wedding to a cousin. After Steerforth deserts her, she emigrates to Australia. *See also* Littimer.

Emma. (1) In Jane Austen's novel *Emma* (1816), an intelligent, proud, spirited, and rather self-centered, but still essentially kind, young woman with an urge to arrange other people's lives; in particular, she insists on arranging overreaching matches for the girl Harriet Smith* which threaten to destroy the girl's life. Emma refuses the vicar's proposal as beneath her, but she ultimately realizes that her own proper match is Knightley,* the only man in the neighborhood to recognize her faults and speak truthfully to her. *See also* Churchill, Frank; Woodhouse. (2) *See* Bovary.

Emmanuel. *See* Immanuel.

Emmaus. In the Bible, *Luke* xxiv, a town near Jerusalem;* it was on the road to Emmaus that the resurrected Jesus* first appeared to two of His disciples and at Emmaus that He broke bread with them.

Empedocles. Historically, a Greek philosopher and disciple of Pythagoras.* Legend says he jumped into the crater of Mt. Etna in order to so completely disappear that people would think he had been made a god, but the volcano threw out his sandal, thus proving his mortality.

Enarete. In Greek legend, wife of Aeolus.*

Enceladus. In Virgil's *Aeneid*, a giant buried under Mt. Etna; when he turns over, he causes earthquakes.

Encolpius. In Petronius's *Satyricon*, the roguish traveller and narrator. *See also* Ephesus, Widow of; Eumolpus; Trimalchio.

Endor. *See* Witch of Endor.

Endymion. (1) In Greek legend, a mortal son of Zeus.* Artemis* saw him naked while he slept and made love to him while he dreamed, which was so pleasant he asked Zeus for perpetual sleep and dreams, in which she continued to visit him. The most famous retelling is in John Keats's poem *Endymion* (1818), which is summarized by the line, "A thing of beauty is a joy forever." (2) In John Lyly's play *Endymion* (1587), a courtier who deserts his lover for Cynthia,* the moon goddess and metaphorically Queen Elizabeth,* and is put under a spell by the witch Dipsas* until awakened by a kiss from Cynthia. *See also* Eumenides.

Engidu. In the Babylonian epic *Gilgamesh*, the great friend whose death sends Gilgamesh* on a long search for him in the land of the dead.

English, Julian. In John O'Hara's novel *Appointment in Samarra* (1934), an American car salesman who seems to have wealth and happiness but who is so alcoholic, confused, and depressed by his unsatisfying marriage and friends that he commits suicide.

Engstrand. In Henrik Ibsen's play *Ghosts* (1881), **Jacob** is a drunken carpenter who pretends to be the father of **Regina**, a servant of Mrs. Alving.* When Osvald falls in love with her, Mrs. Alving tells him that Regina is really Osvald's illegitimate sister.

Enid. In Tennyson's poem *Enid* (1859), Geraint's* faithful wife, who faces with nobility and innocence his many tests of her honesty.

Enobarbus. In Shakespeare's play *Antony and Cleopatra* (1606), the bluff veteran soldier and friend of Antony.* He eventually deserts when he realizes that the Antony who loves Cleopatra* is no longer the Antony he admired, but he then dies of grief. He also gives the famous description of Cleopatra's barge.

Enoch. (1) In the Bible, *Genesis* iv, eldest son of Cain,* born after Cain was driven out by God, and father of Methuselah;* he lived 365 years until "God took him." (2) *See* Arden, Enoch.

Enos. In the Bible, *Genesis* v, a son of Seth.*

Eos. A name sometimes used for Aurora.*

Epanchin. In Dostoevsky's novel *The Idiot* (1868), a general of worldly disposition. The women of the family play an important role in the story of Prince Myshkin:* For the mother, *see* Prokofievna, Lizaveta; for the daughter, *see* Aglaya.

Ephesus, Widow of. In Petronius's *Satyricon*, a widow keeping watch in her husband's tomb who is persuaded by a passing soldier first to eat and then to make love.

Ephraim. In the Bible, *Genesis* xlvii, the second son of Joseph,* brother of Manasseh;* he was blessed by Jacob* as the firstborn because his seed would be a multitude of nations. Although technically Joseph was the father of the twelfth tribe of Israel,* it was usually referred to by the name of Ephraim, or sometimes as Ephraim and Manasseh.

Ephron. In the Bible, *Genesis* xxiii, a Hittite who sold Abraham* a field in which to bury Sarah* and in which Abraham also was later buried.

Epicaste. A name sometimes used for Jocasta.*

Epicene, In Ben Jonson's play *Epicene* (1609), a woman whom Morose* marries because he believes her to be silent; after the marriage, she proves to be anything but, and he pays his nephew to get rid of her, whereupon she is revealed to be a boy.

Epihodov. In Anton Chekhov's play *The Cherry Orchard* (1904), the sad, accident-prone clerk.

Epimenides. In Greek legend, a shepherd who slept for 57 years; after awakening, he was a poet, sometimes listed as one of the Sages.*

Epimetheus. In Greek legend, brother of Prometheus* and husband of Pandora.*

Epirus. *See* Oracle.

Epistemon. In Rabelais's *Pantagruel* (1532), a friend of Pantagruel* noted for his learning and for a trip he makes to the underworld when his head is cut off in battle with the Dipsodes.* *See also* Panurge.

Epona. In Roman mythology, goddess of horses and cattle.

Eppie. In George Eliot's novel *Silas Marner* (1861), the sweet and loving blonde child whom the miserly misanthrope Silas Marner* adopts and whom he comes to regard as his new treasure. To several generations of American schoolchildren, she has been a symbol of boring sentimentality and of drudgery, due to the work's appearance in numerous textbooks for children too immature to read it with interest.

Erasmus, St. A name sometimes used for St. Elmo.*

Erastus. In the Bible, *Acts* xix, a missionary sent to Macedonia by Paul.*

Erato. In Greek mythology, the Muse* of lyric poetry and love poetry, usually symbolized by the lyre.

Erda. In Richard Wagner's operas *The Ring of the Niebelung* (1869–76), the goddess of fate who prophesies the fall of the gods if Wotan* persists in his attempt to keep the ring. She is also the mother of Brünnhilde.*

Erebus. (1) In Greek mythology, god of darkness and father of the day. (2) In Greek mythology, sometimes the same as Hades,* sometimes a place through which the dead must pass on their way to Hades.

Eriboea. (1) A name sometimes used for Aphrodite.* (2) In Greek legend, mother of Ajax.* (3) In Greek legend, mother of Penelope.*

Erigone. (1) In Greek legend, an illegitimate daughter of Clytemnestra;* later the mistress of Orestes,* she brought him to trial for the murder of her mother and hanged herself when he was acquitted. (2) In Ovid's *Metamorphoses*, a woman who hanged herself when her father died and who was changed to the constellation Virgo.*

Erinyes. A name sometimes used for the Furies.*

Eris. In Greek mythology, goddess of strife and discord, daughter of Zeus* and twin sister of Ares.* Her most noted act was to roll the golden apple* engraved "for the fairest" among Aphrodite,* Athena,* and Hera,* which led to the Judgement of Paris* and ultimately to the Trojan War.* *Also called* Discordia.* *See also* Strife.

Erisichthon. In Ovid's *Metamorphoses*, a man who cut trees in Demeter's* sacred grove; as punishment, she gave him such an insatiable appetite that he ate his own body.

Erl-King. In German folklore, king of the elves; in Goethe's poem (1782) and Schubert's song (1821) *Erl-König*, he steals the life of a child in the forest at night.

Erminia. In Tasso's *Jerusalem Delivered* (1580), the heroine who fell in love with Tancred* after he restored her wealth and who nursed him when he was wounded.

Ernest. *See* Earnest; Pontifex.

Eros. (1) In Greek mythology, god of love; although generally equivalent to Cupid,* he is usually portrayed as a somewhat older youth and is associated with a broader range of love than simple romantic attraction. Many British personifications are based on the statue in Piccadilly Circus. (2) In Shakespeare's play *Antony and Cleopatra* (1606), Antony's* servant who kills himself rather than help his master commit suicide.

Erotium. In Plautus's play *Menaechmi*, a slow-witted courtesan. *See also* Menaechmi.

Erycina. A name sometimes used for Venus.*

Erymanthian Boar. In Greek legend, a savage boar that Heracles* killed as one of his labors.

Esau. In the Bible, *Genesis*, the son of Isaac* and Rebecca,* twin brother of Jacob.* The brothers' struggles together began in the womb and continued into maturity. Esau was a hunter, and one day when he came in hungry from the hunt, he traded his rights as firstborn to Jacob for Jacob's pottage of lentils; later, as Isaac was going blind, Jacob, prompted by his mother, disguised himself as the "hairy" Esau and received his blessing, for which Esau threatened to kill Jacob, driving him out to the land of Laban.*

Escamillo. In Bizet's opera *Carmen* (1875), the egotistical toreador who sings the famous Toreador Song and for whom Carmen* deserts Don José.* *See also* Lucas.

Esculapius. *See* Aesculapius.

Esméralda. In Victor Hugo's novel *The Hunchback of Notre Dame* (1831), a gypsy dancer obsessively desired by the priest Frollo,* in whom she has no interest due to her infatuation with the handsome soldier Phoebus.* She gives water to the hunchback Quasimodo* when he is in the stocks, for which he falls in love with her and, when she is to be executed for murder, he rescues her. Mistakenly leaving the sanctuary, she is captured and hanged, and her bones are later found held in an embrace by the bones of a hunchback.

Esmond. In William Makepeace Thackeray's novel *Henry Esmond* (1852), **Henry** is a sensitive and intelligent young man who, through love for his beautiful cousin **Beatrix**, becomes involved in the plot to place James the Stuart Pretender on the British throne. When he realizes that Beatrix is James's mistress, he marries her mother **Rachel**, a quieter and more loyal woman, and they emigrate to America.

Essenes. Historically, a Jewish sect in the time of Jesus* devoted to simplicity and purity, dressing in white and living communally.

Essex. Historically, one of several English earls. The most noted was Robert Devereaux (d. 1601), a favorite courtier and rumored lover of Queen Elizabeth.* After his failure in the Irish wars, he planned a coup to oust Elizabeth's advisers and perhaps her as well, but he failed and was executed. He appears in numerous works, most notably in Walter Scott's novel *Kenilworth* (1821) and Maxwell Anderson's play *Elizabeth the Queen* (1930).

Estella. In Charles Dickens's novel *Great Expectations* (1860), the beautiful but cold-hearted ward raised by Miss Havisham* to break men's hearts. Pip* loves her from childhood, but she can love no one. She marries Drummle,* who mistreats her, and only after his death gains maturity and marries Pip.*

Esther. (1) In the Bible, *Esther*, the Jewish woman taken as queen by the Persian king Ahasuerus;* she used her influence to prevent a plot to have all the Jews massacred. *Also called* Hadassah. *See also* Mordecai; Vashti. (2) *See* Summerson, Esther; Gobseck. (3) *See also* Hester.

Estragon. In Samuel Beckett's play *Waiting for Godot* (1952), one of the two tramps waiting eternally for Godot.* *See also* Vladimir.

Eteocles. In Greek legend, a son of Oedipus* and Jocasta* and brother of Antigone* and Polynices.* When Oedipus was exiled from Thebes, Eteocles and Polynices agreed to share the throne, ruling in alternate years. Eteocles refused to fulfill his part of the bargain, however, and Polynices attacked the city; both brothers were killed in combat. Creon's* decision to bury Eteocles and not Polynices led to Antigone's revolt and her eventual death. *See also* Seven Against Thebes.

Ethan. (1) In the Bible, *I Kings* iv, a wise man with whom Solomon* was compared favorably. (2) *See* Frome.

Ethel. *See* Mertz.

Étienne. In Émile Zola's novel *Germinal* (1883), the unemployed machinist who becomes a miner and organizes a strike. The strike is broken, and he almost drowns when the mine is flooded by Souvarine;* he then leaves to continue socialist organizing. In Zola's multi-novel Rougon-Macquart* family, he is the illegitimate son of Gervaise.*

Ettarre. In Tennyson's poem *Pelleas and Ettarre* (1869), a cold-hearted woman who rejects the love of the innocent knight Pelleas* but allows herself to be seduced by Gawain.*

Euclio. In Plautus's play *Aulularia*, a miser.

Eudora. In Greek legend, one of the Nereids.*

Eudorus. In Homer's *Iliad*, a friend of Achilles* and commander of the Myrmidons.*

Eugene. *See* Gant.

Eugénie. (1) Historically, wife (d. 1920) of the French emperor Napoleon* III, noted for her devotion to fashion and pleasure and her incompetence in political affairs. (2) *See* Grandet.

Eula. *See* Varner.

Eulalia, St.. In Christian legend, a child martyr burned to death for throwing down the idols of the Romans, particularly popular in Spain; her day is December 10.

Eulenspiegel. *See* Till Eulenspiegel.

Eumaeus. In Homer's *Odyssey*, the faithful shepherd who first recognizes Odysseus* on his return home and who then helps him slay Penelope's* suitors.

Eumenides. (1) A name sometimes used for the Furies.* In Aeschylus's play *Eumenides*, they side with the spirit of Clytemnestra,* torment Orestes,* and demand that Athena* punish him. (2) In John Lyly's play *Endymion* (1588), the faithful friend of Endymion.*

Eumolpus. In Petronius's *Satyricon*, a poet who travels with Encolpius* and who also tells the story of the Widow of Ephesus.*

Eunice. In the Bible, *II Timothy* i, mother of Timothy,* noted for her faith.

Eunomia. In Greek mythology, goddess of order; also sometimes listed as one of the Horae.*

Euphelia. In Matthew Prior's poem *Euphelia and Chloe* (1709), a beautiful woman who "serves to grace my measure." *See also* Chloe.

Euphemia, St. In Christian legend, a maiden martyred after much torture—in some stories devoured by wild beasts, in others beheaded after the beasts refused to kill her.

Euphrosyne. In Greek mythology, goddess of joy.

Euphues. In John Lyly's novel *Euphues* (1578), a young Athenian in adventures defining love and friendship. The name is known less for the character than the style, called euphuistic, a complex but mellifluous prose heavily dependent on antithesis and allusion.

Europa. In Greek legend, sister of Cadmus;* to seduce her, Zeus* changed himself into a bull and carried her away on his back to Crete, where she gave him three sons and eventually married the Cretan king.

Euryalus. (1) In Greek legend, one of the Argonauts* who joined with Diomedes* in the Trojan War.* (2) In Virgil's *Aeneid*, a Trojan who came with Aeneas* to Italy, noted for his great friendship with Nisus,* who died trying to rescue him in battle.

Euryclia. In Homer's *Odyssey*, the aged nurse of Odysseus;* she recognizes him from his scar.

Eurydice. (1) In Greek legend, the beloved wife of Orpheus.* When she died, he followed her to Hades* and was allowed to bring her back, provided that he did not look back at her on the return trip. Unable to restrain himself, he did look at her, and she was returned to Hades immediately. (2) In Greek legend, wife of Creon.*

Eurylochus. In Homer's *Odyssey*, a companion of Odysseus;* he refuses to taste Circe's* potion and thus is not turned into a pig, but later steals the Cattle of the Sun.*

Eurymachus. In Homer's *Odyssey*, one of Penelope's* suitors who pretends to reasonableness to mask his devious cunning. *See also* Antinous; Odysseus; Telemachus.

Eurynome. In Homer's *Odyssey*, Penelope's* housekeeper.

Eurypylus. In Homer's *Iliad*, a Trojan* warrior and lover of Cassandra.* In Dante's *Divine Comedy*, he is placed in Hell* among the astrologers.

Eurystheus. In Greek legend, the king of Tiryns who assigned the twelve labors to Heracles.* In Euripides's play *Heracleidae*, he is a proud and murderous king who tries to kill Heracles's children but is defeated by the Athenians, who have given them refuge. *See also* Hyllas.

Eustace, St. In Christian legend, a Roman general who converted when he saw a cross between a stag's antlers and who was roasted to death when he refused to sacrifice to the Roman gods. The patron saint of huntsmen, his day is September 20. *See also* Hubert, St.

Euterpe. In Greek legend, the Muse* of music, usually symbolized by the flute.

Eutycus. In the Bible, *Acts* xx, a young man who fell into such a deep sleep while Paul* was preaching that he was taken for dead until he was revived by Paul.

Eva. (1) Latin form of Eve.* (2) In Harriet Beecher Stowe's novel *Uncle Tom's Cabin* (1852), a daughter of the plantation owner St. Clare,* often called Little Eva. She is pure but frail, and she dies young, her ascension into heaven becoming one of the most admired and then parodied scenes in the numerous stage adaptations of the book.

Evadne. (1) In Greek legend, wife of Capaneus;* when he was killed, she threw herself on his funeral pyre and perished with him. She is a personification of fidelity in Virgil's *Aeneid*, where Aeneas* sees her among the virtuous on his trip through the underworld. (2) In Beaumont and Fletcher's play *The Maid's Tragedy* (1619), the king's mistress who is ordered to marry Amintor* but never consummates the marriage; her brother forces her to murder the king, after which she kills herself.

Evander. In Virgil's *Aeneas*, a king in Italy who befriends Aeneid.*

Evangeline. In Henry Wadsworth Longfellow's poem *Evangeline* (1847), an Acadian maiden separated from her fiancé Gabriel* when they are driven out of Nova Scotia. She searches for him through Louisiana and the American prairie, eventually becoming a nurse and accidentally finding him on his deathbed.

Evangelist. In John Bunyan's *Pilgrim's Progress* (1678), Christian's* guide and trustworthy adviser.

Evans. In Shakespeare's play *The Merry Wives of Windsor* (1598), a Welsh parson with a thick accent and pedantic manner. Tricked into a duel with Dr. Caius,* he talks his way out of it and later aids in the attack of the fairies on Falstaff.*

Eve. (1) In the Bible, *Genesis*, the first woman; made from Adam's* rib, she was Adam's wife and mother of Cain* and Abel.* The serpent* tempted her to eat the fruit of the Tree of Knowledge, and she in turn tempted Adam; as a result, they realized they were naked and covered themselves with fig leaves. When God discovered they had disobeyed Him, He drove them out of the Garden of Eden,* condemning Adam to a life of labor and Eve to the pain of childbirth. In much Christian folklore and literature, she is depicted as the personification of sexual sin, particularly temptation and lust, although not necessarily lustful herself, as well as a proof of the weakness of all women. In John Milton's poem *Paradise Lost* (1667), she is initially gentle and beautiful, but she is tempted when she is left unprotected in order to demonstrate Adam's trust in her, becoming lustful and quarrelsome after the Fall. *Also called* Eva. *See also* Seth. (2) In the movie *All About Eve* (1950), a scheming young actress who hypocritically masks her ambition behind a gentle, servile, and naive exterior. *See also* Channing, Margo.

Everdene, Bathsheba. In Thomas Hardy's novel *Far From the Madding Crowd* (1874), a beautiful and vain young woman, a practical and successful farm owner who is attracted to shallow, flashy men like Sergeant Troy,* whom she marries, bringing unhappiness to herself and tragedy to the sensible Boldwood,* who kills Troy. *See also* Oak, Gabriel.

Everyman. In the anonymous play *Everyman*, a representative man who is called by death and is deserted by all his earthly friends, but is supported by God.

Ewing. In the American television series ''Dallas'' (beg. 1978), a fabulously wealthy Texas family followed through a number of outrageous soap-opera vicissitudes. The most notable members include **J. R.**, the eldest son, a flamboyantly caricatured Texas oilman who revels in power, greed, lust, and the double-cross; **Miss Ellie**, his sweet and long-suffering mother; **Sue Ellen**, his long-suffering wife whose primary expression of displeasure with her husband is to have yet another affair; and **Bobby**, his brother, continually in conflict over

J. R.'s lack of scruples but later more famous for coming back from the dead after two years' absence in what, even by "Dallas's" standards, was a flamboyantly absurd premise. The episode revealing "who shot J. R.?" in 1980 was watched by more Americans than any other television program in history and was treated throughout much of the world as a significant news event.

Excalibur. In Malory's *Morte d'Arthur*, the sword of King Arthur.* At his death, the sword was thrown into the lake, from which a hand rose to catch it and carry it away. There is some disagreement as to its source; Malory says it was given to Arthur by the Lady of the Lake* but also identifies it as the sword that Arthur pulled from the stone in order to prove he should be king.

Exodus. In the Bible, *Exodus*, the escape from Egypt by the Jews under the leadership of Moses.*

Eyre, Jane. In Charlotte Brontë's novel *Jane Eyre* (1847), an orphan girl, mistreated in her aunt Mrs. Reed's* home and in Brocklehurst's* puritanical school, who becomes a governess for the child of Rochester.* She falls in love with him but discovers that he is already married, though the wife is a lunatic, and she leaves the house, only to return to care for and to marry him after a fire blinds him and kills his wife. *See also* Rivers.

Eyre, Simon. Historically, a lord mayor (d. 1459) of London; he is the genial shoemaker in Thomas Dekker's play *The Shoemaker's Holiday* (1599).

Ezekias. A name sometimes used for Hezekiah.*

Ezekiel. In the Bible, *Ezekiel*, a great prophet and priest of the Jews during the Babylonian captivity. He foretold the fall of Jerusalem,* as well as the fall of Tyre and Assyria, and then in a vision described the temple to be rebuilt in Jerusalem. Other noted visions included the cherubim* and the wheels, the sword of the Lord killing the wicked, and the plain of dry bones into which God breathed life.

Ezra. In the Bible, *Ezra*, the priest sent back to Jerusalem* to restore law and order after the Jews returned from the Babylonian captivity. *See also* Nehemiah.

Ezra, Rabbi ben. In Robert Browning's poem *Rabbi ben Ezra* (1864), a learned Jew who describes life as a pot shaped by the master's hand.

F

FDR. *See* Roosevelt.

Fabian. (1) In Shakespeare's play *Twelfth Night* (1599), a servant who aids Sir Toby Belch's* trick against Malvolio.* (2) *See* Fabius.

Fabius. Historically, a Roman general (d. 203 B.C.) famous for the campaign of delay and avoidance that he fought against Hannibal;* hence, any policy or group that avoids direct conflict or immediate action is called Fabian.

Fabrice. *See* Fabrizio.

Fabricius. Historically, a Roman consul (third century B.C.) known for his strict integrity; legend noted his refusal of all gifts.

Fabrizio. In Stendhal's novel *The Charterhouse of Parma* (1839), a romantic, noble Italian youth who idealistically joins Napoleon* and later progresses in ecclesiastical politics. Gentle in private, he becomes enmeshed in a passionate and complex love affair with the beautiful Clelia* and becomes involved in political intrigue and murder before he retires to a monastery. *See also* Mosca; Sanseverina.

Face. In Ben Jonson's play *The Alchemist* (1610), the servant who lets the house to the alchemist Subtle* while his master is gone and who then aids the alchemist in various plots. *See also* Common, Dol; Lovewit.

Factotum, Johannes. In sixteenth-century European usage, a man who claims to do everything; its first English literary appearance is in fact an insulting description of Shakespeare.

Fafner. In Richard Wagner's opera *Siegfried* (1876), Fafnir.*

Fafnir. In the *Volsung Saga* and the *Niebelungenlied*, the dragon who guards the gold of the Niebelung* and is killed by Siegfried.*

Fag. In R. B. Sheridan's play *The Rivals* (1775), Absolute's servant. The use of the name for any junior student acting as a servant for older boys at English public schools may derive from the name, or the name from the usage, as they appeared at the same time, but it seems to have no direct relation to the American use of the term for homosexual males.

Fagin. In Charles Dickens's novel *Oliver Twist* (1837), a sinister, greedy Jew who trains small boys to be criminals, lives from their takings, and fences stolen goods for other criminals. An uneasy partner of Bill Sikes,* he kidnaps Oliver Twist* and is eventually captured and executed. *See also* Artful Dodger.

Fainall. In William Congreve's play *The Way of the World* (1700), the charming but unscrupulous lover of Mrs. Marwood;* he tries to destroy his own wife's reputation in order to gain control of her fortune. Mrs. Fainall is a former mistress of Mirabell* and is still in love with him.

Fairfax, Gwendolen. *See* Gwendolen.

Fairfax, Jane. In Jane Austen's novel *Emma* (1816), a beautiful and mysterious visitor in the neighborhood who is secretly engaged to Frank Churchill.* *See also* Bates, Miss.

Fairy. In European folklore, a small supernatural being, usually able to fly. In early usage, fairies were sometimes malevolent, but by the early nineteenth century they had come to be seen as cute, playful, and completely harmless creatures who lived a life almost unconnected with humans. In modern American lore, they are the bringers of wealth, such as the tooth fairy or Cinderella's* fairy godmother. Among the more significant types are brownie,* elf,* fata,* genie,* gnome,* goblin,* leprechaun,* nymph,* ondine,* peri,* pixie,* sylph,* troll,* and wili.* Among the more significant literary individuals are Ariel,* Mab,* Oberon,* Puck,* Robin Goodfellow,* Sylphide,* Tinker Bell,* and Titania.* In Shakespeare's play *The Merry Wives of Windsor* (1598), Falstaff* is humiliated in an attack by townspeople disguised as fairies, and fairies are principal characters in his play *A Midsummer Night's Dream* (1595). Fairyland appears regularly in numerous works as a place of sweetness and light and perpetual happiness.

Faithful. In John Bunyan's *Pilgrim's Progress* (1678), a brave Christian pilgrim arrested and burned at Vanity Fair.*

Fakir. In traditional Hindu society, an ascetic religious beggar. Westerners associate him particularly with lying on a bed of nails, walking on coals, or performing the Indian Rope Trick, with the result that, in British and American usage, it sometimes means a magician or more specifically a fraudulent magician.

Fall, The. In Christian usage, Adam* and Eve's* fall from God's grace and protection and their eviction from the Garden of Eden.*

Falstaff. In Shakespeare's plays *Henry IV (Parts I & II)*, *Henry V*, and *The Merry Wives of Windsor* (1597–99), a fat, witty, self-indulgent, lustful, and drunken old knight, the epitome of the happy roisterer. A character of considerable complexity, he is intelligent, inventive, and charming as well as a definitive liar, a coward, and a bad influence on character. Whenever he is beaten or ridiculed, he always bounces back with a quick story to suggest he planned things that way. For some, he is a fat, funny, but worthless old fool; for many others, the very spirit of life itself. Prince Hal's* friend, he is beaten by Hal in a robbery on Gad's Hill, the story of which he embellishes into a great battle, then he cynically collects sickly soldiers to be "food for cannon" in the war, makes the famous meditation on the transitory value of honor, pretends to have killed Hotspur,* meditates on youth and the passing of time with Justice Shallow,* and is eventually publicly rejected by the reformed Henry at his coronation. In *Henry V*, his death is reported movingly. In *The Merry Wives of Windsor*, he courts two women, writing identical letters to each, is forced to hide from Mistress Ford's* husband in a basket of laundry that is dumped in the river, and then is assaulted at Herne's Oak by the townspeople disguised as fairies.* *See also* Bardolph; Page; Pistol; Poins; Quickly, Mistress.

Fama. In Roman mythology, goddess of fame. *See also* Pheme.

Fancyfull, Lady. In John Vanbrugh's play *The Provok'd Wife* (1697), a jealous woman of fashion who vainly (and in vain) believes all the men are in love with her.

Fang. In Charles Dickens's novel *Oliver Twist* (1837), a judge who answers for the defendants rather than waste time waiting for their responses.

Fanny. (1) In Henry Fielding's novel *Joseph Andrews* (1742), the virtuous maiden who escapes numerous attempts on her chastity until she is eventually united with her true love Joseph Andrews.* (2) In Alphonse Daudet's novel *Sapho* (1884), a shrewd, feminine, and successful courtesan. (3) In Marcel Pagnol's plays *Marius* (1929), *Fanny* (1931), and *César* (1936), a Marseilles girl who loves the sailor Marius* and has his bastard child but marries the kind, dependable Panisse.* (4) *See* Dashwood; Dorrit; Hill, Fanny; Price, Fanny; Squeers.

Fantine. In Victor Hugo's novel *Les Misérables* (1862), a beautiful woman with an illegitimate child Cosette.* Eventually forced into prostitution and arrested by the policeman Javert,* she dies of tuberculosis and leaves her child to the care of Jean Valjean.*

Farange. In Henry James's novel *What Maisie Knew* (1897), **Maisie** is a young girl forced into peculiar prescience by the pressures of coping with the divorce and shared custody of her parents. Her father **Beale** is a vain and somewhat mercenary minor diplomat, and her mother **Ida** is a charming but tempestuous woman of dubious morality. Maisie sees her governess become the "second

Mrs. Beale,'' to be deserted in her turn, and even for a time lives with the governess and her new lover before opting to live with an ugly and conventional later governess.

Fashion. In John Vanbrugh's play *The Relapse* (1696), **Sir Novelty** is a town fop engaged to the country heiress Miss Hoyden.* His brother, **Young Fashion**, deeply in debt, disguises himself and marries the girl in secret. *See also* Clumsey, Sir Tunbelly.

Fat Boy, The. In Charles Dickens's novel *Pickwick Papers* (1836), Joe, a fat servant boy of Mr. Wardle,* noted for his ability to fall asleep without warning and under any circumstances.

Fata. An Italian term for a fairy;* most noted is Fata Morgana, usually called in English usage Morgan le Fay.*

Fates. In Greek mythology, three goddesses who presided over the lives of individual persons; they were independent even of Zeus* and were usually depicted spinning thread. Clotho held the distaff, Lachesis spun the thread of life, and Atropos cut the thread. *Also called* Moirae; Parcae. *See also* Destiny; Norns.

Father Brown. *See* Brown, Father.

Fatima. (1) Historically, Mohammed's* youngest daughter (d. 632), from whom a dynasty of Egyptian rulers was descended. (2) In folklore, the last wife of Bluebeard.* (3) Historically, a Portuguese town where the Virgin Mary* appeared six times in 1917, much celebrated in modern legend.

Fat Man, The. *See* Gutman, Caspar.

Fatted Calf. *See* Prodigal.

Faulkland. In R. B. Sheridan's play *The Rivals* (1775), Jack Absolute's friend who almost destroys a happy engagement by jealousy and worry about the state of the relationship.

Fauna. In Roman mythology, wife of Faunus* and goddess of fertility.

Fauntleroy, Little Lord. In F. E. H. Burnet's novel *Little Lord Fauntleroy* (1886), a sweet child who inherits an English earldom and reconciles his English grandfather to his American mother; known for his long girlish curls, a cloying unathletic manner, and a suit with velvet breeches and a lacy collar that was much imitated by American mothers and much detested by American boys.

Faunus. In Roman mythology, god of agriculture and fertility, generally equivalent to Pan.* *See also* Fauna; Lupercus.

Faust. Historically, a German conjurer (d. 1540); legend says he made a pact with the Devil.* In literature, he became a symbol of man in search of knowledge, especially in Christopher Marlowe's play *Dr. Faustus** (1592) and in Goethe's poem/play *Faust* (1808–32). In the latter, Faust is the subject of a wager between God and Mephistopheles,* who offers Faust anything he might desire and who will collect Faust's soul if Faust finds anything given to him so beautiful that he asks for it to stay. Faust eventually is shown Gretchen,* whom he seduces and whose brother he murders, and he despairs after she commits suicide. Helen* is brought back to be his mistress, then is taken away, as is their son; Faust at last determines that the only real duty is to help mankind, reclaiming an island which is so fair he asks for it to stay, at which moment he dies, and, although Mephistopheles tries to take him to Hell,* he is carried away by angels.* In Gounod's opera *Faust* (1859), he is carried to Hell as Marguerite's soul flies into Heaven.* *See also* Leverkühn; Melmoth.

Faustus. In Christopher Marlowe's play *Doctor Faustus* (1592), a scientist who turns to magic in order to become "emperor of the world" and sells his soul to Mephistopheles* in return for absolute freedom for 24 years. He calls up Helen,* the "face that launched a thousand ships," and embarks on a sometimes ludicrous and sometimes cruel series of tricks and adventures, eventually facing complete damnation. *See also* Faust; Leverkühn; Melmoth.

Fawkes, Guy. Historically, an English Catholic (d. 1606) who attempted to blow up Parliament; his capture is still celebrated as an annual holiday in England, usually with a great bonfire on which his effigy is burned.

Fawley, Jude. *See* Jude.

Fawlty, Basil. In the British television series "Fawlty Towers" (beg. 1977), an officious, self-important, toadying hotel owner who always manages to make the worst of any crisis.

Fay, Morgan le. *See* Morgan le Fay.

Februus. In Roman mythology, god of purification, to whom the second month was dedicated.

Félicité. In Gustave Flaubert's story *A Simple Heart* (1877), a simple country servant who devotes her life to people who do not return her love; eventually she is left alone with her piety and her stuffed parrot, which she confuses with the Holy Spirit.

Felicity. *See* Félicité.

Felicity, St. Historically, a Christian martyr (d. 203), a slave girl who gave birth in prison and was killed in the arena with St. Perpetua.* Their day is March 7.

Felix. (1) In the Bible, *Acts* xxiii, the Roman governor of Judea when Paul* was arrested and persecuted. (2) In numerous movie cartoons (beg. 1917), a solidly black, upright cat with enormous eyes, noted for the anthropomorphic loneliness and angst of his existence, ever ignored, ever spurned. (3) In Neil

Simon's play *The Odd Couple* (1965), a fanatically neat man. *See also* Oscar. (4) *See* Holt, Felix.

Fenian. In Irish legend, a body of warriors raised by Finn* to drive out invaders; Ossian* refers to them in numerous poems, and the name was revived in the nineteenth century by an Irish and Irish-American organization that attempted to invade Canada in 1866 and staged several abortive rebellions in Ireland against the British. Although the group faded in the early twentieth century, replaced by the Sinn Fein, it remained the subject of much adulatory song and story, and members of the latter group were often still called Fenians.

Fenwick, Grand. In several novels by Leonard Wibberley, beginning with *The Mouse That Roared* (1955), the tiniest country in the world, a place of simplicity and innocence; through a series of accidents, it obtains a doomsday bomb, thereby bringing peace to the world.

Ferdinand. (1) In Shakespeare's play *Love's Labour's Lost* (1595), the idealistic king who swears off all interest in women, only to be immediately enamored of the princess of France. *See also* Berowne. (2) In Shakespeare's play *The Tempest* (1611), a handsome young man shipwrecked on Prospero's* island who falls in love with Miranda.* (3) In John Webster's play *The Duchess of Malfi* (1613), the duke who is obsessed with his sister, a haunted, arrogant man; when she secretly remarries, he drives her insane and has her murdered by Bosola,* then kills the assassin as he is himself killed. *See also* Malfi, Duchess of. (4) In Munro Leaf's story *Ferdinand the Bull* (1936), a gentle bull who is mistaken for a mighty fighter when stung by a bee and is sent to the bullring, where he disgraces all bulls with his gentleness but lives to return to his fields. (5) *See* Isabella.

Fergus. In Irish legend, a minstrel in the time of Finn;* in W. B. Yeats's play *Deirdre* (1907), he is a nobleman and Conchubar's* trusted friend.

Feronia. In Roman mythology, goddess of orchards; in Virgil's *Aeneid*, she is also goddess of childbirth.

Ferrara, Andrew. Historically, a maker of swords so widely admired that the name was often given to any fine seventeenth-century sword.

Ferrars. In Jane Austen's novel *Sense and Sensibility* (1811), **Mrs. Ferrars** is a domineering and temperamental old woman who uses her great wealth to control her children. Her daughter **Fanny** marries John Dashwood* and the selfishness she has learned from her mother makes her turn him against his half-sisters. Her son **Edward** is a weak and gentle soul who has been trapped into an engagement by the mercenary Lucy Steele,* but she deserts him for his foppish brother **Robert** when Mrs. Ferrars disinherits Edward on learning of the engagement. This actually frees Edward for the life he desires, which is to marry Elinor Dashwood and to be a minister.

Ferumbras. *See* Fierabras.

Feste. In Shakespeare's play *Twelfth Night* (1599), the witty clown; he also torments Malvolio* and sings: "hey, ho, the wind and the rain." *See also* Belch, Sir Toby.

Festus. In the Bible, *Acts* xxv, the Roman governor who succeeded Felix* and continued Paul's* trial; he thought Paul mad but would have released him, had Paul not previously requested that he be tried in Rome.

Feverel. In George Meredith's novel *The Ordeal of Richard Feverel* (1859), **Sir Austin** hates women and devises a system for educating his son without any contact with women. His son **Richard** demonstrates the failure of the system by eloping with almost the first girl he meets and then facing seduction and deceit in London and on the continent, his spirit breaking when his first love Lucy Desborough* dies.

Fezziwig. In Charles Dickens's story *A Christmas Carol* (1843), the genial man whose happy party is shown in Scrooge's* "Christmas Past."

Fidelia. In William Wycherley's play *The Plain Dealer* (1677), the faithful woman who follows Manly* to sea dressed as a man and is sent in disguise to woo another woman for him.

Fidelio. In Beethoven's opera *Fidelio* (1805), the name adopted by Leonora* when disguised as a man.

Fides. In Roman mythology, goddess of oaths.

Fidget. In William Wycherley's play *The Country Wife* (1673), a jealous and stupid husband who insists his wife spend time with Horner,* whom he believes is impotent; **Mrs. Fidget** pretends to public propriety while engaging in private bawdy, in particular the famous "china scene."

Fierabras. In medieval European legend, a great giant and sultan of Babylon, defeated and baptized by Oliver.* *Also called* Ferumbras.

Fifi. In de Maupassant's story *Mademoiselle Fifi* (1882), a nickname given to an effeminate Prussian officer who is later killed by a woman for insulting the French flag. As this usage suggests, the name was already a generic term for a French girl and is thus used in unnumerable plays, stories, and dirty jokes for a cute and worldly Frenchwoman.

Figaro. In Beaumarchais's plays *The Barber of Seville* (1775) and *The Marriage of Figaro* (1777), a witty and resourceful servant. In the earlier play, he arranges for his master Almaviva's* marriage, and in the later helps prevent Almaviva's seduction of Figaro's own bride Susanna.* Better known outside France are the operatic versions: Rossini's *The Barber of Seville* (1816) and Mozart's *The Marriage of Figaro* (1786).

Filomena, St. In Christian legend, a martyr whose remains were found in 1802; she was often associated in the nineteenth century with healing. In 1961 the Church determined that the remains were not authentic and removed her name from the Calendar of Saints.

Fina, St. In Christian legend, a paralyzed ten-year-old girl who insisted on resting on a board so that she might share Christ's pain; while ill, she was attacked by rats and, after her death, violets were found covering the board.

Fingal. *See* Finn.

Fink, Mike. In American folklore, a Mississippi boatman with awesome physical appetites and powers.

Finn. In Irish legend, a great hero, leader of the Fenians,* noted for his wisdom and honesty as well as his valor. In the poems of Ossian* (1760), he is called Fingal and is a righter of wrongs who comes from Scotland to help the Irish king drive out the Scandinavian invaders. *See also* Conan; Grainne; Oisin.

Finn, Huck. In Mark Twain's novels *Tom Sawyer* (1876) and *Huckleberry Finn* (1884), a spirited, independent boy who fascinates all the respectable boys because he smokes a pipe and his father does not make him go to school. A friend of Tom Sawyer,* he shares the treasure Tom discovers and as a result is made a ward of Miss Watson* and the Widow Douglas.* The brutality of his father, who tries to kidnap him, and the constraints of small-town respectability weigh heavily on him in the later book, and he runs away, rafting down the Mississippi with Jim,* the runaway slave, on an odyssey that has become one of the fundamental journeys in American culture. Along the way he attempts to disguise himself as a girl; observes the Grangerford*/Shepherdson* feud and a murder by Col. Sherburn,* who subsequently faces down a lynch mob; discovers his father's body in the midst of a storm; and becomes involved in a long escapade with the charlatan Dauphin* and Duke.* Finally, he participates with Tom in an absurdly complex attempt to rescue Jim after the latter has been recaptured. When given the chance to return to his home town, he chooses to "light out for the Territory" rather than be "sivilized" and is usually seen as the personification of the spirit of youth, instinctive goodness, and freedom, as well as a rejection of the hypocrisy of small-town, religious, respectable America.

Finn, Phineas. In several novels by Anthony Trollope, beginning with *Phineas Finn* (1869), a young politician whose experiences in Parliament provide a cross-section of mid-Victorian politics.

Finnegan. (1) In an Irish folksong, a man with whiskers on his "chinnegan;" the song ends "Finnegan, begin again," and is often cited in circular arguments. (2) In James Joyce's novel *Finnegan's Wake* (1939), an Irish hod-carrier killed in a fall; at his wake, he begins to rise at the word whiskey, but he is talked back into the coffin by the men at his wake. *See also* Earwicker.

Fionnuala. In Thomas Moore's song in *Irish Melodies* (1807–35), a beautiful woman changed into a swan that wanders over the waters of Ireland.

Firebird. In the ballet *The Firebird* (1910), a magical bird who gives a feather to a young man and comes to his aid when he is endangered by a wicked magician; the work is often alluded to as one of the principal milestones in modern art due to its startling score by Stravinsky.

Fish. In much Christian symbolism, the fish is used to symbolize Jesus* because of the similarity of the Greek word for fish, Ichthus, to the Greek initials of Jesus Christ, Son of God, Saviour, and to symbolize mankind since so many of the original Apostles* were fishermen, made by Jesus into "fishers of men." To Catholics, Friday is "fish day" because, until 1966, they were expected to abstain from meat on Fridays but could eat fish instead. *See also* Loaves and Fishes.

Fitz-Clare. *See* Clare, Lady.

Flagg. In Anderson and Stallings's play *What Price Glory?* (1924), a U.S. Marine captain who has maintained a perpetual friendship and feud with Quirt;* it is one of the most vivid buddy tandems in literature. *See also* Charmaine.

Flaherty, Pegeen. *See* Pegeen.

Flamborough. In Oliver Goldsmith's novel *The Vicar of Wakefield* (1766), the neighbor who talks incessantly. *See also* Primrose.

Flamineo. In John Webster's play *The White Devil* (1612), an unscrupulous opportunist and brother of Vittoria.* He panders for his sister, murders her husband as a favor to the duke Brachiano,* and kills his own brother; he jests ironically even at his own death.

Flanders, Moll. In Daniel Defoe's novel *Moll Flanders* (1722), an adventuress whose life is a series of amorous and amoral ups and downs; she is variously a prostitute, pickpocket, reputable wife, mother, beggar, and colonial planter.

Flashman. In Thomas Hughes's novel *Tom Brown's School Days* (1857), a school bully, who is eventually expelled for drunkenness. He was later revived in a series of novels by George Macdonald Fraser, beginning with *Flashman* (1969), as a cowardly, lustful scoundrel whose cupidity is invariably interpreted as bravery and patriotism.

Flavius. In Shakespeare's play *Timon of Athens* (1607), Timon's* faithful steward who follows Timon into exile.

Fleance. In Shakespeare's play *Macbeth* (1605), Banquo's* son who escapes from the murderers and whom prophecy says will found a line of kings after Macbeth's* death.

Fleece. (1) *See* Golden Fleece. (2) In Herman Melville's novel *Moby-Dick* (1851), the cook who preaches to the sharks on the nature of greed.

Fleming, Henry. In Stephen Crane's novel *The Red Badge of Courage* (1895), a "Youth" dreaming of heroism who runs away from his first battle, then wanders the rear where he sees his friend Jim Conklin* die and is accidentally hit on the head. Next day, he lives up to the red badge of his wound by distinguishing himself in battle.

Flibbertigibbet. (1) In English folklore, a name given to a fiend that tries to harm humans; one such appears in a vision to Lear* on the heath. Simultaneously and apparently not directly related, it has come to mean a flighty and/or talkative woman. (2) *See* Sludge, Dickie.

Flic. In French slang, a policeman.

Flintwitch. In Charles Dickens's novel *Little Dorrit* (1855), the cold butler whose knowledge of family secrets makes him Mrs. Clennam's* business partner. His wife **Affery** is the cook, a gentle soul who defers to those who are smarter and who is easily convinced by her husband that she is merely dreaming when she overhears evil plans.

Flite, Miss. In Charles Dickens's novel *Bleak House* (1852), a frail old woman whose life has been destroyed by the delays in her chancery lawsuit; nevertheless, she maintains her bright manner and friendly nature, aiding Richard Carstone* and Esther Summerson* when she can. She is noted for the birds she keeps which will be released when the case is settled and which are, instead, released when she dies. *See also* Krook.

Flood, The. In the Bible, *Genesis* vi–ix, God became so upset by mankind's sinfulness that he covered the earth with water, sending rain for 40 days and 40 nights, drowning everyone but Noah,* his family, and the animals he had saved on the Ark.* When the rain stopped, Noah sent out birds to look for land; the Ark came to rest on Mt. Ararat, and God promised never to destroy the earth by water. Similar stories appear in the legends and religious works of almost all ancient peoples. *See also* Deucalion; Utnapishtim.

Flopsy, Mopsy, and Cottontail. In Beatrix Potter's story *The Tale of Peter Rabbit* (1900), the obedient siblings of Peter Rabbit.*

Flora. (1) In Roman mythology, the goddess of flowers, generally equivalent to Chloris,* although sometimes also associated with love. (2) In Charles Dickens's novel *Little Dorrit* (1885), the former fiancée of Arthur Clennam,* noted for her embarrassing reversion to childish flirtatiousness when he returns despite her middle age and his clear lack of response.

Floradora Girls. Historically, six chorus girls in the American musical comedy *Floradora* (1900); five of the six married admiring millionaires during the first year of the show's run, thereby setting the stereotype of the chorus girl that permeated twentieth-century literature and folklore.

Florence. *See* Dombey.

Florestan. In Beethoven's opera *Fidelio* (1805), a Spanish nobleman imprisoned for political reasons and threatened with death until his wife Leonora,* disguised as a boy, secures his release.

Florian, St. In Christian legend, a Roman soldier martyred by being drowned; he is said to have once extinguished a burning city with a single bucket of water and is thus invoked for protection against fire.

Fluellen. In Shakespeare's play *Henry V* (1598), a brave but pedantic and hot-tempered knight; his pride, temper, and long-winded use of language made him a stereotype of the Welsh among the English.

Flute. In Shakespeare's play *A Midsummer Night's Dream* (1595), the bellows mender who plays Thisbe in the "Pyramus and Thisbe"* play in spite of his having "a beard coming." *See also* Quince, Peter.

Flutter, Fopling. In George Etherege's play *The Man of Mode* (1676), the epitome of the stupid fop whose attempts at fashion serve only to demonstrate the shallowness of the man behind the clothes.

Flying Dutchman. In European legend, a ship that is condemned to haunt the earth without ever landing in penance for a crime on board. In Richard Wagner's opera *The Flying Dutchman* (1843), the captain is cursed to roam the seas until he finds a woman who will be faithful; when Senta* shows her faithfulness by drowning herself, he is freed from his curse, the ship sinks, and the two of them ascend to Heaven.*

Fogg. *See* Dodson and Fogg.

Fogg, Phileas. In Jules Verne's novel *Around the World in Eighty Days* (1873), a methodical, emotionless Englishman who wagers that he can go around the world in only 80 days and does so despite numerous adventurous obstacles, accompanied by his servant Passepartout.*

Foigard. In George Farquhar's play *The Beaux' Stratagem* (1707), a man disguised as a priest whose "French shows him to be English, and his English shows him to be French."

Fons. In Roman mythology, the god of springs.

Fonz, The. In the American television series "Happy Days" (beg. 1974), a supposedly teenaged boy who prided himself on his motorcycle, his perfectly greased and combed ducktail haircut, his skill with women, and his "cool;" a sanitized 1970s version of the 1950s "greaser."

Fool. The most noted literary Fool is the jester in Shakespeare's play *King Lear* (1605). His jests are noted for their pointed common sense, for he is the only person who dares tell Lear* the truth; he is also one of the few who remain completely loyal to Lear, going with him out into the storm. One of the favorite conjectures of students is why he disappears without comment halfway through the play. Other noted fools include Dagonet,* Feste,* Rigoletto,* and Yorick.* *See also* Bergamo; Gotham.

Fopling. *See* Flutter, Fopling.

Foppington, Lord. Another name for Novelty Fashion.*

Forbush, Nellie. In James Michener's stories *Tales of the South Pacific* (1947), an American nurse who falls in love with a French South Seas planter but is much disturbed by his previous miscegenous affairs; best known from Rodgers and Hammerstein's musical play *South Pacific* (1949), in which she is "as corny as Kansas in August" and will "wash that man right outta my hair."

Ford. In Shakespeare's play *The Merry Wives of Windsor* (1598), a jealous husband who disguises himself and then hires Falstaff* to try to seduce his wife in order to test her; his attempts to catch them together soon make him a laughingstock. **Mistress Ford** is a practical middle-class woman who with her friend Mistress Page* determines to teach both Falstaff and her husband a lesson; she hides Falstaff in a laundry basket that is carried out beneath Ford's nose and is dumped into the river.

Ford, Henry. Historically, an American manufacturer (d. 1947) who established an automobile factory; its success was due to a cheap, simple car that was made for years without any design changes, the Model T or Tin Lizzie, in "any color you want as long as it's black." In American folklore, he became a hero of the common man, a symbol of the self-made man and of the auto industry itself; to many Europeans, he became an equally potent symbol of American assembly-line culture and anything-for-money attitudes.

Foresight. In William Congreve's play *Love for Love* (1695), the guardian of Angelica,* noted for his devotion to astronomy and astrology.

Forsyte. In several novels by John Galsworthy, beginning with *The Man of Property* (1906), an upper-middle-class Edwardian family whose growth and vicissitudes illustrate English social attitudes of the times. Most notable members are **Soames**, head of the family, a cold and aggressive businessman, and his wife **Irene**, a sensitive and artistic beauty whose happiness is destroyed by the acquisitive nature of her husband and of the society in which she lives.

Fortinbras. In Shakespeare's play *Hamlet* (1600), a neighboring prince who invades as Hamlet* finally kills Claudius* and who becomes the king of Denmark by default, being the only royalty left alive at the play's conclusion. For many, he was a standing theatrical joke, as he was the character always cut from performances to shorten the play.

Fortuna. In Roman mythology, the goddess of destiny or chance, usually symbolized by a wheel, generally equivalent to Tyche.*

Fortunato. In Edgar Allan Poe's story *The Cask of Amontillado* (1846), the man walled up alive.

Fortunatus. (1) In the Bible, *I Corinthians* xvi, a Christian who comforted Paul.* (2) In the fairy tale, a man with a bottomless purse.

Forty Days and Forty Nights. *See* Flood, The.

Forty Days in the Wilderness. *See* Temptation, The.

Forty Thieves. *See* Ali Baba.

Four Just Men. In Edgar Wallace's novel *The Four Just Men* (1906), a group of mysterious, wealthy men who devote themselves to bringing to justice those influential or wealthy criminals whom the law allows to go unpunished. In the course of the novel, however, they assassinate a generally admirable British cabinet minister to prevent the passage of a law they believe will be unjust, in many ways prefiguring the modern terrorist use of violence and media manipulation to influence politics in other nations.

Fox. *See* Rabbit, Br'er; Reynard; Volpone.

Foyle, Kitty. In Christopher Morley's novel *Kitty Foyle* (1939), a Philadelphia working girl who falls in love with a wealthy young man but who is left to make her own way when he can not overcome his aversion to her lower class origins.

Frail, Mrs. In William Congreve's play *Love for Love* (1695), a mercenary and jealous widow tricked into marrying the foolish Tattle* during her attempt to spoil Valentine's* marriage.

Francesca da Rimini. In Dante's *Divine Comedy*, the hunchback Malatesta's* wife who falls in love with her handsome brother-in-law Paolo;* she is usually seen as a symbol of romantic love rather than of adultery, and her story has been expanded in such works as G. H. Boker's play (1855) and Gabriele D'Annunzio's play (1902) of the same name.

Francis, St. (1) Historically, Francis of Assisi, a wealthy young man (d. 1226) who renounced his possessions when he heard a statue of Jesus* speak to him and who then founded an order of traveling preachers noted for their humility, poverty, and simplicity of life. By his example and his preaching, he became one of the most famous and admired of all the saints. Two years before his death, he received the stigmata of the crucifixion.* Legend credits him with numerous miracles illustrating his gentleness and sincerity, the most beautiful of which is perhaps his sermon to the birds. He is usually depicted in the brown robe of his order, with the stigmata, and is often accompanied by animals, especially birds. His day is October 4. (2) Historically, Francis Xavier, a missionary (d. 1552) among the Malay, Japanese, and Chinese; patron saint of missionaries, his day is December 30. (3) Historically, Francis de Sales, a French bishop (d. 1622), a missionary among Calvinists and a model of sensitivity and moderation; author of numerous devotional tracts, he is the patron saint of journalists and writers, and his day is January 24.

Francisco, St. St. Francis.*

Françoise. (1) In Émile Zola's novel *The Earth* (1887), a sensitive peasant girl who leaves her land to the brother-in-law who rapes and kills her rather than to her husband who is not "in the family;" she first appears, in a famous "shocking" passage, aiding a stallion to mount a mare. (2) In Marcel Proust's novels *Remembrance of Things Past* (1913–27), a faithful family servant who actually dictates the daily life of the family. *See also* Marcel.

Frank, Anne. Historically, a Jewish girl who hid in an attic with her family for two years to escape the Nazis until finally captured; she died in a concentration camp (c. 1945). Her diaries were widely read when published in 1947, and she became a symbol both of the sensitive young girl entering her teens and of all Jewish victims of Germany's extermination program.

Frankenstein. In Mary Shelley's novel *Frankenstein* (1817), a scientist who assembles a living creature from the body and organs of the dead; since the creature had no name, it also came to be called Frankenstein, even before the highly successful series of movies using the character. Dr. Frankenstein became a symbol for the scientist as overreacher, and the creature became the quintessential horrific monster and a misunderstood natural creature destroyed by the shallowness and bigotry of so-called civilization.

Frankie. (1) In an American folksong, a woman who shoots her unfaithful lover Johnny* because "he done her wrong." (2) In Carson McCullers's novel *The Member of the Wedding* (1946), a lonely twelve-year-old girl who tries to go on her brother's honeymoon; a much admired portrayal of preteen confusions about life and love. *See also* Brown, Berenice.

Franklin. In Chaucer's *Canterbury Tales*, the wealthy pilgrim who tells the story of Dorigen.*

Franklin, Ben. Historically, an American patriot, writer, and diplomat (d. 1790), author of the Poor Richard* maxims and inventor of the cast-iron stove and bifocal spectacles. He is much noted as an exemplar of commonsensical self-improvement, as described in his *Autobiography*; as a spokesman for American independence, signing the Declaration of Independence; and as something of a rake while serving as ambassador to France. His most remembered act, however, was flying a kite in an electrical storm to determine whether lightning and electricity are related, for which he is credited in folklore as the discoverer of electricity.

Franks. Historically, a tribe in France, but the name was used by Byzantine/ Greeks and Arabs for all Western Europeans.

Franny. In J. D. Salinger's story *Franny and Zooey* (1961), a young woman with an undefined and apparently inexplicable malaise. *See also* Zooey.

Frea. *See* Freya.

Fred and Ethel. *See* Mertz.

Frederic. In Gilbert and Sullivan's operetta *The Pirates of Penzance* (1879), the "slave of duty," a young man mistakenly apprenticed by a nurse who misheard "pilot" as "pirate." *See also* Mabel; Pirate King; Ruth; Stanley, Major General.

Frederick, Duke. In Shakespeare's play *As You Like It* (1599), a usurper and villain who exiles his niece Rosalind;* suddenly converted by a holy man, he becomes a hermit and restores his brother to the throne. *See also* Celia; Oliver; Orlando; Senior, Duke.

Freischütz. In German folklore, a marksman given seven magic bullets by the Devil,* the first six of which would hit anything aimed at, but the seventh of which did only as directed by the Devil. Allusions are usually to Weber's opera on the subject, *Der Freischütz* (1821), in which the Devil uses the last bullet to kill another man who had sold the Devil his soul.

Frey. In Norse mythology, the god of peace and fertility. *See also* Gerda.

Freya. In Norse mythology, the sister of Frey* and the goddess of love and of the night; she was married to Odhir, but he generally ignored her. She is sometimes identified with Frigga.*

Freyr. A name sometimes used for Frey.*

Friar. In Chaucer's *Canterbury Tales*, the genial and venal priest who tells the story of the Summoner* who loses his soul.

Friar Laurence. *See* Laurence, Friar.

Friar Tuck. *See* Tuck, Friar.

Fribble. In David Garrick's play *Miss in Her Teens* (1747), an effeminate man, noted for his exaggerated sensitivity to pain and his devotion to paper dolls of female fashions, which he designs.

Fricks. A name sometimes used for Frigga.*

Friday. In Daniel Defoe's novel *Robinson Crusoe* (1719), a native rescued from cannibals by Crusoe;* Friday becomes Crusoe's faithful servant and friend, the source of the term "man Friday." Recently, in some circles he has become a symbol of colonialist oppression.

Friday, Joe. In the American radio and television series "Dragnet" (1949–70), a phlegmatic police sergeant identified by his deadpan expression and the catch-phrase, "just the facts, ma'am."

Frietchie, Barbara. In John Greenleaf Whittier's poem *Barbara Frietchie* (1864), a 90-year-old woman who bravely brandishes the Union flag in the face of invading Confederate troops, shouting the much-quoted "Shoot if you must this old grey head/ But spare your country's flag."

Frigga. In Norse mythology, the wife of Odin* and the goddess of family life and married love.

Fritz. In American and English usage, a stereotyped name for a German.

Frodo. In J. R. R. Tolkien's novels *The Lord of the Rings* (1954–55), a hobbit who went on a great quest to destroy a ring that could make the wearer all-powerful, lest it fall into the hands of an evil lord; in the 1960s in the United States, "Frodo Lives" was one of the principal signals of the youth movement associated with the period. *See also* Baggins, Bilbo; Gandalph.

Frollo. In Victor Hugo's novel *The Hunchback of Notre Dame* (1831), the archdeacon of Notre Dame; he becomes obsessed with the gypsy Esméralda* and tries to murder the soldier she loves. When she refuses to become his mistress, he allows her to be hanged for the crime; Quasimodo* throws him off the bell tower after he laughs during the hanging.

Frome. In Edith Wharton's novel *Ethan Frome* (1911), **Zeena** is a sickly, loveless, and nagging wife. **Ethan** is a poor farmer trained for a better life who falls in love with Mattie,* his wife's cousin, and the two of them try to commit suicide together by running their sled against a tree; the attempt fails and they are both condemned to a life as invalids treated by the bitter Zeena.

Frontin. In numerous French plays, a generic name for a scheming valet, most notably in Le Sage's play *Turcaret* (1709).

Frosine. In Molière's play *The Miser* (1668), the matchmaker.

Ftatateeta. In G. B. Shaw's play *Caesar and Cleopatra* (1901), Cleopatra's nurse, a domineering bully.

Fulgora. In Roman mythology, the goddess of lightning and thunderstorms.

Fu Manchu. In numerous novels by Sax Rohmer, beginning with *The Mystery of Dr. Fu Manchu* (1913), a brilliant Chinese mandarin* with drooping mustache and long nails who masterminds international criminal plots, the epitome of the "yellow peril." *See also* Smith, Nayland.

Fungoso. In Ben Jonson's play *Every Man Out of His Humour* (1598), the unlucky imitator of Fastidious Brisk.*

Furies. In Greek legend, three spirits of vengeance, usually depicted as winged women. *Also called* Erinyes; Eumenides.* *See also* Alecto.

Furina. In Roman mythology, a goddess whose early function is not clearly understood, but who is later associated with robbers.

G

Gabler, Hedda. In Henrik Ibsen's play *Hedda Gabler* (1890), the bored, self-centered, romantic bride of Tessman;* she plays with other people's dreams and eventually encourages the poet Lovborg* to commit suicide in order to make a beautiful gesture. When Judge Brack* tries to blackmail her for her part in this, she also commits suicide.

Gabriel. (1) In the Bible, *Daniel* ix and *Luke* i, an archangel* who visited Daniel* and who announced to Mary* that she would bear the Son of God. In John Milton's poem *Paradise Lost* (1667), he is the chief archangel in Heaven* and the leader of God's forces in the war against Satan.* In general Christian tradition, it is thought that his trumpet blast will announce the Second Coming;* hence, he is often depicted with a trumpet. He is also often shown with a lily to indicate his participation in the Annunciation.* (2) In Longfellow's poem *Evangeline* (1847), the young man loved by and separated from Evangeline,* reunited with her only when she finds him on his deathbed in a charity hospital. (3) *See* Oak, Gabriel.

Gabrina. In Ariosto's *Orlando Furioso* (1516), a woman who demanded that Philander,* the man who had killed her husband, marry her; when she tired of him as well, she poisoned him, was imprisoned, escaped, and was rescued by a knight who grew to detest her so much that he hanged her.

Gad. (1) In the Bible, *Genesis* xxx, seventh son of Jacob* and founder of one of the twelve tribes of Israel.* (2) In the Bible, *I Chronicles* xxi, the seer who reported to David* God's wrath over the numbering of the tribes, which led to the great pestilence.

Gadarene Swine. In the Bible, *Mark* v, a herd of swine into whom Christ* sent the devils* he cast out of the man possessed; when the devils entered them, the swine rushed off a cliff and drowned in the sea.

Gadshill. In Shakespeare's play *Henry IV, Part I* (1597), both a rowdy tavern friend of Prince Hal* and the site of the famous robbery in which Falstaff* robs a traveler and is robbed in turn by Hal in disguise.

Gaea. *See* Gaia.

Gaev. In Anton Chekhov's play *The Cherry Orchard* (1904), the family name of the owners of the estate and cherry orchard which will be sold. **Leonid** is the brother, a talkative, impractical dreamer who distracts himself with billiards. For others in the family, *see* Anya; Ranevskaya; Varya.

Gaffer. *See* Hexam.

Gaheris. In Malory's *Morte d'Arthur*, a brother of Gawain* who aided Mordred's* machinations and was killed by Lancelot.*

Gaia. In Greek mythology, the most ancient Earth goddess; she gave birth to Uranus* and then with her son produced the Titans.* She is sometimes the same as Terra* (or Rhea) and is sometimes her mother. *Also called* Ge. *See also* Rumor.

Galahad. In Malory's *Morte d'Arthur*, the son of Lancelot* and the purest of the knights at Arthur's* court; after an arduous quest, he does see the Holy Grail.* *See also* Elaine.

Galapas. In Malory's *Morte d'Arthur*, a Roman giant whom Arthur* killed after cutting off his legs to bring him down to size.

Galatea. (1) In Greek legend, a nymph* in love with Acis* but loved in turn by Polyphemus;* when she rejected the latter, he killed Acis. (2) In Ovid's *Metamorphoses*, a statue sculpted by Pygmalion* to represent the perfect woman; she was so perfect that Pygmalion asked Venus* to give the statue life, and Galatea became a woman and his wife.

Galilee. In the Bible, the district in which Jesus* concentrated most of His teaching; He walked on the water in the Sea of Galilee, which is fed by the river Jordan,* and on its shores found several of His Apostles.*

Galotti, Emilia. In Lessing's play *Emilia Galotti* (1771), a soldier's beautiful daughter who is abducted by a lustful prince but is stabbed by her father to prevent her violation.

Gamaliel. In the Bible, *Acts* v, a Pharisee* who convinced the others to let the disciples go free, since a false prophet would be exposed sooner or later and a genuine one could not be fought against.

Game Chicken, The. In Charles Dickens's novel *Dombey and Son* (1846), the parasitic boxer who accompanies Toots.*

Gamp, Sairy. In Charles Dickens's novel *Martin Chuzzlewit* (1843), a fat, drunken, high-spirited Cockney midwife, always accompanied by the smell of liquor and by her umbrella, who tells outrageous lies and attributes them to her imaginary friend Mrs. Harris. *See also* Prig, Betsey.

Gandalph. In J. R. R. Tolkien's novels *The Lord of the Rings* (1954–55), the tall, good magician who sends Frodo* on his quest and who aids him whenever possible.

Ganelon. In the anonymous *Song of Roland*, the traitorous stepfather of Roland;* he betrays Roland to the Saracens and tries to persuade Charlemagne* against coming to Roland's aid; when his treason is discovered, he is drawn and quartered.

Ganesha. In Hindu mythology, the god of wisdom, represented by the head of an elephant.

Gant. In Thomas Wolfe's novel *Look Homeward, Angel* (1929), **Eugene** is the prototypical American writer in youth: shy, awkward, sensitive, and misunderstood. His father **Oliver** is a generous alcoholic stonecutter as devoted to the angel he carves as he is at odds with his wife Eliza, who runs a boarding house where he is not allowed to live. **Eliza** is a gaunt, repressed, repressing, and miserly woman, obsessed by real estate. **Ben**, Eugene's adored brother, dies of pneumonia due to Eliza's refusal to pay for a doctor, but in dreams is Eugene's confidant.

Ganymeda. In Greek legend, the goddess of youth and a wife of Heracles;* she was cupbearer of the gods until one day she fell and exposed herself. *Also called* Hebe. *See also* Ganymede.

Ganymede. (1) In Greek legend, the most beautiful Trojan boy; he was carried away by Zeus's* eagle to replace Ganymeda* as cupbearer for the gods. (2) In Shakespeare's play *As You Like It* (1599), the alias adopted by Rosalind* when disguised as a boy.

Garcia. In Elbart Hubbard's essay *A Message to Garcia* (1899), a Cuban general to whom an American soldier delivers an important message; the arduous journey the soldier experiences became a symbol of the importance of initiative and commitment to duty.

Garden, The. *See* Eden; Gethsemane.

Gareth. In Malory's *Morte d'Arthur*, a young nobleman who joins Arthur's* court as a kitchen scullion until Lynette* comes to seek aid; he asks for the quest and is given it, much to Lynette's dismay, and kills the four knights holding Lynette's sister captive. When Tennyson retold the story in his poem *Gareth and Lynette* (1872), he changed Malory's ending so that Gareth married Lynette rather than her sister.

Gargantua. In Rabelais's *Gargantua* (1534), a giant with enormous appetites for food, drink, and free-spirited living; he travels with a gigantic mare, for whose neck he steals the bells of Notre-Dame, triumphs in a comic war, and receives various types of education satirizing French practices of the time, but is most often noted for his intense pleasure in the crude but free aspects of daily life. His son is Pantagruel.*

Gargery. In Charles Dickens's novel *Great Expectations* (1860), **Joe** is Pip's* brother-in-law and guardian, a gentle, simple, and sincere blacksmith. His wife, called **Mrs. Joe**, is a shrew who continually and unnecessarily berates her husband; she is attacked by Joe's helper and is left paralyzed for years before she dies.

Garland. In Charles Dickens's novel *The Old Curiosity Shop* (1840), the kindly family with the pony with a mind of its own; they give Kit Nubbles* a job and help in the search for Little Nell.*

Gaspar. In Christian legend, one of the Magi,* usually an Ethiopian.

Gastrolaters. In Rabelais's *Pantagruel* (1532–52), the greedy, gluttonous monks whose god is an idol whose eyes are bigger than its belly.

Gatsby. In F. Scott Fitzgerald's novel *The Great Gatsby* (1925), a wealthy and mysterious man who gives lavish parties but whom no one really knows; when he accidentally meets Daisy,* an old love, they begin an affair in which he begins to come out of his shell, but he is killed by a man who mistakenly thinks his wife had an affair with Gatsby, whose car ran her down. A haunting figure, he epitomizes the kind of man who seems to have no real self-esteem and no friends and who uses wealth to demonstrate his value, perhaps most noted in the scene in which he tries to impress Daisy with the number of his silk shirts. *See also* Buchanan; Carraway, Nick; Wolfsheim.

Gaunt, John of. *See* John of Gaunt.

Gautier, Marguerite. *See* Camille.

Gavroche. In Victor Hugo's novel *Les Misérables* (1862), the happy, heroic little guttersnipe whose name is often given to any boy of the streets.

Gawain. In Malory's *Morte d'Arthur*, a great knight, noble, pure, and courageous, whose strength declines after noon; his only failings are beheading a woman and killing one unarmed knight. He becomes Lancelot's* enemy when Lancelot kills his brothers, and he is finally killed in the war with Mordred.* In the anonymous poem *Sir Gawain and the Green Knight*, he agrees to trade blows with a giant, who carries off his own head after Gawain cuts it off and promises to claim his return blow in a year; on the way to the return battle, Gawain is tempted by the wife of the Green Knight but resists, keeping a girdle of invulnerability, and is rewarded with his life. In Tennyson's poem *Pelleas* *and Ettarre* (1869), he promises to help Pelleas* win the love of Ettarre* but instead seduces her for himself.

Gay, Walter. In Charles Dickens's novel *Dombey and Son* (1846), the young man who loves Florence Dombey* but is sent away and thought dead by his grandfather Solomon Gills,* returning at last to marry her.

Gaza. In the Bible, a Philistine* city, known primarily as the town in whch Samson* was imprisoned and pulled down the temple.

Ge. *See* Gaia.

Gedeon. *See* Gideon.

Gehazi. In the Bible, *II Kings* v, a servant of Elisha;* he took a present intended for his master and was punished with leprosy.

Gehenna. In the Bible, *II Kings* xxiii, a valley in which idols were worshipped; after the idols were destroyed, the valley was used as a garbage dump, constantly burning, into which were also cast the bodies of criminals, so that the name came to be associated with Hell.*

Gemini. In Greek legend, the twins Castor* and Pollux;* also, the constellation into which they were changed after their deaths.

Geminianus, St.. In Christian legend, the priest who cast out a demon from the Roman emperor's daughter and frightened away Attila* the Hun from Modena by appearing to him in a vision; he is often depicted holding a mirror.

General, Mrs. In Charles Dickens's novel *Little Dorrit* (1855), she is the "varnished" widow who becomes the mentor of the Dorrit* daughters and originates the formula for pretty lips: "prunes and prism."

Genesis. In the Bible, the first book; although it covers a vast amount of ancient history and myth, most allusions to the name itself are to the account of the creation of the world in six days in *Genesis* i, the central point of conflict between religion and the theory of evolution.

Geneviève, St. Historically, a holy woman (d. 512) whose prayers were said to have turned away the Huns from Paris and whose good works led to her canonization; her relics were said to have ended an epidemic (1129), confirming her position as patron saint of Paris. Her day is January 3.

Genghis Khan. Historically, the great warrior chief (d. 1227) who established the Mongol empire; he is generally associated with brutal warfare. *See also* Kubla Khan.

Genie. In Islamic folklore, a spirit that can work for good or evil and may change its shape, often resembling a man. The most noted is the genie that Aladdin* releases from the lamp, but genies figure in many of the tales of the *Arabian Nights. Also called* djinn; jinn; jinnayah.

Genius. In Roman mythology, the god who determined each man's character or spirit at birth and who later came to be associated with the spirit or character of any person or place.

Genji. In Lady Murasaki's novel *The Tale of Genji* (c. 1000), a handsome, courtly prince and lover.

George. (1) Historically, the name used by six kings of England, most noted of which was George III (d. 1820), the king whose policies led to the American Revolution and whose last ten years were spent under his son's regency due to his own insanity. (2) In John Steinbeck's novel *Of Mice and Men* (1937), a small, agressive vagrant worker who cares for his gentle half-wit cousin Lennie* and is eventually forced to kill him to save him from a lynch mob. (3) *See* Barnwell, George; Gibbs; Pontifex; Primrose; Sedley.

George, St. In Christian legend, a Roman soldier who rescued a princess from a great dragon,* thereby inducing all the onlookers to convert; he was later martyred by being beheaded. The patron saint of England, of boy scouts, and of soldiers, he is usually depicted as a medieval knight in shining armor decorated with a red cross; his day is April 23. *See also* Red Cross Knight; Sabra.

George and Martha. In Edward Albee's play *Who's Afraid of Virginia Woolf?* (1962), a destructive middle-aged couple, best summarized in their own words: "George and Martha, sad, sad, sad." George is an unambitious, undistinguished college professor, and Martha is a spoiled, disappointed, childless woman; both engage in witty, vicious "games" in which each tries to destroy the other's psyche, the most notable being the invention of an imaginary child. Their names in turn are a reference to the historical George and Martha Washington.*

Georgiana. *See* Podsnap.

Geraint. In Tennyson's poem *Enid* (1859), the jealous husband who sends his wife Enid* into danger in his place to test her love.

Gerd. In Henrik Ibsen's play *Brand* (1866), the gypsy girl who sees Brand* as the Lord and follows him up the mountain.

Gerda. In Scandinavian mythology, the goddess of the frozen earth.

Gerhardt, Jennie. In Theodore Dreiser's novel *Jennie Gerhardt* (1911), a poor girl who finds herself forced to sleep with men in order to get help for her family; she almost marries a wealthy man, but she gives him up for his own good, finally nursing him after his heart attack despite his marriage to another.

Germont. In Verdi's opera *La Traviata* (1853), Alfredo is the young man who falls in love with the courtesan Violetta;* his father is a respectable man who convinces her to leave his son in hopes of giving Alfredo a chance at a respectable life. *See also* Camille; Duval.

Géronte. In French comedy, a stock name for a greedy, silly old man, similar to the commedia dell'Arte's Pantalone* character; the most well-known is the father in Molière's play *The Doctor in Spite of Himself* (1666). *See also* Sganarelle.

Gerridge, Sam. In Tom Robertson's play *Caste* (1867), the sturdy gas fitter who marries Polly Eccles* and whose byplay with her was long noted as outstanding comic characterization.

Gershom. (1) In the Bible, *Exodus* ii, a son of Moses.* (2) *See* Gershon.

Gershon. In the Bible, *Genesis* xlvi, eldest son of Levi.* *Also called* Gershom.

Gertrude. (1) In Shakespeare's play *Hamlet* (1600), Hamlet's* mother, who marries Claudius* when he assumes the throne after the death of her first husband, the king. Hamlet accuses her of immorality in a scene which, in the twentieth century, has been interpreted as a prime example of the Oedipus* complex, and she ultimately dies by mistakenly drinking the poison Claudius intends for Hamlet. (2) *See* Morel.

Gervaise. In Émile Zola's novel *L'Assommoir* (1877), the somewhat simple laundress who is deserted by her lover; marries Coupeau,* who becomes a drunkard; and eventually joins him in alcoholism, dying a miserable death. *See also* Étienne; Nana.

Geryon. In Greek legend, a three-headed monster whose herds of cattle were stolen by Heracles* as one of his labors. In Dante's *Divine Comedy*, he is a beast with a human face and a scorpion's tail, symbolizing fraud.

Gestapo. Historically, the German secret police during the time of Hitler;* their leather overcoats and use of vicious torture made them immediate symbols of state brutality and suppression and of evil in general.

Gestas. In Christian legend, the thief crucified with Jesus* who does not repent and ask to be saved. *See also* Dismas.

Gethsemane. In the Bible, *Matthew* xxvi, the garden in which Jesus* prayed alone after the Last Supper* and where he and the Apostles* were walking when Judas* kissed Him to identify Him for arrest.

Ghost. In numerous folklores, a spirit of a dead person. In European traditions, a ghost is translucent, usually white, may fly or pass through walls, and looks like the person whose spirit it represents; in other traditions, a ghost may take on various shapes. The most notable literary ghosts include Marley* and the ghosts of Christmas Past, Present, and Yet-to-Come who visit Scrooge;* the ghost of Hamlet's* father; the Headless Horseman;* Banquo's* ghost who haunts Macbeth's* banquet; Quint;* the Kerbys who haunt Topper;* and Elvira.* *See also* Banshee; Goblin; Larvae.

Giant. In Greek legend, a set of monstrous sons of Gaia* and Uranus,* most notable of which were the Cyclops.* In many allusions, these are often confused with the Titans.* In the Bible, the most noted giant was Goliath,* who was killed by David* and his slingshot, but the hunter Nimrod* was also a giant, as were Behemoth* and Og.* Giants figure in much folklore, in particular the giant whom Jack* finds at the top of the beanstalk and who grumbles "fee, fi, fo, fum, I smell the blood of an Englishman." Other notable folkloric giants include Paul Bunyan,* Cacus,* and Fierabras.* Notable literary giants include Enceladus,* Galapas,* Gargantua,* the people in Brobdingnag,* the Laestrygonians,* Melambruno,* Pantagruel,* Polyphemus,* Ymir,* and the windmill attacked by Don Quixote.*

Giant Despair. In John Bunyan's *Pilgrim's Progress* (1678), a giant who imprisons Christian* in Doubting Castle.

Giant Pope. In John Bunyan's *Pilgrim's Progress* (1678), a giant who once killed many men but is now so stiff and old that he can only sit at his cave and bite his nails in frustration at the men he cannot catch.

Gibbie, Goose. In Walter Scott's novel *Old Mortality* (1816), the half-wit poultry lad.

Gibbs. In Thornton Wilder's play *Our Town* (1938), one of the two representative families depicted. **George** is a typical boy who loves baseball until he falls in love, marries Emily,* and becomes a respectable, responsible farmer and father. **Mr. Gibbs**, his father, is the town doctor, a kindly man whose hobby is the Civil War, and **Mrs. Gibbs** is a hardworking, sensible woman. *See also* Webb.

Gibson Girl. In numerous drawings by Charles Dana Gibson during the 1890s, an idealized American young woman, known for her beauty, fashionableness, athleticism, and romantic sensibility; the style of Gibson's drawings became synonymous with turn-of-the-century fashion.

Giddens. *See* Regina.

Gideon. In the Bible, *Judges* vi–viii, a great warrior who delivered the Israelites from the Midianites.

Gidget. In several novels by Frederick Kohner, beginning with *Gidget* (1957), and especially in a series of movies (beginning 1959), an athletic teenaged girl, one of the first "California girls."

Gigi. In Colette's story *Gigi* (1944) and particularly in the movie version (1958), a beautiful Parisian girl whose innocent charm marks her as an ideal courtesan but who rejects that role and successfully demands marriage instead.

Gilbert. In Marcel Proust's novels *Remembrance of Things Past* (1913–27), the daughter of Swann* and Odette;* the youthful Marcel* loves her but she cannot cope with his constant attentions. When she meets him again as a middle-aged woman, she is stout, and Marcel thinks she looks like an old whore. *See also* Saint-Loup.

Gil Blas. *See* Blas, Gil.

Gilda. In Verdi's opera *Rigoletto* (1851), the innocent young daughter of the jester Rigoletto;* she is seduced by a licentious duke and sacrifices herself to die in the duke's place. She sings the famous "Caro nome." *See also* Sparafucile.

Gilead. In the Bible, an area, including a city and a mountain of the same name, to the east of the river Jordan.* The most noted reference is *Jeremiah* viii, which asks, "Is there no balm in Gilead, is there no physician there?"

Giles, St. In Christian legend, a hermit most noted for a moment when he saved a hind from hunters by taking the arrows in his own arm and stilling the hounds' voices. The patron saint of cripples and of the poor, his day is September 1.

Gilgamesh. In the Babylonian epic *Gilgamesh*, a great king who becomes a close friend of the wild man Engidu.* After Engidu dies, Gilgamesh falls into a deep depression and goes on a quest in search of Utnapishtim,* the man who survived the great flood,* and his secret of eternal life, but Gilgamesh loses it again and dies.

Gilles. In French versions of the commedia dell'Arte, a comic servant with an amorous nature, dressed completely in white, similar to Pierrot,* but generally cruder.

Gilles de Rais. Historically, a French general (d. 1440) who led the forces associated with Jeanne d'Arc;* he was later executed for molesting and murdering children and in folklore is often identified with Bluebeard.*

Gillespie, Dr. In several novels by Max Brand and especially in movies beginning with *Young Doctor Kildare* (1938), the cantankerous old doctor who guides the young intern Kildare.*

Gilligan. In the American television series "Gilligan's Island" (1964–67), an incredibly stupid sailor marooned on a deserted Pacific island along with a set of stock comic characters; he is often cited as a demonstration of the stupidity of American television programming.

Gills, Solomon. In Charles Dickens's novel *Dombey and Son* (1846), Walter Gay's* old-fashioned grandfather, who sells nautical instruments.

Gilpin, John. In William Cowper's poem *John Gilpin* (1783), a draper who borrows a horse that once started cannot be stopped.

Gina. *See* Ekdal.

Gioconda, La. A name sometimes used for the Mona Lisa.*

Giovanni, Don. In Mozart's opera *Don Giovanni* (1787), Don Juan.*

Gipsy. *See* Gypsy.

Giselle. In the ballet *Giselle* (1841), a peasant girl who, her heart broken in love, goes mad and kills herself; after her death, she joins the Wilis,* beautiful female spirits who dance each night away and force any men trapped by them in the forest to dance themselves to death. When Albrecht,* her former lover, comes to her grave, the Wilis trap him too, but Giselle recognizes him and manages to forestall them until dawn, when he will be safe. For balletomanes, this is one of the fundamental roles against which each prima ballerina must ultimately be measured.

Glad Girl. *See* Pollyanna.

Glass Slipper. *See* Cinderella.

Glauce. In Greek legend, Creon's* daughter for whom Jason* intended to desert Medea,* thus precipitating Medea's murder of her children. In Euripides's play *Medea*, Glauce does not appear but is killed by a poisoned robe sent to her as a present from Medea. *Also called* Creusa.

Glaucus. (1) In Greek legend, a son of Sisyphus.* He refused to put his mares to stud in hopes of increasing their speed; Aphrodite* was so offended by this that she stimulated the mares to turn on Glaucus and tear him to pieces. (2) In Homer's *Iliad*, a Trojan* warrior who exchanged his gold armor for Diomedes's* bronze; later he was killed by Ajax.* (3) In Ovid's *Metamorphoses*, a fisherman who wished to join the fish he caught in the sea and was made a minor sea deity.

Glegg. In George Eliot's novel *The Mill on the Floss* (1860), a prudent and wealthy retired merchant. His wife **Jane** is Maggie Tulliver's* aunt, parsimonious and proud.

Glendower. Historically, the Welsh leader of a rebellion against Henry IV* of England; he is most known from Shakespeare's play *Henry IV, Part I* (1597), in which he is a wild pagan magician.

Glick, Sammy. In Budd Schulberg's novel *What Makes Sammy Run?* (1941), the quintessential Hollywood executive, a tasteless, devious opportunist who starts from nothing and worms or blackmails his way to the top of a studio without regard for the movies he makes or the people he destroys on the way up.

Gloriana. In Edmund Spenser's poem *The Faerie Queene* (1590), the name used for Queen Elizabeth,* the perfect queen in whose service the various knights of the poem have their adventures.

Glorvina. *See* O'Dowd.

Glossin. In Walter Scott's novel *Guy Mannering* (1815), the crooked lawyer.

Gloucester. In Shakespeare's play *King Lear* (1605), an earl who remains loyal to Lear;* he is persuaded by his illegitimate son Edmund* to drive out his legitimate son Edgar* and then is brutally blinded by Cornwall* for his attempts to support Lear. He meets Edgar again while wandering about the heath.

Glubdubdrib. In Jonathan Swift's novel *Gulliver's Travels* (1726), the island of sorcerers.

Gnatho. In Roman literature, a name often used for a parasite, the most notable being the cynic of Terence's play *The Eunuch*.

Gnome. In European folklore, a race of tiny creatures who live underground and guard the treasures of the earth, sometimes malevolent, like Alberich,* sometimes cute, like the leprechaun,* and sometimes merely used interchangeably with the dwarf.* *See also* Fairy.

Gobbo, Lancelot. In Shakespeare's play *The Merchant of Venice* (1596), Shylock's* clownish servant who deserts his master as soon as practical.

Goblin. In European folklore, a mischievous and often malevolent spirit, usually distinguished from a ghost* by its ugliness.

Gobseck. In several novels by Balzac, most notably *Gobseck* (1830) and *Père Goriot* (1834), a miserly Jewish moneylender who lives in poverty despite his great wealth. His great-grand-niece **Esther** is "la Torpille," whose career as a courtesan is followed in *A Harlot High and Low* (1838–47). *See also* Nucingen.

Godbole. In E. M. Forster's novel *A Passage to India* (1924), a Hindu mystic and teacher.

Godiva, Lady. In English legend, a woman who rode naked through the streets of Coventry so that her husband would repeal an unjust tax. *See also* Tom, Peeping.

Godot. In Samuel Beckett's play *Waiting for Godot* (1952), a mysterious personage whose appearance is continually awaited by Vladimir* and Estragon,* but who never arrives.

Godunov, Boris. In Pushkin's play *Boris Godunov* (1825), a cruel czar who murders his way to the throne and then, tormented by his guilt, dies during a rebellion.

Godzilla. In numerous Japanese movies, beginning with *Godzilla* (1955), a prehistoric monster revived in the modern world that spends most of its time walking around stepping on cities or battling other similar revived monsters; often cited as a symbol of the kind of movie people enjoy because it is so bad.

Gog. (1) In the Bible, *Ezekiel* xxxviii, a prince who, it is prophesied, will try to destroy the faithful from his land Magog in the north; the name recurs in a confusing passage in *Revelation* xx, in which Gog and Magog may be tribes deceived by Satan* or allied with Satan. (2) In European legend, with Magog, two allies whom Alexander* shut out behind a great wall in the Caucasus. (3) In Edmund Spenser's *The Faerie Queene* (1590), Gogmagog is a great giant in Albion* drowned by Corineus.

Gold, City of. *See* Eldorado.

Goldberg. In the American radio and television series "The Goldbergs" (1929–1954), a typical poor New York Jewish family, dominated by the prototypical protective, food-oriented Jewish Mother.

Goldberg, Rube. In American newspaper cartoons by Rube Goldberg (beg. 1915), a series of incredibly complex and complicated mechanical inventions designed to do very simple things; the name is often given to any unnecessarily complicated solution to a problem.

Golden Age. In Greek legend, the Golden Age existed in the ancient past when all men lived in peace and plenty without war or women; for most other cultures, the Golden Age is that time at which any particular desirable trait seems dominant, as in the "golden age of chivalry," or a skill seems at its peak, as in the "golden age of counterpoint," etc.

Golden Apple. *See* Apple; Hesperides.

Golden Bough. In Virgil's *Aeneid*, a bough of gold sacred to Persephone* which Aeneas* carries in order to obtain safe passage through the underworld.

Golden Calf. In the Bible, *Exodus* xxxii, while Moses* was away on Mt. Sinai,* Aaron* made an idol in the shape of a golden calf, during the worship of which the Israelites fell into an orgy; Moses returned bearing the Ten Commandments,* which he shattered in anger, and then crushed the idol, forcing the Israelites to drink the golden powder mixed in their water, and ordered the Levites to kill some 3,000 offenders, after which God also sent a plague.*

Golden Dustman. *See* Boffin.

Golden Fleece. In Greek legend, a fleece from a golden winged ram that Jason* and the Argonauts* sought and found during their adventure. *See also* Helle.

Golden Rule. In Christian usage, the title given to Jesus's* commandment, given in somewhat different form in each gospel but popularly understood as: "Do unto others as you would have them do unto you."

Golden Touch. *See* Midas.

Goldilocks. In the fairy tale, a self-centered little blonde girl who sneaks into the home of the Three Bears and eats their porridge, breaks their furniture, and falls asleep in their bedroom until they return and frighten her away.

Golgotha. In the Bible, the hill on which Jesus* was crucified, known as the place of the skulls. *Also called* Calvary.*

Golias. In medieval French literature, a stock character, drunken, licentious, and insubordinate, who is also a patron of scholars.

Goliath. In the Bible, *I Samuel* xvii, a giant and a great warrior of the Philistines;* when he challenged the Israelites to send someone out for personal combat, the shepherd boy David* volunteered and killed Goliath with a stone thrown from his sling.

Golovin, Ivan Illyich. *See* Ivan.

Gomer. (1) In the Bible, *Genesis* x, the eldest son of Japheth.* (2) In the Bible, *Hosea*, a "wife of whoredoms" whom God commanded Hosea* to marry because Israel* had committed great whoredoms. (3) *See* Pyle, Gomer.

Gomorrah. *See* Sodom.

Goneril. In Shakespeare's play *King Lear* (1605), Lear's* eldest daughter, a brutal hypocrite who mistreats her father and eventually poisons her sister Regan* in a jealous conflict over the bastard Edmund.* *See also* Albany; Cordelia.

Gonzago. In Shakespeare's play *Hamlet* (1600), the king who is murdered by having poison poured in his ear in the play enacted for the court by the strolling players.

Gonzalo. In Shakespeare's play *The Tempest* (1611), the faithful and sincere, but boringly talkative, courtier.

Good Friday. In Christian usage, the day on which Jesus* was crucified, celebrated on the Friday preceding Easter Sunday.

Goodwin, Archie. In numerous novels by Rex Stout (beg. 1934), the secretary and legman who investigates and reports to Nero Wolfe.*

Goodwin, Lee. In William Faulkner's novel *Sanctuary* (1931), a moonshiner who tries to help Temple Drake* but is burned alive in jail when falsely charged with a murder. *See also* Popeye.

Goodwood. In Henry James's novel *The Portrait of a Lady* (1881), an American who had loved Isabel Archer* and who tries to persuade her to return with him to America; his uncompromising single-mindedness, however, convinces her to return to Gilbert Osmond.*

Goody Two-Shoes. In the anonymous story *Goody Two-Shoes* (1765), often attributed to Oliver Goldsmith, an orphan girl who teaches herself to read and becomes a respected member of the community; her nickname comes from an incident when, so poor she had only one shoe, she was elated to receive two matching shoes from a charitable gentleman. In later usage, she came to signify someone so pure and pious as to be sickening to more "normal" persons, perhaps from confusion over the meaning of "goody."

Google, Barney. In the American newspaper cartoon *Barney Google* (beg. 1919), a little man with a big nose, a top hat, and "goo-goo-googledy eyes," noted for his sports mania, particularly for horse racing.

Goose, Mother. *See* Mother Goose.

Gorbuduc. In Norton and Sackville's play *Gorbuduc* (1562), a king who divides his kingdom between two sons; most allusions, however, are to the play's position as the first English blank verse tragedy.

Gordian Knot. In Greek legend, a knot so complicated no one could untie it, although it was said that whoever should do so would rule all Asia; Alexander* cut it with his sword.

Gordius. In Greek legend, the father of Midas* and the man who tied the Gordian Knot.*

Gorgon. In Greek legend, a female monster with hair made of snakes, a scaly body, wings, and the ability to turn men to stone with her stare. The most famous is Medusa.*

Goriot. In Balzac's novel *Père Goriot* (1835), a kindly, loving old father who sacrifices all his wealth to provide dowries and then to support two spoiled, thoughtless, and selfish daughters. After their marriages into the nobility, they think him beneath them and do not even bother to come to his funeral after he dies in abject poverty. Throughout, his love and indulgence of the daughters never wavers, no matter how cruelly or disdainfully they treat him. *See also* Nucingen; Restaud, Countess de.

Goshen. In the Bible, *Genesis* xlvi, the land in Egypt which Joseph* gave to Jacob* and the Israelites.

Gotham. In English folklore, a village noted as the home of fools. The name was first given to New York City in 1807 by Washington Irving, although in many later usages no particular stupidity seems implied. Similar communities full of fools exist in most folklore, such as Bergamo, the home of Brighella* and Harlequin* in the commedia dell'Arte; Swabia in German folklore; or possibly even Nazareth* in Biblical lore.

Gracchi. Historically, two Roman brothers (second century B.C.) who became great statesmen and social reformers; when young, their mother Cornelia* called them her jewels.

Graces. In Greek mythology, three sisters personifying loveliness and gracefulness, often shown dancing in artistic representations.

Gradgrind. In Charles Dickens's novel *Hard Times* (1854), **Thomas** is a merchant who ruins his childrens' spirit in his school where they are taught nothing but "facts, facts, facts." His daughter **Louisa** has no imagination or sentiment and marries Bounderby* without love; when she is unable to find the courage to run away with a lover, whe returns to her father's house. Her brother **Tom** lapses into melancholy and, in reaction to his education, becomes a drunkard and a thief. *See also* Blackpool, Stephen; Jupe, Sissy; M'Choakumchild.

Grail, Holy. In Christian legend, the cup from which Jesus* drank at the Last Supper* and in which Joseph* of Arimathea collected drops of Christ's blood on the cross. Legend says that it was carried to various places, including Britain, and that it could be found again only by a completely pure knight. In Malory's *Morte d'Arthur*, Arthur's* knights are on quests in search of the Grail, but only Galahad,* Percival,* and Bors* actually see it before it ascends into Heaven.* *See also* Launfal, Sir; Parzival.

Grainne. In Irish legend, a princess loved by Finn;* when she chose another, Finn pursued the two of them and eventually killed her husband.

Grandet. In Balzac's novel *Eugénie Grandet* (1833), a great miser whose love of money destroys all other feelings. **Mme. Grandet** is a long-suffering woman who devotes all the attention her hard lot allows to her daughter **Eugénie**. Eugénie herself is steadfast, loyal, and pure; when she falls in love with her wastrel cousin **Charles**, she gives him her life savings, waits patiently for his return, and, after inheriting from her father, pays all Charles's debts so that he can marry another woman, devoting herself instead to good deeds and helping the poor. *See also* Nanon.

Grandison, Charles. In Samuel Richardson's novel *Sir Charles Grandison* (1753), an honorable and virtuous nobleman.

Granger, Edith. *See* Edith.

Grangerfords. In Mark Twain's novel *Huckleberry Finn* (1885), a family with whom Huck Finn* spends some time during his trip downriver; a daughter writes sentimental poems about death, and the entire family is engaged in a feud with the Shepherdsons,* which eventually results in the brutal murder of the son who is Huck's age.

Granny. *See* Clampett.

Grant, U. S. Historically, the American general who won the Civil War and later became president (d. 1885); he appears in much American literature and folklore, sometimes with patriotic admiration, sometimes as a methodical butcher, sometimes as a genial, simple man easily misled by friends, and most often as a drunkard, due to his rumored bouts with alcohol in the army and Lincoln's* famous remark that he wished all his generals drank whatever Grant drank since he seemed to be the only one able to win a battle.

Gratiae. *See* Graces.

Graustark. In G. B. M'Cutcheon's novel *Graustark* (1901), an imaginary middle European kingdom where romantic events occur, similar to Ruritania,* and often used to signify an operetta-like world of romance.

Gray, Dorian. In Oscar Wilde's novel *The Picture of Dorian Gray* (1891), an unprincipled young man whose portrait ages while he remains young.

Great-heart. In John Bunyan's *Pilgrim's Progress*, Part II (1684), Christiana's* escort on her pilgrimage.

Greek Slave, The. In a sculpture by Hiram Powers (1843), a manacled standing female nude intended to symbolize the spirit of freedom, noted in all "cultured" American nineteenth-century households as an epitome of art itself and noted in many twentieth-century allusions as a prime artistic example of the Victorian mix of high-minded sentiment and prurience.

Green Knight. *See* Gawain.

Gregers. In Henrik Ibsen's play *The Wild Duck* (1884), Hjalmar Ekdal's* friend, a young man who believes the truth must be told at all times and who, by telling what he believes to be the truth about Hjalmar's wife and child, destroys his friend's family.

Gregory. Historically, one of sixteen popes adopting the name. The most noted include **Gregory I** (d. 604), later St. Gregory, whose political skill and religious dedication stabilized northern Italy after Rome's collapse and who established the Church as an independent authority, and **Gregory VII** (d. 1085), whose long conflict with Henry* IV led to Henry's famous capitulation in the snow at Canossa.

Gregory, St. (1) *See* Gregory. (2) Historically, a Greek missionary (d. 270) called the Wonderworker, who had the first recorded vision of the Virgin Mary.* (3) Historically, Gregory of Utrecht (d. 775), a missionary and bishop who is most noted for his refusal to take revenge on the men who murdered his own half-brothers.

Grendel. In the anonymous *Beowulf*, a monster that steals men from the lord's hall and eats them, until the hero Beowulf* arrives and kills it; Grendel's mother is an even greater monster who tries to avenge her son's death but is killed by Beowulf in a desperate underwater battle.

Gretchen. (1) In Goethe's poem/play *Faust* (1808–32), the pure young maiden whom Faust* eventually seduces; she bears him an illegitimate child but is saved from damnation by her natural purity. Her song at her spinning wheel, "meine Ruhe ist hin," is one of the most famous single passages in all of literature, and it has been set to music by numerous composers, most notably Schubert. Her ascent to Heaven* in Gounod's opera *Faust* (1859) was one of the most famous and admired moments in opera for almost a century. *Also called* Margaret; Margareta; Marguerite.* *See also* Mephistopheles; Valentin.

Gretel. *See* Hansel and Gretel.

Grey, Lady Jane. Historically, a young girl (d. 1554) who, through the machinations of her father, was named to succeed to the English throne, where she reigned for nine days until Mary Tudor* asserted her claim. Despite her youth and naïveté, she was executed along with her father and her husband and has since been a popular subject of historical romances.

Greyfriars. *See* Bunter, Billy.

Gride, Arthur. In Charles Dickens's novel *Nicholas Nickleby* (1838), the miserly old man who attempts to buy Madeline Bray* in marriage.

Griffin. In Greek legend, a creature with a lion's body and the head and wings of an eagle that guarded Zeus's* gold. *See also* Gryphon.

Griffiths, Clyde. In Theodore Dreiser's novel *An American Tragedy* (1925), a poor young man on the make who gets the factory girl Roberta Alden* pregnant and then tries to kill her in order to be free to marry a wealthy girl; he has second thoughts, but Roberta drowns nonetheless, and he is convicted of murder.

Grimes, Peter. In George Crabbe's poem *The Borough* (1810), a foul-tempered fisherman who killed his apprentices by such ill-treatment that he was forced to live alone; he was then driven mad by his guilty conscience.

Grimm, Brothers. Historically, two German brothers who collected and retold (1812–22) a number of European folk tales and thus became synonymous with such folklore and fairy tales.

Grimwig. In Charles Dickens's novel *Oliver Twist* (1837), Brownlow's* friend who promises to eat his own head if ever proven wrong.

Grinder, Rob the. *See* Toodle.

Griselda. In Boccaccio's *Decameron*, a young wife subjected to numerous indignities and tests of her fidelity, which she bears so patiently that she is always known as "patient Griselda"; the story is widely known in English from the Clerk of Oxford's Tale in Chaucer's *Canterbury Tales* and is also in Perrault's *Mother Goose* stories.

Grisette. In numerous nineteenth-century French works, a stock name for a hardworking but amorous, lighthearted Parisian milliner, laundress, or worker in a similar profession. *See also* Fifi; Mimi; Musette.

Grove, Lena. *See* Lena.

Grub Street. Historically, an eighteenth-century London street where a number of writers lived; in popular usage, it signifies any literary hackwork.

Grumio. In Shakespeare's play *The Taming of the Shrew* (1593), a long-suffering servant of Petruchio.*

Grundy, Mrs. In Thomas Morton's play *Speed the Plough* (1798), a neighbor who never appears but exerts a powerful influence, since one of the characters constantly worries what Mrs. Grundy will think about anything that happens. Consequently, she has become a symbol of stultifying and thoughtless conventionality.

Grushenka. In Dostoevsky's novel *The Brothers Karamazov* (1880), the earthy mistress of Karamazov;* jealousy over her favors is the ostensible motive for his murder by his son.

Gryphon. In Lewis Carroll's *Through the Looking Glass* (1872), a griffin* who is the friend of the Mock Turtle.*

Guenever. *See* Guinevere.

Guermantes. In Marcel Proust's novels *Remembrance of Things Past* (1913–27), the aristocratic family whose circle Marcel* joins and describes. When he is young, the Guermantes circle seems the epitome of beauty and sophistication, especially the **Duchesse** herself, but, after he is admitted to it as an adult, he comes to see it as trivial, malicious, and decadent, its ultimate decline illustrated by the **Prince's** remarriage to a shallow social climber, the widow Verdurin.* *See also* Charlus; Odette; St.-Euverte, Mme. de; Saint-Loup.

Guerre, Martin. Historically, a French farmer who disappeared in the sixteenth century and was replaced by another man who was completely accepted as Guerre until the original reappeared; the impostor's trial fascinated many writers and it has been the subject of several noted works.

Guido. *See* Franceschini.

Guildenstern. *See* Rosencrantz and Guildenstern.

Guinevere. In English legend, the wife of King Arthur.* As codified in Malory's *Morte d'Arthur*, she is a beautiful young woman who marries Arthur, bringing with her the Round Table,* and lives faithfully until Lancelot* arrives at court. Her passion leads to adultery, to her trial for treason and subsequent rescue by Lancelot, and to the civil war that follows, in which Arthur is killed, after which Guinevere retires to a convent.

Gulliver. In Jonathan Swift's novel *Gulliver's Travels* (1726), a sailor and doctor who goes on a number of voyages to exotic places that serve as satirical portraits of the English world, including Lilliput,* where people are so small that he is treated as a giant; Brobdingnag,* where the inhabitants are so large that he is treated as a small pet; and the land of the Houyhnhnms,* where he sees the humanlike Yahoos* that so disgust him that he can no longer stand human company on his return to England, choosing to live the rest of his life in the stables. *See also* Glubdubdrib; Laputa; Luggnagg; Struldbrugs.

Gummidge, Mrs. In Charles Dickens's novel *David Copperfield* (1849), the widow who calls herself a "lone, lorn creetur."

Gunn, Ben. In R. L. Stevenson's novel *Treasure Island* (1883), the lunatic old pirate marooned with the treasure.

Gunther. In the anonymous *Niebelungenlied*, the king of Burgundy who obtains Siegfried's* help in gaining Brunhild* for a bride and who is impersonated in the marriage bed by Siegfried. He appears essentially the same in Richard Wagner's opera *Götterdämmerung* (1876), although neither he nor Siegfried consummates the marriage before the deception is discovered; Gunther then arranges for Siegfried's death in hopes that Brünnhilde will then accept him. *See also* Gutrune; Hagen.

Guppy. In Charles Dickens's novel *Bleak House* (1852), the law clerk who proposes to Esther Summerson* and then legalistically reneges after she is scarred by smallpox.

Gurth. In Walter Scott's novel *Ivanhoe* (1820), the swineherd who loyally follows Ivanhoe.*

Gutman, Caspar. In Dashiell Hammett's novel *The Maltese Falcon* (1930), "the fat man," a devious crook. *See also* Spade, Sam.

Gutrune. In Richard Wagner's opera *Götterdämmerung* (1876), Gunther's* sister, who falls in love with Siegfried* and gives him the potion of forgetfulness. *See also* Kreimhild.

Guy, The Old. The effigy burned on Guy Fawkes* Day.

Guy Fawkes. *See* Fawkes, Guy.

Guy of Gisborne. In an English ballad, a yeoman who attempts to capture Robin Hood* and is killed.

Gwendolen. In Oscar Wilde's play *The Importance of Being Earnest* (1895), the wealthy and haughty daughter of Lady Bracknell;* she has sworn never to love anyone not named Ernest. *See also* Cecily; Worthing, Jack.

Gwendolyn. *See* Gwendolen.

Gyges. In a story related by Plato, a shepherd who found a brass ring that would make the wearer invisible; he wore the ring to enter the queen's chamber, murdered the king, and then married the queen and became king.

Gynt, Peer. In Henrik Ibsen's play *Peer Gynt* (1867), a young idler and braggart who continually upsets his family and the local farming society with his lies and his escapades, such as stealing a bride from her wedding. He leaves home to find adventure, almost marrying the daughter of the Troll* King, getting rich in the slave trade, and then losing his fortune to the Arab dancing girl Anitra.* At last escaping from an insane asylum and returning to Norway, he first meets the Button Moulder,* who tells him that he does not have enough soul to merit even Hell,* and then sees again the faithful Solveig.* A complex figure, he is part romantic dreamer, part wastrel, and part a symbol of the emptiness of "modern" life. *See also* Aase.

Gypsy. Historically, a member of a tribe of wanderers throughout Europe, noted for their colorful clothing, their ability to tell fortunes, and their dramatic music, usually played on the violin. They are the subject of much folklore, most of it negative, and they are generally said to be crooked horse traders, thieves who steal small children as well as animals, and practitioners of mysterious devilish rites.

H

Habakkuk. In the Bible, *Habakkuk*, a prophet noted for preaching "woe to the wicked."

Hadassah. A name sometimes used for Esther.*

Hades. In Greek mythology, the underworld to which were sent the dead; it was ruled by the god Pluto,* although sometimes the god as well as the place was called Hades. Although descriptions vary, it is generally described as being bordered by the rivers Styx* or Acheron,* across which the dead are ferried by Charon;* the actual entrance is guarded by the dog Cerberus.* Persephone* is queen there, but she resides there only half of each year. In legend and literature, several mortals visit Hades and return, including Heracles,* Orpheus,* Odysseus* in Homer's *Odyssey*, and Aeneas* in Virgil's *Aeneid*; some portions of these visits are adapted by Dante in his description of Hell* in his *Divine Comedy*. *See also* Elysium; Erebus; Lethe; Paradise; Valhalla.

Haemon. In Sophocles's play *Antigone*, the son of Creon* who is in love with Antigone* and kills himself when she is put to death.

Hagar. In the Bible, *Genesis* xvi, xxi, the handmaid of Sarah;* as Sarah continued to be barren, she encouraged her husband Abraham* to lie with Hagar, who then bore Ishmael.* Later, Hagar became arrogant and was driven out by Sarah, returned, and was then driven out again.

Hagen. (1) In the anonymous *Niebelungenlied*, a greedy knight who murders Siegfried.* *See also* Brunhild. (2) In Richard Wagner's opera *Götterdämmerung* (1879), Gunther's* half-brother and Alberich's* son who makes the potion that gives Siegfried* forgetfulness and then kills him in hopes of obtaining Alberich's* ring. *See also* Gutrune.

Haidée. In Byron's poem *Don Juan* (1819), a beautiful child of nature who rescues the shipwrecked Juan* and lives with him in an idyllic island romance until her father, a pirate, returns and sells him into slavery; she dies of a broken heart.

Hajji Baba. In James Morier's novel *The Adventure of Hajji Baba* (1824), a Persian rogue who has numerous picaresque adventures, most notably impersonating a barber, a doctor, and an executioner.

Hal, Prince. In Shakespeare's plays *Henry IV, Parts I & II* (1597–8), the nickname for the English prince who eventually becomes Henry V.*

Halcyone. (1) In Greek legend, one of the Pleiades.* (2) In Ovid's *Metamorphoses*, the daughter of Aeolus;* she was changed into a kingfisher so she could be with her beloved husband Ceyx.*

Haller, Harry. In Hermann Hesse's novel *Steppenwolf* (1927), a lonely, socially isolated middle-aged man who comes to see himself as a wolf of the steppes. Disturbed by his separation of spirit and flesh, he wanders into various vices, almost losing his sanity, until he is restored to some stability through his visits to a "magic theater." For unclear reasons, this became a seminal work for American youth in the sixties.

Ham. (1) In the Bible, *Genesis* v–ix, the youngest son of Noah.* He saw his father drunk and naked, and in punishment God cursed his son Canaan,* ordaining him to live as a servant to the children of Ham's brothers. In the nineteenth century, this was sometimes taken by slavery apologists to indicate God's approval of slavery, and Negroes were sometimes called "children of Ham." *See also* Cush; Shem; Japeth. (2) *See* Peggotty.

Hamadryad. *See* Dryad.

Haman. In the Bible, *Esther*, the prime minister of Ahasuerus;* displeasure with Mordecai* caused Haman to plan to kill all the Jews until the plot was exposed by Esther* and he was himself killed.

Hamilcar. Historically, a great general of Carthage (d. 228 B.C.) and father of Hannibal,* although he may be better known from Gustave Flaubert's novel *Salammbô* (1862).

Hamilton, Emma. Historically, the mistress (d. 1815) of Admiral Nelson.*

Hamilton, Melanie. *See* Melanie.

Hamlet. In Shakespeare's play *Hamlet* (1600), the Prince of Denmark who sees the ghost of his father (also called Hamlet), who in turn tells him that he has been murdered by his brother Claudius,* now king and husband of Hamlet's mother Gertrude,* and demands that his son seek revenge. Hamlet tries to determine the truth of this message, feigning madness (or perhaps going mad), during which he mistreats his love Ophelia,* questions his mother, and stages a play that illustrates the murder to see Claudius's reaction. Determining at last on revenge, he kills Ophelia's father Polonius* by mistake, and he is sent away carrying a letter demanding his execution, which he discovers. He escapes, returning to find Ophelia dead, and he leaps into her open grave. He is then lured into a fencing match with her brother Laertes.* Claudius has poisoned the tip of the foil and, at the end of the match, Hamlet dies, along with Claudius, Gertrude, and Laertes. He is arguably the most widely known, quoted, and analyzed character in our literature, and explications and analyses of his character abound. Since the early nineteenth century, he has been portrayed wearing black tights and doublet, and the image is so firmly fixed that the costume is synonymous with the character. He is also often shown holding a skull, from the "Alas, poor Yorick"* scene in the graveyard. More lines are commonly quoted from *Hamlet* than from any other single work; *the* soliloquy is his "To be or not to be . . . " meditation on suicide. He is often referred to as the Melancholy Dane. The role is generally regarded as the ultimate test of an actor, and the play is considered by many to be the finest play ever written, synonymous with theatrical art. *See also* Fortinbras; Horatio; Osric; Rosencrantz and Guildenstern.

Hamor. *See* Dinah.

Handy Andy. In Samuel Lover's stories *Handy Andy* (1842), a simple and mischievous Irish boy, actually named Andy Rooney.

Hannah. In the Bible, *I Samuel* i, the mother of Samuel.* Barren for many years, she promised that, if she could conceive, the child would be dedicated to God. Eli* mistook her prayers for drunkenness.

Hannay, Richard. In several novels by John Buchan, beginning with *The 39 Steps* (1915), a brave, honorable, and resourceful British engineer and gentleman whose natural gifts allow him to foil various terrible plots.

Hannibal. Historically, a general of Carthage (d. 182 B.C.) whose skill and daring almost defeated Rome; known especially for crossing the Alps with his troops and elephants.

Hanno. *See* Buddenbrook.

Hans. (1) A common Germanic name, often used to indicate a stereotypical German peasant, sturdy and stolid. (2) *See* Brinker, Hans; Castorp, Hans; Sachs, Hans.

Hansa. In Ole Rölvaag's novel *Giants in the Earth* (1924), **Per** is the father of a family that struggles to settle a farm in the American west, an even-tempered and loyal man who dies in a blizzard while trying to bring a minister to a dying friend. His wife **Beret** is a beautiful and superstitious woman almost driven mad by the strains of childbirth and their isolated life, until a traveling preacher revives her religion.

Hansel and Gretel. In the fairy tale, two children abandoned in the forest by their stepmother; there they meet an old lady in a gingerbread house who tries to bake them. Instead, they shove her into the oven and escape.

Happy. *See* Loman.

Harcourt. In William Wycherley's play *The Country Wife* (1673), a friend of Horner* and a clever wit who dupes Sparkish* in order to marry the latter's betrothed.

Hardcastle. In Oliver Goldsmith's play *She Stoops to Conquer* (1773), a hearty country squire who is mistaken by his future son-in-law Marlow* for an innkeeper. **Mrs. Hardcastle** is an overbearing woman blindly devoted to her loutish son by a previous marriage, Tony Lumpkin,* and in an effort to marry him off to a girl he does not want, she is dumped by him in the pond. Hardcastle's daughter **Kate** is an intelligent and charming girl who playfully pretends to be a maid in order to observe Marlow and falls in love with the enthusiastic, romantic person he becomes when he is not faced with an intimidating ''lady.''

Harding, Rev. In several novels by Anthony Trollope, beginning with *The Warden* (1855), a kind, gentle, and completely Christian canon.

Hardy, Andy. In several movies (1937–47), an energetic and perfectly ''nice'' American middle-class teenager, the ideal son in the ideal American family. Sometimes ridiculed for his naïveté, he symbolizes the perfect nostalgic world of the small-town American, a fantasy world where lovers only hold hands, no one ever faces a financial crisis that cannot be solved by the gang's putting on a show, and all personal crises are resolved by the end of the feature.

Hareton. *See* Earnshaw.

Harker. In Bram Stoker's novel *Dracula* (1897), an English lawyer who travels to Transylvania* and meets Dracula.*

Harlequin. In the commedia dell'Arte, the zany* and fool, noted for his delight in tricks, his simplemindedness, and his parti-colored suit. *Also called* Arlequino. *See also* Bergamo; Brighella; Columbine; Gilles; Pantalone; Pierrot.

Harlowe, Clarissa. *See* Clarissa.

Harold, Childe. In Byron's poem *Childe Harold's Pilgrimage* (1812–18), a man who, bored and disgusted with a life of pleasure, begins a long pilgrimage across Europe where the historical associations of each place he visits lead him to meditations on the meaning and purpose of life.

Haroun al Rashid. *See* Harun al Rashid.

Harpagon. In Molière's play *The Miser* (1668), the miser; he buries his money in the garden, orders his servants not to polish the furniture for fear of wearing it out, feeds straw to his horses, and generally illustrates the ridiculous extremes to which the money-mad may go.

Harpy. In Greek legend, a monster with the face of a woman and the body, claws, and wings of a vulture; harpies carried away the souls of the dead and punished criminals. In Virgil's *Aeneid*, they plunder Aeneas* on the way to Italy. *See also* Phineas.

Harriet. (1) In George Etherege's play *The Man of Mode* (1676), a sharp-tongued beauty whom Dorimant* unscrupulously arranges to marry. (2) *See* Ozzie and Harriet.

Harris, Mrs. In Charles Dickens's novel *Martin Chuzzlewit* (1844), the imaginary woman to whom Sairey Gamp* attributes her outrageous lies.

Harris, Zonker. *See* Zonker.

Harun al Rashid. Historically, a caliph of Baghdad (d. 809), noted primarily as the Caliph in many stories of *The Arabian Nights*.

Harvey. In Mary Chase's play *Harvey* (1944), a gigantic but invisible rabbit. *See also* Dowd, Elwood P.

Hastings. (1) Historically, site of the battle (1066) in which William* of Normandy conquered the Anglo-Saxons and gained control of England. (2) In Oliver Goldsmith's play *She Stoops to Conquer* (1773), Marlow's* impetuous, romantic friend who falls in love with Constance Neville.*

Hatfield. Historically, an American family on the Kentucky-Virginia border engaged in a long-running feud, begun after the Civil War, with the McCoy family; the two names are now synonymous with hillbillies and with feuds.

Havisham, Miss. In Charles Dickens's novel *Great Expectations* (1860), a bitter old woman who locks herself in her house and trains her ward Estella* to manipulate and destroy men. She was jilted on her wedding day and as a result still wears her wedding dress and keeps the house exactly as it was at the moment this occurred, including a table set with moldering food and covered with rats and spider webs, until it all burns down around her when her dress catches fire. *See also* Pip.

Hawdon, Capt. In Charles Dickens's novel *Bleak House* (1852), the former lover of Lady Dedlock* and the father of Esther Summerson,* reduced to penury and dying of malnutrition; Lady Dedlock dies of exposure at his grave.

Hawkeye. (1) A nickname of Natty Bumppo.* (2) *See* Pierce, Hawkeye.

Hawkins, Jim. In R. L. Stevenson's novel *Treasure Island* (1883), the boy who joins the hunt for the hidden treasure and narrates the story. *See also* Silver, Long John.

Hawkins, Sadie. In the American newspaper cartoon *Li'l Abner* (beg. 1934), a legendary woman whose day is celebrated by a "race" in which the women pursue the men and get to marry any man they can catch.

Hawkshaw. In Tom Taylor's play *The Ticket-of-Leave Man* (1863), the brilliant detective, also a master of disguise. The climactic moment when he reveals himself was one of the great *coups de théâtre* of the nineteenth century. The name was long synonymous with any detective.

Headless Horseman. In Washington Irving's story *The Legend of Sleepy Hollow* (1819), the headless ghost that is said to haunt the countryside; after seeing what seems to be this ghost, Ichabod Crane* disappears.

Headstone. *See* Hexam.

Heathcliff. In Emily Brontë's novel *Wuthering Heights* (1847), a foundling raised by the Earnshaws* and humiliated by their son, obsessed with revenge for that treatment. This, plus his rejection by Cathy,* whom he had loved passionately, turns him into a brooding, malevolent, and violent man who lives in squalor on the lands he has taken from the ruined Earnshaws. The intensity with which he is described has made him one of the most haunting figures in romantic fiction and an unlikely but powerful symbol of romantic passion. *See also* Linton.

Heathen Chinee. *See* Ah Sin.

Heaven. In Christian belief, the paradise* to which the souls of those who are saved are taken after death and where they reside at one with God, as opposed to those who are condemned to Hell* for their sins. In Dante's poem *Divine Comedy*, it is described as a place of eternal beauty and light, and in folklore it is often depicted as a place where the saved float on clouds and play harps. It is also the home of God and of the angels,* from which God can look down on the earth.

Hebe. (1) A name sometimes used for Ganymeda.* (2) In Gilbert and Sullivan's operetta *H. M. S. Pinafore* (1878), the dominating leader of "Sir Joseph's* sisters and his cousins and his aunts."

Hecaba. *See* Hecuba.

Hecate. In Greek mythology, there are two related aspects. Initially, she seems to have been a triple godess of moon, earth, and underworld, but those roles were assumed respectively by Luna,* Artemis,* and Persephone.* Hecate then was associated with ghosts, witchcraft, and black magic, primarily as an underworld attendant of Persephone, in which guise she appears in Shakespeare's play *Macbeth* (1605).

Hector. In Greek legend, a son of Priam* and Hecuba* and the greatest warrior of Troy.* In Homer's *Iliad*, he is the noblest warrior on either side with human affection for family and friends, controlled passions, and an ideal sense of honor in addition to his battlefield prowess. In the course of the battles, he kills Patroclus;* in revenge, Achilles* kills him, first chasing him three times around the city when he is trapped alone outside the walls and then dragging the body behind his chariot. One of the more memorable passages is Hector's farewell to his wife Andromache.* *See also* Ajax; Astyanax; Polyxena.

Hecuba. In Greek legend, the wife of Priam* and the mother of numerous Trojan children, most notable of which are Hector,* Polyxena,* Cassandra,* Paris,* and Helenus.* In Homer's *Iliad*, she is a pathetic figure forced to see her children killed off one by one. In Euripides's play *The Trojan Women*, she survives the fall of Troy but despairs and is given as a slave to Odysseus.* In Euripides's play *Hecuba*, before she goes into slavery she lures into her tent Polymestor,* the man who killed her son Polydorus,* and puts out his eyes. In Ovid's *Metamorphoses*, the vigor with which she scratches out Polymestor's eyes changes her into a dog.

Hedda. *See* Gabler, Hedda.

Hedvig. *See* Ekdal.

Heep, Uriah. In Charles Dickens's novel *David Copperfield* (1849), the professionally '' 'umble'' clerk with the damp hands and the writhing mannerisms; his unctuous insistence on his humility masks an ambition and malevolence that almost ruins Betsey Trotwood* and Mr. Wickfield* until he is exposed by Micawber.*

Heffalump. In A. A. Milne's stories *Winnie-the-Pooh* (1926), a great beast that is hunted but is never found since the trap for him catches Pooh.*

Heidi. In Johanna Spyri's novel *Heidi* (1881), an orphaned Swiss girl who pines away when she is sent to town but is restored when returned to her mountains and goats, where she also restores her misanthropic grandfather's faith in God.

Hekate. *See* Hecate.

Helen. (1) In Greek legend, the daughter of Leda* and Zeus* and the most beautiful woman in the world. She was wooed by all the chiefs of Greece but chose to marry Menelaus.* Later, Paris* fell in love with her, and she ran away with him to Troy, thus instigating the Trojan War.* In Homer's *Iliad*, she is a beautiful but weak woman who saps the will of Paris unintentionally. In Homer's *Odyssey*, after the war she returns to live happily with Menelaus at Sparta. In Euripides's play *The Trojan Women*, Menelaus intends to kill her but she uses her feminine wiles to change his mind. In Euripides's play *Helen*, however, she was never at Troy, but was in fact carried away by Proteus* to Egypt, where Menelaus and the phantom Helen find her again after the war and where he rescues her from the dead king's son. The description of hers as "the face that launched a thousand ships" is in Christopher Marlowe's play *Doctor Faustus* rather than in the *Iliad*. *Also called* Helena; Hélène. *See also* Deiphobus; Hermione; Odysseus. (2) *See also* Ellen, Helena; Hélène.

Helena. (1) In Shakespeare's play *A Midsummer Night's Dream* (1595), one of the young lovers, the tall blonde, who spaniel-like pursues her love Demetrius.* (2) In Shakespeare's play *All's Well That Ends Well* (1602), a doctor's daughter who cures the king and is rewarded with marriage to the count Bertram.* When he runs away rather than marry beneath him, she pursues him and substitutes herself for another woman in his bed, thereby becoming pregnant, obtaining proof of their marriage, and gaining his agreement to the marriage. She is seen as an independent, intelligent heroine, although her story is problematical or distasteful to many. (3) *See* Serebryakov. (4) *See also* Helen.

Helena, St. Historically, the mother (d. 330) of Constantine;* she converted after her son's conversion. Legend says that she made a pilgrimage to Jerusalem* in old age and there found the True Cross, for which reason her symbol is a cross. Her day is August 18.

Hélène. *See* Helen; Kuragina, Hélène.

Helenus. In Greek legend, a son of Hecuba* and Priam* with the gift of prophecy. It was his prediction after he was captured by the Greeks that led them to bring back Neoptolemus* and the bow of Philoctetes.* After Neoptolemus's death, he married Andromache* and in Virgil's *Aeneid* was visited by Aeneas,* whom he told how to recognize the place where his journey would end.

Helios. In Greek mythology, the sun, usually depicted as driving a shining chariot across the sky; sometimes also a name used for Apollo.* *Also called* Sol.* *See also* Circe.

Hell. In Christian belief, the name of the underworld where the sinful dead or the souls of the sinful dead reside, as opposed to Heaven* where the good who have been saved reside. The name itself is an Anglo-Saxon translation of the Biblical term *Sheol*. It is generally depicted as a place full of great fires presided over by the Devil,* suggested by Gehenna* and by the lake of fire in *Revelation* xx. It also often owes a great deal to Dante's description in his poem *Divine Comedy*, where it is depicted as a place with numerous varied punishments designed to fit the sins of those consigned to reside there, built in descending circles to a center of ice. It is often used synonymously with Hades,* although, in the Greek underworld, both the good and the wicked resided together.

Helle. In Greek legend, a woman who drowned after falling from the back of a ram with golden fleece into what is now called the Hellespont.

Helmer. In Henrik Ibsen's play *A Doll's House* (1879), the hypocritical husband, a lawyer promoted to bank manager, who treats his pretty wife Nora* like a doll; for many, he is a central symbol of male chauvinism.

Héloïse. Historically, a twelfth-century Parisian girl who had an affair with her tutor, the theologian Abélard. After she bore him an illegitimate child, he took her to a convent to protect her from her guardian's rage, and the guardian in return had Abélard castrated. She became a nun and he, a monk. They exchanged a set of famous romantic letters and were buried together in Paris. *See also* Julie.

Henchard. In Thomas Hardy's novel *The Mayor of Casterbridge* (1886), a prosperous merchant and mayor who in his youth had sold his wife and child to a sailor; when this is revealed, he is publicly humiliated and financially ruined, dying friendless.

Henderson. In Saul Bellow's novel *Henderson the Rain King* (1959), a wealthy American who goes to Africa to find himself and temporarily becomes a tribal king and god.

Henri. The French form of Henry.*

Henry. (1) Historically, a name used by eight English kings. *See* Henry II; Henry IV; Henry V; Henry VI; Henry VIII. (2) Historically, a name used by four kings of France, the most noted being **Henry IV** (d. 1610), *also called* Henry of Navarre, a Huguenot prince who converted to Catholicism to take the throne, saying "Paris is worth a mass." He was noted as a wise administrator, a great soldier, the man who established a certain amount of toleration for Protestants, and something of a rake until his assassination. (3) Historically, a name used by seven Holy Roman Emperors, the most noted being **Henry IV** (d. 1106), whose conflicts with Pope Gregory* VII led to his excommunication; they were at least temporarily reconciled after the meeting at Canossa where he knelt in the snow to ask forgiveness. (4) *See* Aldrich, Henry; Fleming, Henry.

Henry, John. *See* John Henry.

Henry, Patrick. Historically, an American patriot (d. 1799) noted for saying, "Give me liberty, or give me death."

Henry II. Historically, king of England (d. 1189), first of the Plantagenets, noted primarily for the murder of Thomas à Becket,* which occurred with his consent if not at his command.

Henry IV. (1) Historically, king of England (d. 1413). In Shakespeare's play *Richard II* (1595), under his family name Bolingbroke, he is an ambitious but honorable man who forces Richard II* to abdicate for the good of the kingdom; in *Henry IV, Parts I & II* (1597–98), he is an ascetic, disturbed by the manner in which he took the throne and by the irresponsibility and rebelliousness of his son Hal;* he puts down Glendower's* revolt and makes plans for a crusade, but he dies before he can leave. *See also* Hotspur. (2) *See* Henry.

Henry V. Historically, king of England (d. 1422), noted for his conquests in France, especially the great victory at Agincourt. In Shakespeare's plays *Henry IV, Parts I & II* (1597–98), as Prince Hal, he is a wild, rebellious young man, living riotously among the taverns and brothels of London with Falstaff,* Pistol,* Poins,* and others. He persuades Falstaff to rob some travelers and in turn robs Falstaff, meanwhile ignoring his father's pleas to act as befits a potential monarch. When Hotspur* and others rise in revolt, however, he puts off his playfulness and shows himself to be a great soldier and an honorable son, saving his father's life and killing Hotspur. When he is crowned, he repudiates Falstaff and, in *Henry V* (1598), shows himself to be the ideal monarch and a great English hero. Famous scenes include his disguised walk among the common soldiers before Agincourt, a witty flirtation with the French princess, and two great speeches, the "once more unto the breach" and the "St. Crispin's* Day" orations.

Henry VI. Historically, king of England (d. 1471) noted for the chaos brought about by the regency during his youth, his loss of all of France but Calais, and the Wars of the Roses that dominated the last years of his reign. In Shakespeare's plays *Henry VI, Parts I, II, & III* (1590–92), he is a pious but weak-willed man dominated by his wife Margaret.*

Henry VIII. Historically, king of England (d. 1547), father of Mary Tudor* and Elizabeth* I. The most famous male monarch in English history, he is known primarily for making the kingdom Protestant when the Pope refused to grant him a divorce from his first wife Catherine* so that he could marry Anne Boleyn;* his six wives, two of whom he divorced, two of whom he had beheaded, one of whom died a natural death; his conflicts with Catholics such as Thomas More, whom he eventually had executed; and his immense appetites that turned him into the gigantic fat man of folklore and popular modern materials. He also wrote poetry and music and in legend is the composer of the song "Greensleeves."

Hephaestus. In Greek mythology, the god of fire and all crafts related to it, such as the forging of metals; thus, he is usually described as a smith working in a forge. He was said to be so ugly that he was thrown out of Olympus,* breaking his leg when he landed, but was nevertheless married to Aphrodite,* of whom he was quite jealous, with quite good reason. *Also called* Vulcan.* *See also* Apollo.

Hephzibah. (1) In the Bible, *II Kings* xxi, wife of Hezekiah* and mother of Manasseh.* (2) *See also* Hepzibah.

Hepzibah. (1) *See* Pyncheon. (2) *See also* Hephzibah.

Hera. In Greek mythology, sister and wife of Zeus,* queen of the gods, and generally the goddess of women and marriage; she is usually depicted as a rather imposing female, although she felt herself qualified to compete for the title of the fairest goddess in the Judgement of Paris* and killed Rhodope* for thinking herself more beautiful. Most legends see her as matronly and deal with her jealous attempts to prevent her husband's numerous liaisons, or failing that, to wreak vengeance on the mortal women involved, such as Alcmena,* Callisto,* Io,* Lamia,* and Leto.* Her own dalliances are more limited; her most noted suitor was Ixion.* *Also called* Juno.* *See also* Argos; Heracles; Hermes; Tiresias.

Heracles. In Greek legend, the son of Zeus* and Alcmena* and the greatest hero of legend. At his birth, Hera* jealously sent two snakes to kill him, but he strangled them in his cradle. He was instructed in all skills and he excelled in music and poetry as well as in the valorous arts. At the age of eighteen, he was sent to tend his mother's flocks, where he was tempted by Pleasure but chose Virtue. When he returned, he married Megara,* a daughter of Creon* of Thebes, but later was driven mad by Hera and killed his wife and their children. The Delphic oracle* told him to serve Eurystheus,* who assigned him the Twelve Labors, which he accomplished with imagination as well as strength. In other legends, he sacked an early city at Troy;* killed Antaeus;* rescued Alcestis* from Hades;* and fell in love with Iole* and killed her brother, for which the gods condemned him to be the slave of Omphale,* who dressed him in women's clothes. He also married Deianeira,* but his passion for Iole continued; when Deianeira gave him the shirt of Nessus,* thinking it would cure his wandering eye, the poison on the shirt burned his flesh so badly he had himself burned to death to escape the pain. He was at last allowed into Olympus,* where he married Ganymeda.* His Labors were: killing the Nemean Lion;* killing the Hydra;* capturing the Erymanthian Boar;* catching the Cerynean Hind;* killing the Stymphalides;* cleaning the Augean Stables;* capturing the Cretan Bull, also called the Minotaur;* taming the horses of Diomedes;* capturing the girdle of the Amazons* worn by Hippolyta;* stealing the cattle of Geryon,* to reach whose land he had to sail so far west that he passed the edge of known land, which he marked with the Pillars of Heracles (thought to be Gibraltar); finding the golden apples of the Hesperides;* and kidnapping Cerberus* from Hades.* He is always depicted wearing a lion's skin, which is variously the skin of the Nemean Lion or of a lion he killed while still a shepherd. There is also a "thirteenth labor" in which he impregnated 49 of the 50 daughters of Thespius in a single night. The 51 children born of that feat were persecuted after his death by Eurystheus, which is the subject of Euripides's play *Heracleidae*; the death of Megara is depicted in Euripides's play *Heracles* and in Seneca's play *Hercules Furens*. *See also* Busiris; Cacus; Hesione; Hylas; Hyllas; Iolaus; Laomedon; Linus; Macaria; Megara; Philoctetes; Prometheus; Sarpedon.

Herbert. *See* Pocket.

Hercules. The Roman name for Heracles.*

Hermaphroditus. In Greek legend, a son of Aphrodite.* He was loved by a nymph* who desired to be united completely with him; the wish was granted, producing a single person both male and female.

Hermes. In Greek mythology, a son of Zeus,* god of luck and wealth and the messenger of the gods. On the day of his birth, he invented the lyre and stole the cattle of Apollo.* He wore winged sandals and a broad-brimmed hat and carried a caduceus, a staff entwined with snakes, and he is always depicted with these items. He was noted for his speed and his playfulness. *Also called* Mercury.* *See also* Argos; Autolycus; Battus; Chione; Daphnis; Io; Maia.

Hermia. In Shakespeare's play *A Midsummer Night's Dream* (1595), one of the young lovers, the short brunette. She loves Lysander,* but her father prefers Demetrius,* so they run away into the forest where the fairy king Oberon* solves everything.

Hermione. (1) In Greek legend, the wife of Cadmus.* (2) In Greek legend, the daughter of Helen* and Menelaus,* promised to Orestes* but given in marriage to Pyrrhus.* In Racine's play *Andromaque* (1667), she is treacherous and self-centered, playing Orestes against Pyrrhus, and committing suicide when the latter is murdered by the former at her own instigation. (3) In Shakespeare's play *The Winter's Tale* (1610), the noble wife of Leontes* who is wrongly accused of adultery; she is thought to have died in prison until a statue of her comes back to life and she is reunited with Leontes and her now-grown daughter Perdita.*

Hernani. In Victor Hugo's play *Hernani* (1830), a Spanish bandit of great personal honor. The complex plot is rarely mentioned, but the play was the cause of one of the great theatrical riots, due to its violations of the French classical rules of the theater, and it is generally noted as the beginning point of French theatrical romanticism.

Hero. (1) In Greek legend, a beautiful priestess loved by Leander;* when she placed a light in a tower, he swam the Hellespont to see her. One night a storm arose, and he drowned, whereupon she drowned herself. (2) In Shakespeare's play *Much Ado About Nothing* (1598), a gentle, pure young woman betrothed to Claudio* until she is falsely accused of having a lover; she swoons away and is thought dead until Claudio repents, at which point she is restored and they are married. *See also* Beatrice.

Herod. (1) In the Bible, *Matthew*, et al., the king of Judea* when Jesus* was born, called Herod the Great. Fearing a prophecy that a child had been born who would become king, he ordered the massacre of all the children of Bethlehem.* He was often represented as a raving ranter in medieval mystery plays, so that his name also became synonymous with overacting. *See also* Mariamne. (2) In the Bible, *Matthew* xiv, Herod Antipas, the son of Herod. He ruled Galilee and had John the Baptist* beheaded to please his stepdaughter Salome;* he was the ruler when Jesus was crucified. (3) In the Bible, *Acts* xii, Herod Agrippa, the son of Herod Antipas, who brutally persecuted the Christians. (4) In the Bible, *Acts* xxv, Herod Agrippa, the son of Herod Agrippa, brother and husband of Bernice;* he listened to Paul* and would have released him had not Paul already appealed to be tried in Rome.

Herodias. In the Bible, *Matthew* xiv, granddaughter of Herod,* mother of Salome,* and wife of Herod Antipas; John the Baptist's opposition to that marriage led to his imprisonment and death.

Hesione. (1) In Greek legend, the daughter of Laomedon* and sister of Priam.* She was captured by a sea monster; when Heracles rescued her, Laomedon refused to reward him, whereupon Heracles sacked their city, taking her to Greece. It was on a journey to negotiate her return that Paris* met Helen.* (2) *See* Hushabye.

Hespera. A name sometimes used for Aurora.* Later, she was said to accompany the sun and thus was associated more with evening than with dawn. She was sometimes included among the Hesperides.* *See also* Hesperus.

Hesperides. In Greek legend, three daughters of Atlas* who lived far in the west and guarded the sacred golden apples in a garden there, aided by a dragon; Heracles* killed the dragon and stole the apples, but they were returned because they withered when taken away. Apples from this garden were used to defeat Atalanta* and were thrown by Eris* to initiate the Judgement of Paris.*

Hesperus. In Greek mythology, the evening star. *See also* Hespera.

Hester. (1) In Nathaniel Hawthorne's novel *The Scarlet Letter* (1850), Hester Prynne, a young woman in Puritan New England who bears the illegitimate child Pearl* and is forced to wear a scarlet letter ''A'' for ''adulteress.'' She lives a life of absolute rectitude but never names the father, Dimmesdale,* even though she is haunted by the reappearance of her presumed-dead husband Chillingworth.* She gradually reveals a spirit of considerable bravery and noble integrity. (2) *See also* Esther; Hetty.

Hestia. In Greek mythology, the goddess of the hearth; as a chaste goddess of the home, she was not the subject of much legend. *Also called* Vesta.*

Hetty. In George Eliot's novel *Adam Bede* (1859), Hester Sorrel, an innocent country girl seduced and abandoned by Donnithorne;* when she abandons her child, it dies, and she is tried for murder. *See also* Bede.

Hexam. In Charles Dickens's novel *Our Mutual Friend* (1864), **Gaffer** is an illiterate boatman who makes his living pulling junk and bodies which he robs from the Thames. His son **Charlie** coolly rejects all his family in an effort to become respectable. Gaffer's daughter **Lizzie** is a quiet but courageous young woman who tries to maintain the family. Depressed by Gaffer's death, Charlie's rejection, and pursuit by her deranged suitor Headstone, she tries to run away from London, but she is pursued both by Headstone and by Eugene Wrayburn,* whom she had nursed back to life after he was fished out of the river and whom she marries after nursing him again when Headstone jealously tries to murder him.

Heyst, Axel. In Joseph Conrad's novel *Victory* (1915), an enigmatic, passionless man who has maintained his virtue by living like a hermit; when he spontaneously rescues Lena,* he is unable to understand any emotions related to her. When later their island is attacked by outlaws, he is unprepared to cope with such evil and, after she is killed, burns the house down around himself and her.

Hezekiah. In the Bible, *II Kings* xviii–xx, the twelfth king of Judah,* whose reign was saved by the intervention of the angel* that killed Sennacherib's* troops in the night and was lengthened on his deathbed in order for him to hear the prophecy of Isaiah.* *Also called* Ezekias.

Hiawatha. In Henry Wadsworth Longfellow's poem *Hiawatha* (1855), an American Indian brave who speaks to the animals, fights his father the west wind, and initiates a period of peace for his tribe after his marriage to Minnehaha. After a later famine, he leaves, telling his people to be prepared to follow the missionary who will come with a new religion. *See also* Nokomis.

Hickey. In Eugene O'Neill's play *The Iceman Cometh* (1946), a loquacious and colorful salesman who brings inspiration to a saloon full of losers only to reveal that his optimism is a mask for his own failure and guilt; noted especially for his very long monologues.

Hickok, Wild Bill. Historically, an American frontiersman and lawman (d. 1876) known in numerous legends as a great gunfighter and gambler.

Hieronimo. In Thomas Kyd's play *The Spanish Tragedy* (1585), a Spanish noble who, to avenge his son's murder, feigns madness, then stages a play in which he, as an actor, murders his son's killer and then commits suicide; noted primarily as a possible inspiration for Hamlet.*

Higgins. In G. B. Shaw's play *Pygmalion* (1913), a temperamental, dominating bachelor and student of accents who makes a bet he can turn the flower girl Eliza Doolittle* into a duchess simply by teaching her to speak like one. He is also noted for the way he treats everyone equally rudely and the fact that he violates theatrical tradition by not falling in love with Eliza. *See also* Pickering.

Hilara. In Greek legend, the sister of Phoebe* and a maiden abducted by Castor* and Pollux.*

Hilarion, St. Historically, the first known Christian hermit in Palestine (d. 371) where he lived near Gaza* for 50 years until the converts he attracted drove him into the desert in search of new solitude.

Hilda. *See* Wangel.

Hill, Fanny. In John Cleland's novel *Memoirs of Fanny Hill* (1749), a vivacious young girl who is introduced into a brothel and enthusiastically pursues a number of erotic adventures. She and the work are both often cited for her almost innocent pleasure in sexual activity and as one of the quintessential erotic/pornographic literary works.

Hill, Harold. In Meredith Willson's musical comedy *The Music Man* (1957), a fast-talking turn-of-the-century con man who sells an entire town on the idea of a band. *See also* Marian.

Hindley. *See* Earnshaw.

Hippodamia. In Greek legend, a woman who arranged for her father's death during a chariot race so that she could marry Pelops;* this crime led to the curse on the family of their son Atreus.*

Hippogriff. A mythical beast part griffin* and part horse, most noted as the creature on which Astolpho* rides to the moon in Ariosto's *Orlando Furioso* (1532).

Hippolyta. (1) In Greek legend, a queen of the Amazons;* for one of his labors, Heracles* took her girdle, variously described as killing her or receiving it after he seduced her. She was also supposed to have been defeated in battle by Theseus,* whom she then either did or did not marry but nevertheless bore him a son Hippolytus.* Sometimes also called Antiope,* and sometimes treated as her sister. (2) In Greek legend, a queen spurned by Peleus.*

Hippolyte. In Jean Racine's play *Phèdre* (1677), Hippolytus.

Hippolytus. In Greek legend, the son of Theseus* and Hippolyta.* His stepmother Phaedra* fell in love with him, but he spurned her; in revenge, she accused him of trying to seduce her. Theseus asked for Poseidon's* punishment, whereupon Hippolytus was drowned while driving his chariot along the shore. The story is most completely related in Euripides's play *Hippolytus*. In Virgil's *Aeneid*, he is reported to have been rescued by Diana* and to have lived to old age in Italy. *See also* Aricie.

Hippona. In Roman mythology, the goddess of horses.

Hiram. In the Bible, *I Kings* v, a king of Tyre who befriended David;* also, in vii, a great artisan sent by that king to Solomon.*

Hitler, Adolf. Historically, dictator (d. 1945) of Germany before and during World War II, which he is generally given credit for starting. No single figure in history, with the possible exception of Napoleon,* has so completely fascinated the general public, his unprepossessing exterior covering a massive megalomania that made him believe he could and should conquer the world. He is noted for his tiny mustache, the stiff-armed salute accompanied by the phrase "Heil Hitler" that he demanded from all his followers, and his penchant for four-hour radio speeches and massive public rallies that underlined his position as "Der Führer" of the Nazi party and of Germany. He is most often associated with his attempt to exterminate the Jews of Europe in the concentration camps and with the Gestapo,* a secret police force he established that used torture and murder to eliminate all opposition to his policies; thus, he is often used as a personification of pure evil.

Hjalmar. *See* Ekdal.

Hobbit. In J. R. R. Tolkien's novels *The Hobbit* (1937) and *The Lord of the Rings* (1954–55), a humanlike creature noted for its short height, large furry feet, and genial disposition. *See* Baggins, Bilbo; Frodo.

Hobgoblin. *See* Goblin.

Hobson. In British legend, a stableman who gave customers the first horse by the door no matter which they asked for; hence, "Hobson's choice," meaning "take it or leave it" or "no choice at all."

Hogganbeck, Boon. In William Faulkner's story *The Bear* (1942), the gigantic, simple part-Indian who takes care of the camp and the dogs on the hunt, misses the bear five times with a shotgun, and finally kills the bear with a knife to keep it from killing a favorite dog.

Holden. *See* Caulfield, Holden.

Holmes, Sherlock. In numerous stories by Arthur Conan Doyle (beg. 1887), the world's greatest detective, who uses purely rational analysis of the evidence to solve mysteries. He is noted for his pipe, his deerstalker cap, his use of drugs when bored, his violin playing, his devoted friend and chronicler Dr. Watson,* and his ability to make startlingly accurate deductions from physical evidence ignored by normal observers, which he sometimes passes off as "Elementary, my dear Watson." There are countless theatrical, movie, and television versions of the originals, as well as new stories by other authors and parodies. *See also* Adler, Irene; Baskerville; Moriarty.

Holofernes. (1) In the Bible, in the Apocrypha, *Judith*, a Babylonian general who was beheaded by the beautiful Judith* after he got drunk celebrating her agreement to sleep with him. (2) In Rabelais's *Gargantua* (1534), an old-fashioned pedagogue who teaches useless information to Gargantua.* (3) In Shakespeare's play *Love's Labour's Lost* (1595), a village schoolmaster noted for his pedantic, repetitious speech.

Holt, Felix. In George Eliot's novel *Felix Holt, the Radical* (1866), a dedicated social reformer who chooses to live as an artisan to be an example to the poor and to demonstrate that social progress cannot be made by legislation.

Homais. In Gustave Flaubert's novel *Madame Bovary* (1857), a small-town promoter and self-styled liberal who knows the solutions to all the world's problems but whose ideas are in fact trite and hypocritical.

Homer. Historically, the name given to the poet who wrote *Iliad* and *Odyssey*, although it is now thought to be the work of several poets over many years; in legend, he is depicted as a blind wanderer. Generally, he is regarded as not only the first great poet but also as the greatest of all poets; the phrase "even Homer nods," by Horace, is used to indicate that even the greatest of writers or persons is not perfect.

Honeycomb, Will. In numerous *Spectator* stories (1711–12), an aging fop who devotes all his time to finding a wife.

Hood, Robin. *See* Robin Hood.

Hook, Capt. In J. M. Barrie's play *Peter Pan* (1904), the vain pirate captain who has a hook in place of a hand and who pursues Peter Pan* and is in turn pursued by the crocodile that ate his hand and liked the taste.

Horace. (1) In Corneille's play *Horace* (1640), the principal brother of the Horatii* who is willing to sacrifice all personal interests for the sake of his patriotism. In the course of the conflict, he kills his sister's fiancé and his wife's brothers and then his sister as well, but he is pardoned by the king because of his feats in battle. (2) *See* Regina.

Horae. In Greek mythology, the seasons (usually only three in number).

Horatii. In Roman legend, three brothers who were selected to fight three champions from a neighboring city with which Rome was at war.

Horatio. (1) In Shakespeare's play *Hamlet* (1600), Hamlet's* friend from school, who is noted for his sincerity and reliability. (2) *See* Horatius.

Horatius. In Roman legend, a great warrior who bravely held off an invading army single-handedly at the bridge across the Tiber and then swam the river in full armor when the bridge had at last been cut through. His story is best known from T. B. Macaulay's poem *Horatius* (1842), although in common usage, this is often misidentified as "Horatio at the Bridge."

Horner. In William Wycherley's play *The Country Wife* (1673), a rake who spreads a rumor that he is impotent, thereby encouraging husbands to leave their wives with him and the wives to try to cure him. He is most famous for the "china scene," in which he must sequentially make love to several ladies under the guise of showing his china collection. *See also* Fidget; Pinchwife; Sparkish.

Horner, Jack. In the nursery rhyme, a little boy who pulls a plum from his pie and thinks, "What a good boy am I."

Hortense. *See* Hulot.

Hortensio. In Shakespeare's play *The Taming of the Shrew* (1593), a suitor of Bianca* who disguises himself as a musician to see her; when she marries Lucentio,* he in turn weds a rich widow.

Hotspur. In Shakespeare's play *Henry IV, Part I* (1597), a brave, honorable, and skilled knight, noted for his short temper and his impetuosity in battle, an admirable counterfoil to the riotous Prince Hal.* When he joins a revolt against Henry IV,* he meets Hal and is killed by him, although Falstaff* later tries to take credit for the dead body. He is also noted for a remarkably gentle and playful scene with his young wife. *Also called* Henry Percy.

Hosea. In the Bible, *Hosea*, a prophet who denounced idolatries in Israel.*

Hoshea. (1) The original name of Joshua.* (2) In the Bible, *II Kings* xv, the last king of Israel,* who was captured by the Assyrians. *See also* Shalmaneser.

Houri. In Moslem legend, a beautiful woman who serves those men who go to Paradise* after their death.

Houyhnhnm. In Jonathan Swift's novel *Gulliver's Travels* (1726), creatures who look like horses but have intelligence, courtesy, and rational behavior; they keep as servants the crude, humanlike Yahoos.* After time spent with them, Gulliver* can no longer stand human companions, and when he returns to England he goes to live in his stable.

Howdy Doody. In the American television series "Howdy Doody" (1948–60), a freckle-faced boy puppet, for many synonymous with children's entertainment and with simpleminded pleasures.

Hoyden, Miss. In John Vanbrugh's play *The Relapse* (1696), a nubile, playful heiress who marries both Young Fashion* and his brother Novelty.

Hrothgar. In the anonymous *Beowulf*, the lord of the Danes whose hall is attacked by Grendel* and saved by Beowulf.*

Hubbard. In Lillian Hellman's play *The Little Foxes* (1939), the quintessential materialistic Southern family, willing to do anything for money and property development, represented by the brothers Benjamin and Oscar and their married sister Regina.*

Hubert, St. Historically, a bishop (d. 727) noted for his missionary activities; in legend, he converted after he saw a cross between the antlers of a stag. *See also* Eustace, St.

Huck. *See* Finn, Huck.

Hudson. In the British television series "Upstairs, Downstairs" (beg 1972), also seen in the United States (beg. 1974), the prototypical butler for the Bellamy* family, noted for his restraint, propriety, and lack of humor. *See also* Rose.

Hugh of Lincoln, St. (1) Historically, a bishop of England (d. 1200) known for his support of the common people against the king's foresters, his ability to calm King Henry II* with a joke, and his stand against rioters out to murder the Jews; he also appears in some versions of the Robin Hood* legends. His emblem is a swan, from a favorite pet, and his day is November 17. (2) Historically, a nine-year-old boy found dead in a well in 1255, whose death was ascribed to ritual murder by Jews; often called Little St. Hugh. *See also* William of Norwich.

Hulot. (1) In Balzac's novel *Cousin Bette* (1847), the **Baron** is a profligate who squanders on courtesans what money he does not lose in speculation, at last giving his faithful and long-suffering wife **Adeline** a heart attack when she discovers his affair with a kitchen maid. His most costly affair is with Mme. Marneffe,* who is introduced to him by Cousin Bette* because she is insanely jealous of his daughter **Hortense**, a beautiful but thoughtless girl who marries the artist Steinbock,* whom Bette herself loves. (2) In several movies, especially *Mr. Hulot's Holiday* (1952), a genial, shy, and awkward middle-aged man who finds himself humorously trapped by the little things of everyday life.

Humbert, Humbert. In Vladimir Nabokov's novel *Lolita* (1955), an intellectual, middle-aged European who suddenly discovers he is passionately in love (and in lust) with Lolita,* an American girl barely in her teens, whom he takes on a long, wandering drive across America.

Humpty Dumpty. In the nursery rhyme, the egg that fell and could not be put back together again.

Hun. Historically, a tribe of barbarians from the Eurasian plains noted for cruelty and barbarianism as a result of their fifth-century marauding led by Attila* that reached even to the gates of Rome. When Kaiser Wilhelm told his troops in China in 1900 to fight like Huns, the story was so widely circulated that, in World War I, the Germans were called the Hun.

Hunchback. The most notable literary hunchback is perhaps Quasimodo,* but such allusions are also made to Richard III,* Rigoletto,* and Igor.*

Hunding. In Richard Wagner's opera *Die Walküre* (1870), Sieglinde's* husband who is allowed by Wotan* to kill Siegmund.*

Hundred Days, The. *See* Napoleon.

Hurstwood. In Theodore Dreiser's novel *Sister Carrie* (1912), **George** is a successful businessman whose love for Carrie* leads him into embezzlement, which begins a long and painful decline that his own pride does not allow him to reverse. **Mrs. Hurstwood** is a cold, conformist woman devoted to social activities.

Hushabye. In G. B. Shaw's play *Heartbreak House* (1919), the "artistic" couple. **Hector** is a handsome romantic who tells outrageous lies about his deeds in order to avoid boasting about his real actions. His wife **Hesione** is a sensitive, attractive, and extremely intelligent woman who uses romance to cope with her own boredom. *See also* Dunn; Mangan; Shotover, Capt.; Utterword, Lady.

Hyacinthus. In Greek legend, a beautiful young man loved by both Apollo* and Zephyrus.* When Apollo threw a discus, Zephyrus jealously blew it off course, and it struck and killed the boy. In Ovid's *Metamorphoses*, the discus glances off a rock, and Hyacinthus is changed into a flower.

Hyde. In R. L. Stevenson's story *Dr. Jekyll and Mr. Hyde* (1886), the evil side of Dr. Jekyll's* personality, released when Jekyll takes an experimental drug. A seducer and murderer, he is often cited as a personification of pure evil.

Hydra. In Greek legend, a great serpent with many heads (sources vary from 7 to 50) that was killed by Heracles.* When he cut off one head, two more grew in its place, so he cauterized each wound with a hot iron until they had all been cut off. The blood of the Hydra was poisonous, and Heracles dipped all his arrows in it. Years later, this backfired when Heracles killed Nessus* with one of the arrows, and the poison mixed with the blood on Nessus's shirt—when the shirt was given to Heracles, the poison killed him.

Hygeia. In Greek mythology, the daughter of Aesculapius* and the goddess of health. *Also called* Salus.* *See also* Iasus; Panacea.

Hylas. In Greek legend, a beautiful page of Heracles.* He was kidnapped for his beauty by water nymphs;* in order to search for him, Heracles abandoned his participation in the search for the Golden Fleece.*

Hyllas. In Greek legend, Heracles's* son and the killer of Eurystheus.*

Hyllus. *See* Hyllas.

Hymen. In Greek mythology, the god of marriage, usually the leader of a celebratory chorus at the wedding feast.

Hyperboreans. In Greek legend, a race of people who lived far to the north in peace and happiness.

Hyperion. In Greek mythology, a Titan,* a son of Uranus* and the father of the sun and moon; the name is often used for the sun.

Hypermnestra. In Greek legend, the only Danaid* not to murder her husband and, with her husband Lynceus, founder of the people of Argos.*

Hypnos. In Greek mythology, the god of sleep and the father of Morpheus.* *Also called* Somnus.*

Hypsipyle. In Greek legend, a princess of Lemnos* who helped her father escape when the women of the island killed all the men there. When the Argonauts* landed, they impregnated all the women, and Hypsipyle bore twin sons to Jason,* who nonetheless deserted her; she was then driven into exile by the remaining women.

I

Iacchus. A name sometimes used for Bacchus.*

Iachimo. In Shakespeare's play *Cymbeline* (1609), a villainous Italian. He unsuccessfully tries to seduce Imogen* and in revenge for her refusal hides in a trunk and steals her bracelet, thereby convincing her husband of her infidelity.

Iago. In Shakespeare's play *Othello* (1604), the consummate villain. Outraged at being passed over for promotion, he plots the downfall of Cassio,* the man promoted, and Othello,* the general who promoted him. Alert, intelligent, malevolent, yet outwardly "honest Iago," he worms his way into Othello's confidence and convinces him that his wife Desdemona* is adulterous. Ultimately, Iago is exposed by his wife Emilia,* but not before Othello has killed Desdemona and has been ruined. Iago is then led away to torture refusing to explain what he had done. Many have seen him as a figure of pure, unmotivated malevolence. *See also* Roderigo.

Iago, St. The Spanish name for St. James.*

Ianthe. In Ovid's *Metamorphoses*, a girl in love with another woman Iphis;* Iphis was changed into a man so that they might be married.

Iapetus. In Greek mythology, a Titan,* the father of Atlas* and Prometheus;* sometimes credited as father of all mankind.

Iasus. In Greek mythology, the goddess of healing. *See also* Hygeia;* Panacea.*

Ibbetson, Peter. In George du Maurier's novel *Peter Ibbetson* (1891), a shy, dreamy young man who kills his uncle in a rage and who retreats into insanity, living in a dream world with his childhood sweetheart Mimsey.*

Ibraham. In the Koran, Abraham.*

Icarius. (1) In Greek legend, a human who received the gift of wine from Dionysus;* when Icarius shared it with others, however, they lost control and killed him. (2) In Homer's *Odyssey*, Penelope's* father.

Icarus. In Greek legend, the son of Daedalus.* When his father made him a set of wings from wax and feathers, he flew, but he ignored his father's warning and flew so near the sun that the wax melted and he crashed into the sea and drowned.

Ichabod. (1) In the Bible, *I Samuel* iv, the child of Phinehas.* His mother delivered him prematurely in shock at the death of her husband and of Eli* and the loss of the ark,* then refused to look at him, naming him for the shame of those events. (2) *See* Crane, Ichabod.

Ichthus. In Christian tradition, an anagram formed from the initial Greek letters signifying Jesus* Christ, Son of God, Savior. As they also spell the Greek word for fish, the fish was used as a secret symbol to identify early Christians to each other.

Ichthys. *See* Ichthus.

Idaea. A name sometimes used for Rhea.*

Idas. In Greek legend, a valiant warrior who loved Marpessa.* Apollo* abducted her and Idas gave chase, challenging the god to battle; given a choice by Zeus,* Marpessa chose Idas.

Iden. In Shakespeare's play *Henry VI, Part II* (1592), the commonsensical country gentleman who kills Jack Cade.*

Ides. In the Roman calendar, in some months the 13th, in others the 15th; the Ides of March, when Julius Caesar* was assassinated, was March 15.

Idomeneus. In Greek legend, the leader of the Cretan forces in the Trojan War.* On his way home, a storm arose, and he promised to sacrifice the first thing he saw on land if Poseidon* would spare him; when he landed, he was met by his son.

Iduna. In Scandinavian mythology, a goddess who kept the golden apples that the other gods ate to maintain eternal youth and who was often associated with fruits and fertility.

Ignatius, St. (1) Historically, Ignatius of Antioch, a second-century martyr who was thrown to the bears; noted for a set of surviving letters describing early Christian life. His day is October 17. (2) Historically, Ignatius of Loyola (d. 1556), a soldier who converted and founded the Society of Jesus, or Jesuits; his day is July 31.

Ignatz. In the American newspaper cartoon *Krazy Kat* (1910–44), the mouse with the love-hate relationship with Krazy Kat,* noted primarily for the bricks he regularly threw at her.

Igor. (1) In the anonymous poem *The Campaign of Igor*, a Russian prince who is defeated, is captured by the Poles, and eventually escapes to return to his wife, who is described in a famous lament. (2) In the movie *Frankenstein* (1931), the hunchback servant of Dr. Frankenstein,* so often imitated as to become a defining cliché of the horror movie genre.

Igraine. In Malory's *Morte d'Arthur*, mother of Arthur;* she was impregnated by Uther Pendragon* when Merlin* the magician changed him into the shape of her husband.

Ilia. In Roman legend, mother of Romulus* and Remus.*

Ilium. A name sometimes used for Troy.*

Illuminati. Historically, one of several secret sects claiming special knowledge or insight, the most noted being a Bavarian group of which Goethe was a member; the term is often used satirically.

Illyria. In Greek legend, the western land where Cadmus* lived after he left Thebes. Shakespeare set his play *Twelfth Night* (1599) there.

Ilych, Ivan. *See* Ivan.

Immanuel. In the Bible, *Isaiah* vii, a name meaning "God is with us," given to the prophesied Messiah* and thus usually signifying Jesus.*

Imogen. In Shakespeare's play *Cymbeline* (1609), the admirable and beautiful daughter of Cymbeline.* Against her father's wishes, she marries the impoverished noble Posthumus,* but he is wrongly convinced of her adultery by the villain Iachimo.* She disguises herself as a man to avoid Posthumus's attempt to kill her and is almost raped by her stepbrother Cloten.* Eventually, she is reconciled to both her husband and her father. The scene in which she awakens beside Cloten's headless body, which she believes to be her husband's, was much admired, particularly in the nineteenth century.

Imp. In European legend, a small devil* or a devil's child.

Indigetes. In Greek mythology, a generic name for gods who were known only in small localities.

Indra. In Hindu mythology, the god of the air and of rain.

Ines. *See* Inez.

Inez. (1) In Byron's poem *Don Juan* (1819–24), Don Juan's* domineering mother who tries to keep him innocent. (2) In José Zorrilla's play *Don Juan Tenorio* (1844), a pure woman with whom Don Juan* falls in love and whose prayers save him from damnation.

Infant Phenomenon. *See* Crummles.

Ingrid. In Henrik Ibsen's play *Peer Gynt* (1867), a neighbor girl whom Peer Gynt* abducts on her wedding day.

Injun Joe. *See* Joe, Injun.

Innisfail. An ancient name for Ireland, often used by poets, not to be confused with the "Isle of Innisfree" in W. B. Yeats's poem of that name, which is an actual small island in Lough Gill in County Sligo.

Innisfree. *See* Innisfail.

Ino. In Greek legend, a daughter of Cadmus* who became a wicked stepmother and tried to murder her stepchildren before they managed to escape on a golden ram. In Euripides's play *The Bacchae*, she helps her sister Agave* tear the body of Pentheus.*

Inspector General. *See* Klestakov.

Invisible Man. (1) In H. G. Wells's story *The Invisible Man* (1897), a scientist who has discovered a formula for invisiblity but who gradually goes insane and becomes a criminal. (2) In Richard Wright's novel *The Invisible Man* (1952), a nameless young American Negro male who feels that his true self is invisible, at first because of his race; ultimately, he perceives that this invisibility is a common aspect of all modern existence.

Io. In Greek legend, a beautiful woman loved by Zeus.* To escape Hera's* observation, Zeus changed Io into a heifer, but Hera then sent Argos* to guard the heifer, and Zeus sent Hermes* to kill Argos. Hera then sent one of the Eumenides* to torment Io, driving her away until she came to Egypt, where she was changed back to a woman and bore Zeus a son.

Iocaste. *See* Jocasta.

Iolaus. In Greek legend, a friend who helps Heracles* kill the Hydra;* he also guards Heracles's children in Euripides's play *Heracleidae*.

Iole. In Greek legend, a woman carried off by Heracles;* in hopes of winning him back from her, his wife Deianeira* gave him the garment that killed him.

Ion. In Greek legend and in Euripides's play *Ion*, an abandoned child of Creusa* and Apollo.* When Creusa later married, she was childless, and her husband promised to adopt the first child to appear, which was Ion. Creusa, however, thought this to be her husband's bastard and tried to kill him, until a priestess revealed the truth and all were reconciled. Ion then became the ancestor of all the Ionians of the Aegean.

Iphigenia. In Greek legend, daughter of Agamemnon* and Clytemnestra.* When the Greeks prepared to attack Troy* from Aulis, the winds were unfavorable, and a seer claimed that the gods wanted Agamemnon to sacrifice Iphigenia in return for a stag of Artemis* that Agamemnon had killed. At the last moment, the gods substituted a stag for her, and she was transported to Tauris where she became a priestess of Artemis. In Euripides's play *Iphigenia at Aulis*, she is tricked into appearing at the sacrifice by a promise of marriage to Achilles,* but she goes bravely to her expected death when she learns the truth. In Euripides's play *Iphigenia at Tauris*, local custom demands that she sacrifice all strange men to Artemis, but when her brother Orestes* arrives on a quest to expiate his guilt, she runs away with him. In Racine's play *Iphegénie en Aulide* (1674), she is willing to go gladly to her death, even though Achilles threatens armed intervention to prevent it, until the seer announces that another Iphigenia is the one required. *Also called* Chrysothemis.

Iphis. (1) In Ovid's *Metamorphoses*, a woman who was raised as a boy and who loved another woman Ianthe;* Iphis was then changed into a man so that the two might marry. (2) In Ovid's *Metamorphoses*, a young man who hanged himself when he was rejected by Anaxarete;* when she was unmoved by the sight of his body, she was changed into a stone.

Iphitus. In Homer's *Odyssey*, the brother of Iole;* he gave Odysseus* his great bow.

Ipthime. In Homer's *Odyssey*, Penelope's* sister; when Athena* wished to speak to Penelope, she took Ipthime's form.

Ira. In the Bible, *II Samuel* xx, a priest who served David.*

Iras. In Shakespeare's play *Antony and Cleopatra* (1606), Cleopatra's* faithful maid, who commits suicide with her. *See also* Charmian.

Irena. *See* Irene; Irina.

Irene. (1) In Greek mythology, the goddess of peace. *See also* Concordia; Pax. (2) *See* Forsyte. (3) *See also* Irina.

Irijah. In the Bible, *Jeremiah* xxxvii, the captain who arrested Jeremiah.*

Irina. (1) In Anton Chekhov's play *Three Sisters* (1901), the youngest and prettiest sister whose chance to leave is lost when her fiancé Tusenbach* is killed in a duel. She is the source of the principal parodied element of the play: her persistent repetitions of her dream of going to Moscow. *See also* Masha; Olga; Prozorov; Solyony. (2) *See* Arkadina, Irina. (3) *See also* Irene.

Iris. (1) In Greek mythology, the goddess of the rainbow, sometimes used as a messenger between the gods and the earth. In Aristophanes's play *The Birds*, she is sent back from Cloudcuckooland* by the birds. (2) *See also* Iras; Irus.

Iron Mask, Man in the. Historically, a mysterious seventeenth-century French prisoner whose identity was hidden by an iron mask; legend says he might have been any one of a number of famous personages. In Alexandre Dumas's novel

The Man in the Iron Mask (1847), he is a twin of Louis XIV* who later becomes Louis XIV himself after he replaces his twin on the throne.

Iron Maiden. Historically, a medieval torture device consisting of a case much like a mummy* case but with spikes in the cover that penetrate the victim when the cover is closed. There is some question as to how many of these were actually used, but in folklore they rank with the rack as the quintessential symbols of torture.

Ironsides. (1) Historically, the admiring nickname for Cromwell's* soldiers. (2) Historically, the nickname for the American ship *Constitution*, rescued from destruction and carried into legend by Oliver Wendell Holmes's poem *Old Ironsides* (1830).

Irus. (1) In Homer's *Odyssey*, a beggar who acts as a messenger for the suitors and whom Odysseus* knocks down when Irus tries to throw him out of the house. *See also* Penelope. (2) In numerous *Spectator* stories (1711–12) featuring Roger de Coverley,* a countryman who saves everything for fear of being thought poor. *See also* Laertes.

Isaac. (1) In the Bible, *Genesis*, the son of Abraham* and Sarah,* born to Sarah after many years of barrenness. When Isaac was young, God demanded that he be sacrificed, and Abraham prepared to do so, but the child was saved when at the last moment God sent a ram to be sacrificed in his place. When Isaac matured, he married Rebecca* and fathered Esau* and Jacob;* when he went to the land of Gerar, he pretended that Rebecca was his sister until he was caught ''sporting'' with her. He also dug the wells of Beersheba. In his old age, he was deceived by Jacob's disguise and blessed Jacob by mistake. (2) In R. B. Sheridan's play *The Duenna* (1775), an odious little Jew who wants to marry the young heiress but is tricked into marrying the duenna. (3) In Walter Scott's novel *Ivanhoe* (1820), a kindly Jew, father of Rebecca* and friend of Ivanhoe;* he is forced to pay an enormous ransom for himself, and, after Rebecca is rescued, he takes her to Spain.

Isabel. (1) *See* Archer, Isabel. (2) *See also* Isabella; Isabelle.

Isabella. (1) Historically, queen (d. 1504) of a united Spain with her husband Ferdinand. She expelled the Jews, conquered the Moors, and took control of the Inquisition, but her most prominent position in literature and legend is as the underwriter of the voyages of Columbus.* (2) In Ariosto's *Orlando Furioso* (1532), the Saracen maiden who loves Zerbino;* after his death, she forces Rodomont* to kill her to protect her reputation. (3) In Thomas Kyd's play *The Spanish Tragedy* (1585), Hieronimo's* wife, who goes insane when her son is murdered. (4) In Shakespeare's play *Measure for Measure* (1604), the noblewoman who emerges from a nunnery to plead for her brother Claudio's* life. When Angelo* demands that she trade her virginity for her brother's life, she refuses, an attitude that has brought much confusion and disagreement to audiences and critics over the years. (5) In John Webster's play *The White Devil* (1612), the patient wife who dies from devotedly kissing a poisoned portrait of her husband. (6) In Thomas Middleton's play *Women Beware Women* (1621), a young woman in love with her uncle Hippolito.* She marries another but continues her affair with him, until her aunt Livia* admits the affair is incestuous, after which Isabella poisons Livia as Livia kills her. (7) In Middleton and Rowley's play *The Changeling* (1622), the bored housewife; in order to court her, Antonio* pretends to be insane. (8) *See* Linton. (9) *See also* Isabel; Isabelle.

Isabelle. (1) In Molière's play *The School for Husbands* (1661), the beautiful young ward whom Sganarelle* keeps secluded and ignorant in hopes that she will marry him. (2) In Walter Scott's novel *Quentin Durward* (1823), the Countess de Croye who becomes a pawn between various French political forces; Durward* rescues her from bandits twice and after the second time marries her. (3) *See also* Isabel; Isabella.

Isaiah. In the Bible, *Isaiah*, one of the greatest of the prophets, noted primarily for his foretelling of the coming of the Messiah,* who should "feed his flock like a shepherd." *See also* Hezekiah.

Isak. *See* Isaac.

Iscariot, Judas. *See* Judas.

Isegrim. In French folklore, the wolf who was forced to give his shoes to Reynard* and who fought a duel with Reynard after the fox tricked Isegrim's wife into dangling her tail into freezing water to catch fish, which instead resulted only in freezing her tail in the ice where she was trapped and almost killed by villagers.

Iseult. *See* Isoud.

Ishmael. (1) In the Bible, *Genesis*, son of Abraham* and Hagar;* he was a "wild man" who became the father of a tribe of nomadic wanderers. (2) In Herman Melville's novel *Moby-Dick* (1851), the narrator, a sailor who goes to sea whenever it is "November in my soul," and who joins Capt. Ahab's* voyage. He is most noted for his meeting with the cannibal Queequeg* when he is forced to share a bed with him in an inn and his solitary escape floating on Queequeg's coffin after Moby Dick* sinks his ship.

Ishtar. (1) Principal goddess of Mesopotamia and Babylonia, the goddess of fertility and war. *Also called* Astarte.* (2) *See also* Esther.

Isis. In Egyptian mythology, the sister and wife of Osiris* and the goddess of fertility.

Ismene. In Greek legend, daughter of Oedipus* and Jocasta* and sister of Antigone.* In Sophocles's play *Antigone*, she is a timid and gentle woman who claims to be too weak to help Antigone bury Polynices,* but she is willing to share in Antigone's punishment, although she is not ultimately punished. In most retellings of the Antigone story, if she appears, it is as a similar, more traditionally feminine, foil for her sister. In Sophocles's play *Oedipus at Colonus*, she is pious and more active, and she follows the wandering Oedipus and Antigone to Colonus.

Isolde. In Gottfried von Strassbourg's poem *Tristram und Isolde*, essentially the same as Isoud;* her story currently is most widely known through Richard Wagner's opera *Tristan und Isolde* (1865).

Isolt. In Tennyson's poem *The Last Tournament* (1871), Isoud.*

Isoud. In Malory's *Morte d'Arthur*, an Irish princess betrothed to King Mark.* When the knight Tristram* is sent to escort her, they fall in love and continue their affair even after she marries the king and he marries a different Isoud. In some other versions, Tristram sends for Isoud with directions that she should show a white sail; when a black sail is shown by mistake, he dies of grief, and she kills herself over his body. *Also called* Iseult; Isolde;* Isolt;* Yseult.

Israel. In the Bible, the name given by God to Jacob* and the name by which all his children and the children of Joseph* were called to indicate their position as God's chosen people. The term meant at various times the twelve tribes or the land controlled and ruled by the twelve tribes (except for the Levites, who were priests and had no fixed land). Noted kings of the land were Saul,* David,* and Solomon.* When Solomon's son Rehoboam* took the throne, the ten northern tribes revolted and retained the name Israel, while the southern part of the land was called Judah. After the Jews were dispersed, the term continued to be used in its earlier Biblical sense by Jew and Christian alike, but it often took on derogatory meanings among Christians and was used as a name for stereotypical Jews. In the twentieth century, it also came to be applied to Palestine and then to the independent Jewish nation established in 1948. The tribes were Asher,* Benjamin,* Dan,* Gad,* Issachar,* Judah,* Levi,* Napthali,* Reuben,* Simeon,* and Zebulon;* Joseph's tribe was variously called by the names of his sons, Ephraim* and/or Manasseh.

Israfel. In Moslem usage, the angel* who will sound the trumpet on judgement day. *See also* Gabriel.

Issachar. In the Bible, *Genesis* xxxv, the son of Jacob* and Leah* and the father of one of the twelve tribes of Israel.*

Ithaca. In Homer's *Iliad* and *Odyssey*, the island home of Odysseus.*

Ithamore. In Christopher Marlowe's play *The Jew of Malta* (1589), a slave of Barabas;* he eagerly assists in his master's crimes and then betrays Barabas for a woman.

Ithuriel. In John Milton's poem *Paradise Lost* (1667), one of the Cherubim,* a touch of whose spear forces anyone to tell the truth.

Itys. In Greek legend, the son of Tereus* and Procne;* he was killed, cooked, and served to his father by his mother after his father had raped Philomela,* Procne's sister.

Ivan. (1) The Russian equivalent of John and, as such, a name often used generically for any Russian. (2) Historically, the name used by several Russian czars, the most noted being **Ivan III**, the Great (d. 1505), who drove out the Tartars; and **Ivan IV**, the Terrible (d. 1584), the first to actually use the title czar, who was noted for a long reign of terror in which he murdered numerous opponents, including his own son. (3) In Tolstoy's story *The Death of Ivan Ilych* (1886), an ordinary middle-class man who dies of internal injuries from a minor fall while decorating the Christmas tree and through whose perceptions the author studies the average man's approach to the meaning of death. (4) *See* Karamazov.

Ivanhoe. In Walter Scott's novel *Ivanhoe* (1819), a brave Saxon knight who joins Richard I* in the Crusade. On their return to England incognito, he fights and is wounded in a tournament; is imprisoned with Isaac,* whom he had befriended earlier and who, along with his daughter Rebecca,* is tending him; is eventually rescued by Richard; and then defends Rebecca at her witchcraft trial. He ultimately marries the "fair Rowena."* *See also* Cedric; Gurth.

Ivanova, Charlotte. In Anton Chekhov's play *The Cherry Orchard* (1904), the enigmatic governess, a woman without a class, a past, or a future; she does magic tricks.

Ivanovich, Alexi. In Dostoevsky's novel *The Gambler* (1866), the compulsive gambler.

Ivanovna, Aglaya. *See* Aglaya.

Ivanovna, Alonya. *See* Alonya.

Ivanovna, Katerina. In Dostoevsky's novel *The Brothers Karamazov* (1880), a passionate, aristocratic woman who is betrothed to Dimitri Karamazov.* Spurned by him, and despite her love for his brother Ivan, she determines to watch over him; at one point, she even tries to bribe Grushenka* to leave Dimitri alone. After Dimitri is arrested, however, she gives the court a letter in which he threatened to kill his father, which clinches the case against him.

Ixion. In Greek legend, the first murderer; he killed his father-in-law. Later, he tried to seduce Hera,* but Zeus* substituted a cloud shaped like Hera, to which Ixion made love and fathered the centaurs.* He was condemned to revolve on a wheel in Hades.*

J

J. R. *See* Ewing.

Jabal. In the Bible, *Genesis* iv, a son of Lamech* and the father of all nomads who "dwell in tents." *See also* Jubal; Noah; Tubalcain.

Jabberwock. In Lewis Carroll's poem *Jabberwocky* (1872), a monster "with eyes of flame."

Jabez. In the Bible, *I Chronicles* iv, a son of Judah,* more honorable to the Lord than his brothers.

Jack. (1) A nickname for John* and hence, in English folklore, a common name for a common man, usually a young man or boy, as in Jack Tar, Jack-in-the-box, and Jack jump over the candlestick. He is the silly country boy who trades his cow for magic beans, which grow into a beanstalk that he climbs to a giant's kingdom; after he kills the giant, he captures a goose that lays golden eggs. Another Jack the Giant-Killer kills numerous giants with the aid of a coat that makes him invisible. Jack and Jill go up the hill and fall down again, and Jack breaks his crown, part of a long usage identifying Jack and Jill as typical young lovers. Such generalized usage continues in the twentieth century in such slang as, "I'm all right, Jack." *See also* Sprat, Jack. (2) *See* Point, Jack; Tanner, John; Worthing, Jack.

Jack, Captain. *See* Boyle.

Jack the Ripper. Historically, a never-captured murderer who stabbed several prostitutes in London (1888–89) and who has captured the public imagination throughout the century since.

Jacob. (1) In the Bible, *Genesis* xxv–1, a son of Isaac* and the father of the Jewish nation. As a youth, he traded his elder brother Esau* a mess of pottage for the latter's birthright and then tricked Isaac into giving him his blessing by disguising himself in hairy robes. While fleeing Esau's wrath, he saw a vision of angels* ascending a ladder to Heaven. In the land of Laban,* he fell in love with Rachel;* he worked seven years to gain her hand but was tricked and was given Leah* and worked another seven to win Rachel anyway. On his return with his family, he wrestled with an angel and was given the name Israel.* In his old age, he went to Egypt, where his son Joseph* had become a powerful figure. For his other sons, *see* Israel. (2) In the Bible, *Matthew* i, the father of Joseph* and the ostensible grandfather of Jesus.* (3) In Latin, Jacobus is generally understood to be the equivalent of James;* hence, James and Jacob are sometimes used interchangeably, particularly in Catholic writings. (4) *See also* Jacques; Jaques.

Jacobin. Historically, a group of radicals in the French Revolution who met in a disused convent of St. Jacques; the term is sometimes used for any radical social reformers.

Jacobite. *See* James.

Jacques. (1) The French form of Jacob,* also related to James* through the Latin form Jacobus, often used in English as a stereotypical name for any Frenchman and in French as a stereotypical name for a peasant since at least the Jacquerie uprisings in 1358. (2) In Molière's play *The Miser* (1668), Harpagon's* outspoken but loyal coachman, given to practical jokes. (3) *See also* Jaques.

Jael. In the Bible, *Judges* iv, a nomadic woman who offered shelter to Sisera* after he lost the battle with Deborah* and who then killed him by driving a nail through his head while he rested.

Jaffier. In Thomas Otway's play *Venice Preserved* (1682), the husband of Belvidera;* left penniless and dishonored by her father, he becomes enmeshed in a complex plot to overthrow the senate and demonstrates his true sense of honor by killing himself and his friend Pierre.

Jaggers. In Charles Dickens's novel *Great Expectations* (1860), the gruff lawyer interested only in provable facts. *See also* Wemmick.

James. (1) In the Bible, two of the apostles* of Jesus.* James "the Greater," the son of Zebedee* and brother of the apostle John,* was the first martyr, killed by Herod* Agrippa. In legend, he visited Spain to preach and later his body was brought to Spain, where he continues to be prominent as St. Iago, and his day is celebrated on July 25. James "the Lesser" became one of the first leaders of the Christians in Jerusalem* until he was stoned to death; his day is May 3. *Also called* Jacob, from the Latin form Jacobus; Jacques. (2) In the Bible, *Matthew* xiii, the son of Joseph* and the brother of Jesus. He is also thought to be the author of the epistle called *James*. In Catholic theology, since Mary* is without sin, the brotherhood expressed here is believed to be a purely metaphorical statement of his close ties with the Apostles. (3) Historically, the name used by six kings of Scotland and two kings of England, the most noted of whom was James I of England (also James VI of Scotland) (d. 1625) who succeeded Elizabeth* I, thereby uniting the thrones of both countries, and who authorized the standardized Bible known as the King James Version. Later claimants of the throne from his family, who had been displaced by William* and Mary, and their followers were called Jacobites, from Jacobus, the Latin equivalent of James. (4) In modern usage, a stereotypical name for a servant, especially a chauffeur. (5) *See also* Iago; Jacob; Jacques; Jim; Jimmy.

James, Jesse. Historically, an American outlaw (d. 1882) whose gang staged the first successful daylight bank robbery in America; in legend, he was seen as the most dangerous outlaw as well as an American Robin Hood.*

James, St. Either James* "the Greater" or James "the Less."

Jane. (1) In numerous novels by Edgar Rice Burroughs (beg. 1914), and especially in numerous movies, Tarzan's* female companion, denoted by the catch-phrase from the movies, "Me Tarzan, you Jane." (2) *See* Bennet; Dick and Jane; Eyre, Jane; Grey, Lady Jane.

Jane, Lady. *See* Grey, Lady Jane.

Janus. In Roman mythology, the god of beginnings and endings, usually represented as a god with two faces; the month of January is named for him.

Japheth. In the Bible, *Genesis* v–ix, the second son of Noah;* he was reputed to be the father of the Gentiles. *See also* Ham; Shem.

Jaques. (1) In Shakespeare's play *As You Like It* (1599), the melancholy follower of the Duke in the Forest of Arden,* noted for his ability to draw melancholy from the most pleasant circumstances and for his Seven Ages of Man* speech. (2) *See also* Jacques.

Jarley, Mrs. In Charles Dickens's novel *The Old Curiosity Shop* (1840), proprietor of the traveling waxworks who simply changes the signs on the dummies when she wants to depict a new character.

Jarndyce. In Charles Dickens's novel *Bleak House* (1852), *Jarndyce vs. Jarndyce* is the name of a lawsuit which drags on so long that the entire estate is paid out in lawyers' fees and the children who began as principals have time to grow old and die. **John** Jarndyce is a distant participant who tries to avoid all contact with the suit, but is drawn back in when he is made the guardian of Ada Clare* and Richard Carstone,* two youthful parties involved; he is genial and generous, retreating to his "Growlery" whenever he is upset and withdrawing his proposal to Esther Summerson* when he realizes she loves another. *See also* Boythorn; Flite, Miss; Skimpole.

Jason. (1) In Greek legend, a hero who sailed with the Argonauts* in search of the golden fleece of a ram of Colchis. In order to obtain that fleece, he had to perform several labors, the most notable of which were to yoke the fire-breathing bulls and to kill the warriors who grew from a set of dragon's teeth sown in a field. The king's daughter Medea* returned with him and bore him two children, but when he decided to desert her in favor of Creon's* daughter, she killed the bride-to-be and Jason's children. In Euripides's play *Medea*, he is condemned as an unfaithful husband and draws sympathy only through his genuine love for his children. In the course of the voyage, he also seduced and abandoned Hypsipyle,* for which he is condemned to Hell* as a seducer in Dante's *Divine Comedy*. (2) In the Bible, *Acts* xvii, a Christian with whom Paul* stayed in Thessalonica. (3) *See* Compson.

Javert. In Victor Hugo's novel *Les Misérables* (1862), the relentless policeman who pursues Jean Valjean* for years; when Valjean eventually risks his own capture by saving Javert's life on the barricades of a revolution, the conflict between Javert's gratitude and his sense of duty leads him to drown himself. *See also* Fantine.

Jean. (1) The French equivalent of John.* (2) In August Strindberg's play *Miss Julie* (1888), the valet who sleeps with Julie,* a crude but complex man who begins to dominate her after their sexual relations. (3) *See* Valjean, Jean.

Jean-Christophe. In Romain Rolland's novels *Jean-Christophe* (1906–12), a genius and composer who epitomizes the creative life of the artist.

Jeanie. *See* Deans.

Jeanne d'Arc. Historically, a French peasant girl (d. 1431), called Joan of Arc in English, who saw visions of the archangel Michael,* who commanded her to save France from the invading English. She talked her way into the French court, identified the disguised Dauphin,* and obtained a commission. Dressed in man's armor, she led the forces in the relief of Orleans and in subsequent battles; eventually she was captured, given first to the English, then to the Church where she was tried as a heretic, convicted, and burned. For a time, she was forgotten, but in the nineteenth century she emerged as a great French patriotic heroine; she was canonized in 1920. She appears in numerous works, most notably in Voltaire's burlesque poem *La Pucelle* (1755), G. B. Shaw's play *St. Joan* (1923), and Jean Anouilh's play *L'Alouette* (1953). She also appears as Joan la Pucelle in Shakespeare's play *Henry VI, Part I* (1590) as a witch whose power is derived from the devils* that possess her. *See also* Dunois.

Jed. (1) *See* Clampett. (2) *See also* Jedidiah.

Jedidiah. In the Bible, *II Samuel* xii, the baby Solomon.*

Jeeter. *See* Lester.

Jeeves. In numerous stories and novels by P. G. Wodehouse (beg. 1919), the perfect valet whose unshakeable aplomb, social rectitude, and resourcefulness rescue his master Bertie Wooster* from many crises.

Jehoshaphat. (1) In the Bible, *II Samuel* viii, David's* recorder. (2) In the Bible, *I Kings* xxii, the religious king of Judah* at the same time as Ahab* was king of Israel.* (3) In the Bible, *Joel* iii, the valley in which the Last Judgement* will occur.

Jehovah. In Christian usage, a medieval transliteration of Yahweh.*

Jehu. In the Bible, *II Kings* ix–x, a corrupt king of Israel,* noted particularly for driving his chariot "furiously": in England, the name was sometimes given to any reckless coachman. He also led the revolt against Jezebel.*

Jekyll. In R. L. Stevenson's story *Dr. Jekyll and Mr. Hyde* (1886), a good and honorable doctor who develops a drug that will alter personality, only to discover that when he takes it, it releases from his own personality a creature of pure malevolence, which he calls Mr. Hyde;* realizing he can never again be only Dr. Jekyll, he kills himself.

Jellyby. In Charles Dickens's novel *Bleak House* (1852), a dominating woman who devotes herself to charity, particularly to projects in Africa, to the complete neglect of her own children and family life.

Jemima. (1) In the Bible, *Job* xlii, the first daughter born to Job* after he was restored; she was noted for her great beauty. (2) In American twentieth-century usage, a jolly, fat Negress, from the labels of a series of the "Aunt Jemima" food products, a personification of the happy slave "mammy." In the latter half of the century, it became a term of insult for Negroes, implying that they were happy to be oppressed by whites.

Jenkyns. In Elizabeth Gaskell's novel *Cranford* (1853), two spinster sisters influential in the village; Deborah is a willful, dominating woman, while Matty, smarter but quieter, is primarily concerned with the effect of poverty on her position.

Jennie. (1) *See* Gerhardt, Jennie. (2) *See also* Jenny.

Jenny. (1) *See* Diver, Jenny; Pirate Jenny. (2) *See also* Jennie.

Jephthah. In the Bible, *Judges* xi–xii, a great judge of Israel.* In return for God's promise to defeat the Amorites, Jephthah vowed to sacrifice the first creature to appear from his tent; when his beloved daughter and only child rushed out to meet him, he hesitated, but with her encouragement, he eventually killed her.

Jereboam. *See* Jeroboam.

Jeremiah. In the Bible, *Jeremiah*, a great prophet particularly noted for his calls for moral reform, his prophecies of the fall of Jerusalem* to Babylon, and the grieving poems about the destruction of Jerusalem in *Lamentations*, which are ascribed to him.

Jericho. In the Bible, *Joshua* v–vi, a city in Canaan* which Joshua* and the Israelites besieged; on the seventh day, the priests blew their trumpets and the walls came tumbling down.

Jeroboam. In the Bible, *I Kings* xi, the first king of Israel* after its separation from Judah,* noted for his size and might. *See also* Rehoboam; Zachariah.

Jerome, St. Historically, a great Christian scholar (d. 420) and principal translator of the "Vulgate" Bible, the Latin version still in use as the common version of the Catholic Church. In legend, he was said to have removed a thorn from the paw of a lion, which then became the monastery's pet, guard, and work animal; hence, he is usually depicted as an old hermit with a lion. His day is September 30.

Jerry. In Edward Albee's play *The Zoo Story* (1959), an unconventional young man who meets and talks with a conventional man on a park bench until he taunts the other into killing him; noted particularly for the story of "Jerry and the dog" that chased him in the halls of his building.

Jerusalem. Historically, the principal city of Israel* and the principal holy city of the Jews and the Christians, as well as a significant holy city for the Moslems. In the Bible, David* made the city his capital and started a temple for the ark* of the covenant, which was finished by his son Solomon.* It was destroyed by the Babylonians and then rebuilt after the Jews returned from a 50-year exile; it was destroyed a second time by the Romans after a Jewish rebellion in 70. In the New Testament, it was the site of Jesus's* triumphant entry on Palm Sunday, trial, Crucifixion,* and Resurrection,* as well as of the Pentecost* during which the Apostles* spoke in tongues. In the centuries since, the name has continued to indicate a city of holy glory, as in *Revelation* xxi, where Heaven* itself is called the New Jerusalem, a usage that is maintained in William Blake's poem *Jerusalem* (1804), which serves as an unofficial English national anthem. Its recapture was the goal of the numerous medieval Crusades, and "next year in Jerusalem" was the rallying cry of the Jewish Zionists who founded modern Israel.

Jesse. In the Bible, *I Samuel* xvii, the father of David.* The geneology of Jesus* generally begins with him and is depicted as the "tree of Jesse."

Jessica. In Shakespeare's play *The Merchant of Venice* (1596), Shylock's* beloved daughter who deserts him, steals his jewels, and elopes with the Christian Lorenzo. In the nineteenth century, almost all actors interpolated a pantomime scene in which Shylock came home to find her gone.

Jesus. In the Bible, New Testament Gospels, the founder of the Christian religion. He was the "Son of God," conceived by the Virgin Mary* after an angel* visited her. He was born in a stable in Bethlehem,* where Mary and her husband Joseph* had gone to be registered for taxation and where they could find no room in any of the inns. At His birth, a new star appeared in the heavens and guided shepherds* and the Magi* to Him. The family escaped the Massacre of the Innocents* by going to Egypt, but then returned to Joseph's village of Nazareth,* where Jesus remained in obscurity until about His thirtieth year. At that time, He was baptized in the Jordan* by John the Baptist,* who recognized Him as the "Lamb of God;" He then spent 40 days in the wilderness, where He rejected all the temptations of the Devil.* He began to preach, gathering the first twelve Apostles,* and to perform miracles, gradually attracting large crowds of followers, whom He taught primarily by means of parables, as well as enemies among the local religious and political powers, particularly after He drove the money changers* from the Temple and preached the Sermon on the Mount.* Finally, when He was about 33, He returned to Jerusalem,* making a triumphant entry amidst a crowd waving palms. At the end of that week, during the Jewish Passover,* He held His Last Supper* with His Apostles, at which He predicted His impending death. Afterwards, He was betrayed in the Garden of Gethsemane* by Judas,* and was arrested, tried, and convicted by the local religious powers. After the conviction was approved by the Roman procurator Pontius Pilate,* Jesus was crucified on Golgotha,* dying after about nine hours on the cross, at which time an earthquake occurred. He was entombed, but three days later, His body rose from the tomb, and shortly thereafter He reappeared to His followers, with whom He stayed until the fortieth day, when He ascended into Heaven.* *Also called* Christ,* The Good Shepherd,* Messiah,* Prince of Peace, Savior. Among His many miracles were the curing of numerous blind, crippled, and leprous persons; for other noted miracles, *see* Bethesda; Cana; Gadarene Swine; Galilee; Lazarus; Loaves and Fishes. For His principal parables, *see* Lazarus; Mustard Seed; Needle, Eye of the; Pearl of Great Price; Prodigal; Samaritan, Good; Servant of Two Masters; Shepherd, Good; Talents; Vineyard; Virgins, Foolish; Woman Taken in Adultery. *See also* Ascension; Calvary; Easter; Herod; Ichthus; Jesse; Mary Magdalene; Olives, Mount of; Passion; Paul; Peter; Resurrection; Second Coming.

Jethro. (1) In the Bible, *Exodus* xviii, the father of Zipporah* and the father-in-law of Moses;* returning to Moses in the desert, he advised him to appoint judges rather than administer all justice alone. (2) *See* Clampett.

Jewel. *See* Bundren.

Jezebel. In the Bible, *I Kings* xviii, *II Kings* ix, the wife of Ahab* and queen of Israel.* She used her seductive power to turn Ahab toward the worship of Baal,* persecuted those who would not worship the idols, even driving Elijah* into the wilderness, and encouraged lascivious pagan rites. The Jews eventually revolted, and she was thrown from a window, her body eaten by the dogs. She is usually seen as the ultimate scarlet woman* who leads pure men into wickedness and is particularly associated with heavy makeup, since she painted her face before her final confrontation with Jehu.* *See also* Athaliah; Naboth; Obadiah.

Jiggs. In the American newspaper cartoon *Bringing Up Father* (beg. 1913), a short, red-haired Irish-American, made a millionaire by winning the Irish sweepstakes, who wants only to continue the simple pleasures of a working man but is constantly forced to repress these by his shrewish, pretentious, and muscular wife Maggie.

Jill. *See* Jack.

Jim. (1) In Mark Twain's novel *Huckleberry Finn* (1885), the simple Negro slave who runs away and whom Huck Finn* decides to aid; the two of them float down the Mississippi together on a raft, and Huck learns to respect him as a human being and friend. In recent years, he has become a very controversial figure because, although he is honorable, sincere, and dignified in his own complex manner, he is also ignorant, superstitious, and both calls himself and is called "Nigger Jim." *See also* Sawyer, Tom; Watson, Miss. (2) In Joseph Conrad's novel *Lord Jim* (1900), a British sailor who, along with the rest of the crew, deserts a ship full of pilgrims, thinking it is sinking, only to discover later that it did not sink. He loses his papers and disappears into the Malayan jungles to prove that he really is a heroic figure. There he becomes a "lord" among a native tribe until a group of pirates arrive; in an attempt to be honorable and to protect his tribe, Jim secures the pirates' release, and they repay him by killing the chief's son. Jim then allows himself to be shot. He is generally regarded as one of the classic depictions of guilt caused by our inability to live up to our dreams in the complex real world. *See also* Marlow. (3) In Kingsley Amis's novel *Lucky Jim* (1954), a young English university lecturer desperately but unsuccessfully trying to find a way to keep his job in an intellectual and cultural environment he detests; noted as one of the most vivid, and funniest, of the "angry young men" of British 1950s literature. (4) *See* Hawkins, Jim. (5) *See also* James.

Jim Crow. In American folklore, a Negro dancer; the name also came to be applied to laws maintaining separate facilities for Negroes in the American South.

Jingle. In Charles Dickens's novel *Pickwick Papers* (1836), an amiable con man noted for his fragmentary discourse; he supports himself by eloping with various spinsters and taking money from their families to send them back before anyone hears of the scandal. *See also* Pickwick; Trotter, Job; Wardle.

Jinks, Capt. In a popular American song of the mid-nineteenth century, a happy-go-lucky playboy.

Jinn. *See* Genie.

Jinnayah. *See* Genie.

Jip. *See* Dora.

Jo. In Louisa May Alcott's novel *Little Women* (1868), the gawky sister who wants to be a writer and who plans entertainments for her family; she grows up to be a governess, marry a teacher, and start her own school. *See also* Amy; Beth; Meg.

Joab. In the Bible, *II Samuel* ii–iii, the captain of David's* army who assassinated Abner.* *See also* Sheba.

Joachim. In Christian legend, the father of Mary.*

Joad. In John Steinbeck's novel *The Grapes of Wrath* (1939), the "Okie" family whose trials are followed through their migration to California. **Tom** is the eldest son who returns from prison to find that his family has lost the farm; he joins their trip west in a single truck, tries to find work as a migrant farm worker, kills another man to protect a friend who is a labor organizer, and disappears into the countryside. **Pa** becomes senile, unable to adjust to the life of a migrant worker. **Ma** is a determined woman who holds the family together through willpower alone, the epitome of the powerful "hillbilly" mother figure. **Rosasharn**, the teenaged daughter, is deserted by her husband, loses her baby, and is last seen breast-feeding a starving man in a boxcar. **Noah**, the second son, wanders away into the desert.

Joan. *See* Darby and Joan; Jeanne d'Arc.

Joan, Pope. In European legend, a brilliant woman who disguised herself as a man and rose to become Pope, only to be exposed when she gave birth to a child during a religious ceremony. The legend's lack of foundation was demonstrated in the late nineteenth century, but the story has revived in the later twentieth century, particularly among feminist writers.

Joan, St. *See* Jeanne d'Arc.

Joanna. In the Bible, *Luke* viii, the wife of a steward of Herod;* with Mary Magdalene,* she followed Jesus* and the Apostles* in their travels, and was later listed among the women who came to Jesus's tomb.

Joan of Arc. The English name for Jeanne d'Arc.*

Job. (1) In the Bible, *Job*, a wealthy, pious man who was given grotesque afflictions by God in order to demonstrate the strength of his piety; despite the loss of his wealth and his family, the desertion of his friends, and his own affliction with painful disease, he refused to "curse God and die," and ultimately all was restored to him. *See also* Jemima; Satan. (2) *See* Trotter, Job.

Jocasta. In Greek legend, the wife of Laius* and the mother, and later wife, of Oedipus.* In Sophocles's play *Oedipus Rex*, she kills herself on learning the true identity of her second husband. Their children were Antigone,* Eteocles,* Ismene,* and Polynices.* *Also called* Epicaste; Iocaste. *See also* Creon.

Joconde, La. *See* Giaconda, La.

Joe. (1) In twentieth-century usage, a generic name for an American man, as in G.I. Joe, a good Joe, Joe Blow, Joe College, etc. (2) In William Saroyan's play *The Time of Your Life* (1939), an eccentric, wealthy man who sits all day every day in a slum bar, drinking, playing with toys, and listening to the stories of strangers who wander in. *See also* Carson, Kit. (2) *See* Fat Boy, The; Gargery; Miller, Joe. (3) *See also* Joseph.

Joe, Injun. In Mark Twain's novel *Tom Sawyer* (1876), a sinister half-breed who tries to kill Tom Sawyer* after the latter witnesses Joe's murder of another man; the boys find his treasure, and he is trapped and starves in the treasure cave.

Joe, Mrs. *See* Gargery.

Joel. In the Bible, a name used for numerous persons, the most noted being the prophet in *Joel*, noted for his description of a plague of locusts.

Johann. The German form of John.*

Johannan. A name sometimes used for John the Baptist.* *See also* Iaokannan; Jokanaan.

John. (1) In the Bible, the brother of James* and one of the Apostles,* traditionally thought to be the author of *John*, *Revelation*, and three epistles of John. In legend, he was unharmed when boiled in oil in Rome. His day is December 27. *See also* Boanerges. (2) Historically, a king of England (d. 1216), known primarily as the king who was forced to ratify the Magna Carta and as the wicked regent during Richard I's* absence on the Crusades in the Robin Hood* legends and in Walter Scott's novel *Ivanhoe* (1820). (3) One of the most common male names, often used to indicate an ordinary, nondescript man, as in John Doe.* In World War II, a "Dear John" letter was a letter in which a sweetheart or wife announced to a soldier that she had found another man. (4) *See* Darling; Doe, John; Prester John; Savage, John; Tanner, John. (5) *See also* Ivan; Jack; Jean; Johann; Johnny; Jonathan; Juan.

John, Don. (1) In Shakespeare's play *Much Ado About Nothing* (1598), the bastard brother of the prince and a malcontent and rebel who maliciously tries to claim that Hero* is not pure and then flees. *See also* Borachio. (2) *See also* Juan, Don.

John, Little. In English legend, one of the followers of Robin Hood* known for his great strength and size.

John, Prester. *See* Prester John.

John, St. (1) John* the Apostle. (2) Historically, John Chrysostomus, one of the great doctors of the Church (d. 407) noted for his homilies and preaching. (3) Historically, John of the Cross, a theologian (d. 1591) and mystical religious poet. (4) Historically, John Bosco (d. 1888), founder of the Salesians and responsible for numerous schools and hospitals, noted for his gentle but effective ways with children.

John Doe. *See* Doe, John.

John Henry. In American legend and song, a man of great strength, noted primarily for the contest in which he out-drilled a steam drill but "died with a hammer in his hand."

John of Gaunt. Historically, a duke of Lancaster (d. 1399) noted primarily for his description of England as "this sceptred isle" in Shakespeare's play *Richard II* (1595).

John the Baptist. In the Bible, New Testament Gospels, a prophet in the wilderness who baptized his followers in the river Jordan* and foretold the coming of Jesus;* when Jesus came to be baptized, he identified Him as "the Lamb of God." He rebuked Herod* Antipas for marrying Herodias,* for which he was arrested and eventually beheaded, his head being given to Salome* as a reward for her dance. He is usually depicted wearing animal skins, and is also noted for living on locusts and honey. *Also called* Johannan; Jokanaan.* *See also* Elisabeth.

Johnny. (1) In an American folksong, the two-timing lover who is shot by his girlfriend Frankie;* in some versions of the song he is called Albert. (2) *See also* John.

Johnson, Dr. Historically, a noted author (d. 1784) and compiler of the first English dictionary; through Boswell's* biography, he became such a legendary wit that he is often automatically credited with any witty saying for which the genuine source is unknown.

Jokanaan. In Richard Strauss's opera *Salome* (1905), John the Baptist.*

Jonadab. In the Bible, *II Samuel* xiii, a nephew of David;* "a very subtle man," he advised Amnon* and arranged for the visit from Tamar* that culminated in her rape, but he managed to extricate himself from the ensuing scandal and revenge.

Jonah. In the Bible, *Jonah*, a prophet sent by God to preach at Nineveh; when he tried to flee God's call by sailing to Tarshish, he was thrown overboard by the other sailors during a storm and swallowed by a great fish, usually depicted as a whale. When released, he preached so successfully that Nineveh repented and was spared, which upset Jonah.

Jonas. (1) A name sometimes used for Jonah.* (2) *See* Chuzzlewit.

Jonathan. (1) In the Bible, *I Samuel*, Saul's* son whose close relationship with David* became synonymous with friendship. Jonathan had been a hero in battle, and after becoming David's friend protected him from Saul's anger and saved his life. Jonathan eventually was killed in battle, leading to Saul's suicide. His name is sometimes used to imply homosexuality due to David's dirge in *II Samuel* i saying, "thy love to me was wonderful, passing the love of women." (2) In American folklore, a commonsensical, shrewd, but unsophisticated New Englander, either used by or patterned after such a character in Royall Tyler's play *The Contrast* (1787). (3) *See* Wild, Jonathan. (4) *See also* John.

Jones. In English, one of the most common surnames, often used to signify a common or average man. *See also* Smith, Mr.

Jones, Brutus. *See* Jones, Emperor.

Jones, Casey. In American folklore, a great railroad engineer devoted to speed and schedule who died at the throttle of a "big eight-wheeler" in a crash with an oncoming train.

Jones, Emperor. In Eugene O'Neill's play *The Emperor Jones* (1920), Brutus Jones, an American Negro who proclaims himself king of a Caribbean island and then, while fleeing the rebels, begins to hallucinate both his personal past and the history of American Negroes until he reverts to savage, superstitious terror and is killed with a silver bullet.

Jones, John Paul. Historically, a Scottish sailor (d. 1792) who commanded the American ship *Bonhomme Richard* during the Revolutionary War, noted primarily for his famous reply when asked to surrender: "I have not yet begun to fight."

Jones, Tom. In Henry Fielding's novel *Tom Jones* (1749), a foundling raised by the honorable Squire Allworthy.* A good-hearted but playful boy, his actions are misrepresented by jealous relations of Allworthy, and Tom is thrown out of the house, embarking on an adventurous journey to London in which he has an affair with Mrs. Waters,* the woman thought to be his mother, befriends a comic highwayman, becomes the lover of a London lady, enjoys the colorful life of London, and is eventually revealed to be the true nephew of Allworthy, after which he marries Sophia Western.* *See also* Blifil; Partridge; Square; Thwackum.

Jordan. The river in Palestine that flows through the Sea of Galilee and into the Dead Sea. In the Bible, this is the river the Israelites must cross to enter the Promised Land,* and is thus in much folklore depicted as surrounding Heaven.* Jesus* was baptized by John the Baptist* in the water of the Jordan, so that it has also come to symbolize holy water.

Jordan, Robert. In Ernest Hemingway's novel *For Whom the Bell Tolls* (1940), a disillusioned American who joins the Spanish civil war where he finds selfishness as well as love and honor, and eventually bravely sacrifices himself to blow up a bridge and allow the rest of his band to escape. Perhaps the most noted moment, however, is when "the earth moved" while Maria* shares his sleeping bag. *See also* Pilar.

Jorrocks. In numerous stories by Robert Surtees, beginning with *Jorrocks' Jaunts and Jollities* (1838), a comic Cockney grocer who yearns to be a sportsman and eventually buys a country house and leads the hunt.

José. The Spanish equivalent of Joseph.*

José, Don. (1) In Byron's poem *Don Juan* (1819), Don Juan's father. (2) In Prosper Mérimée's novel (1847) and Bizet's opera *Carmen* (1875), a soldier who is seduced by the gypsy Carmen,* lured into a life of crime, and then deserted in favor of a bullfighter; José then kills her.

Joseph. (1) In the Bible, *Genesis* xxx–1, the son of Jacob* and Rachel.* The child of a favorite wife long thought barren, Joseph was spoiled in childhood, causing much jealousy from his brothers, particularly after he was given a coat of many colors. His brothers threw him in a well, told Jacob he had been killed, and then sold him into slavery in Egypt. There he served Potiphar* until Potiphar's wife charged him with attempted rape; in prison, he interpreted Pharoah's* dream, as a result of which he rose to become Pharoah's trusted adviser and chief administrator. Many years later, during a famine, his brothers came to Egypt seeking aid, and he gave it to them, finally revealing himself, forgiving them, and welcoming all their families to Egypt. *See also* Ephraim; Manasseh. (2) In the Bible, a carpenter and husband of Mary* and thus the earthly father of Jesus;* his distress at her pregnancy was dispelled by the visit of an angel.* He took the pregnant Mary to Bethlehem* to be registered in the census and then fled with her and the baby to Egypt to escape the slaughter of infants instigated by Herod,* after which they went to live in Nazareth.* In the Bible, he is an honorable and just man, and in legend he is depicted as an old man. (3) In the Bible, *Matthew* xxvii, Joseph of Arimathea, who offered the tomb in which Jesus's body was laid after the Crucifixion;* in Christian legend, he went to Europe, bringing with him the Holy Grail.* (4) *See* Andrews, Joseph; Surface. (5) *See also* Joe.

Joseph, St. Joseph,* the husband of Mary.*

Joseph, Sir. In Gilbert and Sullivan's operetta *H.M.S. Pinafore* (1878), the "ruler of the Queen's navy" who stuck close to his desk and never went to sea.

Josephine. Historically, the first wife (d. 1814) of Napoleon.* Divorced because she had no children and so that he could make a dynastic marriage with Austria, she is often depicted in literature as a romantic victim of love.

Joses. In the Bible, *Mark* vi, one of the "brothers" of Jesus.* *See* James.

Joshua. In the Bible, *Exodus* and *Joshua*, the leader of the Israelites after the death of Moses.* He brought them into the Promised Land;* conquered various native tribes; defeated the city of Jericho,* where the walls came tumbling down after he had the priests blow their trumpets; defeated the Amorites while the sun stood still so that the slaughter could continue until they were wiped out; and allotted the lands to the twelve tribes. *Also called* Hoshea.

Josiah. In the Bible, *II Kings* xxii–xxiii, a king of Judah* who destroyed the idols and reestablished a strict observance of religious laws.

Jourdain. In Molière's play *The Bourgeois Gentleman* (1670), a rich merchant who tries to become a gentleman by displaying his enormous wealth; he is most famous for his joy on learning that he has been speaking prose all his life, but he makes himself ridiculous in all other cultural areas as well. **Mme. Jourdain** is a sensible woman who tries to maintain some level of common sense in the household. *See also* Dorimène.

Joxer. In Sean O'Casey's play *Juno and the Paycock* (1924), the amiable crony of Jack Boyle* noted for his grin, the twinkle in his eye, and his ability to avoid all manner of work.

Jove. A name sometimes used for Jupiter.*

Juan. The Spanish equivalent to John;* often used as a stereotypical name for any man from any of the Spanish-speaking countries.

Juan, Don. In Tirso de Molina's play *El Burlador* (1616), a Spanish rake with an all but unquenchable appetite for women, eventually condemned to Hell* when a statue comes to life to kill him. Although the play disappeared very quickly, Don Juan became a legendary figure throughout Europe, the ultimate great lover, generally seen as handsome, dashing, and irresistable to women, as well as persistently fascinating to writers. His most notable appearances are in Molière's play *Don Juan* (1665), in which his hypocrisy is stressed; Mozart's opera *Don Giovanni* (1787), in which he audaciously challenges the forces of religion and morality; Byron's poem *Don Juan* (1819), in which he is an innocent young man seduced by women who will not leave him alone and a man who would be honorable if only depraved "civilized" society offered any honorable options; José Zorrilla's play *Don Juan Tenorio* (1844), in which he reforms and is saved from Hell by the love of a pure woman; and the *Don Juan in Hell* sequence from G. B. Shaw's play *Man and Superman* (1905), in which he has purposely gone to Hell in order to maintain a contemplative life and to escape the hypocritical wiles of respectable women. *See also* Ana, Doña; Commendatore; Elvira; Haidée; Inez; Leporello.

Jubal. In the Bible, *Genesis* iv, a son of Lamech* and the father of musicians and poets. *See also* Jabal; Noah; Tubalcain.

Jud. In Rodgers and Hammerstein's musical play *Oklahoma!* (1943), the crude hired hand who lusts after Laurey,* is gullibly tricked by Curly,* and is killed during the "shivoree."

Judah. (1) In the Bible, *Genesis*, a son of Jacob* and Leah* and the father of one of the twelve tribes of Israel;* when the Israelites split into two kingdoms, this tribe dominated the southern kingdom, which came to be called Judah. (2) *See also* Judas; Jude.

Judas. (1) In the Bible, *Matthew* and *Luke*, Judas Iscariot, one of the twelve Apostles.* He betrayed Jesus* to the religious authorities for 30 pieces of silver, identified Him to the arresting troops by kissing Him in the Garden of Gethsemane,* relented his betrayal and returned the 30 pieces of silver, and then hanged himself. He is the ultimate traitor, although in the twentieth century there has been some literary effort to interpret him as a radical disappointed by what he saw as Jesus's lack of proper fanaticism. (2) *See* Maccabee. (3) *See also* Judah; Jude.

Jude. (1) In the Bible, *Matthew* xiii, a "brother" of Jesus* (*see* James); some think he is the same Jude who was an Apostle;* others think that was a different Jude who was a brother of James* the Less, since the latter was also the son of a woman named Mary.* The author of the epistle of *Jude* may be either of these, or neither. In legend, he was martyred in Persia. In Christian tradition, he is the saint of the impossible and thus the saint to whom one turns for intercession when faced with dire personal problems; his day is October 28. (2) In Thomas Hardy's novel *Jude the Obscure* (1894), Jude Fawley, a stonemason torn between his desire for a religious life and a sensual temperament that forces him into a youthful marriage. His wife deserts him, and he lives with and has three children by a free-thinking cousin who convinces him to forget about the ministry. They are poor outcasts, the children die, the cousin becomes religiously neurotic and returns to her husband, and Jude dies alone, a disillusioned man. (3) *See also* Judah; Judas.

Jude, St. Jude* the Apostle.

Judea. Historically, the name given by the Romans to the province including Jerusalem* and most of the Jewish tribes.

Judgement, Last. In Christian tradition, the day on which the world will end and God will separate the good and the wicked for all time. *See also* Armageddon; Second Coming.

Judith. (1) In the Bible, in the Apochrypha, *Judith*, a beautiful widow who, when her city was besieged by the Babylonian general Holofernes,* entered his camp and promised to sleep with him, which he celebrated with a feast; when he passed out, she cut off his head and saved her city. (2) *See* Sutpen.

Judy. In the British puppet show, the wife of Punch.*

Juggernaut. In Hindu mythology, a title of Krishna,* especially when depicted in a great cart crushing many people under its wheels.

Jukes. Historically, the pseudonymous name given by Richard Dugdale (d. 1883) to a New York family that illustrated his thesis of hereditary criminality and feeblemindedness. A similar study was made of a New Jersey family called the Kallikaks, and the two names are often used together.

Julia. (1) In the Bible, *Romans* xvi, a Christian woman in Rome to whom Paul* sent greetings. (2) In Shakespeare's play *Two Gentlemen of Verona* (1594), a young woman who disguises herself as a gentleman to follow her lover Proteus* and whose loyalty eventually wins him back. (3) In George Orwell's novel *1984* (1949), the woman who becomes Winston Smith's* mistress. (4) *See also* Julie.

Julian, St. In Christian legend, a nobleman who accidentally killed his parents and in expiation built a hospital by a river in the wilderness, where one day he rescued a leper who was revealed to be an angel;* hence, he is almost always called "the Hospitaller." His day is February 12.

Julie. (1) In Rousseau's novel *The New Héloïse* (1761), the aristocratic girl who falls in love with her commoner tutor Saint-Preux* but rejects him to satisfy her parents; she marries another and acts as a perfect wife despite her continuing love for Saint-Preux. *See also* Héloïse. (2) In August Strindberg's play *Miss Julie* (1888), a self-centered, headstrong daughter of a count who likes to humiliate the men who are attracted to her; having horsewhipped her fiancé, she dances and flirts with the servants and seduces the crude valet Jean.* This reveals her own confusion, passion, and lack of character, the love that makes her want to elope turning to hate after she forces Jean to kill her pet bird; when her father returns, she decides to kill herself. (3) In Ferenc Molnar's play *Liliom* (1909) and in Rodgers and Hammerstein's musical play *Carousel* (1945), the gentle and loyal country girl who marries a criminal carnival barker and after his death continues to idealize him. *See also* Bigelow, Billy; Liliom. (4) *See also* Julia.

Juliet. In Shakespeare's play *Romeo and Juliet* (1595), a young girl who falls in love with Romeo,* a member of a family feuding with her own, and secretly marries him. When her parents want her to marry a nobleman, she takes a sleeping potion that makes her seem dead; then, on waking in her tomb to find that Romeo has believed her dead and has killed himself, she kills herself as well. She is the quintessential young girl passionately in love, and is particularly noted for the romantic "balcony scene" which she begins, "Romeo, Romeo, wherefore art thou Romeo?" *See also* Capulet; Laurence, Friar; Montague; Nurse; Tybalt. (2) *See also* Juliette.

Juliette. (1) In de Sade's novel *Juliette* (1797), a sadistic, licentious woman whose devotion to brutal sexual pleasure and cruelty brings her a life of wealth, pleasure, and happiness, in sharp contrast to her pure "sister" Justine.* (2) *See also* Juliet.

Julius Caesar. *See* Caesar, Julius.

Juno. (1) In Roman mythology, the wife of Jupiter;* generally equivalent to Hera.* (2) *See* Boyle.

Jupe, Sissy. In Charles Dickens's novel *Hard Times* (1854), the sensitive, loving foster child of Gradgrind;* she is never able to face the facts he insists she learn and continues to dream of the circus clown father who deserted her.

Jupiter. In Roman mythology, the principal god, generally equivalent to Zeus.* *Also called* Jove.

Justine. In de Sade's novel *Justine* (1791), a virtuous woman whose virtue only brings her pain and ruin in the licentious world, a figure of ridicule and humiliation rather than of sympathy; the work is often cited as the quintessence of sadistic pornography. *See also* Juliette.

Justinian. Historically, the Byzantine Roman Emperor (d. 565) noted primarily for his codification of Roman law, which served as a foundation for most European law into the present. *See also* Theodora.

Juturna. In Roman mythology, the goddess of springs.

Juventas. In Roman mythology, the goddess of youth, generally equivalent to Hebe.*

K

K., Joseph. In Franz Kafka's novel *The Trial* (1925), a bland, conventional man arrested for an unnamed crime and trapped within an endless and faceless bureaucracy.

Kakia. In Greek mythology, the goddess of vice.

Kali. In Hindu mythology, the wife of Shiva,* noted primarily for her bloodthirstiness and for the sacrifices, and sometimes the murders, made in her name.

Kallikaks. *See* Jukes.

Kama. In Hindu mythology, the god of love.

Kane. In the movie *Citizen Kane* (1941), a newspaper magnate of immense wealth and influence who gradually becomes obsessively self-contained, building a great castle in which he hides from the world; noted for his obsession with "Rosebud," which turns out to have been a childhood sled. Many allusions are made to the film, often called the best movie ever made.

Kaplan, Hyman. In numerous stories by Leo Rosten (beg. 1937), an exuberant Jewish immigrant to America noted for his comic misadventures with the English language and his joy in being an American; he usually writes his name as K*A*P*L*A*N.

Karamazov. In Dostoevsky's novel *The Brothers Karamazov* (1880), **Fyodor** is the crude father, a materialistic libertine, cunning, devious, brutal, and licentious. His eldest son **Dimitri** is brooding and excitable, but he has some goodness at heart; he despises his father for the treatment of his dead mother and is jealous of his father's relationship with the earthy Grushenka.* **Ivan**, a half-brother, is an intellectual atheist. **Alyosha**, Ivan's brother, is more spiritual, and he joins a monastery in pursuit of a pure soul. **Smerdyakov** is Fyodor's bastard son, a sadistic half-wit. Prompted by devious hints from Ivan, Smerdyakov kills Fyodor, but Dimitri is suspected, arrested, and convicted; at his trial, he protests his innocence of that crime yet is willing to be punished for his own impure soul.

Karenin. *See* Karenina, Anna.

Karenina, Anna. In Tolstoy's novel *Anna Karenina* (1875), a beautiful woman who falls in love with the handsome Vronsky,* becomes pregnant during their affair, and leaves her cold-natured but respectable husband **Karenin** to go away with him. When the pair returns, Karenin, who had condoned the affair as long as they were discreet, refuses her access to her first child, a son, and they are ostracized by the same society that had thought their affair so intriguing. Obsessed with her son, her guilt, and her fear that Vronsky will tire of her, she becomes unhinged and begins to drive Vronsky away, at last committing suicide by throwing herself under the wheels of a train. *See also* Dolly; Kitty; Levin.

Kastril. In Ben Jonson's play *The Alchemist* (1610), an angry young man who has come to London to learn how to smoke and quarrel.

Kat, Krazy. In the American newspaper cartoon *Krazy Kat* (1910–44), a strange cat, noted primarily as the target of numerous bricks thrown by the mouse Ignatz.* The cartoons are often cited as examples of art in popular culture and as significant expressions of American character.

Katarina. *See* Katerina; Katharina.

Kate. (1) In Shakespeare's play *The Taming of the Shrew* (1593), the intelligent but shrewish sister of Bianca* whom her father Baptista* has declared must be married before he will let Bianca marry. She meets her match in Petruchio,* who seems to want to marry her for her money, in a scene as much a brawl as a courtship; he then humiliates her at the wedding and proceeds to "kill her with kindness" until at last she relents and agrees to his husbandly dominion. Returning to her father's house, she makes a famous speech on the duties of a wife. *Also called* Katharina; Kit. (2) *See* Corinthian Kate; Croy, Kate; Hardcastle; Nickleby. (3) *See also* Catherine; Cathy; Katharina; Katharine; Katherine; Kathy.

Katerina. (1) *See* Ivanovna, Katerina; Katya; Kitty. (2) *See also* Katharina.

Katharina. (1) *See* Kate; Katusha; Katya. (2) *See also* Catherine; Katerina; Katharine.

Katharine. (1) In Shakespeare's play *Love's Labour's Lost* (1595), one of the witty ladies. *See also* Maria; Rosaline. (2) In Shakespeare's play *Henry V* (1598), the princess of France so quaintly courted by Henry V.* (3) *See also* Catherine; Katerina; Katherine.

Katherine. *See* Catherine; Katerina; Katherina; Katharine.

Kathy. (1) *See* Cathy. (2) *See also* Katharine.

Katisha. In Gilbert and Sullivan's operetta *The Mikado* (1885), a mature woman who hopes to marry the young prince Nanki-Poo* and is wildly jealous when she discovers she has been tricked out of the marriage. *See also* Ko-Ko.

Katusha. In Tolstoy's novel *Resurrection* (1899), a bastard servant girl seduced by Dimitri Neklyudov.* This drives her to prostitution and to her eventual arrest for a murder which she did not commit; he is on the jury that tries and convicts her, but he pressures them to change the sentence to exile. She, however, refuses his offer to marry her in restitution for the terrible life his earlier act drove her to.

Katya. In Turgenev's novel *Fathers and Sons* (1862), the shy, young girl who eventually marries Arkady Kirsanov.* *See also* Odintsov, Anna.

Katzenjammer Kids. In the American newspaper cartoon *The Katzenjammer Kids* (beg. 1897), a set of uncontrollable and destructive twins.

Kay. In Malory's *Morte d'Arthur*, Arthur's* foster brother, a brave but sarcastic knight.

Kelly, Ned. Historically, an Australian outlaw (d. 1880) elevated in legend to a status similar to that of Robin Hood* or Jesse James.*

Kent. In Shakespeare's play *King Lear* (1605), a bluff but loyal earl who is banished by Lear* along with Cordelia* but who returns in disguise to become Lear's loyal servant. *See also* Fool.

Kent, Clark. *See* Superman.

Kenwigs. In Charles Dickens's novel *Nicholas Nickleby* (1838), the genteelly poverty-stricken family upstairs who fawn over their relative Lillyvick* in hopes of an inheritance for their children.

Ketch, Jack. Historically, a British executioner (d. 1686) whose name became synonymous with all executioners.

Kettledrummle. In Walter Scott's novel *Old Mortality* (1816), a fanatical Protestant minister.

Khlestakov. In Gogol's play *The Inspector General* (1836), an opportunistic young man who is mistaken by local politicians for an inspector sent by the czar and is showered with gifts, money, and propositions of various kinds; with the aid of his servant Osip* he realizes when he has taken all he can and disappears just before the real inspector arrives.

Kidd, Capt. Historically, a British pirate (d. 1701) who was eventually hanged, but whom legend said had buried great treasures on deserted islands in the Caribbean. *See also* Morgan.

Kildare, Dr. In several novels by Max Brand, and especially in movies beginning with *Young Dr. Kildare* (1938), a handsome and idealistic young intern. *See also* Gillespie, Dr.

Kilmansegg. In Thomas Hood's poem *Miss Kilmansegg and Her Precious Leg* (1841), a wealthy woman who loses her leg after falling from a horse, has it replaced by a golden leg, and is pursued by many suitors; she ultimately marries a count who beats her to death with her leg.

Kilroy. In American slang, an average guy, rarely used except during World War II, when American soldiers scrawled "Kilroy was here" on what at times seemed to be every wall still standing in Europe.

Kim. In Rudyard Kipling's novel *Kim* (1901), the son of an Irish soldier orphaned and raised as an Indian; he aids a holy man on his journey to the Himalayas and in the process also becomes a spy for the British secret service.

Kingfish. In the American radio and television series "Amos 'n' Andy" (1928–1953), a pompous, conniving head of the lodge of the Mystic Knights of the Sea, noted for his numerous successful attempts to con Andy,* his absolute inability to con his domineering wife Sapphire, and his catchphrase, "Holy mack'rel, Andy."

King of Hearts, The. In Lewis Carroll's story *Alice in Wonderland* (1865), the timid, ineffectual king of the cards and judge of Alice's* trial, much intimidated by his forceful Queen of Hearts;* he is noted for wanting the verdict first and the trial after.

Kirillov. In Dostoevsky's novel *The Possessed* (1867), a nihilistic revolutionary who eventually decides to commit suicide rather than endure ordinary existence, but he is persuaded to confess to the murder of Shatov* in order to protect the other members of the group.

Kirsanov. In Turgenev's novel *Fathers and Sons* (1862), **Arkady** is a naive young man brought under the spell of the revolutionary Bazarov* but unable to work up the necessary ruthlessness. His father **Nikolai** is a gentle music lover and ineffectual liberal who is cheated by the peasants he professes to admire. **Pavel** is the other son, a dandy and aristocrat who despises provincial life and goes eventually to Germany. *See also* Katya.

Kit. *See* Carson, Kit; Kate; Nubbles, Kit.

Kite, Sergeant. In George Farquhar's play *The Recruiting Officer* (1706), the sergeant who pretends to be a fortune-teller to draw recruits into the army; noted for his song "Over the hills and far away."

Kitty. In Tolstoy's novel *Anna Karenina* (1875), the beautiful, cheerful, but naive young sister of Dolly,* loved by the kind but dull Levin* but unfortunately herself in love with the dashing Vronsky;* eventually she realizes the value of Levin and marries him. *See also* Shtcherbatsky.

Klestakov. *See* Khlestakov.

Klingsor. In Richard Wagner's opera *Parsifal* (1882), the pagan magician who wounds Amfortas* and who tries to seduce Parsifal away from his quest with the beautiful Kundry.*

Knickerbocker. In Washington Irving's *History of New York* (1809), a fictitious historian with a sly sense of humor. The popularity of the works made the name synonymous with the Dutch in New York, then with New Yorkers in general.

Knight. Historically, minor European nobility who, during the medieval era, gradually developed a complex code of military skill, chivalry, and personal honor. In legend, the code was stressed far more often than in life, and the knight became synonymous with justice, goodness, and the protection of the weak or meek, as seen in such concepts as the "knight in shining armor," modeled on St. George,* who rescues the virgin or who will restore peace and prosperity to the deserving. In literature, the knight has been the subject of numerous works, both medieval and more modern. The most noted include those who served Charlemagne,* such as Roland;* those who joined Arthur* in Camelot;* those who joined the Crusades, such as Tancred;* the knight who tells the story of Palamon* and Arcite* in Chaucer's *Canterbury Tales*; and those depicted in the operas of Richard Wagner, such as Parsifal* and Lohengrin.* Numerous knights modeled after Walter Scott's depiction of Ivanhoe* appear in historical and romantic fiction. Don Quixote* is often called the Knight of the Woeful Countenance, and sometimes simply the Knight, and Falstaff* is sometimes called the Fat Knight. *See also* Red Cross Knight.

Knightley. In Jane Austen's novel *Emma* (1816), Emma's* sensible and frank neighbor who always tells Emma the truth, which she does not always appreciate. Only when she begins to think that he may be interested in another woman does she realize that she loves him, and the two eventually marry.

Knowell. In Ben Jonson's play *Every Man in his Humour* (1598), a kindly gentleman. His son **Edward** is devoted to poetry and frivolous companions but eventually finds love through the aid of his servant Brainworm.*

Ko-Ko. In Gilbert and Sullivan's operetta *The Mikado* (1885), the Lord High Executioner who cannot execute anyone, since his is the first name on the list of those to be executed; eventually, he marries the imposing Katisha* as an alternative to being boiled in oil. He sings "I've Got a Little List."

230   Kore

Kore. *See* Cora.

Kowalski. In Tennessee Williams's play *A Streetcar Named Desire* (1947), **Stanley** is the crude but dynamic brother-in-law of Blanche DuBois.* When she is forced to live with him and her sister Stella, he ridicules her pretensions, threatens legal actions about her loss of the family estate, destroys her hope of marriage by telling her boyfriend about her sordid personal past, then eventually drives her insane by raping her on the night his wife gives birth to a son. He has become a representative of the power and fascination of natural forces and of masculine strength and brutality, as opposed to Blanche's female frailty and culture. **Stella** is a gentle, unpretentious woman who loves him enough not to admit what she knows must be the truth about him and Blanche.

Kraken. In Scandinavian legend, a great sea monster living off the coast of Norway.

Kreimhild. In the anonymous *Niebelungenlied*, the wife of Siegfried* who accidentally reveals his one vulnerable spot to Hagen* and then vows and executes revenge for Siegfried's murder on Hagen and his sons, after which her second husband has her put to death. *See also* Gutrune.

Kreutzer Sonata. Historically, a sonata for violin and piano by Beethoven (1803), noted in literature for its use in Tolstoy's story of the same name. *See* Pozdnyshev.

Kringle, Kris. A name sometimes used for Santa Claus.*

Krishna. In Hindu mythology, the god of fire and an incarnation of Vishnu.*

Krogstad. In Henrik Ibsen's play *A Doll's House* (1879), the bookkeeper who, in order to keep his job, blackmails Nora* about the bond she forged.

Kronos. *See* Cronos.

Krook. In Charles Dickens's novel *Bleak House* (1852), the owner of a junk shop who saves every piece of paper he can find in the belief that if he is surrounded by enough paper he will learn to read it by osmosis; he dies unexpectedly as a result of spontaneous combustion. He is also the landlord of Miss Flite* and Capt. Hawdon.*

Krystle. *See* Carrington.

Kubla Khan. Historically, Genghis Khan's* grandson (d. 1294) who extended the Mongol Empire to include China, where he established a dynasty of Chinese emperors. His impressive new palace was visited and described by Marco Polo,* which made him synonymous with the Chinese and with great wealth and inspired the "stately pleasure dome" decreed by him in S. T. Coleridge's poem *Kubla Khan* (1797).

Kundry. In Richard Wagner's opera *Parsifal* (1882), a beautiful woman under the power of the magician Klingsor.* Forced to seduce knights from their duties and quests, she tries with Parsifal* but fails.

Kuragin. In Tolstoy's novel *War and Peace* (1865), a prince of dubious character who, although married, plans to elope with the impressionable Natasha* and is prevented only at the last moment, which destroys her life without any appreciable effect on him at all.

Kuragina, Hélène. In Tolstoy's novel *War and Peace* (1865), the most beautiful woman in Petersburg, who marries Bezukov* when he inherits his enormous estate and then continues her round of entertainments and affairs. Apparently superficial and shallow, without any interest in even the war unless it touches her directly, she nonetheless comes to doubt the value of her life and poisons herself. For her brother, *see* Kuragin.

Kurtz, Mr. In Joseph Conrad's novel *Heart of Darkness* (1902), a European trader deep in the Congo who is gradually converted to the savage practices of the natives. He dies on the boat in which Marlow* tries to bring him out, his last words being, ''The horror! The horror!''

Kutuzov. Historically, the Russian general (d. 1813) who opposed Napoleon;* he figures particularly in Tolstoy's novel *War and Peace* (1865).

Kyo. In André Malraux's novel *Man's Fate* (1933), a tormented communist organizer, part French and part Japanese, who is eventually captured and executed by the nationalist Chinese. *See also* Ch'en.

L

Laban. In the Bible, *Genesis* xxiv–xxx, the greedy father of Rachel* and Leah;* after Jacob* worked seven years to win Rachel, Laban substituted Leah and then made Jacob work another seven for Rachel.

Labyrinth. In Greek legend, a vast underground maze in Crete in which was kept the Minotaur.* Theseus* ultimately penetrated to the center of the maze, trailing behind him a long string given him by Ariadne,* the daughter of King Minos,* and killed the beast, escaping by following the string out.

Lacedaemon. In Greek legend, a mortal son of Zeus* who founded Sparta.

Lachesis. *See* Fates.

Ladislaw, Will. In George Eliot's novel *Middlemarch* (1871), the unconventional and energetic artist; he marries Dodo Brooke* and eventually goes to Parliament.

Lady of the Lake. (1) In Malory's *Morte d'Arthur*, the supernatural woman who gives Arthur* his sword Excalibur* and who helps bear him away at his death, although she is also identified with Nimue* and with Morgan le Fay,* Arthur's dedicated enemy (or enemies). (2) *See* Douglas.

Laertes. (1) In Greek legend, the father of Odysseus.* In Homer's *Odyssey*, still vigorous in old age, he aids his son after the killing of the suitors. (2) In Shakespeare's play *Hamlet* (1600), the brother of Ophelia;* he returns to avenge her death and the murder of his father Polonius.* In a duel with Hamlet,* the tip of his sword is poisoned, as a result of which he kills Hamlet and is killed himself. Polonius makes the "To thine own self be true . . . " speech to him as he leaves for school. (3) In numerous *Spectator* stories (1711–12), a countryman who spends thoughtlessly in order not to seem poor. *See also* Irus.

Laestrygonians. In Homer's *Odyssey*, a race of giant cannibals who inhabited Sicily and sank eleven of Odysseus's* twelve ships.

Laetitia. *See* Dale, Laetitia; Snap, Laetitia.

Laius. In Greek legend, king of Thebes, father of Oedipus,* and husband of Jocasta.* When a prophecy said Oedipus would kill his father, Laius abandoned the child; years later, they met at a crossroads without recognizing each other and began arguing over the right of way, during which Laius was killed, thus fulfilling the prophecy.

Lajeunnesse, Gabriel. *See* Gabriel.

Lamech. In the Bible, *Genesis* v, father of Noah,* Jabal,* Jubal,* and Tubalcain.*

Lamia. In Greek legend, a beautiful woman whom Hera* jealously changed into a creature with the body of a serpent and the face and breasts of a woman; Lamia then lured numerous passersby to their death.

Lammle. In Charles Dickens's novel *Our Mutual Friend* (1864), **Alfred** and **Sophronia** are charming scoundrels who insinuate themselves into society in search of a wealthy spouse; each is taken in by the other, and they wed, only to discover that they are both poor. *See also* Podsnap.

Lampito. In Aristophanes's play *Lysistrata*, the Spartan* woman, athletic and resourceful, who joins Lysistrata's* plan.

Lancaster. Historically, a family of English nobles which included several kings whose line ended during the Wars of the Roses against the House of York. Several dukes and earls of the family, as well as the Lancastrian kings Henry IV,* Henry V,* and Henry VI,* appear in Shakespeare's history plays.

Lancelot. In Malory's *Morte d'Arthur*, a great knight originally from France who joins Arthur's* court; he performs numerous great deeds and appears to be the perfect knight until he falls in love with the queen Guinevere.* Their affair leads to civil war and the fall of Arthur. *See also* Ector; Elaine; Gaheris; Galahad.

Languish, Lydia. In R. B. Sheridan's play *The Rivals* (1775), a young woman so deeply enamored of romantic novels that she refuses Jack Absolute* in favor of an impoverished ensign, simply because Jack has been arranged for her and is not suitably romantic, only to discover that the ensign is Jack in disguise. Her guardian is Mrs. Malaprop.*

Laocoön. In Virgil's *Aeneid*, a priest and son of Priam* who warned the Trojans not to bring in the Trojan Horse;* his warning was ignored after a great serpent rose out of the earth and crushed him and his sons. The discovery in 1506 of an ancient statute depicting this scene had an enormous impact on the course of Western art; until the early twentieth century, it was generally thought to be the finest sculpture ever done.

Laodamia. In Greek legend, the wife of the first Greek killed in the Trojan War.* When his ghost visited her, she refused to be separated from it and followed it to Hades.*

Laodice. In Homer's *Iliad*, the most beautiful of all Priam's* daughters.

Laomedon. In Greek legend, the father of Priam* and king of a previous Troy. As punishment for various crimes, Zeus* ordered Apollo* and Poseidon* to build walls around Laomedon's city, but when it was done, the king refused to pay the gods, as a result of which the city was attacked by a sea monster and then destroyed by Heracles,* who also killed Laomedon. *See also* Hesione.

Lapham, Silas. In William Dean Howells's novel *The Rise of Silas Lapham* (1885), a self-made millionaire epitomizing the crudity often associated with the type but also sufficiently honest to turn down a crooked deal that would prevent his bankruptcy, after which he returns to the simple life he really prefers.

Lapiths. In Greek legend, a people ruled by Pirithous* and noted for their great battle with the centaurs.*

Laputa. In Jonathan Swift's novel *Gulliver's Travels* (1726), a floating island peopled by philosophers so involved in abstract thought that they must be followed around by servants with flappers, which are regularly shaken in order to draw their attention back to practical life.

Lares. In Roman mythology, minor gods who presided over the individual home. *See also* Penates.

Larry. *See* Stooges, Three.

Larsen, Wolf. In Jack London's novel *The Sea Wolf* (1904), a vicious sea captain who hunts seals, brutalizes his crew, and fights with his long-hated brother "Death" Larsen.

Larvae. In Roman legend, terrible creatures who emerged from their graves at night to haunt the world, similar to ghosts.* *Also called* Lemures.

Lassie. In Eric Knight's novel *Lassie Come-Home* (1940) and in numerous movies and television programs, a heroic collie dog.

Last, Tony. In Evelyn Waugh's novel *A Handful of Dust* (1934), a young Englishman who, to avoid his wife's wish for divorce, goes on an Amazonian expedition, in the course of which he is captured by a part-English jungle lord who forces Tony to remain with him and read to him from the collected works of Charles Dickens.

Last Judgement. *See* Judgement, Last.

Last Supper. In Christian usage, the name given to the last meal eaten together by Jesus* and his Apostles,* described in the Bible in *Matthew* xxvi et al. He broke bread, saying "this is My Body," and gave them wine, saying, "this is

My Blood,'' from which are taken the fundamental aspects of Christian communion services, and then He told them of His coming arrest and death. Many allusions are to the famous painting of the scene by Da Vinci (1498). *Also called* The Lord's Supper.

Latinus. In Virgil's *Aeneid*, a king in Italy, son of Odysseus* and Circe.* He gave his daughter Lavinia* to Aeneas* to marry; thus, all the Latins were descended from him.

Launce. In Shakespeare's play *Two Gentlemen of Verona* (1594), Proteus's* servant, much given to malapropisms; his beloved mongrel dog is Crab.

Launcelot. *See* Lancelot.

Launfal, Sir. In James Russell Lowell's poem *The Vision of Sir Launfal* (1848), a knight in search of the Holy Grail* who learns that Christ* had been present in a beggar whom he had spurned at the beginning of his quest and that the best Christian spirit is service to mankind.

Laura. (1) In numerous poems by Petrarch, the beautiful woman who inspired his love and his poetry. (2) In August Strindberg's play *The Father* (1887), the mother who torments her husband the Captain.* In her loathing for her life as his wife, she tries to have him declared insane and then drives him mad with the thought that their beloved daughter is not really his. (3) *See* Wingfield.

Laurence, Friar. In Shakespeare's play *Romeo and Juliet* (1595), the well-meaning priest who marries the young lovers and then tries to aid their reunion by providing the potion that makes Juliet* appear to be dead.

Lavinia. (1) In Virgil's *Aeneid*, the daughter of Latinus;* she became Aeneas's* new wife in Italy. (2) In Shakespeare's play *Titus Andronicus* (1592), the chaste daughter of Andronicus;* she is raped in the forest, her tongue is cut out, and her hands are cut off to prevent her from identifying her attackers. *See also* Chiron; Demetrius. (3) *See* Mannon; Wilfer.

Lawrence, Friar. *See* Laurence, Friar.

Lawrence, St. Historically, a Christian bishop and martyr (d. 258); legend says he was roasted on a grid and said, ''Turn me over, I'm done on this side.'' He also assembled the poorest of Rome when ordered to surrender the Church's treasures. Among the most widely venerated of martyrs, his day is August 10.

Lazarillo. In the anonymous novel *Lazarillo de Tormes* (1553), a poor boy who learns to live by his wits but retains his essential goodness of heart and gradually rises to a respectable life with a good wife and a government job. Noted activities include having to steal his own food from a miserly master, having to support a different noble master by begging, and becoming a water carrier to support a priest.

Lazarus. (1) In the Bible, *Luke* xvi, a parable told by Jesus.* The beggar Lazarus lives on the crumbs of a rich man's table and his sores are licked by the dogs; when he dies, he goes to Heaven,* but the rich man goes to Hell.* Abraham refuses the rich man's request that Lazarus go back to warn the rich man's brothers to repent, saying that if they heed not the prophets, they would not heed one who came back from the dead. (2) In the Bible, *John* xi–xii, the brother of Mary* and Martha;* Jesus raised him from the dead. He is sometimes confused with the Lazarus of the parable, but there is no apparent connection between the two.

Leah. In the Bible, *Genesis* xxix–xxxi, the first wife of Jacob* because her father Laban* substituted her for her sister Rachel.* As Jacob loved Rachel more, God made Rachel barren and Leah fertile; she gave birth to Reuben,* Simeon,* Levi,* Judah,* Issachar,* and Zebulun.*

Leander. (1) *See* Hero. (2) *See also* Léandre.

Léandre. (1) In numerous classical French plays, the young man in love, the most noted perhaps being in Molière's *The Doctor In Spite of Himself* (1666). (2) *See also* Leander.

Leantio. In Thomas Middleton's play *Women Beware Women* (1621), the clerk who marries the beautiful Bianca.* When she becomes the duke's mistress, he takes the evil Livia* as his own mistress, and Bianca persuades the duke to have him murdered.

Lear. In Shakespeare's play *King Lear* (1605), an old king who decides to divide his kingdom among his three daughters. When his youngest daughter Cordelia* refuses to make a speech about how much she loves him, he exiles her and divides the kingdom between the other two, Goneril* and Regan,* who soon strip him of his authority, followers, and pleasures. He runs away from them onto the heath during a great storm, in which he is driven mad. When Cordelia invades the kingdom, he is reunited with her only briefly before she is captured and killed, at which his own heart breaks and he dies. Long considered the summit of Shakespeare's work and one of the most demanding roles in the theater. *See also* Albany; Cornwall; Edgar; Fool; Gloucester; Kent.

Leatherstocking. A nickname for Natty Bumppo.*

Lecoq. In Émile Gaboriau's novel *Monsieur Lecoq* (1869), a detective who solves crimes with the use of reason, often cited as a precursor of Sherlock Holmes.*

Leda. In Greek legend, the wife of Tyndarus.* She was seduced by Zeus* while he was in the form of a swan and thus became the mother of Castor,* Pollux,* and Helen.* She was also the mother of Clytemnestra,* but most accounts agree that Tyndarus was the father.

Lee, Annabel. In Edgar Allan Poe's poem *Annabel Lee* (1849), the beautiful woman in "the kingdom by the sea" who was killed by the angels* because they were jealous of her love for the narrator.

Lee, Lorelei. In Anita Loos's novel *Gentlemen Prefer Blondes* (1925), a blonde, jazz-age beauty on the lookout for a millionaire to marry.

Lee, Robert E. Historically, commander (d. 1870) of the Confederate army on the eastern front in the Civil War; appearing in innumerable works and noted as much for being the personification of the ideal Southern gentleman as for his military brilliance.

Leeds, Nina. In Eugene O'Neill's play *Strange Interlude* (1928), a woman tormented by guilt for first the sexual repression and then the sexual promiscuity in her past; she marries, has a son from an affair, and then neurotically watches her son grow to ignore her, her lover desert her, and her husband die. Ultimately, she marries a man who has always loved her "purely" from afar.

Le Fever. In Laurence Sterne's novel *Tristram Shandy* (1759), a soldier who falls deathly ill on his way back to his regiment. When Corporal Trim* tells the story to his master Uncle Toby,* Toby swears, but the recording angel* is so moved by Toby's concern for his fellow man that the angel drops a tear that blots out the notation of Toby's sin.

Legion. In the Bible, *Mark* v, the name used by the demons who were driven out and into the Gadarene Swine.*

Legree, Simon. In Harriet Beecher Stowe's novel *Uncle Tom's Cabin* (1852), the brutal plantation owner who has Uncle Tom* beaten to death; synonymous with all the evil of the Southern slave system and one of the most widely known villains in literature. *See also* Cassy.

Leicester, Sir. *See* Dedlock.

Leigh. In Elizabeth Barrett Browning's poem *Aurora Leigh* (1865), **Aurora** is a studious and poetical woman who initially refuses marriage to **Leigh**, a man with an interest in social causes, due to her pride; she makes her living as a writer in London until reunited with the poor and blind Leigh, whom she marries at last.

Lemnians. *See* Lemnos.

Lemnos. In Greek legend, an island in the Aegean; Hephaestus* is said to have landed there when he was thrown out of Olympus. "Lemnian deeds" were synonymous with blood and murder. The women murdered all the men of the island. When the Argonauts landed there, the women slept with them, but rose up again after they left and drove out queen Hypsipyle,* who had spared her own father from the carnage. Later, the Pelasgians carried off the women but murdered them all for refusing to adopt Pelasgian ways. *See also* Dryope.

Lemuel. In the Bible, *Proverbs* xxxi, a king about whom nothing is known.

Lemures. A name sometimes used for the Larvae.*

Lena. (1) In Joseph Conrad's novel *Victory* (1915), a young female musician rescued by Heyst* and brought to his island; although their relationship is complex and unsatisfying to either, she is shown to have much the stronger character after their island is invaded by the malicious Jones, struggling bravely until she is finally shot. (2) In William Faulkner's novel *Light in August* (1932), Lena Grove is a simple country girl, originally in search of the lover who made her pregnant, but eventually becoming a symbol of female fertility itself.

Lenina. In Aldous Huxley's novel *Brave New World* (1932), the apparently perfectly adjusted woman of the future society, content with her drugs and her materialistic life, until she falls in love with John Savage.*

Lennie. In John Steinbeck's novel *Of Mice and Men* (1937), an enormous but gentle half-wit who does not know his own strength. Attracted by pretty or soft things, such as mice or puppies, he kills them by petting too hard. When he meets the pretty but frustrated wife of the ranch owner's son, he tries to pet her, panics, and breaks her neck; realizing that Lennie cannot be saved from the lynch mob, his cousin and protector George* shoots him while telling him of their dream ranch.

Lenore. (1) In Gottfried Burger's poem *Lenore* (1775), a beautiful woman carried off by the ghost of her lover, which she marries at his graveside. (2) In Edgar Allan Poe's poem *Lenore* (1831), a beautiful maiden who dies young before her marriage, perhaps the same "lost Lenore" of whom the lover dreams in his poem *The Raven* (1845).

Lent. In Christian tradition, the 40 days before Easter,* a period of sacrifice during which Christians are expected to give up something they normally enjoy. In many predominantly Catholic areas, the time immediately before Lent is a period of licentious riot, as in the Mardi Gras or Carnival celebrations.

Leo. (1) In European folklore, the usual name given to a lion, from the Latin word for lion and from the constellation. (2) Historically, a name used by thirteen Popes, the most noted being Leo I (d. 461), who turned the invading Huns* from the gates of Rome, effectively stabilized the Church in a period of great social unrest, and was canonized.

Leonard, St. In Christian legend, a reformed nobleman who devoted himself to aiding prisoners until he became a hermit. The patron saint of prisoners, his day is November 6.

Leonatus, Posthumus. *See* Posthumus.

Leonora. (1) In Beethoven's opera *Fidelio* (1805), a woman who disguises herself as a boy in order to rescue her lover Florestan* from prison. (2) In Verdi's opera *Il Trovatore* (1853), the lady who, after numerous travails, poisons herself to keep from fulfilling her bargain to sleep with the evil Count di Luna* in order to save her true love Manrico.*

Leontes. In Shakespeare's play *The Winter's Tale* (1610), an insanely jealous husband and king. *See also* Hermione; Perdita.

Leporello. In Mozart's opera *Don Giovanni* (1787), the comic servant of Don Giovanni,* noted primarily for his "catalogue song" in which he lists Giovanni's conquests.

Leprechaun. In Irish legend, a fairy* who guards a treasure, sometimes buried, sometimes at the end of the rainbow, noted for his sense of humor and the practical jokes he plays on mortals.

Lesbos. An island in the Aegean noted in legend as the home of a race of beautiful and talented women (the most notable being Sappho*) who were also exceedingly amorous with persons of either sex, thus giving the name Lesbian to female homosexuals.

Lescaut, Manon. *See* Manon.

Lester. In Erskine Caldwell's novel *Tobacco Road* (1932), a Southern hillbilly family living in overwhelming poverty and ignorance. **Jeeter**, the father, is shiftless and lazy, always going to find something tomorrow. His wife **Ada** is simple and long-suffering but, in her way, noble. The last two of seventeen children are still at home: **Dude**, a wild 16-year-old who marries a middle-aged widow because she has a car, and **Ellie May**, a voluptuous hare-lipped girl noted for the scene in which she lures a brother-in-law away from his turnips and for later replacing her runaway sister **Pearl** in his bed. In the novel, the family is killed in a fire, but in the long-running theatrical version, Ada sacrifices herself to give Pearl a chance to run away and Jeeter vows to stay on his land.

Lestrade. In numerous stories by Arthur Conan Doyle, and others, featuring Sherlock Holmes,* the self-important but stupid police inspector who must eventually turn to Holmes for help.

Lethe. In Greek legend, one of the rivers of Hades;* its waters produced forgetfulness.

Leto. In Greek mythology, mother of Apollo* and Artemis* after an affair with Zeus,* for which Hera* pursued her to the floating island Delos.*

Leverkühn. In Thomas Mann's novel *Doctor Faustus* (1947), a composer who comes to believe that, like Faust,* he has sold his soul to the Devil* in return for 24 years of genius. After becoming recognized as one of the eminent composers of the century, he is paralyzed by a stroke from which neither his mind nor his body recovers.

Levi. In the Bible, *Genesis* xxx–xxxix, a son of Jacob* and Leah.* He helped avenge the rape of Dinah,* followed his father into Egypt, and became the father of one of the tribes of Israel.* The Levites became the priests and owned no specific territory. *See also* Gershon.

Levi, Dolly. In Thornton Wilder's play *The Matchmaker* (1954), a New Jersey matchmaker who finally sets out to make a match for herself, noted especially for her depiction in the musical comedy *Hello, Dolly* (1964), where she enters on a staircase to the strains of the title song.

Leviathan. In the Bible, a Hebrew name for a great sea monster; often applied to the whale and to anything of great size or power.

Levin. In Tolstoy's novel *Anna Karenina* (1875), **Constantin** is a decent, simple man who retires to his estates to live a simple life, improve the life of his peasants, and avoid the hypocrisy of city civilization. He is a counterpoint to the complexity and guilt of Anna Karenina* and Vronsky,* as well as Kitty* before she agrees to marry him and share his good and simple life. His brother **Nikolai** is a temperamental wastrel dying of tuberculosis.

Lheureux. In Gustave Flaubert's novel *Madame Bovary* (1857), the corrupt draper and moneylender whose exorbitant terms place Emma Bovary* so deeply in debt that she is driven to suicide.

Ligeia. In Edgar Allan Poe's story *Ligeia* (1838), a mysteriously beautiful woman, deeply interested in metaphysics, who dies after writing the poem "The Conqueror Worm;" her spirit returns to take over the body of her husband's second wife.

Liliom. In Ferenc Molnar's play *Liliom* (1909), a shiftless carnival barker who marries the innocent girl Julie* and is killed in a robbery; he is given a chance to return from the afterlife to atone for his sins. *See also* Bigelow, Billy.

Lilith. In the Bible, *Isaiah* xxxiv, a demon, probably drawn from an Assyrian demon of similar name; in Jewish legend, she was a vampire* and was also Adam's* first consort until she was driven away by Eve.*

Lilliput. In Jonathan Swift's novel *Gulliver's Travels* (1726), a land where the people are so small that they could fit in Gulliver's* pocket; as a giant there, he is a subject of much concern, until he defeats a neighboring state's navy by wading into the straits between the two lands.

Lillyvick. In Charles Dickens's novel *Nicholas Nickleby* (1838), the self-important tax collector fawned over by the Kenwigs* in hope of an inheritance; he almost squanders his savings on an actress, who marries and then deserts him.

Lily. *See* Bart, Lily; Briscoe, Lily.

Limbo. In Catholic usage, a place to which are consigned the souls of those who were good but who never had the opportunity to be baptized, such as children who die at birth or pagans who lived before Jesus.* It is not Heaven,* but since it contains no punishment, it is also not Hell.* In much popular usage, the term has come to mean a place where unwanted things or persons are placed, any place between two more interesting places, or a situation in which one has no opportunity to do anything of interest or value.

Lime, Harry. In the movie *The Third Man* (1949), the mysterious criminal, king of the black market in penicillin, who fakes his own death in order to avoid arrest.

Lincoln, Abraham. Historically, president (d. 1865) during the Civil War, identified by his gaunt appearance, his beard, and his stovepipe hat. He is noted for his conduct of the war, his emancipation of the slaves, and his assassination during a performance at Ford's Theatre. Legend and fact are closely intertwined, but the most common stories say he studied by firelight as a boy, was a rail-splitter before becoming a lawyer, and had a mysterious romance with Ann Rutledge* before marrying his wife Mary. As president, he is famous for the Gettysburg Address, which begins "Four score and seven years ago . . . "; his two inaugural addresses; and countless homespun witticisms, anecdotes, and penetrating insights. For many, he is an icon of the American character and is one of the very few politicians whose iconography has survived the scrutiny of history. *Also called* The Emancipator; Honest Abe; Old Abe.

Linda. *See* Loman.

Linet. *See* Lynette.

Linton. In Emily Brontë's novel *Wuthering Heights* (1847), **Edgar** is the cultured and sensitive neighbor who marries Cathy.* His sister **Isabella** is a spoiled girl who marries Heathcliff* against all advice, almost immediately regrets it, and deserts him.

Linus. (1) In Greek legend, the man who taught Heracles* music and was killed when Heracles hit him on the head with a lyre. (2) In the American newspaper cartoon *Peanuts* (beg. 1950), Lucy's* little brother, noted for his perpetual attachment to his security blanket.

Lion. The lion is generally regarded as the "king of beasts" and appears in numerous works as a symbol of strength, courage, and/or nobility; in this guise, he is also the symbol of Great Britain. Notable lions of literature and folklore include the lion who served St. Jerome,* the lion from whose paw Androcles* pulled the thorn, the lion whom Reynard* tricked, the lion in the "Pyramus and Thisbe"* play, and the cowardly lion who joined Dorothy* on her trip to the Wizard of Oz* in hopes of finding courage. *See also* Leo.

Liones. *See* Lyoness.

Lisa, Mona. *See* Mona Lisa.

Litae. In Greek legend, gentle daughters of Zeus* who might intercede with him for persons in distress.

Littimer. In Charles Dickens's novel *David Copperfield* (1849), Steerforth's* valet, the very picture of respectability but a hypocrite beneath; he helps Steerforth seduce Little Em'ly* and then offers to marry her when Steerforth is tired of her.

Little Boy Blue. In Eugene Field's poem *Little Boy Blue* (1888), a now-dead child whose toys are "covered with dust."

Little Dorrit. *See* Dorrit.

Little Em'ly. *See* Em'ly, Little.

Little Eva. *See* Eva.

Little Flower. *See* Theresa, St.

Little Orphan Annie. *See* Annie, Little Orphan.

Little Orphant Annie. (1) In James Whitcomb Riley's poem *Little Orphant Annie* (1885), a servant girl who tells how "the Gobble-uns 'll git you ef you don't watch out." (2) *See also* Annie, Little Orphan.

Little Prince. In Saint-Exupéry's story *The Little Prince* (1943), a small boy from an asteroid who relates a number of experiences of an allegorical nature, noted for their simplicity and penetration.

Littlewit. In Ben Jonson's play *Bartholomew Fair* (1614), the petty official who struggles to get his Puritan mother-in-law to see the puppet show he has written for the fair; his wife Win-the-Fight is simplemindedly naive and is tricked into seeming to be a prostitute, escaping only at the last moment.

Livia. (1) Historically, the wife of Augustus Caesar.* In much rumor and legend, she was a political manipulator who poisoned numerous relatives, and possibly even Caesar himself, in order to guarantee the succession of her son Tiberius.* (2) In Thomas Middleton's play *Women Beware Women* (1621), a personification of pure evil who participates in various seductions, rapes, thefts, lusts, revenges, and murders. *See also* Bianca; Leantio. (3) *See also* Olivia; Livy.

Livy. (1) *See* Primrose. (2) *See also* Livia; Olivia.

Liza. (1) *See* Drozdov. (2) *See also* Eliza.

Lizaveta. (1) In Dostoevsky's novel *The Brothers Karamazov* (1880), a halfwit girl and mother of Smerdyakov.* (2) *See* Drozdov; Prokofievna, Lizaveta. (3) *See also* Elizabeth.

Lizzie. (1) *See* Hexam. (2) *See also* Borden, Lizzie; Elizabeth.

Loam. In J. M. Barrie's play *The Admirable Crichton* (1903), the earl and his family who are stranded on a desert isle, on which their butler Crichton* demonstrates his superiority and takes benevolent control.

Loaves and Fishes. In the Bible, *Matthew* xiv, a miracle made by Jesus.* After preaching to a multitude, He told the Apostles* to feed the crowd, but they had only five loaves and two fishes; He blessed the food, and it fed 5,000. In *Mark* vi–viii, He did this twice, the second time feeding 4,000 with seven loaves and a few fishes.

Lochinvar. In Walter Scott's poem *Marmion* (1808), a dashing knight who "is come out of the west" to the bridal feast for the woman he loves. He pleads one last dance, and as they near the door of the hall, sweeps her out, onto his horse, and away.

Locksley. In Walter Scott's novel *Ivanhoe* (1820), Robin Hood.*

Loge. (1) In Scandinavian mythology, the god of fire. (2) In Richard Wagner's opera *Das Rheingold* (1869), the god of fire who guides Wotan* into the realm of the Niebelung* and helps him steal the ring from Alberich.*

Lohengrin. (1) In Wolfram von Eschenbach's poem *Parzival*, Parzival's* son. (2) In Richard Wagner's opera *Lohengrin* (1850), a mysterious knight who suddenly appears to champion Elsa* and agrees to marry her if she vows never to ask his name; when she ultimately does, he reveals himself as the son of Parsifal,* but leaves to resume his quest for the Grail.* He is also noted for his arrival and departure in a boat drawn by swans.

Lois. In the Bible, *II Timothy* i, Timothy's* grandmother, noted for her piety.

Loki. In Scandinavian mythology, the spirit of evil, also noted as a great trickster; he provided the mistletoe that killed Baldur.*

Lola. In the musical comedy *Damn Yankees* (1955), the beautiful aide of the Devil;* "whatever Lola wants, Lola gets."

Lolita. In Vladimir Nabokov's novel *Lolita* (1955), a seductive American teenaged girl, the epitome of the nymphet. *See also* Humbert, Humbert.

Loman. In Arthur Miller's play *Death of a Salesman* (1949), **Willy** is an old salesman who has lost his touch and is being squeezed out of his company; his mind is also starting to go, and he wanders off into dreams in which he relives his past with his sons, whom he idolized but who have also turned out to be failures. He kills himself in his car to give his family his insurance money. He is often noted as an illustration of the emptiness of those who pursue the materialistic American Dream without success. His son **Biff** was a great school athlete who became disillusioned with his father after discovering him in a hotel room with another woman and who does not want "success," choosing instead to be a simple ranch hand. **Happy**, the other son, is content to be a minor clerk and a woman chaser. **Linda**, Willy's wife, is patient and loving.

Lonelyhearts, Miss. In American slang, a generic title for anyone who writes personal advice columns for a newspaper. In Nathanael West's novel *Miss Lonelyhearts* (1933), a male reporter assigned to the job is soon destroyed by becoming involved in the pathetic problems of the people who write for his advice.

Lone Ranger, The. In the American radio and television series "The Lone Ranger" (beg. 1933), a former Texas Ranger who fights for justice; he is noted for his mask, his horse Silver, his Indian partner Tonto,* the silver bullets he shoots, and the catch-phrase, "Hi-yo, Silver, away."

Longinus. In Christian legend, the soldier at the Crucifixion* who cried out, "Truly this is the Son of God"; he is supposed to have converted and to have been martyred by beheading.

Lopahin. In Anton Chekhov's play *The Cherry Orchard* (1904), a self-made, wealthy, rising businessman; his frustrated love for the distant and beautiful Ranevskaya* causes him to advise her on ways to save her estate, which she ignores, and he finally buys the estate at auction, making himself the owner of the land on which his family had been serfs. He is a complex and fascinating character who represents the rising middle class of Czarist Russia just prior to the revolution. *See also* Varya.

Lord Jim. *See* Jim.

Lord of Hosts. In the Bible, a name for God.

Lord of the Flies. A name sometimes used for the Devil.* Most contemporary allusions, however, are to William Golding's novel *Lord of the Flies* (1954), in which a group of young English schoolboys are marooned on a jungle isle and revert to a state of nature that is brutal and savage.

Lord's Prayer. In the Bible, the prayer taught to His Apostles* by Jesus;* it has slightly different form in *Matthew* vi and *Luke* xi.

Lord's Supper, The. *See* Last Supper, The.

Lorelei. (1) In German legend, a siren* on the Rhine. (2) *See* Lee, Lorelei.

Lorenzo. (1) In Shakespeare's play *The Merchant of Venice* (1596), the Christian with whom Shylock's* daughter Jessica* elopes. (2) *See* Medici; Renzo.

Lorna. *See* Doone.

Lost Generation. Historically, a general name given to the young adults of the 1920s whose ideals had been destroyed by World War I, and in particular to an artistic community, mostly American, who spent the decade in Europe, especially in Paris.

Lot. In the Bible, *Genesis* xiii, xix, a man who traveled with Abraham* out of Egypt and settled near Sodom* and Gomorrah. When God decided to destroy "the cities of the plain" for their wickedness, he warned Lot to leave and not look back; when Lot's wife looked back she was turned into a pillar of salt. Lot's daughters, thinking they were the only survivors in the world, made Lot drunk and slept with him.

Lothario. (1) In Nicholas Rowe's play *The Fair Penitent* (1703), a dashing but heartless libertine and lover. (2) In Goethe's novel *Wilhelm Meister's Apprenticeship* (1795), the nobleman who deserted Aurelia.*

Lotis. In Greek legend, a nymph* pursued by Priapus;* she was changed into the lotus tree.

Lotophagi. In Homer's *Odyssey*, the inhabitants of an island who ate the sweet lotus and lost all desire for action.

Lotte. *See* Charlotte.

Lotus-Eaters. *See* Lotophagi.

Lou. *See* McGrew, Dangerous Dan.

Louis. Historically, the name used by seventeen kings of France, the last of whom was Louis XVIII, Louis XVII having died in prison during the French Revolution. The most notable include **Louis IX**, canonized as St. Louis;* **Louis XIII**, known in literature primarily from his appearances in Alexandre Dumas's novel *The Three Musketeers* (1844) and related works; **Louis XIV;*** and **Louis XVI** (d. 1793), the king whose inability to control the nobles or his wife Marie Antoinette* eventually led to the French Revolution, in which he was guillotined. *See also* Dauphin; Richelieu.

Louis, St. Historically, Louis IX of France (d. 1270), canonized for his pious and just manner and for his leadership in two Crusades, in the first of which he found what was thought to be the cross on which Jesus* was crucified and His crown of thorns.

Louis XIV. Historically, king of France (d. 1715), noted for his long reign in which he consolidated power from his nobles; extended the wealth and power of France; supported such artists as Molière, Racine, and Lully, who made France the center of European culture; and built the palace and elaborate court ritual at Versailles that came to be seen as the epitome of monarchical celebration.

He is often called the Sun King for his gold and the brilliance of his court life. *See also* Man in the Iron Mask.

Louisa. *See* Gradgrind.

Lovborg. In Henrik Ibsen's play *Hedda Gabler* (1890), Hedda Gabler's* former lover, who has reformed, has become a respectable and talented scholar, and has written a manuscript which he believes will guarantee his future. Hedda encourages him to return to alcohol to release his Dionysian spirit and takes his manuscript. Thinking it lost, he contemplates suicide, and Hedda, rather than restore the manuscript, gives him a gun, telling him to "do it beautifully," and burns the manuscript as he shoots himself. *See also* Elvsted, Mrs.

Love. *See* Cupid.

Loveit, Lady. In George Etherege's play *The Man of Mode* (1676), Dorimant's* demanding mistress who unknowingly complains to his new mistress that he has deserted her.

Lovelace. In Samuel Richardson's novel *Clarissa Harlowe* (1747), a young nobleman who seduces Clarissa,* then places her in a brothel; he repents and offers to marry her, but she refuses, and after she dies, he is killed in a duel with her cousin, repenting again.

Loveless. In John Vanbrugh's play *The Relapse* (1696), a country gentleman, once a rake but now married and reformed, who comes to London to test his reformation and easily relapses into his former libertine ways. *See also* Berinthia.

Lovewit. In Ben Jonson's play *The Alchemist* (1610), the master whose house the alchemists use in his absence; on his return, he drives them out but forgives his servant Face,* after taking a cut and accepting the marriage Face has arranged for him.

Lucas. In Prosper Mérimée's novel *Carmen* (1847), the bullfighter for whom Carmen* deserts José;* in Bizet's opera version, he is Escamillo.*

Lucas, Charlotte. *See* Charlotte.

Lucentio. In Shakespeare's play *The Taming of the Shrew* (1593), the young man who woos Bianca* disguised as a schoolmaster while his servant Tranio* impersonates him to distract her father.

Lucia. (1) In Alessandro Manzoni's novel *The Betrothed* (1825), the simple peasant girl whom a noble attempts to abduct, causing her to run away and be separated from her betrothed Renzo;* she takes refuge in a convent but is driven out again to be kidnapped. (2) In Donizetti's opera *Lucia di Lammermoor* (1835), essentially the same as Lucy Ashton;* she is especially noted for a difficult and dramatic "mad scene." (3) *See also* Lucie; Lucy.

Lucie. (1) *See* Carton, Sidney. (2) *See also* Lucia; Lucy.

Lucien. *See* Chardon, Lucien.

Lucifer. A name sometimes used for Satan,* perhaps from a misreading of a reference in the Bible, *Isaiah* xiv, to the morning star.

Lucina. In Roman mythology, goddess of childbirth, generally equivalent to Eilythyia.*

Lucius. In Apuleius's *The Golden Ass*, a licentious Roman who steals a magic salve, only to discover too late that it was the wrong salve and he has been turned into an ass.

Lucrece. *See* Lucretia.

Lucretia. (1) In Roman legend, a Roman wife who was raped by a prince and who then stabbed herself; public outrage at this crime led to the end of the Roman monarchy and to the institution of the republic. *Also called* Lucrece. (2) *See also* Lucrezia.

Lucrezia. (1) *See* Borgia. (2) *See also* Lucretia.

Lucy. (1) In numerous plays during the English Restoration, a common name for a lady's maid. (2) In William Wordsworth's *Lucy* poems (1799), a child of nature who "dwelt among the untrodden ways," and for whom "strange fits of passion have I known." (3) In Bram Stoker's novel *Dracula* (1897), the beautiful English woman who, repeatedly attacked by Dracula,* becomes a vampire* herself. (4) In the American newspaper cartoon *Peanuts* (beg. 1950), the bossy girl with the black hair, noted for her self-satisfaction, her nagging, and her unrequited love for the piano player. (5) *See* Ashton, Lucy; Desborough, Lucy; Ricardo; Steele, Lucy. (6) *See also* Lucia; Lucie.

Lucy, St. In Christian legend, a Roman Christian woman who gave all her wealth to the poor, which so angered her fiancé that he betrayed her and she was ordered executed; when flames would not touch her, she was stabbed in the throat. She is supposed to be particularly helpful against diseases of the eyes; her day is December 13.

Lucy and Ricky. *See* Ricardo.

Lud. In English legend, a great king and founder of London.

Luddite. Historically, a group of English weavers who, fearing the introduction of new looms would end their jobs, in 1811 tried to destroy the looms; the term quickly came to be used to indicate anyone who tried to oppose new technology or machines by unthinkingly destroying them.

Ludmilla. (1) In Pushkin's poem *Ruslan and Ludmilla* (1820), a beautiful woman abducted by a wicked magician and pursued and rescued by her husband Ruslan.* (2) *See* Rustilova, Ludmilla.

Luggnagg. In Jonathan Swift's novel *Gulliver's Travels* (1726), the land in which Gulliver* meets the immortal Struldbrugs.*

Luke. In the Bible, the author of *Luke* and *Acts*, a Greek physician who converted and became an evangelist, perhaps accompanying Paul* on part of his journeys. The patron saint of doctors and medicine, his day is October 18 and his symbol is a winged ox.

Luke, St. *See* Luke.

Lulu. In Franz Wedekind's *Lulu* play trilogy (1918), a mysterious woman who embodies the spirit of Woman, both mother/nurturer and temptress/destroyer.

Lumpkin, Tony. In Oliver Goldsmith's play *She Stoops to Conquer* (1773), a boisterous, bawdy, and crude country gentleman given to practical jokes. He tells Marlow* that his stepfather Hardcastle's* house is an inn, thus setting in motion the plot of the play, but he also comes into his own as the spoiled son of Mrs. Hardcastle who does not much like the way she spoils him, eventually dumping her into the pond in order to prevent an arranged marriage he does not want. For many, he is one of the supreme comic creations of the English theater. *See also* Neville, Constance.

Luna. In Greek mythology, the goddess of the moon, sometimes identified with Artemis* and sometimes seen as a separate goddess.

Lupercalia. *See* Lupercus.

Lupercus. In Roman mythology, a god of fertility, celebrated in the Lupercalia, and sometimes associated with Faunus.*

Lupin, Arsène. In numerous novels by Maurice Leblanc, beginning with *Arsène Lupin* (1907), a gentleman crook turned detective.

Lycidas. (1) In Virgil's *Eclogues*, a shepherd. (2) In John Milton's poem *Lycidas* (1638), the metaphorical name of the dead friend whose loss Milton mourns.

Lycomedes. In Greek legend, the man who threw Theseus* over a cliff, thus killing him.

Lycurgus. In Greek legend, an impious king of Thrace who drove the worshipers of Dionysus* away and was in turn driven mad by the god; he thought his son was a tree and killed him with an ax, and then he cut off his own legs, thinking they were branches.

Lydgate. In George Eliot's novel *Middlemarch* (1871), a progressive doctor whose career is destroyed after he marries **Rosamund**, a spoiled, spendthrift woman who lives far beyond their means.

Lydia. (1) In the Bible, *Acts* xvi, a "seller of purple" and a woman who converted when she heard Paul* preach. (2) *See* Bennet; Languish, Lydia.

Lynceus. *See* Hypermnestra.

Lyndall. In Olive Schreiner's novel *The Story of an African Farm* (1883), a serious-minded young woman who leaves her African farm to go to the city, where she has an affair, is deserted, and dies, returning to the farm only to be buried. *See also* Waldo.

Lynette. In Malory's *Morte d'Arthur*, a lady who seeks help for her sister Lyoness, who is besieged by four evil knights, and is disdainful when Gareth,* the kitchen boy, is sent on the quest. After he is successful, he marries Lyoness, although in Tennyson's poem *Gareth and Lynette* (1872), he marries Lynette instead. *Also called* Linet.

Lyoness. *See* Lynette.

Lysander. (1) Historically, a Spartan* (d. 395 B.C.) who captured Athens, thus ending the Peloponnesian War. (2) In Shakespeare's play *A Midsummer Night's Dream* (1595), the young lover who elopes with Hermia.* *See also* Demetrius.

Lysistrata. In Aristophanes's play *Lysistrata*, an Athenian woman who, upset by the waste and futility of the war with Sparta, organizes the women of both cities to go on strike and refuse to have sexual relations with any of the men until the war is ended. *See also* Lampito; Myrrhine.

M

Mab. In English folklore, the fairy* who acted as "midwife" to men's dreams; the most famous allusion is Mercutio's* speech in Shakespeare's play *Romeo and Juliet* (1595).

Mabel. In Gilbert and Sullivan's operetta *The Pirates of Penzance* (1880), the ingenue; she sings "Poor Wandering One."

Macaire, Robert. In Benjamin Antier's play *L'Auberge des Andres* (1823), an exuberant con man; he may also be connected to a medieval legend of a murderer of similar name who was sniffed out by the victim's dog. Plays and stories about him became so common and popular for several decades that the name became synonymous with criminals and for some with Frenchmen in general.

Macbeth. In Shakespeare's play *Macbeth* (1605), a Scottish noble whose rise to the throne is prophesied by three witches; under prodding from his wife, he tries to make the prophecy come true by murdering the king Duncan.* He is given the throne, murders his friend Banquo,* whose children were also prophesied to take the throne, and becomes a cruel tyrant. He fears no one because of a second prophecy which says that his castle will stand until Burnham Wood walks and that he cannot be killed by a man born of woman. When the country revolts, the troops are camouflaged by tree branches and he is killed by Macduff,* who was born by Caesarean section. **Lady Macbeth** is initially a tough, ambitious woman who provides the courage Macbeth lacks, but she goes mad with guilt, demonstrated in the sleepwalking scene in which she says, "Out, out, damned spot."

Maccabee. In the Bible, in the Apochrypha, *I & II Maccabees*, a family who led a series of Jewish rebellions against the Syrians lasting approximately a century. The best known was Judas, whose recapture of Jerusalem* is celebrated in the feast of Hanukkah. These wars ended only when Rome conquered both countries (63 B.C.), although the Maccabees led several abortive revolts against the Romans as well.

McCaslin. In several novels and stories by William Faulkner, a Southern family representative of the complex problems of interracial relations. The family is founded by **Luke**, who sires a legitimate, white branch and simultaneously with a slave girl sires an illegitimate, Negro branch, including a son incestuously born from Luke's half-Negro daughter. The most notable later member is **Ike**, in *The Bear* (1942), who gains maturity on a dangerous bear hunt and then renounces his inheritance in order to revive his true communion with nature.

M'Choakumchild. In Charles Dickens's novel *Hard Times* (1854), the fact-oriented master of Gradgrind's* model school.

McCoy. *See* Hatfield.

Macduff. In Shakespeare's play *Macbeth* (1605), an honorable noble who kills and beheads Macbeth,* after the latter had murdered his family, fulfilling the prophecy that no man born of woman could kill him, since Macduff was born by Caesarean section.

McGee, Fibber. In the American radio series *Fibber McGee and Molly* (1935–52), a comic husband and homeowner and his wife Molly, noted for their hall closet, the contents of which crashed around Fibber whenever he opened the door, and Molly's catch-phrase, "Tain't funny, McGee."

Macgregor, Farmer. In Beatrix Potter's story *The Tale of Peter Rabbit* (1900), the farmer who tries to kill Peter Rabbit.*

McGrew, Dangerous Dan. In Robert Service's poem *The Shooting of Dan McGrew* (1907), one of the men "whooping it up in the Malamute saloon" who is killed in a gunfight over the lady Lou.

Macheath. In John Gay's operetta *The Beggar's Opera* (1728), a handsome, sensual highwayman betrayed to the police by Peachum,* his father-in-law. He escapes by promising marriage to the jailer's daughter, is recaptured, and then miraculously is pardoned on the scaffold. In Bertolt Brecht's version *The Threepenny Opera* (1928), he is more vicious, nicknamed "Mack the Knife" for his sadistic murders. *See also* Diver, Jenny.

Machiavelli. Historically, an Italian author (d. 1527) and statesman, most noted for his work *The Prince* (1532), in which he described the practical but often brutal or devious ways the Italian princes of his time obtained and maintained power. Hence, for many, particularly outside of Italy, he became synonymous with devious political machination, assassination, and duplicity.

Mack the Knife. *See* Macheath.

Macmorris. In Shakespeare's play *Henry V* (1598), noted primarily as the only Irishman in Shakespeare's works.

Macquart. *See* Rougon-Macquart.

MacStinger, Mrs. In Charles Dickens's novel *Dombey and Son* (1846), the sharp-tongued widow and landlady who terrifies Capt. Cuttle* and eventually marries Bunsby.*

McTeague. In Frank Norris's novel *McTeague* (1899), a crude and greedy dentist who loses his practice and murders his miserly wife; he himself dies of exposure in Death Valley after he kills a man to whom he is handcuffed.

Madeleine. (1) A small, French, cakelike cookie, noted primarily as the food whose taste prompts the memories from which Marcel* builds the complex recollections of Marcel Proust's novels *Remembrance of Things Past* (1913–27). (2) *See also* Madeline; Magdalene.

Madeline. (1) *See* Bray; Usher. (2) *See also* Madeleine; Magdalene.

Mad Hatter. In Lewis Carroll's story *Alice in Wonderland* (1865), a guest at the tea party who asks Alice* absurd riddles and is extremely rude. *See also* Dormouse; March Hare.

Madonna. An Italian name meaning "my lady" and applied almost exclusively to the Virgin Mary,* usually when considered as the mother of Jesus.* After centuries of paintings depicting the Madonna holding the Christchild, the name is sometimes given to any young mother similarly posed.

Maenads. A name sometimes used for the Bacchae.* *See also* Orpheus.

Maeonides. A name sometimes used for the Muses.*

Maeve, Queen. In Irish legend, a queen noted for her amorousness and for her attempt to conquer Cuchulain's* kingdom.

Magdalene. (1) *See* Mary Magdalene. (2) *See also* Madeleine; Madeline.

Maggie. (1) In Tennessee Williams's play *Cat On a Hot Tin Roof* (1955), the frustrated and sensual wife of the alcoholic Brick.* *Also called* Maggie the Cat. (2) *See* Jiggs; Tulliver. (3) *See also* Maggy; Margaret; Meg.

Maggy. (1) In Charles Dickens's novel *Little Dorrit* (1855), the friend of Little Dorrit,* partially bald, blind in one eye, and destined "never to be older than ten" due to the damage done by a childhood fever. (2) *See also* Maggie; Margaret; Meg.

Magi. In the Bible, *Matthew* ii, the Three Wise Men who brought gifts of gold, frankincense, and myrrh to the baby Jesus* after following a star to the stable in which He was born; legend says their names were Balthazar,* Gaspar,* and Melchior.*

Magog. *See* Gog.

Magwitch. In Charles Dickens's novel *Great Expectations* (1860), the convict who terrifies Pip* in the graveyard then escapes to Australia where he makes a fortune and secretly provides the bequest that puts Pip into a gentleman's life; when he returns to see his young gentleman, he is arrested and dies in prison.

Mahon, Christy. In J. M. Synge's play *The Playboy of the Western World* (1907), a naive young peasant boy who becomes a temporary hero in an Irish village when the villagers believe he has murdered his father. *See also* Pegeen.

Maia. In Greek legend, loveliest of the Pleiades* and mother of Hermes.*

Maid Marian. *See* Marian.

Maigret. In numerous novels by Georges Simenon (beg. 1931), a French police detective who solves crimes by intuition and psychological insight.

Maisie. *See* Farange.

Mak. In the anonymous *Second Shepherd's Play*, a thief who tries to disguise a stolen sheep as one of his children and who is with the shepherds* who are told of Jesus's* birth.

Malabar Caves. In E. M. Forster's novel *A Passage to India* (1924), the site at which the attempted rape of Adela Quested* may or may not have occurred.

Malachi. In the Bible, *Malachi*, a Hebrew prophet whose prophecy is devoted primarily to a coming day of judgement.

Malagrowther. In Walter Scott's novel *The Fortunes of Nigel* (1822), a confidant of the king; also a pseudonym used in correspondence by Scott.

Malaprop, Mrs. In R. B. Sheridan's play *The Rivals* (1775), a domineering, pretentious woman noted for her eccentric mangling of the language, such as the famous ''allegory of the Nile,'' now called malapropisms.

Malatesta. In Dante's *Divine Comedy*, a hunchback count married to Francesca da Rimini;* when he discovers her affair with his brother Paolo,* he kills them both.

Malcolm. In Shakespeare's play *Macbeth* (1605), Duncan's* son who escapes to England and organizes the revolt against Macbeth.* *See also* Donalbain.

Malfi, Duchess of. In John Webster's play *The Duchess of Malfi* (1613), a beautiful widow who marries her chamberlain against her brother Ferdinand's* wishes; refusing to be driven mad by his torture, she is finally strangled by Bosola.*

Malmsey, Butt of. *See* Clarence.

Malvolio. In Shakespeare's play *Twelfth Night* (1599), the pompous puritanical steward who dreams of marrying the lady Olivia.* He is ridiculed by a ruse that encourages him to wear ludicrous "cross-garters" and to smile, for which he is thought to be insane. *See also* Belch, Sir Toby; Feste; Maria.

Mambrino. In Ariosto's *Orlando Furioso* (1516), the owner of an enchanted helmet that made the wearer invulnerable; in Cervantes's novel *Don Quixote* (1605), Don Quixote* mistook a barber's basin for this helmet.

Mame. In Patrick Dennis's novel *Auntie Mame* (1954), and in several stage and movie versions, a flamboyant, scatterbrained woman noted for the madcap gusto with which she enjoys a life full of wild ups and downs.

Mamie. *See* Pocock.

Mammon. In the Bible, *Luke* xvi, a word originally meaning "riches." In medieval usage, the word gradually was transformed into a personification of greed, often called the god of money, as in Edmund Spenser's poem *The Faerie Queene* (1590), in which he has a cave housing a great treasure. In Milton's poem *Paradise Lost* (1667), he is an angel* allied with Satan* noted for his materialism.

Mammon, Sir Epicure. In Ben Jonson's play *The Alchemist* (1610), an arrogant, lustful, and greedy knight.

Manasseh. (1) In the Bible, *Genesis*, the eldest son of Joseph;* one of the twelve tribes of Israel* is sometimes identified by his name, and sometimes shared with his brother Ephraim.* (2) In the Bible, *II Kings* xxi, a king of Judah* noted for his long reign and his idolatry.

Manasses. *See* Manasseh.

Manciple. In Chaucer's *Canterbury Tales*, he tells the story of Phoebus* and the crow.

Mandarin. Historically, a Portuguese name for upper-level bureaucrats in China that soon came to be used for all Chinese rulers; in most instances, they were identified by a long, drooping mustache and extremely long fingernails. In recent usages, the term has come to imply any who devote themselves to complex, intellectual activity and are incapable of any "useful" labor.

Manderley. In Daphne du Maurier's novel *Rebecca* (1938), the mansion owned by de Winter* and the epitome of the mysterious great house so essential to the gothic romance genre.

Manders. In Henrik Ibsen's play *Ghosts* (1881), the self-righteous pastor. *See also* Alving.

Manfred. (1) In Hugh Walpole's novel *The Castle of Otranto* (1764), an usurping prince who tries to marry his dead son's bride until he is driven to conversion by exotic supernatural forces. (2) In Byron's poem/play *Manfred* (1817), a man haunted by the demons of guilt for an unexplained crime; he calls up the spirits of the universe in search of oblivion.

Mangan. In G. B. Shaw's play *Heartbreak House* (1920), a domineering industrialist and political power who is exposed as a weak, unimaginative person without money or authority of his own. *See also* Dunn; Hushabye; Shotover, Capt.

Mania. In Roman mythology, mother of the Lares* and the goddess of the dead, sometimes called the goddess of ghosts.*

Manly. In William Wycherley's play *The Plain Dealer* (1674), a misanthropic sea captain whose attempts at plain dealing make problems for himself and for his associates. *See also* Fidelia; Olivia.

Manna. In the Bible, *Exodus* xvi, the food that God caused to appear on the ground each morning for the Jews to eat while wandering in the desert.

Mannon. In Eugene O'Neill's play *Mourning Becomes Electra* (1931), the New England family whose tragedy is depicted. **Ezra** is a Civil War officer who is murdered by his wife **Christine** and her lover. Her son **Orin** is taunted by his imperious, jealous, and obsessive sister **Lavinia** until he kills the lover; the two children then drive Christine to suicide.

Manoah. In the Bible, *Judges* xiii, the father of Samson* after an angel* appeared to his wife, who had long been barren; he was particularly slow to believe the angel.

Man of Law. In Chaucer's *Canterbury Tales*, the lawyer who tells the story of Constance.*

Manon. In the Abbé Prévost's novel *Manon Lescaut* (1731), a young girl who runs away from a convent to be with her lover Des Grieux,* who continues to love her despite her numerous infidelities. She is transported to Louisiana, where he joins her, and they eventually die together in the wilderness. Her story has inspired two major operas, Massenet's *Manon* (1884) and Puccini's *Manon Lescaut* (1893).

Manrico. In Verdi's opera *Il Trovatore* (1853), a young man, really the son of a count, raised by the gypsy woman Azucena.* When he falls in love with Leonora,* the evil Count di Luna* arranges his death, learning too late that they are brothers.

Mantalini. In Charles Dickens's novel *Nicholas Nickleby* (1838), **Mrs. Mantalini** is an efficient and successful milliner in whose shop Kate Nickleby* works; **Mr. Mantalini** is a fop whose spendthrift ways destroy the business.

Mantee, Duke. In Robert Sherwood's play *The Petrified Forest* (1935), a psychotic criminal who terrorizes a group trapped in a western diner.

Mantua, Duke of. In Verdi's opera *Rigoletto* (1851), a libertine noble who tries to seduce Rigoletto's* innocent daughter Gilda;* he sings the famous ''La donna e mobile.''

Marat. Historically, a radical French revolutionary (d. 1793) and pamphleteer, who called himself the voice of the people; because of a skin disease, he spent much of his time in a bath, where he was assassinated by Charlotte Corday.

Marathon. Historically, the site of a great Athenian victory (490 B.C.) over the Persians. The marathon race is based on the distance run by a messenger from the battle to Athens. In legend, Theseus* killed the great bull on the same site.

Marcel. In Marcel Proust's novels *Remembrance of Things Past* (1913–27), the narrator. *See* Albertine; Charlus; Françoise; Gilberte; Guermantes; Madeleine; Odette; Saint-Loup; Swann.

Marceline. In Beaumarchais's play *The Marriage of Figaro* (1784), a jealous old woman who demands Figaro* repay a loan or marry her, only to discover that he is her long-lost son.

Marcellina. In Mozart's opera *The Marriage of Figaro* (1786), Marceline.*

Marcellus. In Shakespeare's play *Hamlet* (1600), an officer of the guard who first sees the ghost of Hamlet's* father.

Marcellus, St. Historically, a Roman centurion (d. 298) who was executed for refusing to celebrate the emperor's birthday.

March. In Louisa May Alcott's novel *Little Women* (1868), the family described. *See* Amy; Beth; Jo; Meg.

March, Ides of. *See* Ides.

Marchbanks. In G. B. Shaw's play *Candida* (1897), an exaggeratedly sensitive, effeminate, and frail young poet. *See also* Candida.

March Hare. In Lewis Carroll's story *Alice in Wonderland* (1865), the hare who invites Alice* to join the tea party. *See also* Dormouse; Mad Hatter.

Marchmain. In Evelyn Waugh's novel *Brideshead Revisited* (1945), the family name of the people who live at Brideshead. The most noted are **Sebastian**, a beautiful and charming student with whom Charles Ryder* becomes a friend and a lover but who wastes his life in alcoholism; **Julia**, Ryder's mistress, noted for her expression of Catholic guilt; their mother **Lady Marchmain**, whose Catholic devotion is the central aspect of her life; and the **Marquis**, who has lived for years in Italy with his mistress to avoid his wife and her religion.

Margaret. (1) Historically, the "she-wolf of Anjou," wife (d. 1482) of Henry VI,* known for her aggressive partisanship in the Wars of the Roses. She figures prominently as a cruel, dominating woman in Shakespeare's *Henry VI* plays, and is particularly noted in Shakespeare's play *Richard III* (1592), in which she prophesies and curses Richard III.* (2) In Walter Scott's poem *The Lay of the Last Minstrel* (1805), the beautiful maiden. (3) *See* Gretchen; Ramsay. (4) *See also* Maggie; Maggy; Marguerite; Meg; Peg; Pegeen.

Margaret, St. (1) In Christian legend, a young girl who refused to marry a pagan governor, for which she was imprisoned with a fire-breathing dragon that swallowed her; as she was eaten, she made the sign of the cross and that cross grew within the dragon's body until it was split open and she was saved, later to be beheaded. She is often depicted with a dragon, and her day is July 20. (2) Historically, a queen of Scotland (d. 1093) noted for her strength of character and her efforts to bring Scotland firmly into the Christian fold. (3) Historically, Margaret Mary, a French nun (d. 1690) whose four visions of Jesus,* in which He explained the importance of His heart, were instrumental in encouraging the Sacred Heart devotions of the Church.

Margareta. *See* Gretchen.

Marguerite. (1) In Gounod's opera *Faust* (1850), Gretchen.* (2) *See* Camille. (3) *See also* Margaret.

Maria. (1) In Shakespeare's play *Love's Labour's Lost* (1595), one of the witty ladies. *See also* Dumaine; Rosaline. (2) In Shakespeare's play *Twelfth Night* (1599), Olivia's* witty servant who thinks up the plot against Malvolio.* (3) In Laurence Sterne's *A Sentimental Journey* (1768), a young French peasant girl who, when her banns had been forbidden, went mad and sat with her dog by the road singing hymns. (4) In R. B. Sheridan's play *The School for Scandal* (1777), Teazle's* beautiful and patient young ward, who waits for her true love Charles Surface.* (5) In Ernest Hemingway's novel *For Whom the Bell Tolls* (1940), an innocent Spanish girl who is taken into a guerilla band and becomes the American Jordan's* lover; perhaps most remembered for the time "the earth moved" when she shared Jordan's sleeping bag. (6) *See* Bertram. (7) *See also* Marie; Mary; Maurya.

Maria Goretti, St. Historically, a girl (d. 1902) who was stabbed by a rapist when she resisted at the age of twelve. Her name often arises because the assailant was not executed; he later converted and became a prime illustration for those opposed to capital punishment.

Mariamne. (1) Two different wives of Herod* the Great had this name: the first was executed after being accused of adultery by her sister, and the second, a great beauty, was divorced after she joined a plot against him. (2) *See also* Marian; Marianne; Mary; Miriam.

Marian. (1) In English folklore, a noblewoman who aids Robin Hood.* (2) In Meredith Willson's musical play *The Music Man* (1957), the prim librarian who hopes for a white knight* and gets Harold Hill.* (3) *See also* Mariamne; Mariana; Marianne; Mary; Miriam.

Mariana. (1) In Shakespeare's play *Measure for Measure* (1604), the faithful fiancée of Angelo;* although deserted by him, she finally wins him by substituting for Isabella* in Angelo's bed. (2) In Goethe's novel *Wilhelm Meister's Apprenticeship* (1795), Wilhelm's* first love, whom he abandons when he learns of her past affairs with others; she dies of a broken heart after bearing his son. (3) In Tennyson's poem *Mariana* (1830), a woman left alone, all "aweary, aweary," who wishes she were dead. (4) *See also* Mariamne; Marian; Marianne; Mary; Miriam.

Marianne. (1) In Marivaux's novel *Marianne* (1731), an orphan of beleaguered virtue. (2) Historically, a password used by a French secret society planning the overthrow of Napoleon* III and restoration of the republic; the name eventually came to stand for the French Republic itself. (3) *See* Dashwood. (4) *See also* Mariamne; Marian; Mariana; Mary; Miriam.

Marie. (1) In Georg Buchner's play *Woyzeck* (1879), the earthy and unfaithful mistress murdered by Woyzeck.* (2) *See* Desqueyroux. (3) *See also* Maria; Mary.

Marie Antoinette. Historically, the wife of Louis* XVI (d. 1793) noted for her frivolous and spendthrift ways which symbolized all the selfishness and decadence that led to the French Revolution. She is most remembered, however, for saying, "Let them eat cake," when she was told that the poor had no bread.

Marina. In Shakespeare's play *Pericles* (1608), Pericles's* daughter, who is entrusted to the care of Cleon* and Dionyza.* When she is grown, Dionyza jealously tries to have her murdered, but she is saved when she is kidnapped by pirates, who sell her into a brothel where her unassailable virginity bankrupts the brothel keepers.

Mariner, Ancient. In Samuel Taylor Coleridge's poem *The Rime of the Ancient Mariner* (1798), a sailor who kills an albatross, which brings a curse upon his ship, becalming it so that all die of thirst except the mariner; he is given a vision of God's grace and condemned to wander the earth telling his story to strangers. While they are becalmed, his shipmates make him wear the dead albatross around his neck. He is noted especially for "water, water everywhere and not a drop to drink."

Marius. (1) In Victor Hugo's novel *Les Misérables* (1862), the young lawyer in love with Cosette;* he is wounded on the barricades in the revolution, but is saved when Jean Valjean* carries him through the sewers of Paris. (2) In Marcel

Pagnol's *Fanny* play trilogy (1929–36), the handsome sailor with whom Fanny*
falls in love and by whom she has a child after he leaves her to go back to sea.

Mark. (1) In the Bible, *Acts*, a convert and companion of Paul* and author of
the gospel bearing his name, generally regarded as the oldest of the four gospels.
In Christian legend, while proselytizing he was driven among the lagoons of
northern Italy, where an angel* predicted a great city would arise, for which he
became the patron saint of Venice; he was said to have been martyred in Libya.
His symbol is the winged lion, and his day is April 25. (2) In Malory's *Morte
d'Arthur*, the king of Cornwall who marries Isoud* and murders Tristram* when
the latter's affair with her is discovered. (3) *See* Tapley, Mark.

Mark, St. *See* Mark.

Marley. In Charles Dickens's story *A Christmas Carol* (1843), Scrooge's* dead
partner whose ghost comes back to warn Scrooge of the misery that awaits him
after death and of the other ghosts who will visit.

Marlow. (1) In Oliver Goldsmith's play *She Stoops to Conquer* (1773), a young
man terrified of ladies but relaxed and flirtatious with serving girls; he mistakes
Kate Hardcastle* for a servant, woos her effectively, and thus accidentally brings
off the marriage his father had already arranged. *See also* Hastings. (2) In several
novels by Joseph Conrad, a sailor who relates various adventures and
observations. His most notable appearances are in *Lord Jim* (1900), in which
his life interweaves with that of Jim,* whose story he ostensibly relates in one
long, single evening's talk, and in *Heart of Darkness* (1902), in which Marlow
travels up the Congo River to find Kurtz* and recognizes the savage darkness
within himself as well.

Marlowe, Philip. In several novels by Raymond Chandler, beginning with *The
Big Sleep* (1939), a tough, cynical, but honorable and sensitive private detective,
the model for generations of "hard-boiled" detectives.

Marmeladova, Sofia. *See* Sonya.

Marmion. In Walter Scott's poem *Marmion* (1808), an English knight with
spotless reputation who seduces a young nun then abandons her for a wealthy
noblewoman and whose repentance is made as he is dying on the battlefield.
See also Clare, Lady; Constance.

Marneffe, Mme. In Balzac's novel *Cousin Bette* (1847), a beautiful, heartless,
and adulterous neighbor of Bette;* her sexual affairs help to destroy the Hulots.*

Marner, Silas. In George Eliot's novel *Silas Marner* (1861), a misanthropic
weaver and miser whose hoard is stolen but who is led back to human kindness
by the orphan Eppie,* whom he comes to see as his new treasure. In America
in particular, many allusions are not to the character but to the boredom and

agony he represents for several generations of students who were forced to read the novel before they were old enough to be interested in it.

Marpessa. In Greek legend, a beautiful young woman abducted by Apollo* and pursued by her human lover Idas;* when Zeus* gave her a choice between them, she selected Idas.

Marple, Miss. In numerous novels by Agatha Christie (beg. 1928), an elderly Englishwoman of unprepossessing appearance who shows remarkable skill in solving mysteries.

Mars. In Roman mythology, the god of war, generally equivalent to Ares.*

Marschallin. In Richard Strauss's opera *Der Rosenkavalier* (1911), a mature noblewoman who loses her young lover Octavian* to the beautiful young Sophie* and accepts it as a bittersweet fact of life.

Marsyas. In Ovid's *Metamorphoses*, a flute player who challenged Apollo* to a music contest; when he lost, he was flayed alive.

Martext. In Shakespeare's play *As You Like It* (1599), an illiterate vicar.

Martha. (1) In the Bible, *John* xi, the sister of Mary* and Lazarus;* her faith allowed Jesus* to bring Lazarus back from the dead. She is generally associated with household affairs and is shown in art with a ladle or keys in her hand. (2) *See* George and Martha; Trapbois.

Martha, St. *See* Martha.

Martin. *See* Chuzzlewit; Guerre, Martin.

Martin, St. (1) Historically, Martin of Tours, a soldier (d. 397) who converted when Jesus* appeared to him after he had given half his cloak to a beggar. Known for his missionary work and his spiritual integrity, he established the monastic system in France, but was lured back from his monastery and made a bishop. He is patron saint of drunkards, perhaps because his feast day is November 11, the ancient feast of Bacchus;* in England, this was the traditional date at which the winter slaughtering began. (2) Historically, Martin de Porres, a Peruvian mulatto priest (d. 1639) who worked among the poor and became a patron for those working for improved interracial relations.

Martine. In Molière's play *The Doctor In Spite of Himself* (1666), Sganarelle's* nagging wife.

Martins, Holly. In the movie *The Third Man* (1949), a naive American writer who finds himself in a complex web of devious European intrigue in postwar Vienna. *See also* Lime, Harry.

Marwood, Mrs. In William Congreve's play *The Way of the World* (1700), the bitter mistress of Fainall* and jealous former mistress of Mirabell.*

Mary. (1) In the Bible, the mother of Jesus.* Although married to Joseph,* she was a virgin and conceived Jesus when the angel Gabriel* announced to her that she would bear the Son of God; she gave birth in a stable in Bethlehem* because there was no room for her in the inns there. Not much is heard about her after He grows up. In medieval Europe, she gradually came to be seen as the principal intercessor between mankind and God and was believed to have been made the queen of Heaven.* She is depicted as the ideal woman, graceful, merciful, and a loving mother, yet eternally a virgin and without taint of sin, underlined by the tradition of her own Immaculate Conception. She is most often represented as the Madonna* with the Child in her arms or as the Pietà,* holding the dead body of Jesus across her lap. *Also called* Maria; Miriam; the Virgin Mary. *See also* Annunciation; James. (2) In the Bible, *John* xi, the sister of Martha* and Lazarus;* she washed Jesus's feet and wiped them with her hair, and her faith allowed Him to bring Lazarus back from the dead. Sometimes confused with Mary Magdalene.* (3) In the Bible, the mother of the apostle James* the Lesser; she also accompanied Mary Magdalene* to Jesus's tomb. (4) In several poems by Robert Burns, most notably *Highland Mary* (1792), a beautiful Scottish maiden and a figure of love and romance. (5) *See* Elliot. (6) *See also* Maria; Mariamne; Marian; Mariana; Marie; Marya; Masha; Maurya; Miriam; Molly; Polly.

Mary, Bloody. Historically, Mary Tudor, half-sister of Elizabeth* and queen of England (d. 1558), called Bloody Mary for her persecutions of Protestants after restoring Catholicism as the national religion upon assuming the throne. *See also* Philip.

Mary, Queen of Scots. Historically, Mary Stuart, a distant cousin (d. 1587) of Elizabeth,* to whom her Catholicism and claim to the English throne made her a threat. She is a popular figure of history and romance due to her beauty, charm, and impetuosity, especially in the events surrounding the flagrant murder of her husband and her elopement with and immediate marriage to the man assumed to have murdered him. When she fled to England, Elizabeth imprisoned her, but she became involved in a number of both serious and absurd plots to take the throne and was eventually beheaded. Sometimes confused with Bloody Mary.* In Schiller's play *Maria Stuart* (1800), she has a great personal confrontation with Elizabeth, which never in fact occurred but which has since remained the core of almost all other plays and novels about her.

Mary, St. (1) Mary Magdalene.* (2) In Christian legend, Mary of Egypt, a prostitute who joined a pilgrimage to seduce the pilgrims but was converted in Jerusalem* and became a hermit, living for many years on three loaves of bread.

Mary, Virgin. *See* Mary.

Marya. (1) In Dostoevsky's novel *The Possessed* (1867), a lame, half-witted girl who secretly marries Stavrogin* and is eventually murdered at his behest. (2) *See* Bolkonsky; Masha. (2) *See also* Maria; Mary.

Mary Magdalene. In the Bible, New Testament Gospels, a woman possessed of evil spirits which were cast out by Jesus;* she became a follower, was present at the Crucifixion,* was one of the women who discovered His open tomb, and saw Him after His Resurrection.* Christian tradition also identifies her as the prostitute (*Luke* vii) who annointed the feet of Jesus and wiped them with her hair, although she is not named in the passage, and a different Mary, Martha's* sister, also does the same thing (*John* xi). She is seen as the ultimate example of the repentant sinner and is often depicted with beautiful flowing hair. *Also called* St. Mary, her day is July 22.

Marys, Three. The Virgin Mary,* Mary Magdalene,* and Mary,* the mother of James; legend says all three came to Provence, where their joint festival of May 25 became a major celebration.

Mary Stuart. *See* Mary, Queen of Scots.

Mary Tudor. *See* Mary, Bloody.

Mascarille. In several plays by Molière, most notably *Les Précieuses ridicules* (1659), a clever, impudent servant.

Masha. (1) In Tolstoy's novel *Anna Karenina* (1875), the faithful mistress of Nicholas Levin* who, despite his violent temper, nurses him as he nears death. *Also called* Marya Nikolaevna. (2) In Anton Chekhov's play *The Sea Gull* (1896), the dreaming daughter of the estate manager; she is hopelessly in love with Constantin* although married to Medvidenko,* whom she browbeats as a result of her own disappointment. (3) In Anton Chekhov's play *Three Sisters* (1901), the middle sister, the frustrated wife of a schoolteacher she thought brilliant when she married him. Discontented when he turns out to be merely a good man, she has an affair with the philosophical Vershinin.* *See also* Irina; Olga; Prozorov. (4) *See also* Marya.

Maskwell. In William Congreve's play *The Double Dealer* (1694), the double dealer.

Mason, Perry. In numerous novels by Earle Stanley Gardner (beg. 1933) and in the American television series ''Perry Mason'' (beg. 1957), an imaginative criminal lawyer who always solves the murder, saves his client, and reveals the true criminal in brilliant courtroom cross-examinations.

Mason-Dixon Line. Historically, the border between Pennsylvania and Maryland surveyed by Mason and Dixon in 1763; generally denoted as the line dividing slave states from free states and the North from the South.

Massacre of the Innocents. *See* Herod.

Mathias. (1) In Leopold Lewis's play *The Bells* (1871), a respected businessman who is haunted by guilt for a murder he committed in his past; the name is almost invariably associated with Henry Irving, the actor who made the role famous. (2) *See also* Matthias.

Mathilde. In Stendhal's novel *The Red and the Black* (1830), a marquis's daughter whom Julien Sorel* intends to marry until his previous mistress exposes his past. *See also* Renal.

Matthew. (1) In the Bible, a tax collector who becomes one of the twelve Apostles;* he is also traditionally credited as the author of the first gospel. His day is September 21. (2) In Ben Jonson's play *Every Man In His Humour* (1598), the pseudopoet who extemporizes plagiarized verses.

Matthew, St. Matthew* the Apostle.

Matthias. (1) In the Bible, *Acts* i, the man chosen to replace Judas* among the Apostles.* (2) *See* Bede. (3) *See also* Mathias.

Mattie. (1) In Edith Wharton's novel *Ethan Frome* (1911), the simple, gentle cousin with whom Frome* falls in love; they make a suicide pact and purposely crash their sled, but both become cripples who are cared for by Frome's cold wife. (2) *See also* Matty.

Matty. (1) *See* Jenkins. (2) *See also* Mattie.

Mauberly, Hugh Selwin. In Ezra Pound's poem *Hugh Selwin Mauberly* (1920), an esthete and poet-manqué who loves Beauty without ever understanding its true nature.

Maud. In Tennyson's poem *Maud* (1855), the beautiful woman loved by the unnamed and mentally unstable narrator; most widely known from the song "Come Into the Garden, Maud" in the poem.

Maugrabin. In Walter Scott's novel *Quentin Durward* (1823), a devious adventurer who alternately befriends and betrays Quentin Durward* and is ultimately hanged.

Maupin, Mlle. de. In Théophile Gautier's novel *Mademoiselle de Maupin* (1835), a girl who disguises herself as a man in order to move freely among men, whom she regards with contempt; in the nineteenth century, she was a critical figure in the movement for "art for art's sake" and a major literary scandal among general readers.

Maurya. In J. M. Synge's play *Riders to the Sea* (1903), an Irish peasant woman who has lost all her sons to the sea.

Maverick. In the American television series "Maverick" (1957–62), one of two brothers who were gamblers and adventurers in the American West, noted for their sly sense of humor and their avoidance of heroics.

Mazeppa. In Byron's poem *Mazeppa* (1819), a Polish nobleman who was tied naked to a wild horse that ran until it fell dead, almost killing the rider as well. The story was adapted into numerous plays, in which Mazeppa was almost always played by a woman.

Meagles. In Charles Dickens's novel *Little Dorrit* (1855), a benevolent and rather naive retired banker who nonetheless prides himself on his practical sense. **Mrs. Meagles** is cheerful and even-tempered, and their daughter, called **Pet**, is a pretty and terribly spoiled young woman who even so is quite gentle, if rather stupid. *See also* Tattycoram.

Medea. In Greek legend, a great magician and enchantress who helped Jason* win the Golden Fleece;* she followed him back to Athens where she bore him two children, but when he planned to desert her in order to marry Creon's* daughter Glauce,* she killed their children. In Euripides's play *Medea*, she moves from sympathetic sorrow to uncontrollable fury in her thirst for revenge and after the murder escapes on a flying chariot drawn by dragons. In Seneca's play *Medea*, considerably more emphasis is given to her "barbarian" background and her powers as a sorceress.

Médée. *See* Medea.

Medici. Historically, the dominant family in Florence from the fifteenth to the early eighteenth century, noted throughout Europe primarily for their immense wealth and artistic patronage. Principal members include **Lorenzo** "the Magnificent" (d. 1492); his son **Giovanni** (d. 1521), who became Pope Leo X; and **Catherine** (d. 1589), who became queen of France and instigated the St. Bartholomew's* Day Massacre.

Medoro. *See* Angelica.

Medusa. In Greek legend, a Gorgon* with snakes for hair who could turn people to stone with her stare. When Perseus* fought her, he reflected her stare in a mirror, then cut off her head and used it to turn many of his opponents to stone. *See also* Pegasus.

Medvidenko. In Anton Chekhov's play *The Sea Gull* (1896), the dull, impoverished schoolteacher and henpecked husband of Masha.*

Meeber, Carrie. *See* Carrie.

Mefistofele. *See* Mephistopheles.

Meg. (1) In Louisa May Alcott's novel *Little Women* (1868), the eldest sister, who wishes to become a lady. *See also* Amy; Beth; Jo. (2) *See* Murdockson, Meg. (3) *See also* Margaret.

Meg Merrilies. In Walter Scott's novel *Guy Mannering* (1815), a half-crazy fortune-teller.

Megara. In Greek legend, the daughter of Creon* and the first wife of Heracles;* he killed her and their three children when he went mad.

mehitabel. In a series (1916–30) of unrhymed, uncapitalized, and unpunctuated poems by Don Marquis, a female cat dedicated to a life of wild abandon, loved from afar by the cockroach archy.*

Meister, Wilhelm. *See* Wilhelm Meister.

Meistersinger. *See* Sachs, Hans.

Melanie. In Margaret Mitchell's novel *Gone With the Wind* (1936), a sweet, ladylike woman who marries Ashley Wilkes;* she is everything that Scarlett O'Hara* is not, and she is often cited as an example of those women who are too good to be true.

Melanippe. In Greek legend, a daughter of Ares,* sister of Hippolyta,* and queen of the Amazons.* *Also called* Menalippe.

Melchior. In Christian legend, the name of one of the Magi,* usually depicted as a Nubian.

Meleager. In Greek legend, a great hunter and warrior who loved Atalanta* and gave her the head of the great Calydonian boar that he killed; it was foretold that he would live only as long as a particular log was not burned, and he died when his mother Althea* dropped the log on the fire. *See also* Oeneus.

Melibea. In Fernando de Rojas's novel *Celestina* (1501), an innocent young girl who is seduced by the nobleman Calisto* and who then throws herself off the roof after his accidental death.

Mélisande. In Maurice Maeterlinck's play *Pélléas and Mélisande* (1892), a mysterious girl who is discovered beside a stream and seems to have no knowledge of good or evil; she falls in love with her husband's brother Pélléas* and dies after his death and their child's premature birth.

Melissa. In Greek legend, the sister of Amalthea* and a Cretan princess who helped nurse the infant Zeus.* She discovered honey.

Mellors. In D. H. Lawrence's novel *Lady Chatterley's Lover* (1928), the game-keeper who becomes the lover of Lady Chatterley;* noted as a symbol of crude animal spirits and natural sexuality.

Melmoth. In C. R. Maturin's novel *Melmoth the Wanderer* (1820), a man who sold his soul to the Devil* and then was bored by his omnipotence, but who could find no one who would trade souls with him. In 1835, Balzac wrote a sequel, *Melmoth Reconciled*, in which Melmoth could hardly hold off the French businessmen eager to sell their souls for wealth. *See also* Faust.

Melpomene. In Greek legend, the Muse* of tragedy.

Mélusine. In French folklore, a water fairy* who married a human on condition that he never visit her on the one day each week she became a mermaid;* he broke his promise, and she ran away. *See also* Ondine.

Memnon. In Homer's *Odyssey*, the handsomest man in the world; in other Greek legends, he was an ally of Troy* who was killed by Achilles.*

Mena. In Roman mythology, the goddess of women's menstrual period.

Menaechmi. In Plautus's play *Menaechmi*, twin brothers who, separated in youth, many years later accidentally find themselves in the same place, with much confusion resulting.

Menalippe. *See* Melanippe.

Menelaus. In Greek legend, the Spartan* king who married Helen* and who then demanded the aid of the other Greek kings to get her back after she eloped with Paris,* thus instigating the Trojan War.* He is generally portrayed as a rather weak-willed, pompous man in comparison with the other Greek warriors. In Homer's *Iliad*, he is overshadowed by his brother Agamemnon* and is not a particularly successful warrior. In Euripides's play *The Trojan Women*, he attempts to be vengeful with Helen but is rather easily beguiled by her, and in Homer's *Odyssey*, they have returned to Sparta and live contentedly together. *See also* Hermione.

Mentor. In Homer's *Odyssey*, a friend of Odysseus* and the guardian and teacher of Telemachus.*

Mephistopheles. In Christopher Marlowe's play *Doctor Faustus* (1592) and in Goethe's poem/play *Faust* (1808–32), a devil, possibly the Devil,* who offers Faust* a life of power in return for his soul. In Marlowe's play, the bargain is for 24 years, and Mephistopheles even tries to dissuade Faustus* from signing the bargain, but once it is signed, he enforces it without mercy. In Goethe's version, he is a more sophisticated, witty, and cynical creature, extremely attractive and fascinating. The dominant image, however, probably comes from Gounod's opera *Faust* (1859), in which he is a gleeful seducer and villain with a pointed goatee and a red feather in his cap who destroys Marguerite* for the pleasure of it and laughs while dragging Faust to Hell.*

Mera. *See* Maera.

Merchant. In Chaucer's *Canterbury Tales*, the businessman who tells the story of the older husband deceived by his young wife in the pear tree.

Merchant of Venice. In Shakespeare's play *The Merchant of Venice* (1596), Antonio,* although most popular usage gives the name to Shylock.*

Mercury. In Roman mythology, the messenger of the gods, generally equivalent to Hermes.*

Mercutio. In Shakespeare's play *Romeo and Juliet* (1595), the witty, poetic friend of Romeo,* noted for his flamboyant verbal flights, such as the "Queen Mab*" speech, and for one of the great theatrical death scenes following his intervention in Romeo's duel.

Merdle. In Charles Dickens's novel *Little Dorrit* (1855), an ostensible financial wizard whose bankruptcy leads him to suicide and sends Arthur Clennam,* among many, to debtor's prison.

Mère l'Oye. *See* Mother Goose.

Merion, Diana. In George Meredith's novel *Diana of the Crossways* (1885), a witty, beautiful young woman who easily attracts men and who willfully refuses to do the "proper" thing; officially cleared of charges of infidelity, she nonetheless refuses to return to her husband, using her notoriety to establish a brief career as a novelist. Declining into poverty, she gains enough maturity to marry the honorable and long-waiting Redworth.

Merle, Mme. In Henry James's novel *Portrait of a Lady* (1881), a vigorous and perceptive woman who befriends Isabel Archer* and encourages Isabel to marry Mme. Merle's former lover Gilbert Osmond.*

Merlin. In Malory's *Morte d'Arthur*, a great magician who assists Arthur* until, falling in love with Nimue,* he is himself enchanted and trapped under a great stone; in Tennyson's poem *Merlin and Vivien* (1859), Vivien* enchants him and seals him inside a great oak. *See also* Igraine.

Mermaid. In European legend, a creature with the upper body of a woman and the lower body of a fish; the Nereids* were Greek mermaids. *See also* Mélusine; Ondine.

Merope. In Greek legend, one of the seven Pleiades.* She married Sisyphus* and, in some sources, was so ashamed of Sisyphus that she hid her head when the sisters were changed into a constellation, thus accounting for the fact that only six stars are visible in the constellation.

Merrilies, Meg. *See* Meg Merrilies.

Merriwell, Frank. In numerous stories by Burt Standish (beg. 1896), a handsome, wholesome American boy, hero of collegiate sports adventures.

Merry Men. In British legend, the followers of Robin Hood.* *See also* Allan-a-Dale; John, Little; Tuck, Friar.

Merteuil, Marquise de. In Choderlos de Laclos's novel *Les Liasons dangereuses* (1782), a fashionable woman scorned whose heartless manipulations lead to the debauchery of innocents in order to gain the humiliation of her lover Valmont.* *See also* Volanges, Cécile de.

Mertz. In the American television series "I Love Lucy" (1951–61), the couple next door, a feuding middle-aged pair composed of **Fred**, the bald, penny-pinching landlord, and **Ethel**, perennial best friend of Lucy Ricardo.*

Meshach. *See* Shadrach.

Messala. In Lew Wallace's novel *Ben Hur* (1880), the Roman who becomes Ben Hur's* enemy; he is killed in the great chariot race in Rome.

Messalina. Historically, wife (d. 48) of the Roman emperor Claudius,* noted for her flamboyant adultery.

Messiah. In the Bible, the name given to the savior who will come from God to save the Chosen People; Christians believe that the Messiah has come and that He is Jesus;* Jews continue to wait for Him. G. F. Handel's musical setting of the principal prophecies concerning Him in *Isaiah* have become a fundamental part of American Christmas celebrations, particularly the "Hallelujah Chorus."

Mesty. In Captain Marryat's novel *Mr. Midshipman Easy* (1836), a sailor and former African king whose loyal friendship provides Easy* with the advice that gets him through numerous scrapes and saves his life when his own men mutiny.

Methodius, St. Historically, the brother and companion of St. Cyril.*

Methuselah. In the Bible, *Genesis* v, son of Enoch* and grandfather of Noah,* noted for living 969 years.

Metis. In Greek legend, the first wife of Zeus;* when she became pregnant, he swallowed her whole, so that Athena* was born through Zeus's head.

Metternich. Historically, an Austrian statesman (d. 1859) whose negotiations restored and maintained a balance of power in Europe after the defeat of Napoleon.* He appears in numerous works as a symbol of antidemocratic oppression and as the ultimate amoral political animal.

Mezzetino. A name sometimes used for Brighella.*

Micah. In the Bible, *Micah*, a prophet noted for his prophecies of Zion.*

Micawber. In Charles Dickens's novel *David Copperfield* (1849), a shabbily genteel, improvident man given to grandiloquent phraseology and to expressing himself in letters to people in the same room. He is always hopeful that "something will turn up;" in the meantime, he contracts a series of debts which he seems never to understand, once being sent to debtor's prison and often thereafter on the verge of being sent back again. He rents a room to the young

Copperfield* and later works for Uriah Heep,* whose villainy drives him to an unusually focused period of work in order to expose Heep's machinations, and eventually emigrates to Australia. In spite of living continually on other people's money and his overblown speech, there seems not a wicked thought in his head, and all those who meet him continue to be his friends. **Mrs. Micawber** swears regularly that she will "never desert" her husband, meanwhile regularly providing him with new children to support. He is generally seen as a fictionalized portrait of Dickens's own father.

Michael. (1) In the Bible, *Daniel* x, a prince of Persia who aids Daniel* and the Jews. (2) In the Bible, *Jude* i and *Revelation* xii, an archangel* who struggles with Satan.* In Christian tradition, he is the leader of all God's hosts, often depicted with a dazzling sword and shield, the angel who will sound the trumpet announcing the Last Judgement* and weigh the souls of mankind. His day is September 29, and, in England in particular, Michaelmas was a day from which contracts and rents were dated. In John Milton's poem *Paradise Lost* (1667), he commands God's armies against Satan* and is the messenger sent to drive Adam* and Eve* from Eden.* *See also* Gabriel; Jeanne d'Arc.

Michio. In Terence's play *The Brothers*, Demea's* brother, who raises his adopted son using kindness rather than fear.

Mickey Mouse. In numerous movie cartoons (beg. 1928), an anthropomorphic mouse who came to symbolize a world of happiness, wholesome entertainment, and innocent fun. *See also* Disney, Walt.

Midas. In Greek legend, a king of Phrygia; everything he touched turned to gold, and he begged to have the gift taken away when even his food and his daughter were turned to gold. In Ovid's *Metamorphoses*, the same man was asked to judge a music contest between Pan* and Apollo;* when he chose Pan, Apollo gave him the ears of a donkey.

Middleton. In George Meredith's novel *The Egoist* (1879), **Clara** is a beautiful young woman engaged to the egoist Patterne* but who refuses to be manipulated by him. Her father is a warmhearted clergyman who helps her trick Patterne into ending the engagement.

Midian. In the Bible, *Genesis* xxv, a son of Abraham;* his descendants were nomads in the land in the east.

Miggs, Miss. In Charles Dickens's novel *Barnaby Rudge* (1841), a servant obsessed with her own virtue; she eventually finds her true calling as a merciless turnkey in a women's prison.

Mignon. In Goethe's novel *Wilhelm Meister's Apprenticeship* (1795), a dainty child rescued by Wilhelm Meister* from a company of rope dancers; she falls hopelessly in love with him and pines away.

Mikado. In Gilbert and Sullivan's operetta *The Mikado* (1885), the ruler of Japan who tries to establish a society in which "the punishment fits the crime." *See also* Nanki-Poo.

Mildred. *See* Rogers, Mildred.

Miles. *See* Standish, Miles.

Miles Gloriosus. In Plautus's play *Miles Gloriosus*, a braggart soldier; his name is often used to identify that comic type, best summarized in the musical play *A Funny Thing Happened On the Way to the Forum* (1962): "I am a parade." *See also* Braggadocio; Capitano, il; Scaramouche.

Milk and Honey, Land of. In the Bible, *Exodus* iii, a description of the Promised Land* used by Moses* to indicate its fertility and often used to indicate any wonderful place without cares.

Millamant. In William Congreve's play *The Way of the World* (1700), the beautiful, witty, and intelligent young woman who is pursued by and who eventually agrees to marry Mirabell* after she obtains an agreement that she shall never be forced to "decline" into a "wife." *See also* Wishfort, Lady.

Miller. (1) In Chaucer's *Canterbury Tales*, the man who tells the story of the carpenter who is tricked into allowing his wife's adultery by a prediction of a second Flood.* (2) In Chaucer's *Canterbury Tales*, in the Reeve's Tale, the man who cheats two students out of part of their grain, in return for which they sleep with his wife and daughter.

Miller, Daisy. In Henry James's novel *Daisy Miller* (1878), a charming, young American woman who becomes an object of scandal in Italian society due to her inability to grasp the subtleties of public decorum, in particular walking unchaperoned with a man and then meeting him alone at night at the Colosseum.

Miller, Joe. Historically, an English comedian (d. 1738); his name was given to a published collection of jokes and later was given to any old, worn out joke.

Miller of Dee. In a British folksong, a miller who envies no one because "I earn my bread . . . " The king, in turn, envies him and adds that "such men as thou are England's boast."

Milo. *See* Minderbinder, Milo.

Milquetoast, Caspar. In the American newspaper cartoon *The Timid Soul* (beg. 1924), a shy, timid little man, easily imposed upon by anyone.

Mime. In Richard Wagner's operas *The Ring of the Niebelung* (1869–76), Alberich's* brother who forges the Tarncap and who later repairs Siegfried's* sword.

Mimi. In Henry Murger's stories *Scenes of Bohemian Life* (1848), an amorous, young French woman who contracts consumption and dies in a garret. Although the name is almost synonymous with a French girl, it is perhaps best known from Puccini's opera version of this story, *La Bohème* (1896).

Mimsey. In George du Maurier's novel *Peter Ibbetson* (1891), Ibbetson's* frail childhood sweetheart who marries a duke and then dies but who visits Peter in his visions in the asylum.

Minderbinder, Milo. In Joseph Heller's novel *Catch–22* (1961), an American soldier who tries to turn World War II into a business enterprise; noted particularly for contracting with the Germans to bomb his own base.

Minerva. In Roman mythology, the goddess of wisdom, generally equivalent to Athena.*

Miniver, Mrs. In the American movie *Mrs. Miniver* (1942), a stiff-upper-lip Englishwoman who bravely tries to maintain a proper life in the face of World War II, a figure widely, if only temporarily, admired.

Minna. In Lessing's play *Minna von Barnhelm* (1767), a beautiful woman who retains the love of the poor but proud soldier Tellheim* by pretending to be destitute herself.

Minnehaha. In Henry Wadsworth Longfellow's poem *Hiawatha* (1855), the Indian maiden who marries Hiawatha.*

Minos. (1) In Greek legend, a son of Europa* famous as a great lawgiver and wise man. (2) In Greek legend, the son of Minos and the king of Crete who built the Labyrinth* in which was kept the Minotaur.* After his son was killed in Greece, he exacted tribute in the form of seven boys and seven girls to be sacrificed to the Minotaur, until the monster was killed by Theseus* with the aid of Minos's daughters Ariadne* and Phaedra.* *See also* Britomartis; Pasiphae.

Minotaur. In Greek legend, a monster captured by Heracles* and later housed in the Labyrinth* at Crete; it had the head of a bull and the body of a man, since it was the offspring of a great white bull and of Pasiphae,* and it ate humans. It was eventually killed by Theseus.*

Mirabell. In William Congreve's play *The Way of the World* (1700), an ideal young man of fashion, intelligent, handsome, witty, and amorous; he is in love with Millamant,* whom he also pursues for her fortune, a motive he admits as openly as he declares his love. He has attracted much attention, both positive and negative, as he seems to be the summation of the ideal Restoration hero, whose mixture of attractiveness and sexuality, intelligence and cynicism, has often confused and disturbed later generations. *See also* Fainall; Marwood; Wishfort, Lady.

Miranda. In Shakespeare's play *The Tempest* (1611), Prospero's* innocent daughter, who falls in love with Ferdinand.*

Miriam. (1) In the Bible, *Exodus* ii, Moses's* sister who watches when he is floating in the bullrushes; in *Numbers* xii, she encourages a rebellion against the leadership of Moses after he marries an Ethiopian woman. (2) The Hebrew name for Mary.* (3) *See also* Mariamne; Marian; Mary.

Misanthrope, The. The title character in Molière's play *The Misanthrope* (1666) is Alceste;* other notable literary misanthropes include Chatsky,* Manly,* Silas Marner,* and Scrooge.*

Misenus. In Virgil's *Aeneid*, Hector's* piper who followed Aeneas* to Italy and was killed when he challenged the gods to a musical contest.

Miser. The title character of Molière's play *The Miser* (1668) is Harpagon;* other notable literary misers include Noddy Boffin,* Martin Chuzzlewit,* Corbaccio,* Euclio,* Grandet,* Silas Marner,* and Scrooge.*

Mitch. In Tennessee Williams's play *A Streetcar Named Desire* (1947), Stanley Kowalski's* gentle friend who intends to marry Blanche DuBois* until Stanley tells him about her past.

Mnemosyne. In Greek mythology, the goddess of memory and the mother of the Muses.*

Moab. In the Bible, *Genesis* xix, the son of Lot* and of Lot's eldest daughter, father of the Moabites, the most noted of whom was Ruth.*

Moby Dick. In Herman Melville's novel *Moby-Dick* (1851), the great white whale that becomes the object of an obsessive hunt led by Capt. Ahab;* in an earlier meeting the whale had bitten off Ahab's leg. The whale finally kills Ahab and destroys his ship, drowning all the sailors but one, Ishmael,* who tells the story. Moby Dick is one of the most vivid and widely interpreted symbols in American literature and is also often used as a symbol of American literature itself, particularly in relation to the modern urge to interpret the life out of every work under study. For many, he is a symbol depicting literary complexity and obscurity owing to numerous classroom exercises and discussions in their youth. *See also* Queequeg; Tashtego.

Mock Turtle. In Lewis Carroll's story *Alice in Wonderland* (1865), a turtle with a calf's head who cries constantly and inflicts the story of his life on anyone who comes within hearing.

Modred. *See* Mordred.

Moe. *See* Stooges, Three.

Mohammed. Historically, a great Arab prophet (d. 632) and founder of the Islamic, or Moslem, religion.

Mohican. *See* Chingachgook.

Moirae. A name sometimes used for the Fates.*

Molech. (1) In the Bible, *II Kings* xxiii, a Canaanite deity to whom children were sacrificed. (2) *See also* Moloch.

Moll. (1) *See* Flanders, Moll. (2) *See also* Molly.

Molly. (1) A common nickname for Mary.* (2) *See* Bloom; McGee, Fibber. (3) *See also* Polly.

Moloch. (1) In John Milton's poem *Paradise Lost* (1667), one of the principal angels who falls with Satan,* an angel so fierce and desperate that he prefers annihilation to defeat. (2) *See also* Molech.

Momus. In Greek legend, a god banished from Olympus* for his continual satire and criticism.

Mona Lisa. In a painting (1506) by Leonardo da Vinci, a woman with an enigmatic smile that has made her a symbol of enigmatic beauty and femininity and has made it the most famous painting in the world. *Also called* La Gioconda.

Moncrief, Algernon. *See* Algernon.

Money Changers. In the Bible, *John* ii, a group of men who changed money at the Temple so that visitors could pay taxes or buy animals for sacrifice; Jesus* drove them out when He cleansed the Temple.

Monica, St. Historically, the mother of St. Augustine,* noted for her maternal devotion.

Monimia. In Thomas Otway's play *The Orphan* (1680), the orphan girl loved by twin brothers; when she is tricked into adultery, she commits suicide.

Monk. Historically, a man who took a vow of chastity and religious dedication expressed through a life lived away from the profane world, usually in a monastery. As monks and monasteries were a prominent feature of medieval and Renaissance society, monks figure in numerous works from and about those periods in one of three basic types: sincere men of religion; jolly hedonists who have chosen the comparative wealth of the Church over the poverty of daily existence; and sinister, dark-robed creatures with secret societies and secret rites.

Montague. In Shakespeare's play *Romeo and Juliet* (1595), one of two feuding families; its most noted members are Romeo* and Mercutio.* *See also* Capulet.

Montano. In Shakespeare's play *Othello* (1604), the hot-tempered officer who is wounded by Cassio* while the latter is drunk.

Monte-Cristo. *See* Dantes, Edmund.

Montezuma. Historically, the Aztec emperor (d. 1520) who was overthrown by the invading Spaniards in Mexico; his great wealth made him a figure of legend, and he has also been associated in many allusions with cruel human sacrifice.

Moore, Mrs. In E. M. Forster's novel *A Passage to India* (1924), a sensitive and perhaps psychic elderly Englishwoman; her spiritual strength makes her much admired by Aziz* and keeps him from completely breaking all relations with the English after his trial.

Mopsy. *See* Flopsy, Mopsy, and Cottontail.

Mordecai. In the Bible, *Esther*, a cousin of Esther.* He interpreted the king's dreams, then outraged Haman,* who planned to massacre all the Jews; when Mordecai told Esther of Haman's plans, she saved the Jews, and Mordecai became a trusted confidant of the king.

Mordred. In Malory's *Morte d'Arthur*, Arthur's* illegitimate son, who leads a rebellion against Arthur in which both he and Arthur are killed and Camelot* is destroyed.

Moreau. (1) In Gustave Flaubert's novel *A Sentimental Education* (1869), a French law student who lets a romanticized attraction to a married woman lead him into a bland, monotonous, and unimaginative life. (2) In H. G. Wells's story *The Island of Dr. Moreau* (1896), a mad scientist who tries to breed human beings from jungle animals.

Morel. (1) In D. H. Lawrence's novel *Sons and Lovers* (1913), **Paul** is a young man whose powerful attachment to his strong-willed mother **Gertrude** makes other relationshps all but impossible; for many, he is a fictionalized self-portrait of the author. Gertrude is given an overdose of painkiller by Paul to end the misery of her cancer. His father **Walter**, a vital coal miner who is interested only in simple pleasures, is gradually driven to brutality and alienation by Gertrude's puritanism and her obsessive interest in Paul's development. (2) In Marcel Proust's novels *Remembrance of Things Past* (1913–27), the servant's son and violinist who has an affair with Charlus* and whose public insult of Charlus encourages the latter's decline into complete depravity.

Morell. In G. B. Shaw's play *Candida* (1897), a vigorous, powerful, and complacent preacher whose strength, he comes to realize, really resides in his wife Candida.* *See also* Marchbanks.

Morgan. (1) A common Welsh name, often used for a stereotypical Welshman. (2) Historically, a buccaneer (d. 1688) who raided Spanish ships and towns in the Caribbean, including a major raid on Panama; he often appears in literature as the ultimate pirate and is used as a model for most fictional pirates.

Morgana. In European legend, a great sorceress who appears in numerous works under many related names, especially as Morgan le Fay.*

Morgan le Fay. In Malory's *Morte D'Arthur*, Arthur's* evil half-sister and a sorceress who tries to kill Arthur and interferes with the work of many of his knights; she is also on the boat that carries Arthur away.

Morgiana. In *The Arabian Nights*, the servant of Ali Baba* who discovers the 40 thieves hidden in jars, waiting to ambush Ali Baba, kills them, and is rewarded with marriage to his son.

Moriarty. In several stories by Arthur Conan Doyle featuring Sherlock Holmes,* the evil mastermind behind all serious crime in London.

Morlock. In H. G. Wells's story *The Time Machine* (1895), the apelike, predatory creatures who live barbarically underground in mankind's far future.

Mormon. Most precisely, the prophet who wrote *The Book of Mormon*, but in common usage any member of the church founded upon the teachings of that book, more properly called The Church of the Latter-Day Saints. They are known in popular lore and literature primarily for their journey west to Utah and for their practice of polygamy, until heavy U.S. governmental pressure caused its prohibition in 1890.

Moroni. Historically, the angel* claimed by Joseph Smith to have delivered *The Book of Mormon.**

Morose. In Ben Jonson's play *Epicene* (1609), a temperamental man with an aversion to noise of any kind who determines to marry a silent woman; she, in fact, turns out to be neither silent nor a woman, due to a plot of his nephew. *See also* Epicene.

Morpheus. In Greek mythology, the god of dreams. *Also called* Phantastus.

Morris, Dinah. In George Eliot's novel *Adam Bede* (1859), a compassionate and dedicated female preacher who believes her calling must take precedence over any private emotions; she relents somewhat when she falls in love with Adam Bede.*

Mors. In Roman mythology, the god of death, generally equivalent to Thanatos.*

Morta. A name sometimes used for Atropos.*

Mortimer. (1) Historically, an English noble designated by Richard II* as his heir but ignored when Bolingbroke himself took the throne as Henry IV;* he is known primarily from the history plays of Shakespeare. (2) *See* Brewster.

Mosca. (1) In Ben Jonson's play *Volpone* (1605), Volpone's* witty and cynical servant who both carries out Volpone's plots and adds a few humiliating variations of his own. (2) In Stendhal's novel *The Charterhouse of Parma* (1839), the prime minister of Parma, a Machiavellian politician and cynic, but also a generous man who ultimately gives up his power to live in penury as the husband of the Countess Sanseverina.*

Moses. (1) In the Bible, primarily *Exodus*, the great leader who guides the Jews out of Egypt to the Promised Land.* When a baby, he was set adrift in a basket in the Nile and adopted by Pharaoh's* daughter. When he was grown, God appeared to him in a burning bush and appointed him as leader of the Jews. He asked Pharaoh* to release the Jews, and when Pharaoh refused, God sent ten plagues.* Moses led the Jews to the Red Sea and parted the waters for them, which then closed over Pharaoh's pursuing army. Moses led the Jews into the desert, finding water by striking a stone. His brother Aaron* encouraged the Jews to worship a golden calf while Moses was away on Mount Sinai receiving the Ten Commandments.* In punishment, God condemned the Jews to wander in the desert for 40 years, during which Moses led them, until at last they came to the Promised Land. God forbade Moses to enter the Promised Land, and he died after seeing Israel* from a distance. Tradition credits him as the author of the first five books of the Bible. *See also* Gershom; Joshua; Miriam; Pisgah; Zipporah. (2) *See* Primrose.

Moth. In Shakespeare's play *Love's Labour's Lost* (1595), the impudent page who taunts his braggart master Armado.*

Mother Goose. The name given by Perrault to the fictional woman from whom he "collected" the tales he published in 1697; some English sources trace it to a set of poems published by Elizabeth Peters in 1719 which she attributed to her mother Mrs. Vergoose. In either case, she is now the traditional source for all "fairy tales."

Mother Hubbard. In the nursery rhyme, the old woman whose cupboard was bare. The name was also given in America to a plain dress that covered the body from neck to floor.

Mother Shipton. (1) Historically, a highly regarded fortune-teller in the reign of Henry VIII.* (2) In Bret Harte's story *The Luck of Roaring Camp* (1868), the fat prostitute with a heart of gold who starves so that the sick, innocent girl can have food.

Mouse. (1) In Lewis Carroll's story *Alice in Wonderland* (1865), the easily offended animal whom Alice* meets when swimming in her pool of tears. (2) The traditional conflict between cat and mouse has made the mouse a popular character in modern cartoons, particularly Mickey Mouse,* Jerry of Tom and Jerry,* and Ignatz.*

Mouse, Mickey. *See* Mickey Mouse.

Mowcher, Miss. In Charles Dickens's novel *David Copperfield* (1849), the "volatile" dwarf and cosmetician.

Mowgli. In Rudyard Kipling's stories *The Jungle Book* (1894), a boy raised by the animals in the Indian jungles.

Mulligan, Buck. In James Joyce's novel *Ulysses* (1922), a medical student who shares lodgings with Stephen Dedalus* and who provides a more practical and scientific counterpoint to Dedalus; he is often known as "Stately, plump Buck Mulligan," which begins the first sentence of the book, perhaps as far as many who quote it have read.

Mulligan, Dan. In several plays by Harrigan and Hart, beginning with *The Mulligan Guard* (1873), a comic Irish-American epitomizing the stereotypes and chauvinism of the period.

Mulliner. In numerous stories by P. G. Wodehouse (beg. 1925), a garrulous man with an endless supply of distant relatives whose stories he relates, whether his companions wish to hear or not.

Münchausen. In Rudolph Raspe's novel *Travels of Baron Münchausen* (1785), an old soldier whose exaggerated tales of his experiences soon made him synonymous with liars and spinners of tall tales.

Munro. In James Fenimore Cooper's novel *The Last of the Mohicans* (1826), the British colonel. His eldest daughter **Cora**, dark haired, independent, and intelligent, falls in love with Uncas* but is captured and killed by other Indians; her sister **Alice**, blonde and frail, marries the young English officer escorting her. *See also* Bumppo, Natty.

Murdockson, Meg. In Walter Scott's novel *The Heart of Midlothian* (1818), the vicious, vengeful old woman who tries to frame Effie Deans* for the murder of Effie's baby and who is eventually hanged as a witch.

Murdstone. In Charles Dickens's novel *David Copperfield* (1849), the handsome but dour stepfather whose dedication to "firmness" destroys all the spontaneous happiness of Copperfield's* youth. His sister **Jane** is, if possible, even more cold and forbidding.

Murrieta, Joaquin. Historically, a Mexican bandit in California (d. 1853) transformed into a Robin Hood* figure of legend by John Ridge's book *The Life and Adventures of Joaquin Murieta* (sic, 1854).

Muse. In Greek mythology, one of nine daughters of Zeus* who supervised numerous artistic aspects of life. *See* Calliope; Clio; Erato; Euterpe; Melpomene; Polyhymnia; Terpsichore; Thalia; Urania. *Also called* Camenae.

Musetta. In Puccini's opera *La Bohème* (1896), a carefree young woman of the streets, noted particularly for her fickleness and for her waltz.

Musette. In Henry Murger's stories *Scenes of Bohemian Life* (1848), Musetta.*

Musgrove. In Jane Austen's novel *Persuasion* (1818), the sporting country squire; for his wife, *see* Elliot.

Mustard Seed. In the Bible, *Matthew* xiii, a parable told by Jesus,* in which Heaven* is compared to the mustard seed, which looks insignificant when sown but which grows into the greatest of herbs.

Muta. In Roman mythology, the goddess of silence.

Mycenae. Historically, an ancient Greek community; in legend, it is a major site, primarily as the home of Agamemnon.*

Myrmidons. In Greek legend, ants who were turned into warriors, noted for unusual brutality. In Homer's *Iliad*, they accompanied Achilles* to the Trojan War.* *See also* Eudorus.

Myrrha. In Greek legend, the mother of Adonis* by an incestuous relation with her father Cinyras.* In Dante's poem *Divine Comedy*, she is transformed into a swine in Hell.*

Myrrhine. In Aristophanes's play *Lysistrata*, the pretty young woman who joins Lysistrata* and submits her husband to a cruelly funny sexual tease.

Myshkin. In Dostoevsky's novel *The Idiot* (1868), an epileptic nobleman of such simple, selfless goodness that it is mistaken for lunacy by many who meet him. Fascinating to women in general, he particularly attracts Nastasia,* who is murdered by Rogozhin.* The most noted scene describes Rogozhin's repentance to Myshkin over Nastasia's corpse, after which Myshkin deteriorates into real insanity and is committed to an asylum. *See also* Aglaya; Prokofievna, Lizaveta.

N

Naaman. In the Bible, *II Kings* v, a Syrian general who was cured of leprosy when he bathed in the river Jordan.*

Nabal. In the Bible, *I Samuel* xxv, a wealthy shepherd who refused food to David's* men while they were in the hills; Abigail* talked David out of destroying Nabal's flocks, but Nabal died of a stroke when she told him what she had done.

Naboth. In the Bible, *I Kings* xxi, the man whom Jezebel* had stoned to death in order to take his vineyard.

Nahum. In the Bible, *Nahum*, a prophet who preached against the evil of Nineveh.

Naiad. *See* Nymph.

Naisi. *See* Deirdre.

Nana. (1) In Émile Zola's novel *Nana* (1880), a beautiful, cunning, and ignorant courtesan who rises to wealth and popularity, declines to common streetwalking, and rises again, depending on the lovers she obtains, many of whom she destroys, until she dies of smallpox. In Zola's Rougon-Macquart* family, she is the daughter of Gervaise.* (2) In J. M. Barrie's play *Peter Pan* (1904), the Darling's* family dog who acts as the children's nanny.

Nancy. (1) In Charles Dickens's novel *Oliver Twist* (1837), the devoted lover of Bill Sikes*; when she tries to aid Oliver Twist*, Bill believes she is betraying him and beats her to death in a famous and brutal scene. (2) *See* Drew, Nancy.

Nanki-Poo. In Gilbert and Sullivan's operetta *The Mikado* (1885), the Mikado's* son, disguised as the wandering minstrel and in love with Yum-Yum.* *See also* Katisha.

Nanon. In Balzac's novel *Eugénie Grandet* (1833), the mannish female servant who faithfully defends the miserly Grandet* and then loyally manages Eugénie's property.

Naomi. In the Bible, *Ruth*, the mother-in-law of Ruth;* when her husband dies, she decides to return to her homeland, and Ruth forsakes all her relations to accompany her and care for her.

Naphtali. In the Bible, *Genesis* xxx, one of the sons of Jacob* and Bilhah* and founder of one of the twelve tribes of Israel.*

Napoleon. (1) Historically, Napoleon Bonaparte (d. 1821), a Corsican corporal in the French Army who after the Revolution rose to become the most effective and feared military general in his time, perhaps in all modern times, defeating the enemies of the Revolution and establishing a new French empire in Europe. Ostensibly a republican, he eventually crowned himself emperor. After a disastrous campaign in Russia, in which his army was destroyed by the weather as much as by his opponents, he was exiled; however, he returned for the famous Hundred Days until he was again defeated at Waterloo* and exiled on the island of St. Helena until his death. He appears in numerous works, most notably Tolstoy's novel *War and Peace* (1865), in numerous characterizations; no figure prior to Hitler* has had such a complex hold on the public imagination. For some, he was the symbol of freedom, the man who would overthrow the oppressive nobility, at least until his assumption of the throne (Beethoven is said to have scratched out his name from the title page of the Eroica Symphony when that occurred). For others, he was the Devil* incarnate. For others, he was a demonstration of what ability and willpower could accomplish; for still others, he was an equally clear demonstration of the fate of the overreacher. Innumerable legends surround his life, not the least of which involve his romance with Josephine,* his marriage to whom he had annulled so that he could marry the Austrian princess Marie Louise. He is often ridiculed for his short height, and in humorous references is always shown with one hand tucked inside his vest. For many years, lunacy has been indicated in popular materials by the patient's belief that he is Napoleon. (2) Historically, Napoleon III (d. 1873), a nephew of Napoleon who after a coup in 1851 declared himself emperor and presided over a period noted for its military disasters, the great Paris Exposition, and unbridled commercial corruption. *See also* Eugénie. (3) In George Orwell's novel *Animal Farm* (1945), the pig who gradually becomes dictator.

Narcissus. (1) In Ovid's *Metamorphoses*, a beautiful young man who fell in love with his own reflection in the water of a pool, ignored Echo,* and pined away until he was changed into a flower. (2) In the Bible, *Romans* xvi, the head of a Christian household in Rome saluted by Paul.*

Nastasia. (1) In Dostoevsky's novel *The Idiot* (1868), the complex, degraded, and discarded mistress of a merchant with whom Myshkin* becomes involved; when he decides he should marry her as a form of Christian sacrifice, she in turn decides to sacrifice herself to save him and runs away with the brutal Rogozhin,* whom she taunts until he jealously murders her. (2) *See also* Anastasia; Natasha.

Natalia. (1) In Goethe's novel *Wilhelm Meister's Apprenticeship* (1795), a beautiful woman called an Amazon* for her help in rescuing Wilhelm's* acting troupe from bandits and whom he ultimately marries. (2) *See also* Nastasia; Natasha.

Natasha. (1) In Turgenev's play *A Month in the Country* (1850), the intelligent and beautiful but bored wife who falls in love with her son's youthful tutor. *See also* Rakitin. (2) In Tolstoy's novel *War and Peace* (1865), the beautiful, vibrant, and charming young daughter of Rostov.* She is engaged to Andrei Bolkonsky* in what would be a perfect match; however, during the betrothal period, she is charmed by the romantic rake Kuragin* and is prevented from running away with him only at the last possible moment, which ends her marriage prospects. When Andrei is wounded in the war, she accidentally meets him and nurses him, and they are reconciled before his death. Afterward, she agrees to marry Bezukov,* who has loved her from a distance for years. She is one of the most vivid and memorable young women in literature, never more so than in the famous description of her at her first ball. (3) In Anton Chekhov's play *Three Sisters* (1901), the crude and selfish woman who marries Prozorov,* conducts an affair under his very nose, and gradually uses her children to squeeze the rest of the family out of their own house. (4) *See also* Nastasia; Natalia.

Nathan. (1) In the Bible, *II Samuel* v, a son of David.* (2) In the Bible, *II Samuel* vii, a prophet who advises David* to build the temple. (3) In Lessing's play *Nathan the Wise* (1779), the generous and tolerant Jewish merchant who is more ''Christian'' than the Christians who persecute him, kill his family, and steal his fortune.

Nathanael. In the Bible, *John* i, an Apostle* found by Philip;* he at first resisted, saying ''Can there any good thing come out of Nazareth?'' As *John* is the only gospel to mention him, many have assumed this is an alternate name for Bartholomew.* (2) *See also* Nathaniel; Nethaneel.

Nathaniel. (1) In Shakespeare's play *Love's Labour's Lost* (1595), a pedantic curate and companion of Holofernes.* (2) *See also* Nathanael; Nethaneel.

Natty Bumppo. *See* Bumppo, Natty.

Nausicaa. In Homer's *Odyssey*, a Phaeacian princess who befriended Odysseus* when he was shipwrecked.

Nausistrata. In Terence's play *Phormio*, the nagging wife of Chremes.*

Naxos. In Greek legend, the island on which Theseus* abandoned Ariadne.*

Nazarene. A name for Jesus,* from his home in Nazareth.*

Nazareth. In the Bible, the home town of Jesus.* Apparently, in local Jewish lore, the village was also noted for its worthlessness or foolishness, which prompted Nathanael's* comment when told about Jesus.

Nebuchadnezzar. Historically, a great king of Babylon (d. 562 B.C.), builder of the famous hanging gardens and conqueror of much of the Middle East. He figures prominently in the Bible as the king who destroyed Jerusalem* and carried off the Jews into exile. In *Daniel*, where he is depicted as proud and conceited, he builds the golden idol that the Jews refuse to worship, for which he throws Shadrach,* Meshach, and Abednego into the fiery furnace, later going mad and eating grass. *See also* Daniel.

Needle, Eye of the. In the Bible, *Mark* x, Jesus* says that it is easier for a camel to go through the eye of a needle than for a rich man to get into Heaven.*

Nehemiah. In the Bible, *Nehemiah*, the governor of Jerusalem* who helped rebuild the city after the return from exile.

Neklyudov, Dimitri. In Tolstoy's novel *Resurrection* (1899), a prince who, while a juror, recognizes the defendant Katusha* as a girl he had seduced years before; realizing the damage he did to her, he undergoes a conversion and resolves to share her punishment of exile in Siberia.

Nell, Little. In Charles Dickens's novel *The Old Curiosity Shop* (1840), the tiny, sweet, and brave girl who leads her grandfather away into the English countryside to prevent his commitment to an asylum after his gambling bankrupts him and to avoid falling into the clutches of the malignant Quilp.* By the time they finally find a new home with real peace, the hardship of their journey has broken her constitution, and she dies in one of the most popular and admired (and later ridiculed) sentimental death scenes in literature. *See also* Nubbles, Kit.

Nellie. *See* Forbush, Nellie.

Nelson, Horatio. Historically, British admiral (d. 1805) and victor of the battle of Trafalgar. One of the great British folk heroes, he is the epitome of the British sailor, defender against the terror of Napoleon,* until dying on the deck in the arms of his lieutenant, to whom his last words were apparently "Kiss me, Hardy." With the beautiful Emma Hamilton,* he shared in one of the most complex romantic liaisons in history. He is usually depicted with an eye patch and with only one arm, due to his various wounds.

Nelson, Ozzie and Harriet. *See* Ozzie and Harriet.

Nemean Lion. In Greek legend, a great animal killed by Heracles* as one of his labors; since its skin was impervious to all weapons, Heracles squeezed it to death, then skinned it and wore the skin as his mantle.

Nemesis. In Greek mythology, the goddess of vengeance.

Nemo. (1) In Homer's *Odyssey*, the alias Odysseus* uses when captured by Polyphemus* because it means "nobody;" as a result, Polyphemus is unable to obtain help against Odysseus for "nobody" harmed him. (2) In Charles Dickens's novel *Bleak House* (1852), the alias used by Hawdon.* (3) In Jules Verne's novel *20,000 Leagues Under the Sea* (1870), the mysterious, misanthropic genius who builds a great submarine and tours the world's seas wrecking ships.

Neoptolemus. In Greek legend, the son of Achilles;* he joined the Trojan War* after his father's death, killed Priam,* and married Hermione.* In Sophocles's play *Philoctetes*, he tricks Philoctetes* into surrendering Heracles's* great bow, which the Greeks need to defeat Troy, but his sense of decency causes him to try to return the weapon, which is prevented only by Philoctetes's decision to join the Greeks. *Also called* Pyrrhus.*

Nepenthe. In Homer's *Odyssey*, a magic drink that causes cares and sorrows to disappear, given to Telemachus* when he visited Helen* at Sparta.

Neptune. In Roman mythology, the god of the sea, generally equivalent to Poseidon.* *See also* Amphitrite.

Nereids. In Greek legend, 50 daughters of Nereus and Doris* who were attendants of Poseidon.* *See also* Nymph.

Nereus. *See* Nereids.

Nerissa. In Shakespeare's play *The Merchant of Venice* (1596), Portia's* clever waiting woman.

Nero. Historically, a Roman emperor (d. 68), noted primarily for the great fire that burned Rome during his reign, during which he is supposed to have "fiddled." He was also noted for the first persecution of the Christians, for which he is often pictured attending the brutal games in the Colosseum, and for a reign of terror in which he poisoned many of his opponents and much of his own family. He is always depicted as a cruel and depraved egotist and tyrant, usually fat as well.

Nessus. In Greek legend, a centaur* who tried to seduce Deianeira* and was killed by her husband Heracles.* Before dying, Nessus told her that the blood on his shirt would guarantee Heracles's faithfulness when, in fact, it was poisoned and killed the hero when she gave the garment to him.

Nestor. In Homer's *Iliad*, a noble Greek chief distinguished by his maturity, eloquence, prudence, and wisdom.

Nethaneel. (1) In the Bible, *Numbers*, one of the men sent by Moses* to spy out the land of Canaan.* (2) In the Bible, *I Chronicles* ii, one of the sons of Jesse.* (3) *See also* Nathanael; Nathaniael.

Never-Never-Land. In J. M. Barrie's play *Peter Pan* (1904), Peter Pan's* home, a magical isle full of adventures where children never grow up.

Neville, Constance. In Oliver Goldsmith's play *She Stoops to Conquer* (1773), Kate Hardcastle's* friend whom Mrs. Hardcastle* intends her son Tony Lumpkin* to marry. In order to get her own jewels from Mrs. Hardcastle, she pretends to agree to the match, but since Tony dislikes her as much as she dislikes him, he helps her, and she is eventually free to marry Hastings.*

Newgate. Historically, a principal prison in London from the early twelfth century until 1902.

Newsome, Chad. In Henry James's novel *The Ambassadors* (1903), a handsome, intelligent young American whose years in Europe have made him so mature and sophisticated that he does not want to return to Massachusetts to run the family business, even after several different ambassadors bring the request from his mother. *See also* Pocock.

Niamh. In Irish legend, a sea goddess who carried Ossian* away with her to live for 300 years.

Nibelung. *See* Niebelung.

Nicanor. In the Bible, *Acts* v, one of the seven men chosen to care for the widows and the poor.

Nicholas. (1) In the Bible, *Acts* v, one of the seven men chosen to care for the widows and the poor. (2) Historically, a name used by several Popes, the most noted being **Nicholas I** (d. 867), who established many of the important precedents of papal authority, and **Nicholas III** (d. 1280), who is given a prominent place in Hell* in Dante's *Divine Comedy* for appropriating Church resources for personal power and advancement. (3) Historically, a name used by two czars of Russia. Most modern references are to **Nicholas II** (d. 1918), whose vacillation, weakness under the pressure of his wife Alexandra and the monk Rasputin,* and unpredictable oppressions led to the revolution in which he and his family were assassinated. (4) *See* Nickleby. (5) *See also* Nikolai.

Nicholas, St. Historically, a fourth-century bishop around whom a large body of legend accumulated. He was said to have rescued three maidens from prostitution by throwing bags of gold through their window, to have raised from the dead three children drowned in a tub, and to have rescued numerous drowning sailors. He is represented by three gold bags or gold balls, and as a result is the patron saint of pawnbrokers, and is often also represented by an anchor to denote his patronage of sailors. He is also the patron saint of children, and through various complex associations came to be connected with the giving of gifts during Christmas season, so that he is now synonymous with Father Christmas* or Santa Claus.* His day is December 6.

Nicholas's Clerk, St. In English Renaissance slang, a thief, or sometimes an impoverished scholar.

Nick. (1) *See* Carraway, Nick. (2) *See also* Nicholas.

Nick, Old. A nickname for Satan.*

Nick, St. St. Nicholas,* but generally used only in reference to Nicholas as Santa Claus.*

Nick and Nora. *See* Charles, Nick and Nora.

Nickleby. In Charles Dickens's novel *Nicholas Nickleby* (1838), **Nicholas** is a warmhearted young man who tries to support his widowed and ineffectual mother. His first job is at the vicious Dotheboys Hall,* where he rebels along with the students and is followed when he leaves by the pitiful Smike.* He then joins Crummles's* acting company and finally finds congenial employment with the Cheerybles,* rescuing and marrying Madeline Bray.* His sister **Kate** is a refined and honorable young woman who excites much jealousy when she works for the milliner Mantalini,* then is pursued by a rapacious and salacious nobleman, whom she barely escapes. Their uncle **Ralph** is a hardheaded businessman for whom all relationships can be reduced to monetary value; he arranges ignominious jobs for Kate and Nicholas and then tries to use Kate to seduce a wealthy nobleman whose later death in a duel while owing great sums leaves Ralph bankrupt. This, plus the revelation that Smike is his son, leads to his suicide. *See also* Noggs; Squeers.

Nicodemus. In the Bible, *John* iii, a Pharisee* to whom Jesus* explains the meaning of being "born again;" he later tries to defend Jesus to other Pharisees and aids in His burial.

Nicolaus. *See* Nicholas.

Nicole. (1) In Molière's play *The Bourgeois Gentleman* (1670), the sensible maid who laughs so hard at her master's pretensions that she asks for her own beating in order to stop laughing. (2) *See* Diver.

Nicolette. In the anonymous romance *Aucassin and Nicolette*, a slave girl bought by a Christian count, reared as his daughter, and loved by Aucassin.* They run away together, are captured by Saracen pirates, and then are separated by a storm, during which she is taken to Carthage and learns that she is the king's daughter. She remains true to her Aucassin, with whom she is at last reunited.

Niebelung. In Scandinavian and German legend, a race of dwarfs who forge a magic ring that gives the wearer unlimited power; they are best known from Richard Wagner's operas *The Ring of the Niebelung* (1869–76), in which Alberich* has the ring stolen from him by Wotan.*

Nigel. *See* Olifaunt, Nigel.

Nike. In Greek mythology, the goddess of victory. *Also called* Victoria.

Nikolaevna, Lizaveta. *See* Drozdov.

Nikolaevna, Marya. *See* Masha.

Nikolai. (1) *See* Bolkonsky; Kirsanov; Levin; Rostov. (2) *See also* Nicholas.

Nimrod. In the Bible, *Genesis* x, a mighty hunter with a great kingdom. The Tower of Babel* was built in his lands, although the account does not indicate whether he initiated it. In Dante's *Divine Comedy*, he is so credited and is also described as a giant, given a prominent place in the lower reaches of Hell.* A similar story about Nimrod and a great tower appears in Greek legend as well.

Nimue. In Malory's *Morte d'Arthur*, a sorceress who lures Merlin* away and imprisons him beneath a great stone. *Also called* Vivien.*

Nina. (1) In Anton Chekhov's play *The Sea Gull* (1896), the beautiful and ambitious young actress who has an affair with Trigorin* in hopes of helping her career. When he deserts her, she again refuses Constantin's* proposal, even though she has come to understand that she will only be a second-rate actress. (2) *See also* Almayer; Leeds.

Niña, Pinta, and Santa Maria. Historically, the three ships in which Columbus* made his first voyage to America.

Nineveh. *See* Jonah.

Ninus. The supposed founder of the kingdom of the Assyrians; in Ovid's *Metamorphoses*, Pyramus* and Thisbe* are to rendezvous at his tomb.

Niobe. In Greek legend, daughter of Tantalus* and a woman who boasted of her numerous children, for which Apollo* and Artemis* killed the children. She wept unceasingly until turned to a stone, from which the tears continued to flow.

Nipper, Susan. In Charles Dickens's novel *Dombey and Son* (1846), the faithful maid of independent spirit who eventually marries Toots.*

Nisus. In Virgil's *Aeneid*, a brave companion of Aeneas.* He was killed in battle against the Rutulians in an attempt to rescue his great friend Euryalus;* the pair are often cited as ideal friends.

Njal. In the anonymous *Njal's Saga*, a peaceful Icelandic man who is reluctantly drawn into a family feud and who dies stoically when his home is burned down around him.

Noah. In the Bible, *Genesis* v–x, the man chosen by God to build an ark* when He planned the Flood.* In the ark Noah took his family and a male and female of every species of animal. After 40 days and 40 nights, the rain stopped and the creatures on the ark were all that survived. The ark came to rest on the peak of Mt. Ararat and Noah began to send out birds in search of land; when at last the dove returned with an olive leaf, he knew that the waters had subsided and he then released the animals and his children, who repopulated the earth. In medieval European folklore, Noah was often depicted as a henpecked husband and as a drunkard, from the incident after they had resettled in which his son Ham* saw him naked and drunk. *See also* Japheth; Shem.

Noble Savage. Historically, a concept which contended that people in a state of nature were inherently good but were corrupted by "civilization;" most often associated with the philosophy of Jean-Jacques Rousseau. Numerous literary examples exist, the most notable including Chingachgook* and Uncas,* John Savage,* the Tahitian natives met by Fletcher Christian,* Huck Finn,* Tarzan,* and the Wild Child.* *See also* Lord of the Flies; René.

Nod. (1) In the Bible, *Genesis* iv, the land east of Eden* into which Cain* was driven after he murdered Abel.* (2) *See* Wynken, Blynken, and Nod.

Noddy. *See* Boffin.

Noggs. In Charles Dickens's novel *Nicholas Nickleby* (1838), Ralph Nickleby's* clerk, an eccentric and kindhearted man.

Nokomis. In Henry Wadsworth Longfellow's poem *Hiawatha* (1855), Hiawatha's* wrinkled and wise old grandmother, originally a spirit woman who fell from the moon.

Nolan, Philip. In Edward Everett Hale's story *The Man Without a Country* (1863), a brash young man who wishes never to hear the name of the United States of America again and is sentenced to do so, living on ships in which all references to his homeland are removed from all his reading materials and are avoided in conversations.

Nora. (1) In Henrik Ibsen's play *A Doll's House* (1879), the pretty and childish wife of Helmer.* When a past indiscretion is exposed, her husband castigates her and then hypocritically repents when it becomes clear that the charge will never be made public, at which point she realizes the shallowness of their relationship and leaves him. The curtain scene, in which she slams the door on her way out, was seen as both a scandalous rejection of the duties of marriage and motherhood and a major blow for the rejection of the double standard and the movement for equal rights for women; it is arguably the most famous single moment in modern drama, perhaps in all modern literature. *See also* Rank, Dr. (2) *See* Charles, Nick and Nora.

Norma. In Bellini's opera *Norma* (1831), a druid priestess seduced by a Roman soldier. When he prepares to marry another priestess, she contemplates first the murder of her children, then of the other woman, and finally sacrifices herself. She is known primarily for the famous aria, "Casta diva."

Norns. In Scandinavian mythology, three women who spin the threads of life, similar to the Fates.*

Norris, Mrs. In Jane Austen's novel *Mansfield Park* (1814), the sister of Lady Bertram* and a miserly, ill-tempered widow and busybody.

Nosferatu. In German legend, Dracula.*

Nostradamus. Historically, a French astrologer (d. 1566); his prophecies, so obscure as to be interpreted wth contradictory meanings, continue to be circulated even in the present day.

Nostromo. In Joseph Conrad's novel *Nostromo* (1904), a complex Italian living in a Latin American country with a great reputation as an incorruptible man because he had rescued the town's silver during a civil war. Although everyone believes the silver was later sunk in a storm, Nostromo in fact hid it on a nearby island, and regularly returns to it to obtain his own spending money, which makes him wealthy but leaves him with a powerful feeling of guilt. After he is mistakenly shot while courting a young woman, he tries to confess, but no one will listen, and he dies with his reputation intact.

Nottingham. *See* Sheriff of Nottingham, The.

Nubbles, Kit. In Charles Dickens's novel *The Old Curiosity Shop* (1840), a generous and faithful boy who loves Little Nell* from afar and who helps in the search for her and her grandfather; he is accused of theft by Quilp,* but proves his innocence and marries the Garland's* housemaid after Nell's death.

Nucingen. In several novels by Balzac, most notably *Père Goriot* (1835) and *A Harlot High and Low* (1838–47), the **Baron** was a fabulously wealthy German Jew who began his fortune by speculating against Napoleon* at Waterloo,* was made a French baron, and was involved in numerous shady but successful financial dealings. He almost sacrificed his standing and his fortune in an uncharacteristically abandoned fling with Esther van Gobseck,* but he recovered after her death and continued his financial machinations. The **Baroness** was Goriot's* second daughter, self-centered and snobbish, who looked down on the old man now impoverished by the sacrifices he made to find her a wealthy husband. She took Rastignac* for a lover and engaged in a long-running social feud with her sister, the Countess de Restaud.*

Numa Pompilius. In Roman legend, the second king of ancient Rome, successor to Romulus* and founder of the Vestal Virgins.*

Numina. In Roman mythology, a collective name for the various gods of home and fields, especially Pomona* and Vertumnus.*

Nun. Historically, women who make a vow of chastity and live in religious orders, usually in isolated convents, although some Catholic orders also serve within the profane world as nurses or teachers. The term is most often applied to Catholic nuns, but there are similar women in most of the world's religions; the ancient Romans had similar persons in the Vestal Virgins.* As nuns were common in Europe from medieval times, they have necessarily played a significant role in literature and folklore, usually in four basic types: gentle, pure, and sincere "brides of Christ" who live lives of self-effacing purity; "sister of mercy" nurses; lascivious women whose convent walls hid shameful sexual license and orgiastic practices, often lesbian as well as heterosexual (many of the stories in Boccaccio's *Decameron* deal with this type); or repressed spinsters who expressed their frustrations in various forms of jealousy, political infighting, and humiliations.

Nun, Second. In Chaucer's *Canterbury Tales*, a gentle nun who relates the story of St. Cecilia.*

Nun's Priest. In Chaucer's poem *The Canterbury Tales*, the priest who accompanies the Prioress* and tells the story of Chanticleer.*

Nurse. In Shakespeare's play *Romeo and Juliet* (1595), the bawdy old nurse and chaperone of Juliet.*

Nycteus. *See* Nyctimene.

Nyctimene. In Greek legend, the daughter of Nycteus. Disguised, she seduced her father, and when he discovered her identity, he tried to kill her, but she was changed into an owl.

Nymph. In Greek legend, any of a number of lesser female deities, long-lived but not actually immortal, and usually associated with natural objects such as rivers (Naiads), trees (Dryads), mountains (Oreades), the sea (Nereids), etc. Generally, they were known as beautiful, graceful, pleasure-loving creatures, similar to fairies but human in size and appearance. For notable nymphs, *see* Amphitrite; Arethusa; Britomartis; Calypso; Chelone; Daphne; Echo; Galatea; Hermaphroditus; Lotis; Oenone; Sabrina; Scylla; Syrinx; Thetis.

O

Oak, Gabriel. In Thomas Hardy's nov᷉ *Far From the Madding Crowd* (1874), the sturdy farmer who works for Bathshe a Everdene,* whom he adores although she is in love with less worthy men. I'e becomes the manager of her farm; eventually, she realizes his love and marries him.

Obadiah. (1) In the Bible, *I Kings* xviii, Ahab's* minister who tried to protect the Hebrew prophets from Jezebel.* (2) In the Bible, *Obadiah*, a prophet who prophesied the destruction of Edom. (3) In British usage, especially in the eighteenth century, a stereotypical name for a Quaker. (4) In Laurence Sterne's novel *Tristram Shandy* (1759), the awkward but genial servant.

Oberon. In many European folklores, the king of the fairies.* Most English allusions are to Shakespeare's play *A Midsummer Night's Dream* (1595), in which Oberon causes his wife Titania* to fall in love with Bottom,* who has been changed into an ass, and magically sorts out the conflicts of the runaway lovers. *See also* Puck.

Oblomov. In Goncharov's novel *Oblomov* (1858), a Russian landowner living a life of complete indolence and unable to stir out of that laziness for anything, even love.

Oblonsky. In Tolstoy's novel *Anna Karenina* (1875), a robust, popular, and cheerful man who cannot remain faithful to his wife Dolly,* no matter how much he may guiltily regret each affair.

Occam. Historically, a fourteenth-century priest and philosopher noted for a theory called Occam's Razor; although variously phrased, this is essentially the idea that the simplest hypothesis to fit the facts is also the best.

Oceanids. *See* Nymph.

Oceanus. In Greek mythology, the eldest of the Titans* and the great outer body of water that surrounded all the world. *Also called* Pontus. *See also* Doris; Styx; Tethys.

Ochs, Baron. In Richard Strauss's opera *Der Rosenkavalier* (1911), the crude middle-aged nobleman who tries to marry the beautiful young Sophie.*

Ocnus. In Roman folklore, a man who worked industriously and had a wife who just as quickly wasted what he earned; he is sometimes shown making a rope which an ass eats as fast as he can make it.

Octavia. Historically, the sister of Octavius* and the wife deserted by Marc Antony* for Cleopatra.* In Shakespeare's play *Antony and Cleopatra* (1606), she is virtuous and a bit pathetic; in John Dryden's play *All For Love* (1677), she is more matronly, stressing the authority granted her as a result of her children.

Octavian. In Richard Strauss's opera *Der Rosenkavalier* (1911), the handsome young lover of the Marschallin;* he is sent as messenger for the crude Baron Ochs* to the beautiful Sophie* and falls in love with the girl.

Octavius. *See* Caesar, Augustus.

Odette. (1) In the ballet *Swan Lake* (1877), the beautiful swan queen who each night takes the form of a young girl in search of a man who will love her faithfully, for whom she would stay completely human. She meets and loves Siegfried,* but when he is lured away by Odile,* she kills herself. (2) In Marcel Proust's novels *Remembrance of Things Past* (1913–27), a shallow courtesan of whom Swann* becomes enamored; he eventually marries her when she becomes pregnant, despite her affairs with other men and women. She rises in society after Swann's death, ultimately becoming the mistress of the aging Duc de Guermantes.* For her daughter, *see* Gilberte.

Odhir. *See* Freya.

Odile. In the ballet *Swan Lake* (1877), the black swan, an evil enchantress who takes the form of a beautiful princess in order to lure Siegfried* away and thus maintain the evil magician's control of the beautiful swan queen Odette.*

Odin. In Scandinavian mythology, the supreme god, a creator of the world and god of wisdom and of the air; married to Frigga,* he is the father of Thor* and Baldur.* *Also called* Wotan.*

Odintsov, Anna. In Turgenev's novel *Fathers and Sons* (1862), the cold and haughty young beauty whose unfeeling exterior is pierced by no one until Bazarov* is on his deathbed. For her sister, *See* Katya.

O'Dowd. In William Makepeace Thackeray's novel *Vanity Fair* (1847), a relaxed Irish major devoted to his witty, vivacious, and delightfully unaffected wife. His sister **Glorvina** is flirtatious and shallow, all "frocks and shoulders."

Odysseus. In Greek legend, a wise, imaginative, and brave warrior who participated in the Trojan War* as well as in numerous other adventures. In Homer's *Iliad*, he is a warrior chief, cool, cunning, and admirable, who provides much imaginative counsel, particularly in the efforts to get Achilles* back into battle. In Homer's *Odyssey*, his journey home after the war takes ten years, during which he must overcome numerous dangers, including capture by Polyphemus* the Cyclops,* enchantments by Circe,* detention by Calypso,* the lure of the Sirens,* and the dangers of Scylla* and Charybdis.* He also makes a trip to the underworld where his future is told by Tiresias.* During this time, his faithful wife Penelope* fends off numerous suitors until Odysseus arrives in disguise, finally killing the suitors and returning to his family and throne. In Virgil's *Aeneid*, Odysseus devises the plan for the Trojan Horse,* as a result of which he is sometimes depicted in Roman sources as sly, devious, and unscrupulous. In other sources, he is the counselor who binds all Helen's* suitors to support the winner, which ultimately leads them to join the Trojan War; he also tries to avoid joining that war by feigning madness, randomly plowing a field, but the ruse is spoiled when he turns the plow to avoid his baby son Telemachus.* In Dante's *Divine Comedy*, he is imprisoned with Diomedes* in Hell* in an eternal flame as a great false counselor. In some legends, he is killed by his bastard son Telegonus,* but he tells Dante that he drowned while sailing across the Atlantic to the end of the world. *Also called* Ulysses. *See also* Ajax; Cattle of the Sun; Eumaeus; Eurylocus; Hecuba; Laertes; Latinus; Mentor; Nausicaa; Nemo; Palamedes.

Oeax. In Greek legend, the brother of Palamedes;* in revenge for his brother's death, he told Clytemnestra* that she would be forsaken by Agamemnon* for Cassandra,* thereby encouraging her to murder her husband when he returned.

Oedipus. In Greek legend, a king of Thebes. When he was born, it was prophesied that he would kill his father Laius,* whereupon he was abandoned; rescued by a shepherd, he was raised by the King of Corinth until, hearing the prophecy again, he left his foster father to avoid killing him and instead killed his real father on the road. Arriving at Thebes, he solved the riddle of the Sphinx* and married Jocasta,* not realizing she was his mother, siring the children Antigone,* Eteocles,* Polynices,* and Ismene.* When he realized the true nature of his actions, he blinded himself and went into exile. The most widely noted version of his story is in Sophocles's play *Oedipus Rex*, which deals with his discovery of his past while searching for the source of a plague that has struck his city. The story is also the foundation of Freud's "Oedipus complex," used to describe a son's jealousy of his father and love for his mother. *See also* Tiresias.

Oeneus. In Greek legend, father of Meleager* and king of Calydon whose land was ravaged by a great boar when he failed to make proper sacrifices to Artemis.* The boar was eventually killed by Meleager after a great hunt involving many of the Greek heroes. *See also* Althea.

Oenone. (1) In Greek legend, a nymph* who loved Paris* even after he deserted her; she killed herself when she learned of his death. (2) In Racine's play *Phèdre* (1677), the old nurse and friend of Phaedra.*

Og. In the Bible, *Deuteronomy* iii, a giant and king of Bashan who was defeated and destroyed by the Israelites.

Ogier. In medieval legend, a great Danish knight at Charlemagne's court.*

Ogyges. In Greek legend, the first king of Greece, in whose time a great flood* occurred.

Ogygia. In Homer's *Odyssey*, the island where Calypso* lived.

O'Hara, Scarlett. In Margaret Mitchell's novel *Gone With the Wind* (1936), a prototypical Southern belle, beautiful, flirtatious, and romantic; the vicissitudes of the Civil War do little to destroy her romanticism but do reveal an indomitable will to keep Tara,* her plantation home. To do so, she makes opportunistic marriages to a carpetbagger and then to Rhett Butler,* who ultimately deserts her because of her unscrupulous conniving and her persistent love for the aristocratically handsome but weak Ashley Wilkes.* When faced with unpleasant truths, she prefers to "think about that tomorrow."*See also* Melanie.

Oisin. In Irish legend, a warrior and son of Finn.* *See also* Ossian.

Olaf, St. Historically, a Norse king (d. 1030) who was killed during civil wars resulting from his efforts to convert his people to Christianity; the patron saint and national hero of Norway, his day is July 29.

Old Girl, The. *See* Bagnet.

Old Man. *See* Santiago.

Old Man of the Sea. In *The Arabian Nights*, an old man who climbed on Sinbad's* back and could not be removed until Sinbad got him drunk.

O'Leary, Mrs. In American folklore, an old woman whose cow kicked over a lantern and started the great fire that burned down Chicago in 1871.

Olga. In Anton Chekhov's play *Three Sisters* (1901), the eldest sister, a schoolteacher who eventually becomes headmistress. *See also* Irina; Masha; Prozorov.

Olifaunt, Nigel. In Walter Scott's novel *The Fortunes of Nigel* (1822), a young Scottish noble who comes to London in hopes of saving his estates, stumbles into intrigue, hides in a lawless section of the city, and is imprisoned before being saved by the efforts of Margaret Ramsay.*

Olive. In Greek mythology, the olive is sacred to Athena,* serving many symbolic functions: Olive trees were a symbol of wealth and fertility, a bride carried an olive garland, the olive branch was carried as a sign that the bearer came in peace, and the olive crown was the original reward at the Olympics. In the Bible, the olive holds a similar position of importance, signifying fecundity, wealth, and peace; the dove brings an olive leaf to Noah* to indicate that the waters of the Flood* have receded, and in many medieval and Renaissance paintings, Gabriel* gives Mary* an olive branch at the Annunciation.* *See also* Olives, Mount of.

Oliver. (1) In the anonymous *Song of Roland*, the great friend of Roland,* so equally brave and skillful that the phrase "Roland and Oliver" is used to indicate perfectly matched pairs. Oliver dies in battle beside Roland, a ring of dead Saracens around him. (2) In Shakespeare's play *As You Like It* (1599), the tyrannical brother whom Orlando* flees; he reforms when saved from a lion by Orlando, and he marries Celia.* (3) *See* Twist, Oliver; Surface.

Olives, Mount of. In the Bible, *Acts* i, a hill near Jerusalem* from which Jesus* made his Ascension;* also the site of Gethsemane.*

Olivia. (1) In Shakespeare's play *Twelfth Night* (1599), a countess in mourning for her brother. Loved by Orsino,* she falls in love instead with Orsino's page, who is in fact another woman, Viola,* in disguise as a man. *See also* Belch, Sir Toby; Malvolio. (2) In William Wycherley's play *The Plain Dealer* (1674), a shallow, scheming, and adulterous woman. (3) *See* Livia; Livy.

Olivier. *See* Oliver.

Olympia. In Edouard Manet's painting *Olympia* (1865), a striking, direct female nude whose departures from the conventional nude in painting became a symptomatic and symbolic controversial point in the rise of "modern" art.

Olympians. The gods who resided in Olympus.* *See* Aphrodite; Apollo; Ares; Artemis; Athena; Demeter; Hera; Hermes; Hestia; Poseidon; Zeus. Although Pluto* resided in Hades,* he had equivalent power and he is sometimes included in the list. *See also* Hephaestus; Momus.

Olympus. In Greek mythology, the home of the gods; the highest mountain in Greece is given the same name. *See also* Olympians; Pelion.

Omar Khayyám. Historically, a Persian poet and astronomer (d. 1123) noted primarily for the *Rubáiyát*, translated and adapted by Edward Fitzgerald (1859), in which Omar became a popular voice of hedonism ("a loaf of bread . . . a jug of wine . . . and thou . . . ") and modern fatalism ("the moving finger writes, and having writ, moves on . . . ").

Omphale. In Greek legend, a queen of Lydia who bought Heracles* when he had been condemned by the gods into slavery and made him spin and weave and do other women's work while she wore a lion's skin and hunted; she also became his lover.

Omphalos. Historically, a block of stone in Apollo's* temple at Delphi;* regarded by ancient Greeks as the "navel of the universe."

Onan. In the Bible, *Genesis* xxxviii, a son of Judah* who was ordered to marry his dead brother's wife Tamar* and who "spilled his seed upon the ground" in order not to produce a child, for which God killed him.

Ondine. In European folklore, a water nymph;* in many stories, she becomes human when she falls in love with a human but she will die if he ever proves unfaithful to her. *See also* Mélusine; Mermaid.

Onegin, Eugene. In Pushkin's poem *Eugene Onegin* (1833), a witty, aristocratic, but unproductive young man who is disillusioned by numerous affairs; eventually he kills a man in a duel caused by a meaningless flirtation. *See also* Tatiana.

One-Hoss Shay, The. In Oliver Wendell Holmes's poem *The Deacon's Masterpiece* (1858), a carriage built to last forever with all parts of equal strength but which, after a hundred years, fell apart all at once. Originally a parable on the breakdown of American Calvinism, it was later applied to many different topics.

Onuphrius, St. In Christian legend, an Egyptian hermit who lived alone in the desert for 60 years, fed only during weekly visits by an angel.*

Open, Sesame. *See* Ali Baba.

Ophelia. In Shakespeare's play *Hamlet* (1600), the naive daughter of Polonius.* Falling in love with the young Hamlet,* she is manipulated into spying on him, for which he brutally humiliates her in the "get thee to a nunnery" scene. When Hamlet kills Polonius, she goes mad in one of literature's most famous mad scenes ("rosemary for remembrance," etc.) and drowns; Hamlet leaps into her grave with her when he sees her funeral. *See also* Laertes.

Ophir. In the Bible, *I Kings* ix, the site of Solomon's* gold mines.

Ops. In Roman mythology, goddess of the harvest, similar to Rhea.*

Oracle. In Greek culture, a statement or prophecy from the gods delivered by an earthly priest or priestess, as well as the site at which such priests served. The most significant sites were at Delphi,* dedicated to Apollo,* which was famous for telling the future, and at Epirus, dedicated to Zeus,* where the sounds made by a brook and the rustling leaves were interpreted.

Orc. In Ariosto's *Orlando Furioso* (1532), a gigantic sea monster that Orlando* kills by wedging its mouth open and cutting it up from the inside out.

Oreades. *See* Nymph.

Orestes. In Greek legend, the son of Agamemnon* and Clytemnestra;* he kills his mother and her lover Aegisthus* in revenge for their murder of his father. He appears in numerous works, the most fundamental of which are Aeschylus's plays *Oresteia*, in which he hesitates to kill Clytemnestra but is pressured into revenge by the god Apollo,* by his sister Electra,* and by the chorus. He is then driven mad by the Furies,* who torment him and demand that he be tried by the gods for his crime, of which he is eventually acquitted by Athena* in a triumph of reason over fear and blind passion. In Jean Racine's play *Andromaque* (1667), he goes mad after killing Hermione's* husband Pyrrhus* in order to secure her love. *See also* Arsinoé; Erigone; Iphigenia; Pylades.

Orfeo. *See* Orpheus.

Orgon. In Molière's play *Tartuffe* (1664), the credulous wealthy man who supports Tartuffe* and refuses to believe ill of the hypocrite until his wife Elmire* hides him under a table where he can overhear Tartuffe's attempt to seduce her. Unfortunately, Orgon has signed over all his wealth to Tartuffe and is faced with ruin, until he is miraculously rescued by a messenger of the king.

Oriana. In numerous sixteenth-century English poems, a name given to Elizabeth.*

Oriel. *See* Ariel.

Orion. In Greek legend, a great hunter who is transformed into the constellation of that name. *See also* Sirius.

Orlando. (1) A name sometimes used for Roland.* (2) In Ariosto's *Orlando Furioso* (1532), a perfect knight lured away from his duty by the beautiful Angelica* and driven mad when she marries another; he lays waste to the countryside until lured back to Charlemagne's* camp where he is cured and defeats the great Saracen Agramante.* *See also* Rinaldo; Rodomont. (3) In Shakespeare's play *As You Like It* (1599), a noble second son cruelly mistreated by his brother Oliver;* when he defeats the wrestler Charles,* he and Rosalind* fall in love at first sight, but, driven into the woods by his brother, he can only write poems to her which he sticks onto trees. When she, disguised as a boy and also in exile, finds the poems, she arranges that Orlando will court her/him while pretending that she/he is really Rosalind; eventually, all is resolved, and they marry and are restored to fortune. *See also* Adam. (4) In Virginia Woolf's novel *Orlando* (1928), a young Elizabethan gentleman who does not age and progresses through centuries of English experience, waking one day to find he has been transformed into a woman, as which he experiences the modern world.

Orpah. In the Bible, *Ruth* i, Ruth's* sister-in-law who returns to her family after her husband's death rather than remain with Naomi* as does Ruth.

Orpheus. In Greek legend, son of Calliope* and the greatest poet and musician; he could charm the beasts to stillness with his music. When his wife Eurydice* died, he followed her to Hades* to get her back, which he was allowed to do provided he never looked back at her on the journey home; when he turned to check on her, she disappeared. In some versions, he is later torn to pieces by Maenads* outraged by his resulting misogyny.

Orsino. (1) In Shakespeare's play *Twelfth Night* (1599), the duke in melancholy love with the cool Olivia* and loved by Viola;* he says, "If music be the food of love, play on." (2) In Shelley's play *The Cenci* (1819), the scheming, villainous count and priest who assassinates Cenci* and then abandons Beatrice so that she must take the blame.

Osbaldistone. In Walter Scott's novel *Rob Roy* (1818), a family illustrating the Jacobite rebellions. **Frank** is the young hero, his cousin **Rashleigh** an embezzler, his father **William** a Stuart businessman, and his uncle **Hildebrand** a Jacobite plotter who dies in prison. *See also* Rob Roy; Vernon, Diana.

Osborne. In William Makepeace Thackeray's novel *Vanity Fair* (1847), **George** is a dashing officer who, though disinherited for the act, marries Amelia Sedley* but is attracted to Becky Sharp;* he is killed at Waterloo.* His father **John** is testy and narrow-minded and tries to take his grandson away from Amelia.

Oscar. (1) In Ossian's poems, Ossian's* son. (2) Historically, an award given by the American movie industry (beg. 1927). (3) In Neil Simon's play *The Odd Couple* (1965), the quintessential slob. *See also* Felix.

Osee. A name sometimes used for Hosea.*

Oshea. A name sometimes used for Joshua.*

Osip. In Gogol's play *The Inspector General* (1836), the elderly but shrewd servant who capitalizes on his master Khlestakov's* mistaken identity to take numerous bribes.

Osiris. In Egyptian mythology, the moon, husband of Isis,* god of the underworld, and judge of the dead; murdered by his brother, his body was cut into pieces and scattered. He also figures in some Greek materials as a son of Zeus* who was killed by Typhon.*

Osmond, Gilbert. In Henry James's novel *The Portrait of a Lady* (1841), an expatriate American devoting himself to aesthetic pleasure in Rome; he marries Isabel Archer.* *See also* Merle, Mme.

Osric. In Shakespeare's play *Hamlet* (1600), the effeminate courtier who judges the fencing match. *See also* Hamlet; Laertes.

Ossa. *See* Pelion.

Ossian. In a famous literary fraud, the ostensible son of Fingal* and the writer of a number of epic poems depicting Scottish prehistory. The works were "translated" by James M'Pherson (beg. 1760) and were accepted throughout Europe as not only genuine but also among the world's greatest poetry, initiating not only the development of Scottish nationalism but also the Romantic fascination with history epitomized by Walter Scott's novels. When the fraud was exposed, the works all but disappeared. Hence, some allusions are to the warrior-bard and his world of pre-Christian poetry and heroism; others are to the fraud itself.

Osvald. *See* Alving.

Oswald. *See* Osvald.

Othello. In Shakespeare's play *Othello* (1604), a Moor and a general of Venice whose noble character and position are destroyed by his jealousy of his wife Desdemona.* When his ensign Iago* insinuates that Desdemona is adulterous, Othello is quick to seize the suggestion; he loses control of himself until, after seeing her handkerchief in Cassio's hands, he sends Iago to kill Cassio and he himself kills Desdemona, in most productions by suffocating her with her pillow. When it is revealed that she was innocent and that Iago had duped him, he kills himself.

O'Trigger, Lucius. In R. B. Sheridan's play *The Rivals* (1775), the braggart Irishman who challenges a rival to a duel and then withdraws as quickly as possible.

Ottilie. In Goethe's novel *Elective Affinities* (1808), a young woman who falls so passionately in love with the married nobleman Edward* that she starves herself to death. *See also* Charlotte.

Otus. In Greek legend, a giant, sometimes said to be the son of Poseidon,* who tried to attack the gods and, in the vain hope of reaching them in heaven, piled the mountain Pelion* on the mountain Ossa and both on Olympus.* In Homer's *Iliad*, he is also said to have imprisoned Ares* in a jar for thirteen months.

Overdo. In Ben Jonson's play *Bartholomew Fair* (1614), a justice of the peace who disguises himself in order to expose wickedness at the fair and is beaten and humiliated, the ultimate blow being the discovery of his drunken wife in a prostitute's clothes at the puppet show. He repents his zealousness and treats the crowd to a supper.

Overreach, Giles. In Philip Massinger's play *A New Way to Pay Old Debts* (1625), the tyrannical miser whose greed becomes so great that his fortune collapses under his own machinations.

Oxbridge. In British usage, a name formed by combining Oxford and Cambridge and used to indicate the whole realm of intellectual and social attitudes and influences in British life associated with those preeminent schools.

Oyl, Olive. In the American newspaper cartoon *Thimble Theater* (beg. 1919) and in numerous movie cartoons (beg. 1932), a bossy, vain, but exceedingly thin and unattractive woman, becoming the true love of Popeye* shortly after his later appearance in the strip.

Oz. In numerous novels by Frank Baum (beg. 1900), an imaginary kingdom where numerous odd characters and adventures occur. In the first novel, *The Wonderful Wizard of Oz*, the country is ruled by a terrifying wizard living in a castle at the end of the yellow brick road, who is finally revealed to be a simple carnival magician. Most allusions are to the movie version (1939). *See also* Dorothy.

Ozymandias. In Shelley's poem *Ozymandias* (1818), a mighty Egyptian king whose dilapidated statue now ironically reveals the shallowness of earthly power.

Ozzie and Harriet. In the American radio and television series "The Adventures of Ozzie and Harriet" (1944–66), the quintessential American middle-class couple, equally admired and ridiculed for their blandness and lack of emotional conflict and for the simple innocence of their children, who were raised and educated in the course of the series.

P

Paddy. An English corruption of the Gaelic equivalent of Patrick; used as a stereotype name for a comic Irishman.

Paeon. In Homer's *Iliad*, the doctor who treated the gods wounded in the Trojan War.*

Page. In Shakespeare's play *The Merry Wives of Windsor* (1598), **Mistress Page** is one of the merry wives, courted by Falstaff,* who schemes with her friend Mistress Ford* to humiliate him; her daughter **Ann** is an innocent ingenue.

Pagliacci. In Leoncavallo's opera *Pagliacci* (1892), the name commonly associated with the clown played by Canio* in the play-within-the-play, although technically he is called Pagliaccio, a form of Pulchinella.*

Paladin. In medieval legend, a name given to any of the knights in the service of Charlemagne.*

Palamedes. In Greek legend, the man sent to fetch Odysseus* to the Trojan War.* He placed the baby Telemachus* in the path of the plow, thus exposing the false nature of Odysseus's madness and earning his enmity. Later, Odysseus framed him as a traitor, and he was stoned to death; in revenge, his father lit false beacons and lured the Greek fleet onto the rocks on its way home. *See also* Oeax.

Palamon. In Chaucer's *Canterbury Tales*, in the Knight's Tale, a knight who loved the lady Emilia* and challenged Arcite to a joust for her. Palamon prayed to win her, and Arcite prayed for victory; both got their wish: Arcite won but was killed by his horse, and Palamon married Emilia.*

Pales. In Roman mythology, the goddess of cattle and flocks.

Palinurus. In Virgil's *Aeneid*, the steersman who fell overboard in his sleep and was murdered after he swam ashore; Aeneas* found him wandering through the underworld because he had not been properly buried. The name was often applied to any pilot or steersman.

Pallas. A name sometimes used for Athena.*

Pamela. *See* Andrews, Pamela.

Pamina. In Mozart's opera *The Magic Flute* (1791), the beautiful maiden rescued by Tamino.*

Pamphila. A name used for a young girl in numerous plays by Menander and Terence, most notably in the latter's *The Eunuch*.

Pan. In Greek mythology, the god of shepherds, flocks, and fertility; he is part man and part goat, playful and lascivious, and is said to have invented the reed flute. *Also called* Capricorn.* *See also* Faunus; Midas; Panic; Pitys; Satyr; Syrinx.

Pan, Peter. In J. M. Barrie's play *Peter Pan* (1904), a boy who can fly; he lives in Never-Never-Land,* where, accompanied by the fairy Tinker Bell,* he never grows up. He has exciting adventures with pirates, led by Capt. Hook,* and Indians, led by Tiger Lily.* *See also* Darling.

Panacea. In Roman mythology, the goddess of health. *See also* Hygeia; Iasus.

Pancks. In Charles Dickens's novel *Little Dorrit* (1855), Casby's* rent collector, an essentially kindly man forced to play the villain to extract payment from the poverty-stricken renters, until he rebels.

Pancras, St. In Christian legend, a teenaged martyr (d. 304), a patron saint of children.

Pandarus. (1) In Homer's *Iliad*, a great Trojan* warrior who wounds Menelaus* and Diomedes.* (2) In medieval legend, as told by Boccaccio and by Chaucer, the go-between who arranges the affair between Troilus* and Cressida,* thus giving the name "pander" to anyone who acts as a sexual go-between or a finder of whores. In Shakespeare's play *Troilus and Cressida* (1602), he is a lascivious, devious, and foul-mouthed old man.

Pandora. In Greek legend, the first woman, made from clay at Zeus's* command in order to be a wife and punishment for Prometheus.* Despite her attractions, Prometheus refused her, and she married instead his brother Epimetheus.* In her most noted act, she was given a box she was told never to open, but her curiosity overcame her prudence, and she did open it, releasing all the ills of human life.

Pangloss. In Voltaire's novel *Candide* (1759), Candide's* teacher, a philosopher who insists that we are living in the best of all possible worlds and that everything always happens for the best. *See also* Cunegonde; Paquette.

Panic. In Greek mythology, the son of Ares* and the god of the sudden fear named for him; this fear is also sometimes attributed to the god Pan.*

Panisse. In Marcel Pagnol's *Fanny* plays (1929–36), the kindly middle-aged businessman who marries Fanny* after Marius* leaves her.

Pantagruel. In Rabelais's *Pantagruel* (1532–52), the giant son of Gargantua.* Like his father, he has an enormous thirst and appetite. He returns home to defend it against the Dipsodes* and evolves into a good-natured and serene humanist prince who takes a long voyage to Cathay. Other notable adventures include the Gastrolaters,* the furry lawyer cats, and the ship full of sheep; these often involve his friends Panurge* and Epistemon,* as well as such passing acquaintances as the fool Triboulet.* In general, Pantagruel is the voice of human appetites and reason, opposed to medieval scholasticism and religious repression.

Pantalone. In the commedia dell'Arte, the foolish old man, usually wearing the pants for which he was named, spectacles, a white pointed beard, and slippers. He is usually a businessman, often a miser. Whether browbeaten by a wife and father of the ingenue, whose marriage he seeks to prevent, or absurdly lustful for a young maiden, he is eventually tricked by Harlequin* or Brighella.* *Also called* Géronte; Pantaloon.

Pantaloon. *See* Pantalone.

Pantheon. Historically, a great circular temple in Rome dedicated in 27 B.C. to all the gods; hence, any significant collection of godlike or very great persons.

Panurge. In Rabelais's *Pantagruel* (1532–52), the witty yet buffoonish friend of Pantagruel* noted for his long consideration of the question of marriage, which he always changes to the opposite opinion from that offered by any adviser; his comic apologia for borrowing; the stratagems that defeat the Dipsodes;* and his bargaining for a shipload of sheep. *See also* Epistemon; Triboulet.

Panza, Sancho. *See* Sancho Panza.

Paolo. In Dante's *Divine Comedy*, the brother of the count of Ravenna; he fell in love with Francesca da Rimini,* his brother's betrothed, and was killed by his brother. Although condemned to Hell,* their story is usually treated as an illustration of great love and passion rather than of adultery.

Papagena. In Mozart's opera *The Magic Flute* (1791), the bird woman who is given to Papageno* to love.

Papageno. In Mozart's opera *The Magic Flute* (1791), the bird catcher whose mouth is padlocked as punishment for his lies and who is given a set of bells to match the magic flute given to Tamino.* When he wishes for a woman to love, an old hag is revealed to be the bird woman Papagena.*

Paphia. A name sometimes used for Aphrodite.*

Paquette. In Voltaire's novel *Candide* (1759), the maid who gives Pangloss* a venereal disease.

Paradise. A term in Greek signifying a great garden, it gradually came to be applied in Christian culture to Eden.* Later it was used in the King James version of the Bible as a name for Heaven;* from that it was applied to any similar place in other religions and cultures and then to any place where life is comfortable and easy. In Dante's *Divine Comedy*, the third book describes the heavenly paradise as a place of eternal light and beauty. In Milton's poem *Paradise Lost* (1667), he describes both the heavenly paradise and Eden, and also adds a "paradise of fools" in Limbo* for those who had vain hopes of eternal fame or glory. In the Moslem version of Paradise, warriors live a life of ease attended by the beautiful Houri;* similar concepts may be seen in such ancient versions as Valhalla.* *See also* Avalon; Eldorado; Elysium; Shangri-La.

Parcae. A name sometimes used for the Fates.*

Pardoner. Historically, a man who sold indulgences for the Church; in Chaucer's *Canterbury Tales*, he is an avaricious traveling preacher who tells the story of the three young men sworn to friendship who kill each other over a golden treasure.

Paris. In Greek legend, the Trojan prince who was asked to judge which of the goddesses Aphrodite,* Athena,* or Hera* was the most beautiful; when he chose Aphrodite, he earned the enmity of the other two. Later, he abducted the beautiful Helen* from her husband Menelaus,* thereby igniting the Trojan War,* in which the offended goddesses sided with the Greeks. In Homer's *Iliad*, he is a vacillating and weak warrior who is eventually killed by Philoctetes.* *See also* Hector; Hecuba; Oenone; Priam.

Parnassus. Historically, a mountain sacred to Apollo,* long seen as the metaphorical home of the greatest poets.

Parnell. Historically, an Irish patriot (d. 1891) who was on the verge of negotiating home rule for Ireland when he lost his public support because he was named in a divorce action. He is often alluded to as a failed hero, an Irish patriot, or a symbol of irrational Irish puritanism.

Parolles. In Shakespeare's play *All's Well That Ends Well* (1602), a bragging, insulting, and lascivious knave who encourages Bertram* to avoid his responsibilities.

Parsifal. In Richard Wagner's opera *Parsifal* (1882), Parzival.* *See also* Amfortas; Klingsor.

Parsival. *See* Parzival.

Parthenon. Historically, the large temple atop the Acropolis hill in Athens; one of the finest examples of Doric architecture and the symbol of all of Greek culture.

Parthenos. A name sometimes used for Athena.*

Partlet. A name sometimes used for Pertelote.*

Partridge. In Henry Fielding's novel *Tom Jones* (1749), the simple school master, most noted for his visit to the theater where he thought Garrick's Hamlet* was mediocre, since "anyone could be so frightened," but praised the actor playing Claudius* because he was so obviously acting.

Parzival. (1) In Wolfram von Eschenbach's *Parzival*, an innocent young knight who sets out for adventure in search of the Holy Grail* and in the process learns remorse, self-doubt, and concern for others. He eventually finds a mature purity that restores his wife to him and makes him King of the Grail. (2) *See also* Parsifal; Percival.

Pasha. Historically, in the Ottoman Empire a high ranking officer in the bureaucracy.

Pasiphae. In Greek legend, wife of Minos,* the mother of Phaedra* and Ariadne,* and, after a union with a great white bull, also the mother of the Minotaur.*

Pasquariello. *See* Capitano, il.

Passepartout. In Jules Verne's novel *Around the World in Eighty Days* (1873), the imperturbable comic servant who accompanies Phileas Fogg.*

Passion. In Christian usage, the collective name given to the final events in the life of Jesus,* generally beginning with His triumphant entry into Jerusalem* on Palm Sunday, continuing through the Last Supper,* the betrayal in the Garden of Gethsemane,* His trial, the Crucifixion,* and ending with His entombment.

Passover. In Jewish usage, the celebration of the night of the plague* in *Exodus* xii, when God killed the firstborn of all the Egyptians but passed over all the homes of the Jews that were properly marked. For Christians, it is most significant as the day on which, or just before which, the Last Supper* was held.

Patelin. *See* Pathelin.

Pathelin. In the anonymous *Farce of M. Pathelin* (1464), a rascally lawyer. The work is noted as one of the earliest French plays and as the source of "Revenons à nos moutons."

Patrick. *See* Paddy.

Patrick, St. Historically, a priest (d. 461) who converted much of Ireland to Christianity after his escape from youthful slavery there. Legend and fact about him are much intertwined, and he is credited with such deeds as driving all the snakes off the island of Ireland, codifying the Irish laws, and opening a cave that gave a descent into Purgatory.* He is the patron saint of Ireland and his day, March 17, has come to be a patriotic holiday for Irishmen throughout the world. His symbols are the snake and the shamrock.

Patroclus. In Homer's *Iliad*, the close friend of Achilles.* He wore Achilles's armor while the great warrior sulked in his tent; when Patroclus was killed by Hector,* Achilles's rage and desire for revenge was so great that he forgot his pride and reentered the battle. *See also* Sarpedon.

Patterne, Sir Willoughby. In George Meredith's novel *The Egoist* (1879), an austere, sententious, and snobbish nobleman whose egocentricities cause him to lose friends and true love. *See also* Dale, Laetitia; Durham, Constantia; Middleton.

Paul. (1) In the Bible, *Acts*, a Pharisee,* originally named Saul,* who was converted to Christianity by a vision while on the road to Damascus* to persecute the Christians and then became the most important early missionary to the Gentiles, essentially the founder and organizer of the Christian Church and the author of the epistles to various churches which compose the bulk of the New Testament. Eventually, he was arrested and sent to Rome, where he was killed (legend says beheaded). His day is June 29; he is usually represented with a sword and/or a book. *See also* Ananias; Barnabas; Peter; Silas. (2) In Saint-Pierre's novel *Paul et Virginie* (1787), the natural and simple lover of Virginie;* he dies of grief after her death. (3) *See* Dombey; Morel.

Paul, St. (1) *See* Paul. (2) In Christian legend, an Egyptian hermit, generally regarded as the first Christian hermit.

Pauline. (1) In Corneille's play *Polyeucte* (1641), Polyeucte's* wife who pleads with him to worship the Roman idols hypocritically in public; when he refuses and is martyred, she converts to Christianity. (2) In the American movie serial *The Perils of Pauline* (1914), an innocent but brave young woman who imaginatively and often miraculously makes a number of hairbreadth escapes from attempts on her life, epitomizing the cliff-hanger serial.

Pavel. *See* Kirsanov.

Pavlov. Historically, a Russian scientist (d. 1936) famous in folklore for his experiments in which he taught dogs to salivate as if for food at the sound of a bell.

Pavlova. Historically, a great dancer (d. 1931); synonymous with the modern ballerina.

Pax. In Roman mythology, the goddess of peace. *See also* Concordia; Irene.

Peachum. In John Gay's operetta *The Beggar's Opera* (1728), the fence for Macheath's gang's stolen goods and a police informer. His daughter **Polly** falls in love with Macheath* and marries him, much to the dismay of **Mrs. Peachum**, who believes that Polly's love has destroyed her chances for wealth. In Bertolt

Brecht's version, *The Threepenny Opera* (1928), Peachum is the head of the beggars' association, planning the beggars' appearances and then growing wealthy on his cut of their earnings.

Pearl. In Nathaniel Hawthorne's novel *The Scarlet Letter* (1850), the blonde, elfin, illegitimate daughter of Hester* and Dimmesdale.*

Pearl of Great Price. In the Bible, *Matthew* xiii, a parable told by Jesus:* The kingdom of heaven is like a pearl of great price; a wise merchant would sell all he had in order to obtain it.

Pecksniff. In Charles Dickens's *Martin Chuzzlewit* (1843), the epitome of the canting hypocrite who commits the most heartless acts as a "duty" and ascribes only the purest of motives to himself, no matter how dubious or distasteful his own actions. Unlike many literary hypocrites, however, he is so completely unaware of the distance between his words and his deeds, even after he has become a drunkard, that even he himself is taken in. His daughters **Charity** and **Mercy** are misnamed; the first is a shrew, and the latter is a vain, selfish girl who does reform to some degree after mistreatment by her cruel husband. *See also* Chuzzlewit; Pinch, Tom.

Peel, Mrs. In the British television series "The Avengers" (1961–69), the cool, willowy, and witty crime fighter, partner to John Steed;* perhaps noted as much for her clothes as for her great physical and mental skill.

Peep-Bo. In Gilbert and Sullivan's operetta *The Mikado* (1885), one of the three little maids from school, sister of Yum-Yum* and Pitti-Sing.*

Peepers, Mr. In the American television series "Mr. Peepers" (1952–55), a shy, bespectacled science teacher and nice guy.

Peeping Tom. In English legend, a tailor who peeked as Lady Godiva* rode through town naked, for which he was struck blind.

Peer Gynt. *See* Gynt, Peer.

Peg. (1) In J. Hartley Manners's play *Peg o' My Heart* (1912), an Irish-American girl who inherits an English fortune, meets much hostility among the English gentry, and wins them over with her honest heart and good spirits, inspiring numerous accolades and the popular song of the same title. (2) *See also* Margaret; Meg; Pegeen.

Pegasus. In Greek legend, a winged horse, which sprang from the blood of Medusa* after Perseus* cut off her head, on which Bellerophon* defeated the Chimera* and tried to fly to Heaven.* It was also said to have raised the mountain sacred to the Muses* with a stamp of its hoof.

Pegeen. In J. M. Synge's play *The Playboy of the Western World* (1907), the sharp-tongued Irish lass who falls in love with Christy Mahon* when she thinks he has killed his father.

Peggotty. In Charles Dickens's novel *David Copperfield* (1849), the sturdy, loyal female servant who pops her buttons, marries Barkis,* and supports and encourages David Copperfield* throughout his youth. Her brother **Daniel** is a genial, simple sailor whose life is destroyed when his niece Little Em'ly* elopes with Steerforth,* and he spends years on a quest to find her. **Ham**, his nephew, is as simple and genial, until Em'ly deserts him on the eve of marriage, after which he begins to take dangerous chances, eventually drowning while trying to rescue a man shipwrecked in a storm who turns out to be Steerforth. *See also* Trotwood, Betsey.

Pegler, Mrs. In Charles Dickens's novel *Hard Times* (1854), Bounderby's* mother, who is paid by her son to stay out of sight so that no one will know he was not a self-made man.

Pelagia. A name sometimes used for Aphrodite.*

Pelagia, St. (1) In Christian legend, a famous courtesan who repented and, disguised as a man, lived as a hermit in a cave on the Mount of Olives.* (2) In Christian legend, two virgin martyrs have this name: One threw herself off a roof to avoid violation, and another was roasted when she refused to sleep with the Roman emperor.

Peleus. In Greek legend, a mortal husband of Thetis,* the father of Achilles,* and the king of the Myrmidons.* It was at his wedding that Eris* introduced the golden apple* that initiated the Judgement of Paris.*

Pelion. In Greek legend, a wooded mountain in Thessaly; in hopes of reaching the gods, Otus* vainly piled Pelion on top of the mountain Ossa and then put both on Olympus.*

Pelleas. (1) In Tennyson's poem *Pelleas and Ettarre* (1869), a young knight of the Round Table who falls in love with the coldhearted Ettarre* and lends his armor to Gawain* so that the latter may plead his case with the lady, only to discover that Gawain, after gaining entrance to the castle, seduced the lady. (2) In Maurice Maeterlinck's play *Pélléas and Mélisande* (1892), a young hunter who falls in love with his brother's wife Mélisande* and then is killed when they are discovered together; they are depicted as victims of innocent passion rather than of adulterous evil.

Pellinore. In Malory's *Morte d'Arthur*, the father of Percival;* he is usually depicted as a genial bumbler.

Pelops. In Greek legend, the son of Tantalus.* His father killed him, cut him into pieces, and served him to the gods, who all refused to eat except Demeter,* who ate the shoulder. When Pelops was restored to life by Zeus,* he was given an ivory shoulder. After his restoration, he brought a curse upon his house by bribing a charioteer to throw a race so that Pelops could win the hand of the king's daughter Hippodamia* and then murdering the charioteer.

Penates. In Roman mythology, the particular household gods of each home. *See also* Lares.

Penelope. In Homer's *Odyssey*, the wife who waits faithfully for Odysseus* during the ten years of the Trojan War* and the additional ten years of his journey home. Pursued by many suitors who claimed that Odysseus was dead and that she must remarry, she put them off until she should finish weaving a shroud for her father-in-law, which she carefully unraveled each evening so that it should not be finished. *See also* Antinous; Eurymachus; Telegonus; Telemachus.

Peneus. In Ovid's *Metamorphoses*, Daphne's* father, who changed her into a laurel tree to keep her out of the clutches of Apollo.*

Peniculus. In Plautus's play *Menaechmi*, the parasite. *See also* Menaechmi.

Pentecost. In the Bible, *Acts* ii, the day on which the Holy Spirit visited the Apostles* and they began to speak in tongues. This, in turn, was a Jewish festival associated with the giving to Moses* of the Torah.*

Penthesilea. In Greek legend, a queen of the Amazons* who came to the aid of the Trojans* and was killed by Achilles.* In Kleist's play *Penthesilea* (1808), she also falls in love with Achilles.

Pentheus. In Euripides's play *The Bacchae*, a Theban king who attempts to suppress the cult of Dionysus.* The god appears to him, gets him drunk, and then sends him off disguised as a woman to spy on the Bacchae,* who are led by Pentheus's mother Agave.* He is discovered and torn apart by the frenzied females.

Pequod. In Herman Melville's novel *Moby-Dick* (1851), the ship captained by Ahab* which is ultimately sunk by Moby Dick.*

Per. *See* Hansa.

Percival. (1) In Malory's *Morte d'Arthur*, one of the virtuous knights of Arthur's* court; he does see the Holy Grail,* but he dies before returning to the court. *See also* Bors; Galahad; Pellinore. (2) *See also* Parzival.

Percy, Henry. The actual name of Hotspur.*

Perdita. In Shakespeare's play *The Winter's Tale* (1610), the daughter abandoned by Leontes* and Hermione* and raised by a shepherd.

Peri. In Arabic folklore, a fairy,* usually depicted as a female.

Périchole, La. Historically, an eighteenth-century singer with a colorful life in Peru and the subject of numerous works, the most notable being Offenbach's operetta *La Périchole* (1868) and Thorton Wilder's novel *The Bridge of San Luis Rey* (1927).

Pericles. (1) Historically, a great statesman and Athenian leader (d. 429 B.C.), who is noted for his political skill, his advancement of democratic processes, and his patronage of the arts which shaped most of the famous statuary and public buildings of Athens. His "funeral oration," reported by Thucydides, is one of the most famous speeches in history. *See also* Cleon. (2) In Shakespeare's play *Pericles* (1608), a prince of Tyre who is shipwrecked, meets and weds Thaisa,* thinks his wife is dead, leaves his daughter Marina* with his untrustworthy friend Cleon,* and is miraculously reunited years later with both wife and daughter.

Periphetes. In Greek legend, an outlaw who killed travelers with his iron club until he was killed by Theseus.*

Perpetua, St. Historically, a Christian martyr who, while in prison, envisioned a ladder leading to heaven and who was killed in the arena along with St. Felicity.* Her day is March 7.

Perrette. In La Fontaine's *Fables* (1668), a milkmaid who is so excited by her dreams of profit that she drops her milk before reaching market.

Persephone. In Greek mythology, the daughter of Demeter.* When Pluto* saw her, he abducted her, and Demeter threatened to destroy all fertility on earth if she were not found. Zeus* ordered her returned, but only if she had eaten nothing in Hades.* Unfortunately, she had eaten some seeds, with the result that she returned to her mother on earth for half the year and spent the other half as queen of Hades. *Also called* Cora; Kore; Proserpine. *See also* Adonis; Ascalaphus; Golden Bough; Hecate.

Perseus. In Greek legend, the son of Danaë* and Zeus* and a great hero. Sent on a quest by a king who lusted after his mother, Perseus killed Medusa* by reflecting her stare in a mirror and cutting off her head. While returning home, he found Andromeda* chained as a sacrifice to a sea monster, which he turned into a stone by showing it Medusa's head. He married Andromeda after turning another suitor, Phineus,* to stone. He similarly turned Atlas* into a mountain in return for his poor treatment of Perseus, and he returned home, where he rescued his mother. An ancient prophecy had said he would kill his grandfather, which he did accidentally with a discus thrown too far during the games; he retired to Persia rather than take the throne thus vacated. *See also* Pegasus.

Pertelote. In Chaucer's *Canterbury Tales*, in the Nun's Priest's Tale, the hen who ridicules Chanticleer's* dreams of doom, thus encouraging the vainglory that almost leads to his death. *Also called* Partlet.

Pet. *See* Meagles.

Peter. (1) In the Bible, New Testament, the first Apostle* of Jesus,* a fisherman about whom He said, "Upon this rock I will build my Church." When Jesus was arrested, Peter drew his sword to defend Him, for which Jesus chid him;

later, after Jesus's trial, before the cock crowed, he three times denied that he knew Him. After the Crucifixion,* he became the leader of the Christian community, performing various miracles and organizing what would become the Church, for which the Popes claimed to be directly consecutive from him. He debated Paul* and agreed to allow Gentiles into the Church, was imprisoned by Herod* Agrippa until released by divine intervention, and eventually was martyred. Tradition says he was crucified and buried on the site of the Vatican basilica. Jesus also promised him the "keys of the kingdom," for which he is often depicted in Christian tradition as the gatekeeper who determines who will and will not be allowed into Heaven.* He is usually shown with a set of keys, and his day is June 29. He is also the patron saint of fishermen. *Also called* Cephas; Simon; Simon Peter. (2) In Shakespeare's play *Romeo and Juliet* (1595), the stupid servant whose inability to read leads him to ask advice of Romeo* and thus brings Romeo to the party where he will meet Juliet.* (3) *See* Quince, Peter.

Peter, St. (1) Peter* the Apostle. (2) Historically, Peter Damian, a bishop and reformer (d. 1072) noted for his intransigent insistence on poverty in the priesthood and the strictness of religious observance.

Petkoff, Raina. *See* Raina.

Petrouchka. In Russian folklore, a puppet who falls in love with the ballerina, becomes jealous of her and the Moor, and is eventually killed by them; the story is known primarily from Stravinsky's ballet of the same name (1911).

Petrovitch, Porfiry. In Dostoevsky's novel *Crime and Punishment* (1866), the detective who solves the murder but who is more interested in encouraging Raskolnikov's* redemption than in obtaining his conviction.

Petrovna, Natalya. *See* Natasha.

Petruchio. In Shakespeare's play *The Taming of the Shrew* (1593), the impoverished noble who is persuaded to marry the shrew Kate* for her money and then proceeds to tame her shrewishness by a campaign of humiliation, overblown solicitude, and irrationality. He woos her with a fight, appears at the wedding dressed as a fool, throws out all her food and clothes on the grounds that they are not worthy of her, and claims the sun is the moon and that an old man is an old woman.

Petrushka. *See* Petrouchka.

Petya. *See* Rostov.

Pew. In R. L. Stevenson's novel *Treasure Island* (1883), the blind, crippled sailor who delivers the black spot and is trampled to death by the raiding revenue agents.

Peyton Place. In Grace Metalious's novel *Peyton Place* (1956), a small New England town in which numerous scandalous affairs occur; it almost immediately became synonymous with hypocrisy and small towns in which public propriety masks lives of sexual debauchery.

Phaedra. In Greek legend, the sister of Ariadne* and the wife of Theseus* after he had deserted Ariadne. She later fell in love with her stepson Hippolytus* and hanged herself after he rejected her advances. In Euripides's play *Hippolytus*, she struggles against her passion, and Hippolytus only discovers it from her nurse. In Seneca's play *Phaedra*, she is much more brazen, telling him herself and then personally denouncing him to his father. In Racine's play *Phèdre* (1677), her passion is so strong that it actually makes her ill, and she reveals it only when she thinks Theseus is dead. When Hippolytus prefers Aricie,* she has her nurse Oenone* accuse him of attempted rape when Theseus unexpectedly reappears and then poisons herself. In this version, she is generally regarded as one of the greatest female roles in theater. *See also* Pasiphae.

Phaeton. In Greek legend, a headstrong son of Apollo;* when he demanded to drive the chariot of the sun, he lost control and let it come too close to earth, where Zeus* killed him with a thunderbolt.

Phantastus. A name sometimes used for Morpheus.*

Phantom. *See* Ghost.

Phantom of the Opera. In Gaston Le Roux's novel *The Phantom of the Opera* (1911) and especially in several movie versions, most notably (1925), a disfigured composer who haunts the Paris Opera House.

Phantom Ship. *See* Flying Dutchman.

Phaon. In Ovid's *Heroides*, an ugly boatman given great beauty by Venus* after he carried her to Asia for no payment; Sappho* fell in love with him and killed herself after he spurned her.

Pharaoh. Historically, the title of the ruler of ancient Egypt. Most references are to the ruler from whom Moses* sought the release of the Jews from their slavery in Egypt (The Bible, *Exodus*); when Pharaoh refused to release them, God sent ten plagues,* the last of which killed the firstborn son of each Egyptian family, including Pharaoh's. Pharaoh relented and the Jews left, but he changed his mind and pursued with an army which was drowned when the Red Sea parted for the Jews but closed over the Egyptians. Allusions to other pharaohs are usually to their individual names.

Pharisee. In the Bible, one of a group of Jewish holy men who refused to have any contact with those less holy; in the parables of Jesus* and in much Christian teaching, they are often held up with the Sadducees* as illustrations of religious hypocrisy.

Phebe. (1) In the Bible, *Romans* xvi, a faithful servant of the Church. (2) In Shakespeare's play *As You Like It* (1599), the disdainful shepherdess who ignores her rustic lover and dotes on Rosalind,* not realizing the latter is, in fact, a woman disguised as a boy. (3) *See also* Phoebe.

Phèdre. *See* Phaedra.

Pheidippides. (1) Historically, a Greek runner who was reported to have covered the distance from Athens to Sparta, 150 miles, in two days before the battle of Marathon.* He is sometimes credited as the messenger who brought the news of the victory at Marathon, but that was apparently a different runner. (2) *See also* Phidippides.

Pheme. In Greek mythology, the goddess of fame. *See also* Fama.

Phemios. In Homer's *Odyssey*, the minstrel forced to entertain the suitors. *See also* Penelope.

Phidias. Historically, a great Greek sculptor (d. 432 B.C.), often identified as the ultimate sculptor.

Phidippides. (1) In Aristophane's play *The Clouds*, a young man who uses sophistry to explain why it is a good thing to beat one's father and mother. (2) *See also* Pheidippides.

Philammon. In Greek legend, the son of Chione* and a great musician.

Philander. In Ariosto's *Orlando Furioso* (1532), a knight who commits adultery with Gabrina* then is led to kill her husband; after they are married, she tires of him and poisons him. His name is often applied to a male adulterer. A character of the same name also appears in an old English ballad in which he is flirting with Phyllis.*

Philemon. (1) In Ovid's *Metamorphoses*, a faithful husband who asked that he die at the same moment as his wife Baucis;* in old age, they died together, and he was changed into an oak tree. (2) In the Bible, *Philemon*, a convert to whom Paul* sent an epistle.

Philinte. In Molière's play *The Misanthrope* (1666), the tactful, reasonable, sensible friend of Alceste.*

Philip. (1) In the Bible, one of the twelve Apostles,* the man who brought Nathanael* to Jesus.* (2) In the Bible, *Acts* vi, a different Philip, *also called* Philip the Evangelist, who distributed food to the widows and carried the gospel to Samaria. (3) Historically, a name used by several kings of Spain. The most noted is **Philip II** (d. 1598), a puritanical and ascetic defender of Catholicism against heresy and Protestantism and the implacable opponent of England. For a time, he was ostensible king of England due to his long-distance and unconsummated marriage to Mary Tudor;* later, he sent the Armada which failed to conquer England. He appears in numerous works, usually as a cold, merciless tyrant and an evil conspirator.

Philip, St. (1) Philip* the Apostle. (2) Historically, Philip Neri (d. 1595), a Roman who became a priest after years of humble Christian service and organization as a layman and who treated Rome as if a place for missionary work, reinvigorating Christianity so well among all levels of the lay community that he became known as the "apostle of Rome." Noted for his cheerfulness and gaiety, his day is May 26. (3) Historically, a Russian primate (d. 1569) who was smothered on orders of Ivan* the Terrible after he opposed Ivan's massacre of political opponents.

Philistine. In the Bible, a member of a neighboring tribe which was a traditional enemy of Israel;* Goliath* was a Philistine, and Samson* was captured by them. In European usage, it came to be applied, especially by the educated, to anyone who was alien and from that evolved into a term signifying someone without culture or sophistication.

Philoctetes. In Greek legend, the great friend of Heracles* to whom the hero gave his great bow in return for lighting his funeral pyre. Later, on the way to the Trojan War,* Philoctetes was bitten by a snake and the wound smelled so bad that he was deserted on an island. In Sophocles's play *Philoctetes*, the Greeks discover that they cannot defeat Troy without Heracles's great bow, and so they are forced to beg that he rejoin them; he refuses until Heracles appears to him in a dream. *See also* Neoptolemus; Paris.

Philomela. In Greek legend, Procne's* sister, who was raped by Procne's husband Tereus.* After he cut out her tongue, she wove a tapestry identifying him. The two sisters then killed and cooked Tereus's son and served him to his father. In Ovid's *Metamorphoses*, Philomela was then changed into a nightingale, and the name is often used by poets for the bird.

Philomena. A name sometimes used for Philomela.*

Philomena, St. *See* Filomena, St.

Phineas. *See* Phinehas; Phineus.

Phinehas. (1) In the Bible, *Exodus* vi, a grandson of Aaron* and a high priest. In *Numbers* xxv, he saved Israel* from a plague by running through an Israelite and a Moabite woman while they were having sex. (2) In the Bible, *Samuel* iv, the father of Ichabod.* He was killed when the Israelites lost the ark* to the Philistines. (3) *See also* Phineus.

Phineus. (1) In Greek legend, a suitor who lacked the courage to save Andromeda* from the sea monster but who tried to claim her after she was rescued, whereupon Perseus* turned him to stone. (2) In Greek legend, a blind prophet tormented by the Harpies.* (3) *See also* Phinehas.

Phlegyas. In Virgil's *Aeneid*, a king of the Lapiths* who burned Apollo's* temple after the god had seduced his daughter; in punishment, he was placed in Hades* beneath a great rock that always appeared to be about to fall on him.

Phobos. In Greek mythology, son of Ares* and a god of dread or fear.

Phoebe. (1) In Greek mythology, a Titan,* goddess of the moon, and grandmother of Artemis.* (2) In much usage, a name given to Artemis,* particularly when she is associated with the moon. (3) In Greek legend, sister of Hilara* and a maiden abducted by Castor* and Pollux.* (4) *See* Pyncheon. (5) *See also* Phebe.

Phoebus. (1) A name sometimes used for Apollo,* particularly in relation to his position as sun god. (2) In Chaucer's *Canterbury Tales*, in the Manciple's Tale, a man with a white crow which reports to him his wife's infidelity; he kills his wife and pulls out the crow's feathers, as a result of which crows are black. The story is itself adapted from Ovid's *Metamorphoses*. (3) In Victor Hugo's novel *The Hunchback of Notre Dame* (1831), the beautiful captain who trifles with Esméralda's* affections and then allows her to be convicted of his murder although he is alive.

Phoenix. A mythical Egyptian bird that burned itself and then rose again renewed from the ashes. Christians often adopted the bird as a symbol of the Resurrection.*

Phormio. In Terence's play *Phormio*, a cynical and devious lawyer.

Phosphor. In Greek legend, the morning star.

Phryne. Historically, a famous Greek courtesan (fourth century B.C.) said to have been the model for several famous statues of Aphrodite* and one well-known statue of herself.

Phyllis. (1) In Greek legend, a Thracian princess who loved Demophon* and either hanged or drowned herself when he stayed away for a month. (2) In Virgil's *Eclogues*, a simple country girl, a usage very often copied in sixteenth- and seventeenth-century English poetry. *See also* Philander. (3) In several *Spectator* stories (1711–12), a beauty and rival of Brunetta; when she bought a particularly gaudy dress, Brunetta dressed her trainbearer in the same material and so humiliated Phyllis that the latter died of mortification.

Pickering. In G. B. Shaw's play *Pygmalion* (1913), the amiable retired soldier who bets that Higgins* cannot turn Eliza Doolittle* into a duchess, yet who treats her always with consideration and respect.

Pickwick. In Charles Dickens's novel *Pickwick Papers* (1836), a genial, fat gentleman with a generous hand and spirit who travels across England to observe national habits and has numerous comic adventures, most of which involve the members of the Pickwick Club who accompany him. He is so genial that when other club members insult him, all is forgiven when they say that the insult was meant only in the "Pickwickian sense." His own adventures include wandering into a lady's room by mistake when lost in an inn, a warm traditional country Christmas and skating party, and the suit for breach of promise mistakenly brought against him by his landlady Mrs. Bardell* and his refusal to pay the damages demanded, resulting in his imprisonment. *See also* Buzfuz; Fat Boy, The; Dodson and Fogg; Jingle; Trotter, Job; Snodgrass; Snubbin; Stiggins, Rev.; Tupman, Tracy; Wardle; Weller; Winkle.

Picus. In Roman legend, a son of Saturn,* sometimes associated with Mars* and sometimes with agriculture; in Ovid's *Metamorphoses,* he spurns the love of Circe* in favor of his wife Canens* and is changed into a woodpecker.

Pied Piper. In European folklore, a piper hired to lure all the rats from the town of Hamelin; when he did so, the city fathers refused to pay him, so he played again and lured away all the children of the town. The English know the story best from Robert Browning's poem *The Pied Piper of Hamelin* (1845).

Pierce, Hawkeye. In Richard Hooker's novel *MASH* (1968), and more notably from the movie (1970) and television series "M*A*S*H" (1972–83), a wisecracking, antiauthoritarian, antimilitary Army surgeon who uses chaotic black humor and sophomoric sexual pranks to escape from the horrors of war. *See also* Hawkeye.

Pierre. (1) In English usage, a stereotypical name for any Frenchman. (2) *See* Bezukov; Jaffier.

Pierrette. In the French pantomime, the lover of Pierrot,* generally equivalent to the commedia dell'Arte's Columbine,* although in the twentieth century she often became more symbolic of romantic love, particularly sad romantic love, than previously.

Pierrot. In French versions of the commedia dell'Arte, a simple servant character closely related to Harlequin.* Over the years, as the pantomime developed, he remained amoral and artless but adopted white face makeup and the pure white costume once used by Gilles.* In the process, he accumulated a core of sadness beneath his humor, particularly in his often frustrated romantic liaisons with Pierrette,* which is often the aspect of his character most alluded to.

Piers Plowman. In Langland's poem *Piers Plowman,* the honest farmer who appears in a number of visions, in each new vision more closely approximating Jesus.*

Pietà. A name used for a depiction of Mary* holding the body of Jesus* after He was brought down from the cross.

Pietas. One of the central Roman philosophical virtues, sometimes represented as a goddess of such things as filial or patriotic duty.

Piglet. In A. A. Milne's stories *Winnie-the-Pooh* (1926), the tiny, timid pig who shares many of Pooh's* adventures.

Pilar. In Ernest Hemingway's novel *For Whom the Bell Tolls* (1940), the female leader of the Spanish guerilla group which Robert Jordan* joins; tough, committed, yet unable to stop loving her traitorous husband, she leads the assault on the bridge.

Pilate. In the Bible, New Testament Gospels, the Roman governor of Judea* who tried Jesus.* Although he found Him not guilty, he "washed his hands" of the problem, acquiescing to the pressure of Jewish religious leaders, and sentenced Him to be crucified.

Pillars of Hercules. *See* Hercules.

Pinch, Tom. In Charles Dickens's novel *Martin Chuzzlewit* (1843), the meek, trusting, and completely good-hearted student and assistant of Pecksniff.*

Pinchwife. In William Wycherley's play *The Country Wife* (1673), a dour, jealous man who brings his innocent wife **Margery** to London from the country, forces her to dress as a man in hopes of preventing other men from noticing her, and then encourages her loss of innocence by so constantly warning her about the dangers of sin in the city that he makes it sound attractive to her. *See also* Horner.

Pinkerton. (1) Historically, a detective (d. 1884) and founder (1850) of a notable private detective agency whose successes solving train robberies led to his organization of the Northern intelligence service in the Civil War and made the Pinkerton man synonymous in America with the detective; by the 1890s, however, the agency was primarily involved in supplying "security" for mines and factories and Pinkerton men became synonymous with thugs and strikebreakers. (2) In John Luther Long's story *Madame Butterfly* (1897), more especially in David Belasco's play (1900) and Puccini's opera (1904), a handsome but thoughtless American naval officer who seduces the gentle Japanese geisha Butterfly,* goes home, and later returns with an American wife, at which point Butterfly kills herself.

Pinocchio. In Collodi's story *Pinocchio* (1881), a puppet who comes to life and runs away for a series of adventures, including being swallowed by a whale, until he learns wisdom and goodness, in return for which he becomes a real boy; his most noted attribute is his nose, which grows longer each time he tells a lie.

Pip. (1) In Herman Melville's novel *Moby-Dick* (1851), the jolly Negro cabin boy who goes mad when he is temporarily abandoned after falling overboard. (2) In Charles Dickens's novel *Great Expectations* (1860), Philip Pirrip, an orphan boy raised by his brother-in-law Joe Gargery,* the blacksmith. As a young boy, he visits the strange rich woman of the neighborhood, Miss

Havisham,* there falling in love with the beautiful young Estella,* and is frightened in a graveyard by the escaped convict Magwitch.* As a young man, he receives a mysterious and anonymous inheritance and goes to London, where he tries to learn to be a gentleman, reviving hopes of Estella, only to discover that his inheritance in fact came from Magwitch. Chastened of his new pride, he returns to the village and eventually marries a widowed Estella. *See also* Biddy; Jaggers; Pocket; Pumblechook; Wemmick.

Piper, Aubrey. In George Kelly's play *The Show-Off* (1924), a genial pathological liar who somehow manages to remain naive and likeable.

Pippa. In Robert Browning's poem *Pippa Passes* (1841), a pure young girl who wanders singing through the town on her holiday, her songs having unexpected effects on those who overhear her. In the twentieth century, she is often cited as an example of simplemindedness rather than purity, primarily for the song containing "God's in his heaven—all's right with the world."

Pirate Jenny. In Bertolt Brecht's play *The Threepenny Opera* (1928), the subject of a song describing a servant girl who avenges herself for the abuse given her by joining a pirate band that sacks her town; the song is often associated with Jenny Diver,* but is in fact sung by the apparently naive Polly Peachum.*

Pirate King. In Gilbert and Sullivan's operetta *The Pirates of Penzance* (1879), the pirate leader who unfortunately robs no one because he cannot bear to harm anyone who says he is an orphan. *See also* Frederic.

Pirithous. In Greek legend, a king of the Lapiths* who invited numerous heroes to his wedding, where a quarrel with the Centaurs* escalated into a war in which the Centaurs were destroyed.

Pirrip. *See* Pip.

Pisander. In Homer's *Iliad*, several different warriors; the most notable was a captain of the Myrmidons* who accompanied Patroclus* into battle.

Pisgah. In the Bible, *Numbers* xxi, the mountains from which Moses* was allowed to see the Promised Land* which he would not be allowed by God to enter.

Piso. In Seneca's *Dialogues*, a Roman judge who condemned a man for murder. When the supposed victim appeared alive, a centurion stopped the execution, whereupon Piso not only carried out the sentence but also passed a sentence of death on the centurion for disobeying orders and on the supposed victim for causing an innocent man to be killed.

Pistol. In Shakespeare's plays *Henry IV, Henry V,* and *The Merry Wives of Windsor* (1597–99), a compatriot of Falstaff* noted particularly for his bombastic language. *See also* Bardolph.

Pitt, Sir. *See* Crawley.

Pitti-Sing. In Gilbert and Sullivan's operetta *The Mikado* (1885), one of the three little maids from school and sister of Peep-Bo* and Yum-Yum.*

Pitys. In Greek legend, a nymph* pursued by Pan;* she fell and was changed into a pine tree.

Pius. Historically, a name used by twelve Popes, the most noted of which include **Pius V** (d. 1572), a ruthless opponent of Protestantism, excommunicating Elizabeth* among others, and particularly reliant upon the Inquisition; and **Pius XII** (d. 1958) who arranged the Papacy's concordat with the Nazis and later excommunicated all Catholic communists. In recent years, he has come under much attack for his lack of action regarding the extermination of European Jews, yet remains for many the very image of an ascetic Pope.

Pixie. In English folklore, a tiny fairy,* usually of a playful and mischievous nature.

Plagues. In the Bible, *Exodus*, God sent ten plagues to Egypt when Pharaoh* refused to let the Israelites leave: water turning to blood, frogs covering the land, dust turning to lice, infestation of flies, murrain on the cattle, boils, a rain of hail, an invasion of locusts, darkness covering the land, and the death of all the Egyptian firstborn sons. Another plague was visited on Israel* after the Golden Calf,* and again after David* numbered the tribes. In European literature, the plague often refers to the bubonic plague, also called the Black Death, that broke out repeatedly after its first devastating Western appearance in 1348–50. Daniel Defoe's novel *Journal of the Plague Year* (1722) describes life in London during its worst infestation in 1664, and Albert Camus's novel *The Plague* (1947) describes a similar situation in modern Oran while using the disease as a metaphor for Nazi occupation. The plague figures in numerous other works, often as a device that forces people together, as with the nobles who gather in the country and narrate the tales of Boccaccio's *Decameron* or who try to hide from it in revelry in Edgar Allan Poe's story *The Masque of the Red Death* (1842). In Sophocles's play *Oedipus Rex*, Oedipus* begins the inquiry into his past in order to find the cause of a plague infesting his city.

Plato's Cave. In Plato's *Republic*, a famous metaphor in which he compared human knowledge to that which is seen by men in a cave who see only shadows on the wall rather than real life in the sunlight.

Pleiades. In Greek legend, the seven daughters of Atlas,* changed into the constellation; one of them hides her head in shame, which explains why the constellation contains only six visible stars.

Pliant, Dame. In Ben Jonson's play *The Alchemist* (1610), an attractive young widow willing to marry almost anyone.

Plurabelle, Anna Livia. *See* Anna Livia Plurabelle.

Pluto. In Greek mythology, the god who oversees the underworld of Hades,* also noted for his pursuit of Persephone.* *Also called* Ades; Dis;* Hades. *See also* Ascalaphus.

Plutus. In Greek mythology, the god of wealth. In Aristophanes's play *Plutus*, he is blinded by Zeus* but has his sight restored in order to be able to see virtuous people.

Pocahontas. Historically, the daughter of the Indian chief who met the earliest English settlers in Virginia; in John Smith's* autobiography, he claims she loved him and rescued him from death by interposing herself between him and the executioner.

Pocket. In Charles Dickens's novel *Great Expectations* (1860), **Herbert** is the cheerful young man with whom Pip* shares lodgings in London and who teaches Pip about manners. His father **Matthew** is a genial tutor for Pip and the head of a large family, very haphazardly presided over by his flustered and fluttery wife **Belinda**. *See also* Havisham, Miss.

Pocock. In Henry James's novel *The Ambassadors* (1903), the family sent to convince Chad Newsome* to return to America and signally failing to do so. **Jim** is a fat, facetious man epitomizing small-town vulgarity. **Mrs. Pocock** believes nothing good can come of Parisian immorality. Their daughter **Mamie** is a robust American girl with enough perception to understand that Chad will never again be interested in her.

Podsnap. In Charles Dickens's novel *Our Mutual Friend* (1864), a self-important and self-satisfied social leader. **Mrs. Podsnap** is, if anything, even more so. Their daughter **Georgiana** is a silly, naive girl easily preyed upon by social climbers such as the Lammles.*

Poena. In Roman mythology, the goddess of punishment.

Pogo. In the American newspaper cartoon *Pogo* (beg. 1949), a gentle possum, noted for saying, "We have met the enemy and he is us," which was, in fact, said by a different character in the cartoon.

Poins. In Shakespeare's play *Henry IV, Part I* (1597), Prince Hal's* companion who helps in the robbery of Falstaff.*

Point, Jack. In Gilbert and Sullivan's operetta *The Yeomen of the Guard* (1888), a jester who dies of unrequited love; among aficionados, he is regarded as Gilbert and Sullivan's Hamlet.*

Poirot. In numerous novels by Agatha Christie (beg. 1920), a Belgian detective noted for his mustache, precision, and "little gray cells."

Polichinelle. *See* Punch.

Polites. *See* Priam.

Politick Would-be. *See* Would-be, Sir Politick.

Pollux. In Greek legend, a twin son, with Castor,* of Leda* and Zeus.* A great boxer, after his death he joined his brother in the constellation Gemini. *Also called* Polydeuces. *See also* Hilara; Phoebe.

Polly. (1) A stereotype name for a parrot in use in English since the early seventeenth century. (2) *See* Eccles; Peachum; Toodle. (3) *See also* Molly.

Polly, Aunt. In Mark Twain's novel *Tom Sawyer* (1876), Tom Sawyer's* tender, scripture-quoting aunt and guardian; she wishes Tom to "reform" but never can find the way to bring it about. She gives him the job whitewashing the fence.

Polly, Mr. In H.G. Wells's novel *The History of Mr. Polly* (1909), a sensitive draper whose spirit is crushed by his dull existence and a stultifying wife; he tries to commit suicide, fails, runs away during the ensuing fire, and finds happiness as a handyman at a country inn.

Pollyanna. In several novels by Eleanor Porter, beginning with *Pollyanna* (1913), an orphan girl who finally wins her strict aunt's affection by her constant effort to be cheerful; her name is often given to any person insistently or unrealistically optimistic. *Also called* The Glad Girl.

Polo, Marco. Historically, an Italian trader and traveler (d. 1324) who became one of the first Europeans to see China; his published descriptions of his journey gave China the exotic fascination the country has since maintained for Westerners, and his name became synonymous with explorers and adventurers.

Polonius. In Shakespeare's play *Hamlet* (1600), the chamberlain and father of Ophelia* and Laertes;* generally pompous and garrulous, he advises "to thine ownself be true" while he himself plays politics as usual. He is killed by Hamlet,* who mistakes him for Claudius* as he spies from behind an arras, and his death drives Ophelia mad.

Polydeuces. A name sometimes used for Pollux.*

Polydorus. In Greek legend, the youngest son of Priam.* In Homer's *Iliad*, he is killed in battle by Achilles;* in Euripides's play *Hecuba* and in Virgil's *Aeneid*, he is sent away to be kept in safety, but the king Polymestor* entrusted with his care kills him for his treasure.

Polyeucte. In Corneille's play *Polyeucte* (1641), a Roman who is converted to Christianity and martyred.

Polyhymnia. In Greek mythology, the Muse* of the sacred lyric.

Polymestor. In Euripides's play *Hecuba*, a king entrusted with the care of Polydorus;* he kills the boy for his treasure and then his own eyes are torn out by the boy's enraged mother Hecuba.*

Polynices. In Greek legend, the son of Oedipus.* After Oedipus went into exile, Polynices and his brother Eteocles* agreed to alternate on the throne. When Eteocles refused to leave at the end of his year, Polynices raised an army including the Seven Against Thebes.* He and Eteocles killed each other in combat, and it was Creon's* refusal to bury Polynices's body that led to Antigone's* tragedy. The story is best known from Sophocles's play *Antigone*, although it is also central to Aeschylus's play *Seven Against Thebes*.

Polyphemus. In Homer's *Odyssey*, a Cyclops* who traps Odysseus and his men in his cave and begins to eat them; Odysseus escapes by getting him drunk, putting out his eye with a log sharpened in the fire, and then holding onto the belly of the giant's sheep where he cannot be felt in the dark. Odysseus tells Polyphemus that his name is Nemo* (no man) and thus escapes punishment when Polyphemus tries to complain to the gods. In legend, Polyphemus also pursues the nymph Galatea* and kills Acis,* who also loves her.

Polyxena. In Greek legend, a daughter of Priam* who would have married Achilles* had not her brother Hector* interfered. Some versions suggest that she was in love with him and killed herself on his tomb, but most follow Euripides's play *Hecuba*, in which after Troy has fallen the Greeks demand that she be sacrificed at the tomb of Achilles.

Pomona. In Roman mythology, the goddess of fruit.

Pompadour, Madame de. Historically, the mistress of Louis XV of France (d. 1764), often synonymous with aristocratic self-indulgence and sensuality; she said the famous, "Après nous le déluge."

Pompeia. *See* Caesar's Wife.

Pompey. (1) Historically, the name of numerous Roman generals and politicians, particularly during the Republic; the most notable was Julius Caesar's* son-in-law and later principal rival, who was killed (48 B.C.) after Caesar crossed the Rubicon.* (2) In seventeenth- and eighteenth-century England, a generic name for Negro servants; one of the earliest such usages is the prostitute's servant in Shakespeare's play *Measure for Measure* (1604).

Pontia. A name sometimes used for Aphrodite,* particularly when associated with her appearance in the sea foam.

Pontifex. In Samuel Butler's novel *The Way of All Flesh* (1903), the typical English middle-class family whose lives are depicted. **George** is a successful publisher who browbeats his children, particularly his son **Theobald**, whom he forces into the ministry with the threat of disinheritance despite the son's skepticism. Theobald, in turn, finds a submissive, daydreaming wife, **Christina**, and together they repress and stifle their son **Ernest**, who is also ordained, but in such a state of ignorance that he is soon defrauded of his inheritance, sentenced to prison for a misinterpreted advance to a young woman, and apparently launched into perpetual decline with a drunkard wife and a failing clothing business until rescued by a convenient inheritance.

Pontius Pilate. *See* Pilate.

Pontus. In Roman mythology, the sea, generally equivalent to Oceanus.*

Pooh. *See* Winnie-the-Pooh.

Pooh-Bah. In Gilbert and Sullivan's operetta *The Mikado* (1885), the "Lord High Everything Else" who will arrange anything for the right fee.

Poor Richard. The pseudonym adopted by Ben Franklin* in his almanacs (beg. 1732), synonymous with the kind of commonsensical, practical aphorisms contained in those works.

Pooter. In George Grossmith's stories *The Diary of a Nobody* (1892), a typical suburban commuter and husband who struggles to maintain his dignity although both his family and the urban world seem expressly designed to humiliate him in ways that he never quite understands.

Popeye. (1) In the American newspaper cartoon *Thimble Theater* (beg. 1929) and in numerous movie cartoons (beg. 1932), an apparently puny sailor with a corncob pipe, gigantic forearms, and a devotion to canned spinach, which makes him temporarily strong and invincible; his numerous adventures are often undertaken either to impress or rescue his love Olive Oyl.* *See also* Wimpy. (2) In William Faulkner's novel *Sanctuary* (1931), an unusually cold, passionless criminal most noted for his rape of Temple Drake* with a corncob; he is a pimp and a killer, but, ironically, he is arrested and executed for a murder he did not commit.

Poppins, Mary. In several novels by P. L. Travers, beginning with *Mary Poppins* (1934), a strict English nanny who can fly with her umbrella; after the movie version (1964), she was often used to symbolize a refusal to recognize reality.

Poppy. In medieval art, the poppy was sometimes used to symbolize Christ's* blood, due to its red color. After World War I, the Allies, particularly the British, adopted the poppy as a symbol of their soldiers' sacrifice, due to its blood-red color and its prominence on the fields of Flanders where so many soldiers were killed in the war. For decades, no self-respecting Briton would appear on Armistice Day without a poppy in his or her lapel. It is also often used to symbolize sleep and dreams, due to the particular cultivated form of it that is the source for opium. More recently, the poppy has become a symbol of evil, due to the traffic in numerous illicit opium-related drugs, and it is often used to indicate many drugs that bear no relation to it at all.

Porgy. In DuBose Heyward's novel *Porgy* (1925) and especially in Gershwin's opera *Porgy and Bess* (1935), a crippled Negro beggar who falls in love with the beautiful Bess,* stabs the vicious Crown to protect her, is jailed, and follows her when he is released and finds she has left town.

Porsena. *See* Clelia.

Porter, Jimmy. In John Osborne's play *Look Back in Anger* (1956), the quintessential "angry young man" of British literature in the fifties, noted for his brilliant expression of a virulent hatred for what he saw as a betrayal of all that had been good in English life and which seemed to sum up the attitudes of a generation.

Porteus. Historically, a British officer who ordered his guard to fire into an Edinburgh crowd (1736), instigating a riot; the incident is a principal event in Walter Scott's novel *The Heart of Midlothian* (1818).

Porthos. In Alexandre Dumas's novel *The Three Musketeers* (1844), one of the Three Musketeers—the large, strong, and slow-witted one. *See also* Aramis; Athos; D'Artagnan.

Portia. (1) In Shakespeare's play *The Merchant of Venice* (1596), a beautiful heiress courted by Bassanio,* whom she tests by the three caskets. When his friend Antonio* is about to be killed by Shylock,* she disguises herself as a lawyer and pleads his case with the famous "quality of mercy" speech, then shows that Shylock has the right to the pound of flesh but not to any blood that might be taken when trying to cut it out, thereby saving Antonio and ruining Shylock. (2) In Shakespeare's play *Julius Caesar* (1599), the faithful wife of Brutus;* she swallows hot coals when she realizes his cause is lost.

Portnoy. In Philip Roth's novel *Portnoy's Complaint* (1969), an American Jew who is frustrated and repressed by his upbringing; he is noted primarily for his obsession with masturbation.

Poseidon. In Greek mythology, the god of the sea, called Neptune by the Romans; he is also associated with horses and earthquakes. He is usually shown as an imposing figure holding a trident, but he is also known for his violent temper, as seen in his punishment of Laomedon,* his persistent enmity for Odysseus* after the latter blinded Polyphemus,* Poseidon's son, and his destruction of Ajax,* Hippolytus,* and Idomeneus's* son. His other children include Charybdis,* Otus,* and Triton.* *See also* Amphitrite; Caeneus; Nereids; Proteus.

Posthumus. In Shakespeare's play *Cymbeline* (1609), the impoverished noble who marries Imogen* and is banished; when he is tricked by Iachimo* into believing Imogen is unfaithful, he orders her death, but is forgiven by and reunited with her.

Potiphar. In the Bible, *Genesis* xxxix, an Egyptian captain of the guard who was Joseph's* master. His wife tried to seduce Joseph and once even tore off his clothes, after which she claimed that Joseph had tried to rape her, offering his clothes as proof, for which Joseph was imprisoned. In Moslem legend, her name is Zuleika.

Potter's Field. In the Bible, *Matthew* xxvii, the field purchased by the priests with the 30 pieces of silver that Judas* returned to them before he hanged himself; used for the burial of the indigent and of strangers.

Pound of Flesh. *See* Shylock.

Pozdnyshev. In Tolstoy's story *The Kreutzer Sonata* (1889), a man with a miserable marriage, due in no small part to his own insensitivity and lack of moral stability. The marriage begins with intense sexual passion but gradually tapers off into sated boredom until he begins to suspect his wife is having an affair with a neighbor with whom she plays Beethoven's Kreutzer Sonata. Despite numerous demonstrations of her innocence, he remains convinced; finally, he discovers them together and kills her.

Praxagora. In Aristophanes's play *Ecclesiazusae*, a housewife who disguises herself and her friends as men and takes over the Athenian government, instituting a utopian communal society, noted among other things, for giving the old and ugly women first choice of all men.

Prester John. In medieval folklore, a Christian priest-king said to reign in the Orient and to be incredibly wealthy; in Ariosto's *Orlando Furioso* (1516), the name is given to the wealthy, blind king of Ethiopia; and most later usage makes him an African king. In John Buchan's novel *Prester John* (1910), he is a Negro preacher who returns to South Africa to organize a great native uprising.

Priam. In Greek legend, the king of Troy* during the Trojan War.* In Homer's *Iliad*, he is a man of integrity and great physical and moral strength, devoted to his family and his city; most other representations generally follow that lead. In Virgil's *Aeneid*, he is killed during the sack of Troy when he slips in the blood of his son Polites. *See also* Aeneas; Cassandra; Deiphobus; Hector; Hecuba; Hesione; Laocoön; Laodice; Paris; Polydorus; Polyxena; Troilus.

Priapus. In Greek and Roman mythology, a god of fertility, probably adopted from the Middle East, usually represented with an enormous phallus.

Price, Fanny. In Jane Austen's novel *Mansfield Park* (1814), a timid, poor relation in love with the second son of the Bertram* family who have taken her in. She outrages Sir Thomas when she refuses to marry a wealthy outsider, but eventually her true worth is realized; she marries Edmund, and he becomes the minister she has expected he would be. *See also* Norris, Mrs.

Prig, Betsey. In Charles Dickens's novel *Martin Chuzzlewit* (1843), the partner of Sairey Gamp* until she has the nerve to doubt the existence of Mrs. Harris.*

Primrose. In Oliver Goldsmith's novel *The Vicar of Wakefield* (1766), **Dr. Primrose** is the kind, generous, homely Christian, so good-hearted that he is easily duped by many yet is firm in his goodness in the face of numerous calamities, including bankruptcy and his children's disastrous lives. His wife **Deborah** is a vain woman interested only in their daughters' marriages. Their daughter **Livy** is beautiful, strong-willed, and coquettish, seduced and deserted by Thornhill.* The other daughter **Sophy** is quiet and modest and is abducted by the same Thornhill but saved by the revelation of Thornhill's father, whom she ultimately marries. Their son **George** fails at numerous occupations, is imprisoned for trying to fight a duel with Thornhill, and eventually joins the army. Another son **Moses** is talkative and as gullible as his father, going to the fair to sell a horse and returning home with a gross of green spectacles.

Prince, Little. *See* Little Prince.

Prince Charming. In the fairy tale, the prince who awakens Sleeping Beauty;* sometimes, also the prince who awakens Snow White.*

Prince of Darkness. A name sometimes used for the Devil.*

Prince of Peace. A name sometimes used for Jesus.*

Prioress. In Chaucer's *Canterbury Tales*, the sympathetic nun who tells the story of the young Christian boy murdered by vengeful Jews. *See also* Hugh of Lincoln; William of Norwich.

Priscilla. (1) In the Bible, *Acts* xviii, a particularly devout woman. (2) In Henry Wadsworth Longfellow's poem *The Courtship of Miles Standish* (1858), the Pilgrim maiden whom the tongue-tied Captain Standish* sends John Alden* to court; she indicates her preference for Alden by telling him, "Speak for yourself, John."

Prism, Miss. In Oscar Wilde's play *The Importance of Being Earnest* (1895), Cecily's* governess who, many years before, had mistakenly confused the manuscript of her three-volume novel and the baby for which she was nurse, depositing the baby (actually Jack Worthing*) in a leather handbag in the cloakroom of Victoria Station. *See also* Chasuble, Rev.

Procne. In Greek legend, the sister of Philomela;* when her husband Tereus* raped her sister, she killed his son, fed him the cooked remains, and was changed into a swallow.

Procopius, St. Historically, a Christian martyr (d. 303) credited in legend with many marvels, including slaying 6,000 with a cross and being miraculously healed of the wounds received each day in torture.

Procris. *See* Cephalus.

Procrustes. In Greek legend, a brutal robber who tied his victims to a bed; if they were longer than the bed, he cut off their limbs, and if they were shorter, he stretched them until they reached its length. Theseus* eventually killed him. *Also called* Damastes.

Prodigal. In the Bible, *Luke* xv, a parable told by Jesus:* A man had two sons, one of whom asked that his father give him his portion of the estate immediately; when the father agreed, the prodigal son ran away and wasted the wealth on riotous living. Eventually, the son returned in poverty and was welcomed back by his father, who ordered that the ''fatted calf'' be killed to celebrate his return. When the eldest son, who had stayed and worked faithfully, protested, the father replied that we should celebrate whenever one that was dead comes back to life.

Prokofievna, Lizaveta. In Dostoevsky's novel *The Idiot* (1868), the moody mother of Aglaya;* her outlandish behavior sometimes distracts from her essential good nature. Despite her admiration of Myshkin's* purity, she breaks off her daughter's engagement to him for fear of inherited madness.

Prometheus. In Greek legend, a son of Iapetus.* He stole fire from the gods to give to mankind, for which Zeus* chained him to a mountain where a vulture ate his entrails each day, after they grew back each night. He is also sometimes credited with making woman from clay and teaching men how to train horses and how to plant crops. He was eventually freed by Heracles,* and he joined the gods on Olympus.* In Aeschylus's play *Prometheus Bound*, he is a portrait of proud resistance against the tyranny of Zeus, defiant even when stricken by a thunderbolt. In Shelley's poem/play *Prometheus Unbound* (1820), he expresses the Romantic voice of the independent spirit and heralds a period of peace and beauty for mankind when he is finally released. *See also* Bia; Deucalion; Epimetheus; Pandora.

Promised Land. In the Bible, *Exodus*, the land promised by God to Moses* and the Jews after they are delivered from Egypt. In Christian usage, the name is sometimes given to Heaven.*

Prophet, The. (1) A name sometimes used for Mohammed.* (2) In Kahlil Gibran's *The Prophet* (1923), a wise man whose aphorisms lead the reader along the path of self-improvement and self-acceptance; often referred to contemptuously as philosophy for schoolgirls.

Proserpine. A name sometimes used for Persephone.*

Prospero. (1) In Shakespeare's play *The Tempest* (1611), an Italian noble marooned on an island, now become a great magician; he uses his magic to control the monster Caliban* and the faithful spirit Ariel* and brings his usurping brother's ship to the island for a reconciliation and the marriage of his daughter Miranda* to Prince Ferdinand.* His farewell speech is often interpreted as Shakespeare's own farewell to the stage. (2) In Edgar Allan Poe's story *The Masque of the Red Death* (1845), the charming and pleasure-loving prince who takes his court to live merrily in isolation in vain hope of avoiding the plague.*

Protean. *See* Proteus.

Proteus. (1) In Euripides's play *Helen*, a king of Egypt who takes the real Helen* while a phantom Helen goes to Troy* with Paris.* (2) In Roman legend, a herdsman of Neptune* who avoided contact with all people by using his power to change his shape at will; hence, anything that seems to have many different appearances is Protean. (3) In Shakespeare's play *Two Gentlemen of Verona* (1594), the egotistical young man who tries to desert Julia* and take the beautiful Silvia* from his friend Valentine.*

Protopopov. In Anton Chekhov's play *Three Sisters* (1901), the local official who is never seen but whose effect is strongly felt as he maintains an affair with Prozorov's* wife Natasha.*

Prozorov. In Anton Chekhov's play *Three Sisters* (1901), the family trapped in a provincial town where their hopes and ideals gradually erode and from which they never reach their dream of going to Moscow. The ostensible head of the family is **Andrei**, whom his sisters believe will be a great scholar but who is a weakling who marries beneath him to the grasping Natasha,* gambles away the family property, and declines into a minor political functionary and babysitter. For his sisters, *see* Irina; Masha; Olga. *See also* Chebutykin; Protopopov; Tusenbach; Vershinin.

Prue, Miss. In William Congreve's play *Love for Love* (1695), the forthright country-bred daughter whom Tattle* humorously teaches the ways in which city women mean the opposite of what they say.

Prufrock, J. Alfred. In T. S. Eliot's poem *The Love Song of J. Alfred Prufrock* (1915), an uncertain, modern, middle-class man, unable to commit himself to anything—"do I dare to eat a peach?"—and always aware of the disappointments that might be lurking beneath the surface.

Prynne, Hester. *See* Hester.

Psyche. In Greek legend, a beautiful Greek princess loved and abandoned by Cupid* when she insisted on seeing his face; Aphrodite* made Psyche her slave, giving her apparently impossible tasks which she accomplished with Zeus's* help, after which she was restored to Cupid and made a god by drinking ambrosia.

Ptah. In Egyptian mythology, the builder of the world.

Pucelle, La. A nickname for Jeanne d'Arc.*

Puck. In Shakespeare's play *A Midsummer Night's Dream* (1595), a mischievous fairy* and servant of Oberon.* After observing the antics of the humans lost in the forest, he says, "What fools these mortals be." *See also* Robin Goodfellow.

Puff. In R. B. Sheridan's play *The Critic* (1779), the hack writer and self-advertiser whose play is seen in rehearsal.

Pulcinella. *See* Punch.

Pulver, Ensign. In Thomas Heggen's novel *Mister Roberts* (1946), the enthusiastic young naval officer, noted for flooding the ship with soapsuds when he takes over the laundry and for his attack on the captain's prize palm tree.

Pumblechook. In Charles Dickens's novel *Great Expectations* (1860), Joe Gargery's* uncle, much given to platitudes.

Punch. In the traditional English puppet show, a humpbacked, foul-tempered husband given to violent fits; when he kills his child, his wife Judy beats him, and he kills her, and sometimes his dog and the doctor who treats him as well. He also beats the policeman but is arrested, finally escaping either by tricking the hangman or by a miraculous restoration of all his victims. He is a particular favorite of children. *Also called* Polichinelle; Pulcinella; Punchinello. *See also* Pagliacci.

Purgatory. In Catholic Christian usage, a place neither Heaven* nor Hell* in which souls are confined for a time and punished for their sins before being ultimately admitted to Heaven. It is a much debated theological concept, not clearly mentioned in the Bible, and was one of the principal Catholic beliefs that was rejected by Protestants, particularly as the Church was long associated with the selling of "indulgences," which were thought to release souls early from Purgatory.

Purgon. In Molière's play *Le Malade imaginaire* (1673), Argan's* doctor, much devoted to the enema as a universal cure.

Puss in Boots. In the fairy tale as told by Perrault (1697), a cat who tricks an ogre into turning himself into a mouse, and then eats the mouse, so that his master can take the ogre's wealth and win the hand of a princess.

Pygmalion. In Ovid's *Metamorphoses*, a sculptor who falls in love with his statue and prays to Venus* for a woman like her; the goddess brings the statue to life as Galatea,* and Pygmalion marries her.

Pylades. In Greek legend, the constant friend of Orestes.*

Pyle, Gomer. In the American TV series "The Andy Griffith Show" and "Gomer Pyle, USMC" (1963–70), a bumbling, ignorant, and naive country boy, often cited as a demonstration of the stupidity of American television.

Pyncheon. In Nathaniel Hawthorne's novel *The House of the Seven Gables* (1851), the degenerate Puritan family descended from a judge who condemned a man for witchcraft in order to take his house. The last members of the family are **Judge Pyncheon**, who tries to commit the weak-minded **Clifford** to an insane asylum in order to obtain the wealth he is sure is hidden in the house; Clifford, who has served a prison term for killing his uncle and is a broken man; **Hepzibah**, Clifford's sister, a frustrated spinster afraid to meet any outsiders; and **Phoebe**, a cousin from the country, young and lively, who injects some life and spirit into the old house.

Pyramus. In Ovid's *Metamorphoses*, a young man forbidden to speak to his love Thisbe, with whom he has been secretly talking through a crack in the wall separating their houses. They run away to meet at night, but Thisbe is frightened away by a lion. When Pyramus finds her veil with blood on it, he kills himself; she kills herself when she sees his body.

"Pyramus and Thisbe." In Shakespeare's play *A Midsummer Night's Dream* (1595), the "tedious brief" play enacted by the "rude mechanicals," a simplistic and hilariously crude version of the Pyramus* story. *See also* Bottom; Flute; Quince, Peter; Snout; Snug; Starveling.

Pyrrha. In Ovid's *Metamorphoses*, the wife of Deucalion.* After mankind is destroyed in a great flood, they throw stones over their shoulders; those that she throws become new women.

Pyrrhus. (1) A name sometimes used for Neoptolemus,* especially in Virgil's *Aeneid* and in Racine's play *Andromaque* (1667). In the latter, despite his betrothal to Hermione,* he is passionately in love with his slave/concubine Andromache* and is killed by Hermione and Orestes* after his betrothed discovers his intention to renounce her in favor of Andromache. (2) Historically, a cousin of Alexander* (d. 272 B.C.) who tried unsuccessfully to conquer Italy. The phrase "Pyrrhic victory" comes from his own comment after a battle which he had won but in which he had lost his best troops, "Another such victory and we will be lost," and signifies any victory won at too great a cost.

Pythagoras. Historically, a Greek philosopher (sixth century B.C.) and mathematician, identified by generations of school children as a boring taskmaster due to the Pythagorean Theorem about the square of the hypotenuse of a right triangle in geometry.

Pythias. *See* Damon.

Quarles, Philip. In Aldous Huxley's novel *Point Counter Point* (1928), a writer who understands everything but feels nothing.

Quasimodo. In Victor Hugo's novel *The Hunchback of Notre Dame* (1831), a deformed orphan, now deaf from the bells of Notre Dame which he rings. Selected by the mob as King of Fools, he falls in love with the gypsy girl Esméralda* and later rescues her when she is about to be hanged for murder; when she is finally hanged, he throws Frollo* from the bell tower in revenge for his part in her conviction.

Quatermain, Allan. In H. Rider Haggard's novel *King Solomon's Mines* (1886), a great white hunter embodying all the positive qualities of the European hunter/explorer attuned to nature.

Queeg, Capt. In Herman Wouk's novel *The Caine Mutiny* (1951), the psychotic captain who arrests his officers over some missing strawberries and eventually drives them to mutiny; he is noted for the ball bearings he constantly rolls through his fingers.

Queen of Hearts. In Lewis Carroll's story *Alice in Wonderland* (1865), the temperamental and tyrannical queen of Wonderland who plays croquet with flamingoes for mallets and later orders "Off with her head!" Alice* is saved when she points out that the queen and her court are all merely cards. *See also* King of Hearts.

Queen of Heaven. *See* Mary.

Queen of the Night. In Mozart's opera *The Magic Flute* (1791), the vengeful goddess who tries to deceive the lovers; noted primarily for one of the most spectacular (and high) coloratura arias in opera.

Queequeg. In Herman Melville's novel *Moby-Dick* (1851), the South Seas cannibal now a harpooner; he becomes Ishmael's* friend after they share a bed on shore. Increasingly mystical as the ship's journey continues, he insists that the ship's carpenter build him a coffin, in which he sleeps, and on which Ishmael escapes when the ship sinks. *See also* Ahab; Moby Dick; Tashtego.

Quentin. *See* Compson.

Quested, Adela. In E. M. Forster's novel *A Passage to India* (1924), the sexually repressed Englishwoman who claims she was assaulted in the Malabar Caves* by Dr. Aziz*; although she later retracts her charge, she remains a mysterious figure personifying the unbridgeable gulf between the East and European society.

Quetzalcoatl. In Aztec mythology, a great god of civilization and agriculture, often depicted as a serpent with feathers, supposed to have been burned and whose return was eagerly awaited. Unfortunately for the Aztecs, they thought the Spaniards were the servants preparing for the return of the god.

Quickly, Mistress. In Shakespeare's plays *Henry IV* and *Henry V* (1597–99), the talkative, silly hostess of the Boar's Head Tavern, subject of many of Falstaff's* tricks. Eventually she marries Pistol* and movingly reports Falstaff's death. In *The Merry Wives of Windsor* (1598), an old busybody and incompetent matchmaker uses the name, but she is apparently a different character.

Quilp. In Charles Dickens's novel *The Old Curiosity Shop* (1840), the sinister dwarf who lends money to Nell's grandfather in hopes of getting Little Nell.* Unusually vicious and menacing, he mistreats his wife **Betsey** and drowns while trying to escape from the police. *See also* Brass; Nubbles, Kit.

Quince, Peter. In Shakespeare's play *A Midsummer Night's Dream* (1595), a carpenter and the gentle director of the "Pyramus and Thisbe"* play; a victim of stage fright, he mangles his prologue. *See also* Bottom; Flute; Snout; Snug; Starveling.

Quint. In Henry James's story *The Turn of the Screw* (1898), the drunken and brutal valet, now dead, whose ghost seems to be haunting the unnamed governess.

Quirinus. A name sometimes used for Ares* or for Romulus.*

Quirk, Thady. *See* Thady.

Quirt. In Anderson and Stallings's play *What Price Glory?* (1924), a career American Army sergeant, whose lifelong friendship and conflict with Flagg* is noted as the first "realistic" theatrical portrait of soldiers. He successfully maneuvers for the attentions of Charmaine,* but he deserts her for the comradeship of military life, with the famous, "Hey, Flagg, wait for baby!"

Quisling. Historically, the leader of the Norwegian Nazi party who delivered the country to the Germans in 1940; hence, a traitor.

Quixote, Don. In Cervantes's novel *Don Quixote* (1605), a gentle Spaniard who reads so many chivalric romances that he believes he is a medieval knight and embarks on an adventure with his squire, the earthy Sancho Panza,* and his old nag which he calls the charger Rosinante.* His most noted adventures are his battle with the windmill, which he thinks is a giant; his choice of a barber's basin for his golden helmet; a battle with sheep that he believes are armies in combat; his release of the galley slaves; and his idealization of a crude girl as his courtly lady Dulcinea.* Originally a figure of ridicule satirizing the Spanish gentry's refusal to live in the present, he soon became for most readers a symbol of the power and importance of personal dreams and the search for a better world.

R

Ra. In Egyptian mythology, the god of the sun and the strongest of all the gods; usually shown as a hawk.

Rabbi ben Ezra. *See* Ezra, Rabbi ben.

Rabbit, Br'er. In Joel Chandler Harris's stories (beg. 1881), a wily rabbit; his most noted adventure comes when he is trapped by the Tar Baby* and begs Br'er Fox not to throw him in the briar patch; Br'er Fox throws him in the briars, and the rabbit escapes easily where he can not be followed.

Rabbit, Peter. In Beatrix Potter's story *The Tale of Peter Rabbit* (1900), a mischievous rabbit who ignores his mother's warnings and goes into Farmer McGregor's garden, where he is almost killed. *See also* Flopsy, Mopsy, and Cottontail.

Rabbit, White. *See* White Rabbit, The.

Rachel. (1) In the Bible, *Genesis,* the daughter of Laban* and the wife of Jacob.* Jacob loved her and worked seven years for her father to get her, but he was tricked into taking her sister Leah.* He served another seven years and married Rachel as well. Rachel was barren and encouraged Jacob to sleep not only with her sister but also with her servant Bilhah,* until eventually her prayers were answered and she bore Joseph.* As she followed Jacob in his travels, she died giving birth to Benjamin.* (2) In Charles Dickens's novel *Hard Times* (1854), a textile worker hopelessly in love with the already married and honorable Stephen Blackpool.* *See also* Bounderby. (3) In Marcel Proust's novels *Remembrance of Things Past* (1918–27), Saint-Loup's* mistress, a former prostitute turned actress, flirtatious and intentionally provoking his jealousy, while preferring various poseurs and charlatans to the more direct and simple Saint-Loup. Allusions to her are somewhat confusing in some references, since there was also historically a famous French actress called Rachel (d. 1858). (4) *See* Esmond.

Rackstraw, Ralph. In Gilbert and Sullivan's operetta *H.M.S. Pinafore* (1878), the tenor, the smartest sailor in the fleet.

Radames. In Verdi's opera *Aida* (1871), the Egyptian army commander loved by both the princess Amneris* and the slave Aida;* he is sealed alive in a tomb after choosing Aida.

Rafael. *See* Raphael.

Raffles. (1) In George Eliot's novel *Middlemarch* (1871), a blackmailer. *See also* Bulstrode. (2) In stories by E. W. Hornung (beg. 1899), a gentleman thief ("cracksman") noted for his ability to move in the best society.

Ragnel. In numerous medieval mystery plays, a devil.*

Raina. In G. B. Shaw's play *Arms and the Man* (1894), the romantic young woman who wants her soldier-fiancé Sergius* to be heroic but finds herself drawn instead to the unheroic but practical Bluntschli,* whom she meets when he hides in her bedroom after a battle.

Rais, Gilles de. *See* Gilles de Rais.

Rakitin. In Turgenev's play *A Month in the Country* (1850), the sophisticated friend who entertains Natasha* by flirting with her.

Ralegh. *See* Raleigh, Sir Walter.

Raleigh, Sir Walter. Historically, an English courtier of Elizabeth* I, a privateer, adventurer, and occasional poet. In contemporary usage, he is noted as a great gentleman because he threw his cloak over a puddle so that Elizabeth could cross without getting wet, a story probably invented by Walter Scott for his novel *Kenilworth* (1821).

Ralph. *See* Nickleby.

Rama. In Hindu mythology, the seventh incarnation of Vishnu,* in which he won his wife by bending the bow of Shiva.*

Rambo. In several movies, most notably *Rambo* (1985), an overly muscular, extremely violent ex-soldier, considered by some a great patriot and by others the epitome of mindless flag-waving chauvinism and violence.

Rameses. Historically, a name used by several Egyptian pharaohs,* the most notable of whom were **Rameses II**, noted for building the Luxor temple, and **Rameses III**, in tradition thought to be the pharaoh from whom Moses* secured the release of the Jews.

Ramona. In Helen Hunt Jackson's novel *Ramona* (1884), a beautiful, pious, but tragic California Anglo-Indian maiden, raised as a Spaniard, who marries a Christianized Indian. As the Americans colonize California, Ramona and her husband are driven from several homes until, depressed and embittered, her husband develops fits of madness, during one of which he steals a horse and is shot. She eventually marries a Spanish landowner and both emigrate to Mexico to escape the Americans.

Rampion. In Aldous Huxley's novel *Point Counter Point* (1928), an artist risen from the lower class and proud of his freedom from social conventions and restrictions. *See also* Quarles, Philip.

Ramsay. (1) In Walter Scott's novel *The Fortunes of Nigel* (1822), **Margaret** is the beautiful young woman who goes to court disguised as a man to plead for the release of her love, whom she eventually marries. Her father **David** is a whimsical clock maker. *See also* Olifaunt, Nigel. (2) In Virginia Woolf's novel *To the Lighthouse* (1927), the prototypical philosopher, intelligent but not brilliant; his need for support takes his wife's attention from their children while his irony encourages his children to fear rather than love him. **Mrs. Ramsay** is warm, devoted, and old-fashioned, impressing all with her reverence for life.

Ramses. *See* Rameses.

Ran. In Scandinavian mythology, the goddess of the sea, a cruel woman who tried to destroy sailors.

Random, Roderick. In Tobias Smollett's novel *Roderick Random* (1748), a reckless but likeable youth who wanders the world in a series of voyages and adventures, assuming disguises, robbing when he is not being robbed; in short, a quintessential picaresque hero.

Ranevskaya. In Anton Chekhov's play *The Cherry Orchard* (1904), the owner of the orchard, a beautiful but sadly empty woman who manages to fascinate all the men who meet her; a middle-aged woman devoted to love but unable to take responsibility for her own future. *See also* Gaev; Lopahin; Varya.

Ranger, Lone. *See* Lone Ranger.

Rank, Dr. In Henrik Ibsen's play *A Doll's House* (1879), the neighbor, dying from an inherited venereal disease, in love from afar with Nora.*

Ransom, Basil. In Henry James's novel *The Bostonians* (1866), a Southern cousin of Olive Chancellor* who comes to Boston and competes with Olive for the love of a talented young woman, eventually carrying her off to be his wife; for many, the epitome of the most dangerous male chauvinist, an autocratic man with manners, education, and sensitivity.

Raphael. (1) In the Bible, in the Apochrypha, *Tobit*, the archangel* who aids Tobias;* usually depicted carrying a pilgrim's staff or a fish. In John Milton's poem *Paradise Lost* (1667), he is also the angel* sent to Adam* in the Garden of Eden.* *See also* Asmodeus. (2) Historically, a great painter (d. 1520) whose works are so admired that he was often cited as the greatest of all painters and synonymous with art itself.

Raskolnikov. In Dostoevsky's novel *Crime and Punishment* (1866), a student who murders a pawnbroker to prove he has no conscience; he is wrong, and his sense of guilt torments him until he confesses the crime and seeks expiation in Siberia. *See also* Petrovitch; Sonya.

Rasputin. Historically, a Russian monk (d. 1916) who gained extreme influence with Czar Nicholas* and Alexandra before his assassination; noted for his incredible strength and his hypnotic gaze, often called "the Mad Monk."

Rasselas. In Samuel Johnson's novel *Rasselas* (1759), a prince who tires of a life of leisure in Happy Valley and escapes to try to find happiness, only to discover that most people are unhappy with their lives.

Rassendyll, Rudolph. In Anthony Hope's novel *The Prisoner of Zenda* (1894), the perfect English gentleman; a double of the king of Ruritania, he is asked to substitute for him to foil a plot to steal the kingdom, and he does so, saving the king with his true gentlemanly skills.

Rastignac. In numerous works by Balzac, expecially *Père Goriot* (1835) and *Lost Illusions* (1837), a representative young man of ambition in Bourbon France. From an impoverished family, he comes to Paris with some scruples and sensitivity in hope of entering society, which he finally accomplishes, with the help of the master criminal Vautrin,* by sleeping with the married Baroness de Nucingen.* He runs through many novels as a manipulator and a cynic, using any opportunity to enrich himself at the expense of supposed friends or lovers, eventually becoming a minister of government and receiving a barony. He is one of the earliest characters to claim that all virtue depends on circumstances. *See also* Goriot; Restaud, Countess de.

Rastus. In American slang, a version of Erastus,* which, as a common name from the Bible given to slaves, came to be used as a generic name for illiterate Negroes.

Raven, The. In Edgar Allan Poe's poem *The Raven* (1844), the bird who comes into the poet's life and, in response to any question, always answers "Nevermore."

Rawdon. *See* Crawley.

Razumihin. In Dostoevsky's novel *Crime and Punishment* (1866), a young man of good humor and generous nature, a friend of Raskolnikov* and in love with his sister Dounia.*

Rebecca. (1) In the Bible, *Genesis,* Isaac's* wife. She was first seen by his servant with a pitcher on her shoulder, and her willingness to give him water was God's sign she should be Isaac's wife. When she conceived Esau* and Jacob* as twins, they fought in her womb. After they were born, she favored Jacob, the younger, and helped him disguise himself in order to receive his father's blessing. (2) In Walter Scott's novel *Ivanhoe* (1820), the beautiful Jewess who nurses Ivanhoe.* She is kidnapped by a Templar mad with lust for her, for which she is accused of witchcraft, only to be rescued by Ivanhoe. She is the classic case in which convention gives the hero the wrong girl, as he chooses the fair but bland Rowena* in spite of most readers' preference for Rebecca. (3) In Kate Wiggin's novel *Rebecca of Sunnybrook Farm* (1903), the epitome of youth, a girl who spreads joy to all around her; to later generations, she often seemed a symbol of sappy sentimental optimism or of someone completely divorced from reality. (4) In Daphne du Maurier's novel *Rebecca* (1938), the mysterious former wife probably murdered by her husband de Winter* but whose memory haunts the household and the life of the new wife. Some people mistakenly call the narrator, a plain, unnamed young girl swept away by the mysterious, romantic de Winter, by this name. *See also* Danvers, Mrs. (4) *See also* Becky.

Rebekah. *See* Rebecca.

Red Cross Knight. In Edmund Spenser's poem *The Faerie Queene* (1590), St. George,* a symbol of English religion and the gentle knight who goes "pricking on the plain." He sets out to rescue Una* but is seduced away by hypocrisy and Catholicism; he loses his strength in an enchanted stream and contemplates suicide, but he is rescued by Arthur* and reunited with true religion in the House of Holiness. He ultimately kills a dragon in a three-day battle and weds Una. *See also* Archimago; Duessa.

Red Ridinghood, Little. In the fairy tale, a little girl sent to her grandmother's where she is threatened by a wolf, who has eaten the grandmother and tries to eat her as well; variations and parodies abound.

Redworth. *See* Merion, Diana.

Reed, Mrs. In Charlotte Brontë's novel *Jane Eyre* (1847), Jane Eyre's* guardian in childhood who humiliates Jane while spoiling her own children; she eventually sends Jane away to Lowood School. *See also* Brocklehurst.

Reeve, The. In Chaucer's *Canterbury Tales,* a choleric man who, having been a carpenter, takes the Miller's* Tale as an insult and tells the story of a miller cuckolded when two students sleep with both his wife and his daughter.

Regan. In Shakespeare's play *King Lear* (1605), Lear's* second daughter, a vicious, cruel woman who humiliates her father and enjoys seeing Gloucester's* eyes removed. She is poisoned by her sister Goneril* since they both want the same man, the bastard Edmund.* *See also* Cordelia; Cornwall.

Regina. (1) In Lillian Hellman's play *The Little Foxes* (1939), a grasping Southern wife who withholds medicine from her husband Horace Giddens and calmly watches him die in order to get control of the family funds for an investment he opposes. *See also* Hubbard. (2) *See* Engstrand.

Rehoboam. In the Bible, *I Kings* xii, the son of Solomon.* During his reign, ten tribes revolted and established a new kingdom of Israel,* separate from his kingdom, which was called Judah.* *See also* Jeroboam.

Reichenbach Falls. In Arthur Conan Doyle's story *The Final Problem* (1893), a waterfall in Switzerland over which Dr. Moriarty* was presumed to have thrown Sherlock Holmes.* Eventually, however, Holmes reappears in *The Adventure of the Empty House* (1903) and indicates that his death here had been a ruse.

Reign of Terror. Historically, a period (1793–94) during the French Revolution in which a great number of nobles and less radical revolutionaries were guillotined; it ended with Robespierre's* execution. The term is often applied to any period of brutal police-state suppression.

Remus. *See* Romulus.

Remus, Uncle. In Joel Chandler Harris's stories (beg. 1881), the kindly Negro farmer, an ex-slave, who tells a series of folklike tales about the animals, such as Br'er Rabbit.* In the 1960s, many came to see him as a negative stereotype. *See also* Tar Baby.

Renal. In Stendhal's novel *The Red and the Black* (1830), **Mme. de Renal** is a beautiful woman who becomes Julien Sorel's* mistress; torn between her passion and her religiosity, she reveals his background when he seduces another woman, leading him to try to kill her. Three days after his execution, she dies of guilt and remorse. **M. de Renal** is mayor of a provincial town—a vulgar, greedy boor. *See also* Mathilde.

Renaud. *See* Rinaldo; Reynard.

René. In Chateaubriand's novels *Atala* (1801) and *René* (1802), a young man who flees the stultifying culture of Europe to find peace and natural life in the wilds of America, where he tries to join an Indian tribe.

Renzo. In Alessandro Manzoni's novel *The Betrothed* (1825), an Italian peasant who flees his home to keep his fiancée Lucia* out of the clutches of a nobleman, is separated from her, almost starves in Milan, is banished for his part in a food riot, and is eventually reunited with Lucia.

Restaud, Countess de. In Balzac's novel *Père Goriot* (1835), one of Goriot's* daughters who marries into the aristocracy, then shuns and tries to deny her commoner father, in spite of his squandering all his wealth to maintain her and the count. *See also* Nucingen; Rastignac.

Resurrection. In Christian usage, the rising from the dead of Jesus,* occurring on the third day after His Crucifixion* and celebrated in the festival of Easter.* The term is also sometimes used for the time when, at the Second Coming,* the bodies of all those who have been saved will be raised from the dead to rejoin their souls with God in Heaven.*

Reuben. (1) In the Bible, *Genesis,* the first son of Jacob* and the father of one of the twelve tribes of Israel.* He slept with his father's concubine; when his brothers were about to kill Joseph,* Reuben convinced them to throw him in the pit instead. *See also* Leah. (2) A typical young man, as in the American nineteenth-century popular song, *Reuben and Rachel,* beginning "Reuben, Reuben, I've been thinking what a queer world it would be, if the men were all transported . . . " Perhaps related is the slang "Rube," indicating a simple, gullible country boy.

Revere, Paul. Historically, an American silversmith (d. 1818) and patriot in the Revolutionary War. He is most commonly known from Longfellow's poem *Paul Revere's Ride* (1863), in which he rides throughout Massachusetts warning "The British are coming." having seen the signal lights "one if by land, two if by sea" in the church steeple.

Reynard. In French folklore, a cunning fox who depends on his wits to protect him from all crises and is gradually rewarded with the position of bailiff of the animal kingdom. *See also* Bruin; Chanticleer; Grimbert; Isegrim; Lion.

Rhadamanthus. In Greek legend, a man of such probity and wisdom that he became a judge of the dead.

Rhea. In Greek mythology, daughter of Gaia,* wife of Cronos,* and mother of many of the gods. *Also called* Cybele;* Dindymene; Idaea; Ops;* Terra.* *See also* Demeter; Hades; Hera; Poseidon; Zeus.

Rhesus. In Homer's *Iliad,* an ally of Troy;* legend had it that Troy could not fall as long as Rhesus's horses drank in the river there; therefore, the Greeks ambushed and killed him.

Rhoda. In the Bible, *Acts* xii, a housemaid who recognized Peter* by his voice and was so excited by his arrival that she forgot to let him in.

Rhodope. In Greek legend, a woman who thought herself more beautiful than Hera,* who changed her into a mountain.

Riah. In Charles Dickens's novel *Our Mutual Friend* (1864), a generous old Jew.

Ricardo. In the American television series "I Love Lucy" (1951–57), **Lucy** was a silly redhead with a penchant for plots that backfired on her, and her husband **Ricky** was a Cuban bandleader, noted for his thick accent. Typical adventures were built around Lucy's disastrous attempts to penetrate "show business," but the couple also seemed to personify average folks at home in the fifties. The shows were so incredibly popular that they have been synonymous with the television sitcom for decades. *See also* Mertz.

Richard. (1) Historically, the name used by three English kings: *See* Richard I; Richard II; Richard III. (2) *See* Feverel. (3) *See also* Dick; Rick.

Richard, Poor. *See* Poor Richard.

Richard I. Historically, a king of England (d. 1199) and a leader of the Crusades who figures in much literature for his bravery and for the romantic story of his imprisonment for ransom in Austria, where he was finally found by his troubadour. He is the good king in the Robin Hood* legends and a symbol of chivalry in many novels, especially in Walter Scott's *Ivanhoe* (1819). *Also called* Richard the Lion-Hearted. *See also* John.

Richard II. Historically, a king of England (d. 1399), a relatively weak king who was deposed and murdered. He is known primarily from Shakespeare's play *Richard II* (1595) as a self-indulgent and theatrical ruler, as opposed to the more puritanical Henry IV* who takes the throne after a rebellion.

Richard III. Historically, a king of England (d. 1485), known primarily from Shakespeare's play *Richard III* (1592), where he is depicted as a hunchback and as one of the greatest of all stage villains. A brilliant hypocrite, he convinces the wife of a man he murders to marry him, has his brother Clarence* drowned in a cask of liquor, has the princes for whom he is regent murdered in the tower, and then contrives to have the mob offer him the crown which he has schemed to gain. He is a ruthless ruler who soon inspires a rebellion in which he is killed, uttering the famous "My kingdom for a horse." *See also* Anne, Lady; Edward.

Richards. *See* Toodle.

Richards, Mary. In the American television series "The Mary Tyler Moore Show" (1970–77), the quintessential young working woman—bright, attractive, single, but also sensitive and vulnerable—she was a TV news producer.

Richelieu. Historically, a French cardinal (d. 1642) and prime minister for Louis XIII who was primarily responsible for solidifying the power of the French monarchy. He figures in numerous works, usually as a wicked manipulator of people and power as in Alexandre Dumas's novel *The Three Musketeers* (1844).

Richmond. Historically, the leader of the revolt against Richard III* and later crowned as Henry VII. In Shakespeare's play *Richard III* (1592), he sends numerous men into battle wearing his clothes, so that Richard is confused and overwhelmed by the appearance of an enemy who seems unable to be killed.

Rick. In the movie *Casablanca* (1942), the cynical cafe owner who finds his lost love and then gives her up again to her husband, a freedom fighter, before going off to join the war against Hitler.* He is known for saying "Play it again, Sam" (which is not quite what he says) and is one of the principal romantic icons of the American sixties and seventies.

Ricky-Ticky-Tavy. In Rudyard Kipling's story *Ricky-Ticky-Tavy* (1894), a brave little mongoose who guards his people's home and attacks the deadly cobra.

Ridd, John. In R. D. Blackmore's novel *Lorna Doone* (1869), the courageous and honorable hero who destroys the savage Doones* and marries Lorna.

Riderhood, Rogue. In Charles Dickens's novel *Our Mutual Friend* (1864), a brutal criminal who tries to have Gaffer Hexam* convicted of a murder he did not commit to claim a reward and then later tries to murder Eugene Wrayburn.* Finally, he drowns in a fight with his partner.

Ridinghood, Little Red. *See* Red Ridinghood, Little.

Rieux. In Albert Camus's novel *The Plague* (1947), the dedicated, unselfish, and analytical doctor who continues to treat his patients during the plague,* setting a vivid example of common decency.

Rigoletto. In Verdi's opera *Rigoletto* (1851), a jester who swears revenge on his master, the Duke of Mantua,* after the Duke tries to seduce Rigoletto's virginal daughter Gilda.* He arranges for the Duke to be murdered, only to discover too late that Gilda has substituted herself for the Duke. *See also* Sparafucile; Triboulet.

Riley, Chester. In the American radio and television series "The Life of Riley" (1943–58), a bumbling working man, noted for his inability to deal with family crises, his malapropisms, and his catch-phrase, "What a revoltin' development this is!"

Rima. In W. H. Hudson's novel *Green Mansions* (1904), the beautiful, hauntingly mysterious "bird woman" who is found living wild in the Amazonian jungles without fear of or harm to any wild creatures. She comes to love the civilized Abel, but she is burned alive by Indians in revenge for her attempt to keep them from hunting the animals she loves.

Rimini. *See* Francesca da Rimini.

Rinaldo. (1) In Ariosto's *Orlando Furioso* (1532), the brother of Bradamant* and a great knight second only to Orlando.* He is in quest of the beautiful but dangerous Angelica,* from whose spells he finally breaks free. *See also* Bayard. (2) In Tasso's *Jerusalem Delivered* (1580), the bravest of the Crusaders.

Rin-Tin-Tin. In numerous movies (beg. 1923), an Alsatian dog who performed brave and daring tricks to aid his various human friends.

Rip Van Winkle. In Washington Irving's story *Rip Van Winkle* (1819), a lazy, drunken Hudson River farmer who comes upon a group of trolls whose drink puts him to sleep for twenty years.

Rivers. In Charlotte Brontë's novel *Jane Eyre* (1847), the family with whom Jane Eyre* lives when she tries to avoid Rochester.* **St. John** is an honorable, religious man who loves Jane but is willing to live with her platonically if she goes with him to be a missionary.

Rizpah. In the Bible, *II Samuel* xxi, a concubine of Saul;* all her children were crucified as payment to the Gabaonites for Saul's attempt to exterminate them.

Roaring Boys. In sixteenth- and seventeenth-century English slang, wild young men.

Roberts, Mister. In Thomas Heggen's novel *Mister Roberts* (1946), the idealistic, efficient, and idolized second-in-command of a World War II American supply ship. He keeps the ship going despite the presence of a hated and incompetent commander but longs to be transferred to the "real" war. When he finally gets his transfer, he is killed while drinking coffee. *See also* Pulver, Ensign.

Robertson, Geordie. In Walter Scott's novel *The Heart of Midlothian* (1818), the alias of a profligate youth who is redeemed when he tries to admit to a crime to save Effie Deans,* whom he at last convinces to marry him. He becomes respectable and inherits a name and fortune, but he is killed by an outlaw who is one of his earlier illegitimate sons.

Robert the Bruce. Historically, a Scottish noble (d. 1329) who led a revolt against the English that eventually resulted in Scottish independence. Legend says that he was inspired to make his return to begin the successful war after observing the persistence of a spider spinning its web in the cave where the Bruce was hiding out.

Robert the Devil. Historically, the father (d. 1035) of William* the Conqueror; in legend, he was noted for a life of cruelty and violence.

Robespierre. Historically, a French revolutionary and a primary mover behind the Reign of Terror,* himself executed in 1794. He appears in many works as a personification of political fanaticism and state-sponsored terrorism.

Robigo. In Roman mythology, the goddess of grain.

Robin, Christopher. *See* Christopher Robin.

Robin Goodfellow. In English folklore, a merry, prankish elf;* in Shakespeare's play *A Midsummer Night's Dream* (1595), Puck* refers to himself by the name.

Robin Hood. In English folklore, a legendary outlaw who "robbed from the rich to give to the poor." He was said to have lived in the late twelfth century, leading a band of "merry men" in Sherwood Forest. He was a thorn in the side of the evil King John* and his agent the Sheriff of Nottingham* and was famous as a great archer. *See also* Allan-a-Dale; Guy of Gisborne; John, Little; Marian; Scarlett, Will; Tuck, Friar.

Robinson, Mrs. In Charles Webb's novel *The Graduate* (1963), a cool, mature woman who has an affair with the young man who wants to marry her daughter. As a result of the movie (1967) and a related popular song with the refrain, "Here's to you, Mrs. Robinson," she became a symbol of American middle-class values gone awry.

Robinson, Swiss Family. In Johann Wyss's novel *The Swiss Family Robinson* (1813), a sturdy, resourceful middle-class family marooned on a deserted island who improvise a life of such comfort and happiness that they choose not to be rescued.

Robinson Crusoe. *See* Crusoe, Robinson.

Rob Roy. In Walter Scott's novel *Rob Roy* (1818), a Scottish outlaw and Jacobite—a dashing figure of romance, honor, and loyalty. *See also* Osbaldistone.

Robsart, Amy. In Walter Scott's novel *Kenilworth* (1821), the honorable and lovely wife of the Earl of Leicester.* Being the queen's favorite, he keeps the marriage a secret; as a result, Amy is variously imprisoned, poisoned, declared insane, and accused of adultery, but she remains faithful until she is killed in a fall from a castle. *See also* Tressilian; Varney.

Rob the Grinder. *See* Toodles.

Roc. In *The Arabian Nights,* a gigantic bird; Sinbad* escapes from the valley of diamonds by tying himself to its leg.

Rochester. In Charlotte Brontë's novel *Jane Eyre* (1847), the proud and moody master of Thornfield who falls in love with Jane Eyre* when she comes to be governess for his daughter. She runs away when she finds out his first wife is not dead, but is instead insane and living in the attic where she sets the house on fire. He is blinded by the fire, but Jane returns to nurse him and then to marry him.

Rockefeller. Historically, an American family that came to prominence in the late nineteenth century through successful oil holdings. **John D.** (d. 1937) in particular became famous as a fabulously wealthy man, and, in America, the name itself soon was synonymous with immense riches.

Rocky. In several movies, beginning with *Rocky* (1976), an underdog boxer who overcomes great odds through personal determination and American spirit; the series itself also became synonymous with the rage for sequels denoted by roman numerals that swept American movies in the 1980s.

Roderigo. In Shakespeare's play *Othello* (1604), a gullible young man who, in vain pursuit of Desdemona,* allows Iago* to use his money and to trick him into the attempted murder of Cassio* and his own death.

Rodin. (1) In Eugène Sue's novel *The Wandering Jew* (1844), a scheming, villainous Jesuit who destroys people by playing with their passions, until he is himself poisoned. (2) Historically, a French sculptor (d. 1917) whose popular works such as *The Thinker** and *The Burghers of Calais* made him synonymous for many with sculpture itself.

Rodolphe. (1) In Gustave Flaubert's novel *Madame Bovary* (1857), a shrewd but vulgar man who seduces Emma Bovary* but then neglects her because the conquest was so easy; he pretends to go on a journey in order to get rid of her. (2) *See also* Rudolpho.

Rodomont. In Ariosto's *Orlando Furioso* (1532), a great Saracen warrior and boaster who kills Isabella* in a drunken frenzy, then in remorse challenges all comers at a bridge over her tomb; he is thrown into the river by Orlando,* and later killed by Rogero.*

Roe, Richard. *See* Doe, John.

Roger, Sir. *See* de Coverley, Roger.

Rogero. In Ariosto's *Orlando Furioso* (1532), a noble knight, converted to Christianity, who wins Bradamant,* the woman he loves, by being the only man who can stand up to her in battle for a full day. *See also* Angelica; Rodomont.

Rogers, Mildred. In Somerset Maugham's novel *Of Human Bondage* (1915), a vain, ignorant waitress who nearly destroys the young doctor Phillip Carey* through his unrequited passion for her, draining him of money and willpower while engaging in numerous additional ruinous affairs.

Rogers, Mister. In the American television series "Mister Rogers' Neighborhood" (beg. 1967), a gentle, kindly man who introduces small children to various interesting aspects of the world. He is much satirized for his monotone voice, sweater, perpetual smile, and willingness to treat anyone and everything as a potential friend.

Rogozhin. In Dostoevsky's novel *The Idiot* (1868), a sensualist with an uncouth appearance; he jealously murders his mistress Nastasia* and then repents to Myshkin* over the corpse.

Roland. In the anonymous *Song of Roland,* Charlemagne's* finest knight, commander of the rear guard that held off the Saracens' advance into France. He was supposed to summon aid by blowing on his horn, but he refused to do so and was killed along with all his men. It is also told that he and Oliver* were such equals that they had the same adventures until they met in combat and fought to a draw after five days; hence, "Roland and Oliver" or "Roland to Oliver" is used to indicate equals or matched pairs. *Also called* Orlando.* *See also* Ganelon.

Roland, Childe. In a Scottish ballad, a son of Arthur* who rescues his sister from enchantment; known primarily through Shakespeare's quotation of "Childe Roland to the dark tower came" in *King Lear* (1605), but retold by Walter Scott in his poem *The Bridal of Triermain* (1813) and allegorically used by Robert Browning in his poem *Childe Roland* (1855).

Romanovna, Avdotya. *See* Dounia.

Romeo. In Shakespeare's play *Romeo and Juliet* (1595), a young man who falls madly in love with Juliet,* the daughter in a family feuding with his own. They are secretly married but, after a duel in which he kills her cousin Tybalt,* he is exiled. When she feigns death to avoid remarriage, he misunderstands and returns to her tomb to commit suicide and to live with her in eternity. Hence, he has become the quintessential lover, both in admiration and ridicule. *See also* Capulet; Laurence, Friar; Mercutio; Montague.

Romford, Facey. In Robert Surtees's stories *Mr. Facey Romford's Hounds* (1865), a country huntsman who joins the hunt by pretending to be the rich man whose name he happens to have. *See also* Sponge, Soapey.

Romola. In George Eliot's novel *Romola* (1862), the beautiful wife of an adventurer; she tries to desert him when she is shocked by his actions, but she returns and is strengthened by her sufferings. After his death, she devotes herself to helping others.

Romulus and Remus. In Roman legend, the twin brothers who founded Rome. Both were supposedly suckled by a wolf. *See also* Quirinus; Sabine Women, The.

Roo. In A. A. Milne's stories *Winnie-the-Pooh* (1926), the baby kangaroo who travels in the pouch of his mother Kanga.

Rooney, Andy. *See* Andy, Handy.

Roosevelt. (1) Historically, a significant and wealthy American family. The most noted members include **Theodore**, usually called Teddy (d. 1919), who led the Rough Riders in the assault on San Juan Hill. As president, he built the Panama Canal and was noted for the dictum: "Speak softly and carry a big stick." A frail child, he became a devotee of the outdoor life and was caricatured for his stocky build, his big grin, and his glasses. Extremely popular for his colorful image, he is sometimes also said to have had "Teddy Bears" named for him. **Franklin** (d. 1945) was a cousin of Teddy and president for four terms during the Great Depression and World War II; he is noted for the phrase, "We have nothing to fear but fear itself," and liberal policies which made his name anathema to conservative elements of American society. *Also called* FDR; That Man. (2) *See* Brewster.

Rosa. *See* Coldfield; Dartle, Rosa. (2) *See also* Rose.

Rosalia, St. In Christian legend, a woman carried into the Italian mountains by angels,* where her knees wore away the rocks while she was praying.

Rosalind. (1) In Shakespeare's play *As You Like It* (1599), the beautiful, witty woman who runs away to the forest of Arden* disguised as a boy and there gives Orlando,* the young man she loves, lessons in courtship; one of the most charming, intelligent, and pleasantly attractive women in all of Shakespeare's plays. *See also* Celia; Phebe; Touchstone. (2) *See also* Rosaline.

Rosaline. (1) In Shakespeare's play *Romeo and Juliet* (1595), the unseen girl to whom Romeo* writes poetry before he meets his true love Juliet.* (2) In Shakespeare's play *Love's Labour's Lost* (1595), a sparklingly verbal and witty lady, matching and usually outwitting Berowne.* (3) *See also* Rosalind.

Rosamond. (1) Historically, a mistress of the English king Henry II.* Legend has it that Henry built her a house like a labyrinth* that no one could enter, until his wife the queen found a way in and murdered her. The name was much used for any beautiful woman in Tudor and Jacobean poetry. (2) *See also* Rosamund.

Rosamund. (1) *See* Lydgate. (2) *See also* Rosamond.

Rosasharn. *See* Joad; Rose of Sharon.

Rose. (1) In the British television series "Upstairs, Downstairs" (beg. 1972) and also seen in the United States, the repressed maid who serves as the principal "ordinary" participant in the life of the Bellamy* household. *See also* Hudson. (2) *See* Bradwardine. (3) *See also* Rosa.

Rosebud. *See* Kane.

Rosencrantz and Guildenstern. In Shakespeare's play *Hamlet* (1600), friends of Hamlet.* They are persuaded to spy on him but fail to understand him, and are eventually killed in his place as a result of a betrayal gone wrong; essentially, they are two faceless, ineffectual hangers-on. As a result of Tom Stoppard's play *Rosencrantz and Guildenstern Are Dead* (1967), they assumed unusual prominence and became symbols of the modern "nice guy," trying to get along but never understanding what he is caught up in, with comic/tragic results.

Rose of Sharon. In the Bible, *Song of Solomon* ii, a beautiful flower in the midst of the marshland of Sharon; sometimes interpreted as a rose in the desert. The name is sometimes given to Mary.* *See also* Rosasharn.

Rosie. In Somerset Maugham's novel *Cakes and Ale* (1930), the crude but open, vigorous, and lusty barmaid.

Rosina. In Rossini's opera *The Barber of Seville* (1816), Rosine.*

Rosinante. In Cervantes's novel *Don Quixote* (1605), Don Quixote's* horse, a gaunt nag near starvation that Quixote insists on believing is a noble charger.

Rosine. In Beaumarchais's play *The Barber of Seville* (1775), the young maiden who eventually marries Almaviva.*

Rosmer. In Henrik Ibsen's play *Rosmersholm* (1887), a freethinker and a clergyman unwelcome among either group. After his wife has committed suicide, thinking he has made another woman pregnant, he becomes obsessed by both his love and his guilt and talks his mistress into joining him in a suicide pact.

Ross, Betsy. In American legend, the woman who sewed the first American flag for George Washington.*

Rostov. In Tolstoy's novel *War and Peace* (1865), one of the principal families depicted. The **Count** is an essentially kindly, if somewhat scatterbrained gentleman with no business sense at all; the **Countess** is obsessed with arranging good marriages for her daughter and her son but her pretensions and lack of insight lead in fact to disastrous romantic consequences for both. The son, **Nikolai**, is a noble, handsome young man who loves his poor cousin Sonya* but agrees not to marry her and seeks instead a rich noblewoman. The younger son **Petya** is enamored of the romance of war and is killed senselessly in a pointless skirmish. For the daughter, *see* Natasha. *See also* Bezukov; Bolkonsy.

Rothschild. Historically, a family of German Jewish bankers who first came to prominence in the late eighteenth century; in general usage, the name is synonymous with unbelievable wealth. *See also* Rockefeller.

Roualt, Emma. The maiden name of Emma Bovary.*

Rougon-Macquart. In numerous novels by Émile Zola, a representative family whose various members provide a cross-section of French society. Noted individuals include Étienne;* Gervaise,* and Nana.*

Rouncewell. In Charles Dickens's novel *Bleak House* (1852), **George** is a retired soldier who runs a shooting gallery, who resists attempts to get him to reveal the past of the dead Nemo/Hawdon,* and is charged with the lawyer Tulkinghorn's* murder. He is freed and restored to his long-lost mother, a cheerful, friendly housekeeper for the Dedlocks.* His brother is a successful businessman trying to get the Dedlock's approval for his son to marry the lady's maid; he is much ridiculed by the nobles because he was a housekeeper's son and a tradesman, no matter how successful. *See also* Bagnet.

Round Table, Knights of the. *See* Arthur.

Roussillon, Countess of. In Shakespeare's play *All's Well That Ends Well* (1602), a wise and gracious woman who tries to encourage her son Bertram* to love Helena,* the wife arranged for him, to little avail.

Rover. In Aphra Behn's play *The Rover* (1677), an attractive, witty, and particularly libidinous sea captain ashore and one of the quintessential Restoration heroes.

Rowena. (1) In English legend, the princess who married Vortigern.* (2) In Walter Scott's novel *Ivanhoe* (1820), the pale, fair maid whom Ivanhoe* comes to love and marry after she is saved from the fate worse than death. Almost always called "the fair Rowena," she is often referred to as the quintessential bland, simpering nineteenth-century heroine, especially as compared to Rebecca.*

Roxana. (1) In European legend, the first wife of Alexander* the Great, originally a captive Persian princess. She murdered his second wife and thus became synonymous with the jealous wife. (2) In Daniel Defoe's novel *Roxana* (1724), a woman left penniless after her husband's death who supports herself and prospers as a courtesan until she finally becomes a respectable, wealthy wife. (3) *See also* Roxane.

Roxane. (1) In Racine's play *Bajazet* (1672), a sultana who frees the prince Bajazet* from prison to take the throne on the assumption that he will marry her; when she realizes that he loves another, she allows him to be killed, but her husband returns and executes her as well. (2) In Edmund Rostand's play *Cyrano de Bergerac* (1897), the beautiful young woman who falls in love with Christian's* looks and with his words, never realizing that the words are really Cyrano's;* she is a charming but shallow woman concerned with appearances over sincerity. After Christian's death, she matures but retires to a nunnery as a grieving widow, only to realize too late that she had missed the genuine love of her life. (3) *See also* Roxana.

Roy, Rob. *See* Rob Roy.

Royal Nonesuch. In Mark Twain's novel *Huckleberry Finn* (1885), the "entertainment" staged by the Duke* and the Dauphin* in backwoods towns; advertising "women and children not allowed," the show packs the men in but consists of nothing. The men in the audience are so humiliated at being tricked that they tell their friends to come on the second night, so that everyone will be equally bilked, and then the con men skip town before the third performance at which the townsmen plan their revenge.

Rubashov. In Arthur Koestler's novel *Darkness at Noon* (1941), the old Bolshevik imprisoned and gradually induced not only to publicly admit nonexistent crimes but to gradually believe he has committed them and to assist in his own conviction and execution during the Russian communist purges of the 1930s.

Rube. *See* Reuben.

Rubicon. Historically, an Italian river beyond which the armies of Rome were expected to remain. When Julius Caesar* brought his army across, he was undeniably in revolt, and thus "crossing the Rubicon" usually means beginning an action from which one cannot turn back.

Rudge. In Charles Dickens's novel *Barnaby Rudge* (1841), **Barnaby** is a strong but good-hearted half-wit who loves a raven and is condemned for his unthinking participation in riots, but is pardoned. His mother tries to protect her son whenever possible, but she lives in continual hardship. Her husband is a savage criminal who murders several men, one of whom is mistaken for him, which allows him to disappear until he is later recognized during the riots and hanged.

Rudolph the Red-Nosed Reindeer. In a popular American song (1949), a shy reindeer added to Santa Claus's* team on a foggy night because his nose glows.

Rudolpho. (1) In Puccini's opera *La Bohème* (1896), the young poet who falls in love with Mimi.* (2) *See also* Rodolphe.

Rufus. In the Bible, *Mark* xv, son of Simon* of Cyrene.

Rugby, Jack. In Shakespeare's play *The Merry Wives of Windsor* (1598), Dr. Caius's* servant.

Ruggiero. *See* Rogero.

Ruggles. In Harry Leon Wilson's novel *Ruggles of Red Gap* (1915), the perfect English valet won in a poker game by an American millionaire and brought to the American West, where much humor is drawn from his shock at the crudeness of life there. He soon realizes the opportunities of real frontier freedom and sets up as his own man.

Rumor. In Greek mythology, daughter of Gaia,* a tattler and a sinister, obstinate, and swift monster.

Rumplestiltskin. In the fairy tale, an evil dwarf who taught a princess how to spin gold in return for her first child; when the child was born, she tried to renege, and he said she could be saved only if she could guess his name. She did this, having overheard him talking to himself, and he stomped himself into the ground in anger.

Rumpole. In numerous stories by John Mortimer and a simultaneous British television series "Rumpole of the Bailey" (beg. 1978), an old down-at-heels barrister passionately committed to the defense in criminal cases, to wine, and to Wordsworth, but with no reverence for any of the trappings of the law.

Ruritania. An imaginary Eastern European country first mentioned in Anthony Hope's novel *The Prisoner of Zenda* (1894), but soon used generally to mean any romantic but rather comic-opera little country where chivalry, swordplay, and princes in love with peasant girls might be found. *See also* Graustark.

Ruslan. In Pushkin's poem *Ruslan and Ludmilla* (1820), a prince whose wife Ludmilla* is stolen by a magician and who searches over Russia to find and rescue her.

Ruth. In the Bible, *Ruth*, a woman who, when her husband died, left her own homeland to return to her mother-in-law Naomi's* home, there to eke out sustenance by gleaning the fields of Boaz,* who noticed her and married her; she is regarded as a romantic figure for her famous "Whither thou goest, I shall go," although this is, in fact, said to her mother-in-law rather than to her lover or husband. *See also* Orpah. (2) In Gilbert and Sullivan's operetta *The Pirates of Penzance* (1879), a middle-aged nurse who joined the pirates by mistake (she misheard the directions to apprentice her charge to a pilot) and who, now that the boy is grown up, tries to convince him that she is beautiful, a point disproved the moment he meets a young girl. *See also* Frederic; Mabel.

Rutledge, Ann. In American folklore, a woman said to be Abe Lincoln's* true love who died young.

Ryder, Charles. In Evelyn Waugh's novel *Brideshead Revisited* (1945), a painter, rather reserved and intellectual, who finds himself drawn into the complex and confusing world of the Marchmains,* first through love of the son Sebastian and then of the daughter Julia.

S

Sabina. In Thorton Wilder's play *The Skin of Our Teeth* (1942), the maid who also serves as a symbol of the nondomestic, nonmaternal aspects of the female. *See also* Antrobus; Sabine Women, The.

Sabine Women, The. In Roman legend, a group of women raped and carried off by the followers of Romulus and Remus* to provide wives for the founding of Rome.

Sabra. In English legend, the princess of Egypt whom St. George* rescued from the dragon.

Sabrina. In John Milton's poem/play *Comus* (1634), a princess who drowns herself to escape her stepmother and becomes a nymph* of the river Severn.

Sachs, Hans. Historically, a German poet and playwright (d. 1576) noted primarily for his depiction in Richard Wagner's opera *Die Meistersinger von Nürnberg* (1868), in which he is an old and genial shoemaker and a master singer who upholds the idea that true art can be judged not by its ability to follow rules but by its ability to reach and move the people. *See also* Beckmesser.

Sad Sack. In the American newspaper cartoon *Sad Sack* (1942–52), an American soldier whose life was a series of continual disasters.

Sadducees. In the Bible, New Testament, an extremely strict, fundamentalist Hebrew sect, rivals of the Pharisees;* in Christian usage, generally lumped together with the Pharisees as examples of religious hypocrisy.

Sages. In Greek legend, the seven wise men who, when each was sent a golden tripod inscribed ''to the wisest man,'' refused it, their wisdom lying in their understanding of what they still did not know.

Sagittarius. In Greek legend, an archer and a centaur,* depicted in a constellation and in one of the signs of the zodiac.

Saint, The. *See* Templar, Simon.

St. Clare. (1) In Harriet Beecher Stowe's novel *Uncle Tom's Cabin* (1852), the kindly original master of Uncle Tom.* For his daughter, *see* Eva. (2) *See* Clare, St.

Saint-Euverte, Mme. de. In Marcel Proust's novels *Remembrance of Things Past* (1913–27), a society hostess at whose soirees Swann* realizes that his love for Odette* has in fact ended.

St. Evrémonde. In Charles Dickens's novel *A Tale of Two Cities* (1859), a cruel French aristocrat who runs down a child with his coach and is, in turn, killed by the child's father. For his son, *see* Darnay, Charles.

Saint-Loup. In Marcel Proust's novels *Remembrance of Things Past* (1913–27), Marcel's* friend who introduces him to the Guermantes* circle; he is obsessively jealous of his mistress Rachel,* but he eventually marries Swann's* daughter Gilberte.* He is also a serving soldier and is killed in World War I.

Saint-Preux. In Jean-Jacques Rousseau's *The New Héloïse* (1760), the bourgeois Swiss tutor who truly loves Julie* but is never allowed to marry her.

Sairey. *See* Gamp, Sairey.

Sakuntala. In Kalidasa's *Sakuntala,* a beautiful maiden who marries the king Dushyanta* in secret, then, when she unwittingly offends a holy man, is cursed so that the king will forget her. She is carried into the heavens for her safety, where she gives birth to a heroic son; eventually, she is reunited with her husband.

Saladin. Historically, the Arab sultan (d. 1193) whose conquest of Jerusalem* in 1187 stimulated the Third Crusade, in which he was defeated by Richard I.* He was an unusually cultivated, brilliant, and honorable ruler and appears in numerous works as a model of chivalry and learning.

Salammbô. In Gustave Flaubert's *Salammbô* (1862), a Carthaginian priestess who sacrifices her virginity to protect the sacred relics, then realizes she loves her violator and commits suicide as he is tortured.

Sallust. Historically, a Roman senator (d. 34 B.C.) and historian noted primarily for his ejection from the senate for adultery.

Sally. *See* Brass.

Salmoneus. In Greek legend, the son of Aeolus;* he demanded to be treated as a god and addressed as Zeus,* for which he was killed by Zeus with a thunderbolt.

Salome. In the Bible, *Matthew* xiv, the daughter of Herodias* who so pleased Herod* with her dancing that she asked for and received as a reward the head of John the Baptist.* The name is not mentioned in the Bible, but in fact comes from Josephus. Tradition quickly accepted it and added that she danced a form of striptease called the "dance of the seven veils," hence making her a symbol of degeneracy and female guile.

Salus. In Roman mythology, the goddess of health, generally equivalent to Hygeia.*

Sam. *See* Weller.

Sam, Uncle. In popular usage, the symbol of the United States, generally portrayed as a tall, skinny man with white hair and pointed beard, wearing a red, white, and blue tailcoat and top hat.

Samael. In legend, the prince of demons, sometimes the angel* of death. *See also* Devil.

Samaritan, Good. In the Bible, *Luke* x, a parable told by Jesus:* A man was robbed and left by the side of the road, where many respectable persons crossed to the other side to avoid him. Finally, a Samaritan, a member of a tribe hated for centuries by the Hebrews, stopped to give aid; hence, a philanthropist or self-sacrificing person.

Samedi, Baron. In Caribbean voodoo lore, Death.

Sampson, Dominie. In Walter Scott's novel *Guy Mannering* (1815), the tutor who when astonished always exclaims: "Prodigious!"

Samsa. In Franz Kafka's story *The Metamorphosis* (1916), a man who wakes up one morning to discover he has been changed into a cockroach.

Samson. In the Bible, *Judges* xiii-xvi, a man of great strength who once killed a thousand men with the jawbone of an ass. His strength came from a vow never to cut his hair, but Delilah,* on finding this out, cut it and delivered him to his enemies, the Philistines* in Gaza,* who blinded him. As his hair grew back, his strength returned; when put on public display, he pushed down the pillars of the temple, destroying all the Philistines as well as himself. *See also* Manoah.

Samuel. (1) In the Bible, *I Samuel,* the last of the judges of Israel,* a prophet second only to Moses* and the anointer of both King Saul* and David.* *See also* Eli; Hannah; Joel. (2) In Eugene Sue's novel *The Wandering Jew* (1844), the Wandering Jew. *See* Ahasuerus.

Samurai, Seven. *See* Seven Samurai.

Sancho Panza. In Cervantes's novel *Don Quixote* (1605), Don Quixote's* fat squire, an extremely commonsensical peasant widely alluded to as an example of the earthy and pragmatic common man.

Sanhedrin. In the Bible, New Testament, a Jewish religious and political council, sometimes also a court, particularly the court that tried Jesus.*

Sanseverina. In Stendhal's novel *The Charterhouse of Parma* (1839), an unorthodox and sprited beauty of intelligence and political astuteness; the mistress of Count Mosca,* she also encourages the career of her nephew Fabrizio.*

Sans-Gêne, Madame. In Sardou and Moreau's play *Madame Sans-Gêne* (1893), a free-and-easy young woman of the French Revolution, whom circumstances eventually involve in a number of behind-the-scenes palace intrigues, which she overcomes by her native wit, facing down Napoleon* himself with a twenty-year-old laundry bill he owes her.

Santa Claus. A name often used for St. Nicholas,* especially in the United States. A jolly, fat old man who delivers presents at Christmas, he is generally depicted as described in Clement Moore's poem *The Night Before Christmas* (1823) with a white beard, a red nose, and a red suit, and usually with a flying sleigh drawn by eight (or nine) reindeer. *Also called* Kris Kringle; Father Christmas. *See also* Rudolph the Red-Nosed Reindeer.

Santiago. (1) St. Iago.* (2) In Ernest Hemingway's novel *The Old Man and the Sea* (1952), an old Cuban fisherman who catches a great fish, tries to fight off the sharks that attack the carcass, and reaches shore, dying, with only the skeleton as a sign of his victory.

Sapphira. In the Bible, *Acts* v, the wife of Ananias;* the two of them tried to cheat Peter* of part of an offering and were struck dead by God.

Sappho. Historically, a Greek poetess (seventh century B.C.) noted for her passionate love lyrics. Born in Lesbos,* in legend she was said to have been unusually licentious, with lovers of either sex, and is primarily used as a symbol of female homosexuality, even though she was reported to have thrown herself off a cliff when the boatman Phaon* spurned her love. *See also* Fanny.

Sara. (1) In the Bible, in the Apochrypha, *Tobit,* a woman married to seven husbands, each of whom was killed on her wedding night by the demon Asmodeus.* Tobias* won her after the angel Raphael* bound Asmodeus and carried him into the desert. (2) *See also* Sarah.

Sarah. (1) In the Bible, *Genesis* xvii-xxi, Abraham's* wife and mother of Isaac* at the age of ninety, thus demonstrating the power of faith while helping to found the tribe of Israel.* *See also* Hagar. (2) *See also* Sairey; Sara.

Sarastro. In Mozart's opera *The Magic Flute* (1791), the high priest, a figure of justice and the guide on the path to truth and light.

Sardanapalus. In legend, the last king of Assyria, notorious for his effeminacy and life of luxury; when besieged by rebels, he burned himself, his treasures, and his concubines in his palace.

Sarpedon. In Homer's *Iliad,* a friend of Glaucus* and the commander of the Lycians at Troy;* he was slain by Patroclus.* In legend, he was slain by Heracles* for his barbaric treatment of strangers.

Satan. In the Bible, *Job,* a "son of God" whose challenge brings on Job's* tests of faith. In various New Testament references, he is the ruler of all evil forces in the world and tempter of Jesus* and of all mankind. In John Milton's poem *Paradise Lost* (1667), the two usages are combined, so that Satan is the prince of all evil as a result of an attempt to lead a revolt of the angels* against God. He is also traditionally identified as the serpent* who tempts Eve,* but is not so named in *Genesis. Also called* Asmodeus;* Beelzebub;* The Devil;* Lucifer;* Old Nick; The Prince of Darkness; Scratch. *See also* Moloch; Mammon.

Saturn. In Roman mythology, one of the Titans* and the father of Jupiter,* generally equivalent to Cronos.*

Satyr. In Greek mythology, the attendants of Dionysus* who looked like men except for having horns and the legs and feet of goats, known for their lasciviousness; sometimes also the followers of Pan* and gods of the forest.

Saul. (1) In the Bible, *I Samuel,* the first king of Israel.* He was later deserted by God in favor of David,* whom Saul persecuted for many years until his own suicide after all his own sons were killed in battle. *See also* Abner; Jonathan; Rizpah; Samuel; Witch of Endor. (2) In the Bible, *Acts,* a Pharisee* who, while on the road to Damascus* where he intended to persecute the Christians, was converted by a blinding vision. Changing his name to Paul,* he became the chief missionary of Christianity; *also called* Saul of Tarsus to distinguish him from King Saul.

Savage, John. In Aldous Huxley's novel *Brave New World* (1932), a natural man introduced into a futuristic society which has no place for his individualistic ideas, passions, or morality; he kills himself after he has been reduced to a tourist attraction. *See also* Lenina.

Savage, Noble. *See* Noble Savage.

Savior. *See* Jesus.

Savonarola. Historically, an Italian friar (d. 1498) who preached a strict, ascetic life and was excommunicated and executed for his attacks on the Pope; he appears in various works as a character of religious purity or of religious and social suppression and fundamentalism.

Sawyer, Tom. In Mark Twain's novels *Tom Sawyer* (1876) and *Huckleberry Finn* (1885), an all-American small-town boy, a pleasant scamp. His most famous escapades include tricking the other kids into whitewashing his fence for him, finding a treasure cave, and rescuing the slave Jim* with an unnecessarily complex plot. His half-brother **Sid** represents the proper role model much admired by adults and much despised by other boys. *See also* Finn, Huck; Injun Joe; Polly, Aunt; Thatcher.

Scapino. In the commedia dell'Arte, a comic valet—playful, witty, and a trickster, a version of Brighella,* used particularly by Molière.

Scaramouche. In the commedia dell'Arte, generally in French versions, one of the versions of the cowardly soldier—all braggadocio with no bite and usually dressed in black. *See also* Capitano, il.

Scarecrow. In Frank Baum's novel *The Wonderful Wizard of Oz* (1900) and especially in the movie version (1939), a talking, walking scarecrow who is in search of a brain. *See also* Dorothy; Lion; Tin Man.

Scarface. In the movie *Scarface* (1932), the quintessential movie gangster.

Scarlet Letter. *See* Hester.

Scarlet Pimpernel. In the Baroness Orczy's novel *The Scarlet Pimpernel* (1905), a foppish English gentleman who, beneath that disguise, is a daring rescuer of French nobility from the Reign of Terror.*

Scarlett. *See* O'Hara, Scarlett.

Scarlet Woman, The. In much Protestant calumny, the Roman Catholic Church, based on the description of the Whore of Babylon in the Bible, *Revelation* xvii, as a woman dressed in scarlet seated on a scarlet beast and called the mother of harlots. In common usage, the term applies to any whore or woman of questionable morals. *See also* Jezebel; Woman in Red.

Scarpia. In Sardou's play *La Tosca* (1887) and in Puccini's opera *Tosca* (1900), one of the classic villains, a particularly corrupt and venal policeman who tries to seduce Tosca* with a false promise to save her lover, only to be murdered by her.

Scheherazade. In *The Arabian Nights,* the bride of the emperor who marries and executes a new woman each day; she saves herself by telling him a new story each evening, thus telling the thousand and one nights of stories.

Schicchi, Gianni. In Dante's *Divine Comedy,* a sinner condemned to Hell* for his lust and greed and turned into a swine; he is perhaps better known as the subject of Puccini's opera *Gianni Schicchi* (1918).

Schweik. In Jaroslav Hašek's novel *The Good Soldier Schweik* (1920–23), a Czech soldier whose apparent stupidity brings him into constant conflict with authority, thereby bringing the authority into ridicule and making him a representative of the simple, common man who has no interest in power, politics, or war.

Sciron. In Ovid's *Metamorphoses,* a thief who throws his victims into the sea to be eaten by a great sea turtle and is himself killed in the same way by Theseus.*

Scobie. In Graham Greene's novel *The Heart of the Matter* (1948), a scrupulous colonial administrator who is compromised by a shady loan and a mistress. Unable to live with himself in such circumstances, he commits suicide—a weak man, in many ways a victim of his own good intentions.

Scratch. A name sometimes used for the Devil.*

Scrooge. In Charles Dickens's story *A Christmas Carol* (1843), a miser without any apparent signs of human feeling who, after visits from several Christmas ghosts, is converted to Christian goodwill and generosity. *See also* Cratchit, Bob; Marley; Tiny Tim.

Scorpio. A constellation in the zodiac, the scorpion.

Scylaceus. In Greek legend, an ally of Troy* who, when he told the wives at home that their husbands had been killed, was stoned to death by them for bringing such bad news.

Scylla. (1) In Greek legend, a sea nymph* who was changed by her rival Circe* into a monster that snatched sailors from passing ships, a companion hazard with Charybdis.* In Homer's *Odyssey,* Odysseus* only barely manages to maneuver his ship between the two hazards, and thus the phrase "between Scylla and Charybdis" is used to indicate a position between two mutually unpleasant alternatives. (2) In Ovid's *Metamorphoses,* a daughter of Nisus.* She betrays her kingdom to Minos* for love, is scorned by him, and then kills herself and is changed into a lark.

Sebastian. (1) In Shakespeare's play *Twelfth Night* (1599), the twin brother of Viola.* (2) *See* Marchmain.

Sebastian, St. In Christian legend, a martyr executed by being bound to a tree and shot with arrows; he is always pictured with numerous arrows protruding from his body. The patron saint of archers and of soldiers, his day is January 20.

Second Coming. In Christian usage, the time when Jesus* will come back to the earth and institute God's Kingdom on Earth, gathering together all those who will be saved. This is often associated with Armageddon.*

Sedley. In William Makepeace Thackeray's novel *Vanity Fair* (1847), **Amelia** is the gentle and virtuous woman, the ostensible heroine, sometimes seeming so innocent and pure as to be a goose, in sharp contrast to Becky Sharp.* Her father **John** is a generally insensitive and bluff businessman whose grasping ways cannot prevent a business failure with which he is unable to cope. Her mother is sweet and perfectly even-tempered. Her brother **Joseph** is a fat dandy who, for a time, keeps Becky as his mistress; shy among women, selfish and a braggart among men, he refuses to use his wealth to help his family. *See also* Dobbin; Osborne.

Segismundo. In Calderon's play *Life Is a Dream* (1635), a prince who, due to dire prophecies, is locked away as a child, then is released to establish the succession, only to be an ignorant and dangerous prince. He is returned to his cell and is told that his release was a dream, thereby becoming so confused that, when he is released again, he refuses to become king because it must be another dream.

Sejanus. Historically, an aide (d. 31) to the Roman Emperor Tiberius.* He used his position to increase his own power and almost overthrew the emperor; hence, he is a figure of overweening pride and corruption in many works, most notably in Ben Jonson's play *Sejanus, His Fall* (1603).

Selene. A name sometimes used for Artemis.*

Sellars, Col. In Mark Twain and Charles Dudley Warner's novel *The Gilded Age* (1873), an opportunistic speculator, operator, and swindler.

Semele. (1) In Greek mythology, mother of Dionysus;* she prayed that Zeus* would visit her in all his splendor, whereupon he appeared as the lightning that killed her. (2) In John Lyly's play *Endymion* (1588), a witty and sharp-tongued girl.

Semiramis. In Greek legend, a great queen of Assyria, builder of Babylon and the Hanging Gardens.

Senior, Duke. In Shakespeare's play *As You Like It* (1599), the genial, honest duke, banished by his wicked brother Duke Frederick* to hold court in the Forest of Arden.*

Sennacherib. In the Bible, *II Kings* xviii-xix, an Assyrian king who beseiged Judah* only to have more than 5,000 of his soldiers killed in their sleep by an angel,* whereupon he returned to Nineveh, where he was murdered by his sons. *See also* Hezekiah.

Senta. In Richard Wagner's opera *The Flying Dutchman* (1843), a beautiful maiden who falls in love with the Flying Dutchman* and, when he doubts her faithfulness, drowns herself; her sacrifice frees him of his curse, and the two of them ascend together into Heaven.*

Seraph. One of the Seraphim.* *See also* Abdiel; Cherub.

Seraphim. In the Bible, *Isaiah* vi, the angels* who surround God's throne. *See also* Cherubim.

Serebryakov. In Anton Chekhov's play *Uncle Vanya* (1899), a retired professor who is a testy, conceited, and ungenerous old man, in part because all his years of scholarship and learning have never produced anything of real value. **Helena**, his young, second wife, is disillusioned by his lack of fame and has become an idle, directionless woman who fascinates other men, such as Vanya* and Astrov,* but who only toys with their affections.

Sergius. In G. B. Shaw's play *Arms and the Man* (1894), the Bulgarian cavalry officer who stupidly leads a charge against machine guns only to become a hero when they run out of ammunition; he is a figure of mock-heroic bombast. *See also* Bluntschli; Raina.

Sergius, St. (1) In Christian legend, a Roman soldier martyred for refusing to sacrifice to Jupiter;* he is patron saint of nomads. (2) Historically, a Russian monk (d. 1392), a founder of monasteries and a teacher of simple communal life in accordance with nature; a peasant and a mystic, he is the most loved of Russian saints; his day is September 25.

Sermon on the Mount. In the Bible, *Matthew* v-vii, a long discourse delivered by Jesus* to a multitude on a mountainside, noted particularly for the Beatitudes* contained within it.

Sermon on the Plain. In the Bible, *Luke* vi, a discourse delivered by Jesus* to a crowd assembled on the plain, similar to the Sermon on the Mount,* but somewhat briefer and less detailed.

Serpent. In the Bible, *Genesis,* a serpent was Eve's* tempter who convinced her to eat from the Tree of Knowledge; hence, serpents or snakes are generally used to denote temptation or evil and are often synonymous with the Devil.* Other notable serpents include the two serpents in Greek legend sent by Hera* to kill Heracles* in his cradle, which he strangled; and, in Virgil's *Aeneid,* the great serpent that kills Laocoön* and thus convinces the Trojans to take in the Trojan Horse.*

Servant of Two Masters. In the Bible, *Luke* xvi, a parable told by Jesus:* No servant can properly serve two masters, and thus each person must choose between "God and mammon.*"

Seth. In the Bible, *Genesis* iv, the son given to Adam* and Eve* to replace Abel* after he was killed by Cain.*

Seton, Elizabeth. *See* Elizabeth, St.

Seven Against Thebes. In Greek legend, seven heroes who joined Polynices* in a war against his brother Eteocles* after Eteocles refused to step down from the throne as promised; all but one were killed.

Seven Ages. In Shakespeare's play *As You Like It* (1599), in a speech by Jaques:* the infant, the schoolboy, the lover, the soldier, the justice, the pantaloon, the second childhood.

Seven Deadly Sins. Pride, Lust, Envy, Anger, Covetousness, Gluttony, Sloth.

Seven Dwarfs. In the motion picture *Snow White and the Seven Dwarfs* (1937), the dwarfs who try to protect Snow White* and who whistle while they work.

Seven Samurai. In the movie *The Seven Samurai* (1954), seven Japanese warriors who defend a peasant village from bandits and in the process learn something about the true values of life.

Seven Wonders. Historically, a collection of impressive architectural constructions. In the first list, by Antipatros (c. 100 B.C.), they included the Pyramids, the Mausoleum at Halicarnassus, the Hanging Gardens of Babylon, the temple of Artemis, the great statue of Zeus, the Colossus of Rhodes, and the Pharos lighthouse at Alexandria. Later writers have regularly updated such lists to include more modern wonders.

Sganarelle. A name used regularly in Molière's plays. In *The Doctor In Spite of Himself* (1666), he is the earthy peasant who, forced to pretend to be a doctor, succeeds far better than the real doctors; in *The School For Husbands* (1661), he is the guardian who epitomizes jealous, strict control of a young girl but is nonetheless outwitted.

Shadrach. In the Bible, *Daniel,* Shadrach, Meshach, and Abednego were cast into the fiery furnace by king Nebuchadnezzar* but were unharmed due to the protection of an angel.*

Shakuntala. *See* Sakuntala.

Shallow. In Shakespeare's play *Henry IV, Part II* (1598), an old friend of Falstaff* and a Justice now grown senile, babbling about his youth.

Shalott, Lady of. In Tennyson's poem *The Lady of Shalott* (1832), the fair princess, "half sick of shadows," who falls in love with Lancelot* from afar and dies of unrequited love while floating downstream to Camelot.* *See also* Elaine.

Shalmaneser. In the Bible, *II Kings* xvii, the Assyrian king who carried the Israelites of Samaria away as prisoners in the reign of Hoshea.*

Shandy. In Laurence Sterne's novel *Tristram Shandy* (1759), **Tristram** is the ostensible hero of the work; he narrates the story but manages to tell almost nothing about himself, other than that his conception was interrupted by questions about winding the clock, that his name was a mistake, that his nose was broken by the doctor's forceps, and that his member was crushed by a falling window sash. **Toby** is the genial and simple uncle who "rides his hobby-horse"—in this case, military siegeworks—and avoids all uncomfortable situations by whistling "Lillabulero," epitomizing the genial strand of English eccentricity. He is relentlessly pursued by the Widow Wadman* but fails even to notice. **Walter** is Tristram's eccentric and obsessive father who knows everything there is to be known about works and topics of no possible use to anyone and who insists on applying that knowledge to his son's education. *See also* Trim, Corporal.

Shane. In Jack Schaeffer's novel *Shane* (1949) and especially in the movie version (1953), the quintessential gunfighter who can never escape his past and who, after saving the good farmers, must ride off alone.

Shangri-La. In James Hilton's novel *Lost Horizon* (1933), a beautiful land of peace and harmony hidden in the Himalayas, often used to denote an earthly paradise.*

Sharon, Rose of. *See* Rose of Sharon.

Sharp, Becky. In William Makepeace Thackeray's novel *Vanity Fair* (1847), the intelligent, beautiful, greedy, and quintessentially self-centered woman who flirts, connives, and sleeps her way to the top of English and French society. *See also* Briggs, Miss; Crawley; O'Dowd; Osborne; Sedley; Steyne, Marquis of.

Shatov. In Dostoevsky's novel *The Possessed* (1867), an emancipated, educated Russian serf who is first enamored of and then disillusioned by the revolutionary cell controlled by Stavrogin.* He is murdered by Verhovensky* as he is about to break all ties with the revolutionaries, and his wife and child (which may be Stavrogin's) die of neglect and exposure. His sister **Dasha** is a meek servant girl secretly in love with Stavrogin;* he commits suicide, however, before they can leave for Switzerland. *See also* Kirillov.

She. *See* She-Who-Must-Be-Obeyed.

Sheba. In the Bible, *II Samuel* xx, an Israelite who raised a revolt against David;* eventually, he was trapped in the city of Abel by Joab,* and the inhabitants cut off his head.

Sheba, Queen of. In the Bible, *I Kings* x, a queen of great wealth who visited Solomon* and made him lavish gifts of gold, wood, and spices when she was impressed by his wisdom.

Sheik. In E. M. Hull's novel *The Sheik* (1921) and especially in the movie version (1922), an Arab chieftain of irresistible romantic attraction, generally used to signify a great lover.

Shelby, George. In Harriet Beecher Stowe's novel *Uncle Tom's Cabin* (1852), the slaveowner who tries to rescue Uncle Tom* but is too late; he reforms and frees all his slaves.

Shem. In the Bible, *Genesis,* a son of Noah.* After the Flood,* he was blessed when he covered his father's nakedness. *See also* Elam; Ham; Japeth.

Shemuel. *See* Samuel.

Shepherd, Good. In the Bible, *Luke* xv, a parable told by Jesus:* A shepherd with a hundred sheep had one wander away; he left the 99 to look for and save the one, thereby illustrating God's love and rejoicing over the sinner who repents. Jesus* is also often called the Good Shepherd.

Shepherds. In the Bible, *Luke* ii, there were "shepherds abiding in the fields" who were visited by an angel* announcing the birth of Jesus* and who then went to Bethlehem* to worship the Christ-child. *See also* Mak.

Shepherdsons. In Mark Twain's novel *Huckleberry Finn* (1885), one of two feuding families. *See also* Grangerfords.

Sheppard, Jack. Historically, a famous English highwayman (d. 1724), who is the subject of numerous plays and songs.

Sherburn, Col. In Mark Twain's novel *Huckleberry Finn* (1884), an aristocratic Southerner who shoots down a local braggart and then faces down the lynch mob that comes after him.

Sheriff of Nottingham, The. In English legend, the evil sheriff who is Robin Hood's* persistent enemy.

Sherlock. *See* Holmes, Sherlock.

Sherwood Forest. *See* Robin Hood.

She-Who-Must-Be-Obeyed. In H. Rider Haggard's novel *She* (1887), the queen of a hidden African city who has eternal life, which she has spent waiting for the reincarnation of her ancient lover; she is a woman of awesome beauty and power.

Shimerda, Ántonia. In Willa Cather's novel *My Ántonia* (1918), a young immigrant girl, innocent and moral, whose simple strength of character and serenity see her through the pains of immigration, prairie life, and social stigma.

Shipman. In Chaucer's *Canterbury Tales,* the shipbuilder who tells the story of the priest who borrows money from a merchant to give to the merchant's wife for her sexual favors and avoids repayment by claiming the money was returned to the wife, who dares not deny it.

Shipton, Mother. *See* Mother Shipton.

Shiva. In Hindu mythology, the god of destruction, usually pictured with four arms and dancing on a prostrate demon. *See also* Brahma; Devi; Kali; Rama; Vishnu.

Shotover, Capt. In G. B. Shaw's play *Heartbreak House* (1919), a retired sea captain in search of tranquillity in what he sees as a society facing anarchy; an eccentric, drunken, yet perceptive old man, he claims to be designing a foolproof explosive device that will prevent mankind from acting insanely. *See also* Hushabye; Utterword, Lady.

Shpigelski. In Turgenev's play *A Month in the Country* (1850), the doctor who hides his cynicism about the wealthy behind a mask of buffoonery.

Shtcherbatskaya, Katerina. *See* Kitty.

Shtcherbatsky. In Tolstoy's novel *Anna Karenina* (1875), Kitty's* father, a bluff, hearty man of infectious cheerfulness. His wife is ambitious.

Shylock. In Shakespeare's play *The Merchant of Venice* (1596), a Jew who lends money to Antonio* secured by a pound of flesh, which he demands as payment when Antonio defaults. He is thwarted when he cannot take the flesh without also taking blood and, as a result, has his estate confiscated. The name is often used derogatorily of a loan shark and of any Jew, although in recent usage he has come to be seen more positively as a sympathetic Jewish character, especially for his "Hath not a Jew eyes?" speech. *See also* Gobbo, Lancelot; Jessica; Portia.

Sibyl. In Greek legend, one of approximately ten women who were endowed with the power of prophecy and could intercede with the gods on behalf of humans. The one at Cumea was given a year of life for each grain of sand she could hold, but she forgot to ask for continuing youth and so lived for a thousand years as an old hag in a cave.

Sid. *See* Sawyer, Tom.

Sidonia. In Disraeli's novel *Tancred* (1847), a Jew who refuses a seat in Parliament to go in search of mysteries in the Holy Land; sometimes called a "Jewish superman."

Siegfried. (1) In the anonymous *Niebelungenlied,* a great hero, a slayer of dragons, and the man who finds the treasure of the Niebelung.* He is killed by Brunhild* in revenge for his seducing her. (2) In Richard Wagner's operas *The Ring of the Niebelung* (1869–76), the great hero, son of Siegmund* and Sieglinde,* raised by Mime,* who reforges his father's broken sword and kills the dragon Fafner* to find the ring of the Niebelung.* By tasting the dragon's blood, he is able to read minds and understand the birds, who lead him to Brünnhilde,* whom he awakens from a spell after passing through the ring of fire. On a later adventure, he is given a potion that causes loss of memory, whereupon he steals Brünnhilde for the king Gunther, only to redeclare his love when memory returns just before he is murdered, at which point Valhalla* crumbles. *See also* Alberich; Hagen; Wotan. (3) In Tchaikovsky's ballet *Swan Lake* (1877), the noble young prince who is loved by the swan queen Odette.* *See also* Swan, Dying.

Sieglinde. In Richard Wagner's operas *The Ring of the Niebelung* (1869–76), Wotan's* daughter who becomes the mother of Siegfried* when, after her marriage to Hunding,* she runs away with and becomes the lover of her twin brother Siegmund.*

Siegmund. In Richard Wagner's operas *The Ring of the Niebelung* (1869–76), a son of Wotan* and a great hero who is killed by Wotan,* even though he has found a sword that guarantees victory in battle, after he commits incest with his twin sister Sieglinde* and fathers Siegfried.* *See also* Fricka.

Sigismonda. (1) In Boccaccio's *Decameron*, a princess of Salerno whose lover, her squire, was murdered by her father Tancred,* who sent her the lover's heart in a golden cup, whereupon she poisoned herself. (2) In Le Sage's novel *Gil Blas* (1715), a princess promised to Tancred.* She agrees to marry another when it appears that Tancred is also betrothed to another. She dies when her fiancé stabs her after he himself is stabbed by Tancred.

Sigurd. In Scandinavian mythology, a great hero, generally equivalent to Siegfried.*

Sikes, Bill. In Charles Dickens's novel *Oliver Twist* (1837), a violent, vicious criminal who brutally murders the faithful Nancy* and later accidentally hangs himself.

Silas. In the Bible, *Acts* xv, a man chosen by Paul* to travel with him through Syria and Cilicia. *Also called* Silvanus.

Silenus. In Roman legend, both the teacher and follower of Bacchus;* he is usually shown as an extremely fat and jolly old man with a crown of flowers, always drunk, and often riding an ass.

Silvanus. (1) In Roman mythology, a rural god of the woods, half man, half goat, sometimes confused with Silenus* and/or the Fauns* and Satyrs.* (2) *See* Silas.

Silver. *See* Lone Ranger, The.

Silver, Long John. In R. L. Stevenson's novel *Treasure Island* (1883), the pirate chief with a wooden leg and a parrot on his shoulder. *See also* Hawkins, Jim.

Silver, Mattie. *See* Mattie.

Silver, Thirty Pieces of. *See* Judas.

Silvia. (1) In Roman legend, the mother of Romulus and Remus.* (2) In Shakespeare's play *Two Gentlemen of Verona* (1594), a paragon of beauty, known primarily from the song "Who is Silvia?" included in the play and set by numerous composers, most notably Schubert.

Simeon. (1) In the Bible, *Genesis,* a son of Jacob* and Leah* and the father of one of the twelve tribes of Israel.* (2) In the Bible, *Luke* ii, a devout man who was the first to recognize the child Jesus* as the Messiah* and who then died in peace, saying "now lettest thou thy servant depart in peace . . . " (3) A name sometimes used for Peter* the Apostle. *See also* Simon.

Simeon Stylites, St. Historically, a hermit-saint (d. 459) who lived thirty-seven years alone on top of various pillars.

Simeonov-Pishchik. In Anton Chekhov's play *The Cherry Orchard* (1904), the neighboring landowner who is constantly trying to borrow money to pay off previous loans.

Simon. (1) A name sometimes used for Peter* the Apostle. (2) In the Bible, Simon the Canaanite or the Zealot, also one of the twelve Apostles.* (3) In the Bible, *Matthew* xxvii, a man who was forced to carry the cross for Jesus,* usually called Simon the Cyrene or Cyrenian. (4) In the Bible, *Acts* viii, a magician who tried to buy from Peter the power to pass the Holy Ghost to others by the laying on of hands. Tradition calls him Simon Magus, and from his activity is named the sin of simony.

Simon, Simple. In the nursery rhyme, the simpleton who met the pieman on the way to the fair.

Simon Bar Jonah. Peter* the Apostle.

Simon Peter. Peter* the Apostle.

Simple, Peter. In Captain Marryat's novel *Peter Simple* (1834), an innocent, lively young man, thought to be a simpleton, who goes to sea and becomes a gallant officer.

Simplicissimus, Simplicius. In Grimmelshausen's novel *Simplicissimus* (1669), a hero who, after being kidnapped by pillaging soldiers during the Thirty Years War, learns to live by his wits and personal ability, becoming a successful soldier, hunter, and robber as needed until, at last, he is able to live a secluded life of piety.

Sin, Ah. *See* Ah Sin.

Sinai, Mt. In the Bible, *Exodus,* the mountain in the desert on which Moses* spoke to God and received the Ten Commandments.*

Sinbad. In *The Arabian Nights,* a great sailor with many adventures, most notably the discovery of an island that is the back of a monster, the meeting with the giant bird the Roc,* and with the Old Man of the Sea.*

Sindbad. *See* Sinbad.

Sinon. In Virgil's *Aeneid* and in Homer's *Odyssey,* the Greek who, after letting himself be captured, convinced the Trojans to bring in the Trojan Horse.*

Sirens. In Greek legend, three seductive creatures, part bird and part woman, whose beautiful singing lured passing sailors to their deaths on the rocks. In Homer's *Odyssey,* Odysseus* escapes them by plugging the ears of his men and lashing himself to the mast so that he cannot respond.

Sirius. In Greek legend, Orion's* dog, placed in the heavens as the brightest star visible.

Sisera. In the Bible, *Judges* iv, the commander of an army that is defeated by the Israelites under the leadership of Deborah;* when he seeks refuge in the tent of Jael,* she drives a nail through his temple.

Sissy. *See* Jupe, Sissy.

Sister Carrie. *See* Carrie.

Sisyphus. In Greek mythology, a king who, as a result of a number of particularly gross crimes, even by mythology's standards, was sentenced by Zeus* to roll a great stone up a hill forever, since the weight of the stone always forced it to roll back down just before he reached the top. In some versions, his crime was an attempt to chain up Death. His story became a major illustration of modern existentialist philosophy through Camus's *The Myth of Sisyphus* (1942). He is also noted for foiling Autolycus's* attempt to steal his cattle by branding them on the bottom of their hooves. *See also* Merope.

Siva. *See* Shiva.

Skeggs, Miss. In Oliver Goldsmith's novel *The Vicar of Wakefield* (1766), a strikingly vulgar woman who pretends to gentility and aristocratic connections.

Skimpole. In Charles Dickens's novel *Bleak House* (1852), the middle-aged man who, as he regularly protests "I am a child," lives completely on the generosity and hospitality of his friends. He has three daughters, said to represent three virtues—Arethusa (beauty), Laura (sentiment), and Kitty (comedy)—whom he neglects. *See also* Jarndyce.

Skywalker, Luke. In several movies, beginning with *Star Wars* (1977), a youthful space pilot and fighter, attractive and pure of heart.

Sleeping Beauty. In the fairy tale, a beautiful princess who is put to sleep for a hundred years along with everyone in her castle and who can be awakened only by the kiss of a prince who can find his way through the overgrowth to her.

Slick, Aaron. In Beale Cormack's play *Aaron Slick from Punkin Crick* (1919), a hillbilly who goes to the big city, manages to avoid the clutches of the Woman in Red,* and out-slicks the city slickers; he was long an incredibly popular and positive character in rural America but was seen by urban audiences as the nadir of provincial taste.

Slick, Sam. In numerous stories by Thomas Haliburton (beg. 1837), a shrewd Yankee peddler.

Slop, Dr. In Laurence Sterne's novel *Tristram Shandy* (1759), the bungling doctor who crushes the baby Tristram Shandy's* nose with his forceps.

Slope, Rev. In Anthony Trollope's novel *Barchester Towers* (1857), a slimy, hypocritical, politically conniving clergyman.

Sloppy. In Charles Dickens's novel *Our Mutual Friend* (1864), a foundling adopted by the Boffins* and much admired by them for his ability to read the papers and "do the Police in different voices."

Sludge, Dickie. In Walter Scott's novel *Kenilworth* (1821), a mischievous friend, ugly but clever. *Also called* Flibbertigibbet.

Sludge, Mr. In Robert Browning's poem *Mr. Sludge, the 'Medium'* (1864), a fraudulent spiritualist.

Sly, Christopher. *See* Christopher Sly.

Slyme, Chevy. In Charles Dickens's novel *Martin Chuzzlewit* (1843), the dubious fellow with a talent for always being just around the corner. *See also* Tigg, Montague.

Small, Lennie. *See* Lennie.

Smart, Maxwell. In the American television series "Get Smart" (1965–70), an inept spy whose consistent bumbling invariably defeated the evil forces of KAOS; he had several catch-phrases, perhaps the most notable being, "Would you believe . . . ?"

Smee. In J. M. Barrie's play *Peter Pan* (1904), the cuddly, baldheaded pirate with a soft heart.

Smerdyakov. In Dostoevsky's novel *The Brothers Karamazov* (1880), the illegitimate son, a sadistic half-wit, who is eventually encouraged by one of his half-brothers to murder his father Karamazov;* he then cannot live with his guilt and kills himself.

Smike. In Charles Dickens's novel *Nicholas Nickleby* (1838), the painfully starved and retarded boy who runs away from Dotheboys Hall* and finds sanctuary and peace with Nicholas Nickleby.* *See also* Squeers.

Smiley, George. In several novels by John Le Carré, most notably *Tinker, Tailor, Soldier, Spy* (1974), the bland but meticulous spy brought out of retirement to head the British Secret Service; notable for both his complex plans and his complex personality.

Smith, Mr. (1) In common usage, a perfectly bland, anonymous name used when a typical common person is denoted or when an alias is needed for minor peccadilloes, such as signing hotel registers when in the company of a woman not one's wife. (2) In the movie *Mr. Smith Goes to Washington* (1939), the politically naive American legislator who is almost destroyed by dirty politics, but whose basic integrity eventually comes to his rescue.

Smith, Harriet. In Jane Austen's novel *Emma* (1816), a young, simple, pretty, but illegitimate girl; Emma* befriends her and gives her ideas above her station, particularly about potential husbands.

Smith, John. Historically, an English explorer (d. 1631) and founder of a 1606 colony in Virginia; in his own and other writings, he is a romantic fictionalized adventurer, most noted for his rescue from death by the intervention and love of the Indian princess Pocahontas.*

Smith, Nayland. In numerous novels by Sax Rohmer (beg. 1913), the implacable foe of Fu Manchu* and protector of the British way of life against the "yellow peril."

Smith, Septimus. In Virginia Woolf's novel *Mrs. Dalloway* (1925), an extremely sensitive poet and war casualty who cannot adjust to the postwar world or accept love without suspecting ulterior motives and who ultimately kills himself.

Smith, Wayland. In Walter Scott's novel *Kenilworth* (1821), the hero's hardy friend and servant, a skilled smith and alchemist. *See also* Tressilian; Wieland.

Smith, Winston. In George Orwell's novel *1984* (1949), a minor civil servant who takes a mistress illegally and tries to become an individual but is discovered and forced to conform. *See also* Big Brother.

Snake. *See* Serpent.

Snap, Laetitia. In Henry Fielding's novel *Jonathan Wild* (1743), a pickpocket, card sharp, and unfaithful wife, who is eventually hanged.

Snark. In Lewis Carroll's poem *The Hunting of the Snark* (1876), an animal of an obscure nature hunted with no success. *See also* Boojum.

Sneerwell, Lady. In R. B. Sheridan's play *The School for Scandal* (1777), a particularly venomous gossip and ruiner of other women's reputations.

Snevellici. In Charles Dickens's novel *Nicholas Nickleby* (1838), a family of actors, consisting of Mr., Mrs., and Miss, who join Crummles's* company.

Snodgrass. In Charles Dickens's novel *The Pickwick Papers* (1836), Pickwick's* poetic companion who never gets around to writing any poems.

Snoopy. In the American newspaper cartoon *Peanuts* (beg. 1950), a vivacious beagle belonging to Charlie Brown,* known for his ability to play shortstop as well as for a vivid imagination that allows him to impersonate various other characters, most notably "the World War I Flying Ace."

Snopes. In several novels and stories by William Faulkner, such as *The Hamlet* (1940) and *The Town* (1957), a clan that comes to personify the degeneracy and rapacity of the American South in the twentieth century. Most notable of these is **Flem**, a cunning, silent, ruthless, single-minded businessman who cheats his way to economic and political power yet still seems to be almost without personality. His father **Abner** is a crooked horse trader and arsonist. Other family members include **Isaac**, who makes love to a cow, a spectacle to which Flem sells tickets; **Mink**, a convicted murderer; and **Eck**, who is drummed out of the family for suggesting that the dishes served in their restaurant ought to contain the food shown on the menu. *See also* Stevens; Varner.

Snout. In Shakespeare's play *A Midsummer Night's Dream* (1595), a tinker who plays the Wall in the "Pyramus and Thisbe"* play.

Snow White. In the fairy tale, and particularly in the movie *Snow White and the Seven Dwarfs* (1937), a beautiful princess who is threatened by the queen, who is jealous of her beauty; she hides with the Seven Dwarfs,* is poisoned by the queen with an apple, and at last is brought back to life by the kiss of a prince.

Snubbin. In Charles Dickens's novel *Pickwick Papers* (1836), the eloquent barrister who loses Pickwick's* case for breach of promise in spite of an eminence that makes him all but unapproachable. *See also* Buzfuz; Dodson and Fogg.

Snug. In Shakespeare's play *A Midsummer Night's Dream* (1595), the gentle joiner who plays the cowardly lion in the "Pyramus and Thisbe"* play.

Soames. *See* Forsyte.

Socrates. Historically, a Greek philosopher (d. 399 B.C.); for many, he is synonymous with philosophy itself. He is known primarily through the writings of Plato, in which he teaches by asking questions and thus leading the other person to reach the conclusion and convince himself—a process known as the "Socratic method." In Plato's *Apology*, Socrates was tried for impiety, was convicted, and was executed by being given hemlock to drink, which is often cited to illustrate the unwillingness of the majority to accept Truth. *See also* Xantippe.

Sodom. In the Bible, *Genesis* xviii-xix, one of the "cities of the plain" in which Lot* lived; God warned Lot* to leave and not to look back; Lot's wife did look back and was turned into a pillar of salt. There were actually five cities of the plain (ch. xiv), but usage generally speaks only of Sodom and Gomorrah, which were the only two specifically named in the accounts of their destruction. Both were noted for their extreme sinfulness, for not even twenty righteous men could be found to prevent their destruction; "sodomy" is derived from actions supposed to have been common there.

Sofya. (1) *See* Sonya. (2) *See also* Sophia; Sophie; Sophy.

Sol. In Roman mythology, the sun, generally equivalent to Helios.*

Solness. In Henrik Ibsen's play *The Master Builder* (1892), a mature, successful builder who has become fearful of both heights and the younger generation and is killed when, encouraged by Hilda Wangel,* he climbs a tower to hang a wreath and falls.

Solomon. In the Bible, *I Kings, I & II Chronicles,* the son of David* and Bathsheba,* ruler of a stable Israel,* builder of the Temple, and a king renowned for his wisdom and justice. This is most often demonstrated in the case in which two women claim the same baby; Solomon offers to cut it in half, thereby revealing the true mother when she renounces her claim in order to keep the child safe. He was also said to have had 1,000 wives and concubines and to have authored the sensual verses of the *Song of Solomon. See also* Adonijah; Jedediah; Rehoboam; Sheba, Queen of.

Solon. In Greek legend, one of the Sages* and a lawgiver whose name is often given to any lawmaker.

Solveig. In Henrik Ibsen's play *Peer Gynt* (1867), Peer Gynt's* ever-faithful sweetheart—a figure of pure, eternal love.

Solyony. In Anton Chekhov's play *Three Sisters* (1901), the tense, mysterious captain who taunts Tusenbach* and finally kills him in a duel.

Soma. (1) In Hindu mythology, the god of a plant with intoxicating juice sometimes used in religious ceremonies. (2) In Aldous Huxley's novel *Brave New World* (1932), the miracle drug used to keep the populace calm and entertained.

Somnus. In Roman mythology, the god of sleep, generally equivalent to Hypnos.*

Sonia. *See* Sonya.

Sonya. (1) In Tolstoy's novel *War and Peace* (1865), the affectionate cousin who releases Nikolai Rostov* from a childhood vow so that he can marry more advantageously. *See also* Natasha. (2) In Dostoevsky's novel *Crime and Punishment* (1866), the trusting prostitute who nurses Raskolnikov,* urges him to surrender to the police, and then follows him to Siberia, a paragon of devotion and pure spirit. *Also called* Sofya Marmaledova. (3) In Anton Chekhov's play *Uncle Vanya* (1899), Serebryakov's* daughter and Vanya's* niece, a plain girl who has lived on the farm and who loves Astrov,* the local doctor, in vain; she is noted for her faith in the healing value of work.

Sooner. In American usage, a native of Oklahoma, from the people who got to their claims sooner than was legal in the great Oklahoma land rush.

Sophia. (1) See Western. (2) *See also* Sofya; Sophie; Sophy.

Sophie. (1) In Jean-Jacques Rousseau's *Émile* (1762), the natural woman. *See also* Émile. (2) In Richard Strauss's opera *Der Rosenkavalier* (1911), the beautiful young maiden who falls in love with Octavian* when he delivers the betrothal rose from the Baron Ochs.* (3) *See also* Sofya; Sophia; Sophy.

Sophrona. The name used by Terence for a childhood nurse in many of his plays.

Sophronia. (1) In Tasso's *Jerusalem Delivered* (1581), the beautiful Christian maiden who sacrifices herself to save the other Christians from massacre. (2) *See* Lammle; Sphynx, Sophronia.

Sophy. (1) *See* Crewler; Primrose. (2) *See also* Sofya; Sophia; Sophie.

Sorel, Julien. In Stendhal's novel *The Red and the Black* (1830), an intelligent, proud, and extremely ambitious young man who after shrewdly building a career loses it in a fit of jealousy by trying to murder his mistress; long accepted as a devastating portrait of the young man on the make in France during the Bourbon restoration. *See also* Mathilde; Renal.

Sorrel, Hester. *See* Hetty.

Sorrell. In Warwick Deeping's novel *Sorrell and Son* (1926), a loving and self-sacrificing father who takes a menial job so that his son may have the education to become a success and, unusual in literature, manages to retain the love and respect of his son while doing so.

Souvarine. In Émile Zola's novel *Germinal* (1885), an exiled Russian and a nihilist mine worker and labor organizer; when the strike he engineers fails, he floods the mine. *See also* Étienne.

Sower. In the Bible, *Matthew* xiii, a parable told by Jesus:* A sower went into the fields to sow, but some of the seeds fell by the wayside, where they were eaten by birds; some on rocks, where they could not put down roots; some among thorns, where they were choked; and only some fell on good earth, where they grew and bore fruit.

Sowerberry. In Charles Dickens's novel *Oliver Twist* (1837), a meek undertaker who hires Oliver Twist* to be a paid mourner because Oliver is so sickly. **Mrs. Sowerberry** is a shrew.

Spade, Sam. In Dashiell Hammett's novel *The Maltese Falcon* (1930), the quintessential hard-boiled private detective.

Sparafucile. In Verdi's opera *Rigoletto* (1851), the professional assassin hired by Rigoletto* to kill the seducer Duke of Mantua* but who accidentally kills the innocent Gilda* instead.

Sparkish. In William Wycherley's play *The Country Wife* (1673), a boorish fool, duped by all, who nevertheless insists he is a wit.

Sparkler, Edmund. In Charles Dickens's novel *Little Dorrit* (1855), an army officer whose brains were frozen in Canada when he was born, at no serious detriment to his career.

Sparsit, Mrs. In Charles Dickens's novel *Hard Times* (1854), a pretentious housekeeper with a closed mind who intrigues and proves Bounderby* is not really a self-made man.

Spartae. In Greek legend, the men who grew from the teeth of the dragon killed by Cadmus,* all but five of whom were killed when they attacked each other after Cadmus threw a stone in their midst; the five remaining joined Cadmus and helped to found Thebes.

Spartan. Historically, a resident of Sparta, one of the principal city-states of ancient Greece and the traditional enemy of Athens. Sparta eventually triumphed in the long Peloponnesian War. Life there was tightly regimented, and all Spartans were raised communally and taught to live without luxury or even minimal comfort and to devote their lives to military skills, with the result that such a life is still called "a Spartan existence." Symptomatic of the ideal is the legend of the Spartan boy who hid a stolen fox inside his tunic and let the fox eat his entrails rather than cry out in pain.

Speed. In Shakespeare's play *Two Gentlemen of Verona* (1594), an exuberant, intelligent, and extremely long-winded servant.

Spenlow. In Charles Dickens's novel *David Copperfield* (1849), a lawyer with whom David Copperfield* studies; he is noted for claiming that all unpleasant decisions are caused by the intransigence of his partner and for being a specialist in wills who dies without a will himself. For his daughter, *see* Dora.

Spens, Patrick. In a British folksong, a great sailor who is drowned when ordered by the king to go to sea against his better judgement.

Sphinx. (1) In Greek legend and most notably in Sophocles's *Oedipus Rex,* a monster with the head and breasts of a woman, the wings of a bird, the body of a dog, and the paws of a lion; it threatened Thebes by posing an unsolvable riddle ("What walks on four legs in the morning, two at noon, and three in the evening?") and by killing all who tried but could not answer it. Creon* promised both the crown and Jocasta* to the man who solved it and rid Thebes of the monster. Oedipus* solved the riddle (man—as baby, a man, and with a cane), and the Sphinx killed itself. (2) In Egyptian mythology, a god, half man, half lion, whose great monument is still seen along the Nile. In prehistory, the two may be related; in most popular usage, the two are often mixed together, as in "the riddle of the Sphinx" or "the silent Sphinx," both of which usually refer to the Egyptian statue.

Sphynx, Sophronia. In Charles Dickens's novel *The Old Curiosity Shop* (1841), the servant girl who steals food to stay alive under the Brass* family's mistreatment and who runs away to care for Dick Swiveler,* in return for which he educates her, comes to love her, and marries her.

Spina. In Ignazio Silone's novel *Bread and Wine* (1937), a revolutionary who wanders through Fascist Italy disguised as a priest, remaining faithful to his ideals despite his continuous disappointments and failures. *See also* Benedetto, Don.

Spirit of '76. In a painting by A. M. Willard (1876), three American revolutionaries of various ages and wounds marching with drums and fife under an American flag.

Spock, Mr. In the American television series "Star Trek" (1966–69), the lieutenant of the space ship, a creature part human, part alien, who had no emotions but approached all situations with pure logic; he was identified by his pointed ears.

Sponge, Soapey. In Robert Surtees's novel *Mr. Sponge's Sporting Tour* (1853), an uncouth Cockney sportsman who meets a number of comic adventures due to his ignorance of the social customs of fox hunting; he later appears in *Mr. Facey Romford's Hounds* (1865) as a cheat who runs away to Australia, where he becomes a wealthy businessman.

Sportin' Life. In Dubose Heyward's novel *Porgy* (1925) and especially in George Gershwin's opera *Porgy and Bess* (1935), the flashy drug ("happy dust") dealer who lures Bess* away to New York; he is most memorable for his humorous cynicism as expressed in "It Ain't Necessarily So."

Spot. *See* Dick and Jane.

Sprat, Jack. In the nursery rhyme, the skinny man who "could eat no fat," and whose fat wife "could eat no lean."

Square. In Henry Fielding's novel *Tom Jones* (1749), a philosopher engaged in endless debate with Thwackum,* but whose hypocrisy helps to cause Tom Jones's* expulsion from home. *See also* Allworthy, Squire.

Squeers. In Charles Dickens's novel *Nicholas Nickleby* (1838), **Wackford** is the cruel and crude proprietor of Dotheboys Hall,* a "school" that is appallingly brutal and mean, where he primarily mistreats and imprisons unwanted children rather than teaching them. **Mrs. Squeers** is equally cruel, and she is particularly detested for her force-feeding of brimstone. His daughter **Fanny** is a spiteful shrew who pretends to beauty and social prominence. *See also* Nickleby; Smike.

Squire. Historically, a boy who served a knight while he himself was a knight-in-training. Thus, squires often appear in stories concerning knights, and one such tells the incomplete story in Chaucer's *Canterbury Tales* of the princess who can understand the language of the birds. It was also a common literary device for a young woman in love to disguise herself as a squire in order to follow and be with the knight she loved, such as Constance* in Walter Scott's *Marmion*. In more recent English usage, however, the term is often applied to any country gentleman or notable in village life.

Stackpole, Henrietta. In Henry James's novel *The Portrait of a Lady* (1881), a female American journalist of independent mind and manner who seeks the sensations of European travel but disapproves of everything not American.

Stage Manager, The. In Thornton Wilder's play *Our Town* (1938), the genial narrator of the action, noted for his pantomime ice-cream counter and his interruptions of the action for philosophical comment.

Stalky. In Rudyard Kipling's stories *Stalky & Co.* (1899), the ingenious prankster schoolboy, absolutely honorable at heart—an epitome of English boys' stories.

Standish, Miles. Historically, the military commander (d. 1656) of the colony in Massachusetts; he is most famous from Henry Wadsworth Longfellow's poem *The Courtship of Miles Standish* (1858), for the shyness that causes him to send John Alden* to court Priscilla* for him.

Stanhope, Capt. In R. C. Sherriff's play *Journey's End* (1929), the commander of a small British unit in the World War I trenches, sustained primarily by his cynicism and drinking and by the strange desperate unity of men trapped together in hellish circumstances; for many, he is the epitome of the British officer's experience in that war.

Stanley. *See* Kowalski.

Stanley, Major General. In Gilbert and Sullivan's operetta *The Pirates of Penzance* (1879), the "very model of a modern major general," who knows all kinds of scientific information but has never actually commanded troops in battle. For his daughter, *see* Mabel.

Starbuck. (1) In Herman Melville's novel *Moby-Dick* (1851), the first mate, conscientious and superstitious, who has much argument with his conscience about taking action to stop Ahab* from endangering the ship. *See also* Moby Dick; Stubb. (2) In N. Richard Nash's play *The Rainmaker* (1954), a flamboyant con man and seducer.

Stark, Willie. In Robert Penn Warren's novel *All the King's Men* (1946), a demogogic American politician who builds his power on his ruthlessness and his popular image as a poor, ignorant, average man; he is eventually assassinated.

Starveling. In Shakespeare's play *A Midsummer Night's Dream* (1595), the slow-witted tailor who plays Moonshine in the ''Pyramus and Thisbe''* play.

Stations of the Cross. In Catholic usage, the fourteen stages of Christ's* journey to the Crucifixion,* often depicted in Christian art: He is condemned; He takes up the cross; He stumbles under the cross; He meets Mary;* Simon* of Cyrene takes the cross; Veronica* wipes His face; He falls a second time; He speaks to the women of Jerusalem;* He falls a third time; He is stripped; He is nailed to the cross; He dies; He is taken down; and He is laid in the tomb.

Staunton. The real name of Geordie Robertson.*

Stavrogin. In Dostoevsky's novel *The Possessed* (1867), the leader of a revolutionary socialist cell—a complex mixture of the cruel, the sensual, and the sensitive—married to the weak-minded cripple Marya,* whom he eventually has murdered, meanwhile ignoring a mistress carrying his child and seducing a respectable young woman. He seems primarily motivated by boredom and moral sterility, yet, after murdering Shatov,* he commits suicide. His mother **Varvara** is an unsentimental autocrat who spoils her son. *See also* Drozdov; Verhovensky.

Steed, John. In the British television series ''The Avengers'' (beg. 1961), a super-spy and crime fighter who also epitomized gentlemanly British elegance and savoir faire. *See also* Peel, Mrs.

Steele, Lucy. In Jane Austen's *Sense and Sensibility* (1811), a vulgar and mercenary young woman secretly engaged to Edward Ferrars;* when he is disinherited, she dumps him for his now wealthy brother.

Steerforth. In Charles Dickens's *David Copperfield* (1849), a handsome, spoiled, attractive young man whose pleasant exterior hides a devious and sensual nature. When Copperfield,* who has been fascinated by him since they were together at school, introduces him to Little Em'ly,* he seduces her and then abandons her in Italy. He drowns in a storm at sea. *See also* Peggotty; Dartle, Rosa; Littimer.

Steinbock. In Balzac's novel *Cousin Bette* (1847), a Polish count and artist saved from suicide by Bette.* In spite of her possessive love for him, he marries Hortense Hulot,* thereby motivating Bette's complex and subtle campaign of revenge, which includes his seduction by Mme. Marneffe* and destroys his own creativity.

Stella. (1) In Philip Sidney's poems *Astrophel and Stella* (1591), the idealized, beautiful woman loved by Astrophel.* (2) *See* Kowalski.

Stentor. In Homer's *Iliad,* a Greek with a voice as loud as 50 normal men.

Stephano. In Shakespeare's play *The Tempest* (1611), a drunken butler who concocts a rebellion against Prospero* but is foiled by his own drunkenness. *See also* Caliban; Trinculo.

Stephen, St. (1) In the Bible, *Acts,* one of the seven deacons of the Church and the first Christian martyr; he was stoned to death. His day is December 26. (2) Historically, king (d. 1038) and patron saint of Hungary, who was canonized for his efforts to bring Christianity there; his day is August 16.

Steppenwolf. *See* Haller, Harry.

Stevens. In several novels by William Faulkner, most notably *Intruder in the Dust* (1948) and *The Town* (1957), **Gavin** is a gentlemanly lawyer committed more to justice than to the law but whose personal nature often makes him ineffectual, even in his love for Eula Varner.* His nephew **Gowan** is an irresponsible student whose carelessness leads to the kidnapping of Temple Drake* in *Sanctuary* (1931).

Steyne, Marquis of. In William Makepeace Thackeray's novel *Vanity Fair* (1847), the haughty Lord of the King's Powder Closet who is easily seduced by Becky Sharp.*

Stiggins, Rev. In Charles Dickens's *Pickwick Papers* (1836), a hypocritical alcoholic clergyman who bilks the gullible Mrs. Weller.*

Stockmann. In Henrik Ibsen's play *An Enemy of the People* (1883), **Thomas** is a crusading reformist doctor who tries to close the polluted baths that provide the tourist income of his town and is attacked and ostracized by most, including his brother **Peter** the mayor, while supported only by **Petra**, his earnest daughter, and his wife, a weak woman who is easily swayed.

Stone, Jabez. In Stephen Vincent Benét's story *The Devil and Daniel Webster* (1938), a New Hampshire farmer who sells his soul to the Devil* and is rescued from the contract by the legal skills of Daniel Webster.*

Stooges, Three. In innumerable short movies (beg. 1930), three amazingly stupid and exceedingly violent comic friends, originally **Larry**, with wild frizzled hair; **Curly**, short, fat, and bald; and **Moe**, with a cereal bowl haircut, who acted as boss, claimed to have brains, and punched and poked his partners at every opportunity.

Straker, Henry. In G. B. Shaw's play *Man and Superman* (1903), the Cockney socialist chauffeur who sees himself as the wave of the future due to his knowledge of machinery.

Strangelove, Doctor. In the movie *Doctor Strangelove* (1963), an ex-Nazi and crippled super-scientist now working for the Americans but unable to lose his attachment to Hitler.*

Strenua. In Roman mythology, the goddess of strength and vigor.

Strephon. In Philip Sidney's romance *Arcadia* (1590), a shepherd lamenting the loss of his true love.

Strepsiades. In Aristophanes's play *The Clouds,* a stolid citizen who exhausts the patience of the philosopher Socrates* and eventually burns down Socrates's school. *See also* Phidippides.

Strickland, Charles. In Somerset Maugham's novel *The Moon and Sixpence* (1919), a broker who deserts his family in middle age to become a painter, revealing a genuine talent, and who then runs away to Tahiti to paint without the conflicts and distractions of society; he dies unrecognized but is discovered posthumously.

Strife. In Greek mythology, the son of Eris;* also, sometimes a name for Eris.

Strong, Dr. In Charles Dickens's novel *David Copperfield* (1849), the amiable dictionary writer and headmaster of David Copperfield's* school, who dotes on his much younger wife. She is wrongly assumed by all observers to be having an affair with her cousin.

Struldbrugs. In Jonathan Swift's novel *Gulliver's Travels* (1726), a race given eternal life, which is also accompanied by eternal aging, so that they are the most miserable creatures Gulliver* meets in all his travels.

Struwwelpeter. In Heinrich Hoffman's stories *Struwwelpeter* (1847), a boy who came to a ghastly end because he refused to cut his hair or his nails; the name is sometimes used as a representative of all the heavily moralistic tales of children who do not do as their parents say.

Stuart, Mary. *See* Mary, Queen of Scots.

Stubb. In Herman Melville's novel *Moby-Dick* (1851), the happy-go-lucky second mate, rarely seen without his pipe.

Stubbs, Mr. In Robert Surtees's stories *Jorrock's Jaunts and Jollities* (1838), a footloose Yorkshire sportsman who somehow manages to always get others to pay the bill.

Student Prince. In Sigmund Romberg's operetta *The Student Prince* (1924), a middle European prince who falls in love with a barmaid but eventually leaves her in favor of the duties of the kingdom; often used to signify the entire school of romantic operetta.

Stymphalides. In Greek legend, long-legged man-eating birds with bronze claws, which were killed by Heracles* as part of his twelve labors.

Styx. In Greek mythology, a daughter of Oceanus.* She was the first ally of Zeus* when he overthrew the Titans,* for which he rewarded her by making her the goddess by whom one swore inviolable oaths. In a manner never logically explained, her name came to be applied to the river around Hades* across which all the dead had to be ferried by Charon.*

Suada. In Roman mythology, the goddess of persuasion.

Subtle. In Ben Jonson's play *The Alchemist* (1610), the alchemist, a crook who cheats his public through jargon and their own gullibility and greed. *See also* Common, Dol; Face.

Sue Ellen. *See* Ewing.

Suitors. *See* Penelope.

Sullen. In George Farquhar's play *The Beaux' Stratagem* (1707), a rude, drunken, and stupid countryman of property who tries to neither speak nor do anything. **Mrs. Sullen** has an affair with Archer* and, through fortuitous circumstances, is allowed to divorce Sullen in order to marry Archer.

Summanus. In Roman mythology, the god of thunderstorms.

Summerson, Esther. In Charles Dickens's novel *Bleak House* (1852), the apparent orphan, later revealed to be the illegitimate daughter of Lady Dedlock,* and the narrator of part of the story who joins John Jarndyce's* household. Gentle, kind, and honorable, she is proposed to by Guppy,* who withdraws the offer after she is scarred by smallpox, and then by Jarndyce, who withdraws the offer when he realizes she is in love with a young doctor.

Summoner. In Chaucer's *Canterbury Tales,* the pilgrim who tells the story of the greedy friar who so besieges a sick man that the patient tells him a great treasure is hidden in the bed and then defecates on the friar's hand when he reaches for it. In the Friar's Tale, a summoner is sent to Hell* for attempting to extort a gift from a widow.

Sun King. *See* Louis XIV.*

Superman. In the American cartoon *Superman* (beg. 1938), a superhero from another planet, the defender of "truth, justice, and the American way," able to fly and invulnerable except when in contact with the mysterious element Kryptonite. He is disguised as the "mild-mannered reporter" Clark Kent.

Surface. In R. B. Sheridan's play *The School for Scandal* (1777), **Charles** is the worthy young man whose apparent extravagance is the result of his kind heart and generosity; his brother **Joseph**, apparently more respectable, is eventually shown to be a scheming hypocrite in the famous screen scene with the Teazles.* Their uncle **Oliver** assumes several disguises to test their worthiness.

Surly, Pertinax. In Ben Jonson's play *The Alchemist* (1610), a sour skeptic whose skepticism is the means by which he is duped.

Susanna. (1) In the Bible, in the Apocrypha, *Susanna,* a beautiful woman whose bath was observed by two lustful elders who, when she repelled their advances, accused her of adultery, of which she was acquitted due to the wisdom and justice of the judge Daniel.* (2) In Beaumarchais's play (1784) and in Mozart's opera (1786) *The Marriage of Figaro,* Figaro's* betrothed, an intelligent and honorable maid pursued by Count Almaviva.* She tricks the count in order to protect both her marriage and his. (3) In Stephen Foster's song *Oh, Susanna* (1847), the true love that the singer had come from Alabama with a banjo on his knee to see.

Sutpen. In William Faulkner's novel *Absalom, Absalom!* (1936), a family embodying the complex tragedy of the Old South. **Thomas**, the father, is a man of implacable will as well as a bigamist with a part-Negro wife in Haiti. He entertains himself in his mansion by either sleeping with or wrestling with his slaves. He is killed by an outraged grandfather of one of his illegitimate children. **Henry**, the son, is sensitive and honorable and idolizes his best friend in the Civil War, Charles Bon.* Henry is willing to allow Charles to marry his sister Judith even after discovering Charles is his half-brother; however, he murders Charles to prevent the marriage when he learns that Charles is part Negro. **Judith** is a sensual young woman who is nonetheless faithful to Charles, vowing spinsterhood after his death and dying from smallpox caught while nursing Charles's octoroon mistress. Thomas's wife **Ellen** is a meek, helpless, sensitive example of idealized Southern womanhood trapped in her own upbringing.

Suzanne. *See* Susanna.

Svengali. In George du Maurier's novel *Trilby* (1894), a sinister teacher who transforms the tone-deaf artist's model Trilby* into a renowned singer by keeping her under his hypnotic power.

Swan, Dying. In the ballet *Le Cygne* (1905), the death scene of a swan* which, as danced by Pavlova,* came to epitomize for many both the beautiful and the ludicrous aspects of ballet itself.

Swanhild. In Norse legend, the daughter of Sigurd* who falsely accuses Randver of rape, for which he is executed by his own father, and who is then herself executed by being trampled by horses in the main gate of the castle.

Swanilda. In the ballet *Coppélia* (1870), the village girl who impersonates the doll Coppélia* in order to win back her lover.

Swann. In Marcel Proust's *Remembrance of Things Past* (1913–27), a sensitive and wealthy Parisian Jewish broker who moves in the best society until he falls in love with the stupid and unfaithful courtesan Odette,* whom he marries, despite the ridicule resulting from his jealousy and against his own intellectual judgement, gradually drifting down with her into bourgeois society and attitudes and a comfortable but essentially meaningless life. *See also* Charlus; Gilberte; Guermantes; Verdurin; Vinteuil.

Swan Queen. *See* Odette.

Swithin, St. Historically, a bishop of Winchester (d. 862), whose day is July 15; rain on this day in England is said to promise 40 more days of rain.

Swiveler, Dick. In Charles Dickens's novel *The Old Curiosity Shop* (1841), a conniver whose love for the servant girl Sophronia Sphynx* reforms him.

Sycorax. In Shakespeare's play *The Tempest* (1611), the now dead witch and mother of Caliban.*

Sylvia. *See* Silvia.

Sylph. In European legend, a spirit of the air, almost always a virginal young woman. *See also* Wilis.

Sylphide. In the ballet *La Sylphide* (1832), a spirit woman who falls in love with a mortal; visually defined by her diaphanous, multilayered, ankle-length, white dress synonymous for many with ballet itself.

Syrinx. In Greek legend, a nymph* loved by Pan* and transformed into the reed from which Pan fashioned his pipe.

T

Tabitha. (1) In the Bible, *Acts* ix, a woman of goodness and charity raised from the dead by Peter.* *Also called* Dorcas. (2) *See also* Bramble.

Tadeusz. In Adam Mickiewicz's poem *Pan Tadeusz* (1834), a young Polish nobleman whose attempt to marry leads to a war in which the Poles manage to defeat the Russians; the work is often noted as a major depiction of life among the Polish nobility in the last years of their independence.

Talbot. In Shakespeare's play *Henry VI, Part I* (1590), the general who leads the English forces against Joan of Arc.* He tries to send his son John away from the battle, but the son insists that he could not share his father's name if he did not share his father's dangers; both are killed, but Talbot's death scene is particularly noted.

Talents. In the Bible, *Matthew* xxv, a parable told by Jesus:* A man gave five talents (coins) to one servant, two to a second, and one to a third; the first two servants invested and multiplied their master's money, but the third buried his to be safe. When the master returned, he greeted the first two as "good and faithful servants," but the third was cast out, since "to him that hath shall be given."

Talos. In Greek legend, a nephew of Daedalus* whom the latter pushed off a tower in jealousy after he had invented the saw and compass; in Ovid's *Metamorphoses,* he is called Perdix.

Talthybius. In Homer's *Iliad,* Agamemnon's* herald who seems always to be given the most unpleasant messages and missions, such as sacrificing Iphigenia.* This continues in Euripides's play *The Trojan Women,* where, despite his distaste for the job, he must tell the women about their impending slavery and then kill Astyanax.*

Talus. *See* Talos.

Tamar. (1) In the Bible, *Genesis* xxxviii, the wife of Er who, after his death, was given to Onan,* who spilled his seed upon the ground rather than father children with her. After Onan's death, his father Judah* promised her to a younger son but did not fulfill the promise, so she disguised herself as a harlot and slept with Judah; when she became pregnant and was condemned to death, she revealed the father, and Judah saved her but "knew her again no more." (2) In the Bible, *II Samuel* xiii, the beautiful and innocent daughter of David,* raped by her half-brother Amnon* and avenged by her brother Absalom,* who murdered Amnon.

Tamburlaine. In Marlowe's play *Tamburlaine the Great* (1586), a shepherd who becomes an emperor in the Middle East, a ruthless ruler and warrior who kills women and children and even his own son, imprisons in a cage the emperor he conquers, has his chariot drawn by defeated kings, and relishes theatrical speech and posturing—a theatrically compelling villain. The play was also the introduction of iambic pentameter to the English stage, and many allusions are to the magnificent sound of *Tamburlaine*'s language rather than to the character.

Tamino. In Mozart's opera *The Magic Flute* (1791), the tenor hero who rescues the maiden Pamina* and then has his love purified by a mystical process. *See also* Papageno; Queen of the Night; Sarastro.

Tamora. In Shakespeare's play *Titus Andronicus* (1592), the barbarian queen who tries to avenge her son's death at the hands of Titus Andronicus* by arranging for the rape of Titus's daughter Lavinia,* but, in turn, is forced to eat her own children before being executed by Titus. *See also* Aaron; Chiron; Demetrius.

Tancred. (1) In Boccaccio's *Decameron,* Sigismonda's* father who kills her lover and then sends her his heart in a golden cup. (2) In Tasso's *Jerusalem Delivered* (1580), a noble Christian warrior in love with the pagan warrior queen Clorinda;* he kills her by accident in battle. *See also* Erminia; Rinaldo. (3) In Le Sage's novel *Gil Blas* (1715), a Sicilian prince who is tricked into deserting his true love Sigismonda* and who then kills Sigismonda's new fiancé, but not before the fiancé has also stabbed her.

Tanner, John. In G. B. Shaw's play *Man and Superman* (1903), a reluctant English Don Juan,* a revolutionary socialist with no illusions about the "natural" innocence or purity of women who flees to Spain to escape from Ann Whitefield,* who wants to marry him. He ultimately realizes that the "Life Force" is greater than he is and surrenders to marriage.

Tannhäuser. In German legend, a thirteenth-century minnesinger who spent seven years with Venus.* Finally, overcome by his conscience, he left Venusberg* and sought papal absolution, which was refused, whereupon he returned to Venus. Most common allusions will be to Richard Wagner's version of the story in his opera *Tannhäuser* (1845).

Tanqueray, Mrs. In A. W. Pinero's play *The Second Mrs. Tanqueray* (1893), a woman with a dubious sexual past who, marrying a widower, finds that her stepdaughter is engaged to her former lover. When she exposes him, she is in turn attacked by her stepdaughter. Recognizing that she has no socially acceptable position to live for, she kills herself.

Tansley. In Virginia Woolf's novel *To the Lighthouse* (1927), the boorish young man who contends that women are incapable of producing art.

Tantalus. In Greek legend, the father of Pelops* and Niobe.* He killed his son, cooked him, and tried to feed him to the gods, for which he was punished in Hades* by being placed near water or fruit which was always just out of reach. *See also* Niobe.

Tantamount. In Aldous Huxley's novel *Point Counter Point* (1928), **Hilda** is a malicious and promiscuous woman without conscience who toys with any men who amuse her. Her husband **Edward** is a scientist whose scientific attitudes make him a failure at all human relationships.

Tapley, Mark. In Charles Dickens's novel *Martin Chuzzlewit* (1843), a congenitally good-natured young man who seeks miserable situations so that he might find some credit in being good-natured in adversity. *See also* Chuzzlewit; Pecksniff.

Tappertit. In Charles Dickens's novel *Barnaby Rudge* (1841), an apprentice, a leader of the rioters, and a kidnapper who loses both his legs when he is shot. Set up as a bootblack by his former master, he marries, but his wife controls his moods by stealing his wooden legs whenever he tries to beat her.

Tar Baby. In Joel Chandler Harris's story *The Tar Baby* (1904), a doll made of tar by Br'er Fox. When Br'er Rabbit* sees it, it refuses to answer him, and he hits it, getting stuck in the tar, then getting his other legs stuck as he keeps hitting it to make it let go. In the 1960s and 1970s, it was a common metaphor for American involvement in the war in Vietnam.

Tara. (1) In Irish legend, the house of the great Irish Kings. (2) *See* O'Hara, Scarlett.

Tarpeia. In Roman legend, the daughter of a governor of Rome; she was bribed by Tatius of the Sabines to open the gates of the city. After successfully attacking, Tatius ironically repaid her by hurling the promised bracelet at her, followed by the shields of all his men, the force of which crushed her to death. She was buried under the Tarpeian rock, from which afterwards Roman criminals were often thrown to their deaths.

Tarquinius. *See* Lucretia.

Tarshish. *See* Jonah.

Tartarin. In Alphonse Daudet's novel *Tartarin of Tarascon* (1872), an exuberant dreamer of adventures who finds himself living one of them, going to Africa to hunt, where he has numerous accidents. He finally kills a circus lion, which allows him to return home as a successful great hunter.

Tartuffe. In Molière's play *Tartuffe* (1664), the quintessential religious hypocrite who uses his religious posturing to obtain the property of the sincere, wealthy Christian Orgon,* eventually even trying to take his wife Elmire* as well. *See also* Dorine.

Tarzan. In numerous books by Edgar Rice Burroughs, beginning with *Tarzan of the Apes* (1914), the Lord of the Jungle, a white man raised from babyhood by African apes. His numerous adventures showed him as the ideal man in a state of nature, able to commune with the animals around him, intelligent, resourceful, and naturally good. Numerous movie versions, however, altered Burroughs's characterization to make Tarzan illiterate, simple, and nearly monosyllabic, famous for his mighty yell, for swinging on vines, and for saying, "Me Tarzan, you Jane.*"

Tashtego. In Herman Melville's novel *Moby-Dick* (1851), the Indian harpooner who nails a giant bird to the mast of the ship as it sinks. *See also* Ahab; Ishmael; Moby Dick; Queequeg.

Tatiana. In Pushkin's poem *Eugene Onegin* (1833), the simple and pure country girl whom Eugene Onegin* rejects, only to be rejected by her when she is married to a wealthy man because she believes marriage more important than love; she is noted particularly for the youthful love letter she writes to Onegin.

Tattered Man, The. In Stephen Crane's novel *The Red Badge of Courage* (1895), a soldier encountered when Henry Fleming* has run away; he accompanies Jim Conklin* during his death and questions Henry about his wound.

Tattle. In William Congreve's play *Love For Love* (1695), the vain dandy who is known for his secrecy yet somehow always lets slip the names of his various female conquests; he is tricked into marrying the lascivious widow Mrs. Frail,* whom he detests. *See also* Prue, Miss.

Tattycoram. In Charles Dickens's novel *Little Dorrit* (1855), the childish nickname a maid is forced to use despite her distaste for it; she is perpetually ignored and unthinkingly insulted by the essentially kindly but self-centered Meagles* family she serves, until she runs away.

Taurus. The Bull, the second sign of the Zodiac.

Tawdry, Suky. In John Gay's play *The Beggar's Opera* (1728), one of the whores known by Macheath;* she is retained in Bertolt Brecht's version *The Threepenny Opera* (1928), but is noted primarily from her mention in the song "Mack the Knife" from that show. *See also* Diver, Jenny.

Tchebutykin. *See* Chebutykin.

Tchitchikov. *See* Chichikov.

Tearsheet, Doll. In Shakespeare's play *Henry IV, Part II* (1598), a frowsy whore. *See also* Falstaff.

Teazle. In R. B. Sheridan's play *The School for Scandal* (1777), **Sir Peter** is a bluff, gruff, and elderly cuckold who is treated with contempt by his younger wife, **Lady Teazle**, until she learns in the famous "screen scene" that her lover Joseph Surface* is contemptible and false.

Teddy. *See* Brewster; Roosevelt.

Telegin. In Anton Chekhov's play *Uncle Vanya* (1899), the sentimental and simple neighbor, an impoverished landowner, also called "Waffles" because of his pock marks. *See also* Vanya, Uncle.

Telegonus. In Greek legend, the son of Odysseus* and Circe.* Shipwrecked in Ithaca, he killed Odysseus,* whom he did not recognize, then married Penelope.*

Telemachus. In Greek legend, the son of Odysseus* and Penelope.* When his father pretended madness to avoid joining the Trojan War,* Telemachus was laid in the way of his plow, and Odysseus turned, thereby showing his sanity. In Homer's *Odyssey*, he is unable to help his mother with the suitors but he embarks on a search for his missing father; he comes home in time to recognize Odysseus and help him kill the suitors. *See also* Mentor.

Tell, William. A legendary Swiss hero who is supposed to have encouraged Swiss separation from Austria; he is most famous as a great crossbowman who safely shot an apple from his son's head. He is known primarily from the play by Schiller (1804) and the opera by Rossini (1829), in which he also kills the evil governor and sets the rebellion in motion. The overture to the opera is also known as the theme music for the Lone Ranger.*

Tellheim. In Lessing's play *Minna von Barnhelm* (1767), the extremely proud and honorable ex-soldier who gives money to his old sergeant but refuses all aid himself, even rejecting the help of Minna,* whom he loves, until she pretends to be bankrupt as well.

Tempestates. In Roman mythology, the goddess of storms.

Templar, Simon. In numerous novels and stories by Leslie Charteris and others (beg. 1928), an elegant thief who devotes most of his time to arranging justice for the truly villainous. *Also called* The Saint.

Temple. *See* Drake, Temple.

Temptation, The. In the Bible, New Testament Gospels, the 40 days Jesus* spent in the wilderness following His baptism, during which the Devil* tempted Him with all the powers and attractions of the world. The term is also sometimes applied to the travails of St. Anthony,* particularly as a subject for painters.

Ten Commandments. In the Bible, *Exodus* xx, the fundamental laws given by God to Moses.* The exact wording and numbering varies, depending on translations, but they are generally understood as follows. Thou shalt not: (1) have any other gods, (2) make graven images, (3) take the Lord's name in vain, (4) forget the Sabbath day, (5) fail to honor thy parents, (6) kill, (7) commit adultery, (8) steal, (9) lie, (10) covet anything of thy neighbor's.

Ten Thousand, The. Historically, a body of Greek mercenaries who joined the revolt of Cyrus* in 401 B.C. After Cyrus's collapse, they embarked on an arduous ''march to the sea'' across modern Turkey which, as related in Xenophon's *Anabasis,* became a model of heroic endeavor.

Tennessee. In Bret Harte's story *Tennessee's Partner* (1870), a wild Westerner who runs off with his best friend's wife, becomes a robber, and is eventually hanged; he is the progenitor of endless American literary and film Westerners identified by the place they came from rather than by names.

Tenorio, Don Juan. *See* Juan, Don.

Teresa, St. Historically, Teresa of Ávila, the founder of the ''barefoot'' Carmelites (d. 1582) and the author of numerous religious works; she is often noted for the mystical piercing of her heart by the spear of Divine Love; not to be confused with St. Theresa,* her day is October 15.

Tereus. In Greek legend, the king of Thrace who raped Philomela.* Her sister Procne,* also his wife, in revenge killed and cooked his son Itys* and fed him to Tereus.

Terminus. In Roman mythology, the god of boundaries.

Terpander. In Greek legend, the inventor of the seven-stringed lyre; hence, he is the father of music.

Terpsichore. In Greek mythology, the Muse* of the dance.

Terra. In Roman mythology, the goddess of the earth, generally equivalent to Rhea.*

Tertullus. In the Bible, *Acts* xxiv, a lawyer whose accusations against Paul*
ended in Paul's imprisonment.

Tess. In Thomas Hardy's novel *Tess of the D'Urbervilles* (1891), a young country
girl who is seduced and abandoned by D'Urberville.* When she marries the
gentle Angel Clare,* she admits her earlier seduction, and he too deserts her,
forcing her to return to her seducer. Eventually, she murders D'Urberville and
is captured and executed.

Tessman. In Henrik Ibsen's play *Hedda Gabler* (1890), the sincere, loving, but
insensitive husband, blinded both by his love for Hedda Gabler* and his plodding,
scholarly nature that keeps him unaware of emotional nuances. *See also* Brack,
Judge; Elvsted, Mrs.; Lovborg.

Tethys. In Greek mythology, a Titan,* a sea deity, and the wife of Oceanus.*

Teucer. (1) In Homer's *Iliad,* the greatest of the Greek archers. (2) In some
Greek legends, the first king of Troy.*

Teufelsdrockh. In Thomas Carlyle's *Sartor Resartus* (1833), a priggishly witty
German schoolmaster who uses a discussion of clothes and concern for
appearances to lead into numerous philosophical side streets; seen from out of
his period, it is difficult to know what attitude to take about him or his views,
but he made Carlyle a major literary figure.

Tevye. In numerous stories by Sholom Aleichem (beg. 1895), and especially in
the American musical comedy *Fiddler on the Roof* (1964), a warm-hearted
Russian Jewish milkman primarily noted for his persistent failed attempts to
marry off his daughters properly and his simultaneously querulous and pious
attempts to talk with God.

Thaddeus. In the Bible, *Matthew* x, one of the twelve Apostles;* since he is
not listed in all the Gospels, he and Jude* may be the same person.

Thaïs. (1) In Greek legend, Alexander's* mistress who persuaded him to burn
Persepolis; she is known primarily from John Dryden's poem *Alexander's Feast*
(1697). (2) In Christian legend, a wealthy Egyptian harlot who converted and
finished her life in a penitential cell; she is the subject of Anatole France's novel
(1890) and Massenet's opera *Thaïs* (1894), in which the famous "Meditation"
music appears.

Thaisa. In Shakespeare's play *Pericles* (1608), the wife of Pericles.* After giving
birth to their daughter Marina,* she is thought to be dead and is cast adrift in a
sealed casket, from which she is eventually rescued, restored to life, and returned
to her husband and daughter.

Thalassa. In Greek mythology, the mother of Aphrodite* and sometimes a name for the sea. The cry of "Thalassa! Thalassa!" was given by the Ten Thousand* when they finally reached the sea, and it is sometimes quoted when a difficult goal has been reached.

Thalia. In Greek mythology, the Muse* of comedy.

Thamar. *See* Tamar.

Thamuz. A name sometimes used for Adonis.*

Thamyris. In Greek legend, a poet/musician who challenged the Muses* and was blinded for his pride.

Thanatos. In Greek mythology, the god of death. *Also called* Mors.*

Thatcher. In Mark Twain's novel *Tom Sawyer* (1876), **Becky** is the quintessential mid-American girl—pretty, golden-haired, and innocently in love with Tom Sawyer.* Her father, **Judge Thatcher**, is something of a windbag, but he protects Tom's right to the treasure they find and also reappears in *Huckleberry Finn* as Huck Finn's* legal administrator.

That Man. *See* Roosevelt.

Thea. In Greek mythology, a Titan,* the goddess of light and mother of the sun, moon, and dawn.

Theale, Milly. In Henry James's novel *The Wings of the Dove* (1902), a terminally ill American heiress who marries Morton Densher* and, discovering that he married her for her money while he was in love with another, she despairs and dies but magnanimously leaves him the money.

Thélème, Abby of. In Rabelais's *Gargantua* (1534), a castle on the door of which was inscribed, "Do whatever you want."

Themis. In Greek mythology, a Titan,* the goddess of order and mother of the Fates* and of Prometheus.*

Thénardier. In Victor Hugo's novel *Les Misérables* (1862), a greedy and unscrupulous innkeeper who takes Fantine's* money, blackmails Valjean,* and even forces Valjean to bribe him to be let out of the sewers while rescuing Marius.* **Mme. Thénardier** is a virago.

Theobald. *See* Pontifex.

Theodora. (1) Historically, a courtesan (d. 547) and later the wife of Justinian* and empress of Byzantium noted originally for her bravery, intelligence, and administrative skill and later, after the discovery of various "secret" writings, noted for her lascivious profligacy. (2) In Ariosto's *Orlando Furioso* (1532), the Greek emperor's sister who casts Rogero* into a dungeon in revenge for the death of her son.

Theresa, St. Historically, a nun (d. 1897) of gentle, unremarkable life, whose autobiography published in 1895 so demonstrated the sanctity of little things and small lives that she was called "The Little Flower" and became perhaps the most popular of all modern saints; not to be confused with St. Teresa,* her day is October 1.

Thérèse. *See* Desqueyroux.

Thérèse, St. *See* Theresa, St.

Thermopylae. Historically, the battle (480 B.C.) in which a comparative handful of Greeks held off the entire Persian army for three days; long used to symbolize any brave resistance against overwhelming odds.

Thersites. In Homer's *Iliad,* a deformed Greek noted for his scurrilous attacks on the Greek heroes' attitudes; eventually he was killed by Achilles.*

Thésée. *See* Theseus.

Theseus. In Greek legend, the son of Aegeus* and a great hero who became king of Athens by killing the great bull of Heracles* and then traveled to Crete where he killed the Minotaur* and escaped from the Labyrinth* by following a thread given to him by Ariadne.* He then took her away, only to desert her in favor of her sister Phaedra.* He is also said to have previously defeated the Amazons* and married Hippolyta,* which ceremony is the excuse for the celebrations in Shakespeare's play *A Midsummer Night's Dream* (1595). Their son Hippolytus* involved the house in tragedy after Phaedra arrived, for she fell in love with him. *See also* Demophon; Lycomedes; Minos; Periphetes; Procrustes; Sciron.

Thesmophoriazusae. In Aristophanes's play *Thesmophoriazusae,* the women who, while celebrating the women's festival of Demeter,* attack Euripides for criticizing women in his plays.

Thespis. In Greek legend, the first actor.

Thespius. *See* Heracles.

Thestylis. In Greek pastoral poetry, a rustic maiden.

Thetis. In Greek mythology, a sea nymph* and the mother of Achilles.* *See also* Eris; Paris; Peleus.

Thia. *See* Thea.

Thief, The. In the Bible, either of the two men crucified with Jesus.* In *Matthew* and *Mark,* both thieves ridicule Him on the cross, but, in *Luke,* the second thief asks Jesus to remember him and is promised a place in Paradise.* *See also* Dismas; Gestas.

Thinker, The. In Auguste Rodin's* sculpture *The Thinker* (1904), a nude male with his head resting on his right hand, a pose that almost immediately became synonymous with thought itself as well as one of the most widely recognizeable of all works of art.

Thin Man, The. In Dashiell Hammett's novel *The Thin Man* (1934), the murder victim; in common usage, particularly after the American movie version (1934), the name was applied to Nick Charles, the detective who solved the crime. *See* Charles, Nick and Nora.

Thirty Pieces of Silver. *See* Judas.

Thisbe. *See* Pyramus.

Thomas. (1) In the Bible, one of the twelve Apostles,* noted for his skepticism, giving rise to his common description as "doubting Thomas;" legend has it that he went to India. He is often represented among the saints with a carpenter's square; his day is July 3. *Also called* Didymus. (2) *See also* Tom; Tommy.

Thomas, Bigger. In Richard Wright's novel *Native Son* (1940), a young Negro who, while drunk, accidentally smothers a white girl, which releases his pathological hatred of whites, itself resulting from his own symptomatic poverty and position as a victim of racial prejudice. He is eventually discovered and sentenced to death, as much for society's own fears as for his crime.

Thomas, St. (1) Thomas* the Apostle. (2) Thomas à Becket.* (3) Historically, Thomas Aquinas, the greatest theologian (d. 1274) of Catholicism. His day is January 28.

Thomas à Becket. *See* Becket, Thomas à.

Thompson, Sadie. In Somerset Maugham's story *Rain* (1922), an attractive and loose woman trapped on a South Sea island whose appearance drives a missionary to assault her; she ultimately reveals his hypocrisy. For many years she served as a symbol of sexual freedom and honesty, particularly after the success of the play and movie versions that followed.

Thor. In Scandinavian mythology, the god of thunder and the weather, denoted by his hammer.

Thornhill. In Oliver Goldsmith's novel *The Vicar of Wakefield* (1766), the **Squire** is an unprincipled local rake who seduces one of the vicar's daughters with a false wedding and has the vicar imprisoned for debt. His uncle, **Sir William**, is an eccentric who lives in disguise but ultimately sets all to right. *See also* Primrose.

Thoth. In Egyptian mythology, the scribe of the gods, the inventor of numbers, and the god of time; often the god of magic. *See also* Trismegistus.

Three Bears. *See* Goldilocks.

Thug. Historically, a member of an Indian sect who robbed and strangled victims in sacrifice to the goddess Kali.* The sect was suppressed by the British in the 1840s, but it was much revived in British adventure novels and Hollywood movies of later years.

Thumb, Tom. In English folklore, a child no bigger than his father's thumb; hence, a name given to anyone small, most notably to a famous midget with Barnum's circus in the nineteenth century and to a satirical portrait of the politician Walpole in Fielding's play *Tom Thumb* (1730), in which a midget conquers giants and weds King Arthur's* daughter Huncamunca* before being unceremoniously swallowed by a cow.

Thwackum. In Henry Fielding's novel *Tom Jones* (1749), a bigoted, self-righteous minister retained to teach Tom Jones;* his primary teaching methods are beatings. *See also* Allworthy, Squire; Square.

Thyestes. In Greek legend, the grandson of Tantalus* and the brother of Atreus,* whose wife he assaulted and who served him the flesh of his own children in a meal in revenge. He also committed incest with his daughter (accidentally), thus fathering Aegisthus,* and later ruled Mycenae until dethroned by Menelaus.*

Thyrses. In John Milton's poem/play *Comus* (1634), shepherd who is really a spirit in disguise, whose advice and magic charms restore Virtue. *See also* Comus; Sabrina.

Tiberinus. In Roman legend, a king in Italy who drowned in the river that was renamed the Tiber.

Tiberius. (1) Historically, the second Roman emperor (d. 37); he appears in numerous works as the instigator of a brutal reign of terror; also noted and for his exotic sexual proclivities. *See also* Livia; Sejanus. (2) *See* Cornelia.

Tietjens, Christopher. In Ford Maddox Ford's novels *Parade's End* (1924–28), "the last English Tory," an old-fashioned English gentleman whose dignity, integrity, and intelligence continually attract both jealousy and spite. His disappointments include an unfaithful wife, an unrewarding government job, and his relief from his World War I command despite his heroism and the respect of his men. The last leads to a complete breakdown, and he only gradually recovers in the twenties, while saddened by the end of his values in society at large.

Tiger Lily. In J. M. Barrie's play *Peter Pan* (1904), the Indian princess who first is Peter Pan's* enemy and then his ally against the pirates. *See also* Hook, Captain.

Tigg, Montague. In Charles Dickens's novel *Martin Chuzzlewit* (1843), a con man, initially a friend who tries to borrow money for Chevy Slime* and who later organizes a fraudulent insurance firm and blackmails Jonas Chuzzlewit* until Jonas kills him.

Tillet, Ferdinand du. In Balzac's novel *César Birotteau* (1837), the villain who as an apprentice steals from Birotteau* and devotes himself to repaying good with evil when Birotteau forgives him; a seducer and thief, he prospers and becomes a respected member of society.

Till Eulenspiegel. In German folklore, a merry prankster who carries out a number of tricks and vulgar practical jokes, managing even to escape from the gallows.

Tim, Tiny. *See* Tiny Tim.

Time, Father. In American folklore, the symbol of passing time, usually seen in New Year's Eve illustrations as an old man with a beard and a scythe giving way to a cute baby.

Timon. (1) In the Bible, *Acts* vi, one of the first seven deacons, appointed to give aid to the widows. (2) In Shakespeare's play *Timon of Athens* (1607), a wealthy man who gives away all his wealth and then is disillusioned when his former friends refuse him aid, and who then invites all to a banquet where he serves only water before he becomes a hermit in the forest, from which he uses a found treasure to avenge himself upon his former city; one of the most antisocial and cynical of all Shakespeare's characters. *See also* Flavius; Ventidius.

Timothy. In the Bible, a faithful friend of Paul,* a minister at Ephesus, and the recipient of the New Testament epistles called *I and II Timothy. See also* Eunice; Lois.

Tinker Bell. In J. M. Barrie's play *Peter Pan* (1904), the fairy* who accompanies Peter Pan;* she drinks poison intended for Peter but is saved from death by Peter's plea to the audience: "If you believe in fairies, clap your hands."

Tin Man, The. In Frank Baum's novel *The Wonderful Wizard of Oz* (1900), a man made of tin who joins Dorothy* while in search of a heart for himself. *See also* Lion; Scarecrow.

Tiny Tim. In Charles Dickens's story *A Christmas Carol* (1843), Bob Cratchit's* crippled son, whose optimism is constant; known for his "God bless us, everyone." *See also* Scrooge.

Tip. *See* Dorrit.

Tipton, John Beresford. In the American television series "The Millionaire" (1955–60), an eccentric millionaire who each week gave away a million dollars simply to see what effect it might have on the recipient.

Tiresias. In Greek legend, a blind prophet. In some stories, he is blinded for watching Athena* bathing; in others, for siding with Zeus* in an argument with Hera* over whether men or women enjoy sex more, in compensation for which Zeus gave him prophetic sight. He is also supposed to have been both a man and a woman at various times in life. His most prominent appearance is in Sophocles's play *Oedipus Rex,* in which he helps reveal to Oedipus* the nature of his past and crimes. He also figures as the man who vainly warns Pentheus* in Euripides's *Bacchae. See also* Odysseus.

Titan. In Greek mythology, any of several pre-Olympian gods of Greece, children of Gaia* and Uranus,* eventually overcome by Zeus.* For the most notable, *see* Atlas; Coeus; Crius; Cronos; Hyperion; Iapetus; Mnemosyne; Oceanus; Phoebe; Rhea; Tethys; Thea; Themis; Typhon.

Titania. In Shakespeare's play *A Midsummer Night's Dream* (1595), the queen of the fairies* whose feud with her husband Oberon* causes him to put her under a spell in which she falls in love with the cloddish mortal Bottom,* who has been changed into an ass. *See also* Puck.

Tithonus. In Greek legend, a brother of Priam* who was so beautiful Aurora* made him immortal; since he forgot to ask for eternal youth, he grew old and begged to die.

Titus. (1) In the Bible, *Titus,* organizer of the Church in Crete; this may or may not be the same Titus who accompanied Paul* on his trip to Jerusalem* (*Galatians* ii). (2) In Christian legend, a name sometimes given to the penitent thief on the cross. *See also* Dismas.* (3) In Racine's play *Bérénice* (1670), a Roman emperor whose sense of duty and honor causes him to surrender his love for Bérénice.*

Titus Andronicus. In Shakespeare's play *Titus Andronicus* (1592), a Roman soldier of a particularly grisly nature. Having lost 21 sons in war, he has the son of his enemy Tamora* sacrificed; his daughter Lavinia* is raped by Tamora's sons; his son is executed for avenging that rape; and Titus goes increasingly mad, cutting off his own hand and finally serving up Tamora's children baked in a pie to her before killing both her and Lavinia.

Toad. In Kenneth Grahame's novel *The Wind in the Willows* (1908), the profligate lord of Toad Hall who wastes his wealth in fads such as gypsy caravans and motor cars, one of which he steals, for which he is jailed. He finally escapes disguised as a woman, only to need rescuing again by his more sensible friends along the river when Toad Hall is overrun by weasels.

Tobacco Road. In Erskine Caldwell's novel *Tobacco Road* (1932), the road along which the Lesters* live; for many synonymous with the home of any poor and ignorant hillbillies.

Tobias. In the Bible, in the Apocrypha, *Tobit,* a pious man who, with the aid of the angel Raphael,* wins the love of Sara* by defeating the demon Asmodeus.*

Tobit. In the Bible, in the Apochrypha, *Tobit,* the blind father of Tobias,* usually depicted with his dog, the only pet dog in the Bible.

Toby. (1) The dog in the traditional Punch* and Judy* puppet show. (2) *See* Belch, Sir Toby; Shandy.

Toby, Uncle. *See* Shandy.

Todd, Mary. Historically, the wife (d. 1882) of Abraham Lincoln.* She appears in many fictional works variously as a young and ambitious woman who leads or forces Lincoln into politics and as an older madwoman whose lunacies disturb and disrupt Lincoln during the war; both versions have some support in historical record.

Todd, Sweeney. In numerous mid-nineteenth-century stories and plays, a barber who goes mad and murders his customers. In some versions, the customers are then ground up and baked in pies by a neighbor woman. *Also called* The Demon Barber.

Toinette. In Molière's play *Le Malade imaginaire* (1673), the vivacious, intelligent maid who eventually unites the lovers by disguising herself as a doctor too ludicrous even for the hypochondriac Argan.* *See also* Diafoirus.

Tom. (1) In English folk materials, a general name for dullards or fools of various kinds; for example, Tom o' Bedlam, a lunatic; Tom Fool (used both as a noun and an adjective), a particularly stupid person or thing; Tom, Tom, the Piper's Son, a foolish child who stole a pig and could do nothing but cry when caught; Edgar's* alias when feigning madness on the heath in Shakespeare's *King Lear,* and so on. (2) A traditional name for a male cat. (3) A nobody, as in Tom, Dick, and Harry, meaning anyone and everyone. (4) *See* Sawyer, Tom; Tulliver; Wingfield. (5) *See also* Thomas; Tommy.

Tom, Corinthian. *See* Tom and Jerry.

Tom, Peeping. In British folklore, a foolish young man who tried to peek at the naked Lady Godiva,* for which he lost his sight.

Tom, Uncle. In Harriet Beecher Stowe's novel *Uncle Tom's Cabin* (1852), the gentle, kind, and Christian Negro slave, sold to a weak master and beaten to death by Simon Legree.* In the 1960s, his patience and Christian gentleness made the name a pejorative term in the American civil rights movement, signifying a Negro who had no independence, racial pride, or masculinity. *See also* Cassy; Chloe; Eliza; Eva; St. Clare.

Tom and Jerry. (1) In Pierce Egan's stories *Life In London* (1820), Corinthian Tom and Jerry Hawthorn, two merry young scoundrels and men about town; symbols of wild and carefree living. (2) In numerous movie cartoons (beg. 1937), a cat and a mouse, respectively, who engage in traditional chase comedy.

Tommy. In general British and American usage, from the nineteenth century, the British private soldier, ostensibly from the use of the name "Tommy Atkins" in the sample registration form given to all recruits (beg. 1815). *See also* Doe, John.

Tom Thumb. *See* Thumb, Tom.

Toni. *See* Buddenbrook.

Tonio. In Leoncavallo's opera *Pagliacci* (1892), the clown who, spurned by Canio's* young wife, arranges for Canio to find out she is unfaithful with another. *See also* Pagliacci.

Tonto. In the American radio and television series "The Lone Ranger" (beg. 1933), the Indian partner of the Lone Ranger,* famous for his loyalty and the catch-phrase "Kemo sabe;" hence, a quintessential sidekick.

Tony. (1) *See* Last, Tony. (2) *See also* Toni.

Toodle. In Charles Dickens's novel *Dombey and Son* (1846), **Polly** is the kindly nurse hired to care for young Dombey;* she is renamed "Richards" and is fired when Florence is temporarily kidnapped for her hair. **Mr. Toodle** is a stoker and a loyal family man. Their son is called **Rob the Grinder** after he is admitted to the Grinders' School, where he is out of his element and most unhappy.

Tootles. In J. M. Barrie's play *Peter Pan* (1904), the smallest of the orphan boys in Never-Never-Land.* *See also* Pan, Peter; Wendy.

Toots. In Charles Dickens's novel *Dombey and Son* (1846), a rich and eccentric boy who spends his school time writing letters to himself signed by famous names and then later courts Florence Dombey* in an exceedingly shy, vague, and eccentric manner, visiting her dog rather than her. *See also* Game Chicken, The; Nipper, Susan.

Topper, Cosmo. In Thorne Smith's novel *Topper* (1926), a mild-mannered, henpecked bank manager whose life is wildly altered when he is haunted by the fun-loving spirits of the Kerbys, a playboy client and his wife.

Topsy. In Harriet Beecher Stowe's novel *Uncle Tom's Cabin* (1852), the irrepressible young Negro child who "just growed."

Torah. In Jewish usage, the laws handed down by God to Moses;* sometimes interpreted to mean the first five books of the Bible, and sometimes all the teachings of the Old Testament and the Talmud.

Torpille, La. *See* Gobseck.

Torquemada. Historically, an Inquisitor-General of Spain (d. 1498) whose excessive zeal in torturing heretics, Jews, and Moors made him a widely used symbol of cruelty and unreasoning persecution.

Tosca. In Sardou's play *La Tosca* (1887) and in Puccini's opera *Tosca* (1900), a self-centered actress who jealously causes her lover Cavaradossi's* arrest for treason. When she is given an opportunity to trade her sexual favors for his release, she agrees, only to stab the villain Scarpia* before it is consummated. However, she discovers too late that she has been tricked, when her lover is killed in what she thought would be a sham execution, and she throws herself into the Tiber.

Toto. *See* Dorothy.

Touchstone. In Shakespeare's play *As You Like It* (1599), the clown who runs away to the Forest of Arden,* entertaining Rosalind* with witty sayings until he talks himself into marrying the homely Audrey.* *See also* Celia; Jaques.

Tox, Miss. In Charles Dickens's novel *Dombey and Son* (1846), a spinster of drab respectability with designs on Dombey* expressed so drably and respectably that no one notices them; she shifts these designs to Major Bagstock* with no better result.

Tozer. In Charles Dickens's novel *Dombey and Son* (1846), Paul Dombey's* depressed student roommate who hates school but hates holidays even more because his family turns them into continual examinations to test his educational progress. *See also* Blimber; Toots.

Tracy, Dick. In the American newspaper cartoon *Dick Tracy* (beg. 1931), a police detective notable for his square jaw and nose, his tough anticrime stance, a series of futuristic tools such as the two-way radio-TV in the shape of a wrist watch, and a set of criminals and friends with names suitable in their self-descriptiveness for Restoration comedies.

Traddles. In Charles Dickens's novel *David Copperfield* (1849), an unhappy student at school with David Copperfield;* he consoles himself by drawing skeletons. Later, he becomes a lawyer of kindly disposition whose hair always stands on end and who marries Sophy Crewler,* whom he constantly calls the "dearest girl in the world."

Tramp, The Little. In numerous movies (beg. 1915), the character played by Charlie Chaplin, a down-but-never-out tramp, distinguished by his faded frock coat, bowler hat, tiny mustache, cane, and a remarkable shuffle, as well as his inventive resilience in the face of all obstacles and his sentimental attitude toward children and pure young girls.

Tranio. In Shakespeare's play *The Taming of the Shrew* (1593), the servant who disguises himself as his master Lucentio* so that the master in disguise may safely court Bianca.*

Transylvania. Historically, a region in what is now called Rumania, but, since Bram Stoker's novel *Dracula* (1897), in which this was Count Dracula's* homeland, it is inescapably associated with vampires and other related creatures.

Trapbois. In Walter Scott's novel *The Fortunes of Nigel* (1822), an usurious moneylender and landlord who is murdered. His daughter **Martha** is uneducated but is intelligent and resourceful; she saves her father's money chest and eventually marries well after a brief but unhappy marriage to the spendthrift Dalgarno.*

Trent, Nell. *See* Nell, Little.

Treplev, Constantin. *See* Constantin.

Tressilian. In Walter Scott's novel *Kenilworth* (1821), an intelligent and honorable gentleman in love with Amy Robsart.* He mistakes her actions and inadvertently sets in train a series of events that gets her killed and almost results in his own death in a duel. *See also* Smith, Wayland; Varney.

Triboulet. In Rabelais's *Pantagruel* (1546), the lunatic who advises Panurge* to seek advice from the Divine Bottle about marriage.

Tribulation Wholesome. In Ben Jonson's play *The Alchemist* (1610), a Puritan hypocrite willing to trade principles for profit. *See also* Ananias.

Trifle. In Pierce Egan's stories *Life In London* (1821), the skinniest dandy in London. *See also* Tom and Jerry.

Trigorin. In Anton Chekhov's play *The Sea Gull* (1896), a prolific writer bored with writing, a man who uses other people not so much from evil as from restlessness and boredom. Despite being Arkadina's* lover, he elopes with Nina* and then deserts her. *See also* Constantin.

Trilby. In George du Maurier's novel *Trilby* (1894), the pretty artist's model (with the most beautiful feet in the world) who cannot sing until hypnotized by Svengali,* which makes her sing beautifully. Under his influence, she becomes a great singing star but wastes away and dies, having lost control of her soul. *See also* Billee, Little.

Trim, Corporal. In Laurence Sterne's novel *Tristram Shandy* (1759), the faithful but extremely talkative servant of Uncle Toby,* much pursued by Mrs. Bridget.* *See also* Fever, Le; Wadman, Widow.

Trimalchio. In Petronius's *Satyricon,* a vulgar former slave anxious to impress with his wealth; most memorable for an incredibly elaborate banquet and his tortuously confused mythology.

Trinculo. In Shakespeare's play *The Tempest* (1611), a drunken clown in the plot with Caliban* and Stephano.* *See also* Ariel; Prospero.

Trinity. In Christian usage, a doctrine that God is a single unity in three "persons:" God the Father, God the Son (Jesus*), and God the Holy Ghost (or Holy Spirit). The exact nature of that unity has been the subject of much debate and not a few wars.

Triptolemus. In Greek legend, Demeter's* priest, later made a god, who gave mankind grain, the plow, and culture.

Trismegistus. A third-century name given to Thoth* or Hermes.*

Tristan. In Gottfried von Strasbourg's poem *Tristan und Isolde,* essentially the same as Tristram;* this was the primary source for Richard Wagner's opera *Tristan und Isolde* (1865).

Tristram. (1) In Malory's *Morte d'Arthur*, a knight of the Round Table* sent by King Mark* to escort his bride Isoud.* During the journey, they fall in love with each other and continue the affair after she is married to Mark and Tristram is married to another Isoud (la Blanche Mains). Eventually, Mark discovers the affair and murders Tristram. Alternatively, in other sources, Tristram is wounded and sends for his beloved Isoud, who is supposed to show a white sail; when his wife tells him the ship has a black sail, he dies of grief, and his lover arrives and dies beside him. *See also* Tristan. (2) *See* Shandy.

Triton. In Greek mythology, Poseidon's* son, a sea god half man and half dolphin who calmed sea storms; he is often depicted wearing a long beard and holding a trident.

Tritonia. A name sometimes used for Athena.*

Trivia. A name sometimes used for Hecate* or Diana* of the Crossways.

Trofimov. In Anton Chekhov's play *The Cherry Orchard* (1904), the idealistic, perpetual student, always sure of the glory of the future, which in retrospect made him something of a communist prophet in modern Russian interpretation; he is never able to actually finish anything, including his degree, although Anya* does fall in love with him.

Troilus. In Greek legend, a son of Priam* killed by Achilles.* In medieval Europe, he was said to have loved the beautiful but faithless Cressida;* thus, he became a symbol of idealistic love, especially in Chaucer's poem *Troilus and Criseyde* and much more cynically in Shakespeare's play *Troilus and Cressida* (1602). *See also* Pandarus.

Trojan. In Greek legend, an inhabitant of Troy.* Their gallant defense of their city in the Trojan War* made them common symbols of bravery and endurance. In Virgil's *Aeneid,* they are claimed as the progenitors of the Romans. *See also* Aeneas.

Trojan Horse. In Homer's *Odyssey,* the trick by which Odysseus* brings about the fall of Troy. The Greeks pretend to break off the seige of Troy, leaving behind as a gift a great wooden horse which the Trojans bring inside the city walls. Hidden in the horse are Greek warriors who sneak out while the Trojans celebrate, and they let in the remainder of the Greek forces, who defeat the Trojans and burn the city. Virgil also uses the story in the *Aeneid,* which prompts the famous "beware Greeks bearing gifts," adding the story of Laocoön,* who tried to warn the Trojans but was crushed by a great serpent.

Trojan War. In Greek legend, a war between the combined Greek states and the city of Troy.* As depicted in Homer's *Iliad,* it became the most widely known and admired war in literature. The war began when the Trojan prince Paris* abducted the beautiful Helen,* wife of the Greek king Menelaus.* Menelaus then obtained the support of many other Greek kings, and together, under the overall command of Agamemnon,* they beseiged Troy for ten years, until, by the ruse of the Trojan Horse,* the Greeks got inside the city walls and massacred the remaining Trojans. *See also* Achilles; Aeneas; Ajax; Andromache; Briseis; Cassandra; Chryseis; Cressida; Diomedes; Hector; Hecuba; Idomeneus; Iphigenia; Myrmidons; Neoptolemus; Nestor; Paeon; Pandarus; Patroclus; Peleus; Philoctetes; Polyxena; Priam; Rhesus; Troilus.

Troll. In Scandinavian mythology, a race of dwarves with supernatural powers who live underground. Usually wicked, they are most noted for their appearance in Henrik Ibsen's play *Peer Gynt. See also* Rip Van Winkle.

Trotter, Job. In Charles Dickens's novel *Pickwick Papers* (1836), Jingle's* servant and accomplice, noted for his ability to cry on cue. *See also* Pickwick; Weller.

Trotwood, Betsey. In Charles Dickens's novel *David Copperfield* (1849), Copperfield's* eccentric and plainspoken aunt; she originally refuses contact with David when he is born because he is not a girl, but later she becomes his benefactress after he runs away from the job at the wine merchant's. An honest woman who is nonetheless quite kind beneath a severe, angular surface, she is noted particularly for her obsession with the donkeys who graze on the commons before her cottage and for her general distaste for the male sex, with the exception of the genial lunatic Mr. Dick,* whom she cares for and respects. *See also* Heep, Uriah; Peggotty; Wickfield.

Troubleall. In Ben Jonson's play *Bartholomew Fair* (1614), a madman obsessed by the trappings of legal judgement. *See also* Purecraft.

Troy. Historically, an ancient city on the coast of modern Turkey, fabled as the site of the Trojan War.* *Also called* Ilium. *See also* Dardanus; Laomedon.

Troy, Sergeant. In Thomas Hardy's novel *Far From the Madding Crowd* (1874), the soldier of dashing exterior and heartless interior who marries Bathsheba Everdene,* disappears after his seduction of another girl is exposed, then returns and is killed by another man in love with Bathsheba. *See also* Boldwood; Oak, Gabriel.

Truewit. In Ben Jonson's play *Epicene* (1609), a witty but argumentative defender of cosmetics for women and a plotter who helps his friend foil his uncle's plots to disinherit him. *See also* Epicene; Morose.

Tubalcain. In the Bible, *Genesis* iv, a son of Lamech* and the father of all metalworkers. *See also* Jabal; Jubal.

Tuck, Friar. In English folklore, a jolly fat priest who joins Robin Hood's* band; he is first introduced to them when Robin knocks him off a log while crossing a stream. *See also* John, Little.

Tucker, Tommy. In English folklore, the little boy who sang for his supper.

Tudor. Historically, a family of English nobility and, from 1485 to 1603, the country's ruling family. *See* Henry VIII;* Mary Tudor;* Elizabeth* I.

Tulkinghorn. In Charles Dickens's novel *Bleak House* (1852), a particularly cold, conniving, and unscrupulous lawyer, eventually murdered after blackmailing Lady Dedlock* and then refusing to pay blackmail in his turn. *See also* Guppy; Hawdon, Capt.; Jarndyce; Rouncewell.

Tulliver. In George Eliot's novel *The Mill on the Floss* (1860), **Maggie** is an imaginative and generous young woman whose impetuosity causes most people to think her sometimes irresponsible, more often immoral; after an unfounded scandal, she sacrifices herself in an attempt to save her brother Tom from drowning in a flood. **Tom** is industrious and honorable, if somewhat priggish, and treats his sister severely while struggling to pay off the family's many debts. Their father **Edward** is hot-tempered and careless, losing the family mill in a series of lawsuits and finally having a stroke after thrashing the man who took his mill. Their mother **Elizabeth** is a woman proud of her birth but dependent on the advice of others, who has a low regard for her daughter.

Tupman, Tracy. In Charles Dickens's novel *Pickwick Papers* (1836), Pickwick's* middle-aged friend who falls in and out of love with a series of spinsters. *See also* Snodgrass; Wardle; Weller; Winkle.

Turandot. In a tale originally given by Galland as part of *The Arabian Nights* (1704), but more known from Gozzi's play (1762) and from Puccini's opera *Turandot* (1926), a Chinese princess who, having declared revenge on all men for an ancient grievance, offers to marry any noble who can solve three riddles or to kill him if he cannot solve them. When a prince does solve them, she refuses to marry him after all, and then has a change of heart that also changes her mind; the opera's ending was added by other hands after Puccini's death.

Turveydrop. In Charles Dickens's novel *Bleak House* (1852), a selfish man, devoted only to the appearance of good manners. *See also* Jellyby.

Tusenbach. In Anton Chekhov's play *Three Sisters* (1901), a gentle and sentimental young German baron in love with Irina;* he often waxes philosophical about the importance of real work in the future, for which he is ridiculed. He is eventually killed in a duel by Solyony,* a rival for her love. *See also* Prozorov; Vershinin.

Tweedledee. *See* Tweedledum.

Tweedledum. Originally, in English eighteenth-century usage, tweedledum and tweedledee were terms for opposites, supposedly derived from the sounds of low and high musical instruments. In Lewis Carroll's *Through the Looking-glass* (1872), the names are given to two identical fat men who engage in a long and incomprehensible argument. Since then the names have been used to indicate people or things that, whatever their appearance, actually offer no choice between them.

Twist, Oliver. In Charles Dickens's novel *Oliver Twist* (1837), a foundling raised in a workhouse, where he is mistreated for asking for more food. Apprenticed to a mortician who uses him as a mourner at children's funerals because he looks so sickly, he runs away and is introduced to the gang of thieves led by Fagin.* Arrested, he is temporarily rescued by the benevolent Brownlow,* until the thieves force him back into crime, where he is wounded while helping Bill Sikes* and is just saved from death by the kindly intercession of Mrs. Maylie, who takes him in until his true origins are revealed. *See also* Artful Dodger; Bumble; Corney, Mrs.; Fang; Nancy.

Tybalt. In Shakespeare's play *Romeo and Juliet* (1595), Juliet's* hot-headed cousin who kills Mercutio* in a duel and is in turn killed by Romeo.* *See also* Capulet; Montague.

Tyche. In Greek mythology, the goddess of luck. *Also called* Fortuna.*

Tydeus. In Greek legend, one of the Seven Against Thebes* who managed to revolt even the normally unshakeable goddess Athena* by cutting off his enemy's head and eating the brains.

Tyl. *See* Till Eulenspiegel.

Tyndareus. *See* Tyndarus.

Tyndarus. In Greek legend, a king of Sparta and the husband of Leda.*

Typhon. In Greek mythology, the most terrible of the Titans,* with a hundred dragon heads and a body covered with snakes; he was killed by Zeus's* thunderbolt. He was father of most of the Greek monsters, such as Cerberus,* Chimera,* Hydra,* and Sphinx.* *See also* Osiris.

Tyrrheus. In Virgil's *Aeneid,* Latinus's* herdsman, the death of whose pet stag led to a war with Aeneas's* people.

u

Ugly American. In Lederer and Burdick's novel *The Ugly American* (1959), a physically ugly American espionage agent in Southeast Asia; in the novel, he was a hero of the fight against communism, but in popular usage the phrase was quickly adopted to signify the pushy and provincial attitudes of many Americans when dealing with foreigners, from loud-mouthed tourists to business people and governmental figures who refused to accept that other cultures might be different.

Ulloa, Ana de. *See* Ana, Doña.

Ulysses. Latin name for Odysseus.* Many modern allusions to the name, however, refer not to the character but to the novel of that title by James Joyce (1924), which is organized around the travels of Odysseus,* and generally refer to the complexity, the greatness, or the unreadability of that novel. *See also* Bloom; Dedalus, Stephen.

Una. In Edmund Spenser's poem *The Faerie Queene* (1590), a lady who symbolizes the true religion. She is separated from the Red Cross Knight* but is protected by a lion and by the fauns* and satyrs* of the forest until finally she is reunited with her love.

Uncas. In James Fenimore Cooper's novel *The Last of the Mohicans* (1826), a young Indian brave who falls in love with a white woman and is killed avenging her death by an Indian from a rival tribe, thereby ending the line of the Mohicans. *See also* Bumppo, Natty; Chingachgook; Munro.

Uncle Remus. *See* Remus, Uncle.

Uncle Sam. *See* Sam, Uncle.

Uncle Toby. *See* Shandy.

Undershaft. In G. B. Shaw's play *Major Barbara* (1905), **Andrew** is a munitions tycoon who enjoys turning what passes for common sense on its head and wins back his daughter's affections from the Salvation Army by demonstrating that the soul cannot be saved until the poverty of the body is eliminated and that the most productive eliminator of poverty is not charity but his form of aggressive, enlightened capitalism. His wife, **Lady Britomart**, abhors his "death-dealing," although she has no qualms at all about living on the wealth derived from it. For his daughter, *see* Barbara, Major. *See also* Cusins.

Undine. *See* Ondine.

Unicorn. In European fable, an animal like a small horse, usually white, with a single horn projecting from the head; often a symbol of virginity and in medieval legend often associated with the Virgin Mary.* In more recent times, it has become more a symbol of grace, beauty, imagination, and of a beautiful past now gone forever. It also figures in the royal arms of Great Britain and of Scotland.

Urania. In Greek mythology, the Muse* of astronomy; in some Renaissance poetry, she is called the muse of poetry.

Uranus. In Greek mythology, the sky itself, the father of the Titans,* and the most ancient of all gods. *Also called* Coelus. *See also* Gaia.

Uriah. (1) In the Bible, *II Samuel* xi, Bathsheba's* husband, who is sent into battle by David* in order that he might be killed, thus freeing Bathsheba to become David's wife. *Also called* Urijah. (2) *See* Heep, Uriah.

Uriel. (1) In the Bible, in the Apochrypha, *Enoch,* one of the seven archangels.* In John Milton's poem *Paradise Lost* (1667), he is the archangel who supervises the sun and who directs Satan* to Paradise* by mistake, unable to see through his disguise.

Urijah. *See* Uriah.

Urizen. In numerous poems and drawings by William Blake, a grim, moralistic giant, generally equated with Jehovah.*

Ursula. In Ben Jonson's play *Bartholomew Fair* (1614), a fat, filthy, and wildly bawdy pig woman.

Ursula, St. In Christian legend, a virgin martyr who went on pilgrimage to avoid a marriage and who, along with 11,000 virgin followers, was said to have been killed by the Huns.* Her day is October 21.

Usher. In Edgar Allan Poe's story *The Fall of the House of Usher* (1839), **Roderick** is a madman, last of his family line, morbidly sensitive, who dies of terror when his sister **Madeline** reappears to him from her grave. A cataleptic, she has been buried alive and has broken out of her tomb, only to die with her brother as their dark, brooding old house collapses around them.

Uther Pendragon. In British legend, the father of Arthur.* *See also* Igraine.

Utopia. In Thomas More's *Utopia* (1516), an island where the inhabitants have developed the perfect society, named from the ancient Greek word for "nowhere." The work was widely read and has had many imitators, each drawing up a different vision of the perfect society, but all failing, like More, to indicate how mankind might move from present evils to that perfection, with the result that the term "utopian" has come to suggest more a beautiful or impractical dream than any realistic vision of social life. *See also* Atlantis; Eldorado; Shangri-La.

Utterword, Lady. In G. B. Shaw's play *Heartbreak House* (1919), the apparently scatterbrained but actually quite logical and self-controlled wife of an empire builder; she defends both the propriety and efficiency of a firm rule by the squirearchy. Her brother-in-law **Randall** is a selfish, peevish, empty man trapped in the pride of his class and his codes but with no real authority or independence. *See also* Dunn; Hushabye; Mangan; Shotover, Capt.

Utnapishtim. In the anonymous *Gilgamesh,* the ancient man who survived the great Flood* and to whom Gilgamesh* goes to learn the secret of life in hopes of restoring Engidu.*

Uzzah. In the Bible, *II Samuel* vi, a man who touched the Ark* of the Covenant and was struck dead by God.

Uzziah. In the Bible, *II Kings* xv, a king of Judah* made a leper by God because he allowed incense to be burned in the temple.

Uzziel. In John Milton's poem *Paradise Lost* (1667), an angel* second in power to Gabriel.*

V

Vacuna. In Roman mythology, a goddess of leisure and repose; in some sources also a goddess of agriculture.

Vader, Darth. In several movies, beginning with *Star Wars* (1977), a futuristic villain, noted for his black plastic armor and mask.

Valentin. (1) In Goethe's poem/play *Faust* (1790), Gretchen's* brother, a soldier who is killed by Faust.* (2) In Balzac's novel *The Wild Ass's Skin* (1830), a reckless law student who finds a magic ass's skin that grants him anything he wishes, but it shrinks each time it does so, and his death will occur if it shrinks to nothing. He wastes away most of his wishes on frivolous sensual pleasures and then becomes morbidly depressed as the skin shrinks. (3) *See also* Valentine.

Valentine. (1) In Shakespeare's play *Two Gentlemen of Verona* (1594), a witty but faithful lover who is willing to sacrifice anything for friendship, even his love for Silvia. *See also* Proteus. (2) In William Congreve's play *Love for Love* (1695), a profligate young lover who feigns madness to test the love of Angelica* as well as to escape his debts. (3) *See also* Valentin.

Valentine, St. In Christian legend, a martyred Roman Christian. He is associated with young lovers, who give gifts on his day, February 14; however, no one has offered a particularly convincing explanation of how this association came about.

Valerian. In Christian legend, the husband of the virgin martyr St. Cecilia.* As related in Chaucer's *Canterbury Tales,* in the Second Nun's Tale, Cecilia refused him admittance to her bedchamber because she was meeting an angel* there, whereupon he became baptized by the Pope to gain the right to enter the room; there he found the angel, who granted him and his brother the chance to be holy martyrs.

Valhalla. In Scandinavian mythology, the Paradise* to which all great warriors were taken after their death.

Valjean, Jean. In Victor Hugo's novel *Les Misérables* (1862), a simple man who is sent to prison for stealing bread to feed his starving relatives. His numerous attempts at escape turn a five-year sentence into nineteen years; when he is released, his attempts to lead a proper life are disrupted by harrassment from the policeman Javert.* Among many noted incidents are his theft of a bishop's candlesticks, which leads to his conversion when the bishop refuses to have him arrested; his renouncing of his pseudonym to save another man accused in his place; a famous pursuit through the sewers of Paris; and his eventual rescue of Javert himself from the 1830 revolutionaries. *See also* Cosette; Fantine; Marius; Thénardier.

Valkyrie. In Scandinavian mythology, the maids of heaven who rode into battle to select the men who would be admitted into Valhalla.* Richard Wagner uses one of them, Brünnhilde,* as a central figure in his operas *The Ring of the Niebelung,* and their ride and chant of "hoy-yo-to-ho" are among the most exciting moments of opera. As a result, however, they are also often parodied as fat women wearing horned helmets and metal brassieres, the standard illustration of the ludicrous aspects of opera.

Valmont. In Choderlos de Laclos's novel *Les Liaisons dangereuses* (1782), an unscrupulous libertine. *See also* Merteuil, Marquise de; Volanges, Cécile de.

Vampire. In European legend, a creature who lives by sucking the blood of his or her victims; the most famous personification is Dracula.*

Vance, Philo. In numerous novels by S. S. Van Dine (beg. 1926), an American pseudo-English amateur detective, noted for his esoteric habits and his ability to unravel wildly improbable mysteries.

Vandal. Historically, an ancient Germanic tribe that sacked Rome in 455, thereby giving their name to any random, senseless destruction.

Vanderhof. In Kaufman and Hart's play *You Can't Take It With You* (1936), an eccentric family that lives completely as it wishes. **Grandpa** collects snakes and avoids taxes; his daughter **Penny** paints when not writing plays because a typewriter was delivered to the house by mistake; her husband makes fireworks in the basement; and her daughter is the world's worst, but happiest, ballerina.

Van Helsing. In Bram Stoker's novel *Dracula* (1897), the doctor whose specialty is vampire lore and who is brought in to save Lucy* and to destroy Dracula.*

Vanity Fair. In John Bunyan's *Pilgrim's Progress* (1678), a fair set up by Beelzebub* where the shops sold all the forms of vanity; Faithful* is burned to death there, but Christian* manages to escape and continue on his journey.

Van Winkle, Rip. *See* Rip Van Winkle.

Vanya, Uncle. In Anton Chekhov's play *Uncle Vanya* (1899), a poor relation who has devoted his life to running the estate for Serebryakov,* only to learn that Serebryakov is a worthless nobody. Vanya tries in vain to kill him and falls in love in vain with Serebryakov's new wife Helena. *See also* Astrov; Sonya.

Varden. In Charles Dickens's novel *Barnaby Rudge* (1841), **Dolly** is a naive, plump, garrulous, good-hearted girl; her father **Gabriel** is an honest locksmith who defies the mob; her mother is noted for her wildly changeable moods.

Vargas Girl. In numerous paintings by Alberto Vargas (actually called the Varga Girl), particularly those published in *Esquire* magazine (beg. 1940), an idealized, sexy American girl, noted for her large breasts and long legs, associated in particular with the World War II pinup.

Varner. In several novels by William Faulkner, especially *The Hamlet* (1940), **Will** is the Mississippi plantation owner, a bluff dominating Southern gentleman; his daughter **Eula**, from early youth, is an Earth Mother,* a woman of unconsciously potent sexuality who literally draws men like flies, only to be married to the least sexual male available, the money-grubbing Flem Snopes.* *See also* Stevens.

Varney. In Walter Scott's novel *Kenilworth* (1821), a charming but unscrupulous courtier who falsely convinces Sussex that his wife is unfaithful; he commits suicide after being imprisoned. *See also* Robsart, Amy; Tressilian.

Varvara. *See* Stavrogin; Varya.

Varya. (1) In Anton Chekhov's play *The Cherry Orchard* (1904), the plain, competent housekeeper and adopted daughter of Ranevskaya,* unlucky in love and with nothing but daily work to occupy her life. *Also called* Varvara. *See also* Gaev; Lopahin. (2) *See also* Varvara.

Vashti. In the Bible, *Esther* i, the beautiful queen of Persia who held her own women's banquet and refused to go to that given by Ahasuerus,* whereupon he divorced her lest her example encourage Persian women to disobey their husbands. *See also* Esther.

Vathek. In William Beckford's novel *Vathek* (1786), an Arab sultan who, after human sacrifices, makes a deal with a mysterious stranger to learn the pleasures of depravity and black magic, until his heart is consumed by eternal flames.

Vautrin. In several novels by Balzac, particularly *Père Goriot* (1835), a criminal mastermind, unusually mysterious and effective, who eventually ends his life as chief of the French secret police. *See also* Chardon, Lucien; Rastignac.

Veneering. In Charles Dickens's novel *Our Mutual Friend* (1864), a former law clerk who becomes a partner and then, armed with ''everything new,'' buys a Parliamentary seat, never losing his shallow personality.

Venn, Diggory. In Thomas Hardy's novel *The Return of the Native* (1878), initially a figure of mystery and potential terror, since the sheep dye he sells has turned his skin completely red; he reveals himself as a lonely but sincere suitor whose misunderstandings help to trigger tragic events but also to rescue the girl he loves. *See also* Vye, Eustacia; Yeobright.

Ventidius. In Shakespeare's play *Timon of Athens* (1607), a faithless friend who deserts Timon* when the latter's money disappears.

Venus. In Roman mythology, the goddess of love, generally equivalent to Aphrodite* but more closely associated with physical, romantic love in particular than the Greek goddess had been. *Also called* Erycina.

Venusberg. In German legend, a mountain in the caves of which Venus* held her court. In Richard Wagner's opera *Tannhäuser* (1845), Tannhäuser lives there for seven years; the "Venusberg music" is noted for its sensuality.

Verdurin, Mme. In Marcel Proust's novels *Remembrance of Things Past* (1913–27), a pretentious bourgeois wife who tries to maintain an "artistic" salon, never mixing with real society in spite of her pretensions and never really understanding anything the artists say. Swann* meets Odette* at one of her parties. *See also* Guermantes; Vinteuil.

Vere, Capt. In Herman Melville's story *Billy Budd* (1924), the ship's captain, a sensitive intellectual who is trapped between strict naval regulations and his desire to save the pure Billy Budd.* *See also* Claggart.

Verges. In Shakespeare's play *Much Ado About Nothing* (1598), the elderly, bumbling associate and admirer of Dogberry.*

Verhovensky. In Dostoevsky's novel *The Possessed* (1867), **Pyotr** is a fanatic, irreligious, nihilist revolutionary, completely without scruples, himself completely under the spell of Stavrogin;* he is able to charm others into the cause and then lead them to criminal action. His father **Stepan** is an old liberal, rather weak-willed, who gradually is appalled by his son's character; convinced that he has been a fool, he wanders off to find the true Russia and dies. *See also* Shatov.

Verloc. In Joseph Conrad's novel *The Secret Agent* (1907), a foreign spy posing as a shopkeeper in London who tries to bomb Greenwich Observatory. His wife **Vinnie** is a motherly woman who murders him after the bomb goes off accidentally and kills her half-wit brother, who is carrying the bomb. The couple are noted as extremely shabby and realistic persons, some of the earliest such in "spy" literature.

Vernon, Diana. In Walter Scott's novel *Rob Roy* (1818), the outspoken Catholic heroine. *See also* Osbaldistone; Rob Roy.

Veronica, St. In Christian legend, a woman who wiped Jesus's* brow while he carried the cross, her cloth (or veil) thereby receiving an image of His face. Her day is July 12.

Verplaca. In Roman mythology, the goddess of family harmony.

Vershinin. In Anton Chekhov's play *Three Sisters* (1901), the married lover of Masha,* a colonel who endlessly reiterates his belief that the world is constantly improving itself. *See also* Prozorov.

Vertumnus. In Roman mythology, the god of the seasons and of change; in Ovid's *Metamorphoses,* he assumes numerous disguises to win Pomona.*

Vesta. In Roman mythology, the goddess of the hearth, symbol of the home; the Vestal Virgins were maidens of spotless chastity who maintained the fire of her temple in Rome. *Also called* Hestia.

Vestal Virgin. *See* Vesta.

Vicar of Bray. In an eighteenth-century English song, a vicar who boasted that whoever was king and whatever the official church, he remained the Vicar of Bray; hence, a person who changes beliefs whenever profitable.

Vicar of Wakefield. *See* Primrose.

Vice. In the medieval morality plays, a mischievous fool, not directly related to any particular sin.

Victoria. (1) In Roman mythology, the goddess of victory, generally equivalent to Nike.* (2) Historically, a queen of England (d. 1901) whose long reign and the prosperity and triumphs that occurred during it gave her name to the century. Although she reigned from her youth, she is generally portrayed as seen late in life—strict, prudish, frumpy, and reserved, devoid of humor and the embodiment of stodgy, unemotional, unfeeling social propriety and sexual repression. (3) *See also* Vittoria.

Vincent, St. (1) Historically, Vincent of Saragossa (d. 304), the most celebrated of Spanish martyrs, who was killed, after other tortures, by being roasted on a grid. His day is January 22, and he is often called the patron saint of drunkards. (2) Historically, Vincent de Paul, a priest (d. 1660) of notable humility and virtue whose lifelong works of charity led to the founding of the Lazarists and later the extremely visible Catholic charitable societies bearing his name.

Vincentio. (1) In Shakespeare's play *The Taming of the Shrew* (1593), the bombastic father of Lucentio.* *See also* Bianca; Kate. (2) In Shakespeare's play *Measure for Measure* (1604), the Duke of Vienna, an ambiguous figure who pretends to go away in order to test his deputy Angelo* and then in disguise manipulates events to resolve the crisis his earlier pretense made possible. *See also* Isabella.

Vineyard. In the Bible, *Matthew* xx, a parable told by Jesus:* A man hires workers for his vineyard, but he pays all exactly the same, whether they work all day or only the last hour, illustrating that "the last shall be first."

Vinteuil. In Marcel Proust's novels *Remembrance of Things Past* (1913–27), a composer, noted in particular for the violin sonata that introduces and accompanies the romance of Swann* and Odette.*

Viola. In Shakespeare's play *Twelfth Night* (1599), a shipwrecked girl who disguises herself as a man, falls in love with the lord Orsino,* whom she comes to serve, and in turn finds that Olivia,* the woman to whom she carries Orsino's messages of love, has fallen in love with her male disguise. She eventually finds herself trapped in a famous comic duel with Aguecheek* and in much confusion until she is reunited with her twin brother Sebastian.* *See also* Belch, Sir Toby; Malvolio.

Violenta. In Shakespeare's play *All's Well That Ends Well* (1602), a neighbor woman who has no lines; thus, a common example of a nonentity.

Violetta. In Verdi's opera *La Traviata* (1853), the doomed courtesan who falls in love with a respectable young man, renounces that love for his own good, and is only reunited with him on her deathbed. Musically, she is characterized by her aria "Sempre libre." *See also* Camille.

Virgilia. In Shakespeare's play *Coriolanus* (1607), Coriolanus's* sweet, gentle, homebody of a wife, whom he calls "my gracious silence."

Virgin, The. *See* Mary.

Virginia. (1) In Chaucer's *Canterbury Tales,* in the Doctor's Tale, a pure Roman maiden who asks her father to kill her to escape a lascivious judge's designs. (2) *See also* Virginie.

Virginian, The. In Owen Wister's novel *The Virginian* (1902), the model fictional cowboy, tough, brave, simple, and yet a perfect gentleman around women; noted for saying, "When you call me that, smile." He restores law and order even when it means hanging a friend turned cattle rustler.

Virginie. (1) In Saint-Pierre's novel *Paul et Virginie* (1787), a pure maiden who drowns rather than take off her clothes to swim in sight of the sailor trying to rescue her; at the time of publication, a widely admired symbol of natural, uncorrupted innocence. (2) *See also* Virginia.

Virgin Mary. *See* Mary.

Virgin Queen. The literary name given to Queen Elizabeth* I of England, due to her refusal to marry.

Virgins, 11,000. *See* Ursula, St.

Virgins, Foolish. In the Bible, *Matthew* xxv, a parable told by Jesus:* Ten women come to await the return of the bride and groom, but five have their lamps burn out while they wait. While they are gone to get extra oil, the five who brought spare oil meet the wedding party and get invited in, while the five foolish ones are locked out.

Virgins, Wise. *See* Virgins, Foolish.

Virgo. A constellation in the zodiac, represented by a robed woman holding a sheaf of grain. *See also* Astraea; Erigone.

Vishnu. In Hindu mythology, one of the three great gods, the preserver who rides on an eagle. *See also* Brahma; Krishna; Rama; Shiva.

Vittoria. (1) In John Webster's play *The White Devil* (1612), the brave, eloquent, and beautiful lady who is eventually destroyed by the all-consuming passion of Brachiano,* who murders his wife and Vittoria's husband in order to marry her. *See also* Flamineo. (2) *See also* Victoria.

Vitus, St. In Christian legend, a martyr during the reign of Diocletian to whom people often pray for help with illness, particularly epilepsy and chorea (so closely associated with him as to be popularly known as "St. Vitus's dance"). His emblem is a cock or a dog; his day is June 15.

Vivien. In Tennyson's poem *Merlin and Vivien* (1859), the vain coquette who seduces Merlin* into revealing his magic secrets and then casts a spell over him. *Also called* Nimue.* *See also* Lady of the Lake; Morgan le Fay.

Vladimir. In Samuel Beckett's play *Waiting for Godot* (1952), one of the two tramps waiting eternally for Godot.* *See also* Estragon.

Volanges, Cécile de. In Choderlos de Laclos's novel *Les Liaisons dangereuses* (1782), the innocent young woman who is trapped in the lascivious plots of Valmont* and the Marquise de Merteuil.*

Volpone. In Ben Jonson's play *Volpone* (1605), an enthusiastically devious and greedy Venetian who pretends to be dying in order to trick his even greedier neighbors into giving him outrageously valuable gifts in hopes of being named in his will. One of the most cynical and flamboyantly avaricious characters in literature, he is nonetheless attractive due to the gusto with which he approaches his schemes. *See also* Corbaccio; Corvino; Mosca; Voltore; Would-Be, Politic.

Voltore. In Ben Jonson's play *Volpone* (1605), a ruthless, greedy lawyer duped by Volpone.*

Volturnus. An early Roman god of the river Tiber, who generally faded from view after the river came to be called after King Tiberinus.*

Volumnia. In Shakespeare's play *Coriolanus* (1607), the mother of Coriolanus*
and the epitome of the noble Roman matron.

Vortigern. In British legend, a fifth-century king who invited the Jutes to help
him retain his throne only to find that they refused to leave afterward. Notable
primarily as the subject of *Vortigern and Rowena,* claimed to be by Shakespeare
in one of the most famous literary forgeries of the late eighteenth century.

Vronsky. In Tolstoy's novel *Anna Karenina* (1875), the handsome officer who
falls in love with Anna Karenina* and lives with her until her guilt destroys
their affair and she kills herself. *See also* Kitty.

Vulcan. In Roman mythology, the god of fire and metalworking, generally
equivalent to Hephaestus.*

Vye, Eustacia. In Thomas Hardy's novel *The Return of the Native* (1878), a
dark, passionate young woman who falls in love with her idea of Clym
Yeobright* and marries him after first meeting him while disguised as a boy in
the Christmas mummer's play, mistakenly believing that he will take her away
to a romantic life, only to be trapped on the heath she detests. She renews an
earlier affair and is drowned during a storm as she tries to run away with her
lover. *See also* Yeobright.

W

Wadman, Widow. In Laurence Sterne's novel *Tristram Shandy* (1759), the neighbor widow with matrimonial designs on Uncle Toby;* she is much concerned with the nature of Toby's wound.

Waffles. *See* Telegin.

Wagner. (1) In Christopher Marlowe's play *Doctor Faustus* (1592), Faustus's* comic servant. (2) In Goethe's *Faust* (1790), Faust's* servant, a shallow pedant who understands only platitudes and surfaces.

Wait, James. In Joseph Conrad's story *The Nigger of the 'Narcissus'* (1897), the "nigger" of the title, a Negro sailor obsessed with the presentiment of his own death, which slowly demoralizes the crew around him.

Waitwell. In William Congreve's play *The Way of the World* (1700), Mirabell's* servant who humiliates Lady Wishfort* by successfully masquerading as a wealthy man in search of a wife.

Wakefield, Vicar of. *See* Primrose.

Waldo. In Olive Schreiner's novel *The Story of an African Farm* (1883), a studious, serious young man who loves from afar, leaves to wander the world, and eventually returns disillusioned to the farm to die. *See also* Lyndall.

Walker, Bill. In G. B. Shaw's play *Major Barbara* (1905), a tough who refuses to be saved, attacks one of the Salvation Army girls, and is in turn humiliated by Major Barbara's* militant Christianity.

Walküre. *See* Valkyries.

Wallah. Originally, a Hindu term meaning a person connected with a particular duty or job; particularly common in British military slang.

Walpurgis, St. *See* Walpurgisnacht.

Walpurgisnacht. In German legend, a night on which witches* appeared for a night of wild revelry, generally on April 30, the day of St. Walpurgis.

Walter. In Schiller's play *William Tell* (1804), William Tell's* son who holds the apple on his head.

Wally. *See* Cleaver.

Wamba. In Walter Scott's novel *Ivanhoe* (1820), the quick-witted jester who helps Cedric* escape from prison.

Wandering Jew. *See* Ahasuerus; Samuel.

Wangel. In Henrik Ibsen's play *The Lady from the Sea* (1889), **Ellida** is a woman who feels stifled by the mountains and the memory of a sailor she once loved. When he returns, she chooses to stay with her husband; the act of the choice itself seems to restore her sanity. Her husband **Dr. Wangel**, in his concern for her sanity, agrees to let her go if she so desires. In *The Master Builder* (1892), **Hilda**, a stepdaughter of Ellida, now grown-up, is a vivacious but fanciful young woman in love with Solness* from childhood; she pressures him to overcome his fears and exults when he does so, even though he dies.

Warbucks, Daddy. In the American newspaper cartoon *Little Orphan Annie* (beg. 1924), the ultraconservative multimillionaire who often helped Little Orphan Annie.* Physically distinguished by his completely bald head, he is usually synonymous with the unbridled power of money.

Wardle. In Charles Dickens's novel *Pickwick Papers* (1836), the robust and genial owner of Manor Farm, where Pickwick* visits several times, including the memorable Christmas with the ice-skating party. *See also* Fat Boy, The; Jingle; Tupman.

Warlock. In English folklore, a wizard or male witch.*

Warrior Queen. *See* Boadicea.

Washington, George. Historically, the leader of the American forces (d. 1799) in the Revolutionary War and the first President of the United States. He figures in much American legend for such fictional exploits as his refusal to tell a lie when he chopped down his father's cherry tree and his tossing of a coin across the Potomac River, as well as for his historical exploits, for which he is called the Father of His Country.

Waterloo. Historically, the battle (1815) in which Napoleon* was finally and permanently defeated; hence, often used to denote any event that disastrously concludes an ambitious project or plan.

Waters, Mrs. In Henry Fielding's novel *Tom Jones* (1749), a former maid who has an affair with Tom Jones* which, for a time, is thought to have been incestuous, since she is thought by some to be his mother until the truth of his background is revealed. She is sometimes noted for her participation in a salaciously suggestive dinner scene in the movie version (1963), one of the famous moments of film.

Watson, Dr. In numerous stories by Arthur Conan Doyle (beg. 1889), Sherlock Holmes's* stolid companion and chronicler. In the stories, he is a faithful, stalwart friend with somewhat better than ordinary perception, which works as a foil for Holmes's brilliance. In movies, however, particularly in the American series (beg. 1939), he has generally been portrayed as a slow-witted buffoon to whom Holmes must constantly explain that which is "Elementary, my dear Watson."

Watson, Miss. In Mark Twain's novel *Huckleberry Finn* (1885), the spinster sister of the Widow Douglas* who tries to reform Huck Finn* into a God-fearing Christian and a respectable boy; she is also the owner of Jim.*

Waverley. In Walter Scott's novel *Waverley* (1814), **Edward** is a brave British officer who becomes involved with Bonnie Prince Charlie's* army and is charged with treason; eventually, he regains the king's favor and inherits the family fortune. His father **Richard** swears loyalty to King George in hopes of political advantage but is destroyed in political maneuvering; **Everard**, Richard's brother, is a committed Jacobite.*

Wayland. (1) *See* Smith, Wayland. (2) *See also* Wieland.

Webb. In Thornton Wilder's play *Our Town* (1938), one of the two typical families depicted. **Mr. Webb** is the editor of the local newspaper; **Mrs. Webb** is a loving but strict mother. For their daughter, *see* Emily.

Webster, Daniel. Historically, an American senator (d. 1852) noted for his legendary oratorical skills. *See also* Stone, Jabez.

Wegg, Silas. In Charles Dickens's novel *Our Mutual Friend* (1864), a sly and mean-spirited semiliterate who is hired by Boffin* to read to him and then tries to find Boffin's secret hoard by endlessly sifting through a pile of ashes. Finally, he tries to blackmail Boffin and is thrown out with the garbage.

Weird Sisters. In Shakespeare's play *Macbeth* (1605), three witches* who foretell Macbeth's* rise to power and also the circumstances of his death; noted particularly for "double, double, toil and trouble." *See also* Banquo; Fleance.

Welby, Marcus. In the American television series "Marcus Welby, MD" (1969–76), the perfect, kindly family physician.

Wellborn, Grace. In Ben Jonson's play *Bartholomew Fair* (1614), the attractive and intelligent fiancée of Bartholomew Cokes.* She is so upset by his neglect of her that she agrees to marry a man selected at random by a local madman, as a result wedding the only sensible man in the entire play.

Weller. In Charles Dickens's novel *Pickwick Papers* (1836), **Sam** is Pickwick's* imaginative, resourceful servant, noted in particular for his endless stream of aphorisms in the form ''as the _____ said when _____.'' **His father** is a coachman who wants only a simple life with food and drink but, much to his regret, has married a widow who owns a pub and gives free liquor to the hypocritical local minister Stiggins.* *See also* Trotter, Job.

Wemmick. In Charles Dickens's novel *Great Expectations* (1860), the efficient and kindly clerk of Jaggers* who converts his cottage into a miniature castle complete with moat and into which he withdraws after working hours with his father, whom he calls ''the Aged,'' often quoted as ''Aged P.''

Wenceslas. Historically, a king of Bohemia (d. 929) who established Christianity and was killed by his pagan brother. He was canonized and, as St. Wenceslas, is the patron saint of Czechoslovakia. In Britain and America, he is most known as the Good King Wenceslas of the nineteenth-century Christmas carol, all events of which are legendary and which occur on St. Stephen's* day rather than on Wenceslas's (September 28).

Wendy. *See* Darling.

Wentworth. In Jane Austen's novel *Persuasion* (1818), the penniless officer who is persuaded to give up his interest in Anne Elliot* but who later, after becoming a wealthy captain, meets her again and renews his love.

Werewolf. In European legend, much used in American movies, a man who looks like or changes into a wolf when the moon is full and then attacks humans. In some sources, he can be killed only by a silver bullet.

Werther. In Goethe's novel *The Sorrows of Young Werther* (1774), a lovesick young man who sees his dream woman Charlotte* marry another man, tries to forget her, fails, and then tries to force his attentions on her even though she is married. He is so humiliated and guilt-ridden by the episode that he shoots himself. He was the primary model of the Romantic hero—a young man whose heart overwhelms him, who tries to be ruled by Nature rather than by Reason, and who suffers from unrequited love.

Westenra, Lucy. *See* Lucy.

Western. In Henry Fielding's novel *Tom Jones* (1749), **Sophia** is the virtuous maiden whom Tom Jones* loves and eventually marries after her father's attempt to marry her off to someone else makes her run away. Her father, the **Squire**, is a domineering, uncouth countryman who loves his horses, hounds, and drink.

White Rabbit. In Lewis Carroll's story *Alice in Wonderland* (1865), the rabbit whom Alice* follows down the rabbit hole into Wonderland; he wears a waistcoat, carries a pocket watch, and is in a great hurry.

Whitefield, Ann. In G. B. Shaw's play *Man and Superman* (1903), the persistent, intelligent woman, by turns a liar, a coquette, and a bully but with enough charm to get away with it. She always eventually gets what she wants, in this case John Tanner.* *See also* Ana, Doña; Juan, Don.

Whittington, Dick. Historically, a Lord Mayor of London (d. 1423) noted for his great wealth. Legend says he became rich after he sent his cat on a voyage during which it was purchased for an enormous sum by a king plagued by rats. Numerous variations on the story have been played by English pantomimes for several centuries, although a more prosaic version points out that the ships used in the coal trade were also called cats.

Who, Dr. In the British television series "Dr. Who" (beg. 1963), a brilliant time-traveling scientist whose intelligence and daring save him and the Earth in numerous adventures across the galaxies; noted for his Tardis, a time machine/ spaceship disguised as a British police call box, his long scarf, and a playful sense of humor unusual in sci-fi movies or television.

Whore of Babylon. *See* Scarlet Woman.

Wickfield. In Charles Dickens's novel *David Copperfield* (1849), a lawyer who tries to reduce all human action to a single motive, who becomes a quiet alcoholic in his grief over his wife's death, and who is almost destroyed by the machinations of his clerk Uriah Heep.* For his daughter, *see* Agnes.

Wickham. In Jane Austen's novel *Pride and Prejudice* (1813), the charming but unscrupulous officer who lies to the Bennet* girls about Darcy* and then elopes with the naive Lydia.

Widow at Windsor. In Rudyard Kipling's poem *The Widow at Windsor* (1890), Queen Victoria.*

Widow Douglas. *See* Douglas, Widow.

Widow of Ephesus. *See* Ephesus, Widow of.

Widow of Windsor. *See* Widow at Windsor.

Wieland. (1) In Scandinavian legend, a smith so adept that, when he fought a rival with a sword he had made, the rival was cut in two but did not feel a thing until he tried to move, at which point he came apart. (2) *See also* Wayland.

Wife of Bath. In Chaucer's *Canterbury Tales,* a flamboyantly lively, bawdy, much-married (and widowed) woman who tells the story of the knight who learns that women love "sovereignty" more than anything else.

Wife of Usher. In a Scottish ballad, a mother whose sons are drowned at sea and then appear to her again only to disappear from her celebration feast at cockcrow.

Wiggs, Mrs. In Alice Hegan's novel *Mrs. Wiggs of the Cabbage Patch* (1901), a poor tenement widow with five children who nonetheless regards the world through "rose-colored spectacles" and who believes everything works out for the best if you wait long enough.

Wild, Jonathan. In Henry Fielding's novel *Jonathan Wild* (1743), a criminal who seeks greatness through crime, only to be hanged eventually.

Wild Boar of Ardennes. In Walter Scott's novel *Quentin Durward* (1823), a vicious outlaw who twice tries to kidnap Isabelle* and who tries to seize Liège by murdering its bishop.

Wild Child, The. Any of several children found wandering the woods in various parts of Europe during the eighteenth century who were thought to be pure children of nature without any aspects, good or bad, of civilization. *See also* Noble Savage.

Wildfire, Madge. In Walter Scott's novel *The Heart of Midlothian* (1818), a girl who steals Effie Deans's* baby, goes mad after she is seduced, and is harried to death by a mob. *See also* Murdockson, Meg.

Wilfer. In Charles Dickens's novel *Our Mutual Friend* (1864), **Bella** is a beautiful poor girl taken in by the Boffins.* At first a very selfish and self-centered girl, she becomes more natural and caring as she sees Noddy appear to become a miser. Her sister **Lavinia** is a sharp, firm, strong-willed girl. **Mrs. Wilfer** is a shrew; **Mr. Wilfer** is a seedy, cherubically kindly old man.

Wilfred, St. Historically, an English bishop (d. 709) and an ardent missionary. A narrow passage in his crypt at Ripon is called St. Wilfred's Needle, and it was said that only true virgins were able to pass through it.

Wilhelm Meister. In Goethe's novels *Wilhelm Meister's Apprenticeship* (1795) and *Wilhelm Meister's Travels* (1821), a young man who travels after discovering the faithlessness of his first love and who becomes involved with an acting troupe and with numerous adventures that teach him that life is an apprenticeship. In the later work, he renounces commerce and the stage to wander the earth in search of spiritual purification. *See also* Aurelia; Mariana; Mignon.

Wilis. In the ballet *Giselle* (1841), beautiful female spirits who appear at night and force any man they capture to dance until he drops dead from exhaustion. *See also* Giselle.

Wilkes, Ashley. In Margaret Mitchell's novel *Gone With the Wind* (1936), Scarlett O'Hara's* romantic dream man who is sensitive and sophisticated as well as handsome but is much weaker than her romantic view makes him out to be. *See also* Butler, Rhett; Melanie.

William. (1) Historically, the name of several English kings. The most notable include **William I** (d. 1087), called William the Conqueror, who invaded England in 1066 from Normandy, defeated the Saxon armies, and established a line of Norman nobility that altered the shape of English language and culture; and **William of Orange** (d. 1702), originally a Dutch prince, who was offered the throne after his marriage to Mary in order to provide a stable Protestant line of succession, after the bloodless Glorious Revolution of 1688–89. (2) *See* Elliot.

William, Father. In Robert Southey's poem *The Old Man's Comforts* (1799), a representative, upright old man; now much better known from the parody in Lewis Carroll's *Alice in Wonderland* (1865), in which he is a silly old man who stands on his head.

William of Norwich. Historically, a twelve-year-old boy whose body was found mutilated in 1144 and who was locally venerated because he was thought to have been ritually slaughtered by Jews. No evidence was ever found to support this or any subsequent similar charges, but the legends of Jewish ritual killing of Christian children, not completely ended yet, have continued from that date. *See also* Hugh of Lincoln.

Williams. In Shakespeare's play *Henry V* (1598), a soldier who quarrels with the disguised King Henry V* and challenges him to a duel.

Willie, Wandering. In Walter Scott's novel *Redgauntlet* (1824), a blind fiddler.

Willie and Joe. In Bill Mauldin's cartoons from World War II, the quintessential average American private soldiers.

Willoughby. In Jane Austen's novel *Sense and Sensibility* (1811), the handsome but dissipated villain who tries to seduce the emotional Marianne Dashwood* until it is revealed that he has already seduced another girl and married for money.

Willoughby, Sir. *See* Patterne.

Willy. *See* Loman.

Wilson, William. In Edgar Allan Poe's story *William Wilson* (1839), a man embarked on a life of wickedness but constantly foiled by a double, until at last he kills the double and is free to be damned.

Wimpy. In the American newspaper cartoon *Thimble Theater* (beg. 1930) and in numerous movie cartoons (beg. 1932) featuring Popeye,* the round man with the tiny hat who eats nothing but hamburgers and tries to borrow money he will gladly repay on Tuesday.

Wimsey, Peter. In numerous novels and stories by Dorothy Sayers (beg. 1923), an English gentleman amateur detective who puts on an appearance of fatuousity over a brilliant and perceptive mind. *See also* Bunter.

Wingfield. In Tennessee Williams's play *The Glass Menagerie* (1945), **Amanda**, the mother, is a pushy and ultimately stifling woman left in poverty after her husband's desertion, living on dreams of romance for her daughter and her memories of life as a Southern belle. Her daughter **Laura** is a gentle, shy cripple who is afraid even to go to classes and who keeps a menagerie of glass animals. Her son **Tom** finally rebels against the monotony of his job and the dreariness of his family life and runs away. **The father**, never seen, is famous as a telephone man "who fell in love with long distances."

Winifred, St. A legendary Welsh woman who resisted a pagan chieftain's advances until he cut off her head; the earth opened and swallowed him, whereupon her head was restored to her shoulders by St. Beuno, and she came back to life and became a nun. The place where her head fell was said to have become a spring, the water of which cured various diseases. Pilgrimages to Winifred's Well have continued into the twentieth century. Her day is November 3.

Winkle. In Charles Dickens's novel *Pickwick Papers* (1836), the young man who pretends to skills he does not have, getting into situations in which he accidentally shoots his friends, stumbles into duels, falls off of horses, and so on. He also falls in love and marries against his father's wishes but is eventually reconciled by Pickwick's* intercession.

Winkle, Rip Van. *See* Rip Van Winkle.

Winnie-the-Pooh. In A. A. Milne's stories *Winnie-the-Pooh* (1926), a teddy bear belonging to Christopher Robin* that seems to be alive and has numerous fey adventures, most of which somehow manage to involve jars of honey. *See also* Eeyore; Heffalump; Piglet; Roo.

Winston. *See* Churchill, Winston; Smith, Winston.

Winter, de. *See* de Winter.

Wintergreen, ex-PFC. In Joseph Heller's novel *Catch–22* (1961), a lowly soldier who controls the army because he controls the mimeograph machine.

Wiseman, Worldly. In John Bunyan's *Pilgrim's Progress* (1678), a man in the town of Carnal Policy who tries to persuade Christian* not to go on his pilgrimage but rather to seek relief from sin in Legality.

Wise Men, Three. *See* Magi.

Wishfort, Lady. In William Congreve's play *The Way of the World* (1700), the lustful, sex-starved old woman who is ludicrous in her desire for a man and thus is easily gulled by Mirabell's* servant Waitwell,* who pretends to admire her. She is also the guardian of Millamant.*

Witch. In legend and folklore, a human with magical powers, almost always depicted as malevolent and female, and usually ugly and old as well. In general, witches are thought to derive their power from the Devil,* whom they worship in a Black Mass or a Witches' Sabbath, and to use that power to cast spells over those other humans who displease them. In European lore, they are most often depicted wearing conical hats and black garb, riding a broomstick on which they can fly, and accompanied by a black cat, although in other countries they take different forms.

Witch of Endor. In the Bible, *I Samuel* xxviii, the witch* consulted by Saul* when he believes God has forsaken him and who foretells Saul's death.

Witches, Three. *See* Weird Sisters.

Witherington. In the anonymous *Ballad of Chevy Chase,* a knight whose legs are cut off but continues to fight on the stumps.

Witterly. In Charles Dickens's novel *Nicholas Nickleby* (1838), a snobbish, pretentious family. **Henry**, the husband, thinks **Julia**, his wife, is "a hot-house plant" whose fragility must be protected at all costs.

Witwoud. In William Congreve's play *The Way of the World* (1700), an idle fop who prides himself on his witticisms; his brother **Sir Wilful** is a country gentleman with a bluff but honest nature, very raucous but good-natured.

Wizard of Oz. *See* Oz.

Wobegon, Lake. In the American radio series "A Prairie Home Companion" (1974–87) and in Garrison Keillor's novel *Lake Wobegon Days* (1985), a mythical but representative American small "town that time forgot" where it has always "been a quiet week." Because of the good humor of the descriptions of events there, many allusions see it as more simple and sentimentalized than the complex community actually depicted.

Woden. A name sometimes used for Odin.*

Woeful Countenance, Knight of the. *See* Quixote, Don.

Wolfe, Nero. In numerous novels and stories by Rex Stout (beg. 1934), a detective noted for his great weight, his passionate devotion to orchids, and his refusal ever to leave his home to work on various mysteries. He depends on occasional interviews and the evidence dug up by his aide Archie Goodwin* to reveal the solution to his brilliant mind.

Wolfsheim. In F. Scott Fitzgerald's novel *The Great Gatsby* (1925), a mysterious associate of Gatsby* and a gambler who is rumored to have fixed the 1919 World Series.

Wolstan, St. *See* Wulfstan, St.

Woman in Red. In Beale Cormack's play *Aaron Slick from Punkin Creek* (1919), the city woman who tries to seduce the honest country boy Aaron Slick* from the ways of honesty; in some usage, this also identifies the mysterious woman who betrayed the American gangster John Dillinger. *See also* Scarlet Woman.

Woman Taken in Adultery. In the Bible, *John* viii, an adulterous woman brought before Jesus* to see if He would uphold the ancient commandments to have her stoned to death; instead, He said, "He that is without sin among you, let him first cast a stone at her," and she was released. Some legend identifies her as Mary Magdalene,* but there is no Biblical evidence to support this.

Wonderland. *See* Alice.

Wooden Horse. *See* Trojan Horse.

Woodhouse. In Jane Austen's novel *Emma* (1816), an amiable hypochondriac. For his daughter, *see* Emma.

Wooster, Bertie. In numerous stories and novels by P. G. Wodehouse (beg. 1919), a particularly simple and fatuous, but perfectly good-hearted, English gentleman known for his inventive way with a cliché, his terror of aunts and marriage, and his propensity for complicated situations from which only the brilliance of his valet Jeeves* can rescue him.

Wopsle. In Charles Dickens's novel *Great Expectations* (1860), a parish clerk who goes on the stage to play Hamlet* with minimal success.

Worthing, Jack. In Oscar Wilde's play *The Importance of Being Earnest* (1895), the witty young man in love with Gwendolen;* he pretends to be called Ernest,* as that is the only name she could love. *See also* Algernon; Bracknell, Lady; Cecily; Prism, Miss.

Wotan. The German form of Odin.* In Richard Wagner's operas *The Ring of the Niebelung* (1869–76), he is the god who steals the ring of the Niebelung* from Alberich,* thus setting in motion the events that will eventually destroy the gods. He also kills his mortal son Siegmund* for committing incest with Sieglinde* and punishes his Valkyrie* daughter Brünnhilde for her interference by putting her to sleep within the ring of fire. *See also* Erda; Siegfried.

Would-be, Sir Politick. In Ben Jonson's play *Volpone* (1605), a gullible and naive tourist who pretends to be a part of the nation's inner circle by hinting at sinister explanations for simple actions. **Lady Would-Be** is a shallow woman who never stops talking, so much so that even Volpone* is willing to forego cheating her if she will just shut up and leave.

Woyzeck. In Georg Büchner's play *Woyzeck* (1879), a stupid army conscript who has strange visions; driven mad by his mistress's infidelity, he murders her and then accidentally drowns himself while trying to get rid of the weapon. Allusions are perhaps more often to Alban Berg's opera version *Wozzeck* (1925), noted by many as the quintessential ''modern'' opera, the epitome of the kind of opera critics love and audiences hate.

Wozzeck. *See* Woyzeck.

Wrayburn, Eugene. In Charles Dickens's novel *Our Mutual Friend* (1864), a sprightly, intelligent lawyer who falls in love with Lizzie Hexam;* he is nearly murdered by a rival but survives and marries her.

Wren, Jenny. In Charles Dickens's novel *Our Mutual Friend* (1864), the crippled maker of dolls' dresses.

Wulfstan, St. Historically, the only English bishop (d. 1095) to keep his office after William* invaded the country; he was instrumental in ending the practice of slavery in England.

Wycliffe, John. Historically, an English priest (d. 1384) who instituted the first English translation of the Bible and was excommunicated for opposing the power of the Pope; he thus became an occasional symbol of Protestant individuality and religious scruples.

Wynken, Blynken, and Nod. In Eugene Field's poem *Wynken, Blynken, and Nod* (1892), three sailors in a wooden shoe who sail and fish among the stars, eventually revealed to be a child dreaming.

X

Xanadu. In S. T. Coleridge's poem *Kubla Khan* (1797), the site of the "stately pleasure dome" decreed by Kubla Khan.*

Xanthus. In Homer's *Iliad,* a horse as fast as the wind; it could also talk and it foretold Achilles's* death. *See also* Balius.

Xantippe. Historically, the wife of the philosopher Socrates;* tradition has it that she was a great shrew, browbeating the philosopher at home.

Xavier. *See* Francis, St.

Xerxes. Historically, a king of Persia (d. 465 B.C.), Darius's* son, who is noted particularly for his invasion of Greece which was delayed at Thermopylae* and ended at the battle of Salamis. He also appears in the Bible, where he is called Ahasuerus.*

Ximena. In the anonymous *Poem of the Cid,* the wife of the Cid.* *See also* Chimène.

Y

Yahoo. In Jonathan Swift's novel *Gulliver's Travels* (1726), the humanlike creatures in the land of the Houyhnhnms.* Dirty, irrational, and ignorant, their foul appearance and character turn Gulliver* into a recluse who cannot stand human company when he returns to England.

Yama. In Hindu mythology, the god of the dead and the judge who punishes the wicked.

Yankee. Originally, in American usage, a New Englander; in the South, it was used to describe any Americans not from the Confederate States and it is still considered an insult. Outside the United States, it has been regularly used to signify any American. *See also* Connecticut Yankee; Yankee Doodle.

Yankee Doodle. In an eighteenth-century British song, an ignorant young man who stuck a feather in his cap and thought it was high fashion. The song was quickly adopted by Americans during the Revolutionary War and, as the words lost their topicality, the song and the term came to be positive depictions of Americans.

Yasha. In Anton Chekhov's play *The Cherry Orchard* (1904), the insolent footman who prides himself on the time he spent in Paris. *See also* Dunyasha.

Yahweh. In the Bible, the most commonly used Hebrew name for God in the Old Testament books. The common European transliteration was Jehovah.*

Yellow Brick Road. *See* Dorothy.

Yeobright. In Thomas Hardy's novel *The Return of the Native* (1878), **Clym** is a successful diamond merchant who finds that life shallow and returns to the English heath country to be a teacher; he makes a disastrous marriage to Eustacia Vye* and almost loses his sight, becoming a manual laborer until his unjustified guilt after his mother's death destroys the marriage and he becomes a lay preacher. **Mrs. Yeobright** is a strict woman who opposes his marriage; mistakenly locked out when she tries to make up their quarrel, she dies of exposure and heart failure. Her daughter **Thomasin**, a simple and lovely country girl, vainly loves a handsome but weak failure, until he tries to run away with Eustacia and drowns. *See also* Venn, Diggory.

Ymir. In Scandinavian mythology, an ancient giant, the father of the frost giants.

Yokum. In the American newspaper cartoon *Li'l Abner* (beg. 1934), **Mammy**, Li'l Abner's* mother, is a tiny hillbilly woman noted for her powerful fists, her strong will, and her corncob pipe. **Pappy** is a weak and weak-willed little man who bows to Mammy's wishes at all times.

Yonadab. *See* Jonadab.

Yorick. (1) In Shakespeare's play *Hamlet* (1600), the dead jester whose skull is dug up, leading to Hamlet's* "Alas, poor Yorick" and his philosophizing on the transitoriness of life. (2) In Laurence Sterne's novel *Tristram Shandy* (1759), an eccentric and naive parson noted for his spavined nag, his habit of openly telling the truth, and his tombstone, which also reads "Alas, poor Yorick." *See also* Shandy.

York. *See* Lancaster.

Yossarian. In Joseph Heller's novel *Catch–22* (1961), an American pilot who is increasingly unnerved by the horrors of war and the even greater insanity of military life but who is trapped by Catch–22* and can never get shipped back home. He disappears in a rubber raft after he crashes his plane in the ocean.

Youth, The. *See* Fleming, Henry.

Yseult. *See* Iseult; Isolde.

Ysolde. *See* Iseult; Isolde.

Yum-Yum. In Gilbert and Sullivan's operetta *The Mikado* (1885), the beautiful young maiden in love with Nanki-Poo;* she is also one of the three little maids from school. *See also* Peep-Bo; Pitti-Sing.

Ywain. In Chrétien de Troyes's romance *Ywain,* a noble knight, known as the Knight of the Lion.

Z

Zaccheus. In the Bible, *Luke* xix, a tax collector who climbs a tree to see Jesus* and with whom Jesus stays, despite complaints that he is a sinner; he is saved by the experience.

Zachariah. (1) In the Bible, *II Kings* xv, a king of Israel* who continued the sins and wickedness of his father Jeroboam* and was assassinated. *Also called* Zechariah. (2) *See also* Zacharias; Zechariah.

Zacharias. (1) In the Bible, *Matthew* xxii, a prophet stoned for his prophecies, possibly the same as Zechariah.* (2) In the Bible, *Luke* i, the father of John the Baptist.* (3) *See also* Zachariah.

Zachary. *See* Zachariah; Zacharias.

Zaharov. (1) Historically, a wealthy and powerful munitions manufacturer and dealer (d. 1936) whose name became synonymous with all "merchants of death." (2) *See also* Zaroff.

Zanni. *See* Zany.

Zany. In the commedia dell'Arte, a stock character buffoon or fool; significant zanies include Harlequin* and Brighella.*

Zarathustra. A name sometimes used for Zoroaster,* noted most often for its use by Nietzsche in *Thus Spake Zarathustra* (1885), in which he prophesies and describes the coming Nietzschean superman.

Zarietchnaya, Nina. *See* Nina.

Zaroff. (1) In Richard Connell's story *The Most Dangerous Game* (1924), an elegant but cruel Russian who lives on an uncharted island and for entertainment hunts men. (2) *See also* Zaharov.

Zebadiah. (1) In the Bible, *I Chronicles* xii, one of the men who joined David* in his flight from Saul.* (2) In the Bible, *Ezra* viii, the head of one of the families that returned from the captivity in Babylon. *See also* Ezra.

Zebedee. In the Bible, *Matthew* iv, a fisherman and the father of James* and John.*

Zebediah. *See* Zebadiah.

Zebulun. In the Bible, *Genesis* xxxv, a son of Jacob* and Leah* and the father of one of the twelve tribes of Israel.*

Zechariah. In the Bible, a common name for a number of prominent Old Testament leaders; most references are to the prophet in the book of *Zechariah,* the author of a particularly mysterious set of prophecies. *Also called* Zachariah* and often spelled interchangeably.

Zedekiah. (1) In the Bible, *I Kings* xxii, a false prophet who encouraged Ahab* to go into the battle in which he was killed. (2) In the Bible, *II Kings* xxiv-v, the last king of Judah;* he was killed, and his state was destroyed in a revolt against the Babylonians. *See also* Nebuchadnezzar.

Zeena. *See* Frome.

Zephon. In John Milton's poem *Paradise Lost* (1667), a strong and subtle spirit sent to Eden* to search out Satan.*

Zephyrus. In Greek mythology, the west wind. *See also* Hyacinthus.

Zerbinetta. A name sometimes used for Columbine.*

Zerbino. In Ariosto's *Orlando Furioso* (1532), a perfect Scottish knight of whom it was said that they broke the mold when he was made.

Zero. In Elmer Rice's play *The Adding Machine* (1923), an average man, an accountant who loses his job to a machine, goes mad and kills his boss, and then is sent back from Heaven* to serve the machine.

Zeus. In Greek mythology, the most powerful of the gods, the ruler of heaven and earth, called Jupiter by the Romans. He attained power by overthrowing the Titans* and ruled from Olympus.* He was usually depicted as a great bearded figure, carrying a thunderbolt. Although ostensibly the ruler of all gods, he was never omnipotent, often not getting his way in the jockeying among all the other gods, especially in Homer's *Iliad,* in which Zeus favors the Trojans.* He was notorious for his philandering with human women, often changing his appearance to seduce them, despite his marriage to the jealous and strong-willed Hera.* With Hera, he fathered several of the gods; *see* Ares; Eilythyia; Eris; Hephaestus. However, he fathered most of the other gods with various Titans or other goddesses; *see* Apollo; Aphrodite; Artemis; Athena; Dionysus; Hermes; Litae; Muses; Persephone. For his most noted affairs, *see* Alcmena; Callisto; Danaä; Dione; Electra; Europa; Io; Leda; Leto; Metis; Mnemosyne; Semele. For his most noted children, *see* Britomartis; Castor; Dardanus; Endymion; Helen; Heracles; Lacedaemon; Perseus; Pollux. For his most noted acts in relation to humanity, *see* Baucis; Caeneus; Celmus; Ganymede; Marpessa; Pandora; Phaeton; Plutus; Prometheus; Psyche; Sisyphus; Tiresias. For his war with the Titans, *see* Corybantes; Cronos; Pelops; Saturn; Styx; Typhon. *Also called* Jove.* *See also* Amalthea; Amphitryon; Chelone; Cynosura; Melissa; Ixion; Oracle; Salmoneus.

Zillah. In the Bible, *Genesis* iv, the wife of Lamech* and the mother of Tubalcain.*

Zion. In the Bible, a name for the hill on which the temple was built in Jerusalem;* often used metaphorically, in the Bible and in general usage, for the dwelling of God.

Zipporah. In the Bible, *Exodus,* the wife of Moses,* married after Moses rescued her and her sisters from an attack at a well in the desert.

Zonker. In the American newspaper cartoon *Doonesbury* (beg. 1970), the quintessential "hippy," a gentle, innocent, long-haired young man who has no cares in the world.

Zooey. In J. D. Salinger's stories *Franny and Zooey* (1961), a television actor and the sensitive brother of Franny.*

Zophar. In the Bible, *Job,* one of the friends who deserts Job* during his trials.

Zophiel. In John Milton's poem *Paradise Lost* (1667), the swiftest cherub.*

Zoroaster. Historically, a sixth-century B.C. prophet in Persia, the founder of a religion based on the conflict between a god of light and fire and a god of darkness. *Also called* Zarathustra.*

Zossima. In Dostoevsky's novel *The Brothers Karamazov* (1880), the patriarchal holy man whose guidance leads at least Alyosha* to triumph over the evil in his soul. *See also* Karamazov.

Zuleika. (1) In Moslem legend, Potiphar's* wife. (2) *See* Dobson, Zuleika.

About the Author

DAVID GROTE is the author of *Script Analysis, Staging the Musical, The End of Comedy,* and *Theatre: Preparation and Performance* (coauthored with Charlotte Lee). He has also published seven plays. He served as editor of the *Secondary School Theater Journal* for two years, and has published articles in *Dramatics, Dramatists' Guild Quarterly, Publishers Weekly,* and *In These Times.*